ACCA

G000122944

PAPER P4

ADVANCED FINANCIAL MANAGEMENT

P R A C T I C E & R E V I S I O N K I T

BPP Learning Media is the **sole ACCA Platinum Approved Learning Partner – content** for the ACCA qualification. In this, **the only Paper P4 Practice and Revision Kit to be reviewed by the examiner**:

- We discuss the **best strategies** for revising and taking your ACCA exams

- We show you how to be **well prepared** for your exam

- We give you **lots of great guidance** on tackling questions

- We show you how you can **build your own exams**

- We provide you with **three** mock exams including the **new Pilot paper**

Our **Passcard** and **i-Pass** products also support this paper.

FOR EXAMS UP TO JUNE 2014

BPP LEARNING MEDIA

First edition 2007
Seventh edition January 2013

ISBN 9781 4453 6654 8
(previous ISBN 9781 4453 8003 2)

e-ISBN 9781 4453 6957 0

British Library Cataloguing-in-Publication Data
A catalogue record for this book
is available from the British Library

Published by

BPP Learning Media Ltd
BPP House, Aldine Place
London W12 8AA

www.bpp.com/learningmedia

Printed in the United Kingdom by

Polestar Wheatons
Hennock Road
Marsh Barton
Exeter
EX2 8RP

All our rights reserved. No part of this publication may be reproduced, stored in a retrieval system or transmitted, in any form or by any means, electronic, mechanical, photocopying, recording or otherwise, without the prior written permission of BPP Learning Media Ltd.

We are grateful to the Association of Chartered Certified Accountants for permission to reproduce past examination questions. The suggested solutions in the exam answer bank have been prepared by BPP Learning Media Ltd, except where otherwise stated.

©
BPP Learning Media Ltd
2013

Your learning materials, published by BPP Learning Media Ltd, are printed on paper sourced from sustainable, managed forests.

Contents

A note about copyright

Dear Customer

What does the little © mean and why does it matter?

Your market-leading BPP books, course materials and e-learning materials do not write and update themselves. People write them: on their own behalf or as employees of an organisation that invests in this activity. Copyright law protects their livelihoods. It does so by creating rights over the use of the content.

Breach of copyright is a form of theft – as well as being a criminal offence in some jurisdictions, it is potentially a serious breach of professional ethics.

With current technology, things might seem a bit hazy but, basically, without the express permission of BPP Learning Media:

- Photocopying our materials is a breach of copyright

- Scanning, ripcasting or conversion of our digital materials into different file formats, uploading them to facebook or emailing them to your friends is a breach of copyright

You can, of course, sell your books, in the form in which you have bought them – once you have finished with them. (Is this fair to your fellow students? We update for a reason.) Please note the e-products are sold on a single user licence basis: we do not supply 'unlock' codes to people who have bought them second-hand.

And what about outside the UK? BPP Learning Media strives to make our materials available at prices students can afford by local printing arrangements, pricing policies and partnerships which are clearly listed on our website. A tiny minority ignore this and indulge in criminal activity by illegally photocopying our material or supporting organisations that do. If they act illegally and unethically in one area, can you really trust them?

Using your BPP Learning Media products

This Kit gives you the question practice and guidance you need in the exam. Our other products can also help you pass:

- **Learning to Learn Accountancy** gives further valuable advice on revision

- **Passcards** provide you with clear topic summaries and exam tips

- **Success CDs** help you revise on the move

- **i-Pass CDs** offer tests of knowledge against the clock

- **Underlying knowledge CD** offers guidance on assumed knowledge for Options papers P4, P5, P6, P7

You can purchase these products by visiting http://www.bpp.com/acca

Question index

The headings in this checklist/index indicate the main topics of questions, but questions are expected to cover several different topics. Questions have been amended to reflect the new format of the exam from June 2013. Questions set under the old syllabus Paper 3.7 – *Strategic Financial Management* (SFM) and Paper 14 – *Financial Strategy* (FS) are included as their style and/or content are similar to the questions that appear in Paper P4 – *Advanced Financial Management*.

Mock exam 1

Questions 85 to 88

Mock exam 2

Questions 89 to 92

Mock exam 3 (Pilot paper)

Questions 93 to 96

Planning your question practice

Our guidance from page xx shows you how to organise your question practice, either by attempting questions from each syllabus area or **by building your own exams** – tackling questions as a series of practice exams.

June and December 2013 exams

BPP's answers for these exams along with additional questions will be available for free after the exams on http://www.bpp.com/acca

Topic index

Listed below are the key Paper P4 syllabus topics and the numbers of the questions in this Kit covering those topics.

If you need to concentrate your practice and revision on certain topics or if you want to attempt all available questions that refer to a particular subject, you will find this index useful.

Syllabus topic	Question numbers
Acquisitions - regulatory framework and processes	7, 39, 40, 63, 74, 80
Acquisitions and mergers versus other growth strategies	39, 42, 64, 67, 71, 72, 75, 82
Application of option pricing theory in investment decisions	17, 22, 23, 24, 25, 26, 27, 83, 84
Business re-organisation	38, 43, 44, 45, 46, 76, Mock 1 Q4, Mock 3 Q3
Conflicting stakeholder interests	1, 5, 6, 8, 11, Mock 1 Q1
Dividend policy in multinationals and transfer pricing	11, 12, 14, 58, 63, 64, 71, 78, Mock 2 Q4
Environmental issues	4, 7, 8, 73, 83, Mock 3 Q1
Ethical issues	3, 4, 5, 7, 13, 76
Financial planning for multinational organisations	10, 11, 14, 65, 67, 72, Mock 2 Q1
Financial reconstruction	43, 76, Mock 3 Q3
Financial strategy formulation	1, 3, 4, 5, 7, 37, 63, 64, 66, 68, 75, 80, Mock 2 Q4, Mock 3 Q1
Financing acquisitions and mergers	40, 72, 74, 75
Foreign exchange risk hedging	48, 49, 50, 51, 52, 53, 65, 68, 77, 78, 84, Mock 1 Q2, Mock 2 Q2
Impact of financing on investment decisions and adjusted present values	10, 27, 28, 29, 30, 31, 32, 33, 34, 35, 37, 38, 57, 65, 66, 68, 69, 70, 81, Mock 3 Q4
Interest rate risk hedging	27, 47, 49, 54, 55, 56, 57, 75, 77, 79, Mock 2 Q2, Mock 3 Q2
International investment and financing decisions	16, 33, 71, 72, Mock 2 Q1, Mock 3 Q1
International trade and finance	60, 61, 70
Investment appraisal - discounted cash flow techniques	15, 16, 17, 18, 20, 21, 29, 56, 67, 68, 69, 81, 82, 83, Mock 1 Q1, Mock 1 Q3, Mock 2 Q3
Islamic financing	59, 62, 70
Management of international trade and finance	9, 11, 12, 13, 37, 63, 78
The role and responsibility of senior financial executive/advisor	2, 3, 10, 13, 64, 66, Mock 1 Q1
Treasury function	48, 50, 78, 79
Valuation and the use of free cash flows	19, 41, 42, 66, 73, 80, 84, Mock 1 Q3
Valuation for acquisitions and mergers	40, 41, 42, 71, 72, 73, 74, 80, 84
World financial markets	59, 60, 61, 73

BPP
LEARNING MEDIA

Helping you with your revision – the ONLY P4 Practice and Revision Kit to be reviewed by the examiner!

BPP Learning Media – the sole Platinum Approved Learning Partner - content

As ACCA's **sole Platinum Approved Learning Partner – content**, BPP Learning Media gives you the **unique opportunity** to use **examiner-reviewed** revision materials for the 2013 and June 2014 exams. By incorporating the examiner's comments and suggestions regarding syllabus coverage, the BPP Learning Media Practice and Revision Kit provides excellent, **ACCA-approved** support for your revision.

Tackling revision and the exam

Using feedback obtained from ACCA examiners as part of their review:

- We look at the dos and don'ts of revising for, and taking, ACCA exams
- We focus on Paper P4; we discuss revising the syllabus, what to do (and what not to do) in the exam, how to approach different types of question and ways of obtaining easy marks

Selecting questions

We provide signposts to help you plan your revision.

- A full **question index**
- A **topic index** listing all the questions that cover key topics, so that you can locate the questions that provide practice on these topics, and see the different ways in which they might be examined
- **BPP's question plan** highlighting the most important questions and explaining why you should attempt them
- **Build your own exams**, showing how you can practise questions in a series of exams

Making the most of question practice

At BPP Learning Media we realise that you need more than just questions and model answers to get the most from your question practice.

- Our **Top tips** included for certain questions provide essential advice on tackling questions, presenting answers and the key points that answers need to include
- We show you how you can pick up **Easy marks** on some questions, as we know that picking up all readily available marks often can make the difference between passing and failing
- We include **marking guides** to show you what the examiner rewards
- We include **examiners' comments** to show you where students struggled or performed well in the actual exam
- We refer to the **2012 BPP Study Text** (for exams up to June 2014) for detailed coverage of the topics covered in questions

Attempting mock exams

There are three mock exams that provide practice at coping with the pressures of the exam day. We strongly recommend that you attempt them under exam conditions. **Mock exams 1 and 2** reflect the question styles and syllabus coverage of the exam; **Mock exam 3** is the pilot paper.

Revising P4

Topics to revise

Any part of the syllabus could be tested in the compulsory Section A question, therefore it is essential that you learn the **entire syllabus** to maximise your chances of passing. There are no short cuts – trying to spot topics is dangerous and will significantly reduce the likelihood of success.

As this is an advanced level paper, it **assumes knowledge** of the topics covered in Paper F9 – *Financial Management*, including the Capital Asset Pricing Model (CAPM), investment appraisal techniques (such as NPV and IRR), cost of capital and risk management. You should revise these topics if necessary as they have a significant impact on your understanding of the more advanced techniques.

It's also useful to keep reading the business pages during your revision period and not just narrowly focus on the syllabus. Remember that the examiner has stressed that this paper is about how organisations respond to real-world issues, so the more you read, the more practical examples you will have of how organisations have tackled real-life situations.

Question practice

You should use the Passcards and any brief notes you have to revise the syllabus, but you mustn't spend all your revision time passively reading. **Question practice is vital;** doing as many questions as you can in full will help develop your ability to analyse scenarios and produce relevant discussion and recommendations. The question plan on page xxi tells you what questions cover so that you can choose questions covering a variety of syllabus areas.

Make sure you leave enough time in your revision schedule to practise the longer Section A questions, as such questions are compulsory in the exam. The scenarios and requirements of Section A questions are more complex and will integrate several parts of the syllabus, therefore practice is essential. Also ensure that you attempt all three mock exams under exam conditions.

Passing the P4 exam

Displaying the right qualities

The examiner will expect you to display the following qualities.

Qualities required	
Fulfilling the higher level question requirements	This means that when you are asked to show higher level skills such as **assessment or evaluation**, you will only score well if you demonstrate them. Merely describing something when you are asked to evaluate it will not earn you the marks you need.
Identifying the most important features of the organisation and its environment	You must use your **technical knowledge and business awareness** to identify the key features of the scenario.
Sorting the information in the scenario	You will get a lot of information, particularly in the Section A scenario, and will be expected to **evaluate how useful** it is and **use it** to support answers such as comparisons and discussions.
Selecting relevant real-life examples	You will gain credit for using **good examples.**
Arguing well	You may be expected to discuss both sides of a case, or present an argument in favour or against something. You will gain marks for the **quality** and **logical flow of your arguments**.
Making reasonable recommendations	The measures you recommend must be **appropriate** for the organisation; you may need to discuss their strengths and weaknesses, as there may be costs of adopting them. The recommendations should clearly state what has to be done.

Avoiding weaknesses

Our experience of, and examiner feedback from, other higher level exams enables us to predict a number of weaknesses that are likely to occur in many students' answers. You will enhance your chances significantly if you ensure you avoid these mistakes:

- **Failing to provide what the question verbs require** (discussion, evaluation, recommendation) or to write about the topics specified in the question requirements
- **Repeating the same material** in different parts of answers
- **Stating theories and concepts** rather than applying them
- **Quoting chunks of detail** from the question that don't add any value
- **Forcing irrelevancies into answers**, for example irrelevant definitions or theories, or examples that don't relate to the scenario
- **Giving long lists or writing down all that's known** about a broad subject area, and not caring whether it's relevant or not
- **Focusing too narrowly on one area** – for example only covering financial risks when other risks are also important
- **Letting your personal views prevent you from answering the question** – the question may require you to construct an argument with which you personally don't agree
- **Unrealistic or impractical recommendations**
- **Vague recommendations** - instead of just saying improve risk management procedures, you should discuss precisely **how** you would improve them
- **Failing to answer sufficient questions**, or all parts of a question, because of poor time management

Using the reading time

We recommend that you spend the first part of the 15 minutes reading time choosing the Section B questions you will do, on the basis of your knowledge of the syllabus areas being tested and whether you can fulfil all the question requirements. Remember that Section B questions can cover different parts of the syllabus, and you should be happy with all the areas that the questions you choose cover. We suggest that you should note on the paper any ideas that come to you about these questions.

However don't spend all the reading time going through and analysing the Section B question requirements in detail; leave that until the three hours' writing time. Instead you should be looking to spend as much of the reading time as possible looking at the Section A scenario, as this will be longer and more complex than the Section B scenarios and cover more of the syllabus. You should highlight and annotate the key points of the scenario on the question paper.

Choosing which questions to answer first

Spending most of your reading time on the compulsory Section A question will mean that you can get underway with planning and writing your answer to the Section A question as soon as the three hours start. It will give you more actual writing time during the one and a half hours you should allocate to it and it's writing time that you'll need. Comments from examiners of other syllabuses that have similar exam formats suggest that students appear less time-pressured if they do the big compulsory questions first.

During the second half of the exam, you can put Section A aside and concentrate on the two Section B questions you've chosen.

However our recommendations are not inflexible. If you really think the Section A question looks a lot harder than the Section B questions you've chosen, then do those first, but **DON'T run over time on them.** You must leave yourself at least one hour and 30 minutes to tackle the Section A question. When you come back to it, having had initial thoughts during the reading time, you should be able to generate more ideas and find the question is not as bad as it looks.

Tackling questions

Scenario questions

You'll improve your chances by following a step-by-step approach to Section A scenarios along the following lines.

Step 1   Read the background

Usually the first couple of paragraphs will give some background on the company and what it is aiming to achieve. By reading this carefully you will be better equipped to relate your answers to the company as much as possible.

Step 2   Read the requirements

There is no point reading the detailed information in the question until you know what it is going to be used for. Don't panic if some of the requirements look challenging – identify the elements you are able to do and look for links between requirements, as well as possible indications of the syllabus areas the question is covering.

Step 3 Highlight the action verbs that are used in each requirement

These convey the level of skill you need to exhibit and also the structure your answer should have. A lower level verb such as define will require a more descriptive answer; a higher level verb such as evaluate will require a more applied, critical answer. Approximately 75% of the syllabus will be tested at intellectual level 3 (synthesis), 20% at intellectual level 2 (application) and 5% at level one (knowledge). Action verbs that are likely to be frequently used in this exam are listed below, together with their intellectual levels and guidance on their meaning.

Intellectual level		
1	**Identify/describe**	State the meaning of
	Calculate	Perform a specific mathematical technique
2	**Discuss**	Examine in detail by argument
	Analyse	Examine in detail the structure of...
	Evaluate	Use your judgement to assess the value of...
3	**Advise**	Use judgement to recommend a course of action
	Report	Present/justify valid recommendations
	Estimate	Make an approximate judgement or calculation

Step 4 Check the mark allocation to each part

This shows you the depth anticipated and helps allocate time.

Step 5 Read the question slowly, focusing on the initial requirements

Once you know what you are expected to do in the first requirement, read the question in detail, trying to focus on the information that will be needed for your first task.

Step 6 Read the scenario carefully

Put points under headings related to requirements (eg by noting in the margin to what part of the question the scenario detail relates).

Step 7 Consider the consequences of the points you've identified

You will often have to provide recommendations based on the information you've been given. Be prepared to criticize the code, framework or model that you've been told to use if required. You may have also to bring in wider issues or viewpoints, for example the views of different stakeholders.

Step 8 Write a brief plan

You may be able to do this on the question paper as often there will be at least one blank page in the question booklet. However any plan you make should be reproduced in the answer booklet when writing time begins. Make sure you identify all the requirements of the question in your plan – each requirement may have sub-requirements that must also be addressed. If there are professional marks available, highlight in your plan where these may be gained (such as preparing a report).

Step 9 Write the answer

Make every effort to present your answer clearly. The pilot paper and exam papers so far indicate that the examiner will be looking for you to make a number of clear points. The best way to demonstrate what you're doing is to put points into separate paragraphs with clear headers.

Do not be tempted to write all you know about a particular topic in a discussion question. Markers can easily spot when a student is 'waffling' and you will receive little or no credit for this approach. Keep referring back to the question requirement to ensure you are not straying from the point.

To make it easier for the marker to determine the relevance of the points you are making, you could explain what you mean in one sentence and then why this point is relevant in another.

Remember that **depth of discussion** will be important. Always bear in mind how many marks are available for the discussion as this will give you an indication of the depth that is required. Ask yourself the following questions as you are tackling a discussion question:

- **Have I made a point in a coherent sentence?**
- **Have I explained the point** (to answer the 'so what' or 'why' queries)**?**
- **Have I related the point to the company in the scenario?**

Gaining the easy marks

Knowledge of the core topics that we list under topics to revise should present you with some easy marks. The pilot paper suggests that there will be some marks available on certain part questions for definitions, explanations or descriptions that don't have to be related to the scenario. However don't assume that you can ignore all the scenarios and still pass!

As P4 is a Professional level paper, 4 **professional level marks** will be awarded. Some of these should be easy to obtain. The examiner has stated that some marks may be available for presenting your answer in the form of a letter, presentation, memo, report or briefing notes. You may also be able to obtain marks for the style and layout of your answer.

Reports should always have an appropriate title. They should be **formally written**, with an **introductory paragraph** setting out the aims of the report. You should use **short paragraphs** and **appropriate headings**, with a summary of findings as a conclusion.

Memorandums should have the following information at the beginning:

Subject; name of recipient; name of author; date

The language can be **less formal** than a report but the content should still have an introduction and conclusion, and be divided into small paragraphs with appropriate headings.

Letters should be addressed appropriately to the correct person and be dated. They should have a short introductory paragraph, and conclusion and be formally written. Letters beginning with 'Dear Sir/Madam' should end with 'Yours faithfully'.

Exam formulae

Set out below are the **formulae you will be given in the exam**. If you are not sure what the symbols mean, or how the formulae are used, you should refer to the appropriate chapter in this Study Text.

Chapter in Study Text

Modigliani and Miller Proposition 2 (with tax)

$$k_e = k_e^i + (1-T)(k_e^i - k_d)\frac{V_d}{V_e}$$

7a

The capital asset pricing model

$$E(r_i) = R_f + \beta_i(E(r_m) - R_f)$$

2

The asset beta formula

$$\beta_a = \left[\frac{V_e}{(V_e + V_d(1-T))}\beta_e\right] + \left[\frac{V_d(1-T)}{(V_e + V_d(1-T))}\beta_d\right]$$

2

The growth model

$$P_0 = \frac{D_0(1+g)}{(r_e - g)}$$

12

Gordon's growth approximation

$$g = br_e$$

5

The weighted average cost of capital

$$WACC = \left[\frac{V_e}{V_e + V_d}\right]k_e + \left[\frac{V_d}{V_e + V_d}\right]k_d(1-T)$$

7a

The Fisher formula

$$(1 + i) = (1 + r)(1 + h)$$

5

Purchasing power parity and interest rate parity

$$S_1 = S_0 \times \frac{(1 + h_c)}{(1 + h_b)}$$

8

$$F_0 = S_0 \times \frac{(1 + i_c)}{(1 + i_b)}$$

8

Modified internal rate of return

$$\text{MIRR} = \left[\frac{PV_R}{PV_I}\right]^{\frac{1}{n}} (1+r_e) - 1 \qquad\qquad 5$$

The Black-Scholes option pricing model

$$c = P_a N(d_1) - P_e N(d_2)e^{-rt} \qquad\qquad 6$$

$$\text{Where} \quad d_1 = \frac{\ln\left(P_a/P_e\right) + (r + 0.5s^2)t}{s\sqrt{t}} \qquad\qquad 6$$

$$d_2 = d_1 - s\sqrt{t} \qquad\qquad 6$$

The put call parity relationship

$$p = c - P_a + P_e e^{-rt} \qquad\qquad 6$$

Formulae to learn

These are the main formulae that are not given in the exam formula sheet. Make sure you learn these as you may be required to use them in the exam. They are used throughout the Study Text and this Practice and Revision Kit.

$$\mathbf{Ke} = \frac{D_1}{P_0} + g$$

$$\mathbf{K_d} = \frac{i(1-t)}{P_0}$$

$$\mathbf{K_{pref}} = \frac{\text{Preference dividend}}{\text{Market value}_{(ex\,div)}} = \frac{d}{P_0}$$

$$\text{Gearing} \quad = \quad \frac{\text{Book value of debt}}{\text{Book value of equity}}$$

$$\text{Interest cover} \quad = \quad \frac{\text{Profit from operations}}{\text{Interest}}$$

Current ratio   =   Current   :   Current
               assets   liabilities

BPP
LEARNING MEDIA

Exam information

The exam paper

Format of the paper

The format of the exam changes from June 2013 onwards.

Section A comprises one compulsory question. The total for this section will be 50 marks.

Longer questions will cover topics from across the syllabus but will tend to be based on one major area – for example a cross-border merger question (major topic) might bring in ethical issues (smaller topic).

Section B will be 50 marks in total (25 marks per question). There is a choice of two from three questions.

Four professional marks are available. The examiner has emphasised that in order to gain all the marks available, students must write in the specified format (such as a report or memo). Reports must have terms of reference, conclusion, appendices and appropriate headings. Make sure you are familiar with how different types of documents are constructed to improve your chances of gaining maximum professional marks.

Time allowed is 3 hours with 15 minutes' reading time and the **pass mark** remains at 50%.

Exams prior to 2013

Questions and answers for exams prior to 2013 are available on:

http://www.accaglobal.com/en/student/qualification-resources/acca-qualification/acca-exams/p4-exams/students-acca-exams-p4-past_papers.html

Analysis of past papers

The table below provides details of when each element of the syllabus has been examined and the question number and section in which each element appeared.

Covered in Text chapter		D 12	J 12	D 11	J 11	D 10	J 10	D 09	J 09	D 08	J 08	D 07
	ROLE AND RESPONSIBILITY TOWARDS STAKEHOLDERS											
1, 2	Role of senior financial executive/financial strategy formulation		C		O			C, O		C	C	O
3a	Conflicting stakeholder interests											
3b, 3c	Ethical/environmental issues			O	O				O	O	O	O
	ECONOMIC ENVIRONMENT FOR MULTINATIONALS											
4	Trading and planning in a multinational environment	O				O			O			
	ADVANCED INVESTMENT APPRAISAL											
5	Discounted cash flow techniques	O	O	C		C	C	C, O	C, O	C	O	C, O
6	Application of option pricing theory to investment decisions		C		O	O	C	C, O	O			O
7a, 7b	Impact of financing, adjusted present values / Valuation and use of free cash flows	C	C, O	C, O	O	C			C	O	O	O
8	International investment and financing decisions		O	C								
	ACQUISITIONS AND MERGERS											
9, 11, 12	Strategic/financial/regulatory issues	O			C				C		O	C
10	Valuation techniques	O	C		C		C				C	C
	CORPORATE RECONSTRUCTION & REORGANISATION											
13	Financial reconstruction					C						
14	Business reorganisation	C		O		C	O		C			
	TREASURY & ADVANCED RISK MANAGEMENT TECHNIQUES											
15	Role of the treasury function								O			
16	Hedging foreign currency risk	C			C		O		O		O	
17	Hedging interest rate risk		O	C					O	O		
18	Dividend policy & transfer pricing in multinationals					O						
	EMERGING ISSUES											
19	Recent developments and trends in world financial markets and international trade	O	O			O	O	O				

IMPORTANT!

The table above gives a broad idea of how frequently major topics in the syllabus are examined. It should not be used to question spot and predict for example that Topic X will not be examined because it came up two sittings ago. The examiner's reports indicate that the examiner is well aware some students try to question spot. You can assume that he will therefore take care to ensure that the exams avoid falling into a predictable pattern, and may examine the same topic two sittings in a row for example.

BPP LEARNING MEDIA

Useful websites

The websites below provide additional sources of information of relevance to your studies for *Advanced Financial Management*.

- www.accaglobal.com

  ACCA's website. The students' section of the website is invaluable for detailed information about the qualification, past issues of Student Accountant (including technical articles) and interviews with examiners.

- www.bpp.com

  Our website provides information about BPP products and services, with a link to the ACCA website.

- www.ft.com

  This website provides information about current international business. You can search for information and articles on specific industry groups as well as individual companies.

- www.economist.com

  Here you can search for business information on a week-by-week basis, search articles by business subject and use the resources of the Economist Intelligence Unit to research sectors, companies or countries.

- www.invweek.co.uk

  This site carries business news and articles on markets from Investment Week and International Investment.

- www.pwcglobal.com/uk

  The PricewaterhouseCoopers website includes UK Economic Outlook.

- www.cfo.com

  Good website for financial officers.

- www.bankofengland.co.uk

  This website is useful for sourcing Bank of England publications.

- www.yieldcurve.com

  A useful website for research and articles on such areas as interest rate derivatives and securitisation.

Planning your question practice

We have already stressed that question practice should be right at the centre of your revision. Whilst you will spend some time looking at your notes and Paper P4 Passcards, you should spend the majority of your revision time practising questions.

We recommend two ways in which you can practise questions.

- Use **BPP Learning Media's question plan** to work systematically through the syllabus and attempt key and other questions on a section-by-section basis

- **Build your own exams** – attempt questions as a series of practice exams

These ways are suggestions and simply following them is no guarantee of success. You or your college may prefer an alternative but equally valid approach.

BPP Learning Media's question plan

The BPP Learning Media plan below requires you to devote a **minimum of 45 hours** to revision of Paper P4. Any time you can spend over and above this should only increase your chances of success.

Step 1 **Review your notes** and the chapter summaries in the Paper P4 **Passcards** for each section of the syllabus.

Step 2 **Answer the key questions** for that section. These questions have boxes round the question number in the table below and you should answer them in full. Even if you are short of time you must attempt these questions if you want to pass the exam. You should complete your answers without referring to our solutions.

Step 3 **Attempt the other questions** in that section. For some questions we have suggested that you prepare **answer plans or do the calculations** rather than full solutions. Planning an answer means that you should spend about 40% of the time allowance for the questions brainstorming the question and drawing up a list of points to be included in the answer.

Step 4 Attempt **Mock exams 1, 2 and 3** under strict exam conditions.

Syllabus section	2012 Passcards chapters	Questions in this Kit	Comments	Done ✓
Role and responsibility towards shareholders	1-3C	2	Write an answer plan. This is a good way to test your understanding of capital structure issues.	☐
		3	Answer in full. This question, adapted from the December 2007 exam, tests your knowledge of strategic financial issues	☐
		4	Answer in full. This question, adapted from the December 2008 exam, covers ethical issues.	☐
		6	Write an answer plan. This question examines corporate governance issues and is a good test of your knowledge of different corporate governance systems.	☐
		7	Answer in full. This question, adapted from the June 2011 exam, looks at key financial strategy decisions regarding the commercialisation of a new product.	☐
		8	Answer in full. This question, adapted from the December 2011 exam, looks at triple bottom line reporting and also stakeholder conflict.	☐
Economic environment for multinationals	4	11	Answer in full. This question focuses on overseas tax issues.	☐
		13	Answer in full. This question, adapted from the June 2009 exam, focuses on various ethical and strategic issues facing a multinational company.	☐
		65	Write an answer plan. This is a good question on financing issues facing a multinational company.	☐
		14	Answer in full. This question, adapted from the December 2010 exam, covers advantages and disadvantages of a joint venture with a foreign entity.	☐
Advanced investment appraisal	5 - 8	16	Do the calculations in part (a) to ensure you are comfortable with the investment appraisal methods.	☐
		18	Answer in full. This is adapted from the June 2009 paper and examines investment appraisal techniques and duration.	☐
		81	Answer in full. This question, adpated from the June 2010 paper examines NPV, sensitivity analysis and simulations.	☐

Syllabus section	2012 Passcards chapters	Questions in this Kit	Comments	Done ☑
		19	Answer in full. This adapted June 2012 question tests your ability to use the free cash flow model to value a company.	☐
		22	Do the calculations in part (a). This gives you a good opportunity to ensure you are comfortable with Black-Scholes calculations.	☐
		23	Answer in full. This adapted June 2011 question tests your ability to use the Black-Scholes model to value an option to delay.	☐
		24	Answer in full. This adapted December 2010 question covers options contracts, delta hedging and risk management.	☐
		84	Answer part (a) This question, adapted from the June 2010 exam, looks at capital structure and regulation of takeovers.	☐
		29	Answer in full. This adapted June 2008 question gives you the chance to practise APV and MIRR calculations.	☐
		32	Answer in full. This adapted December 2011 question gives you the chance to practise bond valuations and credit ratings.	☐
Acquisitions and mergers	9 - 12	39	Write an answer plan. This is a good discursive question on issues relating to a takeover.	☐
		38	Answer in full. This question requires you to determine an issue price and calculate cost of equity capital and WACC.	☐
		73	Answer in full. This adapted June 2011 question covers various acquisition issues, including effects on capital structure, business valuation techniques and finance requirements.	☐
		75	Answer in full. An adapted December 2009 question which covers risks associated with an acquisition, performance measures and also interest rate risk.	☐
Corporate reconstruction and reorganisation	13 - 14	43	Write an answer plan. This question makes you think about advantages and disadvantages of an MBO.	☐
		44	Answer in full. An adapted June 2010 question that focuses on issues to be considered when disposing of a division.	☐
		45	Answer in full. This question, adapted from the December 2011 exam, tests your skills in analysing a proposed MBO.	☐

BPP LEARNING MEDIA

Syllabus section	2012 Passcards chapters	Questions in this Kit	Comments	Done ☑
Treasury and advanced risk management techniques	15 - 18	47	Write an answer plan. This tests your understanding of the use of options for foreign currency hedging.	☐
		48	Answer in full. This is a good question for practising different hedging strategies.	☐
		51	Answer in full. This question, adapted from the June 2010 paper, examines calculations and discussion relating to multilateral netting.	☐
		78	Answer parts (a) and (b). A question that covers alternative forms of currency hedging.	☐
		57	Answer in full. This question, adapted from the une 2012 exam, covers interest rate swaps.	☐
		53	Answer in full. A question adapted from June 2011 on interest rate hedging, including swaps.	☐
		58	Answer in full. This question, adapted from the December 2010 exam, covers dividend capacity issues.	☐
Emerging issues	19	59	Answer in full. A good question, adapted from the December 2009 paper, on lending issues set against the background of the global debt crisis.	☐
		60	Answer in full. This question, adapted from the June 2010 exam, deals with tranching, credit enhancement and securitisation.	☐
		61	Answer in full. This question, adapted from the June 2012 exam, deals with overseas subsidiaries, dark pool trading and money laundering.	☐

Build your own exams

Having revised your notes and the BPP Learning Media Passcards, you can attempt the questions in the Kit as a series of practice exams using the suggestions we have listed below.

	1	2	3	4	5
Section A					
1	66	82	78	64	65
Section B					
2	11	55	44	28	16
3	62	43	4	54	47
4	49	10	12	36	38

BPP
LEARNING MEDIA

Questions

ROLE AND RESPONSIBILITY TOWARDS STAKEHOLDERS

Questions 1 to 8 cover the role and responsibility towards stakeholders, the subject of Part A of the BPP Study Text for Paper P4.

1 Preparation question - Shareholders and bondholders (6/03)

27 mins

(a) Discuss why conflicts of interest might exist between shareholders and bondholders. (8 marks)

(b) Provide examples of covenants that might be attached to bonds, and briefly discuss the advantages and disadvantages to companies of covenants. (7 marks)

(Total = 15 marks)

2 Preparation question - Capital structure (12/04)   27 mins

Prepare a briefing document for a board of directors discussing issues that might influence a company's capital structure strategy. (15 marks)

3 Multimedia company   45 mins

You have been appointed as the chief financial officer of a multimedia company which is financed by private equity. There is considerable public interest in the company and it continues a very rapid rate of growth under the leadership of its dynamic founder and chief executive officer, Martin Pickle. Martin Pickle owns over 30 per cent of the company's equity and has also loaned the business substantial sums to sustain its overseas development. The balance of the other investors consist of some small shareholdings held by current and past employees and the remainder is in the hands of a private equity company which is represented by two directors on the board.

Recent financial information

Year ending 31 December	Profit for the year after interest and tax $ million	Investment in projects or capital expenditure $ million	Dividend paid $ million
20X5	18	-	9
20X6	21	30	6
20X7	30	-	15
20X8	33	45	6
20X9	48	-	24

You enjoy a substantial salary and package of other benefits. Your role description gives you overall responsibility to the board for the financial direction of the company, the management of its financial resources, direction and oversight of its internal control systems and responsibility for its risk management. After two months in the job you are called to a meeting with Martin Pickle and the company's non-executive chairman. In that time you have made significant progress in improving the financial controls of the business and the current year end, which is three weeks away, looks very promising. The company's underlying earnings growth promises to be in excess of 20 per cent and its cash generation is strong. The CEO tells you that he would like you to put together a plan to take the company to full listing as a first step to him undertaking a substantial reduction in his financial stake in the business. He tells you that this discussion must be confidential, as he expects that the market would react adversely to the news. However, he would like to see what could be done to make sure that the year end figures are as strong as possible. Given your performance, he also tells you that they would like to offer you a substantial incentive in the form of share options.

(a) Prepare a board paper, describing the procedure for obtaining a listing on an international stock exchange such as the London or New York Stock Exchange. **(6 marks)**

(b) Prepare a briefing note, itemising the advantages and disadvantages of such a step for a medium-sized company. **(5 marks)**

(c) Discuss any ethical considerations or concerns you may have concerning this proposed course of action. **(8 marks)**

(d) Evaluate the current dividend policy of the company **(6 marks)**

(Total = 25 marks)

4 Agenda for change (12/07, amended)   45 mins

The chairman of your company has become concerned about the accumulation of cash in hand and in the deposit accounts shown in the company's statement of financial position. The company is in the manufacturing sector, supplying aerospace components to the civil aviation markets in the UK and Europe. For the last 20 years the company has grown predominantly by acquisition and has not invested significantly in research and development on its own account. The acquisitions have given the company the technology that it has required and have all tended to be small, relative to the company's total market capitalisation.

The company has a healthy current asset ratio of 1.3, although its working capital cycle has an average of 24 unfunded days. The company has not systematically embraced new manufacturing technologies nor has it sought to reduce costs as a way of rebuilding profitability. Managerial and structural problems within divisions have led to a number of substantial projects overrunning and losses being incurred as a result. It has also proven difficult to ensure the accountability of managers promoting projects – many of which have not subsequently earned the cash flows originally promised. At the corporate level, much of the company's accounting is on a contracts basis and over the years it has tended to be cautious in its revenue recognition practices. This has meant that earnings growth has lagged behind cash flow.

Over the last 12 months the company has come under strong competitive pressure on the dominant defence side of its business which, coupled with the slow-down in spending in this area across the major western economies, has slowed the rate of growth of its earnings. The company's gearing ratio is very low at 12% of total market capitalisation and borrowing has invariably been obtained in the European fixed interest market and used to support capital investment in its European production facility. In the current year, investment plans are at the lowest they have been in real terms since the company was founded in the 1930s.

In discussion, the chairman comments upon the poor nature of the company's buildings and its poor levels of pay which could, in his view, be improved to reflect standards across the industry. Directors' pay, he reminds you, is some 15% below industry benchmarks and there is very little equity participation by the board of directors. He also points out that the company's environmental performance has not been good. Last year the company was fined for an untreated discharge into a local river. There are, he says, many useful things the company could do with the money to help improve the long-term health of the business. However, he does admit some pessimism that business opportunities will ever again be the same as in previous years and he would like a free and frank discussion at the next board meeting about the options for the company. The company has a very open culture where ideas are encouraged and freely debated.

The chairman asks if you, as the newly appointed chief financial officer, would lead the discussion at the next board.

Required

(a) In preparation for a board paper entitled 'Agenda for Change', write brief notes which identify the strategic financial issues the company faces and the alternatives it might pursue. **(10 marks)**

(b) Identify and discuss any ethical issues you believe are in the above case and how the various alternatives you have identified in (a) may lead to their resolution. **(10 marks)**

(c) Recommend five possible environmental management accounting measures that your company could use to measure whether ii is improving its environmental performance. **(5 marks)**

(Total = 25 marks)

BPP
LEARNING MEDIA

5 Solar Supermarkets (12/08, amended)   45 mins

Solar Supermarkets, a listed company, has one sole financial objective which is to maximise shareholder wealth. It is reviewing the approach that it should take to remunerating its executive directors and other senior managers. Over the years, the company's share price has performed well although there is now concern that price and cost competition from overseas entrants into the domestic market will have a significant impact on the firm's profitability. As a result, the directors believe that large investment in new technologies and markets will be required over the next five years. Traditionally, management has been rewarded by salary, a generous system of benefits, and a bonus scheme that has taken up to 4% of revenue. The directors are considering introducing a generous share option scheme with a five year vesting period.

There is also a view, expressed by some of the company's principal equity investors, that the company should consider returning cash to them through the sale of its property holdings. The company has over 200 stores nationally and 15 overseas, of which all except five are owned by the company. In the domestic economy, growth in the value of commercial property has averaged 8% per annum in recent years whilst retail growth has remained static at 5.5%.

A sale and leaseback, or the flotation of a separate property company that would rent the stores to Solar Supermarkets at commercial rates, are two suggestions that have been made at investor meetings. Either approach, it is suggested, would return value to investors and create a supply of capital for further expansion. There have been press rumours, possibly fed from sources within the investor community, that the company may be a target for a private equity acquisition. However, no formal approach has been made to the company.

The only other area of controversy to emerge about the company which has concerned the directors followed an announcement about the company pension scheme. Although the scheme is well funded the directors took the decision to close the current final salary scheme to new employees and to replace it with a money purchase scheme. Current employees would not be affected.

Required

(a)   Discuss the strategic, financial and ethical issues that this case presents and the merits of the proposed share option and sale and leaseback schemes.   **(20 marks)**

(b)   Briefly discuss whether the sole financial objective is appropriate, with reference to the scenario.   **(5 marks)**

(Total = 25 marks)

6 Preparation question - International corporate governance (SFM, 12/02)   27 mins

The following are extracts from the corporate governance guidelines issued by a UK plc.

(i)   All auditors' fees, including fees for services other than audit, should be fully disclosed in the annual report. In order to ensure continuity of standards the same audit partner, wherever possible, should be responsible for a period of at least three years.

(ii)   The board shall establish a remuneration committee comprising 50% executive directors and 50% non-executive directors. A non-executive director shall chair the committee.

(iii)   The Chairman of the company may also hold the position of Chief Executive, although this shall not normally be for a period of more than three years.

(iv)   The annual report shall fully disclose whether principles of good corporate governance have been applied.

(v)   No director shall hold directorships in more than twenty companies.

(vi)   Directors should regularly report on the effectiveness of the company's system of internal control.

Required

(a) Discuss the extent to which each of points (i) – (vi) is likely to comply with corporate governance systems such as the UK Corporate Governance Code. **(9 marks)**

(b) Prepare a brief report advising senior managers of your company who are going to work in subsidiaries in Germany, Japan and the USA of the main differences in corporate governance between the UK and any TWO of the above countries, and possible implications of the differences for the managers.

(6 marks)

(Total = 15 marks)

7 Mezza Co (6/11, amended)   45 mins

Mezza Co is a large food manufacturing and wholesale company. It imports fruit and vegetables from countries in South America, Africa and Asia, and packages them in steel cans, plastic tubs and as frozen foods, for sale to supermarkets around Europe. Its suppliers range from individual farmers to Government run cooperatives, and farms run by its own subsidiary companies. In the past, Mezza Co has been very successful in its activities, and has an excellent corporate image with its customers, suppliers and employees. Indeed Mezza Co prides itself on how it has supported local farming communities around the world and has consistently highlighted these activities in its annual reports.

However, in spite of buoyant stock markets over the last couple of years, Mezza Co's share price has remained static. Previously announcements to the stock market about growth potential led to an increase in the share price. It is thought that the current state is because there is little scope for future growth in its products. As a result the company's directors are considering diversifying into new areas. One possibility is to commercialise a product developed by a recently acquired subsidiary company. The subsidiary company is engaged in researching solutions to carbon emissions and global warming, and has developed a high carbon absorbing variety of plant that can be grown in warm, shallow sea water. The plant would then be harvested into carbon-neutral bio-fuel. This fuel, if widely used, is expected to lower carbon production levels.

Currently there is a lot of interest among the world's governments in finding solutions to climate change. Mezza Co's directors feel that this venture could enhance its reputation and result in a rise in its share price. They believe that the company's expertise would be ideally suited to commercialising the product. On a personal level, they feel that the venture's success would enhance their generous remuneration package which includes share options. It is hoped that the resulting increase in the share price would enable the options to be exercised in the future.

Mezza Co has identified the coast of Maienar, a small country in Asia, as an ideal location, as it has a large area of warm, shallow waters. Mezza Co has been operating in Maienar for many years and as a result, has a well developed infrastructure to enable it to plant, monitor and harvest the crop. Mezza Co's directors have strong ties with senior government officials in Maienar and the country's politicians are keen to develop new industries, especially ones with a long-term future.

The area identified by Mezza Co is a rich fishing ground for local fishermen, who have been fishing there for many generations. However, the fishermen are poor and have little political influence. The general perception is that the fishermen contribute little to Maienar's economic development. The coastal area, although naturally beautiful, has not been well developed for tourism. It is thought that the high carbon absorbing plant, if grown on a commercial scale, may have a negative impact on fish stocks and other wildlife in the area. The resulting decline in fish stocks may make it impossible for the fishermen to continue with their traditional way of life.

Required:

(a) Discuss the key issues that the directors of Mezza Co should consider when making the decision about whether or not to commercialise the new product, and suggest how these issues may be mitigated or resolved. **(17 marks)**

BPP LEARNING MEDIA

(b)   The recently acquired subsidiary is currently 60% owned by Mezza Co. The shares were purchased, in one transaction, from the previous majority shareholder. $20 million was paid for 3 million shares. Mezza Co wishes to buyout the remaining shareholders.

Required

Using the European Takeover Directive, discuss the regulatory devices that could affect Mezza Co's purchase of the rest of the shares of the subsidiary.   **(8 marks)**

(Total = 25 marks)

8 Kengai Co (12/11, amended)   45 mins

The Chairman and the Chief Executive Officer (CEO) of Kengai Co, a listed mining company, are discussing whether or not the company should adopt a triple bottom line (TBL) reporting system in order to demonstrate Kengai Co's level of sustainable development. Kengai Co's competitors are increasingly adopting TBL reporting and the Chairman feels that it would be beneficial to follow suit. The CEO, on the other hand, feels that pursuing TBL reporting would be expensive and is not necessary.

Required:

(a)   Explain what TBL reporting involves and how it would help demonstrate Kengai Co's sustainable development. Support your explanation by including examples of proxies that can be used to indicate the impact of the factors that would be included in a TBL report.   **(8 marks)**

(b)   Discuss how producing a TBL report may help Kengai Co's management focus on improving the financial position of the company. Illustrate the discussion with examples where appropriate.   **(10 marks)**

(c)   Buranda is a large region with a rugged, beautiful coastline where rare birds have recently settled on undisturbed cliffs. However, today, many communities in Buranda suffer high unemployment. Government initiatives for regeneration through tourism have met with little success as the area has poor road networks, unsightly derelict buildings and dirty beaches. and has discovered substantial tin reserves in Buranda. With new technology, mining could be profitable, provide jobs and boost the economy. A number of interest and pressure groups have, however, been vocal in opposing the scheme including wildlife protection representatives, villagers worried about the potential increase in traffic congestion and noise, environmentalists, and anti-capitalism groups.

Required

Explain the conflicts between the main stakeholder groups in this scenario and discuss how the conflicts could be resolved.   **(7 marks)**

(Total = 25 marks)

ECONOMIC ENVIRONMENT FOR MULTINATIONALS

Questions 9 to 14 cover economic environment for multinationals, the subject of Part B of the BPP Study Text for Paper P4.

9 International trade

45 mins

Required

(a)   Discuss the reasons why governments may not adopt free trade policies.   **(7 marks)**

(b)   Analyse the economic benefits that countries could gain from forming a common market.   **(10 marks)**

(c)   Analyse the potential benefits of international trade to a business.   **(8 marks)**

(Total = 25 marks)

10 Global financial markets

45 mins

The globalisation of financial markets has facilitated the transfer of funds to emerging markets but it has contributed to financial instability.

(a)   Discuss the reasons for the existence of the 'global debt problem'. Explain briefly what is meant by financial contagion and how financial contagion might affect the global debt problem.   **(7 marks)**

(b)   Explain the main attempts that have been made to resolve the global debt problem and how governments might try to limit financial contagion.   **(8 marks)**

(c)   In April 2012 the credit rating of Italy was classified as BBB+ by Standard & Poor's, A– by Fitch and A3 by Moody's. At the same time Germany was rated as AAA by Fitch and S&P and Aaa by Moody's.

You are required to consider whether the Euro Government Bond market can be treated as homogenous so that there is no need to distinguish, from a credit perspective, between bonds issued by different members of the European Monetary Union.   **(5 marks)**

(d)   The following table shows the credit spreads for industrials in basis points

Rating	1 year	2 year	3 year	5 year	7 year	10 year	30 year
AAA	5	10	15	20	25	33	60
AA	15	25	30	35	44	52	71
A	35	44	55	60	65	73	90
BBB	60	75	100	105	112	122	143
BB	140	180	210	205	210	250	300
B	215	220	260	300	315	350	450
CCC	1,125	1,225	1,250	1,200	1,200	1,275	1,400

One Leaf Co, a BB rated company has 15-year bonds in issue. The current yield on equivalent government bonds is 2.8%. One Leaf Co is subject to corporate tax at a rate of 26%.

Calculate One Leaf Co's post-tax cost of debt for these bonds.   **(5 marks)**

(Total = 25 marks)

11 Boxless (SFM, 12/04, amended)

45 mins

(a) Briefly discuss possible benefits and drawbacks to a multinational company from using a holding company based in a tax haven. **(5 marks)**

(b) Boxless plc has subsidiaries in three overseas countries, Annovia, Cardenda and Sporoon. Corporate taxes for the three countries are shown below:

	Corporate income tax rate	Withholding tax on dividends	% of after tax income remitted to the UK
Annovia	40%	10%	70
Cardenda	25%	–	40
Sporoon	20%	5%	80

The UK corporate tax rate is 30%, and bilateral tax treaties exist between the UK and each of the three countries. Under the treaties, any corporate tax paid overseas on income remitted to the UK may be credited against UK tax liability. Boxless currently remits income from its overseas subsidiaries direct to the UK parent company.

The UK government currently only taxes income from multinational companies' overseas subsidiaries when such income is remitted to the UK. UK tax liability is based upon the grossed up dividend distributions to the UK (grossed up at the local tax rate and before deduction of any withholding tax).

The UK government is now considering taxing the gross income earned by overseas subsidiaries. If such gross income were to be taxed, credit against UK tax liability would be available for all corporate tax paid overseas.

Required

(i) Estimate the impact on the cash flows of Boxless if the UK government alters the tax rules as detailed above.

Assume that the taxable income in each of the subsidiaries is the equivalent of £100,000. **(7 marks)**

(ii) For each of the current and possible new tax rules, evaluate what benefit, if any, Boxless would experience if it were to transfer income from its overseas subsidiaries to the parent company via a tax haven holding company. Assume that the UK tax authorities would then treat all income from overseas subsidiaries as coming from a single source, the tax haven holding company. Comment upon your results. **(4 marks)**

(c) Explain the possible risks that a multinational may face with respect to taxes. **(4 marks)**

(d) Boxless is concerned that local management in the overseas countries may not operate in the best interests of the group. Discuss the agency issues that Boxless faces in regard to this problem. **(5 marks)**

(Total = 25 marks)

12 World Trade Organisation (SFM, 12/05, amended)

45 mins

XYZ Inc has recently extended the export of its goods to include certain developing countries that are not currently members of the World Trade Organisation. However, the governments of these countries are anxious to protect domestic industries from foreign competition and have policies in place to restrict the volume of imports. XYZ is concerned that such restrictions will have an adverse effect on its export trade with these countries.

(a) Provide examples of how countries might impose protectionist measures to control the volume of imports. **(5 marks)**

(b) Briefly state the arguments in favour of and against protectionism. **(5 marks)**

XYZ also has foreign direct investment in another developing country whose government until recently had protectionist measures in place. However, the country has just joined the World Trade Organisation (WTO) and XYZ is concerned about the effects that this membership might have on its operations' current protected status.

(c)   Discuss the role and main objectives of the WTO and its potential effect on protectionist measures.

(6 marks)

(d)   Briefly discuss the possible effects of the developing country's membership of the WTO on XYZ's foreign direct investment activities.

(4 marks)

XYZ uses transfer pricing between its foreign direct investment and the parent company and is thinking about manipulating the transfer prices to remit more funds back to XYZ.

(e)   Outline the mechanisms which prevent transfer price manipulation by multinationals.

(5 marks)

(Total = 25 marks)

13 Pharmaceutical Co (6/09, amended)   45 mins

You have been appointed as deputy Chief Financial Officer to a large multinational pharmaceutical company with trading interests in 24 countries in sub-Saharan Africa, South America and the Indian sub-continent. Your company also has important trading links with the United States, Malaysia and Singapore. There have been a number of issues arising in the previous six months which have impacted upon the company's business interests.

(i)   Following an investigation you discover that commissions were paid to a senior official in one country to ensure that the local drug licensing agency concerned facilitated the acceptance of one of your principal revenue earning drugs for use within its national health service.

(ii)   You have discovered that an agent of your firm, aware that the licensing agreement might be forthcoming, purchased several call option contracts on your company's equity.

(iii)   A senior member of the firm's treasury team has been taking substantial positions in currency futures in order to protect the risk of loss on the translation of dollar assets into the domestic currency. Over the last 12 months significant profits have been made but the trades do not appear to have been properly authorised. You discover that a long position in 50, $250,000 contracts is currently held but over the last four weeks the dollar has depreciated by 10% and all the signs are that it will depreciate considerably more over the next two months.

(iv)   One drug company has managed to copy an innovative drug that you have just released for the treatment of various forms of skin cancer. You have patent protection in the country concerned but your company has not been able to initiate proceedings through the local courts. Contacts with the trade officials at your embassy in the country concerned suggest that the government has made sure that the proceedings have not been allowed to proceed.

(v)   There are a number of overseas interests, which are operated under local control, that have been found to be paying local staff significantly less than other similar multinational companies operating in the same country. There is no minimum wage legislation in the countries concerned.

The company's chief financial officer has asked you to look into these issues and, with respect to (iv), any World Trade Organisation (WTO) agreements that might be relevant, and to advise her on how the company should proceed in each case.

Required:

Prepare a memorandum advising the Chief Financial Officer on the issues involved and recommending how she should, in each case and in the circumstances, proceed.

(25 marks)

14 PMU (12/10, amended)   45 mins

Prospice Mentis University (PMU) is a prestigious private institution and a member of the Holly League, which is made up of universities based in Rosinante and renowned worldwide as being of the highest quality. Universities in Rosinante have benefited particularly from students coming from Kantaka, and PMU has been no exception. However, PMU has recognised that Kantaka has a large population of able students who cannot afford to study overseas. Therefore it wants to investigate how it can offer some of its most popular degree programmes in

BPP
LEARNING MEDIA

Kantaka, where students will be able to study at a significantly lower cost. It is considering whether to enter into a joint venture with a local institution or to independently set up its own university site in Kantaka.

Offering courses overseas would be a first from a Holly League institution and indeed from any academic institution based in Rosinante. However, there have been less renowned academic institutions from other countries which have formed joint ventures with small private institutions in Kantaka to deliver degree programmes. These have been of low quality and are not held in high regard by the population or the government of Kantaka.

In Kantaka, government run universities and a handful of large private academic institutions, none of which have entered into joint ventures, are held in high regard. However, the demand for places in these institutions far outstrips the supply of places and many students are forced to go to the smaller private institutions or to study overseas if they can afford it.

After an initial investigation the following points have come to light:

1. The Kantaka government is keen to attract foreign direct investment (FDI) and offer tax concessions to businesses which bring investment funds into the country and enhance the local business environment. However at present the Kantaka government places restrictions on the profits that can be remitted to foreign companies who set up subsidiaries in the country. There are no restrictions on profits remitted to a foreign company that has established a joint venture with a local company. It is also likely that PMU would need to borrow a substantial amount of money if it were to set up independently. The investment funds required would be considerably smaller if it went into a joint venture.

2. Given the past experiences of poor quality education offered by joint ventures between small local private institutions and overseas institutions, the Kantaka government has been reluctant to approve degrees from such institutions. Also the government has not allowed graduates from these institutions to work in national or local government, or in nationalised organisations.

3. Over the past two years the Kantaka currency has depreciated against other currencies, but economic commentators believe that this may not continue for much longer.

4. A large proportion of PMU's academic success is due to innovative teaching and learning methods, and high quality research. The teaching and learning methods used in Kantaka's educational institutions are very different. Apart from the larger private and government run universities, little academic research is undertaken elsewhere in Kantaka's education sector.

Required

(a) Discuss the benefits and disadvantages of PMU entering into a joint venture instead of setting up independently in Kantaka. As part of your discussion, consider how the disadvantages can be mitigated and the additional information PMU needs in order to make its decision. **(20 marks)**

(b) Assuming that there are limits on funds that can be repatriated from Kantaka, briefly discuss the steps PMU could take to get around this, if it setup a subsidiary in Kantaka. **(5 marks)**

(Total = 25 marks)

ADVANCED INVESTMENT APPRAISAL

Questions 15 to 37 cover advanced investment appraisal, the subject of Part C of the BPP Study Text for Paper P4.

15 Jonas Chemical Systems

45 mins

The board of directors of Jonas Chemical Systems Limited has used payback for many years as an initial selection tool to identify projects for subsequent and more detailed analysis by its financial investment team. The firm's capital projects are characterised by relatively long investment periods and even longer recovery phases. Unfortunately, for a variety of reasons, the cash flows towards the end of each project tend to be very low or indeed sometimes negative. As the company's new chief financial officer (CFO), you are concerned about the use of payback in this context and would favour a more thorough pre-evaluation of each capital investment proposal before it is submitted for detailed planning and approval. You recognise that many board members like the provision of a payback figure as this, they argue, gives them a clear idea as to when the project can be expected to recover its initial capital investment.

All capital projects must be submitted to the board for initial approval before the financial investment team begins its detailed review. At the initial stage the board sees the project's summarised cash flows, a supporting business case and an assessment of the project payback and accounting rate of return.

A recent capital investment proposal, which has passed to the implementation stage after much discussion at board level, had summarised cash flows and other information as follows:

Distillation Plant at the Gulf Refining Centre

	Investment phase		Recovery phase	
	Cash flow (tax adjusted, nominal)	Cumulative cash flow	Cash flow (tax adjusted, nominal)	Cumulative cash flow
	$m	$m	$m	$m
1 January 20X6	(9.50)	(9.50)		
31 December 20X6	(5.75)	(15.25)		
31 December 20X7	(3.00)	(18.25)		
31 December 20X8			4.5	(13.75)
31 December 20X9			6.40	(7.35)
31 December 20Y0			7.25	(0.10)
31 December 20Y1			6.50	6.40
31 December 20Y2			5.50	11.90
31 December 20Y3			4.00	15.90
31 December 20Y4			(2.00)	13.90
31 December 20Y5			(5.00)	8.90

Cost of capital	8%
Expected net present value ($m)	1.964
Net present value volatility ($m)	1.02
Internal rate of return	11.1%
Payback (years)	5.015

The normal financial rules are that a project should only be considered if it has a payback period of less than five years. In this case the project was passed to detail review by the financial investment team who, on your instruction, have undertaken a financial simulation of the project's net present value to generate the expected value and volatility as shown above. The board minute of the discussion relating to the project's preliminary approval was as follows:

31 May 20X5 Agenda Item 6

New capital projects – preliminary approvals

Outline consideration was given to the construction of a new distillation facility at the Gulf Refining Centre which is regarded as a key strategic component of the company's manufacturing capability. The cash flow projections had been prepared in accordance with existing guidelines and there was some uncertainty with respect to capital build

BPP
LEARNING MEDIA

and future profitability. Mrs Chua (chief financial officer) had given approval for the project to come to the board given its strategic importance and the closeness of the payback estimate to the company's barrier for long term capital investment of five years. Mr Lazar (non-executive director) suggested that they would need more information about the impact of risk upon the project's outcome before giving final approval. Mr Bright (operations director) agreed but asked why the board needed to consider capital proposals twice. The board was of the view that what was needed was clearer information about each proposal and the risks to which they were exposed. The chair requested the CFO to provide a review of the company's capital approval procedures to include better assessment of the firm's financial exposure. The revised guidelines should include procedures for both the preliminary and final approval stages. Approved (Action CFO to report)

Required

(a)   Recommend procedures for the assessment of capital investment projects, make proposals about the involvement of the board at a preliminary stage and the information that should be provided to inform their decision. You should also provide an assessment of the alternative appraisal methods.   **(8 marks)**

(b)   Using the appraisal methods you have recommended in (a), prepare a paper outlining the case for the acceptance of the project to build a distillation facility at the Gulf plant with an assessment of the company's likely value at risk. You are not required to undertake an assessment of the impact of the project upon the firm's financial accounts.   **(10 marks)**

(c)   Jonas Chemical Systems is looking into the possibility of setting up distillation plants in countries where government support is available for large investment projects.

Required

Discuss why the proposed methods will not give an accurate appraisal of these types of project. Recommend a method to be used and evaluate the benefits and drawbacks of this method.   **(7 marks)**

(Total = 25 marks)

16 CD   45 mins

CD is a furniture manufacturer based in the UK. It manufactures a limited range of furniture products to a very high quality and sells to a small number of retail outlets worldwide.

At a recent meeting with one of its major customers it became clear that the market is changing and the final consumer of CD's products is now more interested in variety and choice rather than exclusivity and exceptional quality.

CD is therefore reviewing two mutually exclusive alternatives to apply to a selection of its products:

Alternative 1

To continue to manufacture, but expand its product range and reduce its quality. The net present value (NPV), internal rate of return (IRR) and modified internal rate of return (MIRR) for this alternative have already been calculated as follows:

NPV	=	£1.45 million using a nominal discount rate of 9%		
IRR	=	10.5%	MIRR =	Approximately 13.2%
Payback	=	2.6 years	Discounted payback =	3.05 years

Alternative 2

To import furniture carcasses in 'flat packs' from the USA. The imports would be in a variety of types of wood and unvarnished. CD would buy in bulk from its US suppliers, assemble and varnish the furniture and re-sell, mainly to existing customers. An initial investigation into potential sources of supply and costs of transportation has already been carried out by a consultancy entity at a cost of £75,000. CD's Finance Director has provided estimates of net sterling and US$ cash flows for this alternative. These net cash flows, in **real** terms, are shown below.

Year	0	1	2	3
US$m	(25.00)	2.60	3.80	4.10
£m	0	3.70	4.20	4.60

The following information is relevant:

- CD evaluates all its investments using nominal sterling cash flows and a nominal discount rate. All non-UK customers are invoiced in US$. US$ nominal cash flows are converted to sterling at the forward rate and discounted at the UK nominal rate.

- For the purposes of evaluation, assume the entity has a three year time horizon for investment appraisals.

- Based on recent economic forecasts, inflation rates in the US are expected to be constant at 4% per annum. UK inflation rates are expected to be 3% per annum. The current exchange rate is £1 = US$1.6.

Note: Ignore taxation.

Required

Assume you are the Financial Manager of CD.

(a) Evaluate alternative 2, using net present value, discounted payback, internal rate of return and the (approximate) modified internal rate of return. **(11 marks)**

(b) Calculate the project duration for alternative 2 and discuss the significance of your results if you are told that the duration for alternative one is 3.2 years. **(4 marks)**

(c) Evaluate the two alternatives and recommend which alternative the entity should choose. Include in your answer a discussion about what other criteria should be considered before a final decision is taken.

(10 marks)

(Total = 25 marks)

17 Slow Fashions Co (6/09, amended)   45 mins

Slow Fashions Ltd is considering the following series of investments for the current financial year 20X9:

Project bid proposals ($'000) for immediate investment with the first cash return assumed to follow in 12 months and at annual intervals thereafter.

Project	Now	20Y0	20Y1	20Y2	20Y3	20Y4	20Y5	NPV	IRR
P0801	−620	280	400	120				55	16%
P0802	−640	80	120	200	210	420	−30	69	13%
P0803	−240	120	120	60	10			20	15%
P0804	−1000	300	500	250	290			72	13%
P0805	−120	25	55	75	21			19	17%
P0806	−400	245	250					29	15%

There is no real option to delay any of these projects. All except project P0801, can be scaled down but not scaled up. P0801 is a potential fixed three-year contract to supply a supermarket chain and cannot be varied. The company has a limited capital budget of $1.2 million and is concerned about the best way to allocate its capital to the projects listed. The company has a current cost of finance of 10% but it would take a year to establish further funding at that rate. Further funding for a short period could be arranged at a higher rate.

Required:

(a) Draft a capital investment plan with full supporting calculations justifying those projects which should be adopted giving:
   (i)   The priorities for investment,
   (ii)   The net present value and internal rate of return of the plan; and
   (iii)   The net present value per dollar invested on the plan. **(14 marks)**

(b) Estimate and advise upon the maximum interest rate which the company should be prepared to pay to finance investment in all of the remaining projects available to it. **(8 marks)**

(c) Assume that there is a real option to delay projects P0802 and P0804 for a further year, when capital will not be restricted. Explain, without further calculations, how this would change the answer to part (a). **(3 marks)**

(Total = 25 marks)

18 Your business (6/09, amended)

45 mins

You have been conducting a detailed review of an investment project proposed by one of the divisions of your business. Your review has two aims: first to correct the proposal for any errors of principle and second, to recommend a financial measure to replace payback as one of the criteria for acceptability when a project is presented to the company's board of directors for approval. The company's current weighted average cost of capital is 10% per annum.

The initial capital investment is for $150 million followed by $50 million one year later. The post tax cash flows, for this project, in $million, including the estimated tax benefit from capital allowances for tax purposes, are as follows:

Year	0	1	2	3	4	5	6
Capital investment (plant and machinery):							
First phase	−127.50						
Second phase		−36.88					
Project post tax cash flow ($ millions)			44.00	68.00	60.00	35.00	20.00

Company tax is charged at 30% and is paid/recovered in the year in which the liability is incurred. The company has sufficient profits elsewhere to recover capital allowances on this project, in full, in the year they are incurred. All the capital investment is eligible for a first year allowance for tax purposes of 50% followed by a writing down allowance of 25% per annum on a reducing balance basis.

You notice the following points when conducting your review:

1. An interest charge of 8% per annum on a proposed $50 million loan has been included in the project's post tax cash flow before tax has been calculated.

2. Depreciation for the use of company shared assets of $4 million per annum has been charged in calculating the project post tax cash flow.

3. Activity based allocations of company indirect costs of $8 million have been included in the project's post tax cash flow. However, additional corporate infrastructure costs of $4 million per annum have been ignored which you discover would only be incurred if the project proceeds.

4. It is expected that the capital equipment will be written off and disposed of at the end of year six. The proceeds of the sale of the capital equipment are expected to be $7 million which have been included in the forecast of the project's post tax cash flow. You also notice that an estimate for site clearance of $5 million has not been included nor any tax saving recognised on the unclaimed writing down allowance on the disposal of the capital equipment.

Required:

(a) Prepare a corrected project evaluation using the net present value technique supported by a separate assessment of the sensitivity of the project to a $1million change in the initial capital expenditure.

(14 marks)

(b) Estimate the discounted payback period and the duration for this project commenting on the relative advantages and disadvantages of each method. **(5 marks)**

(c) Recommend whether this project is acceptable and also which techniques the board should consider when reviewing capital investment projects in future. **(6 marks)**

(Total = 25 marks)

19 Kodiak Company (12/09, amended)

45 mins

Kodiak Company is a small software design business established four years ago. The company is owned by three directors who have relied upon external accounting services in the past. The company has grown quickly and the directors have appointed you as a financial consultant to advise on the value of the business under their ownership.

The directors have limited liability and the bank loan is secured against the general assets of the business. The directors have no outstanding guarantees on the company's debt.

The company's latest income statement and the extracted balances from the latest statement of financial position are as follows:

Income Statement	$'000	Financial Position	$000
Revenue	5,000	Opening non-current assets	1,200
Cost of Sales	3,000	Additions	66
Gross profit	2,000	Non-current assets (gross)	1,266
Other operating costs	1,877	Accumulated depreciation	367
Operating profit	123	Net book value	899
Interest on loan	74	Net current assets	270
Profit before tax	49	Loan	(990)
Income tax expense	15	Net Assets Employed	179
Profit for the period	34		

During the current year:

(1)   Depreciation is charged at 10% per annum on the year end non-current asset balance before accumulated depreciation, and is included in other operating costs in the income statement.

(2)   The investment in net working capital is expected to increase in line with the growth in gross profit.

(3)   Other operating costs consisted of:

	$000
Variable component at 15% of sales	750
Fixed costs	1,000
Depreciation on non-current assets	127

(4)   Revenue and variable costs are projected to grow at 9% per annum and fixed costs are projected to grow at 6% per annum.

(5)   The company pays interest on its outstanding loan of 7·5% per annum and incurs tax on its profits at 30%, payable in the following year. The company does not pay dividends.

(6)   The net current assets reported in the statement of financial position contain $50,000 of cash.

One of your first tasks is to prepare for the directors a forward cash flow projection for three years and to value the firm on the basis of its expected free cash flow to equity. In discussion with them you note the following:

−   The company will not dispose of any of its non-current assets but will increase its investment in new non-current assets by 20% per annum. The company's depreciation policy matches the currently available tax write off for capital allowances. This straight-line write off policy is not likely to change.

−   The directors will not take a dividend for the next three years but will then review the position taking into account the company's sustainable cash flow at that time.

−   The level of the loan will be maintained at $990,000 and, on the basis of the forward yield curve, interest rates are not expected to change.

−   The directors have set a target rate of return on their equity of 10% per annum which they believe fairly represents the opportunity cost of their invested funds.

Required

(a)   Prepare a three-year cash flow forecast for the business on the basis described above highlighting the free cash flow to equity in each year.   **(12 marks)**

(b)   Estimate the value of the business based upon the expected free cash flow to equity and a terminal value based upon a sustainable growth rate of 3% per annum thereafter.   **(6 marks)**

(c)   Advise the directors on the assumptions and the uncertainties within your valuation.   **(7 marks)**

(Total = 25 marks)

BPP
LEARNING MEDIA

20 Tisa Co (6/12, amended)   45 mins

Tisa Co is considering an opportunity to produce an innovative component which, when fitted into motor vehicle engines, will enable them to utilise fuel more efficiently. The component can be manufactured using either process Omega or process Zeta. Although this is an entirely new line of business for Tisa Co, it is of the opinion that developing either process over a period of four years and then selling the productions rights at the end of four years to another company may prove lucrative.

The annual after-tax cash flows for each process are as follows:

Process Omega

Year	0	1	2	3	4
After-tax cash flows ($000)	(3,800)	1,220	1,153	1,386	3,829

Process Zeta

Year	0	1	2	3	4
After-tax cash flows ($000)	(3,800)	643	546	1,055	5,990

Tisa Co has 10 million 50c shares trading at 180c each. Its loans have a current value of $3.6 million and an average after-tax cost of debt of 4.50%. Tisa Co's capital structure is unlikely to change significantly following the investment in either process.

Elfu Co manufactures electronic parts for cars including the production of a component similar to the one being considered by Tisa Co. Elfu Co's equity beta is 1.40, and it is estimated that the equivalent equity beta for its other activities, excluding the component production, is 1.25. Elfu Co has 400 million 25c shares in issue trading at 120c each. Its debt finance consists of variable rate loans redeemable in seven years. The loans paying interest at base rate plus 120 basis points have a current value of $96 million. It can be assumed that 80% of Elfu Co's debt finance and 75% of Elfu Co's equity finance can be attributed to other activities excluding the component production.

Both companies pay annual corporation tax at a rate of 25%. The current base rate is 3.5% and the market risk premium is estimated at 5.8%.

Required:

(a)   Provide a reasoned estimate of the cost of capital that Tisa Co should use to calculate the net present value of the two processes. Include all relevant calculations.   **(8 marks)**

(b)   Calculate the internal rate of return (IRR) and the modified internal rate of return (MIRR) for Process Omega. Given that the IRR and MIRR of Process Zeta are 26.6% and 23.3% respectively, recommend which process, if any, Tisa Co should proceed with and explain your recommendation.   **(8 marks)**

(c)   Elfu Co has estimated an annual standard deviation of $800,000 on one of its other projects, based on a normal distribution of returns. The average annual return on this project is $2,200,000.

Required:

(i)   Estimate the project's Value at Risk (VAR) at a 99% confidence level for one year and over the project's life of five years. Explain what is meant by the answers obtained.   **(4 marks)**

(ii)   Apart from the use of VAR, briefly explain methods that Elfu Co can use to deal with risk and uncertainty in investment appraisal and their drawbacks.   **(5 marks)**

(Total = 25 marks)

21 GDW Co   45 mins

GDW Co is a listed group which operates a number of manufacturing facilities.

GDW Co has $2,450 million funds available for capital investment in new product lines in the current year. Most products have a very limited life cycle. Four possible projects have been identified, each of which can be started without delay.

Initial calculations for these projects are shown below:

Project	Initial investment ($ million)	Net annual cash inflows ($ million)	Project term (years)	PV of cash flows ($ million)	NPV ($ million)
A	350	529.2	1	472.5	122.5
B	525	288.1	4	875.0	350.0
C	1,050	849.1	2	1,435.0	385.0
D	1,225	434.0	6	1,785.0	560.0

Notes:

1. The projects are non-divisible and each project can only be undertaken once in each period, although Projects B, C and D can be undertaken again in subsequent periods.
2. Apart from the initial investment, annual cash flows are assumed to arise at the end of the year.
3. A discount rate of 12% has been used throughout.
4. Ignore taxation.

Required

(a) (i) Prioritise the projects according to each of the following measures:

- Net present value (NPV)
- Profitability index (PI)
- Payback (undiscounted) **(5 marks)**

(ii) Explain the strengths and weaknesses of each of the prioritisation methods used in (a)(i) above as the basis for making investment decisions in the context of capital rationing for non-divisible projects. **(9 marks)**

(b) (i) Explain how the optimal combination of projects would need to be reassessed under EACH of the following circumstances:

- 'Soft' rather than 'hard' single period capital rationing applies.
- The same level of capital rationing and range of projects is expected in the following year. **(8 marks)**

(ii) Formulate the constraints for a linear programming problem covering three years where the available funds decrease by 10% each year. **(3 marks)**

(Total = 25 marks)

22 Preparation question - Cathlynn 27 mins

(a) The current share price of Cathlynn plc is £3.50. Using the Black-Scholes model, estimate the value of a European call option on the shares of the company that has an exercise price of £3.30 and 3 months to run before it expires. The risk free rate of interest is 8% and the variance of the rate of return on the share has been 12%.

Note. The Black-Scholes formula shows call price for a European option P_c where

$$P_c = P_s N(d_1) - Xe^{-rT} N(d_2)$$

Where $N(d)$ = cumulative distribution function

$$d_1 = \frac{\ln(P_s/X) + rT}{\sigma\sqrt{T}} + 0.5\sigma\sqrt{T}$$

$$d_2 = d_1 - \sigma\sqrt{T}$$

P_s = share price

e = the exponential constant 2.7183

BPP LEARNING MEDIA

X = exercise price of option

r = annual (continuously compounded) risk free rate of return

T = time of expiry of option in years

σ = share price volatility, the standard deviation of the rate of return on shares

$N(d_x)$ = delta, the probability that a deviation of less than d_x will occur in a normal distribution with a mean of zero and a standard deviation of one

ln = natural log

Normal distribution tables are in the appendix to this kit. **(10 marks)**

(b) Discuss the main limitations of the Black-Scholes model. **(5 marks)**

(Total = 15 marks)

23 MMC (6/11, amended)   45 mins

MesmerMagic Co (MMC) is considering whether to undertake the development of a new computer game based on an adventure film due to be released in 22 months. It is expected that the game will be available to buy two months after the film's release, by which time it will be possible to judge the popularity of the film with a high degree of certainty. However, at present, there is considerable uncertainty about whether the film, and therefore the game, is likely to be successful. Although MMC would pay for the exclusive rights to develop and sell the game now, the directors are of the opinion that they should delay the decision to produce and market the game until the film has been released and the game is available for sale.

MMC has forecast the following end of year cash flows for the four-year sales period of the game.

Year	1	2	3	4
Cash flows ($ million)	25	18	10	5

MMC will spend $7 million at the start of each of the next two years to develop the game, the gaming platform, and to pay for the exclusive rights to develop and sell the game. Following this, the company will require $35 million for production, distribution and marketing costs at the start of the four-year sales period of the game.

It can be assumed that all the costs and revenues include inflation. The relevant cost of capital for this project is 11% and the risk free rate is 3.5%. MMC has estimated the likely volatility of the cash flows at a standard deviation of 30%.

Required:

(a) Estimate the financial impact of the directors' decision to delay the production and marketing of the game. The Black-Scholes Option Pricing model may be used, where appropriate. All relevant calculations should be shown. **(12 marks)**

(b) Briefly discuss the implications of the answer obtained in part (a) above. **(7 marks)**

(c) Discuss how a decrease in the value of each of the determinants of the option price in the Black-Scholes option-pricing model for European options is likely to change the price of a call option. **(6 marks)**

(Total = 25 marks)

24 Marengo Co (12/10, amended)   45 mins

The treasury division of Marengo Co, a large quoted company, holds equity investments in various companies around the world. One of the investments is in Arion Co, in which Marengo holds 200,000 shares, which is around 2% of the total number of Arion Co's shares traded on the stock market. Over the past year, due to the general strength in the equity markets following optimistic predictions of the performance of world economies, Marengo's investments have performed well. However, there is some concern that the share price of Arion Co may fall in the coming two months due to uncertainty in its markets. It is expected that any fall in share prices will be reversed following this period of uncertainty.

The treasury division managers in Marengo, Wenyu, Lola, Sam have met with CEO Edward, to discuss what to do with the investment in Arion Co and they each made a different suggestion as follows:

1.   Wenyu was of the opinion that Marengo's shareholders would benefit most if no action were taken. He argued that the courses of action proposed by Lola and Sam, below, would result in extra costs and possibly increase the risk to Marengo Co.

2.   Lola proposed that Arion Co's shares should be sold in order to eliminate the risk of a fall in the share price.

3.   Sam suggested that the investment should be hedged using an appropriate derivative product.

4.   Edward does not understand why Marengo Co holds equity investments at all. He believes all shares should be sold.

Although no exchange-traded derivative products exist on Arion Co's shares, a bank has offered over-the-counter (OTC) option contracts at an exercise price of 350 cents per share in a contract size of 1,000 shares each, for the appropriate time period. Arion Co's current share price is 340 cents per share, although the volatility of the share prices could be as high as 40%.

It can be assumed that Arion Co will not pay any dividends in the coming few months and that the appropriate inter-bank lending rate will be 4% over that period.

Required

(a)   Estimate the number of OTC put option contracts that Marengo Co will need to hedge against any adverse movement in Arion Co's share price. Provide a brief explanation of your answer.

Note: You may assume that the delta of a put option is equivalent to N(–d1)   **(7 marks)**

(b)   Discuss possible reasons for the suggestions made by each of the three managers and the CEO. **(18 marks)**

(Total = 25 marks)

25 Digunder (12/07, amended)   45 mins

Digunder, a property development company, has gained planning permission for the development of a housing complex at Newtown which will be developed over a three year period. The resulting property sales less building costs have an expected net present value of $4 million at a cost of capital of 10% per annum. Digunder has an option to acquire the land in Newtown, at an agreed price of $24 million, which must be exercised within the next two years. Immediate building of the housing complex would be risky as the project has a volatility attaching to its net present value of 25%. One source of risk is the potential for development of Newtown as a regional commercial centre for the large number of professional firms leaving the capital, Bigcity, because of high rents and local business taxes. Within the next two years, an announcement by the government will be made about the development of transport links into Newtown from outlying districts including the area where Digunder hold the land option concerned. The risk free rate of interest is 5% per annum.

Required

(a)   Estimate the value of the option to delay the start of the project for two years using the Black and Scholes option pricing model and comment upon your findings. Assume that the government will make its announcement about the potential transport link at the end of the two-year period.   **(12 marks)**

(b)   On the basis of your valuation of the option to delay, estimate the overall value of the project, giving a concise rationale for the valuation method you have used.   **(3 marks)**

(c)   Describe the limitations of the valuation method you used in (a) above and describe how you would value the option if the government were to make the announcement at ANY time over the next two years.

(6 marks)

(d)   Briefly explain TWO other types of real option that may be present, relating to the Newtown housing development.   **(4 marks)**

(Total = 25 marks)

BPP
LEARNING MEDIA

26 AVT (SFM, 12/01, amended)   45 mins

AVT Inc is considering the introduction of an executive share option scheme.

The scheme would be offered to all middle managers of the company. It would replace the existing scheme of performance bonuses linked to the post-tax earnings per share of the company. Such bonuses in the last year ranged between $5,000 and $7,000. If the option scheme is introduced, new options are expected to be offered to the managers each year.

It is proposed for the first year that all middle managers are offered options to purchase 5,000 shares at a price of 500 cents per share after the options have been held for one year. Assume that the tax authorities allow the exercise of such options after they have been held for one year. If the options are not exercised at that time, they will lapse.

The company's shares have just become ex-div and have a current price of 610 cents. The dividend paid was 25 cents per share, a level that has remained constant for the last three years. Assume that dividends are only paid annually. The company's share price has experienced a standard deviation of 38% during the last year. The short-term risk free interest rate is 6% per annum.

Required

(a) (i) Discuss the relative merits for the company of the existing bonus scheme and the proposed share option scheme.   **(7 marks)**

(ii) Evaluate whether or not the proposed share option scheme is likely to be attractive to middle managers of AVT Inc.   **(11 marks)**

(iii) When told of the scheme one manager stated that he would rather receive put options than call options, as they would be more valuable to him.

(1) Discuss whether or not AVT should agree to offer him put options.   **(3 marks)**

(2) Calculate whether or not he is correct in his statement that put options would be more valuable to him.   **(4 marks)**

                                                                        (Total = 25 marks)

27 Alaska Salvage Co (12/09, amended)   45 mins

Alaska Salvage is in discussion with potential lenders about financing an ambitious five-year project searching for lost gold in the central Atlantic. The company has had great success in the past with its various salvage operations and is now quoted on the London Alternative Investment Market. The company is currently financed by 120,000 equity shares trading at $85 per share. It needs to borrow $1.6 million and wants to borrow at a fixed rate. Alaska Salvage is concerned about the level of the fixed rates being suggested by the lenders, which are typically 9%. After lengthy discussions the lenders are prepared to offer finance against a mezzanine issue of fixed rate five-year notes with warrants attached. Each $10,000 note, repayable at par, would carry a warrant for 100 equity shares at an exercise price of $90 per share. The estimated volatility of the returns on the company's equity is 20% and the risk free rate of interest is 5%.

You may assume that the issue of these loan notes will not influence the current value of the firm's equity. The issue will be made at par. The company does not pay dividends to its equity investors.

Alternatively Alaska Salvage is interested in an interest rate swap and has found a willing counterparty, which can borrow at a variable rate of LIBOR + 2% or a fixed rate of 6.5%. The counterparty wants to borrow at a variable rate. Alaska Salvage could borrow at a variable rate of LIBOR + 3%. Bank fees for the swap would be 0.25% each.

Required

(a)   Estimate, using Black-Scholes Option Pricing Model as appropriate, the current value of each warrant to the lender noting the assumptions that you have made in your valuation.

(10 marks)

(b)   Estimate the coupon rate that would be required by the lenders if they wanted a 13% rate of return on their investment.

(4 marks)

(c)   Discuss the advantages and disadvantages of issuing mezzanine debt in the situation outlined in the case.

(6 marks)

(d)   Illustrate how the interest swap could be structured to leave both parties better off than before the swap

(5 marks)

(Total = 25 marks)

28 Strayer (SFM, 6/02, amended)   45 mins

The managers of Strayer Inc are investigating a potential $25 million investment. The investment would be a diversification away from existing mainstream activities of stationery retail and into the printing industry. $6 million of the investment would be financed by internal funds, $10 million by a rights issue and $9 million by long-term loans. The investment is expected to generate pre-tax net cash flows of approximately $5 million per year, for a period of ten years. The residual value at the end of year ten is forecast to be $5 million after tax. As the investment is in an area that the government wishes to develop, a subsidised loan of $4 million out of the total $9 million is available. This will cost 2% below the company's normal cost of long-term debt finance, which is 8%.

Strayer's equity beta is 0.85, and its financial gearing is 60% equity, 40% debt by market value. The average equity beta in the printing industry is 1.2, and average gearing 50% equity, 50% debt by market value.

The risk free rate is 5.5% per annum and the market return 12% per annum. Issue costs are estimated to be 1% for debt financing (excluding the subsidised loan), and 4% for equity financing. The corporate tax rate is 30%.

Required

(a)   Estimate the Adjusted Present Value (APV) of the proposed investment.

(14 marks)

(b)   Discuss the circumstances under which APV might be a better method of evaluating a capital investment than Net Present Value (NPV).

(6 marks)

(c)   Discuss the dangers to Strayer Inc of this diversification.

(5 marks)

(Total = 25 marks)

29 Neptune (6/08, amended)   45 mins

Neptune is a listed company in the telecommunications business. You are a senior financial management advisor employed by the company to review its capital investment appraisal procedures and to provide advice on the acceptability of a significant new capital project – the Galileo.

The project is a domestic project entailing immediate capital expenditure of $800 million at 1 July 20X8 and with projected revenues over five years as follows:

Year ended	30 June 20X9	30 June 20Y0	30 June 20Y1	30 June 20Y2	30 June 20Y3
Revenue ($ million)	680.00	900.00	900.00	750.00	320.00

Direct costs are 60% of revenues and indirect, activity based costs are $140 million for the first year of operations, growing at 5% per annum over the life of the project. In the first two years of operations, acceptance of this project will mean that other work making a net contribution before indirect costs of $150 million for each of the first two years will not be able to proceed. The capital expenditure of $800 million is to be paid immediately and the equipment will have a residual value after five years' operation of $40 million. The company depreciates plant and equipment on a straight-line basis and, in this case, the annual charge will be allocated to the project as a further indirect charge. Preconstruction design and contracting costs incurred over the previous three years total $50 million and will be charged to the project in the first year of operation.

BPP LEARNING MEDIA

The company pays tax at 30% on its taxable profits and can claim a 50% first year allowance on qualifying capital expenditure followed by a writing down allowance of 40% applied on a reducing balance basis. Given the timing of the company's tax payments, tax credits and charges will be paid or received twelve months after they arise. The company has sufficient other profits to absorb any capital allowances derived from this project.

The company currently has $7,500 million of equity and $2,500 million of debt in issue quoted at current market values. The current cost of its debt finance is $LIBOR plus 180 basis points. $LIBOR is currently 5·40%, which is 40 basis points above the one month Treasury bill rate. The equity risk premium is 3·5% and the company's beta is 1·40. The company wishes to raise the additional finance for this project by a new bond issue. Its advisors do not believe that this will alter the company's bond rating. The new issue will incur transaction costs of 2% of the issue value at the date of issue.

Required

(a) Estimate the adjusted present value of the project resulting from the new investment and from the refinancing proposal and justify the use of this technique. **(14 marks)**

(b) Estimate the modified internal rate of return generated by the project cash flows, excluding the effects of refinancing. **(6 marks)**

(c) Briefly discuss the advantages and disadvantages of using MIRR to evaluate the project **(5 marks)**

(Total = 25 marks)

30 Airline Business (12/07, amended)   45 mins

Your company, which is in the airline business, is considering raising new capital of $400 million in the bond market for the acquisition of new aircraft. The debt would have a term to maturity of four years. The market capitalisation of the company's equity is $1.2 billion and it has a 25% market gearing ratio (market value of debt to total market value of the company). This new issue would be ranked for payment, in the event of default, equally with the company's other long-term debt and the latest credit risk assessment places the company at AA. Interest would be paid to holders annually. The company's current debt carries an average coupon of 4% and has three years to maturity. The company's effective rate of tax is 30%.

The current yield curve suggests that, at three years, government treasuries yield 3.5% and at four years they yield 5.1%. The current credit risk spread is estimated to be 50 basis points at AA. If the issue proceeds, the company's investment bankers suggest that a 90 basis point spread will need to be offered to guarantee take up by its institutional clients.

Required

(a) Advise on the coupon rate that should be applied to the new debt issue to ensure that it is fully subscribed. **(4 marks)**

(b) Estimate the current and revised market valuation of the company's debt and the increase in the company's effective cost of debt capital. **(8 marks)**

(c) Discuss the relative advantages and disadvantages of this mode of capital financing in the context of the company's stated financial objectives. **(8 marks)**

(d) Briefly consider company-specific factors that will be used in the credit rating assessment to classify the company as AA. **(5 marks)**

(Total = 25 marks)

31 Fubuki (12/10)

45 mins

Fubuki Co, an unlisted company based in Megaera, has been manufacturing electrical parts used in mobility vehicles for people with disabilities and the elderly, for many years. These parts are exported to various manufacturers worldwide but at present there are no local manufacturers of mobility vehicles in Megaera. Retailers in Megaera normally import mobility vehicles and sell them at an average price of $4,000 each. Fubuki Co wants to manufacture mobility vehicles locally and believes that it can sell vehicles of equivalent quality locally at a discount of 37.5% to the current average retail price.

Although this is a completely new venture for Fubuki Co, it will be in addition to the company's core business. Fubuki Co's directors expect to develop the project for a period of four years and then sell it for $16 million to a private equity firm. Megaera's government has been positive about the venture and has offered Fubuki Co a subsidised loan of up to 80% of the investment funds required, at a rate of 200 basis points below Fubuki Co's borrowing rate. Currently Fubuki Co can borrow at 300 basis points above the five-year government debt yield rate.

A feasibility study commissioned by the directors, at a cost of $250,000, has produced the following information.

1. Initial cost of acquiring suitable premises will be $11 million, and plant and machinery used in the manufacture will cost $3 million. Acquiring the premises and installing the machinery is a quick process and manufacturing can commence almost immediately.

2. It is expected that in the first year 1,300 units will be manufactured and sold. Unit sales will grow by 40% in each of the next two years before falling to an annual growth rate of 5% for the final year. After the first year the selling price per unit is expected to increase by 3% per year.

3. In the first year, it is estimated that the total direct material, labour and variable overheads costs will be $1,200 per unit produced. After the first year, the direct costs are expected to increase by an annual inflation rate of 8%.

4. Annual fixed overhead costs would be $2.5 million of which 60% are centrally allocated overheads. The fixed overhead costs will increase by 5% per year after the first year.

5. Fubuki Co will need to make working capital available of 15% of the anticipated sales revenue for the year, at the beginning of each year. The working capital is expected to be released at the end of the fourth year when the project is sold.

Fubuki Co's tax rate is 25% per year on taxable profits. Tax is payable in the same year as when the profits are earned. Tax allowable depreciation is available on the plant and machinery on a straight-line basis. It is anticipated that the value attributable to the plant and machinery after four years is $400,000 of the price at which the project is sold. No tax allowable depreciation is available on the premises.

Fubuki Co uses 8% as its discount rate for new projects but feels that this rate may not be appropriate for this new type of investment. It intends to raise the full amount of funds through debt finance and take advantage of the government's offer of a subsidised loan. Issue costs are 4% of the gross finance required. It can be assumed that the debt capacity available to the company is equivalent to the actual amount of debt finance raised for the project.

Although no other companies produce mobility vehicles in Megaera, Haizum Co, a listed company, produces electrical-powered vehicles using similar technology to that required for the mobility vehicles. Haizum Co's cost of equity is estimated to be 14% and it pays tax at 28%. Haizum Co has 15 million shares in issue trading at $2.53 each and $40 million bonds trading at $94.88 per $100. The five-year government debt yield is currently estimated at 4.5% and the market risk premium at 4%.

Required:

(a) Evaluate, on financial grounds, whether Fubuki Co should proceed with the project. **(17 marks)**

(b) Discuss the appropriateness of the evaluation method used and explain any assumptions made in part (a) above. **(8 marks)**

(Total = 25 marks)

BPP LEARNING MEDIA

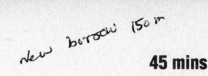 new borrow 150 m

32 Levante Co (12/11, amended)

45 mins

Levante Co is a large unlisted company which has identified a new project for which it will need to increase its long-term borrowings from $250 million to $400 million. This amount will cover a significant proportion of the total cost of the project and the rest of the funds will come from cash held by the company.

The current $250 million unsubordinated borrowing is in the form of a 4% bond which is trading at $98.71 per $100 and is due to be redeemed at par in three years. The issued bond has a credit rating of AA. The new borrowing will also be raised in the form of a traded bond with a par value of $100 per unit. It is anticipated that the new project will generate sufficient cash flows to be able to redeem the new bond at $100 par value per unit in five years. It can be assumed that coupons on both bonds are paid annually.

Both bonds would be ranked equally for payment in the event of default and the directors expect that as a result of the new issue, the credit rating for both bonds will fall to A. The directors are considering the following two alternative options when issuing the new bond:

(i)   Issue the new bond at a fixed coupon of 5% but at a premium or discount, whichever is appropriate to ensure full take up of the bond; or

(ii)   Issue the new bond at a coupon rate where the issue price of the new bond will be $100 per unit and equal to its par value.

The following extracts are provided on the current government bond yield curve and yield spreads for the sector in which Levante Co operates:

Current Government Bond Yield Curve

Years	1	2	3	4	5
	3.2%	3.7%	4.2%	4.8%	5.0%

Yield spreads (in basis points)

Bond Rating	1 year	2 years	3 years	4 years	5 years
AAA	5	9	14	19	25
AA	16	22	30	40	47
A	65	76	87	100	112
BBB	102	121	142	167	193

Required:

(a)   Calculate the expected percentage fall in the market value of the existing bond if Levante Co's bond credit rating falls from AA to A.   **(3 marks)**

(b)   Advise the directors on the financial implications of choosing each of the two options when issuing the new bond. Support the advice with appropriate calculations.   **(8 marks)**

(c)   Among the criteria used by credit agencies for establishing a company's credit rating are the following: industry risk, earnings protection, financial flexibility and evaluation of the company's management.

        Briefly explain each criterion and suggest factors that could be used to assess it.   **(8 marks)**

(d)   The following information is available for the expected situation after the proposed bond issue.

        Total assets = $1,050m
        Monthly net income = $25m
        Annual profit before interest and tax = $450m
        Standard deviation of earnings = 8%

        Assume the new bond is issued with a 5% coupon.

        Use the Kaplan-Urwitz model for unquoted companies to predict whether the credit rating will be AAA, AA or A.   **(6 marks)**

        Note: The model is $Y = 4.41 + 0.0014F + 6.4\pi - 2.56S - 2.72L + 0.006C - 0.53\sigma$

Where

F = total assets
π = net income/total assets
S = debt status (subordinated =1, otherwise 0)
L = gearing (long-term debt/total assets)
C = interest cover
σ = standard deviation of earnings

AAA ratings are given for scores over 6.76, AA ratings are given for scores over 5.19 but less than 6.76, A for scores over 3.28

(Total = 25 marks)

How they use m+m for Ke
+ 60:40 Kd

33 Do-it-Yourself

45 mins

You are the chief financial officer of a multinational company in the Do-It-Yourself (DIY) retail business based in the United States. Your company is considering a major expansion into the rapidly developing China market where one of your competitors has already established a presence with three stores, one in Beijing and two in Shanghai. After conducting local market research and a personal review, you are convinced that, although your competitor has successfully opened a new market in those cities, the demand is considerably greater than its ability to supply. Your overseas operations group report that they can open the appropriate supply chains and that, unlike the competition, you will be able to get a greater variety of goods onto the shelves and maintain supply at competitive prices.

Your assessment is that the company will need to raise the equivalent of $380 million of new finance over 10 years for this venture, of which $80 million could come from the company's existing liquid reserves. You have completed your review of the financial merits of the case and the project offers a rate of return in excess of 80 per cent. The company's current credit rating is assessed at AA–. Its total market capitalisation is $3.5bn, which includes a ten year syndicated loan of $0.5 billion due for retirement in three years. The balance of the firm's capital is in the form of common stock (ordinary shares) trading on the New York and Hong Kong markets.

You wish to undertake a preliminary review of the options for financing this project. Your assessment is that borrowing the money is a possibility but that the increase in gearing would drop your credit rating to A+. You believe that the likelihood of that happening is 60 per cent, with a further 40 per cent chance that the company's rating could fall to A. The company's existing weighted average cost of capital (tax adjusted at the company's average corporation tax rate of 30 per cent) is 6.8 per cent. The current nominal yield curve and credit spreads for the retail sector are shown below:

Exhibit 1: 30 year yield curve

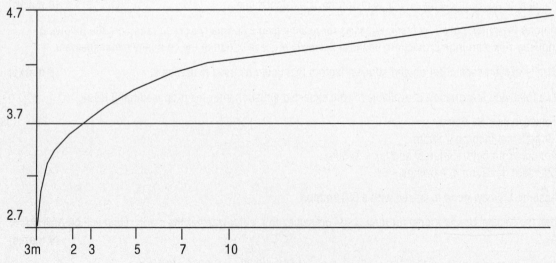

Exhibit 2: Yield spreads for retail sector (in basis points)

Rating	1yr	2yr	3yr	5yr	7yr	10yr	30yr
Aaa/AAA	4	8	12	18	20	30	50
Aa1/AA+	8	12	20	30	32	35	60
Aa2/AA	15	24	30	34	40	50	65
Aa3/AA–	24	35	40	45	54	56	78
A1/A+	28	37	44	55	60	70	82
A2/A	55	65	75	85	95	107	120

Required

(a) Estimate the expected cost of capital for this project on the assumption that the additional finance is raised through a bond issue in the US market. **(10 marks)**

(b) Draft a brief report for the board which outlines the alternative sources of finance that are potentially available for this project. Include, in your report, a brief discussion of the advantages and disadvantages and the likely impact of each alternative source upon the firm's cost of capital. **(9 marks)**

(c) Discuss the key financial and other factors that should be considered by Do-It-Yourself before investing in a foreign country rather than the home country. **(6 marks)**

(Total = 25 marks)

34 AWP Co

45 mins

AWP Co is a multinational listed company which has a credit rating of AA from major credit rating agencies. AWP Co currently has a financial gearing level measured by debt divided by debt plus equity (Debt/ (Debt + Equity)) of 8%. The average gearing ratio for AWP Co's industry is 35%. The Chief Executive understands Modigliani and Miller's theory and wants AWP Co to issue more debt as he believes this will increase the value of AWP Co. The Chief Executive has also been quoted as saying "I don't understand why the industry average gearing ratio is only 35%. Surely companies should be issuing as much debt as possible, as a 100% geared company would have a much greater value."

In response to the Chief Executive's wishes, AWP Co will issue bonds of $200 million. There are two different bonds that it is currently considering.

Option 1

A four-year bond with an annual coupon rate of 5%. The bonds will be redeemable at par.

Option 2

A three-year bond with an annual coupon rate of 4%, redeemable at a premium of 5% to nominal value.

The current annual spot yield curve for government bonds is as follows:

One-year   3.3%
Two-year   3.8%
Three-year 4.5%
Four-year   5.3%

The following table of spreads (in basis points) is given for the retail sector.

Rating	1 year	2 year	3 year	4 year
AAA	12	23	36	50
AA	27	40	51	60
A	43	55	67	80

Required

(a) (i)   Calculate the theoretical issue prices and the duration of the two bonds.   **(12 marks)**

(ii) Analyse the results obtained in part (a) (i)   **(4 marks)**

(b) Evaluate the comments made by the Chief Executive, making reference to other theories of capital structure.   **(9 marks)**

(Total = 25 marks)

35 Preparation question: Somax (FS, 6/96, amended)   22 mins

(a) Somax plc wishes to raise 260 million Swiss Francs in floating rate finance for a period of five years.

The funds are to be used to establish a new production plant in the eastern region of Switzerland. Somax evaluates its investments using NPV, but is not sure what cost of capital to use in the discounting process. The company is also proposing to increase its equity finance in the near future for UK expansion, resulting overall in little change in the company's market weighted capital gearing. The summarised financial data for the company before the expansion are shown below.

Income statement for the year ending 31 March 20X6

	£m
Turnover	1,984
Gross profit	432
Profit after tax	81
Dividends	37
Retained earnings	44

Statement of financial position as at 31 March 20X6

	£m
Non-current assets (net)	846
Working capital	350
	1,196
Medium and long-term loans[1]	(210)
	986
Shareholders' funds	
Issued ordinary shares (50 pence par)	225
Reserves	761
	986

[1]Including £75m 14% fixed rate bonds due to mature in five years time and redeemable at £100. The current market price of these bonds is £119.50. Other medium and long-term loans are floating rate UK bank loans at base rate plus 1% with a cost of debt of 3%.

Corporate rate tax may be assumed to be at the rate of 33% in both the UK and Switzerland. The company's ordinary shares are currently trading at 376 pence.

Somax's equity beta is estimated to be 1.18. The systematic risk of debt may be assumed to be zero. The risk free rate is 7.75% and market return 14.5%. Bank base rate is currently 8.25%.

The estimated equity beta of the main Swiss competitor in the same industry as the new proposed plant in the eastern region of Switzerland is 1.5, and the competitor's capital gearing is 35% equity, 65% debt by book values, and 60% equity, 40% debt by market values.

Exchange rates

Spot	SFr2.3245 – 2.3300/£
6 months forward	SFr2.2955 – 2.3009/£

Required

Estimate the sterling cost of capital that Somax should use as the discount rate for its proposed investment in eastern Switzerland. State clearly any assumptions that you make.   **(12 marks)**

WACC

◊ the ~~dinars devalues about 5,~~

36 Pondhills (FS, 6/01, amended)

Spot

45 mins

Pondhills Inc is a US multinational company with subsidiaries in the UK and Africa. The currency of the African country is pegged against the dollar, with a current exchange rate of 246.3 dinars/$US. In recent months political unrest and an increasing inflation rate has led the finance director of Pondhills to become concerned about a possible devaluation of the dinar. He believes that the dinar could devalue by up to 15% relative to the dollar during the next few months.

Summarised financial data for the African subsidiary, Ponda SA, are shown below:

	Million dinars
Revenue	2,300
Non-current assets	510
Current assets	
Cash	86
Receivables	410
Inventory	380
	876
Short-term payables	(296)
Long-term loans	(500)
	590

Shareholders' equity = 590

Current exchange rates are:

£1 = US$1.5780   US$1 = 246.3 dinars

Notes

(i)   All sales from the African subsidiary are denominated in US dollars, and all receivables are therefore payable in dollars.   *all in dollars*

(ii)   50% of payables are debts owed in sterling to the UK subsidiary by Ponda SA.   *Find £= Dinars*

(iii) The cost of goods sold and other operating expenses (excluding interest) for Ponda SA are 70% of revenue. 40% of this is payable in dollars or sterling and 60% in dinars.

(iv)   The interest rate on loans is 12%.

(v)   No significant changes in exchange rates are expected between the dollar and other major currencies.

Required

Calculate:

(a)   (i)   The statement of financial position transaction exposure of Pondhills Inc, AND the potential profit or loss on translation of the statement of financial position using the current or closing rate method where all exposed assets and liabilities are translated at the current exchange rate.   **(10 marks)**

        (ii)   The expected impact on the dollar value of Ponda SA's annual cash flow in the first full year after devaluation. The time value of money may be ignored.   **(7 marks)**

(b)   Comment upon whether or not Pondhills Inc should hedge against the exposures estimated in (a) (i) and (a) (ii).   **(4 marks)**

(c)   Provide examples of possible longer term economic/cash flow implications of the possible devaluation for Pondhills Inc.   **(4 marks)**

(Total = 25 marks)

37 Ennea (6/12)
Discuss it Properly

45 mins

Three proposals were put forward for further consideration after a meeting of the executive directors of Ennea Co to discuss the future investment and financing strategy of the business. Ennea Co is a listed company operating in the haulage and shipping industry.

Proposal 1

To increase the company's level of debt by borrowing a further $20 million and use the funds raised to buy back share capital.

Proposal 2

To increase the company's level of debt by borrowing a further $20 million and use these funds to invest in additional non-current assets in the haulage strategic business unit.

Proposal 3

To sell excess non-current haulage assets with a net book value of $25 million for $27 million and focus on offering more services to the shipping strategic business unit. This business unit will require no additional investment in non-current assets. All the funds raised from the sale of the non-current assets will be used to reduce the company's debt.

Ennea Co financial information

Extracts from the forecast financial position for the coming year

	$m
Non-current assets	282
Current assets	66
Total assets	348
Equity and liabilities	
Share capital (40c per share)	48
Retained earnings	123
Total equity	171
Non-current liabilities	140
Current liabilities	37
Total liabilities	177
Total liabilities and equity	348

Ennea Co's forecast after tax profit for the coming year is expected to be $26 million and its current share price is $3.20 per share. The non-current liabilities consist solely of a 6% medium term loan redeemable within seven years. The terms of the loan contract stipulates that an increase in borrowing will result in an increase in the coupon payable of 25 basis points on the total amount borrowed, while a reduction in borrowing will lower the coupon payable by 15 basis points on the total amount borrowed.

Ennea Co's effective tax rate is 20%. The company's estimated after tax rate of return on investment is expected to be 15% on any new investment. It is expected that any reduction in investment would suffer the same rate of return.

Required:

(a) Estimate and discuss the impact of each of the three proposals on the forecast statement of financial position, the earnings and earnings per share, and gearing of Ennea Co. **(20 marks)**

(b) An alternative suggestion to proposal three was made where the non-current assets could be leased to other companies instead of being sold. The lease receipts would then be converted into an asset through securitisation. The proceeds from the sale of the securitised lease receipts asset would be used to reduce the outstanding loan borrowings.

Required:
Explain what the securitisation process would involve and what would be the key barriers to Ennea Co undertaking the process. **(5 marks)**

(Total = 25 marks)

 BPP LEARNING MEDIA

ACQUISITIONS AND MERGERS

Questions 38 to 42 cover acquisitions and mergers, the subject of Part D of the BPP Study Text for Paper P4.

38 Mercury Training (6/08, amended)   45 mins

Mercury Training was established in 1999 and since that time it has developed rapidly. The directors are considering either a flotation or an outright sale of the company.

The company provides training for companies in the computer and telecommunications sectors. It offers a variety of courses ranging from short intensive courses in office software to high level risk management courses using advanced modelling techniques. Mercury employs a number of in-house experts who provide technical materials and other support for the teams that service individual client requirements. In recent years, Mercury has diversified into the financial services sector and now also provides computer simulation systems to companies for valuing acquisitions. This business now accounts for one third of the company's total revenue.

Mercury currently has 10 million, 50c shares in issue. Jupiter is one of the few competitors in Mercury's line of business. However, Jupiter is only involved in the training business. Jupiter is listed on a small company investment market and has an estimated beta of 1.5. Jupiter has 50 million shares in issue with a market price of 580c. The average beta for the financial services sector is 0.9. Average market gearing (debt to total market value) in the financial services sector is estimated at 25%.

Other summary statistics for both companies for the year ended 31 December 2007 are as follows:

	Mercury	Jupiter
Net assets at book value ($million)	65	45
Earnings per share (c)	100	50
Dividend per share (c)	25	25
Gearing (debt to total market value)	30%	12%
Five year historic earnings growth (annual)	12%	8%

Analysts forecast revenue growth in the training side of Mercury's business to be 6% per annum, but the financial services sector is expected to grow at just 4%.

Background information:

The equity risk premium is 3.5% and the rate of return on short-dated government stock is 4.5%.
Both companies can raise debt at 2.5% above the risk free rate.
Tax on corporate profits is 40%.

Required

(a)   Estimate the cost of equity capital and the weighted average cost of capital for Mercury Training.   **(8 marks)**

(b)   Advise the owners of Mercury Training on a range of likely issue prices for the company.   **(10 marks)**

(c)   Discuss the advantages and disadvantages, to the directors of Mercury Training, of a public listing versus private equity finance as a means of disposing of their interest in the company.   **(7 marks)**

                                                                        (Total = 25 marks)

39 Saturn Systems (6/08, amended)   45 mins

Mr Moon is the CEO of Saturn Systems, a very large listed company in the telecommunications business. The company is in a very strong financial position, having developed rapidly in recent years through a strategy based upon growth by acquisition. Currently, earnings and earnings growth are at all time highs although the company's cash reserves are at a low level following a number of strategic investments in the last financial year. The previous evening Mr Moon gave a speech at a business dinner and during questions made some remarks that Pluto Limited was an attractive company with 'great assets' and that he would be a 'fool' if he did not consider the possibility 'like everyone else' of acquiring the company. Pluto is a long established supplier to Saturn Systems and if acquired would add substantially to the market capitalisation of the business.

Mr Moon's comments were widely reported in the following morning's financial newspapers and, by 10 am, the share price of Pluto had risen 15% in out-of-hours and early trading. The first that you, Saturn's chief financial officer, heard about the issue was when you received an urgent call from Mr Moon's office. You have just completed a background investigation of Pluto, along with three other potential targets instigated at Saturn's last board meeting in May. Following that investigation, you have now commenced a review of the steps required to raise the necessary debt finance for a bid and the procedure you would need to follow in setting up a due diligence investigation of each company.

On arriving at Mr Moon's office you are surprised to see the chairman of the board in attendance. Mr Moon has just put down the telephone and is clearly very agitated. They tell you about the remarks made by Mr Moon the previous evening and that the call just taken was from the Office of the Regulator for Public Companies. The regulator had wanted to know if a bid was to be made and what announcement the company intended to make. They had been very neutral in their response pending your advice but had promised to get back to the regulator within the hour. They knew that if they were forced to admit that a bid was imminent and then withdrew that they would not be able to bid again for another six months. Looking at you they ask as one: 'what do we do now?' After a short discussion you returned to your office and began to draft a memorandum with a recommendation about how to proceed.

Required

(a) Discuss of the advantages and disadvantages of growth by acquisition as compared with growth by internal (or organic) investment. **(5 marks)**

(b) Assess the regulatory, financial and ethical issues in this case. **(15 marks)**

(c) Propose a course of action that the company should now pursue, including a draft of any announcement that should be made, given that the board of Saturn Systems wishes to hold open the option of making a bid in the near future. **(5 marks)**

(Total = 25 marks)

40 Minprice   45 mins

The directors of Minprice Inc, a food retailer with 20 superstores, are proposing to make a takeover bid for Savealot Inc, a company with six superstores. Minprice will offer four of its ordinary shares for every three ordinary shares of Savealot. The bid has not yet been made public.

Summarised statements of financial position as at 31 March 20X0

	Minprice Inc			Savealot Inc		
	$m	$m	$m	$m	$m	$m
Land and buildings (net)			483			42.3
Non-current assets (net)			150			17.0
			633			59.3
Current assets						
Inventory	328			51.4		
Receivables	12			6.3		
Cash	44			5.3		
		384			63.0	
Payables: amounts falling due in less than one year						
Trade payables*	459			48.1		
Taxation	22			2.0		
		(481)			(50.1)	
			(97)			12.9
Payables: amounts falling due after more than one year						
14% loan stock			(200)			
Floating rate bank term loans			(114)			(17.5)
			222			54.7

BPP LEARNING MEDIA

Shareholders' Funds

Original shares 25 cents par		75	50 cents par	20.0
Reserves		147		34.7
		222		54.7

* Trade payables include dividends of $12m for Minprice and $2m for Savealot.

Summarised income statements for the year ending 31 March 20X0

	$m	$m
Turnover	1,130	181
Earnings before interest and tax	115	14
Net interest	(40)	(2)
Profit before tax	75	12
Taxation	(25)	(4)
Available to shareholders	50	8
Dividend	(24)	(5)
Retained earnings	26	3

The current share price of Minprice Inc is 232 cents, and of Savealot Inc 295 cents. The current loan stock price of Minprice plc is $125.

Recent annual growth trends:	Minprice Inc	Savealot Inc
Dividends	7%	8%
EPS	7%	10%

Rationalisation following the acquisition will involve the following transactions (all net of tax effects):

(a) Sale of surplus warehouse facilities for $6.8 million.
(b) Redundancy payments costing $9.0 million.
(c) Wage savings of $2.7 million per year for at least five years.

Minprice's cost of equity is estimated to be 14.5%, and weighted average cost of capital 12%. Savealot's cost of equity is estimated to be 13%.

Required

(a)   Discuss and evaluate whether or not the bid is likely to be viewed favourably by the shareholders of both Minprice Inc and Savealot Inc. Include discussion of the factors that are likely to influence the views of the shareholders.

All relevant calculations must be shown. **(15 marks)**

(b)   Discuss the possible effects on the likely success of the bid if the offer terms were to be amended to 325 cents per share cash. **(3 marks)**

(c)   The directors of Savealot Inc have decided to fight the bid and have proposed the following measures:

(i)   Announce that their company's profits are likely to be doubled next year.

(ii)   Alter the Articles of Association to require that at least 75% of shareholders need to approve an acquisition.

(iii) Persuade, for a fee, a third party investor to buy large quantities of the company's shares.

(iv)   Introduce an advertising campaign criticising the performance and management ability of Minprice Inc.

(v)   Revalue non-current assets to current values so that shareholders are aware of the company's true market values.

Acting as a consultant to the company, give reasoned advice on whether or not the company should adopt each of these measures. **(7 marks)**

(Total = 25 marks)

41 Fly 4000

Do part ⓑ properly.
How did use Dvm,

45 mins

You are the chief financial officer of Fly4000 a large company in the airline and travel business whose principal market base is in Europe and the Middle East. Its principal hub is a major Northern European airport and Fly4000 has a small holiday business through its partnership with a number of independent tour operators. It has a good reputation as a business carrier within its European market, earned through very high standards of punctuality and service. Following the recent disinvestment of associated interests and a joint venture, it has cash reserves of $860 million.

FliHi is a smaller airline which also has its centre of operations at the same airport as Fly4000. It has, since it was founded in 1988, developed a strong transatlantic business as well as a substantial position in the long and medium haul holiday market. In the year to 31 December 20X5 its reported turnover was in $1.7 billion and its profit after tax for the financial year was $50 million. The company's net assets are $120 million and it has $150 million of long term loans on its statement of financial position. It has recently expanded its fleet of wide bodied jets suitable for its expanding holiday business and has orders placed for the new Airbus 380 super-Jumbo to supplement its long haul fleet. FliHi has route licenses to New York and six other major US cities.

FliHi's cash flow statement for the current and preceding year is as follows:

FliHi Consolidated Cash Flow Statement (extract)
For the year ended 31 December 20X5

	31 December 20X5		31 December 20X4	
	$m	$m	$m	$m
Net cash inflow from operating activities		210.0		95.0
Return on investment and servicing of finance				
Interest received	12.0		6.0	
Interest paid	(4.0)		(3.0)	
Interest element on finance leases	(6.5)		(4.0)	
		1.5		(1.0)
Taxation		(4.1)		(0.2)
Capital expenditure		(120.2)		(75.0)
Acquisitions and disposals				
Proceeds from the sale of interest in joint ventures		10.0		15.0
Cash inflow before management of liquid				
Management of liquid resources				
Decrease/(increase) in short-term deposits		35.5		(32.2)
Financing				
Repayment of secured loans		(31.0)		(25.0)
Increase/(decrease) in cash for the year		101.7		(23.4)

There is no other airline of comparable size and business mix to Fly4000 although analysts regard Rover Airways as a useful comparator. The statement below contains market data relating to Rover Airways:

Key fundamentals

Forward P/E*	11.00	Dividend Yield	0.00
Price to Book value of equity	1.25	1Yr Total Return (%)**	25.07
Price To Cash Flow	3.00	Beta**	2.00
1Yr Sales Growth	-1.67	1Yr EPS Growth	80.50

** Equity Market Cap $3bn
You also note the following:

The current risk-free rate is 4.5 per cent and the equity risk premium is estimated at 3.5 percent. The prevailing share price for Rover Airways is 290¢ per share and its P/E ratio is 10. The corporation tax rate for both companies is 30 per cent.

The gearing ratio for Rover Airways, expressed as total debt to total capital (debt plus equity), is 60 per cent and as total debt to equity is 150 per cent.

BPP LEARNING MEDIA

You may assume that:

1   FliHi has undertaken a consistent programme of reinvestment
2   The debt in both companies is not expected to be sensitive to market risk.

There has been considerable consolidation in the airline industry and you are advising your board of directors of Fly4000 on the value of FliHi as a potential target for acquisition. It is anticipated that over the longer term the domestic airline industry will settle down to a rate of growth in line with GDP growth in the European economy which stands at 4 per cent per annum (nominal). However, the current rates of growth (6.3%) for this company is likely to be sustained for the next five years before reverting to the GDP growth rate from the sixth year forward.

Required

(a)   Estimate the current cost of equity capital for FliHi using the Capital Asset Pricing Model, making notes on any assumptions that you have made.
(9 marks)

(b)   Estimate the value of Flihi on the basis of its expected free cash flow to equity, explaining the limitations of the methods you have used.
(7 marks)

(c)   Write a brief report outlining the considerations your colleagues on the board of Fly4000 might bear in mind when contemplating this acquisition.
(9 marks)

$$\left[V_0 = \frac{\text{free }y/F \text{ at time } 1}{WACC - g} \right]$$

(Total = 25 marks)

42 Burcolene (12/07, amended)

• what is no, of option outstanding?
• NEW formula of valuation.

45 mins

Burcolene is a large European-based petrochemical manufacturer, with a wide range of basic bulk chemicals in its product range and with strong markets in Europe and the Pacific region. In recent years, margins have fallen as a result of competition from China and, more importantly, Eastern European countries that have favourable access to the Russian petrochemical industry. However, the company has managed to sustain a 5% growth rate in earnings through aggressive management of its cost base, the management of its risk and careful attention to its value base.

As part of its strategic development, Burcolene is considering a leveraged (debt-financed) acquisition of PetroFrancais, a large petrochemical business that has engaged in a number of high quality alliances with oil drilling and extraction companies in the newly opened Russian Arctic fields. However, the growth of the company has not been particularly strong in recent years, although Burcolene believes that an expected long term growth of 4% per annum is realistic under its current management.

Preliminary discussions with its banks have led Burcolene to the conclusion that an acquisition of 100% of the equity of PetroFrancais, financed via a bond issue, would not have a significant impact upon the company's existing credit rating. The key issues, according to the company's advisors, are the terms of the deal and the likely effect of the acquisition on the company's value and its financial leverage. Both companies are quoted on an international stock exchange and below are relevant data relating to each company:

Financial data as at 30 November 20X7

	Burcolene	PetroFrancais
Market value of debt in issue ($bn)	3.30	5.80
Market value of equity in issue ($bn)	9.90	6.70
Number of shares in issue (million)	340.00	440.00
Share options outstanding (million)	25.40	–
Exercise price of options ($ per share)	22.00	–
Company tax rate (%)	30.00	25.00
Equity beta	1.85	0.95
Default risk premium	1.6%	3.0%
Net operating profit after tax and new reinvestment ($ million)	450.00	205.00
Current EPS ($ per share)	1.19	0.44

The global equity risk premium is 4·0% and the most appropriate risk free rate derived from the returns on government stock is 3·0%.

Burcolene has a share option scheme as part of its executive remuneration package. In accordance with the accounting standards, the company has expensed its share options at fair value. The share options held by the employees of Burcolene were granted on 1 January 2004. The vesting date is 30 November 20X9 and the exercise date is 30 November 20Y0. Currently, the company has a 5% attrition rate as members leave the company and, of those remaining at the vesting date, 20% are expected not to have achieved the standard of performance required. Your estimate is that the options have a time value of $7·31.

PetroFrancais operates a defined benefits pension scheme which, at its current actuarial valuation, shows a deficit of $430 million.

You have been appointed to advise the senior management team of Burcolene on the validity of the free cash flow to equity model as a basis for valuing both firms and on the financial implications of this acquisition for Burcolene.

Following your initial discussions with management, you decide that the following points are relevant:

1   The free cash flow to all classes of capital invested can be reliably approximated as net operating profit after tax(NOPAT) less net reinvestment.

2   Given the rumours in the market concerning a potential acquisition, the existing market valuations may not fully reflect each company's value.

3   The acquisition would be financed by a new debt issue by Burcolene.

Required

(a)   Estimate the weighted average cost of capital and the current entity value for each business, taking into account the impact of the share option scheme and the pension fund deficit on the value of each company.

(16 marks)

(b)   Write a briefing paper for management, advising them on:

(i)   The validity of the free cash flow model, given the growth rate assumptions made by management for both firms;

(ii)   The implications of an acquisition such as this for Burcolene's gearing and cost of capital.

(9 marks)

(Total = 25 marks)

BPP
LEARNING MEDIA

Questions 43 to 46 cover corporate reconstruction and reorganisation, the subject of Part E of the BPP Study Text for Paper P4.

43 AIR

How ER buy 2m share ? → (may be for warrenty issue)
what is leveraged

45 mins

The directors of ER have decided to concentrate the company's activities on three core areas, bus services, road freight and taxis. As a result the company has offered for sale a regional airport that it owns. The airport handles a mixture of short-haul scheduled services, holiday charter flights and air freight, but does not have a runway long enough for long-haul international operations.

The existing managers of the airport, along with some employees, are attempting to purchase the airport through a leveraged management buy-out, and would form a new unquoted company, AIR. The total value of the airport (free of any debt) has been independently assessed at $35 million.

The managers and employees can raise a maximum of $4 million towards this cost. This would be invested in new ordinary shares issued at the par value of 50c per share. ER, as a condition of the sale, proposes to subscribe to an initial 20% equity holding in the company, and would repay all debt of the airport prior to the sale.

EPP Bank is prepared to offer a floating rate loan of $20 million to the management team, at an initial interest rate of LIBOR plus 3%. LIBOR is currently at 10%. This loan would be for a period of seven years, repayable upon maturity, and would be secured against the airport's land and buildings. A condition of the loan is that gearing, measured by the book value of total loans to equity, is no more than 100% at the end of four years. If this condition is not met the bank has the right to call in its loan at one month's notice. AIR would be able to purchase a four year interest rate cap at 15% for its loan from EPP Bank for an up-front premium of $800,000.

A venture capital company, AV, is willing to provide up to $15 million in the form of unsecured mezzanine debt with attached warrants. This loan would be for a five year period, with principal repayable in equal annual instalments, and have a fixed interest rate of 18% per year.

The warrants would allow AV to purchase 10 AIR shares at a price of 100 cents each for every $100 of initial debt provided, at any time after two years from the date the loan is agreed. The warrants would expire after five years.

Most recent income statement for the airport

	$'000
Landing fees	14,000
Other revenues	8,600
	22,600
Labour	5,200
Consumables	3,800
Central overhead payable to ER	4,000
Other expenses	3,500
Interest paid	2,500
	19,000
Taxable profit	3,600
Taxation (33%)	1,188
Retained earnings	2,412

ER has offered to continue to provide central accounting, personnel and marketing services to AIR for a fee of $3 million per year, with the first fee payable in year one. All revenues and cost (excluding interest) are expected to increase by approximately 5% per year.

Required

Prepare a report for the managers of the proposed new company AIR which:

(a) Analyses the advantages and disadvantages for the management buy-out of the proposed financing mix.

(9 marks)

(b) Evaluates whether or not the EPP Bank's gearing restriction in four years' time is likely to be a problem.

(10 marks)

All relevant calculations must be shown. State clearly any assumptions that you make.

(c) As a possible alternative to obtaining finance from AV, assume that a venture capital company that you are employed by has been approached by the management buy-out team for a $10 million loan. Discuss what information, other than that provided above, would be required from the MBO team in order to decide whether or not to agree to the loan.

(6 marks)

(Total = 25 marks)

44 MandM Co (6/10, amended)   45 mins

The MandM Company, a large listed company, has two divisions. The first, the MoneyMint division produces coins and notes for the national exchequer and generates 80% of the company's revenues. The second, the LunarMint division, manufactures a brand of sweets which are very popular with traders in the financial markets. The company is considering disposing of its LunarMint division. The LunarMint business is no longer viewed as part of the core business of the MandM Company. The Chief Executive Officer commented that he could never understand why the company entered into sweet-making in the first place. The LunarMint business is profitable and low risk, but has not been a high priority for investment.

Required

(a) Outline the issues that should be considered when disposing of the LunarMint division noting the risks that might be involved.

(19 marks)

(b) Briefly discuss THREE appropriate methods of disposal, other than a management buy-out, for the LunarMint division.

(6 marks)

(Total = 25 marks)

45 Proteus Co (12/11, amended)   45 mins

Proteus Co, a large listed company, has a number of subsidiaries in different industries but its main line of business is developing surveillance systems and intruder alarms. It has decided to sell a number of companies that it considers are peripheral to its core activities. One of these subsidiary companies is Tyche Co, a company involved in managing the congestion monitoring and charging systems that have been developed by Proteus Co. Tyche Co is a profitable business and it is anticipated that its revenues and costs will continue to increase at their current rate of 8% per year for the foreseeable future.

without loan

Tyche Co's managers and some employees want to buy the company through a leveraged management buy-out. An independent assessment estimates Tyche Co's market value at $81 million if Proteus Co agrees to cancel its current loan to Tyche Co. The managers and employees involved in the buy-out will invest $12 million for 75% of the equity in the company, with another $4 million coming from a venture capitalist for the remaining 25% equity.

Palaemon Bank has agreed to lend the balance of the required funds in the form of a 9% loan. The interest is payable at the end of the year, on the loan amount outstanding at the start of each year. A covenant on the loan states that the following debt-equity ratios should not be exceeded at the end of each year for the next five years:

Year	1	2	3	4	5
Debt / Equity (%)	350%	250%	200%	150%	125%

BPP LEARNING MEDIA

Shown below is an extract of the latest annual income statement for Tyche Co:

	$'000
Sales Revenue	60,000
Materials and consumables	12,000
Labour costs	22,000
Other costs	4,000
Allocated overhead charge payable to Proteus Co	14,000
Interest paid	2,000
Taxable Profit	6,000
Taxation	1,500
Retained Earnings	4,500

As part of the management buy-out agreement, it is expected that Proteus Co will provide management services costing $12 million for the first year of the management buy-out, increasing by 8% per year thereafter.

The current tax rate is 25% on profits and it is expected that 25% of the after-tax profits will be payable as dividends every year. The remaining profits will be allocated to reserves. It is expected that Tyche Co will repay $3 million of the outstanding loan at the end of each of the next five years from the cash flows generated from its business activity.

Required:

(a) Briefly discuss the possible benefits to Proteus Co of disposing Tyche Co through a management buy-out.

(5 marks)

(b) Calculate whether the debt-equity covenant imposed by Palaemon Bank on Tyche Co will be breached over the five-year period.

(9 marks)

(c) Discuss briefly the implications of the results obtained in part (b) and outline two possible actions Tyche Co may take if the covenant is in danger of being breached.

(5 marks)

(d) Discuss the reasons why a management buy-out may ultimately not succeed.

(6 marks)

(Total = 25 marks)

46 BBS Stores (6/09, amended) 45 mins

BBS Stores, a publicly quoted limited company, is considering unbundling a section of its property portfolio. The company believes that it should use the proceeds to reduce the company's medium-term borrowing and to reinvest the balance in the business (option 1). However, the company's investors have argued strongly that a sale and rental scheme would release substantial cash to investors (option 2). You are a financial consultant and have been given the task of assessing the likely impact of these alternative proposals on the company's financial performance, cost of capital and market value.

Attached is the summarised BBS Stores' statement of financial position. The company owns all its stores.

	As at year end 20X8 $m	As at year end 20X7 $m
ASSETS		
Non-current assets		
Intangible assets	190	190
Property, plant and equipment	4,050	3,600
Other assets	500	530
	4,740	4,290
Current assets	840	1,160
Total assets	5,580	5,450

LIABILITIES

Current liabilities	1,600	2,020
Non-current liabilities		
Medium-term loan notes	1,130	1,130
Other non-financial liabilities	890	900
	2,020	2,030
Total liabilities	3,620	4,050
Net assets	1,960	1,400
EQUITY		
Called up share capital – equity	425	420
Retained earnings	1,535	980
Total equity	1,960	1,400

The company's profitability has improved significantly in recent years and earnings for 20X8 were $670 million (20X7: $540 million).

The company's property, plant and equipment within non-current assets for 20X8 are as follows:

	Land and buildings $m	Fixtures, fittings & equipment $m	Assets under construction $m	Total $m
Year end 20X8				
At revaluation	2,297	4,038	165	6,500
Accumulated depreciation		(2,450)		(2,450)
Net book value	2,297	1,588	165	4,050

The property portfolio was revalued at the year end 20X8. The assets under construction are valued at a market value of $165 million and relate to new building. In recent years commercial property values have risen in real terms by 4% per annum. Current inflation is 2·5% per annum. Property rentals currently earn an 8% return.

The proposal is that 50% of the property portfolio (land and buildings) and 50% of the assets under construction would be sold to a newly established property holding company called RPH that would issue bonds backed by the assured rental income stream from BBS Stores. BBS Stores would not hold any equity interest in the newly formed company nor would they take any part in its management.

BBS Stores is currently financed by equity in the form of 25c fully paid ordinary shares with a current market value of 400c per share. The capital debt for the company consists of medium-term loan notes of which $360 million are repayable at the end of two years and $770 million are repayable at the end of six years. Both issues of medium-term notes carry a floating rate of LIBOR plus 70 basis points. The interest liability on the six year notes has been swapped at a fixed rate of 5·5% in exchange for LIBOR which is also currently 5·5%. The reduction in the firm's gearing implied by option 1 would improve the firm's credit rating and reduce its current credit spread by 30 basis points. The change in gearing resulting from the second option is not expected to have any impact upon the firm's credit rating. There has been no alteration in the rating of the company since the earliest debt was issued.

The BBS Stores equity beta is currently 1.824. A representative portfolio of commercial property companies has an equity beta of 1.25 and an average market gearing (adjusted for tax) of 50%. The risk free rate of return is 5% and the equity risk premium is 3%. Using CAPM the current cost of equity is 10.47%. The current WACC is 9.55%. The company's current accounting rate of return on new investment is 13% before tax. You may assume that debt betas are zero throughout. The effective rate of company tax is 35%.

BPP
LEARNING MEDIA

Required

On the assumption that the property unbundling proceeds, prepare a report for consideration by senior management which should include the following:

(a)   A comparative statement showing the impact upon the statement of financial position and on the earnings per share on the assumption that the cash proceeds of the property sale are used:

    (i)   To repay the debt, repayable in two years, in full and for reinvestment in non-current assets;

    (ii)   To repay the debt, repayable in two years, in full and to finance a share repurchase at the current share price with the balance of the proceeds.   **(13 marks)**

(b)   An estimate of the weighted average cost of capital for the remaining business under both options on the assumption that the share price remains unchanged.   **(8 marks)**

(c)   An evaluation of the potential impact of each alternative on the market value of the firm (you are not required to calculate a revised market value for the firm).   **(4 marks)**

(Total = 25 marks)

TREASURY AND ADVANCED RISK MANAGEMENT TECHNIQUES

Questions 47 to 58 cover treasury and advanced risk management techniques, the subject of Part F of the BPP Study Text for Paper P4.

47 Troder (SFM, 6/03, amended)　　　　45 mins

(a)　Discuss the advantages of hedging with interest rate caps and collars.　　　**(8 marks)**

(b)　Current futures prices suggest that interest rates are expected to fall during the next few months. Troder Inc expects to have $400 million available for short-term investment for a period of 5 months commencing late October. The company wishes to protect this short-term investment from a fall in interest rates, but is concerned about the premium levels of interest rate options. It would also like to benefit if interest rates were to increase rather than fall. The company's advisers have suggested the use of a collar option.

LIFFE short sterling options ($500,000), points of 100%

	Calls		Puts	
Strike price	Sept	Dec	Sept	Dec
95250	0.040	0.445	0.040	0.085
95500	0.000	0.280	0.250	0.170
95750	0.000	0.165	0.500	0.305

LIBOR is currently 5% and the company can invest short-term at LIBOR minus 25 basis points.

Required

(i)　Assume that it is now early September. The company wishes to receive more than $6,750,000 in interest from its investment after paying any option premium. Illustrate how a collar hedge may be used to achieve this. (N.B. It is not necessary to estimate the number of contracts for this illustration).　　**(9 marks)**

(ii)　Estimate the maximum interest that could be received with your selected hedge.　**(3 marks)**

(c)　Briefly discuss the meaning and importance of the terms 'delta', 'theta' and 'vega' (also known as kappa or lambda) in option pricing.　　**(5 marks)**

(Total = 25 marks)

48 MJY (SFM, 12/05, amended)　　　　45 mins

Assume that it is now 31 December. MJY plc is a UK based multinational company that has subsidiaries in two foreign countries. Both subsidiaries trade with other group members and with four third party companies (company 1 – company 4).

Projected trade transactions for three months' time are shown below. All currency amounts are in thousands.

	Payments (read down) '000'						
Receipts (read across) '000'	Co 1	Co 2	Co 3	Co 4	MJY	Subsidiary 1	Subsidiary 2
MJY	$90	£60	€75	–	–	£40	$50
Subsidiary 1	£50	€85	$40	$20	€72	–	€20
Subsidiary 2	£15	–	€52	$30	£55	€35	–
Company 1	–	–	–	–	–	–	–
Company 2	–	–	–	–	$170	–	–
Company 3	–	–	–	–	$120	€50	–
Company 4	–	–	–	–	–	–	€65

Foreign exchange rates	$/£	€/£
Spot 1	1.7982 – 1.8010	1.4492 – 1.4523
3 months forward	1.7835 – 1.7861	1.4365 – 1.4390

Currency options. £62,500 contract size. Premium in cents per £

	Calls		Puts	
Strike price	February	May	February	May
1.80	1.96	3.00	3.17	5.34
1.78	2.91	3.84	2.12	4.20

BPP
LEARNING MEDIA

Required

(a) Discuss the advantages and disadvantages of centralised treasury management for multinational companies.

(5 marks)

(b) Working from the perspective of a group treasurer, devise a hedging strategy for the MJY group, and calculate the expected outcomes of the hedges using forward markets, and, for the dollar exposure only, currency options.

(15 marks)

(c) You have been asked to produce a paper, to be presented at the next board meeting which justifies your proposed hedging strategy for the group. You should also briefly outline the procedural/policy considerations that need to be addressed in order to finalise the strategy.

(5 marks)

(Total = 25 marks)

49 KYT (FS, 6/99, amended)

45 mins

(a) KYT Inc is a company located in the USA that has a contract to purchase goods from Japan in two months' time on 1 September. The payment is to be made in yen and will total 140 million yen.

The managing director of KYT Inc wishes to protect the contract against adverse movements in foreign exchange rates and is considering the use of currency futures. The following data are available.

Spot foreign exchange rate

$1 = 128.15 yen

Yen currency futures contracts on SIMEX (Singapore Monetary Exchange)

Contract size 12,500,000 yen, contract prices are $US per yen.

Contract prices:

September   0.007985
December   0.008250

Assume that futures contracts mature at the end of the month.

Required

(i) Illustrate how KYT might hedge its foreign exchange risk using currency futures. **(3 marks)**

(ii) Explain the meaning of basis risk and show what basis risk is involved in the proposed hedge.

(4 marks)

(iii) Assuming the spot exchange rate is 120 yen/$ on 1 September and that basis risk decreases steadily in a linear manner, calculate what the result of the hedge is expected to be. Briefly discuss why this result might not occur. Margin requirements and taxation may be ignored. **(5 marks)**

(b) In addition, KYT is concerned about its exposure to variable interest rate borrowing. Discuss the relevant considerations when deciding between futures and options to hedge a company's interest rate risk.

(5 marks)

(c) The KYT business plan for the next 5 years shows a significant increase in business with Japan. The general manager tells you that the operations director is presenting the business case for setting up a wholly owned subsidiary in Japan. To that end, he has asked you to prepare a paper, to be presented at the board meeting, explaining the foreign exchange exposure risks which would result from such an investment.

In particular, he tells you he would like to explain transaction and translation exposure as he has heard that translation exposure risk is only a book entry and not a 'real cost' and so can be ignored. **(8 marks)**

(Total = 25 marks)

50 Asteroid Systems (6/08, amended)   45 mins

Asteroid Systems is a German-based company with a subsidiary in Switzerland. The company's treasury manager expects the Swiss business will remit the equivalent of Euros 1.5 million in two months. Her expectations of the future remittance are based upon the current SFr/Euro forward rate.

The current spot and forward rates for Swiss francs against the Euro are extracted from the Financial Times and are shown in the table below.

	Closing mid-point	Change on day	Bid/offer spread	Days mid high	low	One month Rate	annual %	Three month Rate	annual %
Switzerland (SFr/€)	1.6242	0.0107	239–244	1.6261	1.6147	1.6223	1.4	1.6176	1.6

In the Euro money market the company can make fixed interest deposits at LIBOR and can borrow at LIBOR plus 20 basis points for terms of greater than one month but up to six months. The company can borrow at fixed rates in the Swiss money market. LIBOR rates, as quoted in the Financial Times, are as follows:

	EUR	CHF
Spot	3.56688	2.06000
1 week	3.57300	2.06000
2 week	3.58438	2.07000
1 month	3.60900	2.08000
2 month	3.72538	2.17000
3 month	3.78238	2.20000

The company's treasury manager is keen to eliminate transaction risk. However, because of the margin requirements and their impact upon the firm's cash flow, she would prefer not to use exchange traded derivatives. Swiss franc borrowing or lending rates would need to be negotiated with the bank.

The CEO of Asteroid Systems has heard that a local competitor has made substantial gains from using its treasury department to speculate on foreign exchange markets and is interested in adding speculation to the role of the treasury department.

Required

(a) Estimate the lowest acceptable Swiss borrowing or lending rate for a money market hedge maturing in two months. **(10 marks)**

(b) Discuss the relative advantages and disadvantages of the use of a money market hedge compared with using exchange traded derivatives for hedging a foreign exchange exposure. **(6 marks)**

(c) Discuss the extent to which currency hedging can reduce a firm's cost of capital. **(4 marks)**

(d) Discuss the points to consider when deciding whether the treasury department of Asteroid Systems should operate as a profit centre or a cost centre. **(5 marks)**

(Total = 25 marks)

51 Multidrop (6/10, amended)   45 mins

You are the financial manager of Multidrop (Group) a European based company which has subsidiary businesses in North America, Europe, and Singapore. It also has foreign currency balances outstanding with two non-group companies in the UK and Malaysia. Last year the transaction costs of ad-hoc settlements both within the group and with non-group companies were significant and this year you have reached agreement with the non-group companies to enter into a netting agreement to clear indebtedness with the minimum of currency flows. It has been agreed that Multidrop (Europe) will be the principal in the netting arrangement and that all settlements will be made in Euros at the prevailing spot rate.

BPP LEARNING MEDIA

The summarised list of year end indebtedness is as follows:

Owed by:	Owed to:	
Multidrop (Europe)	Multidrop (US)	US$6.4 million
Multidrop (Singapore)	Multidrop (Europe)	S$16 million
Alposong (Malaysia)	Multidrop (US)	US$5.4 million
Multidrop (US)	Multidrop (Europe)	€8.2 million
Multidrop (Singapore)	Multidrop (US)	US$5.0 million
Multidrop (Singapore)	Alposong (Malaysia)	Rm25 million
Alposong (Malaysia)	NewRing (UK)	£2.2 million
NewRing (UK)	Multidrop (Singapore)	S$4.0 million
Multidrop (Europe)	Alposong (Malaysia)	Rm8.3 million

Currency cross rates (mid-market) are as follows:

Currency		UK £	US $	Euro	Sing $	Rm
1 UK £	=	1.0000	1.4601	1.0653	2.1956	5.3128
1 US $	=	0.6849	1.0000	0.7296	1.5088	3.6435
1 Euro	=	0.9387	1.3706	1.0000	2.0649	4.9901
1 Sing $	=	0.4555	0.6628	0.4843	1.0000	2.4150
1 Rm	=	0.1882	0.2745	0.2004	0.4141	1.0000

You may assume settlement will be at the mid-market rates quoted.

Required:

(a) Calculate the inter group and inter-company currency transfers that will be required for settlement by Multidrop (Europe). **(12 marks)**

(b) Discuss the advantages and disadvantages of netting arrangements with both group and non-group companies. **(9 marks)**

(c) Discuss whether Multidrop (Europe) should adopt a policy of invoicing overseas customers in its home currency (Euro). **(4 marks)**

(Total = 25 marks)

52 NTC (SFM, 6/02, amended) 45 mins

NTC plc is a UK multinational with subsidiaries in Spain, Hong Kong and the USA. Transactions between companies within the group have historically been in all of the currencies of the countries where the companies are located and have not been centrally co-ordinated, with the currency of the transaction varying in each deal. Transactions due in approximately three months' time are shown below. All receipts and payments are in thousand units of the specified currencies.

Assume that it is now mid-June.

	Payments (read down)			
Receipts (read across)	*UK*	*Spain*	*Hong Kong*	*USA*
UK	–	E210	$HK720	$US110
Spain	£100	–	E80	–
Hong Kong	$HK400	–	–	–
USA	$US430	E120	$HK300	–

Exchange rates

	$US/£	*Euro/£*	*$HK/£*
Spot	1.4358 – 1.4366	1.6275 – 1.6292	11.1987 – 11.2050
3 months forward	1.4285 – 1.4300	1.6146 – 1.6166	11.1567 – 11.1602

Note. The Hong Kong dollar is pegged against the US dollar.

Interest rates available to NTC and its subsidiaries (annual %)

	Borrowing	Investing
UK	6.9	6.0
Spain	5.3	4.5
Hong Kong	n/a	6.1
USA	6.2	5.4

Currency options

Philadelphia Stock exchange $/£ options, £31,250 contracts. Premium is in cents per £.

		Calls			Puts	
Exercise price	July	August	Sept	July	August	Sept
1.42	1.42	2.12	2.67	0.68	1.42	2.15
1.43	0.88	1.60	1.79	1.14	1.92	3.12
1.44	0.51	1.19	1.42	1.77	2.51	4.35

Option premiums are payable upfront. Contracts may be assumed to expire at the end of the relevant month.

Required

(a) The parent company is proposing that inter-company payments would be settled in sterling via multilateral netting. Demonstrate how this policy would reduce the number of transactions.

(Foreign exchange spot mid-rates may be used for this purpose.) **(5 marks)**

(b) If payments were to continue to be made in various currencies, illustrate three methods by which the UK parent company might hedge its transaction exposures for the next three months. Discuss, showing relevant calculations, which method should be selected. Include in your discussion an evaluation of the circumstances in which currency options would be the preferred choice.

(*Note.* NTC plc wishes to minimise the transaction costs of hedging.) **(15 marks)**

(c) NTC plc has been approached by a Russian company that wishes to purchase goods from NTC plc in exchange for wheat. The Russian currency is not freely convertible.

Discuss the potential advantages and disadvantages of such countertrade to NTC plc. **(5 marks)**

(Total = 25 marks)

53 Casasophia Co (6/11, amended)   45 mins

Casasophia Co, based in a European country that uses the Euro (€), constructs and maintains advanced energy efficient commercial properties around the world. It has just completed a major project in the USA and is due to receive the final payment of US$20 million in four months.

Casasophia Co is planning to commence a major construction and maintenance project in Mazabia, a small African country, in six months' time. This government-owned project is expected to last for three years during which time Casasophia Co will complete the construction of state-of-the-art energy efficient properties and provide training to a local Mazabian company in maintaining the properties. The carbon-neutral status of the building project has attracted some grant funding from the European Union and these funds will be provided to the Mazabian government in Mazabian Shillings (MShs).

Casasophia Co intends to finance the project using the US$20 million it is due to receive and borrow the rest through a € loan. It is intended that the US$ receipts will be converted into € and invested in short-dated treasury bills until they are required. These funds plus the loan will be converted into MShs on the date required, at the spot rate at that time.

Mazabia's government requires Casasophia Co to deposit the MShs2.64 billion it needs for the project, with Mazabia's central bank, at the commencement of the project. In return, Casasophia Co will receive a fixed sum of MShs1.5 billion after tax, at the end of each year for a period of three years. Neither of these amounts is subject to inflationary increases. The relevant risk adjusted discount rate for the project is assumed to be 12%.

BPP LEARNING MEDIA

Financial Information

Exchange Rates available to Casasophia

	Per €1	Per €1
	US$1.3585–US$1.3618	MShs116–MShs128
Spot	US$1.3585–US$1.3618	MShs116–MShs128
4-month forward	US$1.3588–US$1.3623	Not available

Currency Futures (Contract size €125,000, Quotation: US$ per €1)

2-month expiry	1.3633
5-month expiry	1.3698

Currency Options (Contract size €125,000, Exercise price quotation: US$ per €1, cents per Euro)

	Calls		Puts	
Exercise price	2-month expiry	5-month expiry	2-month expiry	5-month expiry
1·36	2.35	2.80	2.47	2.98
1·38	1.88	2.23	4.23	4.64

Casasophia Co Local Government Base Rate	2.20%
Mazabia Government Base Rate	10.80%
Yield on short-dated Euro Treasury Bills	1.80%
(assume 360-day year)	

Mazabia's current annual inflation rate is 9.7% and is expected to remain at this level for the next six months. However, after that, there is considerable uncertainty about the future and the annual level of inflation could be anywhere between 5% and 15% for the next few years. The country where Casasophia Co is based is expected to have a stable level of inflation at 1.2% per year for the foreseeable future. A local bank in Mazabia has offered Casasophia Co the opportunity to swap the annual income of MShs1.5 billion receivable in each of the next three years for Euros, at the estimated annual MShs/€ forward rates based on the current government base rates.

Required:

(a) Advise Casasophia Co on, and recommend, an appropriate hedging strategy for the US$ income it is due to receive in four months. Include all relevant calculations. **(15 marks)**

(b) Given that Casasophia Co agrees to the local bank's offer of the swap, calculate the net present value of the project, in six months' time, in €. Discuss whether the swap would be beneficial to Casasophia Co.

(10 marks)

(Total = 25 marks)

54 HYK (FS, 12/99, amended) 45 mins

The monthly cash budget of HYK Communications plc shows that the company is likely to need £18 million in two months' time for a period of four months. Financial markets have recently been volatile, due to uncertainties about the impact of a major computer bug. If computer problems occur in January 20X0, the finance director of HYK plc fears that short term interest rates could rise by as much as 150 basis points. If few problems occur then short term rates could fall by 50 basis points. LIBOR is currently 6.5% and HYK plc can borrow at LIBOR + 0.75%.

The finance director does not wish to pay more than 7.50%, including option premium costs, but excluding the effect of margin requirements and commissions.

LIFFE £500,000 3 month futures prices. The value of one tick is £12.50

December	93.40
March	93.10
June	92.75

LIFFE £500,000 3 months options prices (premiums in annual %)

Exercise	Calls			Puts		
Price	December	March	June	December	March	June
92.50	0.33	0.88	1.04	–	–	0.08
93.00	0.16	0.52	0.76	–	0.20	0.34
93.50	0.10	0.24	0.42	0.18	0.60	1.93
94.00	–	0.05	0.18	0.36	1.35	1.92

Assume that it is now 1 December and that exchange traded futures and options contracts expire at the end of the month. Margin requirements and default risk may be ignored.

Required

(a) Estimate the results of undertaking *each of* an interest rate futures hedge and an interest rate options hedge on the LIFFE exchange, if LIBOR

  (i) Increases by 150 basis points, and
  (ii) Decreases by 50 basis points.

  Discuss how successful the hedge would have been.

  State clearly any assumptions that you make. **(15 marks)**

(b) Discuss the relative advantages of using exchange traded interest rate options and over-the-counter (OTC) interest rate options. **(5 marks)**

(c) Given investors can diversify away all risks by including the shares of the company in a portfolio, explain why companies would choose to hedge against risk. **(5 marks)**

(Total = 25 marks)

55 Phobos Co (12/08, amended) 45 mins

Following a collapse in credit confidence in the banking sector globally, there have been high levels of volatility in the financial markets around the world. Phobos Co is a UK listed company and has a borrowing requirement of £30 million arising in two months' time on 1 March and expects to be able to make repayment of the full amount six months from now. The governor of the central bank has suggested that interest rates are now at their peak and could fall over the next quarter. However, the chairman of the Federal Reserve in the United States has suggested that monetary conditions may need to be tightened, which could lead to interest rate rises throughout the major economies. In your judgement there is now an equal likelihood that rates will rise or fall by as much as 100 basis points depending upon economic conditions over the next quarter.

LIBOR is currently 6.00% and Phobos can borrow at a fixed rate of LIBOR plus 50 basis points on the short term money market but the company treasurer would like to keep the maximum borrowing rate at or below 6.6%.

Short term sterling index futures have a contract size of £500,000 and a tick size of £12.50. The open and settlement prices of three month futures contracts are shown below (settlement at the end of the month):

	Open	Settlement
March	93.800	93.880
June	93.870	93.940
September	93.890	93.970

You may assume that basis diminishes to zero at contract maturity at a constant rate over time and that time intervals can be counted in months.

Options on short sterling futures have a contract size of £500,000 and the premiums (shown as an annual percentage) available against a range of exercise prices are as follows:

Exercise	Calls			Puts		
	March	June	September	March	June	September
93750	0.155	0.260	0.320	0.045	0.070	0.100
94000	0.038	0.110	0.175	0.168	0.170	0.205
94250	0.010	0.040	0.080	0.300	0.350	0.360

BPP LEARNING MEDIA

Required

(a)   Estimate the effective interest rate cost if the anticipated interest rate exposure is hedged:

   (i)   using the sterling interest rate futures; and

   (ii)   the options on short sterling futures.   **(14 marks)**

(b)   Outline the benefits and dangers to Phobos of using derivative agreements in the management of interest rate risk.   **(6 marks)**

(c)   In addition, Phobos has long-term variable rate borrowing, which is due for repayment in six years. Phobos previously did not consider the risk great enough to hedge the interest rate risk, but with an expectation that interest rates will rise, they are now considering a swap arrangement.

The Finance Director's assistant has suggested that the company should investigate the use of alternatives to a swap, such as forward rate agreements or interest rate options. The Finance Director has stated that there is very little point in such an investigation because the alternatives to swaps tend to be designed to deal with short term interest rate movements and so they would offer very little protection against the movements that could occur over the next six years. The Finance Director does not believe that there is any point in purchasing a sequence of short term instruments over the next six years.

Required
Evaluate the Finance Director's statement that there is no point in purchasing a sequence of short term instruments to lower exposure to interest rate risks over the remaining six years of the loan.   **(5 marks)**

(Total = 25 marks)

56 Katmai Co (12/09, amended)   45 mins

To finance capital investment in its domestic market, the Katmai Company raised $150 million through the issue of 12-year floating rate notes at 120 basis points over LIBOR, interest payable at six month intervals. Following a review of the current yield curve, the company's Chief Financial Officer has become concerned about the potential impact of rising LIBOR on the firm's future cash flows. The loan now has 10 years to maturity. The CFO asks you, his deputy, to examine the choices that are now available to the firm and to recommend the best course of action. She comments that a swap is an obvious choice but that she would appreciate a briefing on the advantages and disadvantages of the alternative approaches to managing the company's interest rate risk and an estimate of the six monthly Value at Risk (VaR) if nothing is done. As part of your investigation you note that 10-year swap rates are quoted at 5.25–5.40. In estimating the VaR you note that the firm has a policy of 95% confidence level on its exposure to non-core risk and that the annual volatility of LIBOR is currently 150 basis points.

Required

(a)   Evaluate the alternative choices the company has for managing its interest rate exposure and recommend, with justification, the course of action the company should follow.   **(9 marks)**

(b)   Estimate the six-monthly interest rate and the effective annual rate payable if a vanilla interest rate swap is agreed.   **(5 marks)**

(c)   Estimate the six monthly Value at Risk on the interest rate exposure associated with this borrowing and comment upon the interpretation of the result.   **(6 marks)**

(d)   Briefly discuss the uses and limitations of Value at Risk.   **(5 marks)**

(Total = 25 marks)

57 Sembilan Co (6/12, amended)   45 mins

Sembilan Co, a listed company, recently issued debt finance to acquire assets in order to increase its activity levels. This debt finance is in the form of a floating rate bond, with a face value of $320 million, redeemable in four years. The bond interest, payable annually, is based on the spot yield curve plus 60 basis points. The next annual payment is due at the end of year one.

Sembilan Co is concerned that the expected rise in interest rates over the coming few years would make it increasingly difficult to pay the interest due. It is therefore proposing to either swap the floating rate interest payment to a fixed rate payment, or to raise new equity capital and use that to pay off the floating rate bond. The new equity capital would either be issued as rights to the existing shareholders or as shares to new shareholders.

Ratus Bank has offered Sembilan Co an interest rate swap, whereby Sembilan Co would pay Ratus Bank interest based on an equivalent fixed annual rate of 3.76¼% in exchange for receiving a variable amount based on the current yield curve rate. Payments and receipts will be made at the end of each year, for the next four years. Ratus Bank will charge an annual fee of 20 basis points if the swap is agreed and will also guarantee the swap.

The current annual spot yield curve rates are as follows:

Year	One	Two	Three	Four
Rate	2.5%	3.1%	3.5%	3.8%

The current annual forward rates for years two, three and four are as follows:

Year	Two	Three	Four
Rate	3.7%	4.3%	4.7%

Required:

(a)   Based on the above information, calculate the amounts Sembilan Co expects to pay or receive every year on the swap (excluding the fee of 20 basis points). Explain why the fixed annual rate of interest of 3.76¼% is less than the four-year yield curve rate of 3.8%.   **(6 marks)**

(b)   (i)   Demonstrate that Sembilan Co's interest payment liability does not change, after it has undertaken the swap, whether the interest rates increase or decrease.   **(5 marks)**

      (ii) Discuss the advantages and disadvantages of the swap for Sembilan Co.   **(5 marks)**

(c)   Discuss the factors that Sembilan Co should consider when deciding whether it should raise equity capital to pay off the floating rate debt.   **(9 marks)**

                                                                              (Total = 25 marks)

58 Lamri Co (12/10, amended)   45 mins

Lamri Co (Lamri), a listed company, is expecting sales revenue to grow to $80 million next year, which is an increase of 20% from the current year. The operating profit margin for next year is forecast to be the same as this year at 30% of sales revenue. In addition to these profits, Lamri receives 75% of the after-tax profits from one of its wholly owned foreign subsidiaries – Magnolia Co (Magnolia), as dividends. However, its second wholly owned foreign subsidiary – Strymon Co (Strymon) does not pay dividends.

Lamri is due to pay dividends of $7.5 million shortly and has maintained a steady 8% annual growth rate in dividends over the past few years. The company has grown rapidly in the last few years as a result of investment in key projects and this is likely to continue.

For the coming year it is expected that Lamri will require the following capital investment.

1.   An investment equivalent to the amount of depreciation to keep its non-current asset base at the present productive capacity. Lamri charges depreciation of 25% on a straight-line basis on its non-current assets of $15 million. This charge has been included when calculating the operating profit amount.

2.   A 25% investment in additional non-current assets for every $1 increase in sales revenue.

3. $4.5 million additional investment in non-current assets for a new project.

Lamri also requires a 15% investment in working capital for every $1 increase in sales revenue.

BPP
LEARNING MEDIA

Strymon produces specialist components solely for Magnolia to assemble into finished goods. Strymon will produce 300,000 specialist components at $12 variable cost per unit and will incur fixed costs of $2.1 million for the coming year. It will then transfer the components to Magnolia at full cost price, where they will be assembled at a cost of $8 per unit and sold for $50 per unit. Magnolia will incur additional fixed costs of $1.5 million in the assembly process.

Tax-Ethic (TE) is a charitable organisation devoted to reducing tax avoidance schemes by companies operating in poor countries around the world. TE has petitioned Lamri's Board of Directors to reconsider Strymon's policy of transferring goods at full cost. TE suggests that the policy could be changed to cost plus 40% mark-up. If Lamri changes Strymon's policy, it is expected that Strymon would be asked to remit 75% of its after-tax profits as dividends to Lamri.

Other Information

1.   Lamri's outstanding non-current liabilities of $35 million, on which it pays interest of 8% per year, and its 30 million $1 issued equity capital will not change for the coming year.

2.   Lamri's, Magnolia's and Strymon's profits are taxed at 28%, 22% and 42% respectively. A withholding tax of 10% is deducted from any dividends remitted from Strymon.

3.   The tax authorities where Lamri is based charge tax on profits made by subsidiary companies but give full credit for tax already paid by overseas subsidiaries.

4.   All costs and revenues are in $ equivalent amounts and exchange rate fluctuations can be ignored.

Required

(a)   Calculate Lamri's dividend capacity for the coming year prior to implementing TE's proposal and after implementing the proposal.   **(14 marks)**

(b)   Comment on the impact of implementing TE's proposal and suggest possible actions Lamri may take as a result.   **(6 marks)**

(c)   Outline the mechanisms that the tax authorities could use to prevent transfer price manipulation by Lamri.   **(5 marks)**

(Total = 25 marks)

Questions 59 to 62 cover Emerging Issues, the subject of Part G of the BPP Study Text for Paper P4.

59 Moose Co (12/09, amended)   45 mins

You are the Chief Financial Officer of Moose Co. Moose Co is a manufacturer of cleaning equipment and has an international market for its products. Your company places a strong emphasis on innovation and design with patent protection across all its product range.

The company has two principal manufacturing centres, one in Europe which has been reduced in size in recent years because of high labour costs and the other in South East Asia. However, Moose Co's development has relied upon ready access to the debt market both in Europe and in South East Asia and the company is planning significant expansion with a new manufacturing and distribution centre in South America. Your company is highly profitable with strong cash flows although in the last two quarters there has been a downturn in sales in all markets as the global recession has begun to take effect.

Since August 20X7, credit conditions have deteriorated across all of the major economies as banks have curtailed their lending following the down rating of US asset-backed securities. In 20X8 and 20X9 many banks recorded significant multibillion dollar losses as they attempted to sell off what had become known as 'toxic debt', leading to a further collapse in their value. In response many banks also attempted to repair their balance sheets by rights and other equity issues.

The founder and executive chairman of the company, Alan Bison, is planning a round of meetings with a number of investment banks in leading financial centres around the world to explore raising a $350 million dollar loan for the new development. It has already been suggested that a loan of this size would need to be syndicated or alternatively raised through a bond issue.

The chairman has also heard about Islamic finance providing an alternative to conventional forms of finance and is keen to find out more about the benefits and drawbacks of using Islamic finance.

In preparation for those meetings he has asked you to provide him with some briefing notes.

Required

(a)   Given conditions in the global debt market as described above, advise on the likely factors banks will consider in offering a loan of this size.   **(7 marks)**

(b)   Assess the relative advantages of loan syndication versus a bond issue to Moose Co.   **(7 marks)**

(c)   Assess the relative advantages and disadvantages of entering into a capital investment of this scale at this stage of the global economic cycle.   **(6 marks)**

(d)   Discuss the benefits and drawbacks for Moose Co of using Islamic finance.   **(5 marks)**

(Total = 25 marks)

60 GoSlo Motor Corp (6/10, amended)   45 mins

The finance division of GoSlo Motor Corporation has made a number of loans to customers with a current pool value of $200 million. The loans have an average term to maturity of four years. The loans generate a steady income to the business of 10.5% per annum. The company will use 95% of the loan's pool as collateral for a collateralised loan obligation structured as follows:

−   80% of the collateral value to support a tranche of A-rated floating rate loan notes offering investors LIBOR plus 140 basis points.

−   10% of the collateral value to support a tranche of B-rated fixed rate loan notes offering investors 11%.

−   10% of the collateral value to support a tranche as subordinated certificates (unrated).

In order to minimise interest rate risk, the company has decided to enter into a fixed for variable rate swap on the A-rated floating rate notes exchanging LIBOR for 8.5%.

Service charges of $240,000 per annum will be charged for administering the income receivable from the loans.

You may ignore prepayment risk.

Required:

(a) Calculate the expected returns of the investments in each of the three tranches described above. Estimate the sensitivity of the subordinated certificates to a reduction of 1% in the returns generated by the pool.

(10 marks)

(b) Explain the purpose and the methods of credit enhancement that can be employed on a securitisation such as this scheme. **(4 marks)**

(c) Discuss the risks inherent to the investors in a scheme such as this. **(6 marks)**

(d) Aside from the securitisation, GoSlo Motor Corporation has a large corporate fleet customer which owes $5 million, to be repaid in 4 years, to GoSlo. Management is worried about the possibility of default by this customer. A credit default swap, trading at 450 basis points, can be obtained. Illustrate the result of hedging using the credit default swap:

(i) In the event of no default

(ii) In the event of a default after 3 years **(5 marks)**

(Total = 25 marks)

61 Kilenc Co (6/12, amended)   45 mins

Kilenc Co, a large listed company based in the UK, produces pharmaceutical products which are exported around the world. It is reviewing a proposal to set up a subsidiary company to manufacture a range of body and facial creams in Lanosia. These products will be sold to local retailers and to retailers in nearby countries.

Lanosia has a small but growing manufacturing industry in pharmaceutical products, although it remains largely reliant on imports. The Lanosian government has been keen to promote the pharmaceutical manufacturing industry

through purchasing local pharmaceutical products, providing government grants and reducing the industry's corporate tax rate. It also imposes large duties on imported pharmaceutical products which compete with the ones produced locally.

Although politically stable, the recent worldwide financial crisis has had a significant negative impact on Lanosia. The country's national debt has grown substantially following a bailout of its banks and it has had to introduce economic measures which are hampering the country's ability to recover from a deep recession. Growth in real wages has been negative over the past three years, the economy has shrunk in the past year and inflation has remained higher than normal during this time.

On the other hand, corporate investment in capital assets, research and development, and education and training, has grown recently and interest rates remain low. This has led some economists to suggest that the economy should start to recover soon. Employment levels remain high in spite of low nominal wage growth.

Lanosian corporate governance regulations stipulate that at least 40% of equity share capital must be held by the local population. In addition at least 50% of members on the Board of Directors, including the Chairman, must be from Lanosia. Kilenc Co wants to finance the subsidiary company using a mixture of debt and equity. It wants to raise additional equity and debt finance in Lanosia in order to minimise exchange rate exposure. The small size of the subsidiary will have minimal impact on Kilenc Co's capital structure. Kilenc Co intends to raise the 40% equity through an initial public offering (IPO) in Lanosia and provide the remaining 60% of the equity funds from its own cash funds.

Required:

(a) Discuss the key risks and issues that Kilenc Co should consider when setting up a subsidiary company in Lanosia, and suggest how these may be mitigated. **(15 marks)**

(b)   The directors of Kilenc Co have learnt that a sizeable number of equity trades in Lanosia are conducted using dark pool trading systems.

Required:

Explain what dark pool trading systems are and how Kilenc Co's proposed Initial Public Offering (IPO) may be affected by these. **(5 marks)**

(c)   Lanosia has a reputation as a country with significant levels of money laundering.

Required:

Explain the steps that Kilenc Co should take to prevent the company being used by money launderers.

(5 marks)

(Total = 25 marks)

62 NRD Co   45 mins

NRD Co is a multinational airport operator, which is considering bidding for a contract to construct and operate a new major international airport for a period of four years. The airport will be in an Islamic country, where the currency is the Dinar. NRD has no experience of airport construction or working in Islamic countries and so this project is considered to be riskier than NRD Co's existing operations.

NRD Co has budgeted 375 million Dinars for the contract bid, which would be paid at the start of the project. The airport will become operational within the first year of the project although all revenue generating aspects will not be completed until the third year of operation. There is considerable uncertainty about the post-tax operating cash flows associated with this project, as it is thought that the state of the economy will have an effect on this. To assess a likely outcome the finance department has constructed a model of expected cash flows in Dinar millions.

		Year			
Economic state	Probability	1	2	3	4
Decline	0.2	84	91	97	98
Stable	0.3	93	102	112	114
Growth	0.5	105	118	130	132

In addition, NRD Co plans to perform a Monte Carlo simulation to determine the likely outcome of the project.

NRD Co would be looking to finance the construction through debt and its bank is prepared to lend the US$ equivalent funds for this project at a pre-tax rate of 7%. NRD Co has investigated the possibility of raising local finance and has been told that only through the use of Islamic finance, specifically if NRD Co issues Sukuk, would it be possible to raise sufficient funds for the project.

Additional information

It is assumed that each economic state applies for a whole period and that each state has the same likelihood of occurring in any given period.

NRD Co pays corporate income tax at a rate of 28%.

NRD Co has a current WACC of 9%.

Required

(a)   Explain how Islamic financial institutions can make money despite being unable to charge interest.**(3 marks)**

(b)   (i)   Calculate, whether NRD Co should proceed with the bid, based on the existing information. Assume that the money is borrowed from the bank for the project. **(5 marks)**

(ii)   Evaluate the use of probability analysis and simulation by NRD Co for this project. **(7 marks)**

(c)   Discuss any issues, financial and non-financial, that may arise from the use of Islamic financing for this project. **(10 marks)**

(Total = 25 marks)

50 MARK QUESTIONS

Questions 63 to 84 are a bank of mixed 50 mark questions which cover a range of syllabus areas.

63 Vadener (SFM, 6/06, amended)   90 mins

Vadener plc, a UK based company, has instigated a review of the group's recent performance and potential future strategy. The Board of Directors has publicly stated that it is pleased with the group's performance and proposes to devote resources equally to its three operating divisions. Two of the divisions are in the UK, and focus on construction and leisure respectively, and one is in the USA and manufactures pharmaceuticals.

Recent summarised accounts for the group and data for the individual divisions are shown below:

Group data
Income statement

	20X3 £m	20X4 £m	20X5 £m
Revenue	1,210	1,410	1,490
Operating costs	800	870	930
Operating profit	410	540	560
Net interest	40	56	65
Profit before tax	370	484	495
Tax (30%)	111	145	149
Profit after tax	259	339	346
Equity dividends	146	170	185
Retained earnings	113	169	161

Statement of financial position

	20X3 £m	20X4 £m	20X5 £m
Tangible non-current assets	1,223	1,280	1,410
Intangible non-current assets	100	250	250
Current assets			
Inventory	340	410	490
Receivables	378	438	510
Cash	10	15	15
Total assets	2,051	2,393	2,675
Less Payables: amounts falling due within one year			
Trade payables*	375	486	523
Short term loans	135	170	201
Taxation	55	72	75
	1,486	1,665	1,876
Financed by			
Long term liabilities	400	410	470
Shareholders' equity	1,086	1,255	1,406
	1,486	1,665	1,876

* Trade payables include dividend of £73m, £85m, and £93m for 20X3, 20X4 and 20X5 respectively.

Note. The 20X5 amount for shareholders' equity includes a £10 million loss on translation from the US division due to the recent weakness of the US$.

Other group data at year end

	20X3	20X4	20X5
Share price (pence)	1,220	1,417	1,542
Number of issued shares (million)	300	300	300
Equity beta			1.10

The company's share price has increased by an average of 12% per year over the last five years.

Other data at year end

	20X3	20X4	20X5
FT 100 index	3,700	4,600	4,960
PE ratio of similar companies	15:1	14:1	15:1
Risk free rate (%)			5
Market return (%)			12

Divisional data 20X5

	Construction	Leisure	Pharmaceuticals
Revenue (£m)	480	560	450
Operating profit	160	220	180
Estimated after tax return (%)	13	16	14

Data for the sector

Average asset beta 20X5	0.75	1.10	1.40

Required

As senior financial manager you have been asked to write a report for the Board of Vadener plc in which you:

(a) Evaluate and comment on the performance of Vadener plc and each of its divisions. Highlight performance that appears favourable, and any areas of potential concern for the managers of Vadener. Comment upon the likely validity of the company's strategy to devote resources equally to the operating divisions.

All relevant calculations must be shown. **(28 marks)**

(b) Discuss what additional information would be useful in order to more accurately assess the performance of Vadener plc and its divisions. **(7 marks)**

(c) Discuss the possible implications for Vadener plc of the £10 million loss on translation, and recommend what action, if any, the company should take as a result of this loss. **(6 marks)**

Professional marks for format, structure and presentation of report **(4 marks)**

(d) Briefly discuss the possible objectives of transfer pricing strategies used by multinational companies, such as Vadener plc. **(5 marks)**

(Total = 50 marks)

64 International Enterprises (12/07, amended)   90 mins

You are the chief financial officer of International Enterprises, a multinational company with interests in Europe and the Far East. You are concerned about certain aspects of the company's financial management. The company has enjoyed a high rate of growth over the last three years as a result of a single product's development. This product has had a big impact in the fast moving mobile communications industry. However, the company does not have any new products in development and is relying on expanding its market share and developing upgraded versions of the current product.

As part of your preparation for the board meeting to discuss the 20X7 draft accounts, you have prepared a projected income statement and Statement of financial position for the year ending 31 December 20X8. These projections are based upon a number of agreed assumptions taken from the company's strategic plan. As part of the agenda, the board will also consider its dividend target for the forthcoming year.

International Enterprises

Income statement for the year ended 31 December	20X8 (projected)	20X7 (draft)	20X6 (actual)
	$m	$m	$m
Revenue	288.1	261.9	220.0
Cost of sales	143.2	132.6	104.0
Gross profit	144.9	129.3	116.0
less other operating costs	36.1	27.0	24.0
Operating profit	108.8	102.3	92.0
Finance costs	1.8	2.3	2.3
Profit before tax	107.0	100.0	89.7
Income tax expense (at 30%)	32.1	30.0	26.9
Profit for the period	74.9	70.0	62.8

BPP LEARNING MEDIA

Statement of financial position as at 31 December	20X8 (projected) $m	20X7 (draft) $m	20X6 (actual) $m
Non-current assets (see note)			
Buildings, plant and machinery	168.0	116.0	96.0
Current assets			
Inventories	3.2	3.7	2.3
Receivables	25.6	29.1	19.6
Cash	151.8	155.8	121.7
Total current assets	180.6	188.6	143.6
Total assets	348.6	304.6	239.6
Equity and liabilities			
Paid up share capital			
Ordinary shares (25c)	25.0	25.0	20.0
Other reserves	12.0	12.0	10.0
Retained earnings	216.9	170.0	120.0
less dividends payable	0.0	−28.0	−20.0
	216.9	142.0	100.0
Total equity	253.9	179.0	130.0
Current liabilities			
Trade payables	8.8	7.7	6.4
Tax payable	28.5	25.6	23.3
Interest	1.8	2.3	2.3
Dividends payable	0.0	28.0	20.0
Total current liabilities	39.1	63.6	52.0
Non-current liabilities			
Loans	35.0	45.0	45.0
Provisions (deferred tax)	20.6	17.0	12.6
Total non-current liabilities	55.6	62.0	57.6
Total liabilities	94.7	125.6	109.6
Total equity and liabilities	384.6	304.6	239.6

Note	20X8 $m	20X7 $m	20X6 $m
Non-current assets	280.0	200.0	160.0
less accumulated depreciation	112.0	84.0	64.0
Net book value of non-current assets	168.0	116.0	96.0

The projected figures assume:

(i) $10 million of the existing loans will be repaid during the year.

(ii)   Capital investment in plant and equipment of $80 million will be undertaken.

The company is quoted on an international stock exchange and its beta value (based upon three years of monthly return data) is 1.40. The current risk free rate is 3% and the equity risk premium is 5%. The current share price is $16.20 and the sector price/earnings ratio is 24. The company's cost of debt capital remains at its current rate of 5%. You may assume that the current cost of equity capital remains unchanged over the term of the projection.

Required

(a)   Prepare a cash flow forecast for the year ended 31 December 20X8. Note: the format does not need to comply with accounting standards. **(7 marks)**

(b)   (i)   Estimate the company's maximum dividend capacity after the target level of capital reinvestment is undertaken and making any working capital adjustments you deem necessary. **(6 marks)**

      (ii)   Discuss whether International Enterprises dividend policy is sustainable and whether dividends should be paid at the maximum capacity level or not. **(7 marks)**

(c) Draft a report for senior management which:

(i) reviews the potential performance of the business in the year ended 31 December 20X8 if the expectations contained within the strategic plan are fulfilled. You should use the Economic Value Added (EVA™) and any other performance measures you think appropriate and; **(16 marks)**

(ii) addresses the benefits and drawbacks of growth by acquisition and organic growth for International Enterprises and makes a recommendation for the most suitable method of growth. **(10 marks)**

Professional marks for format, structure and presentation of report **(4 marks)**

(Total = 50 marks)

65 McTee (SFM, 6/05, amended)   90 mins

McTee plc is a Scottish manufacturer of golf clubs. The company has decided to purchase an existing golf club manufacturer in the State of Florida, USA. The purchase will cost an agreed $72 million for fixed assets and equipment, and in addition $8 million of working capital will be needed. No additional external funding for the proposed US subsidiary is expected to be needed for at least five years, and sales from the subsidiary would be exclusively to the US market. McTee has no other foreign subsidiaries, and the company's managers are considering how to finance the US investment. McTee's bank has advised that, taking into account McTee's credit rating, the following alternatives might be possible, with finance available up to the amount shown:

(a) A one for four rights issue, at a price of 280 pence per share. Underwriting and other costs are expected to be 5% of the gross amount raised.

(b) Five-year Sterling 7% fixed rate secured bank term loan of up to £50 million, initial arrangement fee 1%.

(c) $15 million one-year commercial paper, issued at $US LIBOR plus 1.5%. This could be renewed on an annual basis. An additional 0.5% per year would be payable to a US bank for a back-up line of credit.

(d) 80 million Swiss Franc five-year fixed rate secured bank loan at 2.5%. This may be swapped into fixed rate $ at an **additional** annual interest rate of 2.3%. An upfront fee of 3.0% is also payable.

(e) £42 million 10-year Sterling Eurobond issue at 6.85%. This may be swapped into $ at an annual interest rate of 4.95%. Eurobond issue costs of 2%, and upfront swap costs of 1.7% would also be payable.

(f) $40 million floating rate six-year secured term loan from a US bank, at $US LIBOR plus 3%.

No currency swaps are available other than those shown. Currency swaps would involve swapping the principal at the current spot exchange rate, with the reversal of the swap at the same rate at the swap maturity date.

$US LIBOR is currently 3%.

Exchange rates:

	Spot	One year forward
$/£	1.7985 – 1.8008	1.7726 – 1.7746
SF/£	2.256 – 2.298	2.189 – 2.205

McTee's current statement of financial position is summarised below.

	£m
Non-current assets	117.8
Investments	8.1
Current assets	98.1
Payables: amounts falling due within one year	
Loans and other borrowings	(38.0)
Other payables	(48.6)
	137.4
Payables: amounts falling due after more than one year	
Medium and long-term bank loans	30.0
8% Bond 20X9 (par value £100)	18.0
	48.0
Capital and reserves	
Ordinary shares (25 pence par value)	20.0
Reserves	69.4
	137.4

A covenant exists that prevents the book value of McTee's debt finance from exceeding 50% of total assets. McTee's current dividend per share is 22.2 pence and dividend growth is approximately 4% per year. The company's current share price is 302 pence.

The directors are also concerned about a possible devaluation of the US dollar affecting remittances to the parent company in the UK.

Interest payments on debt financing may be assumed to be made annually at the end of the year. Corporate tax in the UK, USA and Switzerland is at a rate of 30%. Issue costs and fees such as swap fees are not tax allowable.

Required

(a)   Discuss the factors that McTee should consider before deciding how to finance the proposed US subsidiary.

(10 marks)

(b)   Prepare a report discussing and evaluating each of the six possible sources of finance, and provide a reasoned recommendation of which source, or combination of sources, McTee should use. Supporting calculations, including costs, should be provided wherever relevant.   **(20 marks)**

Professional marks for format, structure and presentation of report   **(4 marks)**

(c)   Discuss the significance to a multinational company of translation exposure and economic exposure.

(8 marks)

(d)   Briefly discuss the possible longer-term economic/cash flow implications of the possible devaluation of the US dollar for McTee.   **(4 marks)**

(e)   Briefly discuss whether or not the overseas subsidiary should use the same capital structure as the group as a whole.   **(4 marks)**

(Total = 50 marks)

66 Wurrall (SFM, 6/04, amended)   90 mins

The board of directors of Wurrall Inc has requested the production of a four-year financial plan. The key assumptions behind the plan are:

(a)   Historically, sales growth has been 9% per year. Uncertainty about future economic prospects over the next four years from 20X5–20X8 however implies that this growth rate will reduce by 1% per year after the financial year 20X5 (eg to 8% in 20X6). After four years, growth is expected to remain constant at the 20X8 rate.

(b)   Cash operating costs are estimated to be approximately 68% of sales.

(c)   Tax allowable depreciation for the past few years has been approximately 15% of the net book value of plant and machinery at year end. This is expected to continue for the next few years.

(d)   Inventories, receivables, cash in hand and 'other payables' are assumed to increase in proportion to the increase in sales. Investments are expected to remain constant.

(e)   Investment in, and net book value of, plant and machinery is expected to increase in line with sales. No investment is planned in other non-current assets other than a refurbishment of buildings at an estimated cost of $40 million in late 20X7.

(f)   Any change in interest paid as a result of changes in borrowing may be assumed to be effective in the next year. Wurrall plans to meet any changes in financing needs, with the exception of the repayment of the fixed rate loan, by adjusting its overdraft.

(g)   Wurrall currently pays 7% per annum interest on its short-term borrowing.

(h)   Corporation tax is expected to continue at its present rate over the next four years.

(i)   For the last few years the company's dividend policy has been to pay a constant percentage of earnings after tax. No changes in this policy are planned.

(j)   Wurrall has borrowed extensively from the banking system, and covenants exist that prevent the company's gearing (book value of total loans to book value of total loans plus equity) exceeding forty percent for a period of more than one year.

(k)   The company's managing director has publicly stated that both profits before tax and Wurrall's share price should increase by at least 100% during the next four years.

Summarised financial accounts of Wurrall Inc
Income statement for the year ended March 20X4

	$m
Revenue	1,639
Operating costs before depreciation	(1,225)
EBITDA	414
Tax allowable depreciation	(152)
EBIT	262
Net interest payable	(57)
Profit on ordinary activities before tax	205
Tax on ordinary activities (30%)	(62)
Dividends	(80)
Amount transferred to reserves	63

Statement of financial position as at 31 March 20X4

	$m	$m
Non-current assets		
Land and buildings	310	
Plant and machinery (net)	1,012	
Investments[1]	32	
		1,354
Current assets		
Inventories	448	
Receivables	564	
Cash in hand and short-term deposits	20	
		1,032
Payables: amounts falling due within one year:		
Short term loans and overdrafts	230	
Other payables	472	
		(702)
Payables: amounts falling due after one year:		
Borrowings (8% fixed rate)[2]		(580)
		1,104
Capital and reserves		
Called up share capital (10 cents par)		240
Reserves		864
		1,104

1   The investments yield negligible interest

2   Borrowings are scheduled to be repaid at the end of 20X6 and will be refinanced with a similar type of loan in 20X6.

The company's current share price is 210 cents, and its weighted average cost of capital is 11%.

Required

(a)   You are required to write a report for the Board of Directors which includes:

(i)   Calculated pro forma statements of financial position and income statements for each of the next four years. Clearly state any assumptions that you make.   **(12 marks)**

(ii)   A critical discussion of any problems or implications of the assumptions that are made in each of points (i) to (iv) and point (ix) in the question.   **(8 marks)**

(iii)   A free cash flow analysis, which evaluates and discusses whether or not the managing director's claims for the future share price are likely to be achievable. (The operating cash flow element of free cash flow may be estimated by: EBIT(1 – t) plus depreciation.)   **(10 marks)**

Professional marks for format, structure and presentation of report   **(4 marks)**

BPP LEARNING MEDIA

(b) The managing director believes that growth in profits before tax and the share price should be the objectives of Wurrall Inc.

Discuss whether these objectives are suitable for Wurrall Inc. **(9 marks)**

(c) Discuss the advantages and disadvantages of using EVA™ for assessing the performance of Wurrall Inc.

(7 marks)

(Total = 50 marks)

67 Blipton International (12/08, amended) 90 mins

It is now 1 December 20X3. You have been hired as a financial consultant to the Blipton International Entertainment Group which is evaluating a proposal from its hotel division to build a 400 bedroom hotel in the East End of London.

Blipton is based in Dubai and both reports and accounts for all its transactions in dollars. The current dollar/sterling spot rate is $1.4925/£. The operating costs for the hotel are expected to be £30 per occupied room per day (variable) and a fixed cost of £1.7 million per annum expressed in current prices. The proportion of bedrooms occupied, on the basis of opening for 365 days a year, is expected to be as follows:

Year ended	occupancy	Year ended	occupancy
31 December 20X4	construction	31 December 20X7	90%
31 December 20X5	40%	31 December 20X8	60%
31 December 20X6	50%	31 December 20X9	60%

UK inflation is currently projected by the Bank of England as 2.5% per annum and inflation in the United States is 4.8% per annum. These rates are expected to be constant over the term of the project. Blipton's real cost of capital is 4.2%. UK hotel property values within the London area are expected to rise in real terms by 8% per annum.

The construction cost for this hotel is estimated to be £6.2 million and it will be built over the 12 months to 31 December 20X9. A 50% first year capital allowance is available for tax purposes on building projects. The balance of the capital expenditure can be claimed in equal instalments over the following three years. UK profit tax is 30% and is levied and paid on profits in the year they arise. There is no additional tax liability on remittance to or from Dubai. The company has sufficient UK profits on its other activities to absorb the capital allowances on this project.

In making investment decisions of this type the company operates the following procedure:

1. All cash flows including construction costs are assumed to arise at the end of the year concerned and are to be projected in nominal (money) terms over the six year period.

2. The residual value of the investment at the end of six years is assumed to be the open market value of the property less a charge for repairs and renewals.

3. The charge for repairs and renewals is expected to be £1.2 million in current prices payable on disposal.

4. The net present value of the project should be based upon a 100% remittance of net cash flows to Dubai and should be calculated in dollars.

5. Average room rates are set at the level required to recover variable cost plus 100%.

Required

(a) Prepare a report for management to include the following:

(i) A six-year nominal dollar projection of the after tax cash flow for this project distinguishing between cash flows arising from its investment phase and those arising from its return phase. **(12 marks)**

(ii) An estimate of the project's dollar net present value and the modified internal rate of return.

Note: you may use the following formula $MIRR = \left[\dfrac{PV_R}{PV_I}\right]^{\frac{1}{n}}(1+r_e)-1$

Where PV_R is the present value of the return phase of the project, PV_I is the present value of the investment phase and r_e is the firm's cost of capital. **(8 marks)**

(iii)   An assessment of the viability of the project with a summary of the relative advantages and disadvantages of the net present value and modified internal rate of return methods in investment appraisal. **(8 marks)**

Professional marks for format, structure and presentation of report   **(4 marks)**

(b)   Blipton is considering a further project to take place in South East Asia, which would involve expanding its hotel business. These hotels would either be newly constructed and run through a joint-equity venture with a local hotel chain or by refurbishing existing hotels which are then licensed to the existing hotel operators.

Required

Discuss the advantages and disadvantages to Blipton of the above proposals.   **(10 marks)**

(c)   Evaluate whether Blipton should undertake capital investment monitoring and use post-completion audits for its large investment projects.   **(8 marks)**

(Total = 50 marks)

68 Jupiter Co (12/08, amended)   90 mins

Rosa Nelson, the Chief Financial Officer (CFO) of Jupiter Co, has been in discussion with the firm's advisors about refinancing the capital of the firm. She is considering a scheme to repay current borrowings of $800 million and raise new capital through a bond issue of $2,400 million. The current debt consists of several small loans raised in the Euro market with differing maturities and carrying an average rate of interest of 5.6%. The average term to maturity of the existing debt is four years. The new debt would be in the form of 10 year, fixed interest bonds with half being raised in the Yen and half in the Euro market. The yield to maturity of an appropriate government bond and the relevant credit risk premium for a company of Jupiter's credit rating in the Japanese and the European market is shown below:

	Yield to maturity		Credit risk premium (basis points)	
	4 years	*10 years*	*4 years*	*10 years*
Japanese Government Bonds	1.00%	1.80%	35	50
European Government Bonds	4.20%	4.60%	45	85

Jupiter's current beta is 1.50. The current risk free rate is 4.0% and the equity risk premium is 3.0%.

The company currently earns a free cash flow to equity of $400 million after interest, tax and net reinvestment. The company consistently reinvests 30% of that free cash flow within the firm and makes the balance available for distribution to investors. The free cash flow to equity model has provided a reasonable estimate of the company's equity market valuation in the past. The current share price, based upon 500 million fully paid, 25¢ equity shares, is 1,380¢. The current rate of tax on corporate profits is 25%. Management is of the view that the additional borrowing will lead to the company being able to increase its earnings growth rate to 4%.

You may assume:

1.   Interest on the firm's debt is paid annually.
2.   The debt in issue and proposed has a zero beta.
3.   The firm's share price will be unaffected by the alteration in gearing.
4.   Foreign exchange risk may be ignored.

Jupiter imports goods from Europe for sale in its home market, where the currency is the US$.

The directors of Jupiter are aware that the company is subject to significant economic exposure to movements on the euro because any appreciation of the euro will increase the cost of goods for resale. Jupiter has attempted to create a partial hedge against this by placing cash reserves in a euro bank account. That way the losses associated with any increase in cost prices will be partially offset by a gain on the bank account.

The directors are concerned that the translation gains and losses on the euro bank balance are visible to shareholders, whereas the offsetting of economic exposure is not and so their hedging policy may be misunderstood.

The Euro bank account has a balance of €70m. The exchange rate is presently €1.3 to US$1. The daily standard deviation of the balance when it is translated to $ is $650,000.

BPP LEARNING MEDIA

Required

As Deputy Chief Financial Officer prepare a briefing note for Rosa Nelson. Your note should include:

(a) An assessment of the firm's current cost of debt, cost of equity and weighted average cost of capital.

(6 marks)

(b) An assessment of the firm's expected cost of debt, cost of equity and weighted average cost of capital after the redemption of the existing debt and the issue of the new bonds. **(8 marks)**

(c) An assessment of the minimum rate of return that the company needs to earn on the new debt capital before interest is paid. **(6 marks)**

(d) A comparison of the proposed method of raising capital for investment purposes with alternative means of raising the debt finance required. **(8 marks)**

Quality and presentation of the briefing note. **(2 marks)**

(e) Evaluate the validity of the directors' concern that "the translation gains and losses on the US$ bank balance are visible to shareholders, whereas the offsetting of economic exposure is not and so their hedging policy may be misunderstood". **(10 marks)**

(f) (i) Calculate the 95% daily value at risk (VaR) of Jupiter's euro bank balance. **(3 marks)**

(ii) Use your answer to (c)(i) to calculate the 95% 30-day VaR of Jupiter's euro bank balance. **(2 marks)**

(iii) Advise the directors on the relevance of the VaR statistic to their consideration of the risks associated with retaining this euro bank balance. **(5 marks)**

(Total = 50 marks)

69 Trosoft (SFM, 12/04, amended) 90 mins

Trosoft pte Ltd is an unlisted Singapore based company specialising in the development of business software. Although Trosoft currently has significant surplus cash balances as a result of the success of its products over the last few years, the company's managers believe that its future growth potential in the software sector is limited, and are considering diversifying into other activities either through developing other activities internally, or through acquisition or merger. One suggestion is to start offering Internet auctions, and a member of the management team has produced the following draft financial proposal.

Internet auctions project

Year	0	1	2	3	4
	S$'000	S$'000	S$'000	S$'000	S$'000
Auction fees	–	4,300	6,620	8,100	8,200
Outflows:					
IT maintenance costs	–	1,210	1,850	1,920	2,125
Telephone	–	1,215	1,910	2,230	2,420
Wages	–	1,460	1,520	1,680	1,730
Salaries	–	400	550	600	650
Allocated head office overhead	–	85	90	95	100
Marketing	500	420	200	200	–
Royalty payments for use of technology	680	500	300	200	200
Market research	110	–	–	–	–
Rental of premises	–	280	290	300	310
Total outflows	1,290	5,570	6,710	7,225	7,355
Profit before tax	(1,290)	(1,270)	(90)	875	665
Tax	316	311	22	(214)	(163)
Other outflows:					
IT infrastructure	(2,700)	–	–	–	–
Working capital	(400)	(24)	(24)	(25)	(26)
Net flows	(4,074)	(983)	(92)	636	476

Additional information

(a) All data include the estimated effects of inflation on costs and prices wherever relevant. Inflation in Singapore is forecast to be 2% per year for the foreseeable future.

(b) The investment in IT infrastructure and the initial working capital will be financed by a 6 year 5.5% fixed rate term loan. Other year 0 outlays will be financed from existing cash flows.

(c) The Singapore government is expected to give a 1% per year subsidy to the cost of the loan to support the creation of jobs associated with this project.

(d) Highly skilled IT staff would need to be taken from other activities resulting in a loss of S$80,000 per year pre-tax contribution for three years.

(e) Head office cash flows for overheads will increase by S$50,000 as a result of the project in year one, rising by S$5,000 per year after year one.

(f) Corporate tax is at a rate of 24.5% per year, payable in the year that the tax liability arises. The company has other profitable projects.

(g) Tax allowable depreciation on IT infrastructure is 20% for the first year, and straight line thereafter. The IT infrastructure has an expected working life of six years after which major new investment would be required.

(h) The company's current weighted average cost of capital is 7.8%.

(i) The company's equity beta can be assumed to be 1.05.

(j) The average equity beta of companies in the Internet auctions sector is 1.42.

(k) The market return is 9.5% per year and the risk free rate 4% per year.

(l) Trosoft's capital gearing is:

Book value 55% equity, 45% debt
Market value 70% equity, 30% debt

(m) The average gearing of companies in the Internet auction sector is 67% equity, 33% debt by market values.

(n) The market research survey was undertaken three weeks ago.

(o) After tax operating net cash flows after year 4 are expected to stay approximately constant in real terms. The royalty payment will remain at S$200,000 in money terms.

(p) Issue costs on debt are 1.5%. These costs are not tax allowable.

Required

(a) Acting as an external consultant you have been asked to prepare a report on the proposed diversification of the company into Internet auctions.

The report must include a revised financial analysis. You should use the adjusted present value method for this purpose.

Include in your report discussion of the limitations of the method used and other financial and non financial factors, including real options, that Trosoft might consider prior to making the investment decision.

(32 marks)

Professional marks for format, structure and presentation of report **(4 marks)**

(b) Discuss whether it is necessary for Trosoft to diversify to reduce its risk when its shareholders can diversify the risk themselves, if they wish to do so. **(7 marks)**

(c) Diversification is one source of financial synergy resulting from an acquisition. Discuss other sources of financial synergy following an acquisition or merger. **(7 marks)**

(Total = 50 marks)

70 Your company (FS, 6/99, amended)   90 mins

Your company is reviewing its policies on funding and cost of capital. The company has extensive global operations. Several issues are under review.

(1)   The company wishes to issue a policy statement for board approval on the sourcing of debt capital from bond markets around the world. There is a proposal that the company should make much more use of developing bond markets, and in particular the market for 'dim sum' bonds and the markets for Islamic bonds ('sukuk'). Dim sum bonds are bonds issued in the Hong Kong bond market and denominated in renminbi (or yuan), the Chinese currency which is becoming more internationalised.

(2)   The company has bank accounts with several European banks. Some of these are in the euro currency zone (the eurozone). Senior management of the company are concerned about the financial stability of European banks in eurozone countries, following the onset of the European Sovereign Debt Crisis from late 2010. They want to review the banking policy.

(3)   Senior management also wish to establish a formal policy for the calculation of company's cost of capital for the purpose of investment appraisal. This will be issued in a guidance manual. An initial draft of the guidance manual has been produced. Extracts from the draft manual, which includes worked examples, are reproduced below.

Guidance manual for estimating the cost of capital

(1)   It is essential that the discount rate used reflects the weighted average cost of capital of the company.
(2)   The cost of equity and cost of debt should always be estimated using market values.
(3)   Inflation must always be included in the discount rate.
(4)   The capital asset pricing model or the dividend valuation model may be used in estimating the cost of equity.
(5)   The cost of debt is to be estimated using the redemption yield of existing debt.
(6)   Always round the solution up to the nearest whole percentage. This is a safeguard if the cost of capital is underestimated.

Illustrative examples

The current date is assumed to be June 20X9, with four years until the redemption of the loan stock.

Relevant data

	Book values $m	Market values $m
Equity (50 million ordinary shares)	140	214
Debt 10% loan stock 20Y3 $80m	80	85

	Per share	Annual growth rates
Dividends	24 cents	6%
Earnings	67 cents	9%

The beta value of the company (asset beta) is 1.1

Other information

Market return	14%
Risk free rate	6%
Current inflation	4%
Corporate tax rate	30%

Illustration 1 – When the company is expanding existing activities

Cost of equity

Dividend valuation model: $\dfrac{D}{P} + g = \dfrac{24}{428} + 0.09 = 0.146$ or 14.6%

Capital asset pricing model:

$$k_e = R_f + (R_m - R_f) \beta$$
$$= 6\% + (14\% - 6\%) \, 1.1$$
$$= 14.8\%$$

Cost of debt

To find the redemption yield, with four years to maturity, the following equation must be solved.

Debt is assumed to be redeemed at par value and interest to be payable annually. Estimates are based upon total interest payments of $80m at 10% or $8m per year.

$$85 = \frac{8}{(1+k_d)} + \frac{8}{(1+k_d)^2} + \frac{8}{(1+k_d)^3} + \frac{88}{(1+k_d)^4}$$

By trial and error

At 9% interest

8 × 3.240	25.92
80 × 0.708	56.64
	82.56

9% discount rate is too high

At 7% interest

8 × 3.387	27.10
80 × 0.763	61.04
	88.14

Interpolating:

$$7\% + \frac{3.14}{3.14 + 2.44} \times 2\% = 8.13\%$$

The cost of debt is 8.13%

Market value of equity $214m
Market value of debt $85m

Weighted average cost of capital:

(CAPM has been used in this estimate. The dividend valuation model would result in a similar answer.)

$$14.8\% \times \frac{214}{299} + 8.13\% \times \frac{85}{299} = 12.90\%$$

Inflation of 4% must be added to the discount rate.

The discount rate to be used in the investment appraisal is 12.90% + 4% = 16.90% or 17% rounded up to the nearest whole percentage.

Illustration 2 – When the company is diversifying its activities

The asset beta of a similar sized company in the industry in which your company proposes to diversify is 0.90.
Gearing of the similar company

	Book values ($m)	Market values ($m)
Equity	165	230
Debt	65	60

Cost of equity

The beta of the comparator company is used as a measure of the systematic risk of the new investment. As the gearing of the two companies differs, the beta must be adjusted for the difference in gearing.

BPP
LEARNING MEDIA

Ungearing

Beta equity = beta assets $\times \dfrac{E}{E + D(1-t)}$

Beta equity = $0.90 \times \dfrac{230}{230 + 60(1 - 0.3)} = 0.76$

Using the capital asset pricing model:

$ke = R_f + (R_m - R_f)$ beta
  $= 6\% + (14\% - 6\%)\ 0.76$
  $= 12.08\%$

Cost of debt

This remains at 8.13%

Market value of equity $214m
Market value of debt $85m

Weighted average cost of capital:

$12.08\% \times \dfrac{214}{299} + 8.13\% \times \dfrac{85}{299} = 10.96\%$

The discount rate to be used in the investment appraisal when diversifying into the new industry is 10.96% + 4% inflation, 14.96% or 15% rounded up to the nearest %.

Required

(a) Discuss the appropriateness of the proposal that the company should make use of the dim sum bond market and the Islamic bond markets as future sources of financing. **(8 marks)**

(b) Discuss the origins of the European Sovereign Debt Crisis and its implications for many banks in the eurozone, and recommend measures that the company could take to reduce its exposure to 'bank risk'. **(8 marks)**

(c) Produce a revised version of the draft manual for estimating the cost of capital. This should include revisions to both the written guidance notes and the illustrative examples. Where revisions are made to any of the six guidance notes, or to the illustrations, a brief discussion of the reason for your revision should be included. State clearly any assumptions that you make.

(30 marks)

Professional marks for format, structure and presentation of the manual for part (c). **(4 marks)**

(Total = 50 marks)

71 Omnikit (FS, 6/97, amended)   90 mins

Omnikit plc is a manufacturer of kitchen furniture in the UK. The company's senior management have believed for several years that there is little opportunity to increase sales in the UK market and wish to set up a manufacturing subsidiary in Switzerland or the USA. Because of high transportation costs, exporting from the UK is not financially viable.

The Swiss subsidiary would involve the construction of a new factory on a 'green field' site. The projected costs are shown below.

Swiss subsidiary

	Now SFr'000	Year 1 SFr'000
Land	2,300	–
Building	1,600	6,200
Machinery	–	6,400
Working capital	–	11,500

Production and sales in year two are estimated to be 2,000 kitchens at an average price of SFr20,000 (at current prices). Production in each of years 3-6 is forecast at 2,500 units. Total local variable costs in Switzerland in year two are expected to be SFr11,000 per unit (at current prices). In addition a fixed royalty fee of £750,000 per year would be payable to the UK parent company. Tax allowable depreciation in Switzerland on machines is at 25% per year on a reducing balance basis. No tax allowable depreciation exists on other non-current assets.

The US investment would involve the purchase, via a takeover bid, of an existing kitchen furniture manufacturer based in Boston. The cost is not precisely known but Omnikit's managers are confident that a bid within the range $8m-10m will be successful. Additional investment of $2 million in new machines and $4 million in working capital would immediately be required, resulting in forecast pre-tax net cash flows (after tax savings from depreciation) in year one of $2 million (at current prices) rising to $3 million (at current prices) in year two and subsequent years.

All prices and costs in Switzerland and the USA are expected to increase annually by the current rate of inflation. The after-tax realisable value of the investments in six years' time is expected to be approximately SFr16.2 million and US$14.5 million at price levels then ruling, excluding working capital.

Inflation rates for each of the next six years are expected to be:

USA	6%
UK	3%
Switzerland	5%

Exchange rates

	SFr/£	$/£
Spot	2.3140 – 2.3210	1.5160 – 1.5210

Omnikit can borrow funds for the investment at 10% per year in the UK. The company's cost of equity capital is estimated to be 15%. After either proposed investment Omnikit's gearing will be approximately 50% debt, 50% equity by book value, and 30% debt, 70% equity by market value.

Corporate tax in Switzerland is at 40%, in the UK 33% and the USA 30%, Full bilateral tax treaties, exist between the UK and both Switzerland and the USA. Taxation is payable, and allowances are available, one year in arrears.

The CEO is interested in transfer prices that can be charged between group companies. She understands the idea of the arm's length standard, but wants to know more about the following terms she has heard mentioned: Comparable uncontrolled price method, resale price method and profit split method.

Required

(a)   Discuss the advantages and disadvantages of organic growth and growth by acquisition.   **(7 marks)**

(b)   Produce a report which:

Evaluates which, if either, of the two subsidiaries should be established by Omnikit. Use the net present value method for this evaluation. Include discussion of the limitations of your evaluation. State clearly any assumptions that you make.   **(24 marks)**

Professional marks for format, structure and presentation of report   **(4 marks)**

(c)   Discuss the non-financial issues that Omnikit plc should consider before making the final decision to set up an overseas manufacturing subsidiary.   **(7 marks)**

(d)   Explain the transfer pricing terms: comparable uncontrolled price method, resale price method and profit split method and the difference between transactions-based and profit-based approaches.   **(8 marks)**

(Total = 50 marks)

72 Intergrand (SFM, 12/02, amended)   90 mins

The Board of Directors of Intergrand Inc wishes to establish an operating subsidiary in Germany through the acquisition of an existing German company. Intergrand has undertaken research into a number of German quoted companies, and has decided to attempt to purchase Oberberg AG. Initial discussions suggest that the directors of Oberberg AG may be willing to recommend the sale of 100% of the company's equity to Intergrand for a total cash price of 115 million Euro, payable in full on acquisition.

BPP LEARNING MEDIA

Oberberg has provided the managers of Intergrand with internal management information regarding accounting/cash flow projections for the next four years.

The projects are in money/nominal terms.

Oberberg AG, financial projections
Euro (million)

Year	20X3	20X4	20X5	20X6
Sales	38.2	41.2	44.0	49.0
Labour	11.0	12.1	13.0	14.1
Materials	8.3	8.7	9.0	9.4
Overheads	3.2	3.2	3.3	3.4
Interest	2.5	3.0	3.5	3.8
Tax allowable depreciation	6.3	5.8	5.6	5.2
	31.3	32.8	34.4	35.9
Taxable profit	6.9	8.4	9.6	13.1
Taxation (25%)	1.7	2.1	2.4	3.3
Incremental operating working capital	0.7	0.9	1.0	2.0
Replacement investment	4.2	4.2	4.2	4.2
Investment for expansion	–	–	9.0	–

Oberberg AG, pro forma summarised income statement for the year ending 31 December 20X2

	Euro (million)
Revenue	35.8
Operating expenses	21.1
Interest expense	3.4
Depreciation	6.2
	30.7
Taxable profit	5.1
Taxation (25%)	1.3
Profit after tax	3.8

Oberberg AG, pro forma summarised statement of financial position as at 31 December 20X2

	Euro (million)
Non-current assets	73.2
Current assets	58.1
Current liabilities	(40.3)
	91.0
Financed by:	
Ordinary shares (100 Euro par value)	15.0
Reserves	28.0
Medium and long term bank loans	30.0
8% Bond 20X9 (par value 1,000 Euro)	18.0
	91.0

Notes

(a)   The spot exchange rate between the Euro and dollar is Euro 1.625/$.

(b)   Inflation is at 4% per year in the US and 2% per year in the Euro bloc. This differential is expected to continue.

(c)   The market return is 11% and the risk free rate is 4%.

(d)   Oberberg's equity beta is estimated to be 1.4.

(e)   Oberberg's 8% bond is currently priced at 1,230 Euro and its ordinary share price is 300 Euro.

(f)   Post-merger rationalisation will involve the sale of some non-current assets of Oberberg in 20X3 with an expected after tax market value of 8 million Euro.

(g)   Synergies in production and distribution are expected to yield 2 million Euro per annum before tax from 20X4 onwards.

(h) $175,000 has already been spent researching into possible acquisition targets.

(i)   The purchase of Oberberg will provide publicity and exposure in Germany for the Intergrand name and brand. This extra publicity is believed to be the equivalent of Intergrand spending 1 million Euro per year on advertising in Germany.

(j)   The weighted average cost of capital of Intergrand is 10%.

(k)   After tax cash flows of Oberberg after 20X6 are expected to grow at approximately 2% per year.

(l)   Oberberg does not plan to issue or redeem any equity or medium and long-term debt prior to 20X6.

(m)   After tax redundancy costs as a result of the acquisition are expected to be 5 million Euro, payable almost immediately.

(n)   Operating working capital comprises receivables and inventory less payables. It excludes short-term loans.

(o)   Current liabilities include negligible amounts of short-term loans.

(p)   The corporate tax rate in Germany is 25% and in the US 30%. A bilateral tax treaty exists between the two countries whereby tax paid in one country may be credited against any tax liability in the other country.

(q)   If Intergrand acquires Oberberg existing exports to Germany yielding a pre-tax cash flow of $800,000 per annum will be lost. It is hoped that about half of these exports can be diverted to the French market.

Required

(a)   Intergrand has suggested that Oberberg should be valued based upon the expected present value (to infinity) of the operating free cash flows of Oberberg. These would be discounted at an all-equity rate and adjusted by the present value of all other relevant cash flows, discounted at an appropriate rate(s).

Acting as a consultant to Intergrand Inc, prepare a report evaluating whether or not Intergrand should offer the 115 million Euro required to acquire Oberberg AG. Include in your report discussion of other commercial and business factors that Intergrand should consider prior to making a final decision.

Assume that it is now mid-December 20X2.

State clearly any other assumptions that you make.   **(30 marks)**

Professional marks for format, structure and presentation of report   **(4 marks)**

(b)   Discuss the reasons why acquisitions and mergers are not always successful and suggest steps that Intergrand can take to reduce the risk of failure.   **(10 marks)**

(c)   Some companies use eurobonds to raise finance for overseas expansion. Discuss the advantages and disadvantages of using eurobonds for this purpose.   **(6 marks)**

(Total = 50 marks)

73 Pursuit Co (6/11, amended)   90 mins

Pursuit Co, a listed company which manufactures electronic components, is interested in acquiring Fodder Co, an unlisted company involved in the development of sophisticated but high risk electronic products. The owners of Fodder Co are a consortium of private equity investors who have been looking for a suitable buyer for their company for some time. Pursuit Co estimates that a payment of the equity value plus a 25% premium would be sufficient to secure the purchase of Fodder Co. Pursuit Co would also pay off any outstanding debt that Fodder Co owed. Pursuit Co wishes to acquire Fodder Co using a combination of debt finance and its cash reserves of $20 million, such that the capital structure of the combined company remains at Pursuit Co's current capital structure level.

Information on Pursuit Co and Fodder Co

Pursuit Co

Pursuit Co has a market debt to equity ratio of 50:50 and an equity beta of 1.18. Currently Pursuit Co has a total firm value (market value of debt and equity combined) of $140 million. Pursuit Co makes sales in America, Europe and Asia and has obtained some of its debt funding from international markets.

Fodder Co, Income Statement Extracts

Year Ended All amounts are in $'000	31 May 2011	31 May 2010	31 May 2009	31 May 2008
Sales revenue	16,146	15,229	14,491	13,559
Operating profit (after operating costs and tax allowable depreciation)	5,169	5,074	4,243	4,530
Net interest costs	489	473	462	458
Profit before tax	4,680	4,601	3,781	4,072
Taxation (28%)	1,310	1,288	1,059	1,140
After tax profit	3,370	3,313	2,722	2,932
Dividends	123	115	108	101
Retained earnings	3,247	3,198	2,614	2,831

Fodder Co has a market debt to equity ratio of 10:90 and an estimated equity beta of 1.53. It can be assumed that its tax allowable depreciation is equivalent to the amount of investment needed to maintain current operational levels. However, Fodder Co will require an additional investment in assets of 22c per $1 increase in sales revenue, for the next four years. It is anticipated that Fodder Co will pay interest at 9% on its future borrowings.

For the next four years, Fodder Co's sales revenue will grow at the same average rate as the previous years. After the forecasted four-year period, the growth rate of its free cash flows will be half the initial forecast sales revenue growth rate for the foreseeable future.

Information about the combined company

Following the acquisition, it is expected that the combined company's sales revenue will be $51,952,000 in the first year, and its profit margin on sales will be 30% for the foreseeable future. After the first year the growth rate in sales revenue will be 5.8% per year for the following three years. Following the acquisition, it is expected that the combined company will pay annual interest at 6.4% on future borrowings.

The combined company will require additional investment in assets of $513,000 in the first year and then 18c per $1 increase in sales revenue for the next three years. It is anticipated that after the forecasted four-year period, its free cash flow growth rate will be half the sales revenue growth rate.

It can be assumed that the asset beta of the combined company is the weighted average of the individual companies' asset betas, weighted in proportion of the individual companies' market value.

Other information

The current annual government base rate is 4.5% and the market risk premium is estimated at 6% per year. The relevant annual tax rate applicable to all the companies is 28%.

SGF Co's interest in Pursuit Co

There have been rumours of a potential bid by SGF Co to acquire Pursuit Co. Some financial press reports have suggested that this is because Pursuit Co's share price has fallen recently. SGF Co is in a similar line of business as Pursuit Co and, until a couple of years ago, SGF Co was the smaller company. However, a successful performance has resulted in its share price rising, and SGF Co is now the larger company.

The rumours of SGF Co's interest have raised doubts about Pursuit Co's ability to acquire Fodder Co. Although SGF Co has made no formal bid yet, Pursuit Co's board is keen to reduce the possibility of such a bid. The Chief Financial Officer has suggested that the most effective way to reduce the possibility of a takeover would be to distribute the $20 million in its cash reserves to its shareholders in the form of a special dividend. Fodder Co would then be purchased using debt finance. He conceded that this would increase Pursuit Co's gearing level but suggested it may increase the company's share price and make Pursuit Co less appealing to SGF Co.

Required:

(a)   Prepare a report to the Board of Directors of Pursuit Co that

    (i)   Evaluates whether the acquisition of Fodder Co would be beneficial to Pursuit Co and its shareholders. The free cash flow to firm method should be used to estimate the values of Fodder Co and the combined company assuming that the combined company's capital structure stays the same as that of Pursuit Co's current capital structure. Include all relevant calculations; **(16 marks)**

    (ii)   Discusses the limitations of the estimated valuations in part (i) above; **(4 marks)**

(iii) Estimates the amount of debt finance needed, in addition to the cash reserves, to acquire Fodder Co and concludes whether Pursuit Co's current capital structure can be maintained; **(3 marks)**

(iv) Explains the implications of a change in the capital structure of the combined company, to the valuation method used in part (i) and how the issue can be resolved; **(4 marks)**

(v) Assesses whether the Chief Financial Officer's recommendation would provide a suitable defence against a bid from SGF Co and would be a viable option for Pursuit Co. **(5 marks)**

Professional marks will be awarded in this question for the format, structure and presentation of the report.

(4 marks)

(b) Assess how the global debt crisis may affect Pursuit Co. **(8 marks)**

(c) The CEO has heard that many companies in the industry use environmental reporting. Discuss what this would involve for Pursuit Co and the advantages and disadvantages to Pursuit Co of adding environmental reporting to its annual report. **(6 marks)**

(Total = 50 marks)

74 Laceto (FS, 6/01, amended)   90 mins

(a) Laceto Inc, a large retail group specialising in the sale of clothing and electrical goods is currently considering a takeover bid for a competitor, in the electrical goods sector, Omnigen Inc, whose share price has fallen by 205 cents during the last three months.

Summarised data for the financial year to 31 March 20X1

	$ million	
	Laceto	Omnigen
Revenue	420	180
Profit before tax (after interest payments)	41	20
Taxation	12	6
Non-current assets (net)	110	63
Current assets	122	94
Current liabilities	86	71
Medium and long-term liabilities	40	12
Shareholders' funds	106	74

The share price of Laceto is currently 380 cents, and of Omnigen 410 cents. Laceto has 80 million issued ordinary shares and Omnigen 30 million. Typical of Laceto's medium and long-term liabilities is 12% loan stock with three years to maturity, a par value of $100, and a current market price of $108.80.

The finance team of Laceto has produced the following forecasts of financial data for the activities of Omnigen if it is taken over.

	$ million			
Financial year	20X2	20X3	20X4	20X5
Net sales	230	261	281	298
Cost of goods sold (50%)	115	131	141	149
Selling and administrative expenses	32	34	36	38
Capital allowances (total)	40	42	42	42
Interest	18	16	14	12
Cash flow needed for asset replacement and forecast growth	50	52	55	58

Corporate taxation is at the rate of 30% per year, payable in the year that the taxable cash flow occurs.

The risk-free rate is 6% per year and market return 14% per year. Omnigen's current equity beta is 1.2. This is expected to increase by 0.1 if the company is taken over as Laceto would increase the current level of capital gearing associated with the activities of Omnigen. Laceto's gearing post acquisition is expected to be between 18% and 23% (debt to debt plus equity by market values), depending upon the final price paid for Omnigen.

BPP LEARNING MEDIA

Post-takeover cash flows of Omnigen (after replacement and growth expenditure) are expected to grow at between 3% and 5% per year after 20X5.

Additional notes

(i)   The realisable value of Omnigen's assets, net of all repayments, is estimated to be $82 million.

(ii)   The PE ratios of two of Omnigen's quoted competitors in the electrical industry are 13:1 and 15:1 respectively.

Required

Produce a report which:

(i)   discusses and evaluates what price, or range of prices, Laceto should offer to purchase the shares of Omnigen. State clearly any assumptions that you make.   **(25 marks)**

(ii)   analyses the factors to consider when deciding whether to make a cash or a paper bid   **(7 marks)**

(iii)   discusses the methods by which Laceto could finance a cash offer   **(6 marks)**

Professional marks for format, structure and presentation of report   **(4 marks)**

(b)   Before making a bid for Omnigen the managing director of Laceto hears a rumour that a bid for Laceto might be made by Agressa.com Inc, an Internet retailer specialising in the sale of vehicles and electrical goods. Summarised financial data for Agressa.com are shown below.

Agressa.com	$m
Revenue	190
Operating profit	12
Interest	4
Taxation	2
Non-current assets (net)	30
Current assets	80
Current liabilities	30
Medium and long-term liabilities	40
Shareholders' funds	40

Agressa's current share price is $26.50 and the company has 15 million issued ordinary shares.

Required

Prepare a brief report for the managing director of Laceto which analyses how Laceto might defend itself from a takeover bid from Agressa.com.   **(8 marks)**

(Total = 50 marks)

75 Anchorage Retail Co (12/09, amended)   90 mins

Anchorage Retail Company is a large high street and on-line retailer that has lost its position as the premier quality clothes, household goods and food chain in the European market. Five years previously there had been speculation that the company would be a takeover target for any one of a number of private equity firms. However, a newly appointed and flamboyant Chief Executive Officer, John Bear, initiated a major capital reconstruction and a highly aggressive turnaround strategy.

The reaction to that turnaround strategy was an improvement in the company's share price from $3 to $7 per share over the subsequent three years. The private equity firms who had been interested in acquiring the company were deterred for two principal reasons. First John Bear had a reputation for his aggressive style and his history of defending his companies against takeover. Second the share price of Anchorage had reached a record high.

In recent months a belief in the investment community had become widespread that the revival of the company's performance had more to do with the reorganisation of the firm's capital than the success of John Bear's turnaround strategy. John Bear insisted, however, that the improvements in the reported 'bottom line' reflected a sustainable improvement in the performance of the business. However, the recession in the European retail market following the 'credit crunch' led to a sharp reduction in Anchorage's share price reinforced by concerns in the financial markets that John Bear has become too dominant in the board of the company.

The most recent accounts for Anchorage Retail, in summary form, are as follows:

Anchorage Retail Company

	20X9 $m	20X8 $m
Income statement		
Sales Turnover	9,000	8,500
Cost of Sales	5,500	5,250
Gross Profit	3,500	3,250
less other operating costs	2,250	2,220
Operating profit	1,250	1,030
Finance Costs	80	110
Profit before tax	1,170	920
Income tax expense (at 30%)	310	270
Profit for the period	860	650

	2009 $m	2008 $m
Statement of financial position		
Assets		
Non-current assets	4,980	4,540
Current assets	1,220	850
Total assets	6,200	5,390
Equity and Liabilities		
Ordinary share capital (25c)	400	425
Share premium	230	200
Capital redemption reserve	2,300	2,300
Other reserves	(6,540)	(6,500)
Retained earnings	5,990	5,400
Dividends payable	(350)	(270)
Total equity	2,030	1,555
Non-current liabilities	1,900	1,865
Current liabilities	2,270	1,970
Total equity and liabilities	6,200	5,390

	20X9 $m
Summary cash flow statement	
Operating cash flow	1,610
less interest	(110)
less taxation	(270)
Free cash flow before reinvestment	1,230
Dividend paid	(270)
CAPEX	(740)
Financing	(70)
Net cash flow	150

The management of Polar Finance, a large private equity investment fund, has begun a review following the sale of a substantial part of its investment portfolio. It is now considering Anchorage as a potential target for acquisition. They have contacted you and asked if you would provide a brief report on the financial performance of Anchorage Retail and give an independent view on a bid the company is considering for the business. The suggested bid would be in the form of a cash offer of $3.20 a share which would represent a 60¢ premium on the current share price. Reviewing the fund's existing business portfolio prior to acquisition you estimate that its asset beta is 0.285. Polar Finance has equity funds under management of $1,125 million and a market based gearing ratio (debt as a proportion of total capital employed) of 0·85. This acquisition would be financed from additional cash resources and by additional borrowing of $2·5 billion. It is expected that Anchorage's proportion of the total post-acquisition cash flows will be 20%. Polar Finance does not pay tax on its income.

During your investigations you discover the following:

1. The equity beta for Anchorage is 0.75. The current risk free rate is 5%. In order to estimate the rate of return on the market using the dividend growth model you note that the current dividend yield on a broadly based market index is 3·1% and the growth in GDP is 4% nominal. The growth of the firms in the index is fairly represented by growth in GDP.

2. Anchorage has a gearing ratio based upon market capitalisation of 24%. You estimate that its current cost of debt capital is 6·2%. You may assume that Anchorage's cost of finance has been constant over the last twelve months.

You may use year end statement of financial position values when calculating performance ratios.

BPP LEARNING MEDIA

Required

Prepare a report for Polar Finance:

(a)   Outlining the principal risks that Polar Finance should consider when assessing an acquisition of this size.
        (6 marks)

(b)   Summarising the performance of Anchorage in 20X9 compared with 20X8 on the basis of the EVA® for each year and using two other ratios you consider appropriate.   **(12 marks)**

(c)   Estimating the impact of this acquisition upon the required rate of return of equity investors in Polar Finance.
        (6 marks)

(d)   Evaluating the argument that this company may have been systematically undervalued by the market and therefore a suitable target for acquisition.   **(4 marks)**

Professional marks will be awarded for the appropriateness of the format and presentation of the report and the effectiveness with which its advice is communicated.   **(4 marks)**

Anchorage will need to renew its long-term loan facility in the next couple of months. The bank has suggested a five-year interest rate swap. Anchorage would issue a five-year sterling fixed rate bond, and make the following swap with a Swiss company that is also a client of the bank.

Anchorage would pay the Swiss company SFr LIBOR + 1% per year. The Swiss company would pay Anchorage 9.5% per year.

A 0.2% per year fee would also be payable by each company to the bank. There will be an exchange of principal now, and in five years' time, at today's middle spot foreign exchange rate. The Swiss company can borrow fixed rate sterling at 10.5% per annum, and floating rate SFr finance at SFr LIBOR + 1.5%.

Anchorage can borrow in SFr at a floating rate of between 5.75% and 6% depending upon which form of borrowing is selected (ie in the euromarkets or the Swiss domestic markets). SFr LIBOR is currently 5%.

Required

(e)   (i)   Estimate the annual interest cost to Anchorage of issuing a five-year sterling fixed rate bond, and calculate whether the suggested swap would be of benefit to both Anchorage and the Swiss company.   **(10 marks)**

        (ii)   Excluding cheaper finance, discuss the possible benefits and the possible risks of such a swap for the two companies and the intermediary bank.   **(8 marks)**

        (Total = 50 marks)

76 Romage (FS, 6/00, amended)   90 mins

Romage Inc has two major operating divisions, manufacturing and property sales, with revenues of $260 million and $620 million respectively

Statement of financial position for Romage Inc

	$m
Land and buildings	80
Plant and machinery	140
Current assets	250
Current liabilities	180
	290
Financed by:	
Ordinary shares (25 cents par)	50
Reserves	130
Secured term loan	60
13% loan stock ($100 par)	50
	290

Summarised cash flow data for Romage Inc:

	$m
Cash revenue	880
Divisional operating expenses	803
Central costs	8
Interest	11
Taxation	14
Dividends	15

The company's current share price is 296 cents, and the market value of a loan stock is $131.

Projected real (ie excluding inflation) per tax financial data ($ million) of the two divisions are:

Year	1	2	3	4	5	6 onwards
Manufacturing:						
Operating net cash flows	45	48	50	52	57	60
Allocated central costs	4	4	4	4	4	4
Tax allowable depreciation	10	8	7	8	8	8
Property sales:						
Operating net cash flows	32	40	42	44	46	50
Allocated central costs	4	3	3	3	3	3
Tax allowable depreciation	5	5	5	5	5	5

Corporate taxation is at the rate of 31% per year, payable in the year that the relevant cash flow arises.

Inflation is expected to remain at approximately 3% per year.

The risk free rate is 5.5%, and the market return 14%.

Romage's equity beta is 1.15.

The company is considering a demerger whereby the two divisions are floated separately on the stock market. The loan stock would be serviced by the property division and the term loan by the manufacturing division. The existing equity would be split evenly between the divisions, although new ordinary shares would be issued to replace existing shares.

The average equity betas in the manufacturing and property sectors are 1.3 and 0.9 respectively, and the gearing levels in manufacturing and property sales by market values are 70% equity 30% debt, and 80% equity 20% debt respectively.

Notes

(1)   Allocated central costs reflect actual cash flows. If a demerger occurs these costs would rise to $6 million per year for each company.

(2)   A demerger would involve a one-off after tax cost of $16 million in year one which would be split evenly between the two companies. There would be no other significant impact on expected cash flows.

(3)   The current cost of the loan stock and term loan are almost identical.

(4)   The loan stock is redeemable at par in fifteen years' time.

Required

(a)   Discuss the potential advantages for Romage Inc of undertaking the divestment of one of its divisions by means of:

    (i)   A sell-off
    (ii)   A demerger and
    (iii)   A divestment   **(8 marks)**

BPP
LEARNING MEDIA

(b)   Write a report to the board of director which:

(i)   Using real cash flows, evaluates whether or not it is expected to be financially advantageous to the original shareholders of Romage Inc for the company to separately float the two divisions on the stock market. Your evaluation should use both a 15 year time horizon and an infinite time horizon.

In any gearing estimates the manufacturing division may be assumed to comprise 55% of the market value of equity of Romage Inc, and the property sale division 45%. State clearly any additional assumptions that you make.   **(24 marks)**

(ii)   Includes a discussion of the limitations of your evaluation.   **(7 marks)**

Professional marks for format, structure and presentation of report   **(4 marks)**

(c)   Assume that there is a proposal to sell the property sales to an existing property sales company. Outline the ethical issues that Romage Inc should consider before agreeing to the sale.   **(7 marks)**

(Total = 50 marks)

77 Galeplus (SFM, 12/04, amended)   90 mins

(a)   From the perspective of a corporate financial manager, discuss the advantages and potential problems of using currency swaps.   **(8 marks)**

(b)   Galeplus plc, a UK-based multinational company has been invited to purchase and operate a new telecommunications centre in the republic of Perdia. The purchase price is 2,000 million rubbits. The Perdian government has built the centre in order to improve the country's infrastructure, but has currently not got enough funds to pay money owed to the local constructors. Galeplus would purchase the centre for a period of three years, after which it would be sold back to the Perdian government for an agreed price of 4,000 million rubbits. Galeplus would supply three years of technical expertise and training for local staff, for an annual fee of 40 million rubbits, after Perdian taxation. Other after-tax net cash flows from the investment in Perdia are expected to be negligible during the three year period.

Perdia has only recently become a democracy, and in the last five years has experienced inflation rates of between 25% and 500%. The managers of Galeplus are concerned about the foreign exchange risk of the investment. Perdia has recently adopted economic stability measures suggested by the IMF, and inflation during the next three years is expected to be between 15% per year and 50% per year. Galeplus's bankers have suggested using a currency swap for the purchase price of the factory, with a swap of principal immediately and in three years' time, both swaps at today's spot rate. The bank would charge a fee of 0.75% per year (in sterling) for arranging the swap. Galeplus would take 75% of any net arbitrage benefit from the swap, after deducting bank fees. Relevant borrowing rates are:

	UK	Perdia
Galeplus	6.25%	PIBOR + 2.0%
Perdian counterparty	8.3%	PIBOR + 1.5%

Note. PIBOR is the Perdian interbank offered rate, which has tended to be set at approximately the current inflation level. Inflation in the UK is expected to be negligible.

	Exchange rates
Spot	85.4 rubbits/£
3 year forward rate	Not available

Required

Write a report for the board of directors which:

(i)   Estimates the potential annual percentage interest saving that Galeplus might make from using a currency swap relative to borrowing directly in Perdia.   **(7 marks)**

(ii)   Assuming the swap takes place as described, provide a reasoned analysis, including relevant calculations, as to whether or not Galeplus should purchase the communications centre. The relevant risk adjusted discount rate may be assumed to be 15% per year.   **(8 marks)**

(iii) Discusses and evaluate the relative merits of the following alternatives to the currency swap which the bank has suggested for Galeplus.

    (1) A swaption with the same terms as the currency swap, and an upfront premium of £300,000.

    (2) A European style three year currency put option on the total expected net cash flow in year 3 at an exercise price of 160 rubbits/£, and an upfront premium of £1.7 million. **(8 marks)**

Professional marks for format, structure and presentation of report **(4 marks)**

(c) As a result of increased foreign currency transactions, Galeplus is considering setting up a treasury department. Discuss the advantages for Galeplus of having a treasury department which is separate to the finance function. **(7 marks)**

(d) (i) The treasury department will operate in the money markets. Describe what money markets are and their main characteristics. Also discuss the differences between a certificate of deposit and a commercial paper. **(6 marks)**

    (ii) Calculate the selling price, 3 days after issue, of a 60-day, €1 million certificate of deposit with a 7% yield. **(2 marks)**

(Total = 50 marks)

78 Polytot (SFM, 6/04, amended)　　　　　　　　90 mins

Assume that it is now 1 July. Polytot plc, a UK-based multinational company, has received an export order valued at 675 million pesos from a company in Grobbia, a country that has recently been accepted into the World Trade Organisation, but which does not yet have a freely convertible currency.

The Grobbian company only has access to sufficient $US to pay for 60% of the goods, at the official $US exchange rate. The balance would be payable in the local currency, the Grobbian peso, for which there is no official foreign exchange market. Polytot is due to receive payment in four months' time and has been informed that an unofficial market in Grobbian pesos exists in which the peso can be converted into pounds. The exchange rate in this market is 15% worse for Polytot than the 'official' rate of exchange between the peso and the pound.

Exchange rates

	$/£
Spot	1.5475 – 1.5510
3 months forward	1.5362 – 1.5398
1 year forward	1.5140 – 1.5178
	Grobbian peso/£
Official spot rate	156.30
	Grobbian peso/$
Official spot rate	98.20

Philadelphia SE £/$ options £31,250 (cents per pound)

	CALLS			PUTS		
	Sept	Dec	March	Sept	Dec	March
1.5250	2.95	3.35	3.65	2.00	3.25	4.35
1.5500	1.80	2.25	2.65	3.30	4.60	5.75
1.5750	0.90	1.40	1.80	4.90	6.25	7.35
1.6000	0.25	0.75	1.10	6.75	8.05	9.15

£/$ Currency futures (CME, £62,500)

September	1.5350
December	1.5275

Assume that options and futures contracts mature at the relevant month end.

Required

Produce a report which:

(a) Discusses the alternative forms of currency hedge that are available to Polytot plc and calculate the expected revenues, in £ sterling, from the sale to the company in Grobbia as a result of each of these hedges. Provide a reasoned recommendation as to which hedge should be selected. **(19 marks)**

Professional marks for format, structure and presentation of report **(4 marks)**

(b) The Grobbian company is willing to undertake a countertrade deal whereby 40% of the cost of the goods is paid for by an exchange of three million kilos of Grobbian strawberries. A major UK supermarket chain has indicated that it would be willing to pay between 50 and 60 pence per kilo for the strawberries.

Discuss the issues that Polytot should consider before deciding whether or not to agree to the countertrade. **(6 marks)**

(c) The Grobbian company has asked for advice in using the Euromarkets to raise international finance.

Required

Provide a briefing memo for the company discussing the advantages of the Euromarkets, and any potential problems for the Grobbian company in using them. **(7 marks)**

(d) Polytot also has subsidiaries in three countries – Umgaba, Mazila and Bettuna.

    (i) The subsidiary in Umgaba manufactures specialist components, which may then be assembled and sold in either Mazila or Bettuna.

    (ii) Production and sales volume may each be assumed to be 400,000 units per year no matter where the assembly and sales take place.

    (iii) Manufacturing costs in Umgaba are $16 per unit and fixed costs (for the normal range of production) $1.8 million.

    (iv) Assembly costs in Mazila are $9 per unit and in Bettuna $7.50 per unit. Fixed costs are $700,000 and $900,000 respectively.

    (v) The unit sales price in Mazila is $40 and in Bettuna $37.

    (vi) Corporate taxes on profits are at the rate of 40% in Umgaba, 25% in Mazila, 32% in Bettuna and 30% in the UK. No tax credits are available in these three countries for any losses made. Full credit is given by the UK tax authorities for tax paid overseas.

    (vii) Tax allowable import duties of 10% are payable on all goods imported into Mazila.

    (viii) A withholding tax of 15% is deducted from all dividends remitted from Umgaba.

    (ix) Shegdor expects about 60% of profits from each subsidiary to be remitted direct to the UK each year.

    (x) Cost and price data in all countries is shown in US dollars.

Required

Evaluate and explain:

    (i) If the transfer price from Umgaba should be based upon fixed cost plus variable cost, or fixed cost plus variable cost plus a mark up of 30%.

    (ii) Whether assembly should take place in Mazila or Bettuna. **(10 marks)**

(e) Comment upon the likely attitude of the governments of each of the four countries towards the transfer price and assembly location selected in (d)(i) and (d)(ii) above. **(4 marks)**

(Total = 50 marks)

79 FNDC (SFM, 12/06, amended)   90 mins

Several months ago FNDC plc, a television manufacturer, agreed to offer financial support to a major sporting event. The event will take place in seven months' time, but an expenditure of £45 million for temporary facilities will be necessary in five months' time. FNDC has agreed to lend the £45 million, and expects the loan to be repaid at the time of the event. At the time the support was offered, FNDC expected to have sufficient cash to lend the £45 million from its own resources, but new commitments mean that the cash will have to be borrowed. Interest rates have been showing a rising trend, and FNDC wishes to protect itself against further interest rate rises when it takes out the loan. The company is considering using either interest rate futures or options on interest rate futures.

Assume that it is now 1 December and that futures and options contracts mature at the relevant month end.

LIBOR is currently 4%. FNDC can borrow at LIBOR plus 1.25%.

Euronext. LIFFE STIR £500,000 three-month sterling futures. Tick size 0.01%, tick value £12.50
December 96·04   March 95·77   June 95·55

Euronext. LIFFE options on three-month £500,000 sterling futures. Tick size 0.005%, tick value £6.25. Option premiums are in annual %.

	CALLS			PUTS		
	December	March	June	December	March	June
9400	1.505	1.630	1.670	–	–	–
9450	1.002	1.130	1.170	–	–	–
9500	0.502	0.630	0.685	–	–	0.015
9550	0.252	0.205	0.285	0.060	0.115	0.165
9600	0.002	0.025	0.070	0.200	0.450	0.710

The following FRAs are also available

FRA 2-5   4.95%
FRA 3-6   5.30%
FRA 5-7   5.85%

Required

(a)   Discuss the relative merits of using short-term interest rate futures and market traded options on short-term interest rates futures to hedge short-term interest rate risk.   **(8 marks)**

Write a report to the board of directors which shows:

(b)   If LIBOR interest rates were to increase by 0.5% or to decrease by 0.5% estimate the expected outcomes from hedging using:
(i)   An interest rate futures hedge; (ii)   Options on interest rate futures; (iii) FRA

Briefly discuss your findings.

Note: In the futures hedge the expected basis at the close-out date should be estimated, but basis risk may be ignored.   **(18 marks)**

Professional marks for format, structure and presentation of report   **(4 marks)**

(c)   (i)   Calculate and discuss the outcome of a collar hedge which would limit the maximum interest rate paid by the company to 5.75%, and the minimum to 5.25%. (These interest rates do not include any option premium.)   **(6 marks)**

       (ii)   Discuss the advantages and disadvantages of an over the counter option to cap interest rates.
                                                                                                           (5 marks)

(d)   (i)   The company has been advised that it can increase income by writing (selling) options. Discuss whether or not this is correct, and provide a reasoned recommendation as to whether or not FNDC plc should adopt this strategy.   **(3 marks)**

       (ii)   Discuss the advantages for FNDC of having a specialist centralised treasury department.   **(6 marks)**

                                                                                                 (Total = 50 marks)

80 Nente Co (6/12, amended)   **90 mins**

Nente Co, an unlisted company, designs and develops tools and parts for specialist machinery. The company was formed four years ago by three friends, who own 20% of the equity capital in total, and a consortium of five business angel organisations, who own the remaining 80%, in roughly equal proportions. Nente Co also has a large amount of debt finance in the form of variable rate loans. Initially the amount of annual interest payable on these loans was low and allowed Nente Co to invest internally generated funds to expand its business. Recently though, due to a rapid increase in interest rates, there has been limited scope for future expansion and no new product development.

The Board of Directors, consisting of the three friends and a representative from each business angel organisation, met recently to discuss how to secure the company's future prospects. Two proposals were put forward, as follows:

Proposal 1

To accept a takeover offer from Mije Co, a listed company, which develops and manufactures specialist machinery tools and parts. The takeover offer is for $2.95 cash per share or a share-for-share exchange where two Mije Co shares would be offered for three Nente Co shares. Mije Co would need to get the final approval from its shareholders if either offer is accepted;

Proposal 2

To pursue an opportunity to develop a small prototype product that just breaks even financially, but gives the company exclusive rights to produce a follow-on product within two years.

The meeting concluded without agreement on which proposal to pursue.

After the meeting, Mije Co was consulted about the exclusive rights. Mije Co's directors indicated that they had not considered the rights in their computations and were willing to continue with the takeover offer on the same terms without them.

Currently, Mije Co has 10 million shares in issue and these are trading for $4.80 each. Mije Co's price to earnings (P/E) ratio is 15. It has sufficient cash to pay for Nente Co's equity and a substantial proportion of its debt, and believes that this will enable Nente Co to operate on a P/E level of 15 as well. In addition to this, Mije Co believes that it can find cost-based synergies of $150,000 after tax per year for the foreseeable future. Mije Co's current profit after tax is $3,200,000.

The following financial information relates to Nente Co and to the development of the new product.

Nente Co financial information

Extract from the most recent income statement

	$'000
Sales revenue	8,780
Profit before interest and tax	1,230
Interest	(455)
Tax	(155)
Profit after tax	620
Dividends	Nil

Extract from the most recent statement of financial position

	$'000
Net non-current assets	10,060
Current assets	690
Total assets	10,750
Share capital (40c per share par value)	960
Reserves	1,400
Non-current liabilities: Variable rate loans	6,500
Current liabilities	1,890
Total liabilities and capital	10,750

In arriving at the profit after tax amount, Nente Co deducted tax allowable depreciation and other non-cash expenses totalling $1,206,000. It requires an annual cash investment of $1,010,000 in non-current assets and working capital to continue its operations.

Nente Co's profits before interest and tax in its first year of operation were $970,000 and have been growing steadily in each of the following three years, to their current level. Nente Co's cash flows grew at the same rate as well, but it is likely that this growth rate will reduce to 25% of the original rate for the foreseeable future.

Nente Co currently pays interest of 7% per year on its loans, which is 380 basis points over the government base rate, and corporation tax of 20% on profits after interest. It is estimated that an overall cost of capital of 11% is reasonable compensation for the risk undertaken on an investment of this nature.

New product development (Proposal 2)

Developing the new follow-on product will require an investment of $2,500,000 initially. The total expected cash flows and present values of the product over its five-year life, with a volatility of 42% standard deviation, are as follows:

Year(s)	Now	1	2	3 to 7 (total)
Cash flows ($'000)	-	-	(2,500)	3,950
Present values ($'000)	-	-	(2,029)	2,434

Required

(a) Prepare a report for the Board of Directors of Nente Co that:

(i) Estimates the current value of a Nente Co share, using the free cash flow to firm methodology;

(7 marks)

(ii) Estimates the percentage gain in value to a Nente Co share and a Mije Co share under each payment offer; **(8 marks)**

(iii) Estimates the percentage gain in the value of the follow-on product to a Nente Co share, based on its cash flows and on the assumption that the production can be delayed following acquisition of the exclusive rights of production; **(8 marks)**

(iv) Discusses the likely reaction of Nente Co and Mije Co shareholders to the takeover offer, including the assumptions made in the estimates above and how the follow-on product's value can be utilised by Nente Co. **(8 marks)**

Professional marks will be awarded for the presentation, structure and clarity of the answer. **(4 marks)**

(b) Evaluate the current performance of Nente Co and comment on what this will mean for the proposed takeover bid. **(8 marks)**

(c) Since the approach to Nente Co, Mije Co has itself been the subject of a takeover bid from Tianhe Co, a listed company which specialises in supplying machinery to the manufacturing sector and has a market capitalisation of $245 million.

Required

Evaluate the general post-bid defences and comment on their suitability for Mije Co to try and prevent the takeover from Tianhe Co. **(7 marks)**

(Total = 50 marks)

81 Seal Island (6/10, amended) 90 mins

The Seal Island Nuclear Power Company has received initial planning consent for an Advanced Boiling Water Reactor. This project is one of a number that has been commissioned by the Government of Roseland to help solve the energy needs of its expanding population of 60 million and meet its treaty obligations by cutting CO_2 emissions to 50% of their 2010 levels by 2030.

The project proposal is now moving to the detailed planning stage which will include a full investment appraisal within the financial plan. The financial plan so far developed has been based upon experience of this reactor design in Japan, the US and South Korea.

The core macro economic assumptions are that Roseland GDP will grow at an annual rate of 4% (nominal) and inflation will be maintained at the 2% target set by the Government.

BPP
LEARNING MEDIA

The construction programme is expected to cost $1 billion over three years, with construction commencing in January 2012. These capital expenditures have been projected, including expected future cost increases, as follows:

Year end	20X2	20X3	20X4
Construction costs ($ million)	300	600	100

Generation of electricity will commence in 20X5 and the annual operating surplus in cash terms is expected to be $100 million per annum (at 1 January 20X5 price and cost levels). This value has been well validated by preliminary studies and includes the cost of fuel reprocessing, ongoing maintenance and systems replacement as well as the growth. The plant is expected to have an operating life of 30 years.

Decommissioning costs at the end of the project have been estimated at $600 million at current (20X2) costs

Decommissioning costs are expected to rise in line with nominal GDP growth.

The company's nominal cost of capital is 10% per annum. All estimates, unless otherwise stated, are at 1 January 20X2 price and cost levels.

Required

(a)   Produce a report for the board of directors which includes:

   (i)   An estimate of the net present value for this project as at the commencement of construction in 2012.   **(11 marks)**

   (ii)   A discussion of the principal uncertainties associated with this project.   **(7 marks)**

   (iii) A sensitivity of the project's net present value (in percentage and in $), to changes in the construction cost, the annual operating surplus and the decommissioning cost. (Assume that the increase in construction costs would be proportional to the initial investment for each year.)   **(6 marks)**

   (iv)   An explanation of how simulations, such as the Monte Carlo simulation, could be used to assess the volatility of the net present value of this project.   **(4 marks)**

Note: the formula for an annuity discounted at an annual rate (i) and where cash flows are growing at an annual rate (g) is as follows:

$$A_n = \left[\frac{1 - \left(\frac{1+g}{1+i}\right)^n}{i-g} \right](1+g)$$

Professional marks for format, structure and presentation of report   **(4 marks)**

(b)   Discuss the merits and potential problems of using each of the weighted average cost of capital and adjusted present value to aid the evaluation of proposed capital investments.   **(9 marks)**

(c)   Seal Island is considering the possible effect on its cost of capital if conversion of a convertible loan stock occurs. Stock market prices have recently been very volatile, and could easily rise or fall by 10% or more during the next two months. The convertible is a $20 million 8% loan stock with four years to maturity, which was originally issued at its par value (face value) of $100. The loan stock may be converted into 20 ordinary shares during the next two months only. The loan stock's current market price is $110. Redemption in four years' time would be at the par value of $100. Seal Island currently has other debts with a market value of $23 million.

Seal Island could currently issue straight debt at par of $100 with a redemption yield of 9%.

Seal Island's current share price is 520 cents, the market value of ordinary shares is $180 million, and financial gearing 80% equity to 20% debt (by market values).

The systematic risk of the company's equity is similar to that of the market, and is thought to be unlikely to change in the near future.

The market return is 15%.

The corporate tax rate is 30%.

Required

Assuming that no major changes in interest rates occur during the next two months, estimate the impact on the company's cost of capital if:

(i)   Seal Island's share price in two months' time is 470 cents, and no conversion takes place.

(ii)   Seal Island's share price in two months' time is 570 cents, and conversion takes place.

State clearly any other assumptions that you make.

Comment on your findings.   **(9 marks)**

(Total = 50 marks)

82 Sleepon (SFM, 12/05, amended)   90 mins

Sleepon Hotels Inc owns a successful chain of luxury hotels. The company is considering diversifying its activities through the construction of a theme park. The theme park would have a mixture of family activities and adventure rides. Sleepon has just spent $230,000 on market research into the theme park, and is encouraged by the findings. The CEO believes that this diversification will help to create a stronger brand, reduce risk and also deliver value to the shareholders.

The theme park is expected to attract an average of 15,000 visitors per day for at least four years, after which major new investment would be required in order to maintain demand. The price of admission to the theme park is expected to be $18 per adult and $10 per child. 60% of visitors are forecast to be children. In addition to admission revenues, it is expected that the average visitor will spend $8 on food and drinks, (of which 30% is profit), and $5 on gifts and souvenirs, (of which 40% is profit). The park would open for 360 days per year.

All costs and receipts (excluding maintenance and construction costs and the realisable value) are shown at current prices; the company expects all costs and receipts to rise by 3% per year from current values.

The theme park would cost a total of $400 million and could be constructed and working in one year's time. Half of the $400 million would be payable immediately, and half in one year's time. In addition working capital of $50 million will be required from the end of year one. The after tax realisable value of non-current assets is expected to be between $250 million and $300 million after four years of operation.

Maintenance costs (excluding labour) are expected to be $15 million in the first year of operation, increasing by $4 million per year thereafter. Annual insurance costs are $2 million, and the company would apportion $2.5 million per year to the theme park from existing overheads. The theme park would require 1,500 staff costing a total of $40m per annum (at current prices). Sleepon will use the existing advertising campaigns for its hotels to also advertise the theme park. This will save approximately $2 million per year in advertising expenses.

As Sleepon has no previous experience of theme park management, it has investigated the current risk and financial structure of its closest theme park competitor, Thrillall Inc. Details are summarised below.

Thrillall Inc, summarised statement of financial position

	$m
Non-current assets (net)	1,440
Current assets	570
Less current liabilities	(620)
	1,390
Financed by:	
$1 ordinary shares	400
Reserves	530
	930
Medium and long term debt	460
	1,390

BPP
LEARNING MEDIA

Other information

(a) Sleepon has access to a $450 million loan at 7.5% fixed rate to provide the necessary finance for the theme park.

(b) $250 million of the investment will attract 25% per year capital allowances on a reducing balance basis, available with a one year lag.

(c) Corporate tax is at a rate of 30%.

(d) The average stock market return is 10% and the risk free rate 3.5%.

(e) Sleepon's current weighted average cost of capital is 9%.

(f) Sleepon's market weighted gearing if the theme park project is undertaken is estimated to be 61.4% equity, 38.6% debt.

(g) Sleepon's equity beta is 0.70.

(h) The current share price of Sleepon is 148 cents, and of Thrillall 386 cents.

(i) Thrillall's medium and long term debt comprises long term bonds with a par value of $100 and current market price of $93.

(j) Thrillall's equity beta is 1.45.

Required

(a) Prepare a report, for the board of directors, which:

(i) analyses whether or not Sleepon should undertake the investment in the theme park using the NPV, MIRR and duration methods **(29 marks)**

(ii) includes a discussion of what other information would be useful to Sleepon in making the investment decision. **(9 marks)**

All relevant calculations must be included. State clearly any assumptions that you make.

Professional marks for format, structure and presentation of report **(4 marks)**

(b) Briefly evaluate the benefits for Sleepon of this diversification and comment on the views of the CEO.
(8 marks)

(Total = 50 marks)

83 Fuelit (FS, 12/00, amended) 90 mins

Fuelit plc is an electricity supplier in the USA. The company has historically generated the majority of its electricity using a coal fuelled power station, but as a result of the closure of many coal mines and depleted coal resources, is now considering what type of new power station to invest in. The alternatives are a gas fuelled power station, or a new type of efficient nuclear power station.

Both types of power station are expected to generate annual revenues at current prices of $800 million. The expected operating life of both types of power station is 25 years.

Financial estimates:	Gas	Nuclear
	$m	$m
Building costs	600	3,300
Annual running costs (at current prices)		
Labour costs	75	20
Gas purchases	500	–
Nuclear fuel purchases	–	10
Customer relations	5	20
Sales and marketing expenses	40	40
Interest expense	51	330
Other cash outlays	5	25
Accounting depreciation	24	132

Other information

(a) Whichever power station is selected, electricity generation is scheduled to commence in three years' time.

(b) If gas is used most of the workers at the existing coal fired station can be transferred to the new power station. After tax redundancy costs are expected to total $4 million in year four. If nuclear power is selected fewer workers will be required and after tax redundancy costs will total $36 million, also in year four.

(c) Both projects would be financed by Eurobond issues denominated in Euros. The gas powered station would require a bond issue at 8.5% per year. The bond for the nuclear project would be at 10%, reflecting the impact on financial gearing of a larger bond issue.

(d) Costs of building the new power stations would be payable in two equal instalments in one and two years' time.

(e) The existing coal fired power station would need to be demolished at a cost of $10 million after tax in three years' time.

(f) The company's equity beta is expected to be 0.7 if the gas station is chosen and 1.4 if the nuclear station is chosen. Gearing (debt to equity plus debt) is expected to be 35% with gas and 60% with nuclear fuel.

(g) The risk free rate is 4.5% per year and the market return is 14% per year. Inflation is currently 3% per year in the US and an average of 5% per year in the member countries of the Euro bloc in the European Union.

(h) Corporate tax is at the rate of 30% payable in the same year that the liability arises.

(i) Tax allowable depreciation is at the rate of 10% per year on a straight line basis.

(j) At the end of twenty-five years of operations the gas plant is expected to cost $25 million (after tax) to demolish and clean up the site. Costs of decommissioning the nuclear plant are much less certain, and could be anything between $500 million and $1,000 million (after tax) depending upon what form of disposal is available for nuclear waste.

Required

(a) Estimate the expected NPV of each of investment in a gas fuelled power station and investment in a nuclear fuelled power station.

State clearly any assumptions that you make.

(*Note.* It is recommended that annuity tables are used wherever possible) **(20 marks)**

(b) Discuss other information that might assist the decision process. **(8 marks)**

Professional marks for format, structure and presentation of report **(4 marks)**

(c) An external advisor has suggested that the discount rate for the costs of decommissioning the nuclear power station should be adjusted because of their risk. Discuss whether or not this discount rate should be increased or decreased. **(4 marks)**

(d) Explain the significance of the existence of real options to the capital investment decision, and briefly discuss examples of real options that might be significant in the power station decision process.

(8 marks)

(e) Discuss the steps that Fuelit could take to improve its reputation for dealing with environmental issues with the general public. **(6 marks)**

(Total = 50 marks)

84 Aggrochem Co (6/10, amended)   90 mins

Aggrochem Co, a pharmaceutical company, is undertaking a due diligence investigation of LeverChem Co, a competitor in the same industry, and is reviewing the sources of finance to fund the acquisition. You have been appointed as a consultant to advise the company's management on various aspects of the bid.

Aggrochem is a fully listed company financed wholly by equity. LeverChem is listed on an alternative investment market. Both companies have been trading for over 10 years and have shown strong levels of profitability recently. However, both companies' shares are thinly traded. It is thought that the current market value of LeverChem's shares at $33\frac{1}{3}$% higher than the book value is accurate, but it is felt that Aggrochem shares are not quoted accurately by the market. As a result of this perceived undervaluation, Aggrochem is only considering a cash offer for LeverChem. It is felt that the equity of LeverChem can be purchased from existing shareholders for a cost of around $2 million.

The following information is taken from the financial statements of both companies at the start of the current year:

	Aggrochem	LeverChem
	$'000	$'000
Assets less current liabilities	4,400	4,200
Capital Employed Equity	4,400	1,200
5-year floating rate loan at yield rate plus 3%		3,000
Total capital employed	4,400	4,200
Net operating profit after tax (NOPAT)	580	430
Net amount retained for reinvestment in assets	180	150

The assets of both companies are stated at fair value. Discussions with the AtReast Bank have led to an agreement that the floating rate loan to LeverChem can be transferred to the combined business on the same terms. The current yield rate is 5% and the current equity risk premium is 6%. It can be assumed that the risk free rate of return is equivalent to the yield rate. Aggrochem's beta has been estimated to be 1.26.

The Chief Executive is concerned that Aggrochem Co does not have an optimal capital structure and believes that the choice of finance for the acquisition can be used to adjust this. In addition the Chief Executive has heard about 7 regulatory devices for acquisition and would like to know more about them.

Required:

(a)   Prepare a report for the management of Aggrochem on the valuation of the combined business following acquisition and the maximum premium payable to the shareholders of LeverChem. Your report should:

(i)   Using the free cash flow model, estimate the market value of equity for Aggrochem Co, explaining any assumptions made.   **(9 marks)**

(ii)   Evaluate the capital structure of Aggrochem and analyse potential sources of finance available to finance the acquisition of LeverChem.   **(12 marks)**

(iii)   Analyse the regulatory devices that could apply to the takeover of LeverChem.

(9 marks)

Professional marks will be awarded for the clarity and presentation of the report.   **(4 marks)**

(b)   Aggrochem Co is negotiating an export contract with a customer in a developing country, Xeridia. Aggrochem has not exported to the country before, and is concerned both about the risk of late or non-payment for the exports, and about the foreign exchange risks associated with the Xeridian peso. The contract specifies that Aggrochem should receive 55 million Xeridian pesos in three months' time. Discos will require short-term finance for the full value of the exports.

Exchange rates (peso/$)

Spot	32.34 – 32.89
3 months forward	33.82 – 34.55
6 months forward	35.17 – 35.90

Current short-term domestic interest rates available to Aggrochem Co

Borrowing	6.5%
Investing	5.3%

Aggrochem is considering three different ways of protecting against the foreign trade risk:

(i)   Insure the deal with Protect Trade plc and undertake a forward market hedge. An insurance policy is available at a cost of 1.25% of the spot dollar equivalent of the export value. The policy gives the following protection: 95% cover against non-payment as a result of political actions by a foreign government; 90% cover against other nonpayment. Any payment by the insurer would be after six months.

(ii)   Use the services of a non-recourse export factor. The factor will guarantee that $1,590,000 is paid in three months' time if the customer pays on time, or $1,530,000 in six months' time if the customer makes a late payment or defaults. The factor is prepared to provide immediate trade finance of up to 80% of the value of the guaranteed sum, at an interest rate of 6.3%. The factor charges an administration fee of 2.5% of the sum guaranteed.

(iii)   Use a confirmed, irrevocable, documentary letter of credit. The letter of credit would include a 90-day bank bill of exchange that may be immediately discounted in the Xeridian money market at an annual rate of 25%, which is the short-term borrowing rate in Xeridia. The fees associated with the letter of credit are $30,000.

Aggrochem has been advised that there is at least a 5% chance of late payment after six months or default by the client. The Xeridian government is not expected to take any action that is detrimental to foreign trade during the next six months.

Required

Discuss the advantages and disadvantages of each alternative, and recommend which should be selected. Relevant calculations should support your discussion. State clearly any assumptions that you make.

(16 marks)

(Total = 50 marks)

Answers

BPP
LEARNING MEDIA

1 Preparation question – Shareholders and bondholders

> **Text references.** Chapter 3a.
>
> **Top tips.** The key to (a) is realising the different attitudes to risk and return of bondholders and shareholders. Bondholders will be willing to take the company into liquidation if they believe it is the only certain way of realising their loan, but will be less willing if bankruptcy costs mean there is insufficient money left to repay loans. Hence it is fine to say that in some circumstances bondholders will prefer liquidation, but not others.
>
> In (b) covenants can be broadly grouped as positive (company must do something), negative (company is prevented from doing something) and quantitative (essentially the accounting covenants, fulfilling financial limits).

(a)   (i)   **Different attitudes to risk and return**

Shareholders may want the company to undertake **risky projects** with correspondingly **high expected levels of returns**. Bondholders will want the company to undertake projects that guarantee sufficient returns to pay their interest each year, and ultimately to repay their loans.

(ii)   **Dividends**

Large (albeit) legal dividends may be preferred by shareholders, but may concern bondholders, because the payments leave low cash balances in the company and hence **put at risk** the **company's ability** to meet its commitments to the bondholders.

(iii)   **Priority in insolvency**

Bondholders may wish to take the company into **liquidation** if there are problems paying their interest, to guarantee their investment. Shareholders however may wish the company to **continue trading** if they expect to receive nothing if the company does go into liquidation.

(iv)   **Attitudes to further finance**

Shareholders may prefer the company to **raise additional finance** by means of loans, in order to **avoid having to contribute themselves** in a rights issue, or the risk of dilution of their shareholding and hence power if an open stock market issue is made. Bondholders may **not wish the company** to take on the burden of additional debt finance, because it may increase the risk that the **interest** that they are **due** will not be paid, or the company will have problems repaying their loans, particularly if the new loans rank above theirs.

(v)   **Restrictions imposed by bondholders**

Restrictions imposed by bondholders to protect their loans, such as charges preventing the company from selling assets or covenants, may limit the company's ability to maximise returns for shareholders.

(vi)   **Bankruptcy costs**

If the **costs of bankruptcy**, such as receivers and lawyers' fees, are likely to be **significant**, bondholders may be much less willing than shareholders for the company to bear any risk. Significant bankruptcy costs may mean that there is insufficient money left to repay their loans.

(b)   A covenant in a loan agreement is an obligation placed on the borrower over and above repaying the loan according to terms.

The three types of covenant are:

Positive covenants

These require a borrower to do something, for example to **provide the bank** with its regular management accounts. This would allow the bank to **check** on the **financial performance** of the company, and to ensure that it is likely to be able to repay the loan as planned.

Loan covenants

The borrower may pledge **not to take out further loans** until the current loan has been repaid, or not to take further loans ranking above existing loans. The purpose of this is to protect the position of the lender, and to ensure that the risk of default is not increased, or the level of security diluted.

Asset covenants

There may be restrictions on the company's ability to **acquire, or dispose of, assets**.

Accounting covenants

These set **limitations on the borrower's financial position**. For example, the company might agree that its total borrowings should not exceed 100% of shareholder's funds. The purpose of this is to keep the gearing, and hence the level of risk to the lender, within certain limits.

Dividend covenants

Covenants may **restrict the levels of dividends** borrowers can pay, or restrict the company's ability to purchase its own shares.

Investment covenants

Covenants may **limit the investments** the borrower can undertake, or prevent the borrower merging or making an acquisition.

Repayment covenants

The lender may be required to **build up a fund over time** to be drawn on to redeem bonds at the end of their life.

Advantages of covenants

(i)   The main advantage of covenants is that lenders may be prepared to lend **more money** to the company if it provides the security of a covenant.

(ii)   Covenants may mean that the costs at which the company can **borrow money** are **lower**.

Disadvantages of covenants

(i)   The main disadvantage of a covenant is that the company's actions may be **constrained**; it may not be able to raise further funds beyond the covenanted loans or undertake profitable investments

(ii)   Covenants may require the borrower to bear **monitoring costs** such as provision of information, auditors' fees or trustee expenses.

2 Preparation question - Capital structure

> **Text references.** Chapter 1.
>
> **Top tips.** There are a number of ways in which you could have approached this question. We've focused on the appeal of debt, the theories and management attitudes. Whatever you discuss, you needed to include pros and cons of the views you put forward.

To: Board of Directors
From: Financial Manager

Briefing document

Issues that might influence capital structure strategy

Capital structure strategy is concerned with the relative proportions of equity and debt financing a company's operations.

(a)   **Features of debt**

    (i)   **Advantages of debt**

        (1)   It has a **cheaper direct cost** than equity, as it is less risky to the funds provider.

        (2)   It **attracts corporate tax relief**, which lowers its cost.

    (ii)   **Disadvantages of debt**

        As a counter to this, when a company borrows, **debt interest takes precedence** over **equity returns**, resulting in some disadvantages:

        (1)   **Returns to equity** become **more volatile**, indicating an increase in equity systematic risk (the gearing, or leverage effect). As a result the cost of equity increases.

        (2)   At **high levels of gearing**, the company is at risk of **financial distress**: the probability of bankruptcy increases, too much management time is used up managing financial emergencies, cost of emergency finance may be high, and customers and suppliers may lose confidence.

(b)   **Effect on company valuation**

    (i)   **Modigliani and Miller**

        In the 1960s Miller and Modigliani developed a theory that shows that, under the perfect capital market assumptions that they make, the cheap direct cost of debt will be exactly counter-balanced by the increased cost of equity due to borrowing. This theory therefore suggests that the **only advantage of borrowing** is the **corporate tax relief**.

        Using Miller and Modigliani's theory, the value of a firm which borrows will therefore exceed the value of an equivalent ungeared firm by the present value of tax relief on borrowings, which is known as the 'tax shield'. As a result, the firm's weighted average cost of capital (WACC) is predicted to fall steadily with **increased gearing**.

        Limitations of Modigliani and Miller

        However in practice at high levels of gearing, any further fall in WACC is **limited by increases to costs of both equity and debt** that set in because of **financial distress**. The situation is also complicated by the existence of **different personal tax treatments** for equity and debt investments that cause investors to have a preference for one or other type of capital, which varies over time and location.

    (ii)   **Traditional theory and optimal gearing levels**

        Overall, however, the theory's predictions are not far removed from those of the traditional view, which predicts that the **weighted average cost of capital falls** with **increased borrowing** at **low gearing levels**, **reaches a minimum** and then rises as borrowing exceeds the safety level. If this is true, then there should be an optimum level of gearing for each company at which its cost of capital is lowest, and in theory companies should aim for this gearing.

        Limitations of traditional view

        In practice companies often have **lower gearing** than would be predicted by these theories. The existence of an optimal gearing is difficult to prove or disprove because a company's level of borrowings is limited by other factors, such as the **amount of surplus cash** it generates compared with investment opportunities, the **operating risk** of its business (high risk will deter too much borrowing) and the **value of tangible assets** which it can offer as security for borrowing.

(c)   **Manager viewpoints**

    Other explanations of capital structure come from theories that are primarily concerned with **managerial decision making, human behaviour** and **the existence of information asymmetry** between management and shareholders.

    (i)   **Pecking order theory**

        In pecking order theory it is suggested that managers use the **most convenient sources of funds first. Retained earnings** and **sale of securities** are preferred because no explanation has to given to shareholders about their use. When these are exhausted, **borrowing** is used as opposed to share issues because of the lower issue costs, the speed with which it can be arranged and the absence of the need to prepare an explanatory prospectus. **Share issues** are used only as a **last resort**, for major expansions. Because of information asymmetry, dividend policy is important, so quite often borrowing will increase or decrease simply to maintain stable dividends in a period of fluctuating profitability.

(ii) **Management attitudes**

Capital structure can also be affected by the attitude of the managers to risk. For example a risk averse management may **prefer low borrowing**. It may also be indirectly affected by managers' personal goals, for example making unwise acquisitions to create expansion and increase status.

(d) **Conclusion**

Capital structure has been **widely debated** for half a century and in general there are no easy conclusions. It is clear, though, that provided the **basic risks** of debt are **understood** and that funds are obtained at **competitive costs**, the gains or losses from varying capital structure are not really significant compared with those that result from capital investment decisions.

3 Multimedia company

Text references. Chapter 3b for ethics; Chapter 2 for stock market listings and dividends.

Top tips. Both parts (a) and (b) are quite general but remember to relate your answer specifically to a medium-sized company. Part (c) is more specific to the scenario – ensure your answer is too. Part (d) requires you to look at the dividend payout ratio and take into account whether capital investment has occurred in that year or not.

Easy marks. If you are familiar with the procedure for obtaining a listing and the advantages and disadvantages of doing so you can pick up the majority of the marks in parts (a) and (b).

Marking scheme

		Marks
(a)	Outline of the three step procedure: registration, listing and admission to trading (2 marks for each step).	6
(b)	Note of the advantages: capital market access, reputation effects.	2
	Note of the disadvantages: compliance costs, vulnerability to takeover, public scrutiny.	3
		5
(c)	Identification of the principal ethical issues involved.	2
	Note on the issue of transparency and the protection of minority rights.	2
	Discussion of alternative ways that the CFO could proceed and the ethical implications of each.	2
	Commentary on the ethical issues involved in earnings management .	2
		8
(d)	Calculation of payout ratio	2
	Comment on difference when investment occurs/does not occur	2
	Comment on sustainability	2
		6
		25

BPP
LEARNING MEDIA

(a)   **Procedure for obtaining a listing on an International Stock Exchange**
       Paper prepared for the Board of Multimedia Company

This paper describes the necessary procedures for obtaining a listing on an international stock exchange.

Obtaining a listing on an international stock exchange such as the London or New York stock exchange consists of satisfying requirements in **three broad areas**; namely **registration, listing and admission to trading**.

In the UK, a firm seeking a listing must first **register** as a public limited company to ensure that it is entitled to issue shares to the public. This will require a change to the company's memorandum and articles of association agreed by the existing shareholders at a special meeting convened for the express purpose of agreeing this change.

The company must meet the regulatory requirements of the **Listing Authority** which is part of Financial Services Authority in the UK. These regulatory requirements impose minimum size restrictions on a company and other conditions concerning length of time trading (normally audited accounts must exist for a three year period). An issue of particular concern here is that the CEO has a controlling interest in the business – this will have to be addressed. Once these requirements are satisfied the company is placed on an official list and is allowed to make an initial public offering of its shares.

Once the company is on the official list it must then seek approval from the Stock Exchange to allow its shares to be traded. Exchanges such as the London Stock Exchange impose strict requirements which invariably mean that the applicant company will need the services of a sponsoring firm specialising in this area. The regulatory requirements of the London Stock Exchange include:

- compliance with corporate governance regulations (for example, 50% of the Board should be independent non-executive directors)

- quality and experience of the executive directors and the business plan, all of which must be carefully laid out in a prospectus.

This tends to be costly and therefore prohibitive for all but the larger companies. The restrictions (and costs) of obtaining a listing on a junior market (eg AIM in the UK) may be lower.

(b)   **Briefing note prepared for Martin Pickle, CEO**

       Subject: Advantages and disadvantages of a stock market listing for a medium-sized company

Following on from our discussion regarding a stock market listing for the company, I have detailed below the main advantages and disadvantages of taking such a step for a company of our size.

For a **medium sized firm**, the principal advantage of obtaining a public listing is the **additional sources of finance** available. A listed company would have access to **equity capital** from both institutional and private investors, and the sums that can be raised are usually much greater than through private equity sources. In addition, the presence of a firm as a limited company on a major exchange, such as the London Stock Exchange enhances the **credibility** of the firm both to potential investors and to the general public as it has opened itself to a much greater degree of public scrutiny than a privately financed firm.

The **disadvantages** are significant; the distributed shareholding places the firm in the market for investors seeking corporate control and also increases the likelihood that the firm will be subject to a takeover bid. The higher degree of public scrutiny imposes a significant **regulatory burden** on the firm as it must comply with a range of **disclosure requirements** and financial accounts must be prepared in accordance with relevant accounting standards. In the UK, this means in accordance with IFRS and the relevant GAAP as well as the Companies Acts. Under the rules of the London Stock Exchange companies must also comply with the governance requirements of the **UK Corporate Governance Code** and have an effective and ongoing business planning process in place. The requirement to comply or explain can impose a significant regulatory burden and can expose the company to critical comment.

(c)   Martin Pickle is a large shareholder, holding over 30% of the company's equity and thereby has certain duties towards other shareholders. He should not undertake any action which is prejudicial to them. It is unclear whether he has discussed his intentions with the other shareholders. Any move towards listed status would require their consent so he will need to provide them details of his future plans and intentions. It may well be that the private equity firm involved has its own exit strategy in mind and his proposed course of action is acceptable to them.

If the decision was made to go public then Martin Pickle's intention would be a **material factor in the valuation of the firm** and the offer price to subscribers. An immediate decision to disinvest would need to be disclosed.

At this stage, there would appear to be nothing wrong with asking the CFO to investigate the matter on a **confidential** basis. The request to enhance the earnings of the business should be resisted in so far as it represents an instruction to engage in earnings manipulation beyond that required to represent a **true and fair view** of the affairs of the business. Earnings management techniques whereby revenues and costs are accelerated/decelerated to achieve desired earnings are strictly limited by GAAP.

The proposal that the CFO would be offered share options places the CFO in a **difficult position**. The CFO must make it clear that he or she must **act in the interests of all the shareholders and all the directors**. An invitation to participate in a share option scheme appears to be a fairly crude attempt to win support for the proposed course of action and should be resisted.

(d)   **Evaluation of current dividend policy**

Year	Profit after interest and tax $m	Capital expenditure / investment in projects $m	Dividend paid $m	Payout ratio (as % of profit)
20X5	18	Nil	9	50%
20X6	21	30	6	29%
20X7	30	Nil	15	50%
20X8	33	45	6	18%
20X9	48	Nil	24	50%

Given the figures above, the current dividend policy appears to be as follows.

No investment takes place

When no investment or capital expenditure takes place, the company pays out 50% of its profits after interest and tax as dividends.

Major investment or capital expenditure takes place

When major investment or capital expenditure takes place, the company appears to pay out $6m, regardless of the level of profit or the size of the investment.

Comments on current dividend policy

The current dividend policy appears to be quite **unstable** and does not give the shareholders a predictable level of income. Given that it is currently a private company, this is not surprising. Private companies' payout policies tend to be influenced by the needs of the companies and the expectations of individual shareholders.

Shareholders are guaranteed a minimum payout of $6m but the maximum payout over the five-year period has been $24m. The shareholders are apparently amenable to the policy of reinvesting all surplus cash above $6m in the business (assuming there are profitable investment opportunities available). Reinvesting in such profitable projects will **increase shareholders' wealth** and will reduce the need to depend on debt finance. This has the effect of keeping gearing ratios at a minimum, thus **reducing risk** and therefore the cost of capital.

BPP
LEARNING MEDIA

4 Agenda for change

Text references. Chapter 1 for the role and responsibilities of management; chapter 3c for environmental issues; chapter 4 for agency issues.

Top tips. There are plenty of issues in the scenario that you can address but make sure to relate your answer to part (a) to strategic financial issues. Make sure that the issues you identify are quite specific as you are required to provide potential actions that could resolve these issues.

Ethics have been identified by the examiner as being an important part of the syllabus and these are dealt with in part (b). Some of the issues can be easily identified. Others, such as the earnings management issue, are more subtle; don't worry if you haven't mentioned that one as it is only worth 2 marks.

As both parts of this question link quite closely to one another, you should carefully plan your answer to ensure that the alternatives you identify in (a) can be used to resolve the ethical issues in (b).

Easy marks. As mentioned above, there are some easy marks to be gained in part (b) by identifying some of the more obvious ethical issues in the scenario. Part (c) is also a fairly straightforward requirement.

Examiner's comments. This question gave candidates a wide degree of latitude in identifying the strategic, financial and ethical issues faced by the company concerned. A wide variety of answers were provided by candidates.

Many candidates demonstrated skills in planning and layout. However relatively few candidates focused on the perspective of a chief financial officer which was the role they were asked to assume. The selection of issues and details of alternative courses of action were generally limited and sometimes inconsistent. Candidates should also pay attention to the simple points. For example, this company has surplus cash and the overriding question is whether there is any prospect that the cash could be used effectively through new value-adding investment. If that is not the case then the company has an ethical duty to return that cash to the shareholders.

Candidates should also note that points should not be repeated unless it is relevant to the development of new lines of argument or mentioned in the conclusion.

Marking scheme

			Marks
(a)	Setting the scene and identifying core problem and its source	2	
	Principal alternatives:		
	Acquisition strategy	2	
	Reorganisation, organic growth with cost minimisation	2	
	Return cash to investors	2	
	Incentives for management with share option scheme	2	
			10
(b)	Identification of core ethical issue	2	
	Social policy and property rights arguments underpinning ethical dimension	2	
	Resolution and advice	4	
	Note on ethics of earning management	2	
			10
(c)	One mark per relevant objective	Max	5
			25

(a)   **Briefing notes for the 'Agenda for Change' board paper**

Strategic financial issues

The company appears to have lost some of its competitive edge due to a slow-down in spending on defence-based components which are a major part of the company's business. The company has failed to invest in research and development although it has adopted a strategy of growth by acquisition. Significant problems appear to be the lack of expenditure on new investment projects and the lack of accountability of managers who sponsor poorly performing projects and whose remuneration is relatively low.

Financial position

The company's financial position appears to be strong, with low gearing and a comfortable current assets ratio, as well as an abundance of cash in hand and on deposit. However such a financial position makes the company ripe for a takeover bid.

Possible alternatives

I have identified four alternatives that could be pursued to address these strategic financial issues. These are not necessarily mutually exclusive.

(i)   **Acquiring research and development expertise by acquisition**

As the company already has a 'growth by acquisition' strategy it could extend this to its research and development facility. As research and development growth by internal investment can take years – and time is not something that the company has – this strategy is much more viable, particularly as the necessary cash is available. An improvement in the essential research and development facility will allow the company to develop new and improved products to appeal to more lucrative markets. This is particularly important as the 'dominant' defence side of the business appears to be in decline.

(ii)   **Returning cash to shareholders**

An excess of cash can make a company vulnerable to a takeover bid. One way of avoiding this – particularly if there are few, if any, profitable investment opportunities available – is to return cash to the shareholders, either in the form of a special dividend or via a share buy-back. As there is currently a problem with ensuring the accountability of managers who are sponsoring projects, there is a risk that managers will enter into unprofitable projects just to be seen to be spending money (but at the expense of shareholder wealth). One way of avoiding such a misuse of funds would be to give the money back to the shareholders directly.

(iii)   **Actively pursuing the adoption of advanced manufacturing technologies**

The manufacture of aerospace components requires the use of the most up to date technology. As the company has not actively pursued the use of such techniques it is placed at a competitive disadvantage and is unlikely to be operating at maximum efficiency or minimum cost. The company should be aware of the potential adverse long-term consequences of continuing to avoid the adoption of advanced technologies. To promote cost efficiency, managers should be made more accountable for the performance of their sponsored projects with specified budgets and targets. To promote operational efficiency, the company should be more aggressive in its adoption of up to date production techniques.

(iv)   **Motivating managers**

At the moment managers' remuneration levels are poor and whilst high salary levels should not be the only motivational factor, they do help to promote the company's appreciation of its staff. Low remuneration packages have resulted in difficulties for the company in attracting a suitably qualified management team. The company could move towards rectifying this situation by offering an incentive package such as a share option scheme. If managers know they will benefit financially from increasing shareholder wealth they are more likely to pursue only those projects with positive NPVs and keep tighter control over costs.

BPP LEARNING MEDIA

(b)   **The key issues**

Lack of investment opportunities

One key issue for the company is the lack of profitable investment opportunities which has led to a slow-down in earnings growth that could soon lead to an actual decline. The main reasons for this appear to be the failure to adopt advanced manufacturing technologies and lack of management accountability.

From an ethical point of view if there are no profitable investments available the company should ensure that shareholders' funds are not wasted on loss-making projects.

Environmental footprint

A second issue is the company's approach to environmental issues. It has already been fined for polluting a river – without resolution, such occurrences are likely to increase.

Earnings management

Earnings management is another key issue. There should be a close examination of the company's ratio of EBITDA to operational cash flow. A ratio that is consistently lower than that of a growing firm suggests that earnings are being hidden. This may discourage shareholders from putting pressure on management to return excess funds to them. Managers themselves may feel unable to press for higher salaries in the light of these artificially reduced earnings. Alternatively it may be an attempt to smooth earnings to enable more consistent performance indicators to be reported. If earnings are being artificially reduced then an ethical issue arises in the form of trying to deceive company stakeholders.

How can these be resolved?

(i)   **Return excess funds to the shareholders**

The ethical issue that shareholders' funds should not be wasted can be resolved by returning the excess funds to the shareholders themselves (as suggested in alternative (ii) above). Such funds should not be used by management – regardless of how poorly they feel they are paid – to enhance their own perks. It could be argued that if money was used to improve managers' remuneration packages then this would motivate them to pursue the overriding company objective of maximising shareholders' wealth. However if funds were returned to the shareholders, they could make their own decisions as to how best to use these funds. The critical factors here are ownership of resources and the efficient use of these resources. Shareholders own the company – any surplus funds legally belong to them and they are therefore entitled to have such funds returned to them.

(ii)   **The use of advanced manufacturing technologies**

The company has been fined for an untreated discharge into a local river. With increased focus on environmental problems and the ethical issues attached to environmental pollution the company should be avoiding such publicity at all costs.

One potential reason for the pollution could be the use of inferior manufacturing techniques. This could be resolved through active pursuit of and investment in advanced manufacturing technologies. Not only could this serve to reduce environmental pollution it may also reduce energy consumption.

(iii) **Internal audit**

In order to ensure as far as possible that managers are disclosing all figures correctly, an internal audit function could be set up if it is not already in evidence. Such governance procedures improve the transparency of the reported figures and can highlight any system issues that prevent figures being reported correctly. It is a company's duty to make full and correct disclosure of its results – the existence of an effective internal audit function should help to ensure that this is the case.

(c)   **Possible environmental management accounting objectives**

(i)   **Eco-balance**

The company should identify the raw materials it uses and outputs such as noise, to which it attributes a notional value. These outputs can then be identified as social 'costs'.

(ii)   **Cleaner technology**

This can be used in the manufacturing process to avoid waste. The company can look at changes in waste levels as a result of adopting new technology.

(iii) **Performance appraisal**

This can include steps taken to reduce pollution, backed up by scientific measures of emissions.

(iv) **Life cycle assessments**

The total environmental impact of a product is measured, from the resources it consumes, the energy it requires in use, and how it is disposed of, if not recycled. It may be that a product's poor ecological impact (and consequent liability or poor publicity) can be traced back to one component or material, which can be replaced.

(v) **Budgetary planning and control system**

These can be used to develop variances analysing environmental issues.

5 Solar Supermarkets

Text references. Directors' duties are covered in Chapter 1. Ethics are covered in Chapter 3b. Stakeholders are covered in Chapter 3a.

Top tips. It is useful at the beginning of your answer to summarise the main issues briefly so that you do not forget to address them all. This does not mean writing out the whole question again however! Remember to address all three types of issues – headings will be useful here to divide your answer and make it easier for the marker to identify each issue.

Part (b) requires a discussion about balancing stakeholder interests with reference to Solar Supermarkets.

Easy marks. You should be able to identify that money purchase pension schemes are less generous than final salary schemes and comment on the ethical issues associated with this perception.

Marking scheme

		Marks
(a)	Overarching duty of directors	3 - 4
	Commentary on the threat of acquisition by private equity	3 - 4
	Merits or issues of sale/leaseback (cost of breakup and risk effects)	3 - 4
	Commentary on share option schemes and redistribution of risk	3 - 4
	Labour market reactions to the move to a money purchase scheme	3 - 4
	Ethical commentary on distribution of risk between stakeholders	5 - 6
		Max 20
(b)	Shareholder importance in running company to be recognised in objectives	2 - 3
	Argument that other stakeholders need to be recognised	2 - 3
	Reference to pension scheme	1
		Max 5
		25

(a) **What are the main issues?**

(i) Management compensation that will provide a sufficient incentive for management to continue to seek profitable investment opportunities.

(ii) Price and cost pressure.

(iii) The potential provision of a final salary pension scheme and the costs of doing so.

(iv) Pressure from investors to release the value tied up in property and the threat of acquisition.

Strategic

At all times, the over-riding duty of directors is to the **shareholders**. The main objective of any company is to **maximise shareholders' wealth** and all decisions taken should be with the fulfilment of this objective in mind. However this is often confused with directors' duty to **the company** itself and their aim to always act in **the company's best interests**.

The issue of sale and leaseback of the stores or the flotation of a separate company that would rent the stores back to Solar Supermarkets is a delicate one. The market has valued the company on the basis that it has its own stores and is **both a retail and property organisation**. If the stores were sold, **the value of the firm may fall** as its now primarily retail focus will be exposed to greater competition which will not be shielded by the property portfolio. Shareholders will suffer as firm value falls, thus contradicting the over-riding objective of companies to maximise firm value.

It is unclear whether the threat of acquisition is real or is just a ploy by investors to ensure the sale of the property to release funds for their benefit. Either way, if the property is sold, the risk of the business will undoubtedly increase. It may therefore be worth reviewing the share option scheme.

The current management reward package allows risk to be shared between the owners and the management team. One of the problems with a share option scheme is that managers are more inclined to take more risks to increase the value of the firm. The risk is then shifted more heavily onto the shareholders.

The movement from a final salary pension scheme to a money purchase scheme may lead to greater difficulties in terms of staff recruitment. Such a move for already lowly paid workers may lead to good quality staff leaving the organisation in favour of companies offering final salary schemes. High staff turnover will lead to increased inefficiencies and ultimately to reductions in profits.

Financial

A **money purchase** pension scheme is perceived as being **less generous** that a final salary scheme. The use of a money purchase scheme brings benefits in terms of fund management and financing. The members of the scheme face greater exposure to future returns and annuity rates. However a final salary scheme could leave the company with significant liabilities in the event of adverse economic conditions and falling share prices, leading to the scheme no longer being "well funded".

Although it may be cheaper to offer a money purchase scheme, **wage rates may have to rise** to compensate for the perceived reduction in benefits. The company may therefore experience few if any financial gains from this alternative scheme.

Ethical

Shop workers are often paid low wages therefore the replacement of a final salary pension scheme with a money purchase scheme may be perceived as **exploitation**. They are now at the mercy of movements in the stock markets rather than having a guaranteed pension, an issue that is often high in the minds of those who have few savings and lower wages.

The various schemes involve the **shift of risk** between stakeholder groups. Employees face higher risks for reasons mentioned above. **Shareholders** have higher risk exposure as managers become **less risk averse** in pursuit of value-adding activities due to their participation in share option schemes. The directors should not take advantage of their position by agreeing to changes that will have a favourable effect on their benefits and risk exposure, or reduce those of other stakeholders, without taking into account the impact on shareholders and employees.

(b)   The maximisation of shareholder wealth is often seen as the primary objective of companies. However an organisation's objectives should recognise that there will always be a number of **stakeholder groups** interested in a company's operations, including shareholders, loan creditors, directors and managers, other employees, customers, suppliers, government (including tax authorities), and the communities in which the company is based. These stakeholder groups will have different needs, for example employees may want job security, customers may want low prices and local communities are likely to want to local environment to be preserved.

The primary stakeholders are the **shareholders,** who are the owners of the company. They appoint **directors as agents** to run the company on their behalf. Therefore, private sector companies **must have a primary objective** that is related to the needs of shareholders. However, there can still be a conflict between **short and long-term** fulfilling of an objective to maximise returns to shareholders. To fully maximise returns now, may involve compromising sustainability and therefore reduce total returns in the long term.

However a company should not necessarily pursue policies that are purely in the interest of the shareholders. Even those who assert that a company's **sole objective** should be to benefit shareholders will agree that this is best done by considering the needs of other stakeholder groups. For example Solar Supermarkets may be able to generate additional shareholder wealth by attracting higher calibre employees. This may be easier with a better benefits package, such as offering a final salary pension scheme, although this may appear, in the short term, to have a negative impact on shareholder wealth - as it may be more expensive and riskier to the company.

6 Preparation question – International corporate governance

Text references. Chapter 3a.

Top tips. It's obviously helpful in this question if you can quote the provisions of the Combined Code but detailed knowledge of the provisions isn't necessary for high marks. Provided you judge, using the principles of the reports, whether the company has gone far enough, you should score well. In (b) we have given guidance for all three countries rather than just the two you were required to give in the question. Key issues in (b) are the role of boards, stakeholders and principles v detailed rules.

Easy marks. If you know the principles of the UK Corporate Governance Code, it should be easy to apply them to (a). Note the stress in the marking scheme on **reasoned** answers.

Marking scheme

			Marks
(a)	Correct comment on each point, 1-2 marks		
	For 2 marks a good reasoned answer is necessary		Max 9
(b)	Contrasts between UK and each country, 2-3 marks per country	4–5	
	Do not give extra credit for comparison with all three countries		
	Implications for managers	1–2	
			Max 6
			15

(a) (i) **Audit fees and audit partner**

The company is **complying** with the **corporate governance codes** in disclosing fees, but should clearly differentiate between audit and non-audit fees. The Combined Code also recommends that the annual report should explain to shareholders how, if the auditor provides **non-audit services**, auditor objectivity and independence is safeguarded.

Governance guidance suggests that partners should not be in charge of a client's audit for too many years, to avoid over-familiarity and hence loss of independence. Therefore as well as setting a minimum period, the guidance should also set a **maximum period** of around five years.

(ii) **Remuneration committee**

The Codes recommend that a remuneration committee with responsibility for recommending executive remuneration policy and directors' packages should be set up. However it should consist entirely of **independent non-executive directors** (NEDs). Independent NEDs should have no connections with the company other than fees and shareholdings.

(iii) **Chairman and chief executive**

This provision, although it is short-term, goes against the recommendations that there should be a **clear division of responsibilities** at the head of a company so that one individual does not have unfettered powers of decision. The Combined Code states that the roles of chairman and chief executive should not be exercised by the same individual.

BPP
LEARNING MEDIA

(iv)   **Disclosures**

The company's provision is fine provided that:

(1)   It fully discloses any **departures** and the **reasons for those departures**, from the principles of the corporate governance codes.

(2)   It makes the **specific disclosures** required by the corporate governance reports including presentation of a balanced and understandable view of the company's prospects, disclosures about the directors, and details about the directors' review of internal controls.

(v)   **Directorships**

This provision is not sufficiently rigorous to fulfil the general principle of the corporate governance reports that directors should devote **sufficient time and attention** to the company's affairs. In particular the Combined Code recommends that the board should not agree to a full-time executive director taking on more than one non-executive directorship in a FTSE 100 company. Non-executive directors who do not hold any executive directorships may take on more than one non-executive directorship, but they should promise to have sufficient time available to discharge their responsibilities. It is very difficult to believe that if they hold as many as twenty directorships, that they will have sufficient time to devote to each one.

(vi)   **Internal control reporting**

This requirement needs to define what is meant by regularly. The Combined code requires a **report on internal controls** to be made to shareholders at least annually. The report should be based on a **review of internal control effectiveness** carried out by the board at least annually, and also consideration of internal controls as a regular part of board meeting agendas. The company's guidance needs to make clear that these procedures will happen.

(b)   **Main differences between the UK and Germany**

Germany has a **two-tier board system** in contrast to the UK's single-tier system. In Germany the **executive board** consists of managers who are responsible for the **running of the business**. The **supervisory board** is responsible for **reviewing the company's direction** and **safeguarding stakeholder interests**. **Banks** are often represented on the supervisory board as they are the most significant providers of long-term finance.

Implications for managers

Managers will be running the company in the knowledge that strategy has to be approved by the supervisory board. This means in particular that the stakeholders represented on the supervisory board, employees, shareholders and finance providers have to **agree with the direction** the company is taking.

Main differences between the UK and Japan

The Japanese system has a lower level of regulation than other major jurisdictions. The emphasis is on **collaboration with other stakeholders**, and less stress than in the UK on keeping shareholders satisfied. As with Germany, many Japanese companies have more than one tier of board. **Policy boards** are concerned with long-term strategic direction, **functional boards** consist of senior executives with operational functions, **monocratic boards** have mainly symbolic roles. Also in common with Germany, **other stakeholders** such as banks may be represented on the policy board.

Implications for managers

Managers in Japan seek to establish **long-term consensual business relationships** with banks, suppliers and customers. In many companies they will also be concerned primarily with **long-term objectives** such as **market share** rather than short-term profit maximisation.

Main differences between the UK and USA

The main differences between the UK and USA is that the USA is more based on **legal rules and regulations**, which companies have to fulfil in order to maintain a listing. In addition the American system requires **certification of the appropriateness** of the financial statements by the chief executive and chief finance officer.

Implications for managers

Managers working in the USA will need to ensure that internal procedures are in place to fulfil the **rigorous and other reporting requirements** of USA regulations. Audit committees need to discuss with external auditors **critical accounting policies** and **appropriate alternative treatments**.

7 Mezza Co

> **Text references.** Ethical and environmental issues are covered in Chapters 3b and 3c. Takeover regulation is in Chapter 11.
>
> **Top tips.** Read the entire requirement before starting your answer – as you will note from the examiner's comments below, a number of students failed to address how issues could be mitigated. Part (b) specifically refers to the European Directive, so you need to know the relevant regulatory devices to include in your answer.
>
> **Easy marks.** There are numerous easy marks to be gained from the environmental and ethical issues surrounding the project, as such issues are extremely topical.
>
> **Examiner's comments.** This question was well answered with many students gaining a high proportion of the marks for their answers. Answers that gained fewer marks did not give many points or lacked adequate discussion. Some answers considered the issues but not how these could be mitigated.

Marking scheme

		Marks
(a)	Over-arching corporate aim	1 – 2
	Discussion of the project adding value and issues relating to return and risk	3 – 4
	Possible suggestions for mitigating the negative issues to above discussion	3 – 4
	Discussion of the ethical and environmental issues	3 – 4
	Possible suggestions for mitigating the ethical and environmental issues	3 – 4
	Other relevant key issues and suggestions for mitigation	2 – 3
		Max 17
(b)	Explanation of European Takeover Directive devices	4 – 5
	Application to scenario	4 – 5
		Max 8
		25

(a) **Over-arching corporate aim**

The main aim of the directors is to maximise shareholder value and any decisions should be taken with this objective in mind. However the company has other stakeholders and directors should be sensitive to potential negative implications from implementing the project.

Key issue (1) – will the project add value?

The first issue to consider is whether the project will add value to the company.

Positive factors

At first glance it would appear that the project would be adding value, as it is meeting an identifiable market need (tackling climate change). There are likely to be positive effects on the company's reputation and ultimately its share price as Mezza Co is demonstrating a desire and ability to tackle climate change. If Mezza Co champions the work being done by its subsidiary, there are likely to be future opportunities for the subsidiary to work on similar projects.

Other factors to consider

Before progressing with the project, further investigation into its likely value is required. Whilst there is no doubt that such a project should be well received there are risks that must be considered, not just from the project itself but also from the behaviour of the directors. Share options form part of the directors' remuneration package and they may be tempted to take greater risks as a result, in order to try boosting the share price. This may be against the wishes of shareholders and other stakeholders who may have a more risk-averse attitude.

The project appears to use new technology and ideas which, by their very nature, will be risky. There will therefore be uncertainty surrounding the income stream from the project – the extent of the risk should be assessed prior to progressing with the project. Are the current revenue and cost estimates realistic? What is the likelihood of competitors entering the market and the potential effects on revenue and market share? A full investigation, using such means as sensitivity analysis and duration, is required to answer such questions.

When assessing the extent of the value added by the project, it is important that risk is factored into the process. By doing so, directors will be in a better position (if necessary) to show stakeholders that they are not taking unacceptable risks in proceeding with the project. Other factors that must be investigated include the length of time it will take to get the product to market, any additional infrastructure required and potential expertise needed.

Key issue (2) – plant location

Positive factors

Mezza Co has identified an 'ideal' location for the plant, namely Maienar in Asia. This is due to Mezza already having a significant presence in Maienar and thus a well-developed infrastructure exists. There are also strong ties with senior government officials in this country and the government is keen to develop new industries. All of these factors are very positive for the potential development of the project. The ties to senior government officials are likely to be particularly useful when trying to deal with legal and administrative issues, thus reducing the time between development and production actually starting.

Other factors to consider

Despite the positive factors mentioned above, there are ethical and environmental issues to consider prior to making a final decision regarding plant location. The likely effect on the fishermen's livelihood could produce adverse publicity, as could potential damaging effects on the environment and wildlife. Environmental impact tends to generate considerable debate and Mezza will want to avoid any negative effects on its reputation (particularly as the project is supposed to be 'environmentally friendly').

The fact that Mezza has close ties with senior political figures and the government in general may create negative feeling if it is felt that Mezza could influence the government into making decisions that are not in the best interests of the locality and the country as a whole. This is a relationship that will have to be managed very carefully.

Risk mitigation

Given that Mezza has an excellent corporate image, it is unlikely that it will want to ignore the plight of the fishermen. It could try to work with the fishermen and involve them in the process, pointing out the benefits of the project to the environment as a whole (without ignoring the effects on their livelihood). It could offer the fishermen priority on any new jobs that are created and emphasise the additional wealth that the project is likely to create.

Mezza could also consider alternative locations for the plant, although this is likely to be expensive, given the need for certain infrastructure already present in Maienar. Alternatively the company could try to find an alternative process for growing and harvesting the plant that would not have adverse effects on wildlife and fish stocks. Again, this is an expensive option and any such costs would have to be set against expected revenues to determine value added.

As mentioned above, Mezza will have to manage its relationship with Maienar's government very carefully as it does not want to appear to be influencing government decisions. Mezza needs to make it very clear that it is following proper legal and administrative procedures - and is working with the government to protect and improve the country, rather than exploit it for its own gains.

Conclusion

It is important that Mezza considers all of the likely benefits and costs related to the project, not just to itself but also the country and its inhabitants. While gaining prompt approval from the government will allow the project to proceed and become profitable more quickly, it is important that Mezza focuses on the effects of the project and alternative ways to proceed, in order to avoid an overall negative impact on its reputation.

(b)   **Takeover regulatory devices**

Mandatory bid rule

Based on the UK threshold, Mezza Co has passed the mandatory bid limit level of share ownership, which would allow the minority shareholders to sell their remaining shares at a fair price. This means Mezza Co would have to make a bid for the remaining shares at a price that is not lower than the $6.67 per share ($20m/3m) from the initial purchase of shares.

The principle of equal treatment

The principle of treating all shareholders equally does not differ too much from the provisions of the mandatory bid rule. In general terms, the principle of equal treatment requires the bidder to offer to minority shareholders the same terms as those offered to the majority shareholder from whom the controlling block was acquired. Note that this would include any alternatives that the previous shareholder was offered also being offered to the remaining shareholders.

The squeeze-out rule

The squeeze-out rule gives the bidder who has acquired a specific percentage of the equity (usually 90%) the right to force minority shareholders to sell their shares. The rule enables the bidder to acquire 100% of the equity once the threshold percentage has been reached and eliminates potential problems that could be caused by minority shareholders.

Note that sell-out rights are not applicable here as Mezza Co wishes to buy all of the remaining shares.

The break- through rule

There is no suggestion that this applies here, since Mezza Co bought a block of shares from a majority shareholder. If differentiated voting rights did exist allowing the remaining minority shareholders to control the subsidiary or frustrate Mezza Co, the break-through rule could be used to allow Mezza Co to exercise control.

Board neutrality

This device does not apply in this situation as Mezza Co is assumed to have full control of the subsidiary so the board is unable to implement any defensive tactics at this stage.

8 Kengai Co

Text references. Triple Bottom Line reporting is covered in Chapter 3c. Stakeholder conflict is in Chapter 3a.

Top tips. Don't forget to relate your answer to the company in the scenario. You are not given a great deal of information in the scenario but you are expected to make your answer relevant. Don't be tempted to write everything you know about TBL in part (a) – you have to relate your answer to sustainable development. There are numerous examples of proxies in the Study Text.

Even if you do not know a great deal about TBL you should be able to make a fair attempt at part (b) by using common sense and information you may have obtained from newspapers and web sites.

Part (c) requires you to think about which group of stakeholders is most important to Kengai.

Easy marks. If you have studied TBL there are numerous easy marks to be picked up here, particularly in part (a).

Examiner's comments. Quite a number of candidates were able to discuss what TBL reporting involves, giving relevant examples of proxies and how TBL reporting helps management to focus on improving financial strength of the company. However, some candidates repeated points that had previously been made, gaining few marks.

Marking scheme

			Marks
(a)	Explaining TBL and relation to sustainability	4 – 5	
	Examples of proxies (up to 2 marks for proxies per TBL factor)	4 – 5	
			Max 8
(b)	Discussion of long-term shareholder wealth maximisation and benefits exceeding costs	2	
	2 – 3 marks per well-discussed example focusing on financial impact	8 – 9	
			Max 10
(c)	Explanation of stakeholder conflicts	4 – 5	
	Resolution of conflict	2 – 3	
			Max 7
			25

(a) Triple Bottom Line reporting

Triple Bottom Line reporting (TBL) is an external reporting approach that gives consideration to economic (financial) outcomes, environmental quality and social equity. The principle of this approach is that the true performance of a business should be measured in terms of the balance between social (people), economic (profits) and environmental (planet) factors – no one factor should grow at the expense of the others.

Sustainable development

A company's sustainable development is concerned with how the three TBL factors can work together and grow to ensure the company is viewed as being a good corporate citizen with concern for social and environmental factors. Whilst shareholders are primarily interested in maximisation of wealth, other stakeholders are concerned with the environment and a company's impact on people. A company that can combine these factors with the ability to improve shareholders' wealth will be satisfying the needs of its wider stakeholders.

Whilst TBL is backward-looking – that is, it provides a quantitative summary of corporate performance in the three factors over a previous time period – sustainable development is forward-looking and qualitative. TBL provides a measurement tool to assess corporate performance against its objectives.

Proxies

Each TBL factor can be measured using a number of proxies.

Economic impact can be measured by such factors as gross operating surplus, dependence on imports and the extent to which the economy is stimulated by the purchase of locally produced goods and services.

Social impact can be measured by such factors as the extent of the company's tax contribution, working conditions, the use of an appropriate labour force that receives a fair wage and looking after the welfare of animals (such as no animal testing or humane transportation of livestock).

Environmental impact can be measured by such factors as the ecological footprint, water and energy use and emissions to soil, water and air.

(b) **Improving the financial position of the company**

In order to improve the financial position of the company, the benefits from the assessment and production of a TBL report must exceed the costs of producing the report. The costs are often easy to measure but the financial benefits may take place over a longer time period and be more difficult to assess.

Environmental and social factors are becoming increasingly important in today's society. If Kengai focuses on these areas it is likely to enhance its reputation which may lead to increased revenues. If it does not bother about these factors its reputation may be damaged and its revenue stream (and corporate value) may decrease as a result.

If Kengai offers good working conditions and fair pay, whilst at the same time consulting with its employees during this process, it is more likely to attract high calibre employees who will be loyal to the company. Kengai will benefit from this in the long-term as employees will be willing to work hard and perform well. Having such a workforce may reduce risk management costs as there is less likelihood of good staff leaving the organisation, resulting in loss of expertise and business knowledge.

If the performance of employees and managers is regularly assessed as part of the TBL reporting requirements this may identify areas where effectiveness and efficiency can be improved. New processes may be introduced to make such improvements that will benefit the financial position of the company in the long-term.

By assessing and improving the environmental factor in the TBL report, Kengai may reduce its carbon footprint as it reduces reliance on imports and instead develops local expertise in producing the necessary inputs. This may reduce the risk of problems with suppliers and potential inventory shortages. In the long-term this will improve Kengai's financial position as losses related to such issues are reduced.

The economic factor assessment should improve due diligence procedures and thus reduce the costs of maintaining stakeholder relationships (for example legal costs). Communication with stakeholders and improvements in reporting may lead to improved governance procedures, which would in turn lead to a reduction in risk management costs.

The extent to which the above opportunities are successful in improving financial performance will depend on the quality of assessment of the three TBL factors and Kengai's ability to enable positive changes to happen.

(c) **Conflicts between main stakeholder groups**

Conflict between economic interests and environmental pressure groups

Kengai's focus on maximising shareholder returns is legitimate within its own terms. It may also be supported (although this is not stated in the scenario) by community groups on the grounds of creating employment, and benefiting the community through taxation, investment and the 'trickle down' affect of economic activity.

Environmental pressure and interest groups, however, focus on a different set of priorities: the need to protect rare species from extinction, the need to preserve scenic beauty for future generations and so on.

Mining is a worldwide target of such groups, because of its often traumatic impact on environments (eg through open cast mines, pollution of river systems and watersheds and so on). These groups may or may not be representative of local community interests: supporting the 'bigger picture' of the environment at the expense of local economic sustainability.

Conflict between local residents and Kengai

A second conflict arises from the fear of loss of residential amenity on the part of the local residents of Buranda as a result of the mining activity. This may partly be legitimately focused on the risk of traffic congestion and noise, but there may also be an underlying fear of change and cultural erosion. Economic progress and development (desirable to some) may represent the loss of a way of life.

While Kengai may agree that congestion and noise should be minimised as part of its social responsibilities, it is clearly committed to industrial development and resource exploitation, and would presumably argue that such a position benefits not only its shareholders, but the local community as well.

Conflict resolution

The resolution of the stakeholder conflict will depend on the relative importance of the stakeholders. If Kengai decides that the local residents are more important than the environmental pressure groups, then the final decision will rest on whether the local residents are generally in favour of, or against, the mining project. If Kengai decides that its shareholders' interests are the sole responsibility it has then it will proceed with the mining if it makes financial sense to do so.

9 International trade

Text references. International trade is covered in Chapter 4

Top tips. Part (a) requires you to discuss how and why governments frequently ignore the advantages of free trade and engage in various forms of protectionism. It is necessary to discuss what individual governments can gain from protectionism.

In part (b) bear in mind that a common market such as the European Union (EU) is a localised free trade area, which may (as the EU does) adopt protectionist measures which militate against freedom of trade with countries outside the common market area.

In (c) the important point is that domestic markets are too limited for the application of much modern technology and the high minimum efficient scale of much production. Consumers want value-for-money products together with some product innovation: both of these are dependent on, or facilitated by, international trade.

Easy marks. Part (a) offers some relatively straightforward discussion marks and gives the opportunity for real world examples.

(a)   There are several reasons why free trade is not pursued by all countries. Firstly, countries attempt to preserve their own weak industries by **restricting imports**. Very few countries are prepared to see whole industries sacrificed to free trade and will always seek to maintain some part of all their traditional industries. This involves some form of protection as the more efficient countries will be able to outsell them even in their own domestic market.

Secondly, the theory of free trade assumes that all countries play fair. This is not always the case. Many countries will seek an **unfair advantage** by expanding certain industries to gain significant economies of scale and dumping the excess production on the other countries at less than a commercial cost. In this way they hope to eliminate competition and eventually become monopoly suppliers. The other countries naturally defend themselves against this sort of threat.

Developing countries protect their so-called 'infant industries' by **protection** until the industries are strong enough to compete on the world markets.

Finally, countries will always wish to maintain their strategic industries without which they would feel threatened. These industries range from those that are absolutely essential to survival to those that are necessary if the country is to maintain any sort of modern industrial base.

For all these reasons countries do not follow the logic of the free trade argument to the letter. However, the various trade liberalisation talks (the General Agreement on Tariffs and Trade being the best known example) are aimed at freeing world trade and do have significant effects given a long enough time scale for implementation.

(b)   The most obvious benefits which countries might gain from forming a common market are associated with free trade between them. The benefits of free trade are illustrated by the law of comparative advantage, which states that countries should specialise in producing those goods where they have a comparative advantage. Specialisation, together with free trade, will result in an **increase in total output** and all countries will be able, to a greater or lesser extent, to share in the benefits.

In particular, different countries have different factor endowments. As the international mobility of these factors tends to be severely limited, trade increases the range of goods and services available in a particular country. By becoming part of a common market, imports from other member countries are available more cheaply and easily. Imports of certain raw materials or types of capital equipment not otherwise available in a particular country will improve its productive potential, enabling a faster rate of economic growth to be achieved. Similarly, improvements in the range and quality of consumer goods available will tend to enhance a country's standard of living.

In addition, there is a larger market for domestic output and firms may be able to benefit from economies of scale by engaging in export activities. Economies of scale improve efficiency in the use of resources and enable output to be produced at lower cost. This also raises the possibility of benefits to consumers if these **cost savings are passed on in the form of lower prices**. In addition, the extension of the market in which firms operate increases the amount of competition they face and hence should improve efficiency.

Establishment of a common market is often accompanied by some form of exchange rate agreement between members and this in turn is likely to encourage further trade as it reduces uncertainty for both exporters and importers. Stability of exchange rates is also beneficial to a government in formulating its domestic economic policies.

Membership of a common market may be particularly **beneficial to smaller or weaker economies** as, in addition to increasing the availability of essential factors of production and the range of goods and services available to domestic consumers, it also enables them to benefit from any economic growth experienced by their fellow members. Spin-offs may be in the form of larger markets for their exports, lower import prices, improved employment opportunities and so on.

As well as fostering economic ties between countries, common markets provide the basis for stronger political links. Again, this may be particularly important for smaller countries, enabling them to benefit from an enhanced position in the world economy. It may also encourage further international economic co-operation, in turn providing an additional stimulus to growth.

(c)   The potential benefits to business from international trade arise from the opportunities available to those operating in world markets as well as from the increased competition. Restrictions on trade may not permit the movement into a country of certain goods but may permit the setting up of subsidiaries by foreign-owned companies in order to manufacture and market within the host country. The removal of trade (and financing) restrictions enable companies to make more **rational decisions** as to how they will develop and operate throughout the world.

For domestic producers, the existence of competition from abroad can be turned to advantage. It can help to keep home suppliers 'on their toes' and so compel the use of more efficient methods and the adoption of innovatory ideas for both products and means of production and supply.

The availability of world markets can enable a firm, already the leader of its industry in the home market, to expand abroad and so exploit economies of scale. It is then more likely to expand its core activities, in which its strengths are greatest, rather than attempt to diversify into more peripheral activities, in which it may have noticeable weaknesses.

Domestic producers will also find it easier to **locate optimal means of fulfilling resource needs**. A wider range of suppliers will be available, and they will need to compete with each other on price, quality and reliability of supply. New ideas on product and component design and development are more likely to be forthcoming. In a closed economy some input needs might not be met or could only be supplied at excessively high prices.

Thus, **input costs should fall as world trade increases**, while export possibilities facilitate expansion of sales. The resulting economies of scale and enhanced efficiency should result in lower (real) selling prices. This in turn provides the basis for further expansion. In addition, if world trade is supported by the free movement of investment funds, it will enable firms to raise funds where the cost is most favourable. Constraints upon business expansion are thus lessened or removed.

BPP
LEARNING MEDIA

10 Global financial markets

Text references. Global financial crisis is covered in chapter 4 and chapter 19. Credit rating is covered in chapter 7a.

Top tips. This question underlines the importance of keeping up-to-date with financial management issues. If you did not know the answer to parts (a) and (b) it is important that you learn about the global debt crisis as it could be part of an exam question.

Easy marks. Part (c) offers some fairly straightforward discussion marks. If you are comfortable with the credit spread table, the calculation in part (d) should also be relatively easy.

(a)   **The global debt problem**

The 'global debt problem' which has affected some developing countries for nearly thirty years is essentially the result of **domestic economic deficit** in these countries, necessitating the borrowing of money to meet basic requirements such as the import of food and fuel. This was combined with an **overoptimistic risk assessment** on the part of international banks. As a result, the level of debt in these developing countries rose and their ability to repay decreased as increasing amounts of the GDP were absorbed in servicing the debt rather then financing development.

Causes of global debt problem

The deficits of developing countries were caused by the considerable **price increases of fuel** and other commodities in the 1970s and 1980s, **widespread recession**, **reduction in import demand** from more developed countries, relatively **high international interest rates** and the propensity for such perceived financial crises to encourage **capital flight**. All this led to levels of expenditure impossible to sustain without borrowing internationally.

Bank lending

The willingness of major banks to lend vast amounts of money, based on the historical premise that sovereign nations are unlikely to default, meant that many countries in South America and Sub Saharan Africa were able to borrow to the extent that **debt servicing payments exceeded 50%** of total export earnings. Insufficient domestic savings made debt repayment impossible.

Financial contagion

The term 'financial contagion' is used to describe the **potential international proliferation** of **financial and economic problems**, a phenomenon made more prevalent by the easing of investment restrictions, lifting of trade barriers and the general trend towards globalisation. It is possible that problems affecting even a small economy can have a critically damaging effect on the economies of its neighbouring countries, as was seen with the spreading South East Asia crisis in 1997, which started in Thailand.

Interaction of global debt and financial contagion

The financial problems that countries contract from their neighbours can prove crippling where those countries are already in debt, increases in deficit making **debt servicing conditions** progressively **more difficult to meet**.

(b)   **Resolution of global debt crisis**

A number of attempts at resolving global debt have been made, some seeking primarily to **alleviate the difficulties** of the **countries in debt**, some providing a **solution for the lender** alone and some endeavouring to **address the problems faced by both parties**.

(i)   **Write-off of debt**

One solution, for example, is the partial or complete writing off of debt, an approach which clearly **aids borrower nations**, at least in the short term, but involves considerable **cost to lending institutions**. The write-offs are normally combined with conditions imposed by the IMF and by the World Bank on channelling funds towards poverty alleviation.

(ii) **Sale of debt**

Another method of resolution is the **sale of debt** from one institution to another for less than face value, a means which ensures that the original lender sees at least some return on its loan but which offers no relief to indebted states given that the debt remains intact.

(iii) **Macroeconomic reforms**

Capital flight can be reduced by creating an economic climate in which investors can see that **funds invested** are **secure** and **produce real returns**. This implies **reforming property** laws and **controlling the macro-economy**, using appropriate fiscal and monetary policies. **The supply side** of the economy can also be improved by methods such as introducing a more flexible market and making the country more internationally competitive.

(iv) **Other methods**

Attempts to tackle the problems of both borrower and lender have included:

- The **extension of repayment periods** in order to moderate cash outflow
- The **lending of further funds** to countries unable to meet interest payments in order to prevent default, such loans in the main being conditional upon IMF provisos for economic reforms
- **Swapping of debt** into alternative types of commitment, ranging from the equity of local companies to the securing of promises that steps will be undertaken to reduce pollution

(v) **Limitation of financial contagion**

Given that economic crises commonly arise in countries with fixed exchange rates and subsequently overvalued currencies, it is apparent that the risk of such occurrences and their possible contagion could be significantly lowered if governments implemented **floating exchange rates**.

(c) The **globalisation** of the financial markets has been **buoyed** by the **creation of the Euro** and the **expansion of the European Union**.

When the European Union began the process of monetary union in the 1990s, the performance of the various member states' economies was noticeably different and there were marked differences in bond yields. However, since that time, many of the disparities have been removed, with the result that **yields have converged significantly**.

The Eurozone bond markets are now highly correlated and, at present, react very much like a homogeneous unit. For example, if the yield on the 10-year German bond rose 100 basis points, then we would expect yields on 10-year bonds from France, Spain, Italy and elsewhere to also rise by around 100 basis points. If this were not the case, then investors would not be indifferent to the investment opportunities available in the Eurozone bond market. Thus, investors would move out of the Italian bond market into Euro Government bonds of countries with stronger economics. It should be noted, however, that this cohesion may come under pressure if the Italian government bond suffers any further downgrades. The strongest core markets in the Eurozone are currently those of German, France, the Netherlands and Spain and the weakest is Italy.

(d) The expected yield on One Leaf Co's bonds is

$$\text{Credit spread} = 250 + \frac{(300 - 250)}{(30 - 10)} \times (15 - 10) = 262.5$$

Expected yield = 2.8% + 2.625% = 5.425%

The post-tax cost of debt is therefore

$k_d = (1 - 0.26) \times 5.425 = 4.01\%$

BPP
LEARNING MEDIA

11 Boxless

Text references. Chapters 4, 8.

Top tips. Detail can help you score well in (a), not just commenting that a tax haven reduces tax, but how it can be used (to avoid certain taxes eg capital gains and reduce other taxes such as withholding taxes).

Planning a proforma such as (b) is helpful as the best format will depend on how the tax is charged. The key stages are

- Calculating the income on which the three taxes (local corporate, withholding and UK income) are charged
- Calculating what these tax liabilities are
- As the last stage of the proforma calculating how much foreign tax can be set off against the UK tax
- Finally, adding the three tax liabilities

Easy marks. You need good understanding of how transfer pricing works to answer parts of this question well. Part (d) is a relatively easy discussion of the agency problem.

(a)   **Inability to offset tax burden**

Taxable income coming from several overseas subsidiaries is treated separately for UK tax purposes. It is likely that for subsidiaries in high tax countries the **local tax suffered** is too high to be **fully relieved** against the UK corporate tax liability, and also cannot be offset against UK tax liabilities of other foreign subsidiaries.

Benefits of tax haven

If a **tax haven holding company is used**, and all remittances to UK are made from this company, the **income is pooled and treated** as if it all comes from this single source. This can allow the total of foreign tax paid to be offset against the total UK tax liability of the tax haven holding company. This result is often that foreign tax credits are more **effectively used**.

In addition the use of tax haven may **enable capital gains to escape tax free** and a **reduction in withholding** tax on dividends if they are paid by the tax haven holding company. It is also often more **tax efficient** to channel cash from cash-rich subsidiaries to those requiring finance via a tax haven, rather than via the parent company. The use of tax havens may mean that the company's affairs may be less transparent as most tax havens have tough privacy laws and often bank secrecy arrangements.

Drawbacks of tax haven

There may be risks to post tax earnings levels as governments seek to close tax loopholes affecting tax havens. In addition, there are some annual incorporation costs involved in registering a tax haven. Finally, a political climate that is becoming more unfavourable to tax avoidance, and scandals involving companies registered in tax havens, may mean that there is a degree of risk to reputation involved in using them.

(b) (i) **Existing tax position**

	Annovia £'000	Carden £'000	Sporoon £'000	Total £'000
Taxable income (as given)	100.0	100	100.0	300.0
Local corporate income tax (40%/25%/20%) (1)	40.0	25	20.0	85.0
After-tax income	60.0	75	80.0	215.0
Dividend remitted to UK (70%/40%/80%)	42.0	30	64.0	136.0
Withholding tax on dividend (10%/–/5%) (2)	4·2	–	3·2	7.4
Dividend remitted to UK	42.0	30	64.0	136.0
Grossed up for UK tax purposes: × 100/(100 – local corporate tax rate):	70.0	40	80.0	190.0
UK tax liability (30%)	21.0	12	24.0	57.0
Foreign tax offset: 70%/40%/80% of local corporate tax charge	28.0	10	16.0	54.0
Withholding tax	4.2	0	3.2	7.4
Total	32.2	10	19.2	61.4
Offset against UK tax liability	21.0 (max)	10	19.2	50.2
UK tax payable (3)	–	2	4.8	6.8
Total tax payable (1) + (2) + (3)	44.2	27	28.0	99.2

Total taxation is £99,200.

UK government taxes total income

	Annovia £'000	Cardenda £'000	Sporoon £'000	Total £'000
Income	100.0	100	100.0	300.0
Local corporate income tax (1)	40.0	25	20.0	85.0
Available for distribution	60.0	75	80.0	215.0
Dividend remitted to UK	42.0	30	64.0	136.0
Withholding tax on dividend (2)	4·2	–	3·2	7.4
Income for UK tax purposes	100.0	100	100.0	300.0
UK tax liability (30%)	30.0	30	30.0	90.0
Foreign tax offset: corporate tax	40.0	25	20.0	85.0
withholding tax	4.2	–	3.2	7.4
Total	44.2	25	23.2	92.4
Offset against UK tax liability	30.0 (max)	25	23.2	78.2
UK tax payable (3)	–	5	6.8	11.8
Total tax payable (1) + (2) + (3)	44.2	30	30.0	104.2

Total taxation is £104,200, an increase of £5,000.

BPP LEARNING MEDIA

(ii)   **Using a tax haven holding company**

Figures are extracted from the total columns above.

	Existing tax position £'000	Total income taxed £'000
Taxable income	300.0	300.0
Local corporate income tax (1)	85.0	85.0
Total dividend to UK from holding company	136.0	136.0
Withholding tax (2)	7.4	7.4
Grossed up income for UK tax purposes	190.0	300.0
UK tax liability (30%)	57.0	90.0
Foreign tax offset:		
[92.4 but max 57; 92.4 but max 90]	57.0 (max)	90.0 (max)
UK tax payable (3)	–	–
Total taxation	92.4	92·4

Total tax payable in both cases is £92,400.

The tax haven holding company enables Boxless plc to **offset all the foreign tax** against UK tax payable. Without the tax haven, tax credits available from Annovia are too high to be fully usable against UK tax.

(c)   **Multinational companies investing or trading aboard** may **risk** a **high tax burden** through suffering local taxes that are particularly heavy on foreign investors or through tariffs and customs charges.

In many instances a multinational will establish a **branch** and utilise its initial losses against other profits and then turn the branch into a subsidiary when it starts making profits.

In some cases, there may be a risk that the company's profits may be **taxed twice**, once in the country in which they are earned, the other in the company's country of residence. However, most countries give **double taxation relief**, a tax credit for taxes on income paid to the host country to prevent this. In addition, in many countries the remitted profits of a subsidiary will be taxed at a higher rate than those of a branch, as profits paid in the form of dividends are likely to be subject to withholding tax. However the double tax treaty existing between most countries means that foreign tax credits are available for withholding taxes on sums paid to other countries as dividends, interest and royalties.

(d)   As is the case with all **corporate governance** mechanisms, monitoring by boards of directors can be costly, both in terms of cost and time. **Subsidiary boards** of directors have similar characteristics to the **corporate boards** of directors. However, it must be noted that, in the subsidiary boards, the role of non-executives may be taken not only by directors who are not affiliated with the parent company or the subsidiary in any way, but also by **directors** who are **employees** of Boxless but not of the **subsidiary**.

Managerial compensation packages can also be used to align the interests of the subsidiary managers to those of the parent company. However, one problem with establishing compensation arrangements for subsidiaries is that most subsidiaries of multinational corporations are not publicly traded companies. As a result, market value based standards and rewards cannot be used in subsidiary compensation schemes.

As a result, any single mechanism cannot mitigate the agency problem of subsidiaries completely. In order to address the agency problem a firm faces, a number of mechanisms need to work in unison.

12 World Trade Organisation

Text references. Chapter 4 and Chapter 18.

Top tips. Hopefully your discussion in (a) got beyond quotas and tariffs as the more subtle measures have become more significant because of the development of GATT and WTO. (c) links in with this; there has been more progress with elimination of the direct restrictions rather than the indirect measures. Remember in (d) to take account of the impact not only on the multinational's investment within the country, but its other activities as well.

Easy marks. If you've revised international trade, (a) should be quite straightforward and part (e) is pretty much a textbook discussion of methods to prevent transfer price manipulation.

(a) **Tariffs or customs duties**

Tariffs or customs duties are taxes on imported goods. The effect of a tariff is to **raise the price paid for the imported goods** by domestic consumers, while leaving the price paid to foreign producers the same, or even lower. The difference is transferred to the government.

Import quotas

Import quotas are restrictions on the **quantity** of a product that is allowed to be imported into the country. Both domestic and foreign suppliers enjoy a **higher price,** while consumers buy less. This should mean **domestic producers supply more** and there are **fewer imports** (in volume). The government collects no revenue.

Export subsidies

Export subsidies include **export credit guarantees** (government-backed insurance against irrecoverable debts for overseas sales), **financial help** (such as government grants to the aircraft or shipbuilding industry) and **state assistance**.

Import restrictions

Import restrictions include **complex import regulations** or **special safety standards** demanded from imported goods and so on

Bureaucratic procedures

Governments may prefer delay rather than restrictions so that importers expend resources in **supplying complex documentation** or are **forced to wait for licences** or **customs clearance.**

(b) **Arguments in favour of and against protection**

Arguments for protection

(i) **Imports of cheap goods**
Measures can be taken against imports of cheap goods that compete with higher priced domestically produced goods, and so preserve output and employment in domestic industries.

(ii) **Dumping**
Measures might be necessary to counter dumping of surplus production by other countries at an uneconomically low price. Although dumping has short term benefits for the countries receiving the cheap goods, the longer term consequences would be a reduction in domestic output and employment, even when domestic industries in the longer term might be more efficient.

(iii) **Retaliation**
Any country that does not take protectionist measures when other countries are doing so is likely to find that it suffers all of the disadvantages and none of the advantages of protectionism.

(iv) **Infant industries**
Protectionism can protect a country's 'infant industries' that have not yet developed to the size where they can compete in international markets. Less developed countries in particular might need to protect industries against competition from advanced or developing countries.

BPP
LEARNING MEDIA

(v)   **Declining industries**

Without protection, these industries might collapse and there would be severe problems of sudden mass unemployment amongst workers in the industry.

(vi)   **Reduction in balance of trade deficit**

Due to retaliation by other countries, the success of such measures by one country would depend on the demand by other countries for its exports being inelastic with regard to price and its demand for imports being fairly elastic.

Arguments against protection

(i)   **Reduced international trade**

Since protectionist measures taken by one country will almost always provoke retaliation by others, protection will reduce the volume of international trade. Therefore the following benefits of international trade will be reduced:

- Specialisation
- Greater competition, and so greater efficiency amongst producers
- Advantages of economies of scale amongst producers who need world markets to achieve their economies and so produce at lower costs.

(ii)   **Retaliation**

If a country applies protectionist measures then other countries will tend to retaliate and thus protectionist measures to reverse a balance of trade deficit are unlikely to succeed. Imports may be reduced, but so too would exports.

(iii)   **Effect on economic growth**

Widespread protection will damage the prospects for economic growth amongst the countries of the world. Thus protectionist measures ought to be restricted to special instances which have been discussed and negotiated with other countries.

(iv)   **Political consequences**

From a nation's own point of view, protection may improve its position, protectionism leads to a worse outcome for all. Protection creates political ill-will amongst countries of the world and so there are political disadvantages in a policy of protection.

(c)   **The World Trade Organisation (WTO)**

The **World Trade Organisation (WTO)** was formed in 1995 to continue to implement the General Agreement on Tariffs and Trade (GATT) to promote free trade. Its aims include:

(i)   To **reduce existing barriers** to free trade
(ii)   To **eliminate discrimination** in international trade and **distortions** such as subsidies
(iii)   To **prevent the growth of protection** by getting member countries to consult with others before taking any protectionist measures
(iv)   To act as a **forum** for assisting free trade by for example administering agreements and helping countries negotiate

One difference is that GATT focused mainly on goods, whereas the WTO also covers trade in services.

The most favoured nation principle

The WTO encourages free trade by applying the **'most favoured nation'** principle where one country (which is a member of GATT) that offers a reduction in tariffs to another country must offer the same reduction to all other member countries of GATT.

Impact on protectionist measures

Although the WTO has helped reduce the level of protection, some problems still remain:

(i)   Special circumstances (for example economic crises, the protection of an infant industry) have to be **admitted** when protection or special low tariffs between a group of countries are allowed.

(ii)   A country in the WTO may **prefer not to offer a tariff reduction** to another country because it would have to offer the same reduction to all other GATT members.

(iii)   In spite of much success in reducing tariffs, the WTO has had **less effect** in dealing with **many non-tariff barriers** to trade which countries may set up.

(d) **Impact on investments in that country**

Removal of barriers as a result of WTO membership may **remove the favoured status** that XYZ's investment has enjoyed. It may be more exposed to **competition** from other countries. However by promoting trade with that country, WTO membership may **improve the economic environment** within which it operates, leading to more opportunities to export and the chance to take advantage of improvements in the supply of resources.

Impact on other investments

On the other hand, XYZ's investments elsewhere may themselves be able to **take advantage** of the **reduction in barriers** and improve trade with that country.

Time lag - WTO conditions will require the removal of barriers **gradually over a period of time**, hence XYZ will have time to adjust to the new circumstances.

(e) Transfer price manipulation is said to occur when multinationals use transfer prices to evade or avoid payment of taxes and tariffs, or other controls that the government of the host country has put in place.

The most common solution that tax authorities have adopted to reduce the probability of transfer price manipulation is to develop particular transfer pricing regulations as part of the corporate income tax code. These regulations are based on the concept of the arm's-length standard, which states that all intra-firm activities of multinationals should be priced as if they took place between unrelated parties acting at arm's-length in competitive market.

The arm's-length standard is defined as the prices which would have been agreed upon between unrelated parties engaged in the same or similar transactions under the same or similar conditions in the open market. In the absence of the existence of data to allow a reasonable estimate of the arm's-length standard then the alternative methods used to establish the arm's-length transfer price include:

(i)   **Comparable uncontrolled price**
       This method looks for a comparable product to the transaction in question being traded by the multinational in a comparable transaction with an unrelated party, or the same or similar product being traded between two unrelated parties.

(ii)   **Resale price method**
       This method focuses on one side of the transaction, either the manufacturer or distributor, and to estimate the transfer price using a functional approach.

(iii) **Cost-plus method**
       This method starts with the costs of production, measured using recognised accounting principles and then adds an appropriate markup over costs. The appropriate markup is estimated from those earned by similar manufacturers.

(iv)   **Comparable profit method**
       This method is based on the premise that companies in similar industries will tend to have similar financial performance, and have similar financial characteristics. This similarity in performance will be indicated by a similarity in financial ratios.

(v)   **Profit split method**
       This method allocates the profit earned on a transaction between related parties.

13 Pharmaceutical Co

Text references. Ethics are covered in Chapter 3b. See Chapter 4 for information on the World Trade Organisation (WTO).

Top tips. Remember to answer the question and address each issue in turn. There are marks available for both identifying the issue and making suitable recommendations so tackle both parts of the problem in each case.

Easy marks. Even if you are not familiar with the intricacies of each case, you should be able to recognise some of the basic issues such as insider dealing.

Marking scheme

	Marks
Discussion of problems of paying commission, principles, ethics and recommendation	5
Discussion of scope of insider trading and application to agents and options markets	5
Discussion of relevance of hedging, authority for trading and action to be taken	5
Advice on position with respect to abuse of patent with reference to TRIPS	5
Discussion of wage ethics and degree of local control	5
	25

Memorandum

To:	Chief Financial Officer
From:	Deputy Chief Financial Officer
Re:	Various issues

Please see below for a summary of the various issues that have arisen in the past six months and recommendations on how we should proceed.

(i) **Payment of commission to a senior official**

This could be viewed as **bribery** in return for ensuring that our drugs are used in that country's National Health Service. This is a **serious breach** of the ethical code of pharmaceutical companies. The official was not in a position to be entitled to this money and the payment should not have been authorised by us. It is assumed that a substantial sum was involved and as such the Chief Executive should be informed with a view to carrying out a **full investigation** of how this transaction was allowed to take place. **Disciplinary action** should be taken if necessary. In addition, we should consider taking this issue up with the health department of the country concerned with a view to full disclosure once the details have been clarified.

(ii) **Potential insider dealing**

The agent could be guilty of insider dealing if it can be proved that the call options were purchased in direct response to the knowledge about potential licensing agreements. Before any accusations can be made, a full investigation is required to establish the facts. Was the agent aware of the forthcoming licensing agreements prior to purchasing the call options or were they purchased purely on speculation? If the former is true then insider dealing could be said to have taken place, although only if the information regarding the licensing agreements was gained purely through the agent's relationship with the company. If the information was already in the public domain then insider dealing can be assumed not to have taken place.

(iii) **Hedging positions**

There appears to be an issue with (or lack of) authorisation procedures in place with regard to taking substantial hedging positions. If there are specific procedures in place and the employee in question was aware of them, disciplinary action may be necessary for breach of these procedures. If there are no such procedures in place, this situation has exposed the need to establish them as soon as possible.

At the moment there is the possibility of a $1.25 million loss against a dollar position of $12.5 million. Even if this is not material from the overall company point of view, it is a loss that could have been prevented. To hedge against further losses on this position, we should reverse the trade by shortening the contract in question. If the loss is material, disclosure should be made to the shareholders of the magnitude of the loss and the action taken.

There is also the issue that translation risk cannot be hedged against. It results from the conversion of results in one currency to the domestic currency for reporting purposes. It does not result in a cash flow movement as no transaction has actually taken place. A policy should be put in place which requires risk management decisions to be taken at Board level rather than by Treasury staff, no matter how senior.

(iv) **Patent protection**

There appears to have been a serious breach of copyright in this case. The actions of the competitor suggest a contravention of the World Trade Organisation's **Trade Related Aspects of Intellectual Property Rights** agreement (TRIPS). However before we can make such an accusation we have to be sure that we had made the drug publicly available. If we had been withholding access to the drug then the country in question may have had the right to issue a 'compulsory licence' – that is, a competitor would have been entitled to produce the drug under licence to make it available to the public.

We should investigate the potential reasons why the government appeared to prevent the progression of the patent protection proceedings through the local courts. If there are no public health policy issues then we should attempt to persuade our own government to intervene to try to resolve the issue.

(v) **Level of overseas wages**

Although there is no legislation being broken here, our company could be seen as exploiting workers and paying a wage that is lower than warranted, particularly as the wages are less than those offered by comparable multinational companies. This seems to be unethical behaviour and could create adverse publicity and a loss of customer goodwill, too.

The cause of this issue comes from the fact that there is local control, which includes the setting of wage levels. To solve this there should be greater central control of the the overseas interests, so that wage levels can be set at an appropriate level. The greater level of central control should also prevent other possible abuses by local management, help to remove the agency problem and ensure goal congruence throughout the group.

If you wish to discuss any of these issues further, just let me know.

14 PMU

Text references. Joint ventures are steps to free up blocked funds are covered in Chapter 4.

Top tips. The question is asking for benefits and disadvantages of entering into a joint venture rather than setting up independently. It is not asking you to discuss whether or not PMU should venture in Kantaka. If you enter into such discussions you will gain no credit.

Make sure your answer is balanced. You are given no indication in the question about the number of marks available for each element of the requirement – it is up to you to address the issues that arise in the scenario. Don't just provide a list of benefits and disadvantages – at this level you are expected to expand each issue and provide potential ways in which disadvantages can be dealt with.

Don't forget to suggest additional information that is required before a final decision can be made.

Easy marks. Even without detailed knowledge of joint ventures, the scenario is sufficiently detailed for you to pick out a number of points that will earn marks.

Examiner's comments. This question was well answered with many candidates gaining a high proportion of the marks for their answers. Answers that gained fewer marks did not give many points or lacked adequate discussion because they were in note form.

		Marks
(a)	Benefits of joint venture (1 to 2 marks per well explained point)	4 – 6
	Disadvantages of joint venture, including ways of mitigating disadvantages (2 – 3 marks per well explained point)	10 – 12
	Additional information (1 mark per point)	3 – 5
		Max 20
(b)	One point per method explained	Max 5
		25

(a) **Benefits and disadvantages of PMU entering into a joint venture**

Benefits of joint venture

A joint venture with a local partner would give PMU relatively **low cost access** to an overseas market. The Kantaka government is offering tax concessions to companies bringing FDI into the country and PMU would benefit further by having to borrow less money if it entered into a joint venture.

Given that PMU has no experience of overseas investment and doing business in foreign countries, having a joint venture partner would be beneficial. Such a partner could assist with such issues as **marketing, cultural and language issues and dealing with government restrictions and bureaucracy**.

A joint venture partner could also give easier access to **capital markets** which would reduce any **foreign currency risk** for PMU. If its investment is funded in Rosinante currency but fee income is in Kantaka currency, this will result in long-term foreign currency risk exposure. We have been told that the Kantaka currency has been depreciating against other currencies over the past two years. If this continues the fee income will be worth less when converted into Rosinante currency and could lead to a shortfall in funds available to cover the cost of the investment borrowings.

A joint venture would give PMU the chance to share costs with the local partner. Academic institutions already exist in Kantaka which would eliminate the need to source new premises and a whole new team to run the degree programmes.

Disadvantages of joint venture

The most significant problem with entering into a joint venture for PMU is the potential effects on **reputation**. PMU is a member of the prestigious Holly League and is world-renowned as being of the highest quality. The Kantaka government has a history of being reluctant to approve degrees from overseas institutions that enter into joint ventures with local partners and those who do graduate with such degrees have been unable to seek employment in national or local government or nationalised organisations. In addition degree programmes emerging from joint ventures are not held in high regard by Kantaka's population.

With this in mind, PMU could suffer from **negative publicity** if it chooses a poor academic institution with which to have a joint venture. It will have to carry out significant research into potential partners before making a decision. The academic institution chosen should ideally have a high reputation for quality teaching and qualifications to protect PMU's own reputation. It may also be worthwhile for PMU to meet with the Kantaka government to try to obtain a commitment from the government to back its degree programmes. All such efforts take time but it is important to do sufficient groundwork before making such a major commitment. PMU should also determine whether the government will recognise its degrees if it sets up on its own rather than entering into a joint venture.

PMU should also be mindful of the potential impact on the **quality** of its degree programmes. We are told that the teaching and learning methods used in Kantaka's educational institutions are very different to the innovative methods used by PMU (which are instrumental in its academic success). In addition, students will have certain very **high expectations** of the quality of infrastructure, such as IT facilities, halls of residence and lecture halls. Any joint venture partner should be able to adapt to match such expectations.

Existing staff will require **sufficient training** to ensure that teaching quality is not compromised. As far as possible, Kantaka students should have the same overall experience that PMU's home-based students in Rosinante enjoy. This may require a higher proportion of Rosinante staff being brought in initially until local staff acquire the necessary skills.

Cultural differences present major challenges to businesses setting up overseas. Steps should be taken to minimise such differences between local staff and expats from Rosinante. We have been told about the differences in teaching and learning methods – there are also differences in **attitudes** towards research, a major activity in Holly League universities. PMU will have to put strategies in place to deal with these and other cultural differences and ensure the availability of programmes to help expat staff settle into a new country. At all costs, a 'them and us' culture should be avoided as this will create resentment and alienation of local staff. One idea might be to encourage **staff exchange programmes** to expose both sets of staff to each other's cultures.

Joint ventures can restrict **managerial freedom of actions** as opinions of both sets of managers may differ. It is important that PMU listens to the opinions of the joint venture partner regardless of how different these may be to the underlying principles of its own managers. Clear guidelines should be developed regarding the aims and objectives of the joint venture and both sets of managers should be involved in the decision-making process.

It is important that PMU considers **government restrictions** on such factors as visas for key staff from Rosinante, proportion of total staff that has to be made up of local employees and repatriation of funds from Kantaka to Rosinante. A meeting with government officials is essential to clarify such issues.

Legal issues must be addressed properly and with due care and attention. Terms and conditions of the joint venture, roles and responsibilities of both parties, profit sharing percentages and ownership percentages must all be discussed by legal representatives of both sides of the contract.

Other information required

- Will tax concessions be lost if PMU decides to 'go it alone' rather than enter into a joint venture? If so the impact on funding required will have to be determined.

- What government restrictions might be imposed on repatriation of funds and visas for key staff?

- Outcome of discussions with the Kantaka government regarding whether it will recognise PMU degrees and thus allow graduates to gain employment in government and nationalised industries.

- Outcome of research into the availability of potential joint venture partners that will fulfil students' expectations regarding infrastructure, facilities and teaching methods.

- What is the likelihood of PMU's degrees being recognised by Kantaka's own people?

- Will PMU be able to raise funds locally to finance the venture, thus reducing exposure to foreign currency risk?

- Will local staff be willing to undergo training in PMU's teaching and learning methods and to what extent is this likely to breed resentment?

- Will PMU be able to source experts in Kantaka to help set up the venture if it decides to 'go it alone'?

(b) There are a number of ways PMU could deal with the issue of blocked funds

(i) PMU could sell goods or services to the subsidiary and obtain payment. This could be for course materials or teaching staff supplied. The amount of this payment would depend on the volume of sales and also on the transfer price for the sales.

(ii) PMU could charge a royalty on the courses that the subsidiary runs. The size of the royalty could be adjusted to suit the wishes of PMU's management.

(iii) PMU could make a loan to a subsidiary at a high interest rate, which would improve PMU's company's profits at the expense of the subsidiary's profits.

(iv) Management charges may be levied by PMU for costs incurred in the management of international operations.

(v) The subsidiary could make a loan, equal to the required dividend remittance to PMU.

BPP LEARNING MEDIA

15 Jonas Chemical Systems

Text references. Value at risk and appraisal methods are covered in Chapter 5.

Top tips. Beware of just treating this question as another investment appraisal problem. At the professional level you are expected to demonstrate a much higher level of understand of the issues surrounding investment decisions. Part (c) requires a discussion of the advantages and disadvantages of using APV as an appraisal method.

Easy marks. Calculations of present values and discounted payback period should be straightforward as these techniques are assumed knowledge from Paper F9.

Marking scheme

		Marks	
(a)	Clear definition of a two stage process for Board involvement in capital expenditure decisions	2	
	Recommendation for the stage 1 appraisal procedure and metrics focusing on the role of payback and viable alternatives	3	
	Stage 2 appraisal focusing on the business plan, value and accounting impact and cash recovery.	3	
			8
(b)	Calculation of the project VAR and assessment of its significance	4	
	Estimation of the potential value impact using MIRR and the assumptions that underpin it.	3	
	Estimation of the potential cash recovery using procedures recommended in (a)	3	
			10
(c)	Problems with existing methods	2 – 3	
	Use of APV	2 – 3	
	Problems with APV	1 – 2	
		Max	7
			25

(a) **Board Paper Presenting Proposal Procedures for Large Capital Expenditure Projects.**

This paper proposes revised guidelines for the board approval of large capital investment projects. The current two stage process of preliminary and final approval is retained because it serves an important role in ensuring that any initial concerns of the board in terms of strategic fit and risk are brought to the attention of the Financial Appraisal Team. In addition, it helps to ensure that this team does not waste time in detailed analysis of projects that do not survive the first (preliminary) stage.

Stage 1 – preliminary approval

- An outline business proposal including assessment of strategic importance, business fit and identified risks.

- Outline financial appraisal to include capital requirement and modified internal rate of return to give an assessment of the project's economic return that takes into account the time value of money. This is likely to be important for investments with a long life span that are not assessed by accounting rate of return (which is currently being used).

- It is recommended that conventional payback is dropped because it ignores the cost of finance and the magnitude of post payback cash flows. Duration is recommended as this measures the time required to recover approximately half of the project's weighted average present value.

Stage 2 – final approval stage

- For projects that have passed the initial screening in stage 1, a detailed business plan must be presented, giving the business case with a rigorous assessment of strategic benefits and risks (including environmental analysis and possible competitor response, finalised capital spend and capital sources).

- A project specific cost of capital should be estimated that reflects both the business risk and financial risk of the project under consideration. This assessment should be used to analyse the project's net present value and should be supported by a calculation of the project's value at risk (VaR). The NPV of the project represents our best estimate of the likely impact of the investment on the value of the firm and the VaR should show the downside of the project (for example, a 95% VaR would show the maximum downside with only a 5% risk of being exceeded).

- NPV is the key statistic from the capital market perspective in that, unless we are assured that the project NPV is positive, the investment will reduce and not enhance the value of the firm. This net present value calculation should be supported by a modified internal rate of return which measures the additional economic return of the project over the firm's cost of capital where intermediate cash flows are reinvested at that cost of capital. In a highly competitive business the reinvestment assumption implicit in the MIRR is more realistic than that assumed with IRR where intermediate cash flows are assumed to be reinvested at the IRR. This may be satisfactory for near-the-money projects but is far less satisfactory for projects which offer high levels of value addition to the firm.

- An accounting impact assessment including the differential rate of return on capital employed and a short term liquidity assessment. Although positive NPV projects are value enhancing, they may not do so in ways that are readily apparent in the financial reports. To manage investor expectations effectively the firm needs to be aware of the impact of the project on the firm's reported profitability and this is most accurately reflected by the differential rate of return measure. Accounting rate of return as normally calculated does not examine the impact of the project on the financial position of the firm but is restricted to the rate of return the investment offers on the average capital employed.

(b) The proposed business case concludes that this is a key strategic investment for the firm to maintain operating capacity at the Gulf Plant. The financial assessment is detailed in the Appendix to this report (excluding an assessment of impact of the project on the financial reports of the firm).

(i) The net present value of this project calculated using a discount rate of 8% gives a value of $1.965 million (Appendix 3). The volatility attaching to the net present value of $1.02 million (given) indicates that there is (Z) standard deviations between the expected net present value and zero as follows:

$$Z = \frac{1.965 - 0}{1.02} = 1.9265$$

This suggests that this project has a 97.3 per cent probability that it will have a positive net present value or conversely a 2.7 per cent probability of a negative net present value.

The project value at risk relies upon an assessment of the number of years that the project cash flow is at risk (10 years), the annual volatility ($1.02m) and the confidence level required by the firm. The formula for the project VaR is:

Project VaR = $\sigma \sqrt{t}$

At the 98% level σ = 1.645 giving

Project VaR = 1.645 x $1.02m x 3.162 = $5.3 million

This assumes a 95% confidence level, at 99% the project VaR is $7.51 million. This value reflects the fact that the capital invested is at risk for ten years and assumes that the volatility of the project is fairly represented by the volatility of its net present value.

BPP LEARNING MEDIA

(ii) **Project return**

The internal rate of return is given as 11.0%. The modified internal Rate of Return is calculated by

- Projecting forward the cash flows in the recovery stage of the project at 8% to future value of $41.7983 million. (Appendix 4)

- Discounting back the investment phase cash flows to give a present value of the investment of $17.3955 million. (Appendix 1)

The Modified Internal Rate of Return is therefore:

$$\text{MIRR} = \sqrt[10]{\frac{41.7983}{17.3955}} - 1 = 0.09162 \text{ or } 9.162\%$$

This rate suggests that the margin on the cost of capital is rather small with only a 1.162% premium for the strategic and competitive advantage implied by this project

(iii) **Project liquidity**

With a present value of the recovery phase of $19.3607 million and of the investment phase of $17.3955 million this suggests that the project will have recovery period of:

$$\text{Recovery} = 2 + \frac{17.3955}{19.3607} \times 8 = 9.1879 \text{ years}$$

In practice the actual recovery is shorter than this because the expected cash in flows occur earlier rather than later during the recovery phase of the project. The above calculation effectively assumes that the recovery cash flows arise evenly through the recovery period. The actual discounted payback period is just over 6 years. (Appendix 5)

The project duration of 4.461 years (Appendix 2) reveals that the project is more highly cash generative in the early years notwithstanding the two year investment phase.

In summary, the analysis confirms that this project is financially viable as it will be value adding to the firm. There is, however, substantial value at risk given the volatility of the net present value quoted. In terms of return, the premium over the firm's hurdle is small at 1.162% and any significant deterioration in the firms cost of capital would be damaging to the value of this project. The liquidity statistics reveal that the bulk of the project's cash returns are promised in the earlier part of the recovery phase and that value invested in the project should be recovered by year six. Taking this into account acceptance is recommended to the board.

Appendix

Note: All calculations have used the discount factor tables. If formulae are used unrounded on a calculator slightly different figures would arise.

1 **PV of investment/base**

Time	Cash flow	DF	PV
	$m		$m
0	(9.50)	1.000	(9.5000)
1	(5.75)	0.926	(5.3245)
2	(3.00)	0.857	(2.5710)
			(17.3955)

2 PV and duration of recovery phase

The recovery phase duration is calculated by multiplying the present value of the cash recovered in each year by the relevant time from project commencement. The sum of the weighted years gives the recovery phase duration.

Time T	Cash flow $m	DF	PV @ 8%	tPV
3	4.50	0.794	3.5730	10.7190
4	6.40	0.735	4.7040	18.8160
5	7.25	0.681	4.9372	24.6860
6	6.50	0.630	4.0950	24.5700
7	5.50	0.583	3.2065	22.4455
8	4.00	0.540	2.1600	17.2800
9	(2.00)	0.500	(1.0000)	(9.0000)
10	(5.00)	0.463	(2.3150)	(23.1500)
	27.15		19.3607	86.3725

$$\text{Project duration} = \frac{\text{Sum of time weighted present value of recovery phase}}{\text{Present value of recovery phase}} = \frac{86.3725}{19.3607} = 4.461 \text{ years}$$

3 PV of project

	$m
PV investment phase	(17.3955)
PV recovery phase	19.3607
	1.9652

4 TV if recovery phase cash flow

$PV \times (1+r)^n$ = TV
19.3607×1.08^{10} = 41.7983

5 Discounted payback period

Time	PV ($m)	Cumulative PV ($m)
0	(9.5000)	(9.5000)
1	(5.3245)	(14.8245)
2	(2.5710)	(17.3955)
3	3.5730	(13.8225)
4	4.7040	(9.1185)
5	4.9372	(4.1813)
6	4.0950	(0.0863)
7	3.2065	3.1202
8	2.1600	5.2802
9	(1.0000)	4.2802
10	(2.3150)	1.9652

(c) The proposed new investments might attract government support, which may take the form of subsidised loans for part of the investment. This makes selecting a single discount rate for the net present value evaluation difficult, as the government loan will be significantly cheaper than any other form of finance for the project.

This means that none of the existing or proposed methods of project evaluation would satisfactorily take into account this cheaper financing and may lead to a project being rejected that would actually enhance shareholder wealth.

BPP LEARNING MEDIA

Adjusted present value

Adjusted present value (APV) is a more advanced method that can be used for any project appraisal exercise, but it is in the more complex cases (involving a **change in capital structure** and/or **other complex finance problems**) that it is the most useful.

(i) The first stage is to **evaluate the base case NPV** of operating cash flows by discounting at the ungeared cost of equity.

(ii) The **present value of each individual financing side effect** is then evaluated separately. The sum of the base case NPV and the PV of financing side effects is the APV.

The method has the advantage over basic net present value using WACC that it allows **each different type of cash flow** to be **discounted at a rate specific to the risk** of that cash flow. It also allows the effects of more complex financing situations to be considered.

Problems with APV

The main practical problem is to **identify correctly the financing side effects** and their appropriate discount rates. Theoretical weaknesses of the method stem from simplifications introduced by the Modigliani and Miller model of capital structure. For example:

- It is assumed that the only effect of debt issued at market rates is the tax relief on debt interest
- The computation of an asset beta assumes that **cash flows** are perpetuities

16 CD

Text references. Investment appraisal methods are covered in Chapter 5.

Top tips. You need to look carefully for the important information in this question. You are given inflation rates in both countries so your first step should be to calculate expected exchange rates using the purchasing power parity formula. The net cash flows are in **real** terms so need to be converted into **nominal** cash flows. Use your knowledge of business strategy from P3 in the discussion in part (c).

Easy marks. The twelve marks for the calculations in part (a) are relatively easy to achieve if you have done enough practice on questions involving inflation and exchange rates and are confident with MIRR.

(a) **Appraisal of alternative 2**

Exchange rates

The future dollar/pound exchange rates for years 1 to 3 can be predicted using the purchasing power parity formula.

Future exchange rate $/£ = current exchange rate $/£ x [(1 + US inflation rate)/(1 + UK inflation rate)] ^{n} where n is the number of years in the future.

Thus, future exchange rate $/£ = 1.600 x [1.04/1.03] ^{n}

Year	0	1	2	3
Exchange rate forecast US$ / £	1.600	1.616	1.631	1.647

Net present value

Year	0	1	2	3
US$m real cash flows	(25.00)	2.60	3.80	4.10
US$m nominal cash flows (inflation 4% p.a.)	(25.00)	2.70	4.11	4.61
Exchange rate	1.600	1.616	1.631	1.647
US nominal cash flows in £m	(15.63)	1.67	2.52	2.80
£m real cash flows		3.70	4.20	4.60
£m nominal cash flows (inflation 3% p.a.)		3.81	4.46	5.03
Total nominal cash flows in £m	(15.63)	5.48	6.98	7.83
9% discount factors	1	0.917	0.842	0.772
Present value £m	(15.63)	5.03	5.88	6.04
Net present value £m	1.32			

The NPV of the project is **£1.32 million** positive.

Payback

Year	0	1	2	3
Total nominal cash flows in £m	(15.63)	5.48	6.98	7.83
Cumulative cash flow £m	(15.63)	(10.15)	(3.17)	4.66

Payback = 2 + (3.17/7.83) = 2.40 years

Discounted payback

Year	0	1	2	3
Present value £m	(15.63)	5.03	5.88	6.04
Cumulative present value £m		(10.60)	(4.72)	1.32

Discounted payback = 2 + (4.72/6.04) = 2.78 years

Internal rate of return

The IRR can be found by trial discount rates and interpolation. If the discount rate is 15%, the NPV is £(0.43) million.

Year	0	1	2	3
Total nominal cash flows in £m	(15.63)	5.48	6.98	7.83
15% factors	1	0.870	0.756	0.658
PV	(15.63)	4.77	5.28	5.15
NPV	(0.43)			

By interpolation the IRR is 9% + (15% − 9%) × 1.32/(1.32 + 0.43) = **13.5% p.a.**

Modified internal rate of return

We can find MIRR using the formula given in the formula sheet.

$$MIRR = \left[\frac{PV_R}{PV_I}\right]^{\frac{1}{n}} \left(1 + r_e\right) - 1$$

Year	0	1	2	3
Total nominal cash flows in £m	(15.63)	5.48	6.98	7.83
9% factors	1	0.917	0.842	0.772
PV	(15.63)	5.03	5.88	6.04
NPV	1.32			

BPP LEARNING MEDIA

PV (return phase – years 1 – 3) = £16.95m

PV (investment phase) = £(15.63)m

MIRR = $(16.95m/15.63m)^{1/3} \times (1 + 0.09) - 1 = 12\%$

(b) **Project duration for Alternative 2**

Present value of cash flows = NPV + initial investment = £1.32m + £15.63m = £16.95m

Year	1	2	3
PV of cash flow	5.03	5.88	6.04
% of total PV	30%	35%	36%
Year × %	1 × 30%	2 × 35%	3 × 36%
	= 0.3	= 0.7	= 1.08

Duration = 0.3 + 0.7 + 1.08 = 2.08 years

Significance of results

On average it will take 2.08 years to recover half the present value of alternative 2. Compared with alternative one this is a good result as it would take over one year longer to recover half the present value for this project. Generally, the longer the duration, the more risky the project as there is greater uncertainty attached to future returns.

(c) **Evaluation of the two alternatives**

Summary of the appraisal results

Alternative	1	2
NPV at 9%	£1.45 m	£1.32 m
IRR	10.5%	13.5%
MIRR	13.2%	12.0%
Duration	3.2 years	2.08 years
Payback	2.6 years	2.40 years
Disc. payback	3.05 years	2.78 years

All other things being equal, the project to be accepted should be the one with the higher NPV, which is Alternative 1. NPV shows the absolute amount by which the project is forecast to **increase shareholders' wealth**, and is theoretically sounder than the IRR and MIRR methods.

In this case the MIRR method backs up the NPV, but the IRR gives the opposite indication. This 'conflict' arises because IRR makes the wrong **assumption** about reinvestment rates (see (ii) above).

The duration of the alternatives shows that alternative 1 is more risky as it takes longer to recover half the present value. This is also backed up by the payback figures showing that Alternative 1 takes longer to recover the original outlay.

Before making a decision, however, there are a number of other important factors that must be taken into consideration.

Alternative 1

- Alternative 1 has a high risk of lowering the firm's reputation for quality and causing confusion among the customer base. The overall effect may be to **lose existing customers** but not to gain many new ones.

- It also removes the **focus** from the business. Marketing a wider range of products may be more difficult than is anticipated and may stretch resources.

- Duration is longer, which might put management off, particularly if they are averse to risk.

Alternative 2

- Alternative 2 represents a fundamental change in the nature of the business from a niche manufacturer to a **value added** distributor.

- The firm may be able to add successfully its **brand reputation for quality** to mass market products, but this will only be possible if the US 'flat packs' are of guaranteed quality and consistency, and the varnishing and assembly work are carried out to a high standard.

- The change in the nature of the firm's work may require **substantial new equipment**.
- This alternative may also result in a **loss of skilled workers**, with the risk of lower quality.
- However, the shorter duration of the project suggests lower financial risk to the firm, which may be a deciding factor if management are struggling to distinguish between the alternatives in other ways.

Given the similarity in the NPVs between the two projects, the decision will almost certainly depend on non-financial factors.

17 Slow Fashions Co

Text references. NPV and IRR are covered in Chapter 5. Capital rationing is covered briefly in Chapter 5 but is assumed knowledge from Paper F9.

Top tips. This question highlights the importance of assumed knowledge as a large proportion of the technical knowledge was originally covered in Paper F9. In part (a), take careful note of restrictions relating to each project (one of the projects cannot be varied for example). By doing this at the start you are less likely to make incorrect recommendations relating to individual projects and the capital investment programme as a whole.

NPV is not a sufficient criterion with which to rank projects when capital is limited. The profitability index (PI) should be used. Make sure you perform a full evaluation of the alternatives in part (a) and recommend the investment programme that will result in the highest overall NPV.

In part (b), the cost of additional finance should not exceed the original cost of capital plus the profitability index of the 'rejected' projects.

For part (c) consider how projects could be undertaken to maximise total NPV, given that two projects can be delayed for one further year.

Easy marks. Capital rationing is assumed knowledge so you should be able to pick up some easy marks in part (a).

Marking scheme

		Marks	
(a)	Comment on the rationale for the use of PI under capital rationing	2	
	Rank ordering of projects	3	
	Alternative treatment of non-divisible project	4	
	Calculation of overall NPV	3	
	Calculation of project IRR graphically or by interpolation	2	
			14
(b)	Calculation of the proportions of investment in each project	2	
	Calculation of the PI for the rejected projects	2	
	Combination of result with current cost of capital to give overall	2	
	opportunity cost		
	Summary comments and advice	2	
			8
(c)	Project PO804 comments	1 – 2	
	Project PO802 comments	1 – 2	
	Max		3
			25

(a) **Capital investment plan**

Restrictions:

(i)   Project PO801 cannot be scaled down – this project cannot be varied.
(ii)   No project can be scaled up.
(iii) Capital budget is $1.2 million.

In capital rationing situations, projects should be ranked according to the profitability index (PI) which is the NPV per $ of invested capital at year zero. Before we can rank the projects, we must calculate the PI for each.

Project	Initial investment	NPV	IRR	PI	Ranking
	$'000	$'000			
PO801	(620)	55	16%	0.0887	3
PO802	(640)	69	13%	0.1078	2
PO803	(240)	20	15%	0.0833	4
PO804	(1,000)	72	13%	0.072	6
PO805	(120)	19	17%	0.1583	1
PO806	(400)	29	15%	0.0725	5

Now that we have established the order in which investments should be made, we have to determine how many of the projects we can afford, subject to the restrictions above.

Project	Initial investment	NPV	IRR	PI	Cumulative investment
	$'000	$'000			$'000
PO805	(120)	19	17%	0.1583	(120)
PO802	(640)	69	13%	0.1078	(760)
PO801	(620)	55	16%	0.0887	(1,380)
PO803	(240)	20	15%	0.0833	(1,620)
PO806	(400)	29	15%	0.0725	(2,020)
PO804	(1,000)	72	13%	0.072	(3,020)

The marginal project is PO801. Our problem is that this project cannot be scaled down – it is the supermarket project that cannot be varied. We now have two choices. We can move PO801 above PO802 (which can be scaled down) in the ranking – this would allow us to undertake the supermarket project in its entirety. Alternatively, we could remove PO801 from the problem completely and ignore it. This would move the other projects up the rankings. The choice with the higher overall NPV should be undertaken.

Choice 1 – move PO801 above PO802

Project	Initial investment	NPV	Cumulative investment	Proportion of project	NPV from investment
	$'000	$'000	$'000		$'000
PO805	(120)	19	(120)	1	19.00
PO801	(620)	55	(740)	1	55.00
PO802	(640)	69	(1,380)	0.71875	49.59
				Total NPV	123.59

Note: the proportion of PO802 that is undertaken is calculated as follows:

Proportion = (Capital budget - cumulative investment to date) / investment required
= ($1,200 - $740) / $640
= 0.71875

Choice 2 – ignore PO801

Project	Initial investment	NPV	Cumulative investment	Proportion of project	NPV from investment
	$'000	$'000	$'000		$'000
PO805	(120)	19	(120)	1	19.00
PO802	(640)	69	(760)	1	69.00
PO803	(240)	20	(1,000)	1	20.00
PO806	(400)	29	(1,400)	0.5	14.50
				Total NPV	122.50

Choice 1 is preferable as it earns the higher NPV. PO801 should therefore be ranked above PO802 to allow the entire project to go ahead.

NPV per $ invested (PI) = $123.59 / $1,200 = 0.1030

Internal rate of return

IRR must be calculated on the NPV of the full projects – it cannot be calculated on proportions of projects. Therefore we must determine the IRR of the optimum investment plan on the assumption that we can invest in the whole of PO802.

We'll try calculating NPV at 14%.

Project	Now $'000	20X0 $'000	20X1 $'000	20X2 $'000	20X3 $'000	20X4 $'000	20X5 $'000
PO005	(120)	25	55	75	21		
PO001	(620)	280	400	120			
PO002	(640)	80	120	200	210	420	(30)
Total cash flow	(1,380)	385	575	395	231	420	(30)
Discount factor	1.000	0.877	0.769	0.675	0.592	0.519	0.456
DCF	(1,380)	337.65	442.18	266.63	136.75	217.98	(13.68)

NPV = 7.51

We'll now try calculating NPV at 17% using the same method as above.

NPV = (80.84)

Using interpolation we can now estimate the IRR of the optimum investment plan.

$$IRR = a + \left[\left(\frac{NPV_a}{NPV_a - NPV_b} \right)(b-a) \right]\%$$

where a   = the lower of the two rates of return used
       b   = the higher of the two rates of return used
       NPV_a = the NPV obtained using rate a
       NPV_b = the NPV obtained using rate b

IRR = 14 + [7.51 / (7.51 + 80.84)] × (17 – 14) = 14.26%

(b)   Maximum rate for additional financing

We cannot use the IRR here as this is the rate that results in NPV = 0 for investment over the life of the projects themselves. We can again make use of the profitability index, based on the NPVs of the rejected projects (including the proportion of PO802 that had to be foregone).

Project	Now $'000	20X0 $'000	20X1 $'000	20X2 $'000	20X3 $'000	20X4 $'000	20X5 $'000
PO802 (balance)	(180)	22.50	33.75	56.25	59.06	118.04	(8.44)
PO803	(240)	120.00	120.00	60.00	10.00		
PO806	(400)	245.00	250.00				
PO804	(1,000)	300.00	500.00	250.00	290.00		
Cash flow of rejected projects	(1,820)	687.50	903.75	366.25	359.06	118.04	(8.44)
Discount factor 10%	1.000	0.909	0.826	0.751	0.683	0.621	0.564
DCF	(1,820)	623.94	746.50	275.05	245.24	73.30	(4.76)

NPV of 'rejected' projects = 139.27
PI = 139.27 / 1,820 = 0.07652

Current cost of capital = 10%
Maximum cost of capital acceptable for the additional finance required = 10% + 7.652% = 17.652%

(c)   The option to delay project PO804 will have no effect on the answer to part (a) as the project would not have been undertaken as it had the lowest profitability index. It could now be undertaken in the second year when capital is not restricted, although the net present value would be lower than $72,000, as all associated cash flows would be delayed by one year.

BPP
LEARNING MEDIA

PO802 can now be delayed until the second year, which would allow the whole of project PO803 to be undertaken as well as (220/400 = 55%) of Project PO806. Again the NPV from project PO802 will be lower than $69,000 as all cashflows are delayed, but Slow Fashions Co is highly likely to generate additional overall shareholder wealth from undertaking the two extra projects. Detailed calculations would need to be performed to support this analysis.

18 Your business

> **Text references.** NPV, sensitivity analysis and duration are covered in Chapter 5. Discounted payback is assumed knowledge from Paper F9.
>
> **Top tips.** When making the adjustments to cash flows in part (a), make sure these are made net of tax as you are given the post-tax cash flows. There is only one mark available for discussion in part (b) so don't write too much. Discounted payback should be familiar to you from previous studies. Part (c) requires two types of recommendation – on the project and on the techniques used - so this gives you a useful structure for your answer.
>
> **Easy marks.** A lot of this question covers techniques that were previously covered in Paper F9. You should be able to pick up a number of relatively easy marks in all parts of the question.

Marking scheme

		Marks	
(a)	Add back net interest	1	
	Add back depreciation	1	
	Add back indirect cost charge	1	
	Deduct infrastructure costs	1	
	Estimation of site clearance	1	
	Calculation of tax on unrecovered capital allowances	3	
	Deduct site clearance and reinstatement	1	
	Calculation of NPV	1	
	Sensitivity to change in CAPEX	4	
			14
(b)	Calculation of discounted payback	2	
	Calculation of duration	2	
	Comparative assessment of the techniques	1	
			5
(c)	Review of techniques and recommendation	2	
	Definition and interpretation of duration measure	2	
	Review of sensitivity and its deficiencies	2	
			6
			25

(a) The first thing to do in this question is to determine how to correct the errors of principle.

    (1) Interest should not be included as this is already accounted for in the discount rate. The annual interest charge of $4 million (less tax of 30%) should be added back to the cash flow in each year.

    (2) Depreciation is NOT a cash flow and should be ignored in NPV calculations. The annual charge of $4 million (less tax at 30%) should be added back to the cash flow in each year.

    (3) Indirect allocated costs are not relevant. These should be added back to the annual cash flows (net of tax). Corporate infrastructure costs are relevant to the project and should have been included. These costs should be deducted from annual cash flow figures (net of tax), as should the estimates for site clearance.

(4)   Capital allowances in year 6 should be accounted for.

Corrected project evaluation

Year	0	1	2	3	4	5	6
	$m	$m	$m	$m	$m	$m	$m
Project post-tax cash flow	(127.50)	(36.88)	44.00	68.00	60.00	35.00	20.00
Add: net interest			2.80	2.80	2.80	2.80	2.80
Add: depreciation net of tax			2.80	2.80	2.80	2.80	2.80
Add: indirect costs			5.60	5.60	5.60	5.60	5.60
Add: capital allowances (W1)							3.68
Less: site clearance costs							(3.50)
Less: infrastructure costs			(2.80)	(2.80)	(2.80)	(2.80)	(2.80)
Revised cash flows	(127.50)	(36.88)	52.40	76.40	68.40	43.40	28.58
Discount factor 10%	1.000	0.909	0.826	0.751	0.683	0.621	0.564
DCF	(127.50)	(33.52)	43.28	57.38	46.71	26.95	16.12

NPV = $29.42m

Working 1 (W1) – Calculation of unclaimed capital allowances

	$m	Tax benefit at 30% $m
Year 0: Capital investment	150.00	
First year allowance (50%)	(75.00)	
Tax written down value	75.00	
Year 1: New investment	50.00	
First year allowance on new investment	(25.00)	
WDA on year 0 investment (25%)	(18.75)	
Tax written down value	81.25	
Year 2: WDA	(20.31)	
Tax written down value	60.94	
Year 3: WDA	(15.24)	
Tax written down value	45.70	
Year 4: WDA	(11.43)	
Tax written down value	34.27	
Year 5: WDA	(8.57)	
Tax written down value	25.70	
Year 6: WDA	6.43	
Tax written down value	19.27	
Proceeds from sale	7.00	
Balancing allowance	12.27	3.68

BPP
LEARNING MEDIA

Sensitivity analysis of project to a $1m increase in initial capital expenditure

Extra capital expenditure will affect not only the cash outflow of the project but also the capital allowances.

Year	0	1	2	3	4	5	6
	$m	$m	$m	$m	$m	$m	$m
Purchase cost/Tax WDV	(1.0)	0.5	0.37	0.28	0.21	0.16	0.12
FYA (50%)	(0.5)						
WDA (25%)	___	(0.13)	(0.09)	(0.07)	(0.05)	(0.04)	(0.03)
Balance	0.5	0.37	0.28	0.21	0.16	0.12	0.09
Impact on cap ex	(1.0)						
Tax saved on capital allowances	0.15	0.039	0.027	0.021	0.015	0.012	0.009
Unrecovered allowance at year 6							0.027 ?
Impact on cash flow	(0.85)	0.039	0.027	0.021	0.015	0.012	0.036
DCF at 10%	(0.85)	0.0355	0.0223	0.0158	0.0102	0.0075	0.0203

Net impact on NPV = $(0.738)m

This means that every additional $1m spent on capital equipment will only cost the project $0.738m due to tax savings resulting from capital allowances.

(b) **Discounted payback and duration**

Discounted payback is used to determine how long it will take the project to repay its original investment. As the name suggests this method uses discounted cash flows in the calculations.

Year	0	1	2	3	4	5	6
	$m	$m	$m	$m	$m	$m	$m
Discounted cash flow	(127.50)	(33.52)	43.28	57.38	46.71	26.95	16.12
Cumulative DCF	(127.50)	(161.02)	(117.74)	(60.36)	(13.65)	13.30	29.42

The discounted payback period is approximately 4.5 years.

Project duration is the time it takes the project to recover approximately 50% of its initial investment. It is calculated by weighting each year of the project by the percentage of the present value recovered in that year.

Year	0	1	2	3	4	5	6
	$m	$m	$m	$m	$m	$m	$m
Discounted cash flow			43.28	57.38	46.71	26.95	16.12
PV of return phase	190.44						
Proportion of PV			0.2273	0.3013	0.2453	0.1415	0.0846
Weighted years			0.4546	0.9039	0.9812	0.7075	0.5076

Duration = sum of weighted years = 3.55 years

Discounted payback overcomes one of the problems of the ordinary payback technique – that is, it uses discounted cash flows rather than ignoring the time value of money. However the problem with payback (discounted or not) is that it **ignores** cash flows that occur beyond the payback period. Thus projects that have very high initial cash flows but few (if any) in later years may be favoured over those projects that might add greater value to the firm but over a longer period.

The advantage of **duration** is that it considers the cash flows over the **entire life** of the project. It measures how long it will be before the project recovers the bulk of its present value. However it can be more **difficult to understand** the concept behind duration and for this reason it may not be widely used.

(c)   **Recommendation on capital investment project**

The current project under review has a net present value (NPV) of **$29.42m** which means that the value of the business will be increased by this amount if the project is undertaken. It has also been found that for every additional $1m spent on capital equipment for this project, the project's NPV will be reduced by $0.738m (due to tax savings made on the capital allowances available on capital expenditure). However given the size of the NPV it is expected that any variations in capital expenditure should not significantly affect the value added to the firm.

By using **discounted payback**, it has been found that the project will wholly recover its investment within 4.5 years. As the majority of the cash flows occur in the earlier years of the project's life, there is an average recovery of total present value of 3.55 years.

On the basis of the above analysis, it is recommended that the Board **approves** this project for commencement.

Investment appraisal techniques

Payback is a technique that has been employed in the appraisal of this project. However, although the discounted version of payback reflects the cost of finance in the results, there is still the problem that it ignores any cash flows that occur after the payback period has been reached. This may result in vital information being missed, such as very few or no cash flows beyond the payback point. **Duration** removes this problem as it focuses on all cash flows of the project, regardless of when they occur. It is a measure of the time taken to recover 50% of the initial investment or, alternatively, earn 50% of the present value. It is a superior technique to payback and its implementation should be considered for future investment appraisal exercises.

Whilst sensitivity analysis is highly useful, there is the problem of **high degrees of correlation** between variables. There is a risk that concentrating too much on one variable will be at the expense of other variables whose movements may be more critical to the project's profitability. The use of **simulation** would help to alleviate this problem. This technique generates thousands of values for the variables of interest and uses those variables to derive the NPV for each possible simulated outcome. The priority of each individual variable in the determination of the overall NPV can then be established.

It is therefore recommended that simulation is incorporated into the investment appraisal in future.

19 Kodiak Company

Text references. Valuing a firm using free cash flow to equity and terminal values is covered in Chapter 5.

Top tips. In part (a), layout is very important, not just to make things clear for the marker, but also for you to ensure that no figures are missed. There are numerous workings involved in this part of the questions therefore you need to be able to keep track of where figures are coming from. Remember that cash flow statements never include depreciation so ensure you account for this when calculating the free cash flow to equity. Make sure you answer the question – you are asked for the free cash flow to equity so you will have to deduct any new investment in non-current assets.

Part (b) is straightforward if you can remember the formula but remember to show your workings. Also write the formula in notation form in your answer to show the marker which formula you are using!

Part (c) is testing your understanding of how estimates can affect the valuation figure. Two of the more important figures are growth rates and required rate of return so make sure you comment on those. There are several other factors you can comment on but remember this part is only worth 6 marks so don't get carried away!

Easy marks. The calculations in part (a) should be quite straightforward and you should be expecting to gain all, or almost all, of the available marks. As mentioned above, part (b) is also quite straightforward if you remember the formula for calculating terminal value.

			Marks
(a)	Estimation of depreciation	1	
	Estimation of taxation	1	
	Estimation of changes in working capital	2	
	Projection of income statements	4	
	Projection of cash flows	<u>4</u>	
			12
(b)	Calculation/identification of free cash flow	1	
	Calculation of terminal value	2	
	Calculation of present values and business value	<u>3</u>	
			6
(c)	Commentary on required rate of return	2 - 3	
	Assumptions about the growth rates	2 - 3	
	Other relevant points	<u>1 - 2</u>	
		Max	<u>7</u>
			25

(a) Using the information in the question it is clear that in order to produce a projected cash flow statement we must first produce a projected income statement for each of the next three years.

Projected income statement

	Year 1 $'000	Year 2 $'000	Year 3 $'000
Revenue (9% growth per annum)	5,450	5,941	6,476
Cost of sales (9% growth per annum)	3,270	3,564	3,885
Gross profit	2,180	2,377	2,591
Other operating costs (W1)	2,013	2,160	2,318
Operating profit	167	217	273

Projected cash flow statement

	Year 1 $'000	Year 2 $'000	Year 3 $'000
Operating profit	167	217	273
Add: Depreciation (W2)	135	144	155
Less: Incremental working capital (W3)	(20)	(22)	(24)
Less: interest	(74)	(74)	(74)
Less: taxation (W4)	(15)	(28)	(43)
	193	237	287
Less: new additions to non-current assets (W2)	(79)	(95)	(114)
Free cash flow to equity	114	142	173

Workings

(1) **Operating costs**

	Year 1 $'000	Year 2 $'000	Year 3 $'000
Variable costs (9% growth per annum)	818	892	972
Fixed costs (6% growth per annum)	1,060	1,124	1,191
Depreciation (10%) (Working 2)	135	144	155
Total operating costs	2,013	2,160	2,318

(2)   **Depreciation and non-current assets**

	Year 1 $'000	Year 2 $'000	Year 3 $'000
Non-current assets at start of year	1,266	1,345	1,440
Additions (20% of last year's additions)	79	95	114
Non-current assets at end of year	1,345	1,440	1,554
Depreciation (10%)	135	144	155

(3)   **Working capital**

	Year 1 $'000	Year 2 $'000	Year 3 $'000
Working capital requirements (9% growth pa)	240	262	286
Incremental working capital	(240 – 220) =	(262 – 240) =	(286 – 262) =
	20	22	24

Note that the working capital figure excludes cash, therefore the current (year 0) working capital figure is $270,000 - $50,000 = $220,000.

(4)   **Taxation**

	Year 1 $'000	Year 2 $'000	Year 3 $'000
Charged on previous year's profit after interest			
Given in question	15		
Previous year's operating profit (from projected income statement)		167	217
Interest		74	74
Profit before tax		93	143
Tax at 30%		28	43

(b)   **Value of business using free cash flow to equity and terminal value**

	Year 1 $'000	Year 2 $'000	Year 3 $'000
Free cash flow to equity (from (a))	114	142	173
Terminal value (W1)			2,546
			2,719
Discount factor (10%)	0.909	0.826	0.751
Present value	104	117	2,042

Value of the business = $2,263,000

Working

(1)   **Terminal value**

$$\text{Terminal value} = \frac{FCF_N(1+g)}{k-g}$$

where g = growth rate
    k = required rate of return

$$\text{Terminal value} = \frac{173(1+0.03)}{0.10-0.03} = \$2,546$$

(c)   **Assumptions and uncertainties within the valuation**

Whilst the valuation of the business is a useful estimate, it should be treated with caution as it is subject to certain assumptions.

Rate of return

The rate of return of 10% is assumed to fairly reflect the required **market rate of return** for a business of this type, which compensates you for the business risk to which you are exposed. Whilst the required return for an investment held in a widely diversified portfolio should only compensate you for **market risk**, if you hold the same investment individually you may expect a higher return due to your increased exposure to risk.

BPP
LEARNING MEDIA

Growth rates

The growth rate applied to terminal value is assumed to be **certain** into the indefinite future. In the case of a three year projection this is unlikely to be the case, due to unexpected economic conditions and the type of business. In order to reduce the effects of such uncertainties, different growth rates could be applied to the calculations to determine business valuation in a variety of scenarios.

Interest rates and tax rates

Similar to the growth rate, it has been assumed that interest rates and tax rates will remain **unchanged** during the three year period. If economic conditions suggest that changes may take place revised calculations could reflect different possible rates to update the estimate of business valuation.

Costs, revenues and non-current assets

It has been assumed that the figures used for these factors are certain and that the business is a going concern. It may be worth investigating the **potential variability** of these factors and the range of values that may result for such variability. Changes in estimates will obviously affect operating profit and projected cash flows, which in turn will affect the estimated value of the business.

20 Tisa Co

Text references. Investment appraisal is covered in Chapter 5.

Top tips. For part (a) you need to calculate the WACC. This can be done by to estimating the project's asset beta then using Tisa Co's capital structure to estimate the equity beta to then calculate the WACC.

Part (c) (i) requires an understanding of how to calculate VAR, but you could still get marks from the explanations of what the figures mean even if you have not calculated them correctly.

For part (b) do not neglect the requirement to explain the recommendation you have made.

Easy marks. Part (c) (ii) offers some straightforward discussion marks, some of which will be brought forward knowledge from F9.

Examiner's comments. In part (a) most candidates made a reasonably good attempt at determining the cost of capital, although few candidates were able to calculate the asset beta of other activities and therefore the component asset beta. A small number of candidates used an average of equity and debt weightings, and where this was done correctly, appropriate credit was given. Many responses did not give reasons for the approach taken and thereby did not achieve some relatively easy marks.

Few responses calculated the annual and five-year value-at-risk figures in part (c), and very few provided explanations of the values obtained.

Marking scheme

			Marks	
(a)		Reasoning behind cost of capital calculation	2	
		Calculation of component asset beta	3	
		Calculation of component equity beta, and Ke and WACC	3	
				8
(b)		Calculation of IRR for Process Omega	3	
		Calculation of MIRR for Process Omega	1	
		Resolution and advice	4	
				8
(c)	(i)	Annual and five-year VAR	2	
		Explanation	2	
				4
	(ii)	1 mark per relevant discussion point	Max	5
				25

(a) Use the information for Elfu Co to estimate the component project's asset beta. Then use Tisa Co's capital structure to estimate the project's equity beta and WACC. It is assumed that the beta of debt is zero.

Elfu Co MV_e = $1.20 × 400m shares = $480 million
Elfu Co MV_d = $96 million
Elfu Co portfolio asset beta = 1.40 × $480m/($480m + $96m × (1 − 0.25)) = 1.217
Elfu Co asset beta of other activities = 1.25 × $360m/($360m + $76.8m × (1 − 0.25)) = 1.078
1.217 = component asset beta × 0.25 + 1.078 × 0.75
Component asset beta = (1.217 − (1.078 × 0.75))/0.25 = 1.634

Component equity beta based on Tisa Co capital structure
1.634 × [($18m + $3.6m × 0.75)/$18m] = 1.879

Using CAPM
K_e = 3.5% + 1.879 × 5.8% = 14.40%

WACC = (14.40% × $18m + 4.5% × $3.6m) / ($18m + $3.6m) = 12.75%

(b) Process Omega

Year	Cash flow (S'000)	Discount factor 12.75%	PV (S'000)	Discount factor 30%	PV (S'000)
0	(3,800)	1.000	(3,800)	1.000	(3,800)
1	1,220	0.887	1,082	0.769	938
2	1,153	0.787	907	0.592	683
3	1,386	0.698	967	0.455	631
4	3,829	0.619	2,370	0.350	1,340
			1,526		(208)

IRR is approximately 12.75% + (1,526/(1,526 + 208)) × (30% − 12.75%) = 27.9%

MIRR

Year	Cash flow (S'000)	Multiplier	Re-invested amount (S'000)
1	1,220	1.1275^3	1,749
2	1,153	1.1275^2	1,466
3	1,386	1.1275	1,563
4	3,829	1.0000	3,829
			8,607

MIRR = $(8,607/3,800)^{1/4}$ −1 = 22.7%

Internal rate of return (IRR) assumes that positive cash flows are **reinvested at the IRR** and so Process Omega, which has higher initial cash flows compared to Process Zeta has a slightly higher IRR. The modified internal rate of return (MIRR) assumes that positive cash flows are reinvested at the cost of capital. The assumption is more **reasonable** and the result produced is consistent with the net present value. Process Zeta should be adopted as a result, although the difference between the two projects is not significant.

(c) (i) A 99% confidence level requires the value at risk to be within 2.33 standard deviations from the mean, based on a single tail measure.

Annual VAR = 2.33 × $800,000 = $1,864,000
Five year VAR = $1,864,000 × $5^{0.5}$ = $4,168,031

This means that Elfu Co can be confident 99% confident that the cash flows will not fall by more than $1,864,000 in any one year or $4,168,031 in total over the five year period. This means that it can be 99% sure that the returns will be at least ($2,200,000 − $1,864,000) = $336,000 each year. The company can also be 99% sure that the total five-year returns will be at least ($11,000,000 − $4,168,031) = $6,831,969. There is only a 1% chance that the returns will be less than $336,000 each year or $6,831,969 in total.

BPP
LEARNING MEDIA

(ii) Risk is most commonly dealt with by using **expected value** analysis, which involves assigning probabilities to all possible outcomes. The major drawback is that the assignment of probabilities is highly subjective. This method is also not suitable for a one-off project, as it may give an expected value that is not possible. It also does not indicate the maximum loss or the probability or making a loss, factors which will impact managers' decision-making when they consider project risks.

Uncertainty can be dealt with using a variety of methods. One of these is **sensitivity analysis**. This involves altering the variables in the investment appraisal and seeing how this affects the outcome. The main drawbacks are that variables are looked at in isolation, but in reality they may be **interdependent** and that it does not assess the likelihood of the changes in the variables occurring.

Payback and **discounted payback** can be used to determine how long it will take to recover the initial cost of the investment. The major drawback is that any cash flows after payback has occurred are ignored.

21 GDW Co

> **Text references.** Investment appraisal techniques and capital rationing are covered in Chapter 5.
>
> **Top tips.** This is a good question if you are comfortable with the limitations of investment appraisal methods.
>
> In part (b) (i) you should include the fact that a soft capital rationing limit can potentially be changed to allow further investment to take place. If capital rationing is still in place in the following year, then a project that will payback before then becomes more attractive.
>
> **Easy marks.** The calculations in part (a) (i) are fairly straightforward and the formulation of the constraints in part (b) (ii) should provide easy marks for a well prepared student.

(a) (i)

Project	Investment $m	PV of post year 1 cash flows $m	NPV $m	PI	Annual cash flows $m	Term (Years)	Payback (Years)
A	(350)	472.5	122.5	35%	529.2	1	0.7
B	(525)	875.0	350.0	67%	288.1	4	1.8
C	(1,050)	1,435.0	385.0	37%	849.1	2	1.2
D	(1,225)	1,785.0	560.0	46%	434.0	6	2.8

Payback calculations

Project A   350/529.2 = 0.7

Project B   525/288.1 = 1.8

Project C   1,050/849.1 = 1.2

Project D   1,225/434 = 2.8

Ranking of projects

Project	NPV	PI	Payback
A	4	4	1
B	3	1	3
C	2	3	2
D	1	2	4

(ii) The **NPV method** gives an absolute figure which shows the increase in shareholders' funds as a result of the investment in a particular project. If capital is unlimited then this is the measure that should determine the projects to be invested in. If capital is limited then it is also necessary to consider the amount of limited capital required by the project.

The **profitability index** is a measure that can be used when capital rationing is in place. It is most useful where projects are divisible, but is **less useful**, as in this case, **where projects are indivisible**. It can be of some help to rank non-divisible projects and can help to identify the optimum combination of projects, or at least a combination that is close to the optimum. However in this particular case it has not produced such a combination.

The **payback method** takes into account the **timing of the cash flows**. Project A is therefore prioritised as it returns the initial investment within the first year. This can be useful in a multi-period scenario as it will indicate that funds could be reinvested in a different project in the following year. This may be an advantage where projects planned for the following period will deliver greater shareholder wealth than those in the current period. However, if capital rationing is only in place for the current period, then this is less useful. Payback helps to **identify riskier projects** as the uncertainty of future cash flows increases with time and therefore a project with a lower payback period will be less risky.

All of these methods have drawbacks. Capital rationing decisions are often **more complicated** than identifying the ranking by such methods. Some of the complications of capital rationing problems are as follows:

(1)   If capital is restricted in one period that it is highly likely to also be restricted in the next and **subsequent periods** as well. A multi-period model will therefore be required.

(2)   Projects are unlikely to possess the same characteristics. For example, some projects may contain real options with follow on opportunities. Other projects may have greater **strategic significance**, which outweigh other financial considerations.

(3)   Some projects may be **'one-off' opportunities** which can only be undertaken in a particular period. Other projects may be able to be delayed and then commence in the following period.

No one method is likely to provide the best solution to a capital rationing scenario on its own. Each method provides useful information which can help the decision making process

(b)   (i)   **Project combinations**

Combination	Investment	NPV
	$m	$m
ABC	1,925	857.5
ABD	2,100	1,032.5
CD	2,275	945.0

The best combination is from projects A, B and D. This only uses $2,100m of the available funds.

Soft or hard capital rationing?

Soft capital rationing occurs when the capital restriction is internally imposed by the company, usually for budgeting purposes. The capital limits are targets and there is the **potential to adjust them according to particular circumstances**.

Hard capital rationing is externally imposed, for example due to restrictive debt covenants, and the **limits cannot be adjusted**.

If GDW Co applies soft capital rationing, it may seek to increase the limit on capital to $2,800 million as this would mean that projects B, C and D could be undertaken. They would generate an NPV of $1,295 million which is $262.5 million higher than the current optimum combination of $1,032.5 million. This is an increase of 25%, with an increase in capital of 14% (350m/2,450m).

If the limit could be increased further, it would be **beneficial** to the shareholder to **undertake all of the available projects**.

Capital rationing in the following year

The optimal combination depends on **whether capital is rationed in the following year**. If this is the case, project A becomes more attractive as the payback period is less than one year and so this capital is **available to be reinvested in the next year**.

BPP
LEARNING MEDIA

Assuming that the limit of $2,450 million applies again in the next year, this will then greatly enhance the funds available for investment at that time.

(ii)   Let X_A be the investment in project A
                    X_B be the investment in project B
                    X_C be the investment in project C
                    X_D be the investment in project D

Year 1 constraint

$$X_A \times 350 + X_B \times 525 + X_C \times 1,050 + X_D \times 1,225 \leq 2,400$$

Year 2 constraint

$$X_B \times 525 + X_C \times 1,050 + X_D \times 1,225 \leq 2,160$$

Year 3 constraint

$$X_B \times 525 + X_C \times 1,050 + X_D \times 1,225 \leq 1,944$$

Tutorial note: In this question the projects are indivisible so the output for the variables would be either 0 or 1. In the case of divisible (but not expandable) projects the outputs would be between 0 and 1.

---

22 Preparation question – Cathlynn

Text references. Chapter 6.

Top tips. If you can work your way through the formula and are able to use the normal distribution table, this question is actually not that bad. In (i), we need the standard deviation, σ, so therefore we need to take the square root of the variance which we are given in the question. We have used interpolation to find the values in (ii).

(a) (i)   Find (d_1) and (d_2)

$$d_1 = \frac{\ln(3.50/3.30) + (0.08 \times 0.25)}{\sqrt{0.12}\sqrt{0.25}} + (0.5 \times (\sqrt{0.12} \times \sqrt{0.25}))$$

$$= 0.4552 + 0.0866 = 0.5418$$

$$d_2 = 0.5418 - (\sqrt{0.12}\sqrt{0.25})$$

$$= 0.5418 - 0.1732 = 0.3686$$

(ii)   Find N (d_1) and N (d_2) using normal distribution tables

N (0.5418)   = 0.5 + 0.2060 = 0.7060
N (0.3686)   = 0.5 + 0.1438 = 0.6438

(iii)   Using the Black-Scholes formula

$$C_0 = (3.50 \times 0.7060) - ((3.30e^{-0.08 \times 0.25}) \times 0.6438)$$
$$= 2.4710 - 2.0825 = 38.85p$$

(b)   The main limitations of the Black-Scholes model are:

(i)   The model is **only designed** for the valuation of **European call options**.

(ii)   The basic model is based on the assumption that **shares pay no dividends**.

(iii)   The model assumes that there will be **no transaction costs**.

(iv)   The model assumes knowledge of the **risk-free rate of interest,** and also assumes the risk-free rate will be constant throughout the option's life.

(v)   Likewise the model also assumes accurate knowledge of the **standard deviation of returns**, which is also assumed to be constant throughout the option's life.

23 MMC

Text references. Real options and the Black-Scholes model are covered in Chapter 6.

Top tips. The key to part (a) is determining the values for the variables in the Black-Scholes equation. P_a is the current 'price' of the project (in this case the present value of its cash flows without the option to delay) and P_e is the 'exercise price'. P_e in this scenario is how much you will pay in production, distribution and marketing costs once the project actually starts (that is, the costs that can be delayed if the option to delay is exercised).

Don't forget to show all workings as it is very easy to make a mistake in putting numbers into your calculator. You will be awarded marks for workings even if you don't get the correct answer.

If you are unsure what some of the variables should be (eg P_a and P_e), make an assumption and use the figures you have assumed to be correct. Remember to state your assumptions in your answer so that the marker will see what you are doing.

Easy marks. The calculations in part (a) are not difficult as you are already given the formulae therefore you should be able to pick up some marks here. Part (c) is straightforward discussion if you understand the determinants within the Black-Scholes model.

Examiner's comments. Most students were able to determine the value of the option in part (a) but few students were able to identify the P_a and P_e values. In part (b) a significant number of students did not identify and discuss real options but merely talked about financial options in a general sense. However some students did recognise that the value of the real option obtained in part (a) is not an actual value.

Marking scheme

		Marks
(a)	Value of project without considering option to delay decision and conclusion	2
	Current price variable (P_a) for Black-Scholes formula	1
	Additional cost (P_e) for Black-Scholes formula	1
	Other variables for Black-Scholes formula	1
	Calculation of $N(d_1)$	3
	Calculation of $N(d_2)$	1
	Value of option to delay decision	1
	Revised value of project and conclusion	2
		12
(b)	1 to 2 marks per well explained point	Max 7
(c))	1 to 2 marks per well explained point	Max 6
		25

(a) Financial impact of option to delay

First of all we calculate the PV of the project without the option to delay.

Year	0	1	2	3	4	5	6
	$m	$m	$m	$m	$m	$m	$m
Cash flows	(7.0)	(7.0)	(35.0)	25.0	18.0	10.0	5.0
Discount factor (11%)	1.000	0.901	0.812	0.731	0.659	0.593	0.535
DCF	(7.0)	(6.31)	(28.42)	18.28	11.86	5.93	2.68

NPV = $(2.98)m

Without the option to delay the project would be rejected.

Option to delay – use the Black-Scholes model to value this option

$$c = P_aN(d_1) - P_eN(d_2)e^{-rt}$$

$$\text{Where } d_1 = \frac{\ln(P_a/P_e) + (r + 0.5s^2)t}{s\sqrt{t}}$$

$$d_2 = d_1 - s\sqrt{t}$$

P_a = current value of the project (that is the PV of its cash inflows)
    = $18.28m + $11.86m + $5.93m + $2.68m
    = $38.75m

P_e = 'exercise price' of the project (that is, the cost of production etc that can be delayed)
    = $35m

t = exercise date (that is when the exercise price is paid) = 2 years

r = risk-free rate = 3.5%

s = standard deviation = 0.3

d_1 = [ln(38.75/35) + (0.035 + 0.5 x 0.3²) x 2]/[0.3 x $\sqrt{2}$] = 0.617

d_2 = 0.617 – (0.3 x $\sqrt{2}$) = 0.193

Using the Normal Distribution tables:

N(d_1) = 0.5 + 0.2291 + 0.7 x (0.2324 – 0.2291) = 0.7314

N(d_2) = 0.5 + 0.0753 + 0.3 x (0.0793 – 0.0753) = 0.5765

Value of option to delay = (38.75 x 0.7314) – (35 x 0.5765 x $e^{(-0.035 \times 2)}$) = $9.529m

Total value of project = $9.529m - $2.98m = $6.549m

The project would therefore be accepted with the option to delay included.

(b) **Implications of the results**

The option to delay the project gives management time to consider and monitor the potential investment before committing to its execution. This extra time will allow management to assess the popularity of similar launches and also to monitor competition. The success of the film will be heavily reliant on the marketing campaign launched by the film's promoters prior to its release – management will be able to monitor the extent of this campaign before committing to an expensive (and potentially unsuccessful) project.

However the calculations of the value of the option to delay are subject to several limiting assumptions, primarily the volatility of the cash flows. The value of the option to delay ($9.529m) is not an exact figure but rather an **indication** of how much management would value the opportunity to delay. The result shows that management should not dismiss the project immediately, despite the current negative NPV.

There may be other options embedded within the project. The technology used to develop the game may be used for other projects in the future (option to **redeploy**). Alternatively the project could lead to follow-on projects if the film is successful enough to generate sequels.

(c) The value of the option depends on the following variables.

(i) **The price of the security**

A decrease in the price of the security will mean that a call option becomes **less valuable.** Exercising the option will mean purchasing a security that has a lower value.

(ii) **The exercise price of the option**

A decrease in the exercise price will mean that a call option becomes **more valuable**; the profit that can be made from exercising the option will have increased.

(iii) **Risk free rate of return**

A decrease in the risk free rate will mean that a call option becomes **less valuable.** The purchase of an option rather than the underlying security will mean that the option holder has spare cash available which can be invested at the risk free rate of return. A decrease in that rate will mean that it becomes less worthwhile to have spare cash available, and hence to have an option rather than having to buy the underlying security.

(iv) **Time to expiry of the option**

A decrease in the time of expiry will mean that a call option becomes **less valuable,** as the time premium element of the option price has been decreased.

(v) **Volatility of the security price**

A decrease in volatility will mean that a call option becomes **less valuable.** A decrease in volatility will decrease the chance that the security price will be above the exercise price when the option expires.

24 Marengo Co

Text references. Option pricing is covered in Chapter 6.

Top tips. There are several ways in which part (b) can be approached and the examiner stated that he would award marks for alternative relevant approaches. What is important is that you assess the advantages and disadvantages of each suggestion to provide a balanced discussion.

Easy marks. Part (a) offers some easy marks for calculating the delta of options and the number of options required.

Examiner's comments. Part (a) was either done well with candidates calculating the delta and then applying it correctly, or done poorly where candidates went on to calculate the value of a call and put option (which were not required). Very few candidates explained the numerical answer. Candidates need to be aware that some question parts may have more than a single requirement and all the requirements need to be addressed correctly in order to achieve full marks. Some reasonable points were made in part (b) but in many cases these lacked depth or substance.

Marking scheme

			Marks
(a)	Identifying the need to calculate $N(d_1)$ for hedge ratio	2	
	Calculation of d_1	2	
	Calculation of $N(-d_1)$	2	
	Calculation of number of put options required	1	
			7
(b)	Discussing the theoretical argument for not hedging	3 – 4	
	Discussing the limitations/risks/costs of selling the shares	3 – 4	
	Discussing the risks/costs of using OTC options to hedge	2 – 3	
	Discussing whether to hold shares at all	2 – 3	
	Discussing the potential benefits of hedging and application to scenario	2 – 3	
	Relevant concluding remarks	1 – 2	
		Max	18
			25

BPP
LEARNING MEDIA

(a)   The number of put options to be purchased depends on the hedge ratio, which in turn is determined by the option's delta. We can estimate delta using $N(-d_1)$.

$$d_1 = \frac{\ln\left(P_a/P_e\right) + \left(r + 0.5s^2\right)t}{s\sqrt{t}}$$

$d_1 = [\ln(340/350) + (0.04 + 0.5 \times 0.4^2) \times 2/12]/(0.4 \times \sqrt{(2/12)})$

$d_1 = (-0.0290 + 0.02)/0.163$

$d_1 = -0.0552$

$-d1 = 0.0552$

$N(-d1) = 0.5 + [0.0199 + (0.0239 - 0.0199)/2] = 0.5219$

Number of put options needed = 200,000 shares/(0.5219 × 1,000 shares) = 383.2 (say 383) contracts

(b)   **Possible reasons for the suggestions made by each of the three managers**

(1)   *No hedging at all*

This argument is based on the theory that corporate risk should not be hedged. This theory states that, where a company holds a well-diversified portfolio and securities are priced correctly, unsystematic risk will be at least reduced to a minimal level or eliminated completely. There is, therefore, no apparent gain to shareholders of any further hedging or management of corporate risk (that is, unsystematic risk cannot be reduced further). Should hedging take place in a perfect market it is likely that shareholders will actually lose out, as the benefits derived from hedging will be outweighed by the costs of doing so.

In an imperfect market, however, shareholders are more likely to benefit from hedging. By reducing the volatility of the firm's earnings, cash flows are likely to increase, which will increase shareholders' wealth. Such a situation is likely to arise

(i)   If stable earnings increase the certainty of being able to pay for future investments which would encourage a more stable investment policy

(ii)   If tax rates are increasing

(iii)   If a high volatility of earnings could lead to financial distress for the company.

None of the above reasons for hedging appears to exist for Marengo Co and the case for hedging seems to be weak. Marengo is a large company with numerous investments, therefore it is unlikely that reducing the volatility of one such investment will have a significant effect on its cash flows.

(2)   *Sell Arion Co's shares in order to eliminate risk of a fall in share price*

This is based on the assumption that Marengo will be protected from a fall in Arion's share price if it gets rid of the shares in Arion. However there are a few issues with this proposal.

It is assumed that Marengo holds shares in Arion as an investment and generates a return greater than the risk-free rate. If Marengo sells these shares, an alternative investment offering similar returns should have to be found for the surplus funds, to prevent a reduction in Marengo's shareholder value. If such investments are not available, the shares should not be sold.

Another issue is the potential effect on Arion's share price if Marengo does 'dump' a large number of shares on the market. Managers have to ask whether they are likely to be able to sell such a large proportion of Arion's shares, although there is the chance that investors want to take the opportunity of purchasing shares at a lower price now, in the expectation that the price will increase again following the projected period of uncertainty.

(3)   *Hedge the investment using an appropriate derivative product*

If this proposal was undertaken, Marengo would be required to purchase 383 OTC put options from the bank (see calculations above). This could prove to be expensive, as Marengo will have to pay a premium on each option for the flexibility of having the right, but not the obligation, to exercise the options. Should the option not be exercised, Marengo will have suffered the cost of the premiums for no reason. However if the options are exercised, Marengo will have protected itself again downside movements in the share price.

Hedging using options involves several risks. Delta is not stable, which means that the number of options that should have been taken out may change (thus Marengo may not be fully protected). Option values also change, the closer they come to the exercise date (measured by theta) and the underlying asset's volatility changes (measured by vega).

Despite the risks associated with derivative products, a stable hedging policy can be used to reduce agency conflicts between shareholders and managers. A single hedging transaction is unlikely to have much impact, but it is important to maintain a consistent approach to hedging against investment risks. This not only protects shareholders' wealth but also managers, who may not be as well diversified as the shareholders.

(4)   *Do not hold any equity investments at all*

Edward may be correct that Marengo Co should not hold equity investments. This is not a core area of business for Marengo Co and it may be best not to focus on it and therefore sell all the shares. However, it is the job of the treasury department to manage excess funds and liquidity and it may be that the equity holdings deliver a valuable dividend stream which contributes to a healthy cash flow for the business. The treasury department will be able to show if their investment choices outperform the market return.

There is no easy way to justify or discourage hedging. Each case should be examined on its individual merits, but it is important for a company to have a risk management strategy on which such decisions can be based.

25 Digunder

Text references. The Black-Scholes model and its use in the valuation of real options are covered in Chapter 6.

Top tips. If you have studied – and are comfortable with – the valuation of real options using the Black-Scholes, this question should be relatively straightforward. The main issues you have to deal with are recognising that you are dealing with real options rather than traded options and appreciating that the option to delay is a call option.

Part (a) is a straightforward application of the Black-Scholes model to value the option to delay. Make sure you make it clear to the marker the value you are attaching to each of the components of the formulae being used. Remember to comment on your findings at the end – an easy thing to forget in the midst of large calculations!

Part (b) simply asks you for the overall value of the project so make sure you clarify how you arrive at your answer. The second requirement of part (b) relates to the Black-Scholes model you used in part (a) – as there are only 3 marks in total for this (including the calculation of the overall value of the project) your comments should be brief.

Part (c) should be fairly brief. A couple of limitations are fine, but make them relevant to the question – the examiner is not looking for general limitations here. The key to this part is recognising that the real option will change to an American option if the government could make the announcement at any time in the next two years.

For part (d) do not waste time by explaining more than two further real options.

Easy marks. If you can identify the figures that match the individual elements within the Black-Scholes formulae, then part (a) will give you a number of easy marks.

BPP
LEARNING MEDIA

Examiner's comments. The majority of candidates were able to specify all but one of the inputs to the Black Scholes option pricing model. Nearly all were able to identify the exercise 'price' – the capital investment – the volatility of the cash flows, the risk-free rate and the time to exercise. Only a few candidates identified the present value of the project as the value of the underlying investment asset.

Part (b) was missed by many candidates who failed to recognise that all that was required was to add the option value derived in (a) to the net present value of the project and to provide a rationale for this approach.

In part (c), candidates could have achieved much higher marks by detailing the assumptions of the Black Scholes model, questioning the logic of using such a model in this context and discussing the problems of estimating the necessary data inputs.

Marking scheme

			Marks
(a)	Identification of inputs into Black-Scholes model	4	
	Calculation of d_1 and d_2 respectively	4	
	Calculation of real option value	2	
	Conclusion on value of the option to delay	2	
			12
(b)	Estimation of overall project value	2	
	Justification of use of Black-Scholes model	1	
			3
(c)	Outline of the limitations of the Black-Scholes model	4	
	Identification of specific option being American style	1	
	Note on appropriate technique for solving American style option	1	
			6
(d)	Explanation of option to expand	Max 2	
	Explanation of option to withdraw	Max 2	
			4
			25

(a) **Value of option to delay**

This involves the use of the Black-Scholes option pricing model. The various components required by the model are:

Volatility = 25%

Current price (value of project including option exercise price) = $24 million + 4 million = $28 million

Exercise price (capital expenditure) = $24 million

Exercise date = 2 years

Risk free rate = 5%

Calculate d_1 and d_2

$$d_1 = \frac{\ln(Pa/Pe) + (r + 0.5s^2)t}{S\sqrt{t}}$$

Where:

Pa	= present value of project	Pe	= capital expenditure
r	= risk free rate	s	= volatility
t	= time period (years)		

$$d_1 \frac{\ln\left(\frac{28}{24}\right) + (0.05 + 0.5 \times 0.25^2) \times 2}{0.25 \times \sqrt{2}}$$

$$= \frac{0.1542 + (0.08125) \times 2}{0.3536} = 0.8956$$

$$d_2 = d_1 - s\sqrt{t}$$

$$= 0.8956 - 0.25 \times \sqrt{2}$$

$$= 0.5421$$

Determine $N(d_1)$ and $N(d_2)$

Using the normal distribution tables:

$N(d_1) = 0.5 + 0.3159 = 0.8159$ (using 0.90 as an approximation for d_1)

$N(d_2) = 0.5 + 0.2054 = 0.7054$ (using 0.54 as an approximation for d_2)

Calculate the value of the option

Value of call option $= P_a \times N(d_1) - P_e \times N(d_2) \times e^{-rt}$

$= (28 \text{ million} \times 0.8159) - (24 \text{ million} \times 0.7054 \times e^{-0.05 \times 2}$

$= 22.85 \text{ million} - 15.32 \text{ million}$

$= \$7.53 \text{ million}$

The value of the option to delay arises as it allows the company to avoid the downside risk of undertaking the project immediately if it does not look advantageous to do so.

(b) **Overall value of the project**

The overall value of the project is the NPV of \$4 million plus the value of the option of \$7.53 million – that is, \$11.53 million. This indicates the considerable payoff from having the option to delay the commencement of the project.

The Black-Scholes model was used in part (a) to determine the value of the real option. The payoff of an option to delay is the same as the payoff of a call option, hence the use of the Black-Scholes model, although this model is more often used for the valuation of financial options. It is a good approximation for the value of real options however and allows companies to determine how valuable having such options available actually are.

(c) **Limitations of the Black-Scholes model**

Volatility

One of the main limitations of using the Black-Scholes model for valuing real options is the estimation of volatility. Real options and their underlying assets are not traded, therefore it is very difficult to establish the volatility of the value. In addition this volatility is assumed to be constant throughout the life of the option.

Risk free rate

Likewise, the model assumes knowledge of the **risk-free rate of interest,** and also assumes the risk-free rate will be constant throughout the option's life, which may not be the case over a longer time period such as two years.

Style of option

The Black-Scholes model assumes that the option is a European style option – that is, it can only be exercised at the maturity date. Where the option can be exercised at any point up to the maturity date (that is, an American style option), the results of the Black-Scholes model are invalid.

BPP LEARNING MEDIA

Which model should be used if the government made its announcement at any time during the two year time period?

If this were the case then the option could be exercised at any point during the next two years – that is, it would become an American style option. As mentioned above, the Black-Scholes model ceases to be accurate in such circumstances. As a result, the binomial option pricing approach would have to be used.

(d)   **Option to expand**

There may be an option to expand if further planning permission for additional housing on the same land can be obtained. Alternatively, a successful development may lead to more demand for housing in the area, which could lead to further housing development opportunities for Digunder.

Option to withdraw

Digunder may discover more profitable opportunities elsewhere that can only be pursued at the expense of this project. Digunder may be able to find another developer willing to take on the development and so it could withdraw and sell the land and the development to another party.

26 AVT

> **Text references.** Chapter 6 for Black-Scholes; Chapter 3a for share option schemes.
>
> **Top tips.** This question illustrates how the data that you need to use in the Black-Scholes formula may be given in an exam question.
>
> The key issues in (a)(i) are how well remuneration is linked to controllable results and problems with the figures used for controllable results.
>
> The data given in the question indicates you can use simple discounting to adjust the value of future dividends in (a)(ii). In a more complex scenario, you may have to adjust future dividends by e-rT.
>
> You need a scientific calculator for the Black-Scholes formula. In is also known as log e and should be on your calculator.
>
> $e^{-0.06} = 1/e^{0.06}$. Again you need your calculator for this.
>
> As d_1 and d_2 are both positive, we need to add 0.5 to the value obtained from the normal distribution tables.
>
> The main Black-Scholes calculation would probably be worth 6-7 marks; you should achieve most of these marks by demonstrating clearly that you were putting the correct figures into the correct place in the formula, even if your figure slipped on your calculator when you carried out the calculation. A good conclusion would have earned you a couple more marks. The put-call parity formula is given in the exam.
>
> **Easy marks.** The discussion in part (a) (i) offers some straightforward marks for advantages and disadvantages.

(a)   (i)   **Advantages for the company**

To the company's shareholders the main advantage of any employee incentive scheme should be that employees are highly **motivated** to improve their own wealth and that in doing so they also increase shareholder returns.

Basic salary plus bonus related to the pre-tax profit of the employee's department

Advantages for the company

The main advantage is that **salary costs** will automatically be **lower** in **years of poor performance**. In other words, the conversion of a fixed salary cost to a variable one lowers the company's operating risk.

Disadvantages for the company

(1)   The measure is based upon **accounting profits** rather than **cash flows** and may be distorted by the **accounting policies chosen** or **manipulation** by the senior managers.

(2)   Middle managers can be encouraged to take a **short-term view of profits** (eg a cost-cutting approach, minimising new investment). This may cause the share price to drop.

A basic salary plus a share option scheme

Advantages for the company

(1) Middle managers will be **motivated** to work towards the **same goal** as **shareholders**, ie maximising share values.

(2) The scheme will **not motivate a short-term outlook** unless the time to maturity is too short. From a shareholder's point of view the longer the time horizon the better, but there must be a trade-off with the manager's reduction in motivation if the time horizon is too long. A typical compromise period would be two to three years.

Disadvantages for the company

(1) Earnings will be **diluted** when the options are exercised.

(2) Middle managers may believe that their decisions will have **little effect** on the share price. This will depend on the extent of the responsibility they are given, and how much the share price is influenced by **factors other than the company's actions**.

(ii) The Black Scholes formula is:

Call price = P_s N (d_1) – Xe^{-rT} N (d_2)

The **share price** must be adjusted by the dividends expected to be paid during the option period discounted at the risk-free rate.

$$P_s = 610 - \frac{25}{1.06}$$
$$= 586.42$$

$$d_1 = \frac{\ln(P_a/P_e) + (r + 0.5s^2)t}{s\sqrt{t}}$$

$$= \frac{\ln(586.42/500) + (0.06 + 0.5 \times 0.38^2)}{0.38 \times \sqrt{1}} \times 1 = \frac{0.1594 + 0.1322}{0.38} = 0.7674$$

d_2 = 0.7674 – (0.38 × $\sqrt{1}$) = 0.3874
N(d_1) = 0.5 + 0.2786 = 0.7786, using interpolation
N (d_2) = 0.5 + 0.1507 = 0.6507, using interpolation

Call price = (586.42 (0.7786)) – (500 e$^{-0.06 \times 1}$ (0.6507))
$$= 456.59 - 306.40$$
$$= 150.19$$

The expected option call price is 150.19c per share, giving a current option value of 5,000 × 150.19 = $7,510.

This is some way above the bonuses that would have been paid over the last few years. The options are in the money and would appear to be more attractive to employees. However their attitude to **risk** will also influence their decisions, as the two schemes have different risks. The value of the Black-Scholes model is very dependent on the assumption that the **previous volatility** of the share price will **continue,** and this may not be the case.

(iii) (1) **Put options**

AVT should not grant the manager put options, allowing shares to be sold at a fixed price. A holder of a put option will benefit from the company's **share price value falling** below the exercise price of the option, and therefore has an incentive to take actions that will **decrease the company's value**.

(2) Pp = Pc – Ps + Xe^{-rT} = 150.19 – 586.42 + 470.88 = 34.65c

Call options are thus **more valuable** in this situation.

27 Alaska Salvage Co

> **Text references.** Black-Scholes Option Pricing Model is covered in Chapter 6. Mezzanine debt is covered in Chapter 2.
>
> **Top tips.** In part (b), treat the problem like an NPV calculation. The only difference is that you are trying to find the discount rate rather than the NPV. Remember that the call value of the option was calculated in part (a).
>
> **Easy marks.** Part (a) offers some easy marks as you are already given the Black-Scholes formulae in the formula sheet. Part (d) is a relatively straightforward illustration of an interest rate swap.

Marking scheme

		Marks
(a)	Calculation of:	
	d_1	3
	d_2	1
	value of the warrant	2
	Assumptions (one mark each to a maximum of 4 marks)	_4_
		10
(b)	Estimation of the coupon rate	4
(c)	Identification of mezzanine debt as a source of high risk finance	2
	Disadvantage for equity investors (reduction in equity value on exercise)	2
	Advantages – low coupon, additional equity participation	_2_
		6
(d)	Calculation of gain	2
	Construction of swap	_3_
		_5_
		25

(a) **Estimation of current value of a warrant**

Using the Black-Scholes model:

$$d_1 = \frac{\ln\left(P_a/P_e\right) + (r + 0.5s^2)t}{s\sqrt{t}}$$

$d_1 = [\ln(85/90) + (0.05 + 0.5 \times 0.2^2) \times 5] / (0.2 \times \sqrt{5})$

$d_1 = [-0.0572 + 0.07 \times 5] / 0.447$

$\mathbf{d_1 = 0.6550}$

$d_2 = d_1 - s\sqrt{t}$

$d_2 = 0.6550 - (0.2 \times \sqrt{5})$

$\mathbf{d_2 = 0.2078}$

$c = P_aN(d_1) - P_eN(d_2)e^{-rt}$

$c = 85 \times N(0.6550) - 90 \times N(0.2078) \times e^{-0.05 \times 5}$

$c = (85 \times 0.7454) - (90 \times 0.5832 \times e^{-0.05 \times 5})$

$c = 63.359 - 40.878$

c = 22.48

This means that the value of each warrant is $2,248 (as each warrant represents an option on 100 equity shares.

Assumptions

- The formulae used above are suitable for 'European' style options therefore it is assumed that the warrants are of the 'European' style.

- There are no taxes or transaction costs

- The share is continuously traded and the share price has a log-normal distribution

- Volatility of returns will remain constant

- No dividends are paid during the warrant's lifetime

- Interest rates are constant and certain

(b) **Estimation of coupon rate**

> **Tutorial note.** The calculations required here are similar to a NPV calculation – the main difference is that we are trying to find the discount (coupon) rate rather than the net present value. We start with what we know and then rearrange the equation to find the rate.

Let c% = the coupon rate

Year	0	1	2	3	4	5
	$	$	$	$	$	$
Coupon	(10,000)	100 × c%	100 × c%	100 × c%	100 × c%	100 × c%
Repayment						10,000
Call value (see (a) above)	2,248					
Cash flow to lender	(7,752)	100 x c%	100 x c%	100 x c%	100 x c%	100 x c% + 10,000

Let A = the five-year annuity factor at 13%

D = the discount factor at 13%

$7,759 = (100 \times c\% \times A) + 10,000 \times D$

$7,759 = (100 \times c\% \times 3.517) + 10,000 \times 0.543$

$7,759 = (351.7 \times c\%) + 5,430$

$c\% = (7,759 - 5,430) / 351.7$

c% = 6.62%

(c) **Advantages and disadvantages of issuing mezzanine debt**

Mezzanine debt is a method of financing where the debt has embedded equity instruments (in this case, warrants) attached. This increases the **value of the debt**.

One of the problems that this proposal has for current equity holders in Alaska Salvage is that the value of their total holding will be **reduced** by the value of the warrants. The extent of this problem will depend on the amount by which the value of the company is likely to rise if the project proceeds using the suggested method of financing.

Another potential problem of mezzanine financing is that the lenders may insist on some degree of **restrictive covenants**, such as restrictions on future borrowing or meeting targets on certain financial ratios.

BPP
LEARNING MEDIA

The nature of Alaska Salvage's business suggests that future borrowing is critical to continued success therefore such restrictions may be damaging in the long-term.

An advantage of mezzanine debt is that it offers more **flexibility** in terms of coupon rates. Providers of mezzanine finance tend to be long-term investors rather than those trying to make a quick return therefore they are less likely to demand very high coupon rates.

Mezzanine debt also provides the company with a means of raising finance for ventures that might not be attractive to commercial banks (due perhaps to the level of risk involved).

(d)

	Alaska Salvage	Counterparty	
Wants	Fixed	Variable	
Without swap	9%	LIBOR + 2%	LIBOR + 11%
Could obtain	LIBOR + 3%	6.5%	LIBOR + 9.5%
Fees	0.25%	0.25%	0.5%
Gain			1.0%
	(LIBOR + 3%)	(6.5%)	
Swap floating	LIBOR + 3%	(LIBOR + 3%)	
Swap fixed*	(8.25%)	8.25%	
Fee	(0.25%)	(0.25%)	
Total post swap	(8.50%)	(LIBOR + 1.50%)	

* If gains are to be shared evenly then each party needs to get a total post swap result of 0.5% lower than the without swap amounts. For example Alaska Salvage needs to finish up with a rate of 8.5%. Therefore, including the bank fee of 0.25% a fixed rate swap of 8.25% is required here.

Note: There are other possible solutions to this requirement, which would receive full credit.

28 Strayer

Text references. Adjusted Present Value is covered in Chapter 7a.

Top tips. A potential trap in (a) is using the information about Strayer to try to calculate its ungeared cost of equity to be used in the base case NPV calculation. As Strayer is diversifying into the printing industry, you have to calculate a base case NPV for that industry. This demonstrates how the examiner expects you to be flexible; although the question is about using adjusted present value, you also have to use gearing and ungearing of betas.

Another trap is including the pre-tax income flows in the base case NPV calculation. As you are not given any information about when tax is paid, you can assume it is paid in the same year as the income or expense to which it relates.

To calculate the annuity factor used in the tax shield calculation (5.5% for 10 years), we have taken the average of the 5% and 6% factors. You could have used the formula given in the annuity table, or rounded up to 6% and used the annuity tables. When calculating the benefit of the subsidy, remember to include the after-tax benefit. You could calculate the tax relief on the $9 million at the full 8% as this represents the increase in the debt capacity.

The issue costs for debt are only for the unsubsidised loan. Remember for (b) that adjusted present value is particularly useful where WACC is difficult to calculate or where the capital structure changes at the start of the decision.

Part (c) requires you to think about whether the diversification will benefit Strayer and the dangers that this strategy could present.

Easy marks. The points in (b), though this question is fundamentally a test of your ability to cope with the complications of APV calculations. It really is worth reviewing (a) carefully if you did struggle.

(a) **Base case NPV**

Use the beta of the printing industry to estimate the cost of capital

$$\beta_a = \beta_e \frac{V_e}{V_e + V_d(1-T)} + \beta_d \frac{V_d(1-T)}{V_e + V_d(1-T)}$$

Assuming debt is risk free

$$\beta_a = 1.2 \frac{0.5}{0.5 + 0.5(1-0.3)} = 0.706$$

Using CAPM : $k_e = 5.5 + (12 - 5.5)\ 0.706 = 10.09\%$, say 10%

Alternative method of ungearing

You would use the following method if beta is not given.

k_e in the printing industry = $R_f + \beta(R_m - R_f) = 5.5 + 1.2\ (12 - 5.5) = 13.3\%$

This can be ungeared using the following formula, assuming that the k_d in printing is the risk free rate.

k_e (geared) = $k_e^1 + (1-t)(k_e^1 - k_d)V_d/V_e$

13.3 (printing) = $k_e^1 + (0.7 \times [k_e^1 - 5.5]\ 50/50)$

$13.3 = k_e^1 + 0.7k_e^1 - 3.9$

$17.2 = 1.7k_e^1$

$k_e^1 = 17.2/1.7 = 10\%$

This is the ungeared cost of equity and is used in the base case NPV.

Years		Cash flow £'000	Discount factor	Present value $'000
0	Investment	(25,000)	1.000	(25,000)
1–10	After tax cash flows [5,000 (1- 0.3)]	3,500	6.145	21,507.5
10	Residual value	5,000	0.386	1,930
				(1,562.5)

Tax shield

Tax relief = ($5 million × 0.08 × 30%) + ($4 million × 0.06 × 30%) = $192,000
Present value of tax shield discounted at the risk free rate　　　= $192,000 × 7.541* = $1,447,872

$$*7.541 = \frac{(7.722 + 7.360)}{2}$$

Subsidy

Benefits of lower interest rate,
discounted at risk free rate　= $4 million × 0.02 × 0.7 × 7.541 = $422,296

Issue costs

Debt $5 million × 1% = $50,000　　Equity $10 million × 4% = $400,000

Adjusted present value

	$
Base case NPV	(1,562,500)
Tax shield	1,447,872
Subsidy	422,296
Issue costs	(450,000)
Adjusted present value	(142,332)

The adjusted present value is negative, and therefore the project is not worthwhile.

BPP LEARNING MEDIA

(b)   A typical NPV will use the **weighted average cost of capital** (WACC) as the discount rate. This will **not be suitable** if a significant project is funded mainly by **debt**.

The use of debt finance can bring distinct advantages in terms of the **tax savings** on the interest payments and also disadvantages in terms of the **issue costs** of such finance. Both issues should be included in the assessment of projects funded mainly by debt. Only the **adjusted present value** (APV) technique does this.

APV is a Modigliani and Miller (MM) technique and **ignores the financial distress costs** associated with high levels of gearing. Financial distress costs are often triggered by a fall in the credit rating of the company and include **falling sales** and **higher costs** from suppliers.

(c)   **Expertise**

This investment is outside the existing mainstream activities of Strayer and there may be a lack of knowledge of, and expertise in, the printing industry within the company. This could affect the ability to make the investment successful.

Change of focus

The investment in the printing industry may make management lose focus on its core mainstream activities. If this is the case the mainstream activities may suffer from reduced profitability and/or increased customer dissatisfaction.

Additional risk

Using the average equity beta for the printing industry and the existing equity beta of Strayer, it looks as though the printing industry is riskier than the existing operations of Strayer Inc. Given Strayer's relatively low asset beta, its shareholders may not be happy with a diversification into a riskier area.

29 Neptune

Text references. Adjusted present value is covered in Chapter 7a. Modified internal rate of return is covered in Chapter 5.

Top tips. The APV calculation may seem rather lengthy but we have laid it out in a step-by-step format to make it as clear as possible.

Remember the objective of APV is to separate the investment decision from the financing decision, therefore the tax shields from the extra debt should be discounted separately. Tax shields are discounted at the pre-tax cost of debt and the information to calculate this rate is given in the question. The 'basic case' NPV is discounted at the cost of equity which must be calculated separately.

Probably the most complicated calculation in part (a) is determining the ungeared cost of equity. If you are struggling to calculate this rate, just assume a figure and use that in your calculations (make sure you make it clear that you have assumed this figure). If the rest of your answer is correct, you will only lose a couple of marks. However the BPP approach is to assume that the tax saving occurs a year later, and our answer reflects this. This illustrates the importance of stating your assumptions when a question is not particularly clear.

The MIRR can be calculated in two different ways – either using the formula given in the exam formula sheet or by using terminal values. Both methods have been demonstrated for completeness – you would obviously only have to use one method in the exam.

Easy marks. The tax effects on NPV calculations should be familiar from your F9 – *Financial Management* studies therefore the calculations should be quite straightforward. The advantages and disadvantages of MIRR is also a relatively easy requirement.

Examiner's comments. Many candidates attempted this question, producing answers that reflected a good understanding of the mechanics of the method, but showing less understanding of its underlying principles or rationale. Unless a project (and its financing) are marginal to the firm's current position it is likely that the decision to proceed with the investment will disturb the firm's cost of capital. This will lead to a situation where an appropriate discount rate cannot be calculated before the impact of the project on the value of the firm or its gearing has been established.

		Marks
(a)	Note of the two approaches to adjusted present value	2
	Projection of relevant cash flows	4
	Identification and calculation of appropriate discount rates	4
	Calculation of value of project and tax shield using APV	4
		14
(b)	Calculation of MIRR using 8.97% as the reinvestment rate	6
(c)	Advantages of MIRR	3
	Disadvantages of MIRR	2
		5
		25

(a) **Calculation of adjusted present value (APV)**

Step 1 – calculate tax allowances

Year	Cost/WDV	Tax saved at 30%	Year of tax benefit
	$m	$m	
20X8	800		
FYA (50%)	(400)	120	20X9
	400		
20X9	(160)	48	20Y0
	240		
20Y0	(96)	28.8	20Y1
	144		
20Y1	(57.6)	17.3	20Y2
	86.4		
20Y2	(34.6)	10.4	20Y3
	51.8		
20Y3	(20.7)	6.2	20Y4
Tax WDV	31.1		
Residual value	(40.0)		
Balancing charge	(8.9)	(2.7)	20Y4

Step 2 – Tax calculations

	20X9	20Y0	20Y1	20Y2	20Y3
	$m	$m	$m	$m	$m
Revenue	680	900	900	750	320
Direct costs	(408)	(540)	(540)	(450)	(192)
Redeployment of labour	(150)	(150)			
Taxable cash flow	122	210	360	300	128
Tax at 30%	36.6	63	108	90	38.4

Remember that the tax charge will be paid the year after it occurs.

BPP
LEARNING MEDIA

Step 3 – Calculate ungeared cost of equity and pre-tax cost of debt

Ungeared cost of equity

$$\text{Current level of gearing} = \left(\frac{V_d}{V_d + V_e}\right) = \frac{2{,}500}{(2{,}500 + 7{,}500)} = 25\%$$

$$\text{Tax-adjusted gearing} = \left(\frac{V_d(1-T)}{V_d(1-T) + V_e}\right) = \frac{2{,}500 \times (1-0.3)}{(2{,}500 \times 0.7 + 7{,}500)} = 0.1892 \text{ or } 18.92\%$$

$$
\begin{aligned}
\text{Asset beta } (\beta_a) \quad &= \text{Equity beta } (\beta_e) \times (1 - \text{tax adjusted market gearing}) \\
&= 1.4 \times (1 - 0.1892) \\
&= 1.1351
\end{aligned}
$$

$$
\begin{aligned}
\text{Cost of equity (ungeared)} \quad &= \text{Risk free rate} + \text{Asset beta x market risk premium} \\
&= 5 + 1.1351 \times 3.5 \\
&= 8.97\%
\end{aligned}
$$

[Note that the risk free rate is $LIBOR (5.4%) – 40 basis points (0.4%) = 5%. This is the one month Treasury Bill rate which is the risk free rate.]

Pre-tax cost of debt

$$
\begin{aligned}
\text{Current cost of debt finance (from question)} \quad &= \$\text{LIBOR} + 180 \text{ basis points} \\
&= 5.4\% + 1.8\% = 7.2\%
\end{aligned}
$$

Step 4 – Discount cash flows using ungeared rate

	20X8	20X9	20Y0	20Y1	20Y2	20Y3	20Y4
	$m	$m	$m	$m	$m	$m	$m
Cash flow		122	210	360	300	128	
Tax at 30%			(36)	(63)	(108)	(90)	(38.4)
Capital costs	(800)					40	
Tax benefit – cap. allowance		120	48	28.8	17.3	10.4	3.5
Cash flow	(800)	242.0	222.0	325.8	209.3	88.4	(34.9)
Dis. Factor at 8.97%	1.000	0.918	0.842	0.773	0.709	0.651	0.597
DCF	(800)	222.0	187.0	251.8	148.4	57.5	(20.8)

NPV if equity financed = $45.9m

Step 5 – Discount value of tax shield on interest using pre-tax cost of debt

New capital introduced = $800m + transactions costs (2% of total amount raised)

$800m will be 98% of total amount raised, so total new capital = $\dfrac{\$800m}{0.98} = \$816.33m$

Interest rate = $LIBOR + 180 basis points = 5.40% + 1.8% = 7.2%

Annual interest = 7.2% of $816.33m = $58.78m

Annual tax saving = $17.63m (30% of $58.78m)

	20X9	20Y1	20Y2	20Y3	20Y4
	$m	$m	$m	$m	$m
Tax saving	17.63	17.63	17.63	17.63	17.63
Discount factor 7.2%	0.870	0.812	0.757	0.706	0.659

Total discount (annuity) factor for five years = 3.804

Present value of tax shield = $67.06m

Step 6 – Calculate APV

APV = NPV (equity financed) + present value of tax shield – cost of financing (transactions costs)

= $45.9m + $67.06m - $16.33m = **$96.63m**

Justification of use of the APV method

APV is justified in the appraisal of this investment as the **financial risk** of Neptune is likely to change as a result of the increased debt financing. The APV method separates the investment decision (NPV assuming equity finance) from the financing decision (PV of tax shields from debt interest). This will allow Neptune to evaluate the gain or loss associated with the costs and benefits of the new finance.

Of the gain in value if the project was to proceed, you will notice that a substantial part is due to the **present value of the tax shields**. This indicates that the **choice of debt finance** contributes a considerable amount to the increase in firm value. This information would not be available if only NPV was used. It would be **inappropriate** to use only NPV to appraise this project anyway, due to the change in financial risk.

(b) **Modified internal rate of return**

Use the formula provided in the formula sheet.

$$MIRR = (PV_R/PV_I)^{1/n}(1 + r_e) - 1$$

Where PV_R = present value of the return phase   n = number of years
PV_I = present value of capital invested r_e = reinvestment rate

$$MIRR = (845.9m/800m)^{1/6}(1 + 0.0897) - 1 = 9.98\%$$

Alternative solution

Calculate the terminal value of the cash flows received each year assuming a reinvestment rate of 8.97%.

	20X9 $m	20Y0 $m	20Y1 $m	20Y2 $m	20Y3 $m	20Y4 $m	Total $m
Cash flow	242	222	325.8	209.3	88.4	(34.9)	
Interest rate multiplier(W1)	1.537	1.410	1.294	1.187	1.0897	1.000	
Terminal value	371.95	313.02	421.59	248.44	96.33	(34.9)	1,416.43

Working

For example, the cash flow received at the end of 20X9 could be reinvested for five years at 8.97%. The interest rate multiplier would therefore be $(1.0897)^5 = 1.537$.

Total return = Terminal value/initial investment

= $1,416.43m/$800m = 1.771

$$MIRR = \sqrt[6]{(1.771)} - 1 = 9.98\%$$

(c) **Advantages of MIRR**

MIRR has the advantage over IRR that it assumes the **reinvestment rate** is the **company's cost of capital**. IRR assumes that the reinvestment rate is the IRR itself, which is usually untrue.

In many cases where there is conflict between the NPV and IRR methods, the MIRR will give the same indication as NPV, which is the **correct theoretical method**. This helps when explaining the appraisal of a project to managers, who often find the concept of rate of return easier to understand than that of net present value.

Disadvantages of MIRR

However, MIRR, like all rate of return methods, suffers from the problem that it may lead an investor to reject a project which has a **lower rate of return** but, because of its size, generates a **larger increase in wealth**.

In the same way, a **high-return** project with a **short life** may be preferred over a **lower-return** project with a longer life.

BPP LEARNING MEDIA

30 Airline Business

Text references. Chapter 7a for theories of capital structure, for credit spreads and the effects on cost of debt.

Top tips. The wording in part (a) suggests that you need to calculate a coupon rate – in fact the only calculation required is that of the yield of the four year government bond. You have to recognise the effects of incorrect estimations of the credit spread and explain these effects.

There is quite a bit of work involved in part (b) for 8 marks, compared with what is required for the same number of marks in part (c). The question does not give you the current value of debt therefore you will have to calculate that first before you can calculate the effect on this value. One of the more complex calculations (not the calculation itself but recognising what you have to do) is working out the percentage effect on current value.

Remember to answer the actual requirement in part (b) – it is easy to forget to determine the *increase* in the effective cost of debt capital.

Part (c) is not particularly difficult but is complicated by the confusing statement about the company's stated financial objectives, when in fact there are no objectives stated in the question. As mentioned above, there is not much to be done for 8 marks but make sure you relate your answer to the specific company in the scenario.

Easy marks. There are some relatively easy marks to be gained in part (c) regarding the advantages and disadvantages of debt. Part (d) is fairly straightforward, but ensure that you only discuss company specific factors.

Examiner's comments. Candidates with an understanding of the principles behind debt and the debt market gained high marks.

In part (a), very few candidates appreciated that the investors' required return would be the coupon rate on a new issue to ensure that it is fully subscribed at par.

In part (b) very few candidates managed to navigate a relatively simple set of calculations. The current gearing ratio and the market capitalisation of equity leads directly to an estimate of the current market value of debt and, given that the market yield is the current coupon, its par value. The alteration in the company's credit rating leads to a revised market value for this equity and at this point candidates had sufficient information to estimate the average cost of debt capital.

In part (c) few candidates appeared to have an understanding of ways in which large amounts of debt can be raised through a bond issue, leasing, syndicated borrowing or single source finance.

Marking scheme

			Marks
(a)	Advice on the appropriate coupon rate		4
(b)	Estimate of current value of debt	2	
	Estimate of market value of debt following new issue	3	
	Calculation of revised cost of debt capital	3	
			8
(c)	Relative advantages and disadvantages		
	Asset specificity and matching	2	
	Agency effects	2	
	Static trade-off arguments	2	
	Pecking order	2	
			8
(d)	One mark per explained factor	Max	5
			25

(a) The appropriate coupon rate for the new debt issue should be the same as the yield for the four year debt, which is calculated as follows:

Yield for 4 year debt   = risk free rate + credit spread

                            = 5.1% + 0.9% (0.9% is the 90 base point spread) = 6%

The investment bankers have suggested that at a spread of 90 base points will guarantee that the offer will be taken up by the institutional investors. If the spread was set too high, the debt would be issued at a premium; if it was too low then it would have to be issued at a discount as there would not be a full take-up.

(b) **Impact of new issue on the company's cost of debt and market valuation**

When new debt is issued this will increase the risk of the company, resulting in a reduction in the company's credit rate and/or an increase in the company's cost of debt.

Current amount of debt in issue

Using the company's current gearing ratio of 25%, we can calculate the current amount of debt in issue:

$$\text{Gearing} = \frac{\text{MV of debt}}{\text{MV of debt} + \text{MV of equity}}$$

$$0.25 = \frac{\text{MV of debt}}{1.2\text{bn} + \text{MV of debt}}$$

$0.25\ (1.2\text{bn} + \text{MV of debt}) = \text{MV of debt}$

$0.25 \times 1.2\text{bn} + 0.25\text{MV of debt} = \text{MV of debt}$

$0.3\text{bn} = 0.75\text{MV of debt}$

$\text{MV of debt} = 0.4\ \text{bn}$

Thus the current market value of debt in issue is $0.4 billion. This is actually the par value as well, given that the coupon rate of 4% and the market yield (3.5% + 50 basis points) are the same.

Effect of new debt on market value of current debt

As mentioned in part (a) above, the yield on the new debt will be 6% (5.1% + 90 basis points). If we assume that this new debt is issued at par at 6%, the market value of existing debt will be reduced by the reduction in credit rating and the increase in yield to 4.4% (that is, original yield of 4% + [90 – 50] basis points).

$$\text{Effect} = \frac{0.4}{1.044} + \frac{0.4}{1.044^2} + \frac{0.4}{1.044^3} = 110 \text{ basis points reduction}$$

This means that the new market value of current debt will be 98.9% (100 – 1.1%) of the current market value.

New market value = 98.9% of $400 million = $395.6 million

If the new debt of $400 million is – as expected – taken up at the par value then total market value of debt in issue will be:

$395.6 million + 400 million = $795.6 million

Effect of new debt on cost of debt capital

Using the yields calculated above (6% for new debt; 4.4% for existing debt), the revised cost of debt capital can be calculated on a weighted average basis, adjusted for the effect of tax:

$$\text{Cost of debt} = \left[\frac{400\,\text{million}}{(400\text{m} + 395.6\text{m})} \times 6\% + \frac{395.6\,\text{million}}{(400\text{m} + 395.6\text{m})} \times 4.4\% \right] \times (1 - 0.30)$$

$$= [3.02\% + 2.19\%] \times 0.7 = 3.64\%$$

Current cost of debt = 4% × (1 – 0.30) = 2.8%

The effect of the new debt issue on cost of debt is to increase it by 84 basis points (3.64% – 2.8%).

BPP
LEARNING MEDIA

What should be borne in mind is that part of this increase will be due to the longer term to maturity (4 years rather than 3 years).

(c) **Advantages and disadvantages of debt as a method of financing**

Relative lower cost of debt compared with equity

One of the advantages of debt is that, due to the tax shield on interest payments, it is a relatively cheaper form of financing than equity (whose dividends are paid out of earnings *after* tax). As such we would expect the higher level of gearing to lead to a fall in the weighted average cost of capital.

Appropriate to the industry and specific assets

The company is in the airline industry where debt tends to be a more appropriate method of finance, given that many of the assets can be sold when they are being replaced. In this case, the company is using debt to acquire new aircraft where a second-hand market does exist.

Signalling and agency effects

Companies tend to prefer debt to equity as a method of financing. This is mainly due to the tax shield offered by interest payments on debt. If the company increases its level of debt financing, the market could interpret this as meaning that management believe the company is undervalued. There is a significant agency effect arising from the legal obligation to make interest payments. Managers are less inclined to divert money towards financing their own incentives and perks if they know they have such legal obligations to meet.

Alteration of capital structure

One of the problems with debt financing is that it could be viewed as increasing the risk of the company to equity holders, given that there is a legal obligation to pay interest before dividends can be paid. As a result, investors may require a higher rate of return before they will be tempted to invest money in the company.

(d) **Management evaluation**

The rating agencies will look at the overall quality of management and succession planning, as well as performance from mergers and acquisitions and financial performance based on financial statements.

Financial gearing

The level of financial gearing will be considered; typically, companies with a low level of gearing will have a higher credit rating.

Position in the airline industry

The relative position of the company within the airline industry in terms of operating efficiency will be taken into account.

Accounting quality

There will be a general consideration of the accounting policies which could be used to manipulate profits (such as goodwill and depreciation) and whether there have been any qualifications to the audit report.

Earnings protection

Existing and projected measures such as return on capital and profit margins will be considered. Sources of future earnings growth will also be taken into account.

Cash flow adequacy

The relationship between cash flow and gearing and the ability to finance the cash needs of the business are important factors to be considered.

Financial flexibility

Financing needs will be evaluated, including alternatives in situations of financial stress. Agencies will also consider banking relationships and any restrictive debt covenants.

31 Fubuki

Text references. NPV is covered in Chapter 5 and APV in Chapter 7a.

Top tips. It is not immediately obvious that APV calculations are required – at this level of examination you are expected to recognise the potential impact of the method of financing. You will still gain marks for calculating the base case NPV but will fail to gain any of the marks available for the APV aspect of part (a).

Be careful which discount rate you use to calculate NPV – you should be making use of the information given on the company in a similar line of business to the new venture. When calculating the tax shield and subsidy effects for APV, make sure you state which rate you use as there are two rates that are feasible.

Part (b) demonstrates the importance of assumptions as you are required to explain any assumptions that you have made. Don't just state the assumptions you think require more explanation – make sure you list all the assumptions made, regardless of how obvious you think they might be.

Easy marks. There are easy marks to be gained in part (a) when calculating base case NPV.

Examiner's comments. The computational element of (a) was done well, but common errors occurred when calculating the working capital requirement (where many answers got the timing wrong) and when calculating the tax shield and value of the subsidy for the APV. Many candidates derived the cost of equity using geared and ungeared betas, whereas using the MM formula would have been less time consuming.

Answers that gained high marks in part (b) gave a detailed discussion of the method used and explanation of the assumptions made. Weaker answers tried to answer this part in brief note form and these did not gain many marks. Many answers did not discuss the link between APV and MM.

Marking scheme

		Marks	
(a)	Sales revenue, direct costs and additional fixed costs	4	
	Incremental working capital	1	
	Taxation	2	
	Estimation of k_e (ungeared)	2	
	Net cash flows, present value and base case NPV	2	
	Issue costs	1	
	Calculation of tax shield impact	2	
	Calculation of subsidy impact	1	
	Adjusted present value and conclusion	2	
			17
(b)	Discussion of using APV	2 – 3	
	Assumption about Haizum as proxy and MM proposition 2	3 – 4	
	Other assumptions	2 – 3	
		Max	8
			25

BPP
LEARNING MEDIA

Value of 5% fixed coupon bond

Year		
1	5×1.0385^{-1}	4.815
2	5×1.0446^{-2}	4.582
3	5×1.0507^{-3}	4.311
4	5×1.0580^{-4}	3.991
5	105×1.0612^{-5}	<u>78.019</u>
	Total value	<u>95.718</u>

This means that the bond would have to be issued at a discount if a 5% coupon was offered.

(ii) *New coupon rate for bond valued at $100 by the market*

As a 5% coupon means that the bond would have to be issued at a discount, a higher coupon must be offered. The coupon rate can be calculated by finding the yield to maturity of the 5% bond discounted at the yield curve given above. This will then be the coupon of the new bond to ensure the face value is $100.

$$\$5 \times (1 + YTM)^{-1} + \$5 \times (1 + YTM)^{-2} + \$5 \times (1 + YTM)^{-3} + \$5 \times (1 + YTM)^{-4} + \$5 \times (1 + YTM)^{-5}$$

$$= \$95.718$$

We solve this equation by trial and error – it doesn't have to work out exactly but we are looking for a coupon rate that will be close to $95.718.

If we try 6%, we obtain a result of $95.78 which is close enough to the target of $95.718.

This means that if the coupon payment is $6 per $100 (6%) the market value of the bond will be equal to the face value of $100.

$$\$6 \times 1.06^{-1} + \$6 \times 1.06^{-2} + \$6 \times 1.06^{-3} + \$6 \times 1.06^{-4} + \$6 \times 1.06^{-5} = \$100$$

Advice to directors

If a coupon of 5% was chosen then the bond would be issued at a discount of approximately 4.28%. Rather than having to issue 1.5 million $100 units in order to raise the required $150 million, the company would have to issue ($150 million/95.718) 1,567,103 $100 units. When the bonds come to be redeemed in five years' time, Levante will have to pay an additional $6,710,300 to redeem the extra 67,103 units.

However a higher coupon rate of 6% means that Levante will have to pay an additional $1,500,000 interest each year for the next five years.

The choice depends on whether the directors feel that that project's profit will be sufficient to cover the additional redemption charges in five years' time. If they are reasonably confident that profits will be sufficient then they should choose the lower coupon rate bond. If they wish to spread the cost rather than paying it in one lump sum then the higher coupon rate should be chosen.

(c) **Industry risk**

Industry risk refers to the strength of the industry within the country and how <u>resilient</u> it is to changes in the country's economy. Industry risk could be assessed using such factors as the impact of economic forces on **industry performance**, the **cyclical nature** of the industry (and the extent of the peaks and troughs) and the extent to which **industry demand** is affected by economic forces.

Earnings protection

Earnings protection refers to how well the industry will be able to protect its earnings in the wake of changes in the economy. This could be assessed using such factors as **diversity** of the customer base, sources of **future earnings growth** and **profit margins** and return on capital.

Financial flexibility

Financial flexibility refers to the ease with which companies can raise finance in order to pursue profitable investment opportunities. This could be assessed by **evaluating future financial needs**, the range of **alternative sources of finance** available, the company's **relationship with its bank** and any **debt covenants** that may restrict operations.

Evaluation of the company's management

This refers to how well management is managing the company and planning for its future. This could be assessed by looking at the company's **planning, controls, financing policies and strategies**; merger and acquisition performance and **record of achievement** in financial results; the **overall quality** of management and succession planning.

(d)   Here

$F = 1,050$

$\pi = (25 \times 12)/1,050 = 0.286$

$S = 0$

$L = 400/1,050 = 0.381$

$\text{Interest} = (250 \times 0.04) + (150 \times 0.05) = 17.5$

$C = 450/17.5 = 25.7$

$\sigma = 0.08$

$Y = 4.41 + (0.0014 \times 1,050) + (6.4 \times 0.286) - 0 - (2.72 \times 0.381) + (0.006 \times 25.7) - (0.53 \times 0.08)$

$Y = 4.41 + 1.47 + 1.830 - 1.036 + 0.154 - 0.042 = 6.79$

The Kaplan-Urwitz model predicts that the credit rating will be AAA.

33 Do-it-Yourself

Text references. Chapter 7a for WACC and Modigliani and Miller; Chapter 8 for International investment decisions and financing.

Top tips. The key to part (a) is recognising that the proposed finance will alter the gearing level, which will determine your approach to ungearing cost of activity and regearing to reflect new debt levels.

The report to the board should relate to the specific project rather than being just a general discussion about sources of finance.

Easy marks. Part (b) should allow you to pick up a number of marks on sources of finance and part (c) offers some marks for some straightforward observations about investing overseas.

BPP
LEARNING MEDIA

		Marks
(a)	Estimation of the current cost of debt capital at 4.324 per cent	3
	Calculation of the existing cost of equity capital at 7.48 per cent	2
	Ungearing and regearing cost of equity capital using M&M proposition 2	3
	Calculation of revised WACC and comment thereon	2
		10
(b)	Note of the theoretical issues in the selection of finance source (M&M, pecking order theory)	3
	Clear description of the potential sources of capital within the context of the Chinese economy, regulation and capital market	2
	Evaluation of the likely advantages and disadvantages of the principal sources of finance	2
	Discussion of the risk management strategies available	2
		9
(c)	One mark per well explained point	Max 6
		25

(a) Current Financing

Debt (3 year)

	%
Yield from yield curve[1]	3.80
Spread of AA – debt	0.40
Cost of debt k_d	4.20

[1] This yield has been estimated using the yield curve (note that the yield for 3 year debt is slightly above the line marked 3.7)

Finance structure	Current	Now
	$bn	$bn
Equity	3.0	3.0
Debt – 3 year	0.5	0.5
– 10 year	–	0.3
	3.5	3.8

WACC and cost of equity

Current WACC = 6.8%

$$\text{WACC} = \frac{E}{V} \times k_e + \frac{D}{V} \times k_d(1-T)$$

$$6.8 = \frac{3.0}{3.5} \times k_e + \frac{0.5}{3.5} \times 4.2 \times 0.7$$

$$6.8 = \frac{3.0}{3.5} \times k_e + 0.42$$

$$6.38 = \frac{3.0}{3.5} \times k_e$$

$$k_e = 6.38 \times \frac{3.5}{3.0} = 7.443\%$$

Ungeared cost of equity

Since the proposed finance will alter the gearing level, the approach is to:

- Ungear from the current level to get the ungeared cost of equity.

- Re-gear to the new debt level.

Now using Modigliani and Miller we have:

$$k_e = k_u + (k_u - k_d) \times \frac{D}{E} \times (1 - T)$$

$$k_e = k_u + k_u \frac{D}{E}(1 - T) - k_d \frac{D}{E}(1 - T)$$

$$k_e = k_d \frac{D}{E}(1 - T) = k_u \left(1 + \frac{D}{E}(1 - T)\right)$$

And so

$$7.443 + 4.20 \times \frac{0.5}{3.0} \times (1 - 0.30) = \left(k_u \left(1 + \frac{0.5}{3.0} \times (1 - 0.30)\right)\right)$$

$$7.933 = 1.1167 \, k_u$$

$$k_u = \frac{7.933}{1.1167} = 7.104\%$$

New cost of debt

Following the new issue there is a 60% chance the credit rating will fall to A+ and a 40% chance it will fall to A. For the 3 and 10 year bands we have:

		3 year	10 year
Spread	– A+	0.440	0.700
	– A	0.750	1.070
	– 60:40 ⟶	0.564	0.848
Yield from yield curve		3.800	4.200
Yield		4.364	5.048

Term	Value $m	Cost %	Weight	Weighted %
3 years	0.5	4.364	⅝	2.7275
10 years	0.3	5.048	⅜	1.8930
	0.8			4.6205

Re-gearing

$$k_e = k_u + (k_u - k_d) \frac{D}{E}(1 - T)$$

$$k_e = 7.104 + (7.104 - 4.6205) \times \frac{0.8}{3.0} \times 0.7 = 7.5676$$

New WACC

$$\text{WACC} = 7.5676 \times \frac{3.0}{3.8} + 4.6205 \times \frac{0.8}{3.8} \times 0.7 = 6.655\%$$

Alternative approach

An acceptable alternative approach is to regear k_e, assuming an unchanged k_d, which is the approach taken by the ACCA examiner. This is a quicker, though less accurate, approach and would be suitable under exam conditions.

BPP LEARNING MEDIA

(b)   **Briefing note on alternative sources of finance**

The choice of finance is partly down to the cost and availability of various sources and partly down to the method the company chooses to hedge its FOREX exposure.

Ignoring foreign exchange considerations, the weighted average cost of capital suggest that the firm should **increase its gearing** to capture further tax shield effects which are not currently being offset by increased default risk. Thus debt finance should be preferred to equity finance. Raising $300 million of debt by bond issue is at the low end of the scale for a new debt issue of this type, although it may be possible to arrange a syndicated issue. The **issue costs** in terms of commission and underwriting fees are likely to be high. If finance is raised on the US market it will be necessary to consider **entering into a swap arrangement** to hedge against the currency risk for the ten year term. Finding a swap of this type would require the services of a financial institution specialising in such transactions.

Alternatively, it may be possible to **raise finance directly in China**. This has the benefit that this would eliminate the need to consider methods of hedging against currency risk. However, as with any emerging market, there are **risks** associated with inward investment and capital entry. These risks may be sufficient to raise the overall risk assessment and as a result the advantages of increased gearing mentioned above may not be realised in practice. In addition, given that Do-it-yourself is a US based company the **cost of debt finance is likely to be higher** than if it was raised in the US. The issue costs associated with a Chinese bond issue are likely to be as high as those for the US market.

A third source available would be to **take out a loan in China** to finance the project. Once again, this would avoid the need to consider entering into any hedging arrangements to reduce foreign exchange risks. However, given the lack of business history and performance in China the company is likely to be charged a **premium** for the debt finance. In addition, the lending institution may also insist upon a **guarantee** from the US company. The last two sources have the advantage of **matching** the borrowing and income flows and hence eliminating foreign currency exposure risk. Any appreciation in the Chinese currency, however, would increase the dollar value of the translated debt in the firm's statement of financial position. If the borrowing is used to purchase matching assets in China then the **translation risk** is mitigated along with the **transaction risk**.

Final source of debt finance is on the **sale and leaseback of assets**. This could be either by the sale and leaseback of existing assets in the US or by the sale and leaseback of new assets purchased for the operation in China. If the assets are not owned but leased or rented then **translation effects** will impact upon the statement of financial performance and may be misread by the market. There are reporting implications for reporting under FASB 13 depending upon whether the leases are financing or operating leases.

Other sources of finance would be to raise equity capital by a **rights or new issue**. This would have the effect of increasing the weighted average cost of capital and would not provide any additional benefits of the tax shield. Finally, the finance can be raised by reducing the dividend payment policy and thereby using retained cash to finance part of the project. The change in the dividend policy is **unlikely to be viewed favourably** and could cause problems in the future.

(c)   **Key financial factors**

Increase in shareholder wealth. The main factor to consider is whether the investment will increase shareholder wealth. Investment appraisal methods can be carried out to determine this.

Foreign exchange risks. Any movement in exchange rates will have an impact on future cash flows. DIY may have to consider hedging against any foreign exchange risks that result from investing overseas, in China.

Political and country risks. DIY should investigate any potential political issues it may encounter when investing in China. There may be pressure from the government to keep any profits in China, by use of withholding taxes which could have an effect on the attractiveness of this project.

Country risks. In addition, DIY will have to consider the challenges in finding suitable staff who speak Chinese. There may be an issue of quality control if local staff do not fully appreciate the levels at which services should be delivered.

Shareholders' attitudes towards risk. Current shareholders may be averse to investing in China, depending on the mix of shareholders in the organisation.

Tax implications. DIY should investigate whether there is a tax treaty in place with China that will protect its earnings from being taxed twice.

34 AWP Co

Text references. Duration and theories of capital structure are both covered in Chapter 7a.

Top tips. This question covers some parts of the syllabus that students typically struggle with.

In part (a) (i) you need to calculate the yield to maturity to get the discount rate for the duration calculation. Don't forget to adjust the spot rate with the AA credit spread. Part (a) (ii) requires you to know the general features of duration and to comment on the results you have found.

Easy marks. Part (b) offers some relatively straightforward discussion marks as long as you have covered these topics.

(a) (i) **Issue price**

The spot yield curve should be used to calculate a likely issue price. This government bond yield curve needs to be adjusted by the credit spread for an AA rated company.

	1 year	2 year	3 year	4 year
Gov't bond annual spot yield curve	3.30	3.80	4.50	5.30
AA rated spread	0.27	0.40	0.51	0.60
	3.57	4.20	5.01	5.90

Each of the bonds can be separated into separate bonds

Option 1

	1 year	2 year	3 year	4 year
Bond 1	5			
Bond 2		5		
Bond 3			5	
Bond 4				105

Option 2

	1 year	2 year	3 year
Bond 1	4		
Bond 2		4	
Bond 3			109

The present values of these payments (using the yield curve calculated above will be the likely issue price.

Option 1

Issue price = $(5 \times \frac{1}{1.0357}) + (5 \times \frac{1}{1.0420^2}) + (5 \times \frac{1}{1.0501^3}) + (105 \times \frac{1}{1.0590^4}) = \$97.24$

Option 2

Issue price = $(4 \times \frac{1}{1.0357}) + (4 \times \frac{1}{1.0420^2}) + (109 \times \frac{1}{1.0501^3}) = \$101.68$

Yield to maturity (YTM)

The yield to maturity for each bond can be calculated as follows

BPP LEARNING MEDIA

Option 1

Year	Cash flow	DF 5%	PV	DF 6%	PV
0	(97.24)	1.000	(97.24)	1.000	(97.24)
1 - 4	5	3.546	17.73	3.465	17.33
4	100	0.823	82.30	0.792	79.20
			2.79		(0.71)

For option1 the YTM is $5 + \left[\left(\dfrac{2.79}{2.79 + 0.71}\right)(6 - 5)\right] = 5.80$

Option 2

Year	Cash flow	DF 4%	PV	DF 5%	PV
0	(101.68)	1.000	(101.68)	1.000	(101.68)
1 - 3	4	2.775	11.10	2.723	10.89
3	105	0.889	93.35	0.864	90.72
			2.77		(0.07)

For option 2 the YTM is $4 + \left[\left(\dfrac{2.77}{2.77 + 0.07}\right)(5 - 4)\right] = 4.98$

Duration

Option 1

	Year 1	Year 2	Year 3	Year 4	
Cashflows	5	5	5	105	
Discount factor (5.80%)	0.945	0.893	0.844	0.798	
Present value	4.725	4.465	4.220	83.790	97.20
Duration weighting	1	2	3	4	
Weighted total	4.725	8.93	12.66	335.16	361.475

Duration = 361.475/97.24 = 3.72 years

Option 2

	Year 1	Year 2	Year 3	
Cashflows	4	4	109	
Discount factor (4.98%)	0.953	0.907	0.864	
Present value	3.812	3.628	94.176	101.616
Duration weighting	1	2	3	
Duration	3.812	7.256	282.528	293.596

Duration = 293.596/101.68 = 2.89 years

(ii) Duration gives each bond an overall risk weighting which allows bonds of different maturities and coupon rates to be directly compared. Duration is a composite measure of risk expressed in terms of years. In general terms longer-dated bonds will have longer durations and lower-coupon bonds will have longer durations. A bond that is redeemed at a premium will also have a longer duration to one redeemed at par or even at a discount.

The first of these general points is shown by the calculations in part (a) (i) where the longer-dated bond has the longer duration. The points about lower coupons and bonds redeemed at a premium is also shown as the duration of option 2 is only marginally less than the three-year length of the bond. This is because the vast majority of the returns are in the redemption payment received in year 3.

(b) The Chief Executive understands that the use of debt financing can increase the value of a company due to the tax relief available on the debt. This comes from Modigliani and Miller's theory which assumes that debt is risk-free.

However, an increase in debt financing will also result in an **increase in the chance of bankruptcy** because of the increased commitment in interest payments. Failure to meet those interest payments because of inadequate cash on hand will cause the firm some financial distress, and the ultimate form of financial distress is bankruptcy.

As a result of these **increased distress costs** the gearing-adjusted value of the firm should be decreased. The value of the company in this case will be: Value of the ungeared company + (tax rate × interest payments) – present value of the bankruptcy costs.

Starting from the empirical observation that firms in AWP Co's industry **do not have 100 percent gearing ratios**, it is plausible that a firm's WACC will start to increase and its value will start to decrease after a certain value of the gearing ratio, to reflect the increasing costs of gearing.

The conclusion is that a company should gear up to take advantage of any tax benefits available, but only to the extent that the **marginal benefits exceed** the **marginal costs** of **financial distress**. After this point, the market value of the firm will start to fall and its WACC will start to rise. This is known as the **static trade-off theory** of capital structure. In this scenario it may well be that the optimum point is around the average industry gearing ratio.

Agency theory provides a rationale for an optimal structure based on the existence of agency costs associated with the issue of debt and equity. There are agency problems in directors trying to reconcile the interests of debtholders and equityholders as well as potentially trying to reconcile the interests of new and old shareholders following an issue of equity. Agency theory states that the optimal capital structure of the company will be formed at the particular level of debt and equity where the benefits of the debt that can be received by the shareholders equal the costs of debt imposed by the debt holders. It could be argued that, given AWP Co's relatively low level of gearing, it has not reached this optimum point.

Pecking order theory states that the preferred order for sources of finance is initially retained earnings, then debt and lastly equity. It is this order that the Chief Executive appears to want AWP Co to move towards, although in the past it seems likely that equity was preferred to debt.

35 Preparation question – Somax

Text references. Chapter 7 on manipulating betas.

Top tips. (a) is a typical ungearing and gearing beta calculation.

(a)   **Use of WACC**

The discount rate that should be used is the **weighted average cost of capital (WACC)**, with weightings based on market values. The cost of capital should take into account the **systematic risk** of the new investment, and therefore it will not be appropriate to use Somax's existing equity beta. Instead, the estimated equity beta of the main Swiss competitor in the same industry as the new proposed plant will be ungeared, and then the capital structure of Somax applied to find the WACC to be used for the discount rate.

Ungearing of Swiss beta

Since the systematic risk of debt can be assumed to be zero, the Swiss equity beta can be **ungeared** using the following expression.

$$\beta_a = \beta_e \left(\frac{V_e}{V_e + V_d(1-T)} \right)$$

where: β_a = asset beta
β_e = equity beta
V_e = value/proportion of equity in capital structure
V_d = value/proportion of debt in capital structure
T = tax rate

For the Swiss company:

$$\beta_a = 1.5 \times \frac{60}{60 + 40(1 - 0.33)} = 1.037$$

BPP
LEARNING MEDIA

We will now **calculate the debt and equity of Somax** based on market values.

		£m
Equity:	2 × 225m = 450m shares at 376p	1,692.00
Debt:	Bank loans	135.00
	Bonds (75m × 1.195)	89.63
	Total debt	224.63

Total market value = £1,692m + £224.63m = £1,916.63m

The beta can now be regeared to reflect Somax's capital structure

$$\beta_e = \beta_a \left(\frac{V_e + V_d(1 - T)}{V_e} \right)$$

β_e = 1.037 x [((1,692 + [224.63 x 0.67])/1,692] = 1.129

This can now be **substituted** into the **capital asset pricing model (CAPM)** to find the cost of equity.

$k_e = r_f + [E(r_m) - r_f] \beta_a$

where: k_e = cost of equity

        r_f = risk free rate of return

      $E(r_m)$ = market rate of return

k_e = 7.75% + (14.5% − 7.75%) × 1.129 = 15.37%

The next step is to calculate the cost of the fixed rate bonds.

Year		Cash flows $	Discount factor 10 %	Discounted cash flow $	Discount factor 4%	Discounted cash flow $
0	Market value	(119.50)	1.000	(121.00)	1.000	(119.50)
1–5	Interest	14.00	3.791	53.07	4.452	62.33
5	Redemption	100.00	0.621	62.10	0.822	82.20
				(5.83)		25.03

k_d = 4 + [25.03/(25.03 + 5.83) x (10 − 4)] = 8.87%

Weightings of debt and equity in capital structure

Equity	(1,692/1,916.63) = 88.3%
Bank loans	(135.00/1,916.63) = 7.0%
Bonds	(89.63/1,916.63) = 4.7%

$$WACC = \left[\frac{V_e}{V_e + V_d} \right] k_e + \left[\frac{V_d}{V_e + V_d} \right] k_d(1 - T)$$

WACC = [(1,692/1,916.63) x 15.37] + [(135/1,916.63) x 3] + [(89.63/1,916.63) x 8.87(1 − 0.33)] = 14.06%

36 Pondhills

Text references. Chapters 4, 8.

Top tips. An illustration that questions about the risks of international exposure can cover risks other than transaction risks, although translation risk should only be a problem if stock markets are not very efficient. Remember that translation and transaction risks are different, and transaction risk is part of the wider category of economic risk.

Translation risk will only be a problem if market efficiency is limited and investors don't understand the impact on the accounts. Note that the main economic risks involve long-term factors and hence have consequences for strategic decisions.

The most important aspect of (a) is identifying which assets and liabilities are exposed. If you worked on the principle that all assets and liabilities were exposed unless question details indicated otherwise (receipts or payments in dollars or sterling) you should have gained the necessary marks. The shareholders' equity is the balancing figure.

Easy marks. Part (b) should be straightforward as this has also been covered in F9 Financial management.

(a)   (i)

	Dinars m	Exposed	$'000 at current rate	$'000 if dinar devalues
Non-current assets	510	Yes	2,071	1,801
Current assets				
Cash	86	Yes	349	304
Receivables	410	No	1,665	1,665
Inventory	380	Yes	1,543	1,342
	876		3,557	3,311
Short-term payables	(296)	50%	(1,202)	(1,123)
Long-term loan stock	(500)	Yes	(2,030)	(1,766)
	590		2,396	2,223
Shareholders' equity	590	Residual	2,396	2,223

Rate if dinar devalues = 246.3 × 1.15 = 283.2

Statement of financial position exposure = 510 + 86 + 380 – 148 – 500 = 328mm dinars

Expected loss on translation = 2,396 – 2,223 = $173,000

Alternative working

Loss = 328 × (1/283.2 – 1/246.3 = $174,000 difference due to rounding

(ii)

	Dinars m	Exposed	$'000 at current rate	$'000 if dinar devalues
Revenue	2,300	No	9,338	9,338
Cost of goods sold and operating expenses				
Dinars (2,300 × 60% × 70%)	966	Yes	3,922	3,411
Overseas (2,300 × 40% × 70%)	644	No	2,615	2,615
Interest (500 × 12%)	60	Yes	244	212
Net cash inflows	630		2,557	3,100

Gain in cash flow = 3,100 – 2,557 = $543,000

BPP
LEARNING MEDIA

(b) **Translation exposure**

There should in theory be no need to hedge against the translation exposure in (b) (i) as it does not represent actual cash flows. Hedging might be undertaken if markets are **not efficient,** and transaction exposure has a detrimental effect on share price.

Economic exposure

(b) (ii) demonstrates that Pondhills is expected to make a gain based on the current predictions of exchange rates. However Pondhills should consider the **likelihood** of the dinar strengthening against the US dollar. Pondhills might also **settle hard currency cash liabilities** by **reducing dinar cash holdings** before devaluation.

(c) **Examples of long-term consequences**

  (i) **Effect on production factor prices**

  A devaluation of the exchange rate might be accompanied by an **increase in inflation,** increasing the cost of sales of Ponda.

  (ii) **Effect on sales in Africa**

  The devaluation should give Ponda scope to reduce its prices without decreasing its overall sales revenues. The extent to which Ponda can do this will depend on its **elasticity of demand.**

  (iii) **Pricing**

  Pondhills may use the devaluation to consider its overall pricing strategy, to decide whether **different prices** should be **charged** in **different markets**.

37 Ennea Co

Text references. Chapter 1 for the role and responsibilities of management; chapter 7a for sources of finance; chapter 19 for securitisation.

Top tips. In part (a) it is important to include the discussion as well as the forecast statements of financial position and ratios. Don't just state what has happened, but also what this means for Ennea Co to get more marks.

Remember to relate the answer in part (b) to the scenario and the relatively small amount of finance makes a securitisation less likely to be appropriate.

Easy marks. There are some easy marks to be gained in part (a) in the forecasts under each of the three different proposals.

Examiner's comments. Part (a) revolved around the impact of changes in financing of a company and how the impact of changing financial structure affected the financial position, earnings per share and the gearing of the company.

The answers to this part tended to be varied. Candidates, who presented the changed financial position and calculated the changes in earnings for each proposal, which were then incorporated into the calculations of EPS and gearing, gained the majority of marks. However, overall this part of the question was not done well.

Many responses tended to discuss or try to explain the changes and therefore gained fewer marks. Many responses did not consider the impact on interest of increased or reduced debt financing, and therefore did not incorporate the impact into the profit after tax and the financial position. In a notable minority of responses, candidates did not calculate the EPS and gearing correctly. Such responses gained few marks.

Part (b), tested what securitisation was and the key barriers to Ennea Co undertaking the process. This part was done poorly by most candidates. Few responses gave an adequate explanation of the securitisation process, often confusing it with what leasing was and/or assuming securitisation meant providing asset security or collateral for a loan. Very few responses considered the barriers to Ennea Co in any detail.

		Marks
(a)	Financial position calculations: proposal 1	3
	Financial position calculations: proposal 2	2
	Financial position calculations: proposal 3	3
	Adjustments to forecast earnings	
	Interest payable on additional borrowing and higher coupon	2
	Interest saved on lower borrowing and lower coupon	1
	Return on additional investment	1
	Return lost on less investment and profit on sale of non-current assets	1
	Gearing and EPS calculations	2
	Discussion of the results of the proposals	2 – 3
	Discussion of the implications (eg risk, market reaction, etc)	2 – 3
		Max 20
(b)	Explanation of the process	2 – 3
	Key barriers in undertaking the process	2 – 3
		Max 5
		25

(a) **Forecast financial position**

Amounts in $'000	Current	Proposal 1	Proposal 2	Proposal 3
Non-current assets	282,000	282,000	302,000	257,000
Current assets	66,000	64,720	67,720	63,682
Total assets	348,000	346,720	369,720	320,682
Current liabilities	37,000	37,000	37,000	37,000
Non-current liabilities	140,000	160,000	160,000	113,000
Total liabilities	177,000	197,000	197,000	150,000
Share capital (40c per share)	48,000	45,500	48,000	48,000
Retained earnings	123,000	104,220	124,720	122,682
Total equity	171,000	149,720	172,720	170,682
Total equity and capital	348,000	346,720	369,720	320,682

Amounts in $'000	Current	Proposal 1	Proposal 2	Proposal 3
Initial profit after tax	26,000	26,000	26,000	26,000
Interest payable on additional borrowing ($20m × 6% × (1 – 0.2))		(960)	(960)	
Additional interest payable ($160m × 0.25% × (1 – 0.2))		(320)	(320)	
Interest saved on reduced borrowing ($27m × 6% × (1 – 0.2))				1,296
Interest saved on lower coupon ($113m × 0.15% × (1 – 0.2))				136
Return on additional investment ($20m × 15%)			3,000	
Return lost on reduced investment ($25m × 15%)				(3,750)
Profit on sale of non-current assets				2,000
Total assets	26,000	24,720	27,720	25,682

BPP
LEARNING MEDIA

	Current	Proposal 1	Proposal 2	Proposal 3
Gearing (non-current liabilities / non-current liabilities + equity)	40.2%	46.1%	43.3%	35.2%
Number of shares ('000)	120,000	113,750	120,000	120,000
Adjusted earnings per share	21.67c	21.73c	23.10c	21.40c

Note: Other calculations of gearing would be acceptable

Tutorial note: These explanations are not required for the answer, but are presented here to aid understanding

Explanations of figures above

Proposal 1

Non-current liabilities are increased by $20m from the additional debt and capital is reduced by the same amount. The split between share capital and retained earnings is $20m × 40c/320c = $2.5 million to share capital and the balance of $17.5 million to retained earnings.

The additional interest payable of $1.28 million is taken off retained earnings due to the reduction in profit after tax and also deducted from cash as it is assumed to be paid in cash. It would be acceptable to include as a current liability if it was assumed to be unpaid.

Proposal 2

Non-current liabilities and non-current assets are increased by $20m from the additional debt and purchase of assets. Additional interest is payable as for Proposal 1 and the new investment will generate an additional return of 15% which is $3 million in income. The net impact is income of $1.72 million, which is added to retained earnings and to current assets as it either represents cash or a receivable.

Proposal 3

Non-current assets are reduced by the net value at disposal ($25 million) and the proceeds of $27 million are used to reduce non-current liabilities. The profit of $2 million is added to retained earnings.

The reduction of investment in non-current assets means there will be a lower return on investment of 15% of the $25 million. However, interest will be saved on the non-current liabilities which will be paid off. The net impact is a loss of $2.318 million which is subtracted from retained earnings and deducted from current assets as a cash expense. Again it would be acceptable to include as a current liability if it was assumed to be unpaid.

Discussion

Proposal 1 would lead to a small increase in earnings per share, due to the reduction in the number of shares since earnings fall by about 5% because of the higher interest payments from the additional debt. However gearing significantly increases by approximately 6%.

Under proposal 3 earnings per share will fall, although total earnings will be higher than under Proposal 1. Total earnings fall because the interest saved and the profit on disposal are less than the loss of the return on the non-current asset investment. Gearing would also reduce significantly, by 5%.

Proposal 2 significantly increases EPS, which the other proposals do not. This is due to the return on the additional non-current asset investment. However, gearing will also increase by just over 3%, although this is less than under Proposal 1.

Proposal 1 is the least attractive. The choice between Proposals 2 and 3 will depend on whether the Board of Ennea Co would prefer a higher EPS figure or a lower level of financial gearing. This may depend on industry averages for both of these figures, how the stock market would react to the proposals and the implications of the proposals on changes to the risk profile of the company and whether this would change the overall cost of capital. It should also be noted that the above forecasts and estimates and actual results may well differ from those stated.

(b)   Asset securitisation for Ennea Co would involve converting the future lease income, from the non-current asset leases, into assets and **selling these assets as bonds** now. The future income is then used to pay the coupons on the bonds. In effect Ennea Co foregoes the interest payments on the leases in favour of the bond sale proceeds.

The lease income would be aggregated and pooled and new bonds would be created based on these. The pooled assets are divided into **tranches** and the tranches are **credit rated**. The higher rated tranches would carry less risk and also have a lower return than tranches with a lower rating. If default occurs, the income of the lower tranches gets reduced first and any subsequent defaults is applied to the lowest tranche with any income left. This process means an asset with a low level of liquidity can be transformed into a security with high liquidity.

There are a number of barriers to undertaking a securitisation process. It is **very expensive** due to management costs, legal fees and ongoing administration and compliance costs. Ennea Co is looking at selling a relatively small amount of non-current assets and therefore the costs would be a significant proportion of the potential income. This high cost means that securitisation is **not feasible for a small asset pool**.

It is usual to not offer the full value of the asset in the form of securities, but to leave say 10% of the asset value as a buffer against default and converting the other 90% into securities. The method of credit enhancement would give the tranches a **higher credit rating** and therefore **improve their marketability**. However, if Ennea Co was to use this method they would not be able to take advantage of the full value of the assets.

38 Mercury Training

Text references. Cost of equity and WACC are covered in Chapter 2. Valuation of shares is covered in Chapter 10. Financing methods are discussed in Chapter 2.

Top tips. In part (a), the asset beta of Mercury is calculated using the revenue weightings from Jupiter and the Financial Services sector. This is quite a tough section for 8 marks and it is important to show all your workings to ensure you gain as many marks as possible.

Part (b) requires the use of the dividend valuation model to calculate share price at the higher end of the range of possible prices. There are three possible growth rates that could be used. You should recognise that the historic earnings growth rate actually exceeds the cost of equity capital and therefore cannot be sustained in the long run. As you are calculating the higher end of the range, use the higher of the other two possible growth rates.

Part (c) requires knowledge of the advantages and disadvantages of public listings and private equity finance. Remember to make it relevant to the scenario.

Easy marks. The discussion in part (c) is more straightforward than some of the calculations. However it can be seen from the examiner's comments below that the easiest way of losing marks is not to read/answer the question set.

Examiner's comments. Candidates were invited to combine market risk measures for the two aspects of Mercury Training. Another company is publicly quoted and has a beta that matches two thirds of the business of Mercury Training. The remainder of its business has a beta matching that of the financial services sector. Using the portfolio beta concept, a combined beta can be estimated. Given the different levels of gearing involved, candidates faced the common problem of ungearing the risk measures for the proxies to create an asset beta. They must then be combined and geared again to match the business profile of Mercury Training. Tax also complicated matters as this affected both the cost of debt and its weighting in the calculation of the respective asset betas.

A substantial majority of candidates understood what the question required and made a good attempt at answering it. Similarly in part (b) many candidates attempted to calculate a likely issue price but did not 'advise' the owners of Mercury Training on the range that might be negotiable in the event of an issue or sale of the business. The overall lesson for candidates here is to focus carefully on the verbs expressing what is required in each part of the question and to construct their answers in a way that clearly focuses on the requirements of the question.

Common problems or issues in candidates' answers were:

(a)   Ignoring tax in the estimation of asset betas.
(b)   Failing to recognise the application of the portfolio beta concept in creating a proxy estimate for the company.

(c)   Using long term growth estimates that were in excess of the equilibrium rate of equity return generated by the CAPM and therefore unsustainable.

(b)   Lack of understanding of the advantages and disadvantages of private equity finance.

Marking scheme

		Marks	
(a)	Calculation of tax adjusted gearing for Jupiter and the FS sector	2	
	Calculation of the proxy asset beta for Mercury and its estimated equity beta	4	
	Estimation of Mercury's equity cost of capital and WACC	2	
			8
(b)	Lowest rate set at liquidated value of the business	2	
	Calculation of reinvestment rate and growth	3	
	Estimation of upper boundary price per share	3	
	Identification of control premium	2	
			10
(c)	Advantages and disadvantages of listing (regulatory, takeover, process)	4	
	Nature of private equity finance and its advantages and disadvantages	4	
		Max	7
			25

(a) ## Step 1

Ungear beta of Jupiter and Financial Services sector

$$\beta_a = \beta_g \frac{V_e}{V_e + V_d (1-T)}$$

Jupiter $= 1.5 \times \dfrac{88}{88 + (12 \times 0.6)} = 1.3865$

FS sector $= 0.9 \times \dfrac{75}{75 + (25 \times 0.6)} = 0.75$

Step 2

Calculate average asset beta for Mercury

$\beta_a = (0.67 \times 1.3865) + (0.33 \times 0.75) = 1.175$

Step 3

Regear Mercury's beta

$$\beta_a \quad = \beta_e \times \frac{V_e}{V_e + V_d(1-T)}$$

$$1.175 \quad = \beta_e \times \frac{70}{70 + 30(1-0.4)}$$

$1.175 \quad = \beta_e \times 0.795$

$\beta_e \quad = 1.48$

Step 4

Calculate cost of equity capital and WACC

Using CAPM:

Cost of equity capital $= R_f + \beta_i(E(r_m) - R_f) = 4.5 + 1.48 \times 3.5 = 9.68\%$

WACC $= \left[\dfrac{V_e}{V_e + V_d} \right] k_e + \left[\dfrac{V_d}{V_e + V_d} \right] k_d (1 - T)$

$= (0.7 \times 0.0968) + (0.3 \times [0.045 + 0.025]) \times 0.6$

$= 8.04\%$

Where k_d = risk free rate (4.5%) + premium on risk free rate (2.5%)

When to use cost of equity and WACC

Cost of equity is the rate of return required by the company's ordinary shareholders. The return includes **a risk free rate** (to reflect that investors are rational) and a **risk premium** (to reflect that investors are risk averse). Cost of equity is used to value income streams to the **shareholders** (that is, dividends).

WACC is the average cost of capital of the business and is based the company's **level of gearing**. WACC is used to value income streams to the **business as a whole** ie free cash flow (for example, it is used as the **discount rate** to appraise potential investments).

(b) **Range of likely issue prices**

Lower range of issue price will be the net assets at fair value divided by the number of shares

= $65 million /10 million shares
= $6.50 per share

Upper range – use **dividend valuation model**

Three possible earnings rates:

(i) **Historical earnings growth rate** of 12% is greater than the cost of equity capital, therefore cannot be sustained in the long run

(ii) The **weighted anticipated growth rate** of the two business sectors in which Mercury operates (0.67 × 6% + 0.33 × 4% = 5.34%)

(iii) **The rate implied from the firm's reinvestment** (9.68% – see part (a) step 4 above)

$g = br_e = \dfrac{(100 - 25)}{100} \times 0.0968 = 7.26\%$

The higher of the two feasible rates – that is, 7.26% - should be used to calculate the higher issue price.

$P_0 = \dfrac{d_0(1+g)}{(k_e - g)}$

$P_0 = \dfrac{25(1 + 0.0726)}{(0.0968 - 0.0726)} = \$11.08$ per share

If the company was floated, the higher price above (which is based on a minority shareholding earning a dividend from the shares) could be achieved. This implies that a portion of the equity and **effective control** are retained. **Private equity investors** are likely to be willing to pay a premium for the benefits of control (**control premium**) – often as much as 30 – 50% of the share price. In this case negotiations may start at a share price of $16.62 ($11.08 × 1.5).

(c) To: Directors of Mercury Training
   From: Treasury department
   Subject: Public listing versus private equity finance

As you are currently considering either a flotation or an outright sale of Mercury Training, I would like to outline the relative advantages and disadvantages of a public listing versus private equity finance.

BPP
LEARNING MEDIA

Public listing

This is the traditional method of raising finance by firms who have reached a certain size. Where a public listing is sought, owners will be looking to **release their equity stake** in the firm (either partially or in total). A public listing gives the company access to **a wider pool of finance** and makes it easier to grow by acquisition. As owners, you will be able to release your holding and use the money to fund other projects.

However, public listings lead to the company being subject to **increased scrutiny, accountability and regulation.** There are greater **legal requirements** and the company will also be required to adhere to the **rules of the stock exchange**.

Obtaining a public listing is **expensive** – for example brokerage commission and underwriting fees.

New investors may have **more exacting requirements** and different ideas of how the business should progress. This may put additional strain on the directors responsible for the company's overall strategy.

Private equity

Private equity finance is raised via **venture capital companies** or private equity businesses. There are **fewer regulatory restrictions** attached to private equity finance than there are to public listings. The cost of accessing private equity finance is lower and in certain jurisdictions there are **favourable tax advantages** to private equity investors.

Directors of a company seeking private equity finance must realise however that the financial institution will require an **equity stake** in the company. The directors responsible for the overall company strategy will still be subject to **considerable scrutiny** as the finance providers may want to have a **representative** appointed to the company's board to look after their interests. They may even require the appointment of an **independent director**.

Private equity providers will need to be convinced that the company can **continue its business operations successfully**, otherwise there will be no incentive to invest.

I hope this information is useful but please contact me if you wish to discuss further.

39 Saturn Systems

Text references. Ethics are covered in Chapter 3b. Regulations relating to takeovers are covered in Chapter 11.

Top tips. This is a relatively straightforward question if you can identify the issues involved.

Requirement (b) is divided neatly into three types of issues so deal with each type under a separate heading to make it easy for the marker to identify your points.

The solution given relates to the UK City Code but you can refer to your own country's codes instead and still gain the available marks.

Make sure you relate your answer to the specific scenario and do not just write everything you know about takeover and acquisition regulations.

Easy marks. Part (a) is a fairly straightforward discussion. Also it should have been easy to identify that the financial risk of Saturn could change if more debt was introduced into the capital structure to fund the acquisition of Pluto.

Examiner's comments. Under most jurisdictions, what was said could be taken as notice of intention to bid, whereas the company had neither estimated the value nor undertaken a due diligence study of the potential target.

The many good answers to this question recognised the significance of the CEO's remarks and the weak position of the company both in terms of its state of preparation for an announcement and the regulatory implications of the remarks. A small minority of candidates did not recognise that there was a problem with the CEO's comments and spent considerable space discussing ways in which the bid might be defended.

Overall many candidates performed well on this question, providing well written and well argued answers. More attention to the wider implications, and particularly those relating to the ethical issues concerning the transparency and availability of price sensitive information, would have earned more marks.

Marking scheme

			Marks
(a)	Per explained point	1 – 2	
			Max 5
(b)	Identification of the problems created by Mr Moon's remarks	3	
	Significance of the price reaction	3	
	The firm's current position and identification of the holding option on the PR	4	
	Ethical problems of insider information, fairness to stakeholders, avoidance of dissembling	5	
			15
(c)	Issue of immediate press release	2	
	Draft of statement reserving the company's position under the six month rule	1	
			5
			25

(a) **Advantages of growth by acquisition**

Acquiring an **existing company** is a speedier method of entering a new business than setting up a project using internal resources, because an acquired business will already have **customers** and, hopefully, **goodwill**. An acquisition may also effectively **eliminate a competitor** and may **allow higher profitability**. Other advantages may come from the **combination of complementary resources** of the acquiring and acquired companies.

Also because Pluto is a **major supplier** of Saturn, the acquisition will help to secure Saturn's supply chain and could help reduce costs, which can be important in a competitive industry such as telecommunications. The acquisition could also mean that competitors are forced to seek alternative and perhaps lower quality suppliers.

Problems of growth by acquisition

Frequently, a **significant premium** must be **paid** in order to **encourage existing shareholders** to sell, or to outbid, a rival. This may make it difficult to show a **respectable return** on the cost of the acquisition.

The acquired company may **not produce the exact product or service** that the acquirer needs, or may need **significant investment** before it conforms to quality requirements.

Management problems are also quite common, particularly when the acquiring and acquired companies have different organisational cultures. **Disputes** may cause the loss of key staff members, resulting in reduced quality or even in the establishment of competing businesses.

(b) There are several **regulatory, financial and ethical issues** that must be considered if Saturn Systems wants to make a bid for Pluto Ltd.

BPP LEARNING MEDIA

Regulatory issues

As a large listed company we have an obligation to ensure that any remarks made in the public domain will not mislead investors. The **City Code** in the UK requires the maintenance of **absolute secrecy** prior to an announcement being made. This requirement falls on the person or persons who hold **confidential information** (particularly information that might affect share price) and every effort should be made to prevent **accidental disclosure** of such information.

The City Code specifically states that a **false market must not be created** in the shares of the 'target' company. The remarks made last night no doubt contributed to the 15% rise in Pluto's share price. In accordance with the City Code, Saturn Systems will be expected to make a **statement of intention** in the light of the effect of the remarks at the dinner.

If it is stated that Saturn Systems are not interested in making a bid, it not be able to make another bid **for six months**, unless Pluto's board **recommends** a bid that might be made by Saturn Systems. Another way in which this restriction could be waived is if another offer is made by a **third party**.

Financial issues

Saturn Systems are in a strong **financial position** at the moment which may be one of the reasons the market interpreted the remarks as being significant. The 15% increase in Pluto's share price indicates that the market now sees Pluto as being a **target for takeover** and that Saturn may be interested in buying the company.

One problems is that Saturn Systems are only in the early stages of investigating Pluto and have not yet conducted a **due diligence** study. It does not know what the company is worth as a valuation has not yet taken place. As the remarks apparently contributed to a 15% increase in share price, Saturn Systems will now have to pay more for Pluto if it decides to make a bid. This could affect the financial position as it may be unable to raise the extra finance required to cover the additional cost.

As well as the issues above, there is also the likelihood of the extra debt affecting the **financial risk profile**. The acquisition of Pluto could also affect the **business risk exposure**. As a result, Saturn Systems cannot value Pluto without revaluing the existing business. If Pluto's value exceeds the increase in Saturn's value if the acquisition took place, it should not proceed with the purchase.

Ethical issues

There is now a dilemma of how to proceed. Saturn Systems have made no secret of the fact that we want to growth by acquisition rather than organically therefore it would not be ethical to deny any interest in Pluto. It was one of four potential targets discussed at the last Board meeting and investigations have been conducted into the company as well as reviewing the steps necessary to raise the finance for acquisition. In order to maintain our commitment to transparency of information, it is recommended that Saturn Systems clarifies its intentions.

(c) **Proposed course of action**

Saturn Systems should release a statement to **clarify the position** regarding Pluto. It should confirm that it is looking into the possibility of an acquisition of Pluto but make it clear that the Board has decided not to make a bid at this time. However, it should be made it clear that Saturn Systems **reserve the right** to make a bid or take any action that would otherwise be prohibited under the **six-month rule** should Pluto's Board agree to an acquisition or if any other company announced their intention to make an offer. This means Saturn Systems still have the chance to complete our investigations and develop a bid proposal before entering into negotiations with Pluto's Board.

40 Minprice

Text references. Chapters 10 to 12.

Top tips. Roughly one third of the marks for (a) would be for estimating the effect on EPS and share price of the takeover Also important are existing share price valuation using the dividend valuation model and a discussion of gearing.

Don't be too disheartened if you did not cope very well with the discussion about market efficiency. Although this topic is important, the other calculations plus reasonable discussion would have gained you more than half marks.

Important points in the discussion in (a) which will often need to be brought into discussions on takeovers and mergers include:

- Views of shareholders
- State of market efficiency
- Valuation of shares using one or more methods and problems of methods used. Consider whether market is under or overvaluing shares
- Combined company issues – gearing, dividend policies, post-acquisition strategies

In (b) remember of course that companies have to find the cash for a cash offer!

Easy marks. Scoring a very feasible 6–7 marks in (c) would only have left you needing 6–7 out of 18 on the other parts to pass this question.

(a)   **Views of shareholders**

Since the terms of the bid involve a share-for-share swap, shareholders will be highly interested in the fundamentals underlying the current market value of shares in both companies, in the **potential economic gains** that can be made by combining the companies and the likely effect of the takeover on share prices, including the proportion in which the gains are likely to be split between the two sets of shareholders.

Shareholders of Savealot are unlikely to accept unless they receive a **premium** over their existing share price, whereas Minprice shareholders will not wish to offer **too high a premium** because this will cause them to lose out. Other factors are also at play in this proposed takeover, one of which is that Minprice may be seeking to reduce its high gearing by taking over the comparatively ungeared Savealot.

Existing share prices

The reasonableness of each company's existing share price can be tested against the dividend valuation model:

Latest dividend per share: Minprice: $24m/300m = 8 cents.
                                             Savealot: $5m/40m = 12.5 cents.

Share values from the dividend valuation model: $D_0(1 + g)/(Ke - g)$:

Minprice: $8 \times 1.07/(14.5\% - 7\%) = 114$ cents
Savealot: $12.5 \times 1.08/(13\% - 8\%) = 270$ cents

If the stock market is efficient, the companies' current market share prices provide the best indicator of the 'true' value of their shares. However, on the basis of the **dividend valuation model** (using past growth rates as an indicator of expected future growth) Minprice's actual share price of 232 cents is more than twice as high as it 'should' be. Although the DVM is a simplistic model, this might signal caution to Savealot's shareholders, whose actual price of 295 cents seems comparatively reasonable. It is clear that future growth for both companies is expected to be better than the past. This may reflect expectations of a general upturn in the sector, or may be the effect of general market feelings that takeovers will be taking place.

Earnings per share are: Minprice: $50m/300m = 16.67c. Savealot: $8m/40m = 20c.

The **P/E ratios are;** Minprice: 232/16.67 = 13.9. Savealot: 295/20 = 14.75.

Unfortunately, no P/E ratios or other statistics for the food retail industry are available for comparison. However, the P/E of Minprice, which is nearly as high as that of Savealot, seems over-rated on the basis of its poorer growth record and higher cost of equity capital.

Potential economic gains from the takeover

The present value of the proposed rationalisation transactions following the takeover is $7.5 million:

	$m
Warehouse sale	6.8
Redundancy	(9.0)
Wage savings for 5 years: $27m $\times$ 3.605*	9.7
	7.5

must use AF

* The annuity factor for 5 years at 12%, the WACC of Minprice. Wage savings may last for more than 5 years, giving a higher present value.

Assuming this gain in value from combining the companies is achievable, it indicates that the takeover is economically worthwhile.

The bid has not yet been made public. The effect of the potential gains from the takeover terms is **unlikely** to have been **reflected** in the share prices of either company. However, it is just as probable that shareholders already have some expectations of takeovers in the industry, in which case synergetic gains would already have been anticipated in share prices, even under the semi-strong view of market efficiency.

Effect of the takeover announcement on share prices

There are a number of different ways of examining the effect of the takeover information being made public.

(i)   **Poor market efficiency**

Assume first that shareholders had **no previous expectations** that the takeover would take place and are taken totally by surprise when the synergetic gains of $7.5 million are announced.

They will estimate the value of the combined business as:

	$m
Value of firms before takeover:	
Minprice: 300m $\times$ 232 cents	696.0
Savealot: 40m $\times$ 295 cents	118.0
	814.0
Post takeover synergy	7.5
Estimated value after takeover	821.5

Minprice will issue $4/3 \times 40m$ new shares = 53.333m new shares to the shareholders of Savealot. The total number of shares in Minprice will rise to 353.333m.

The **expected share price** for Minprice after the takeover is announced will be $821.5m/353.333m = 232.5 cents. This is only a 0.5c gain to Minprice shareholders, who will have allowed all the advantage of synergy to accrue to Savealot.

Savealot shares will be expected to reflect the announcement by rising to $4/3 \times 232.5c = 310c$, giving them a 15c gain, an increase of 5%.

The **reconciliation** of the gains is: Minprice 300m shares $\times$ 0.5c = $1.5m and Savealot 40m shares $\times$ 15c = $6m, giving a total of $7.5m.

On this assumption, shareholders of Savealot would be fairly happy with the terms of the offer and Minprice shareholders would not lose from their existing position.

Total equity earnings from the combination will be $50m + $8m = $58m, assuming that wage savings are offset against redundancy cost write-offs and before any expected earnings growth.

This will give an **expected earnings per share** of $58/353.333 = 16.4 cents. This represents a drop from Minprice's existing 16.67c, but Savealot shareholders would receive the equivalent of $4/3 \times 16.4c = 21.9c$ compared with their existing 20c.

(ii)   **Stronger market efficiency**

Suppose however that shareholders had **already guessed** that the takeover would take place and share prices had **already increased** to reflect expected gains (a stronger view of market efficiency).

The **value of the combined business** would then be $814m and the expected value of Minprice's shares after the terms of the offer were announced would be $814/353.333 = 230.3 cents, a drop of nearly two cents.

Minprice shareholders would be disappointed with the terms of the offer. Savealot shareholders would still be better off, with an expected increase in share price to $4/3 \times 230.3c = 307$ cents (a premium of 4%).

(iii) **Over-valuation of Minprice shares**

As a third possibility, Minprice's shares may be **temporarily over-valued** by the market, as indicated by the high share price compared with that predicted from the DVM.

Such an over-valuation might occur, for example, if investors had false hopes of Minprice's opportunities in the takeover market. A fair price for Minprice's shares based on its existing business might be 114c, giving a total value of 300m × 114c = $342m.

Then the value of the combined company would be $342m + $118m + $7.5m = $467.5m, giving an expected share price after the takeover announcement of $467.5/353.333 = 132.3 cents.

This would represent very favourable takeover terms to Minprice, but would be unacceptable to Savealot, whose equivalent share value would fall from 195c to 4/3 × 132.3c = 176.4c.

Conclusion

In summary, the takeover terms appear to be fair and acceptable, provided that Minprice's shares are not temporarily over-valued by false expectations. Savealot shareholders need to evaluate the stability of Minprice's share price before accepting the offer.

Other factors

(i) **Gearing**

Minprice is very highly geared. Even if only long term debt is considered, gearing (D/E) in terms of book value is 314/222 = 141% and in terms of market value is 364/696 = 52%.

By comparison, Savealot's gearing is only 17.5/54.7 = 32% in book terms and 17.5/118 = 15% in market value terms.

In addition, Minprice has high current payables resulting in net current liabilities. While this is not unusual for a supermarket chain, it indicates that gearing in real terms is even higher. The shareholders of Minprice will favour the share issue terms for the takeover of Savealot which should reduce their gearing substantially, whereas Savealot's shareholders are unlikely to see this as an advantage.

(ii) **Dividend policy**

The companies have different dividend yields and covers, which may influence the views of some shareholders.

	Minprice	Savealot
Dividend yield	3.4% ✓	4.2%
Dividend cover	2.1	1.6

(iii) **Management plans**

The composition of the board of directors and senior managers will be fundamental to the success of the business after the takeover. Savealot seems to have been performing better than Minprice recently and may be able to argue for more than proportional representation on the board. Shareholders of both companies will be interested in these plans.

(b) **325 cents per share cash offer**

For the shareholders of Savealot this represents a **premium of 10%** over the current market price of 295c and is significantly better than the most optimistic estimate of the share offer's value, which was 310 cents.

The **cash offer** gives a **risk free return** compared with the risk of shares. For this reason cash offers are usually less in value than the equivalent share offers. Since this offer is *more* than the share offer it represents good value to Savealot shareholders. However, they will suffer immediate capital gains tax on the disposal.

From Minprice's point of view, the cash offer is **unlikely** to be **feasible**, given its high gearing and weak liquidity position.

(c) To: Board of Directors of Savealot Inc
     From: Consultant

In most countries, defences made by a publicly quoted company against a takeover bid must be legal and be allowed by the codes on Takeovers and Mergers and Stock Exchange regulations. Our advice on your proposals is as follows.

(i)   **Doubling profits**
      If your profits are likely to double, then **now** is a good time to **announce** the fact. You will need to substantiate your claims with clear evidence that can be verified by shareholders. This is very likely to halt the bid, or at least secure better terms.

(ii) **Alteration of articles**
      UK Stock Exchange regulations **prohibit** the alteration of articles of association to require more than a 51% majority to accept an offer for acquisition – you should check on the regulations of your own stock exchange to determine whether the proposed alteration of articles will be permitted.

(iii) **Third party investor**
      This defence, which was used for example in the Guinness case, is illegal as it is tantamount to the company **purchasing its own shares**.

(iv) **Advertising campaign**
      As with defence (i) this can be a very effective form of defence provided that the **information** is **true** and can be substantiated, otherwise a libel action might result.

(v)   **Revaluation of non-current assets**
      Revaluation of non-current assets is a good idea, provided that it is carried out by an independent valuer and the values can be **substantiated**. However, the effect on share values may be less significant than might be thought as, in an efficient market, these true asset values will already have been estimated by institutional shareholders.

41 Fly 4000

Text references. Cost of equity and CAPM are covered in Chapter 2. Free cash flows and the Gordon model are covered in Chapter 5. Valuation of companies is covered in Chapter 10. Financing methods are discussed in Chapters 2 and 12. Synergy evaluation is covered in Chapter 9.

Top tips. In part (a), you can assume that all three companies have the same asset betas as they all operate in the same sector. You can estimate FliHi's equity beta using the information available for Rover Airways and thus calculate the cost of equity using the CAPM. Don't forget to state your assumptions as there are four marks available for this.

You can use the dividend valuation model in part (b). The limitations of the method used stem from the assumptions made in the course of your calculations.

For part (c) the solution given is longer than the one you would be expected to produce but it covers all the main points.

Easy marks. You can pick up marks for displaying knowledge of how to ungear and regear betas in part (a). The calculations in part (b) are also quite straightforward.

		Marks
(a)	Calculation of the asset beta for Rover Airways	2
	Regear asset beta for FliHi	1
	Calculate FliHi's cost of equity	2
	Notes on the assumptions relating to the CAPM	2
	Notes on the assumptions of more practical significance	2
		9
(b)	Calculation and projection of the free cash flow to equity with explanations	2
	Discount these values at the rate of return to equity	2
	Calculation of the present value of the perpetuity with explanations	2
	Calculation of the present value of the firm's equity	1
		7
(c)	Discussion of synergies and their capture	3
	Examination of the risk exposure and the potential real options	3
	Review of the financing options	2
	Summary of valuation and recommendations for the next steps	1
		9
		25

(a) **FliHi cost of equity**

Since all three companies (Fly 4000, FliHi, Rover Airways) operate in the same sector it is reasonable to presume that they will all have the same asset beta.

Based on the information for Rover Airways we have

$\beta_e = 2.0$

D:E = 1.5:1.0 So using

$$\beta_a = \beta_e \left(\frac{V_e}{V_e + V_d(1-T)} \right) + \beta_d \left(\frac{V_d(1-T)}{V_e + V_d(1-T)} \right)$$

and assuming zero systematic risk to the debt ($\beta_d = 0$), we have

$$\beta_a = 2.0 \left(\frac{1}{1 + 1.5(1 - 0.3)} \right) = 2 \times \frac{1}{2.05} = 0.9756$$

To obtain the **equity beta** (β_e) for FliHi we now need to **re-gear** based on the market values of FliHi's equity and debt. Since this information is not available we will use the book values as a proxy.

So using a rearrangement of the above formula to solve for β_e

$$\beta_e = \beta_a \left(\frac{V_e + V_d(1-T)}{V_e} \right) - \beta_d \left(\frac{V_d(1-T)}{V_e} \right)$$

and assuming again that $\beta_d = 0$, we have for FliHi

$$\beta_e = 0.9756 \times \left(\frac{120 + 150(1 - 0.3)}{120} \right) = 0.9756 \times \frac{225}{120} = 1.82925$$

Now, applying CAPM gives

$r_e = r_f + \beta (r_m - r_f) = 4.5 + 1.82925 (3.5) = 10.90\%$

BPP LEARNING MEDIA

Assumptions made in this calculation are:

- That we can use book values of equity and debt as proxies for market values, this may be a reasonable assumption in a capital intensive business such as an airline, but certainly not in a service business where much of the value is in intangibles.

- All of the assumptions inherent in the theories of Modigliani and Miller whose gearing formulae we have applied, ie
  - Investors are rational and risk averse
  - Capital markets are perfect
  - Investors and companies can freely borrow at the same risk-free rate, hence individuals are indifferent between personal and corporate borrowings.

- All of the assumptions inherent in CAPM
  - Investors are rational and risk-averse
  - Investors are diversified
  - Capital markets are perfect, efficient and in equilibrium
  - All investors have the **same expectations** regarding the probability distribution of returns from each security
  - All investors can freely invest or borrow at the same risk-free rate

- Specific assumption noted in the question that debt is not sensitive to market risk, ie $\beta_d = 0$.
  - That since all three companies operate in the same sector they will have the same asset beta, unless their operations are exactly the same this is unlikely to be true. Since it is a smaller company and will, therefore, be less internally diversified and at greater risk of default, perhaps a premium should be applied to its cost of capital through such variants of CAPM as the Fama and French 3 factor model.

(b) **Value of FliHi**

Applying DVM ideas based on the 20X5 FCFE post reinvestment of $87.2m, which represents a surrogate for the dividend that could be paid, we have the following:

Time	Cash flow			DF	PV $
1	$d_1 = 87.2 \times 1.063$	=	92.69	$\dfrac{1}{1.109}$	83.58
2	$d_2 = 87.2 \times 1.063^2$	=	98.53	$\dfrac{1}{1.109^2}$	80.11
3	$d_3 = 87.2 \times 1.063^3$	=	104.74	$\dfrac{1}{1.109^3}$	76.79
4	$d_4 = 87.2 \times 1.063^4$	=	111.34	$\dfrac{1}{1.109^4}$	73.61
5	$d_5 = 87.2 \times 1.063^5$	=	118.35	$\dfrac{1}{1.109^5}$	70.55
5	$E_5 =$	=	1,783.91	$\dfrac{1}{1.109^5}$	1,063.45
					1,448.09

Where E_5 is the share price at time 5 which can be calculated from the constant growth formulation of DCF as

$$E_5 = \frac{d_6}{r_e - g} = \frac{87.2 \times 1.063^5 \times 1.04}{0.1090 - 0.04} = \frac{123.09}{0.0690} = 1,783.91$$

The assumptions made here are:

- The FCFE post reinvestment is a valued surrogate for the dividend payable.
- The growth pattern of dividends is correct and the FCFE is sustainable.
- The company is a going concern and will trade indefinitely into the future (the constant dividend growth model is a perpetuity).
- The required return of 10.9% will remain constant into perpetuity.

The limitations of our method hinge on the reality of the assumptions made. For example the 10.9% required was based (via CAPM) on a 4.5% risk-free rate and a 3.5% premium. It is most likely that these figures will vary as, say, the central bank charges interest rates in response to inflationary pressures. An interest rate of 4.5% is very low and may be expected to rise. Is a growth rate of 40% sustainable indefinitely into the future?

(c)

To:	Whom it may concern
From:	Chief financial officer
Date:	December 20X5
Subject:	**Proposed acquisition of FliHi**

Having completed the divestment of various associated interests and joint ventures, we now have cash reserves of $860m. One of the alternative proposals for these funds is to partially finance the acquisition of FliHi, though the total cost of that acquisition may be of the order of $1,450m and hence require a further $590m finance. The factors I believe we should consider here, each of which I discuss below are:

Strategic objectives	Risk exposure	Other factors
Operating synergies	Valuation	
Financial synergies	Financing	

Strategic objectives

A takeover should only be considered if it helps satisfy some strategic objectives of the business. Fly 4000's principal markets are in Europe and the Middle East from a Northern European hub. FliHi uses the same hub but has developed a strong transatlantic business as well as a substantial business in long-haul and medium-haul markets. As such, the business of FliHi is a good strategic fit with that of Fly 4000, allowing us to diversity into new markets.

In addition, FliHi is currently generating superior growth which helps to satisfy our strategic objective of achieving long-term growth in shareholder wealth.

Finally, from a strategic objective, the acquisition would provide defensive qualities since, as a larger more diversified operation, we would be able to compete more efficiently and effectively through offering a broader service range.

Operating synergies

Operating synergies that are likely to arise from a takeover would include:

- Revenue gains from being able to offer a broader range of flights, which is likely to enhance market share beyond that of the simple sum of the two entities.
- Cost savings and efficiency gains through the removal of any duplication (currently competition) between Fly 4000 and FliHi, resulting in planes operating with higher capacity loads.
- Revenue gains from the re-deployment of any planes released through this process.
- Cost savings from merging maintenance operations in our Northern European hub.
- Economies of scale with respect to fuel purchasing, in-flight catering, maintenance and ticketing operations.

Financial synergies

As a larger entity operating in a greater number of markets we are liable to be able to increase our borrowing capacity offering the opportunity for further expansion. In addition to this there may be tax benefits arising from how and when FliHi operates and the group structure it has.

Risk exposure

There is no reason why the market risk of our operations should be altered by this merger since both businesses operate in broadly the same sector.

We would need to recognise, however, that by increasing our geographical coverage we increase our exposure to overseas markets and exchange rates. There are obviously some diversification benefits to be gained from this, though we must also consider the associated risks, most particularly political risk, economic risk, exchange rate exposure (transaction risk, translation risk) as well as the increased risks of terrorism and the costs of anti-terrorist requirements especially on transatlantic markets.

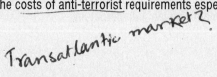

Transatlantic market?

BPP
LEARNING MEDIA

Valuations

Our initial valuation of $1,450m for FliHi is a pessimistic figure based on our far from in-depth knowledge of the business based on FliHi's published accounts. This value has been established using discounted cash flow techniques.

Using a simple earnings based valuation gives a figure of $550m ($50m × 11.00) when applying the PE ratio of Power Airways to the earnings of FliHi. This is, however, very simplistic since the PE of 11.0 reflects the growth, management, prospects etc of Power, not FliHi which has achieved very strong recent growth.

As a result, a value in this range ($550m – $1,450m) would probably be achievable, but this is a very broad range and would be difficult to narrow without further information.

Financing

Clearly if we are at the lower end of this price range then we will need no additional finance to achieve this acquisition. If, however, we are at the higher end of this range then additional finance would be needed.

Consideration should be given to the practicability of raising new debt finance in the current economic circumstances for airlines, especially since many of our assets and many of those being acquired are subject to operating losses and cannot be offered as security for any debt.

On balance a combined cash plus shares offer would probably be advisable for this acquisition.

Other factors

- What is FliHi's reputation in its markets of operation?

- FliHi has recently expanded its fleet with the modern Airbus 380 super-Jumbo, which is ideal for its long-haul and transatlantic markets, with the result that little new investment is likely to be needed in aircraft.

- Are there any unique features to FliHi's offering such as limousines to and from the airport? We would need to assess the business case for any such items.

- Is FliHi dependent on a few key entrepreneurial individuals, and if so do we need to take any action to maintain their services?

- What is the age and experience of their flight crews and their industrial relations record?

42 Burcolene

Text references. Mergers and acquisitions are covered in Chapters 9 – 12. Valuations are in Chapter 10, financing issues are in Chapter 12.

Top tips. There are a substantial number of marks attached to each of the two parts of this question which makes it appear quite daunting. However in part (a) if you take a methodical approach you can score reasonably highly. Do not be put off by the information regarding the share option scheme – the attrition rate simply means that the number of options will decline by 5% each year (remember it will be on a compound basis).

Part (b) is a written report for which professional marks are available so make sure your layout is correct and your lines of reasoning clear. When asked for the validity of the free cash flow model, give both sides of the argument (that is, the pros and cons of the model).

One thing you should note in the marking scheme is the small number of marks available for option valuation (only 4). You should not spend too much time on these calculations.

Easy marks. The calculation of the WACC and dealing with the pension fund deficit in part (a) should provide some easy marks.

Examiner's comments. Common errors in the first part of the question were as follows.

- Not recognising that the equity risk premium is the difference between the rate of return on the market and the risk-free rate.
- Incorrect adjustment of the cost of debt with many candidates not making the correct adjustment for the default risk premium.
- Ignoring the tax shield of 30% on debt, or applying the tax correction to the value of debt in the market gearing calculation as opposed to adjusting the cost of debt capital.
- Using the cost of equity capital rather than the WACC in the valuation of each firm as a whole.
- Adding, rather than deducting, the value of the share options to the value of the firm.

Apart from these issues, many candidates were able to demonstrate a reasonable level of competence in handling this type of valuation question.

In part (b) candidates should note the importance of focusing on the requirements of the question and refrain from presenting irrelevant material such as the defence tactics that might be used by the target company.

Few candidates recognised a critical valuation issue in that the pre-existing cost of capital is likely to remain unchanged as a result of the bid. Combining two companies of significantly different exposure to market risk will lead to a combination of intermediate betas and it is the cost of capital of the combination that needs to be established before an overall value of the post acquisition company can be determined. In addition the mode of financing is likely to have a significant impact on the firm's gearing. Few candidates recognised that the impact on the market gearing, as opposed to the book gearing of the business, will depend on the distribution of shareholder value between investors in each firm.

Marking scheme

		Marks	
(a)	Calculation of WACC	3	
	Calculation of the value of both companies	6	
	Deduction for option value	4	
	Deduction for pension liability	3	
			16
(b)	Identification of Type II acquisition, using market risk measures	1	
	Comparison of FCF model with market capitalisation	2	
	Note on the estimation error and likely causes	3	
	Indeterminate outcome for market gearing following acquisition	2	
	Likely outcome on the firm's WACC	2	
			Max 9
			25

BPP
LEARNING MEDIA

(a) **WACC and current entity value for both Burcolene and PetroFrancais**

We will calculate WACC first (post tax):

	Burcolene	*PetroFrancais*
Cost of equity (using CAPM)	$0.03 + 1.85 \times 0.04$ $= 10.4\%$	$0.03 + 0.95 \times 0.04$ $= 6.8\%$
Market gearing	$3.30/(3.30 + 9.90)$ $= 25\%$	$5.80/(5.80 + 6.70)$ $= 46.4\%$
Cost of debt	$0.03 + 0.016$ $= 4.6\%$	$0.03 + 0.03$ $= 6\%$
WACC	$(1 - 0.25) \times 0.104$ $+ 0.25 \times 0.046 \times 0.7$ $= 8.6\%$	$(1 - 0.464) \times 0.068$ $+ 0.464 \times 0.06 \times 0.75$ $= 5.7\%$

The valuation of a company can be calculated using the following formula:

$$V_0 = \frac{\text{Free cash flow at time 1}}{\text{WACC} - g}$$

Where:

V_0 is the value at time 0
g is the annual growth rate

As Free Cash Flow = NOPAT − net reinvestment, the formula can be rewritten as:

$$V_0 = \frac{(\text{NOPAT} - \text{net reinvestment}) \text{ at time 1}}{\text{WACC} - g}$$

Burcolene

$$V_0 = \frac{450 \times 1.05}{0.086 - 0.05} = \$13{,}125 \text{ million}$$

PetroFrancais

$$V_0 = \frac{205 \times 1.04}{0.057 - 0.04} = \$12{,}541 \text{ million}$$

Share option scheme adjustments – Burcolene

Option value = Intrinsic value + time value

Where:

Intrinsic value = Actual price − exercise price

$$\text{Actual price} = \frac{\text{Value of equity}}{\text{No of shares outstanding}} = \frac{\$9{,}900 \text{ million}}{340 \text{ million}} = \$29.12 \text{ per share}$$

Option value = ($29.12 − 22) + 7.31 = $14.43

Number of options to be exercised:

We have to take into account the attrition rate of 5% per annum and the percentage not expected to achieve the standard of performance required (20%).

Number of options   = 25.4 million $\times (1 - 0.05)^3 \times (1 - 0.2)$ = 17.42 million

Value of options outstanding = 17.42 million × $14.43 = $251.4 million

Burcolene's market valuation   = $13,125 million − 251.4 million = $12,873.6 million

BPP LEARNING MEDIA

Pension scheme deficit adjustment – PetroFrancais

The deficit on the pension scheme of $430 million will reduce the market value of PetroFrancais by the same amount:

PetroFrancais' market valuation = $12,541 million – 430 million = $12,111 million

(b) **Briefing paper to management of Burcolene**

Valuation and financial implications of acquisition of PetroFrancais

The proposed acquisition of PetroFrancais is likely to affect both the business and financial risk of Burcolene, therefore it can be viewed as a potential type III acquisition. This means that the combined business entity should be valued using the free cash flow model – that is, a combination of the cash flows of the acquiring and target companies plus the cash flows resulting from any synergies net of acquisition costs.

The problem with trying to value a type III acquisition using the above model is that the cash flows cannot be estimated until we know the post-acquisition rate of return – which in turn cannot be estimated until the cash flows are known. This can be solved using suitable spreadsheet packages.

Validity of free cash flow model

The current market values of Burcolene and PetroFrancais are $13.2 billion and $12.5 billion respectively. The free cash flow model values the companies at $12.874 billion and $12.111 billion respectively, resulting in respective estimation errors of 2.5% and 3.1%. Such low levels of error suggest that the free cash flow model is appropriate for valuing the combined entity.

The errors may have arisen due to any combination of the following:

- Inefficient capital markets
- Positive market reaction to the acquisition announcement
- Growth estimates being over-optimistic
- The model used to estimate the cost of capital not taking all elements of risk into consideration, perhaps rendering it invalid.

Implications of acquisition for Burcolene's gearing and cost of capital

Burcolene intends to finance the acquisition via a bond issue. This will have an effect on the book gearing of the firm although what effect this method of financing will have on market gearing is more difficult to estimate. A lot will depend on how much (if any) surplus shareholder value is generated and how it is distributed. Market gearing is likely to increase if the majority of the benefits fall to PetroFrancais' shareholders; the reverse will be the case if Burcolene's shareholders enjoy the bulk of the benefits.

The implications for the cost of capital will depend on the bid price and the way in which the acquisition value is distributed amongst the two groups of shareholders.

43 AIR

Text references. Financial reconstruction is covered in Chapter 13 and management buyout issues in Chapter 14.

Top tips. Don't fall into the trap of discussing the advantages and disadvantages of buyouts; the question asked for an assessment of the financing mix.

The answer starts by:

- Quantifying the financing mix
- The main features and conditions attached to the leveraged buy-out
- It then, as directed by the question, spends most time considering the advantages and disadvantages in the context of gearing.

The discussion starts by:

- Showing the initial effect on gearing
- Then showing how gearing will be reduced, quantifying the effects of each method.

However the answer then goes on to show that these methods will not be enough, and the limited effect they do have is dependent upon certain assumptions. The appendix details these **assumptions** but you also need to discuss the key ones in the main body of the report.

As the report has identified a problem, it needs to conclude by assessing:

- How serious the problem will be
- What can be done to solve it.

Easy marks. It's best to do the calculations first, but don't spend more than around 10 minutes on them. That should give you enough to make sufficient reasonable points in the discussion to pass. Part (c) should also provide some easy marks.

(a) **Financing mix**

If the airport can be purchased for $35 million, **the financing mix** is proposed as:

Equity: 50 pence ordinary shares

	$m
8 million purchased by managers and employees	4
2 million purchased by ER	1
EPP Bank: secured floating rate loan at LIBOR + 3%	20
AV: mezzanine debt with warrants (balancing figure)	10
Total finance	35

Up to $15 million of the mezzanine debt is available, which could be used to replace some of the floating rate loan. However, this possibility has been rejected because its cost is 18% compared with 13% and the warrants, if exercised, could dilute the manager/employee shareholding.

Leveraged buyout

A **leveraged buyout** of the type proposed allows managers and employees to own 80% of the equity while only contributing $4m out of $35m capital (11%). However, it is important that the managers and employees agree on the company's strategy at the outset. If the shareholders break into rival factions, **control** over the company might be **difficult to exercise**. It would be useful to know the disposition of shareholdings among managers and employees in more detail.

Gearing

The initial **gearing** of the company will be extremely **high**: the **debt to equity ratio** is 600% ($30 million debt to $5 million equity). Clearly one of the main medium-term goals following a leveraged buyout is to **reduce gearing** as rapidly as possible, sacrificing high dividend payouts in order to repay loans. For this reason EPP

Bank, the major creditor, has imposed a covenant that capital gearing (debt/equity) must be reduced to 100% within four years or the loan will be called in.

Repayment of mezzanine finance

The gearing will be reduced substantially by steady repayment of the unsecured mezzanine finance. This carries such a **high interest** rate because it is a very risky investment by the venture capital company AV. A premium of 5% over secured debt is quite normal. The debt must be repaid in five equal annual instalments, that is $2 million each year. If profits dip in any particular year, AIR might experience cash flow problems, necessitating some **debt refinancing**.

Warrants

If the **warrants** attached to the mezzanine debt are exercised, AV will be able to purchase 1 million new shares in AIR for $1 each. This is a cheap price considering that the book value per share at the date of buyout is $3.50 ($35m/10 million shares). The **ownership** by managers and staff will be **diluted** from 80% to approximately 73%, with ER holding 18% and AV holding 9%. This should not affect management control provided that managers and staff remain as a unified group.

(b) **Gearing at period-end**

Using these assumptions and ignoring the possible issue of new shares when warrants are exercised, the **gearing** at the end of four years is predicted to be 132%, which is **significantly above the target** of 100% needed to meet the condition on EPP's loan. If warrants are exercised, $1 million of new share capital will be raised, reducing the year 4 gearing to 125%, still significantly above the target.

No dividends

A key assumption behind these predictions is that **no dividends are paid** over this period. This may not be acceptable to managers or employees. It is also assumed that cash generated from operations is sufficient to repay $2 million of mezzanine debt each year, which is by no means obvious from the figures provided.

Increase in LIBOR

Results will be worse if **LIBOR rises** above 10%, over the period. However the purchase of the cap will stop interest payments on EPP's loan rising above 15%. Conversely if **LIBOR falls**, the **increase in profit** could be **considerable**, but it is still very unlikely that the loan condition will be met by year 4.

Problems in meeting loan condition

There will therefore definitely be a problem in meeting the EPP's loan conditions. However, if the company is still showing steady growth by year four, and there have been no problems in meeting interest payments, EPP bank will probably **not exercise its right** to recall the loan. If the loan condition is predicted to be a problem, the directors of AIR could consider:

(i) Aiming for **continuous improvement** in **cost effectiveness**

(ii) **Renegotiating** the **central services** contract with ER, or providing central services in-house, in order to save costs

(iii) **Renegotiating** the **allowed gearing ratio** to a more realistic figure

(iv) Going for further expansion after, say, one or two years (eg extension of a runway in order to handle long-haul flights); financing this expansion with an **issue of equity funds**. However, this may affect control of the company

(v) Looking **for possible alternative sources** of debt or equity finance if the EPP loan is recalled, including the possibility of flotation on the stock market

APPENDIX

AIR: forecast income statements for the first four years and computation of debt/equity gearing ratios

	Estimates from				
	Year 0	Year 1	Year 2	Year 3	Year 4
	$'000	$'000	$'000	$'000	$'000
Landing fees	14,000				
Other revenues	8,600				
	22,600				
Labour	5,200				
Consumables	3,800				
Other expenses	3,500				
	12,500				
Direct operating profit growing at 5% pa	10,100	10,605	11,135	11,692	12,277
Central services from ER		(3,000)	(3,150)	(3,308)	(3,473)
EPP loan interest at 13% on £20m		(2,600)	(2,600)	(2,600)	(2,600)
Mezzanine debt interest at 18%					
on $10m		(1,800)			
on $8m			(1,440)		
on $6m				(1,080)	
on $4m					(720)
Profit before tax		3,205	3,945	4,704	5,484
Tax at 33%		1,058	1,302	1,552	1,810
Profit after tax		2,147	2,643	3,152	3,674
Reserves b/f		0	2,147	4,790	7,942
Reserves c/f		2,147	4,790	7,942	11,616
Share capital + reserves		7,147	9,790	12,942	16,616
Total debt at end of year		28,000	26,000	24,000	22,000
Gearing: debt/equity		392%	266%	185%	132%

If warrants are exercised, $1 million of new share capital is issued, reducing the gearing at year 4 to 22,000/17,616 = 125%.

Assumptions

(i) The **central services** will be **provided** by ER for the full 4-year period.

(ii) **No dividend** will be paid during the first four years.

(iii) **Sufficient cash** will be **generated** to repay $2 million of mezzanine finance each year and to fund increased working capital requirements.

(iv) **LIBOR** is **assumed to remain at 10%**.

(v) Tax is payable one year in arrears.

(c) In order to decide whether the management buy-out can be considered for a $10 million loan, the venture capital company would need the following information:

(i) The **purpose** of the buy-out

(ii) Full **details of the management team**, in order to evaluate expertise and experience and to check that there are no 'gaps' in the team

(iii) The company's **business plan**, based on a realistic set of strategies (apparently most approaches to venture capital companies fail on this criterion)

(iv) **Detailed cash flow forecasts** under different scenarios for economic factors such as growth, and interest rates. Forecasts of profit and balance sheets

(v) Details of the **management team's investment** in the buy-out. Venture capital companies like to ensure that the team is prepared to back their idea with their own money

(vi)   Availability of **security** for the loan, including personal guarantees from the management team. Any other 'sweeteners' that could be offered to the lender, such as warrants

(vii)   The possibility of appointing a representative of the venture capital company as a director of AIR.

44 MandM Co

Text references. Sell-off of parts of a business is covered in Chapter 14.

Top tips. Don't be tempted to give a generic answer for part (a) – make sure you relate your points to the scenario where possible. You are also asked to note any risks involved so remember to do so where relevant.

For part (b) it is important to relate your answer to the scenario, for example a spin-off is unlikely to be appropriate here and so should not be included as a possible method.

Easy marks. The marking scheme is quite flexible in this question therefore you should be able to pick up some easy marks along the way. Don't be afraid to state what you might think are obvious points as you will gain marks for these.

Marking scheme

		Marks
(a)	Clarification of assets under sale and purpose	1 – 2
	Status of IP and extent and remedy of defects in protection	1 – 2
	Valuation and note on recursion problem	2 – 3
	Identification of regulatory issues	1 – 2
	Search for, and resolving issues involving, potential buyers	2 – 3
	Due diligence: both seller and buyer	3 – 4
	Contracting and legal issues	1 – 2
	Price negotiation	2 – 3
	Employment and transfer of rights and pension	2 – 3
	Investor agreement	1
	Contract and completion	1
		Max 19
(b)	For each method explained	2
		Max 6
		25

(a)   **Issues to be considered when disposing of the LunarMint division**

This is a disposal situation where the division being sold off does not appear to fit in with the core business of the company. However the determination of what constitutes 'core business' is often a subjective matter.

The first important issue is the **reason for sell-off**. Whilst the question suggests that there is no business case for retaining the LunarMint division, there is no question that this division is profitable and low risk. Should management be considering the sell-off of a profitable part of the business? Why did management decide to invest in such a diverse activity in the first place? Answers to these questions should be sought before any further decisions are taken regarding the proposed sell-off.

There are numerous further issues that should be considered when disposing of the LunarMint division.

Intellectual property

Management will be required to check the status of LunarMint's intellectual property. There is a risk that valuable corporate knowledge and brand symbols may be sold off unknowingly. It is essential that such knowledge and brands are patented or protected by copyright.

Assets of LunarMint

There may be joint assets owned by both LunarMint and MoneyMint and a decision must be taken as to how, and if, these assets should be sold. Once this decision has been finalised, the fair value of the assets being disposed of should be established on a going concern basis. Depending on the type of assets being sold, there may be a risk of a lack of available market making it difficult to establish a fair value.

Regulatory issues

There is a risk that such a disposal to certain purchasers may constitute a **conflict with public interest** and as such result in problems in gaining approval for the acquisition. It is important to clarify any regulatory issues that may give rise to such issues.

Valuation of LunarMint's contribution to the business

The valuation of the division should assess the **impact on shareholder value** that would result from the sale of LunarMint. This will help to establish a **minimum disposal value** that should result in no loss to shareholders. Management should establish whether it intends to sell the division in its entirety or only elements of the division.

Where the sale will significantly impact upon MandM Company's **systematic risk**, the valuation must be more sophisticated. Modelling the group's potential cash-flow loss and the impact on its **asset beta** will be necessary in such circumstances.

Seeking potential buyers

The search for potential buyers can be conducted either through an intermediary or via an open tender. If several potential buyers are being sought, the business may be auctioned. However, depending on the nature of the assets being sold, a single buyer may be sought. There is the risk when seeking potential buyers that the value of the business may be threatened. Where there is a dominant competitor seeking to gain control of the business, a price war may result that will force down prices and hence LunarMInt's value prior to a bid being made.

Due diligence

When a potential buyer has been found, the division's up-to-date accounts and legal documentation relating to transfer of assets should be made available to the interested party. This access will allow the potential party to conduct its own due diligence.

MandM Company should also conduct its own due diligence to determine the **potential buyer's ability** to complete such a sizeable transaction. Issues such as how the transaction will be financed, how long it will take to raise the necessary funds and any other factors that might hinder a straightforward sale should be investigated.

Legal issues

Legalities pertaining to the transfer of intellectual property, employment rights and contractual issues relating to the sale should be investigated and settled by MandM Company's legal team. The transfer should be absolute unless only certain elements of the division are being sold.

Negotiation of price

MandM Company's responsibility regarding the sale lies with ensuring that its shareholders get the best possible deal. Negotiations regarding the selling price of LunarMint should be conducted by a professional team of negotiators that has been thoroughly briefed on all aspects of the sale. Other factors that will be subject to negotiation will include the transfer of employees and accrued pension rights and deeds pertaining to the transfer of assets (both tangible and intangible).

Employment issues

It is essential that employees are kept up to date with how the sale may affect them. Issues such as protection of rights, reasons for sale and incentive payments (such as share options) should be fully discussed with employee representatives and, where relevant, union representatives.

Agreement by shareholders

Before the sale can be finalised, it may be necessary to gain shareholder approval (particularly given the size of the transaction). There is a risk that shareholders will vote against the sale therefore if management feels very strongly in its favour, necessary processes should be put in place to encourage their approval.

Finalisation of sale

Once any necessary approval has been secured, management can go ahead with the sale and the necessary contracts can be exchanged.

(b)   A **divestment** would involve disposing of the assets of the LunarMint division. This may seem an attractive prospect, as there is less need to find a specific buyer interested in the whole division, so marketing costs should be lower. However, the funds raised may be lower than from a sale as a going concern, especially since the division is profitable.

A **sell-off** to a third party for cash would be a good way of raising funds, given that the LunarMint division is profitable and would not attract negative publicity that may accompany a divestment which also includes job losses.

A **carve-out** could be used to raise some funds by selling shares in LunarMint to the public, but MandM would retain a substantial amount of the shares, which seems unlikely to achieve the objective of disposing of the division.

A **demerger** would not help to raise funds for MandM, but would split the divisions into two separate corporate bodies. There would seem to be only limited loss of synergies or economies of scale, given the two diverse operations of MandM. Existing shareholders, who may have wanted the diversification offered by MandM, will still be shareholders in both companies and therefore will not have lost any of their diversification.

45 Proteus Co

Text references. Management buyouts are covered in Chapter 14.

Top tips. The key to part (b) is recognising that you have to prepare an income statement to determine retained earnings per annum and then you have to calculate book value of equity before being able to compute the debt/equity ratio for each year. Once you have established this the calculations are not difficult. Be careful to omit the allocated overhead charge that Tyche Co has to pay to Proteus Co – this will no longer be payable if there is an MBO. Remember to use the year end debt and equity figures when calculating the D/E ratios.

Easy marks. You should be able to pick up some relatively easy marks in part (a). The calculations in part (b) are not difficult therefore you may gain some easy marks here. Part (d) also provides some relatively straightforward discussion marks.

Examiner's comments. Generally part (a) was done well and many responses gained high marks. Some responses discussed the benefits to the management team and not just Proteus Co, which was not asked for. Part (b) was done well, when candidates knew that they had to calculate the future earnings, in order to calculate the future level of equity and therefore the debt-equity ratio, to assess whether or not it would be breached. It was surprising that many answers included payment of debt capital within earnings, before calculating retained earnings. This is clearly incorrect and resulted in an incorrect debt-equity ratio being calculated. In part (c), most answers clearly identified possible actions that could be taken if the covenant was breached, but few discussed the implications of such a breach.

			Marks
(a)	1 – 2 marks for each point discussed	Max	5
(b)	Calculations to get to profit before tax for the next five years	3	
	Calculations to get to the reserves figures for each year	2	
	Calculation of the equity amount each year	1	
	Calculation of debt to equity for year and conclusion when the covenant is breached and when it is not	<u>3</u>	
			9
(c)	Discussion of implications	3	
	Actions Tyche Co may take	<u>2</u>	
			5
(d)	1 – 2 marks for each point discussed		<u>6</u>
			<u>25</u>

(a) Benefits to Proteus Co of disposing of Tyche Co through an MBO

It already has a potential buyer therefore there will be no costs involved in looking for an investor to purchase the company.

As the new owners are already known there should be less resistance from managers and employees to the sale than if the new owner was not known.

Proteus may secure a better price for the company. The managers and employees have very sound knowledge of the company and know how to build on its success therefore may be willing to pay more.

Proteus will provide management services for the first year of the MBO – this relationship may continue in the future which will be beneficial to both parties. This may not happen if an 'external' investor bought the company.

If it handles the disposal successfully and efficiently, Proteus may find its reputation increasing amongst external stakeholders, as well as such internal stakeholders as management and employees.

(b) Is the debt covenant breached over the five-year period?

In order to answer this question we will have to calculate the proportion of debt to equity each year. Debt will decrease by $3 million each year as Tyche repays the loan in instalments. Equity will increase by reserves each year. We therefore have to calculate the amount being added to reserves each year (using forecast income statements), as well as determining the book value of equity and outstanding debt at the end of each year. This will allow us to calculate the debt/equity ratio for each year and compare this ratio to the loan covenant maximum.

Forecast Income Statement (Tyche)

Year	1	2	3	4	5
	$000	$000	$000	$000	$000
Operating income before mgt fee (W1)	23,760	25,661	27,714	29,931	32,325
Management fee (increasing by 8% pa)	(12,000)	(12,960)	(13,997)	(15,116)	(16,326)
Interest payable (W2)	(5,850)	(5,580)	(5,310)	(5,040)	(4,770)
Profit before tax	5,910	7,121	8,407	9,775	11,229
Tax at 25%	(1,478)	(1,780)	(2,102)	(2,444)	(2,807)
Profit after tax	4,432	5,341	6,305	7,331	8,422
Dividend (25%)	(1,108)	(1,335)	(1,576)	(1,833)	(2,106)
Retained earnings transferred to reserves	3,324	4,006	4,729	5,498	6,316

Book value of equity

Year	1	2	3	4	5
	$000	$000	$000	$000	$000
Opening equity balance	16,000	19,324	23,330	28,059	33,557
Reserves (see above)	3,324	4,006	4,729	5,498	6,316
Closing equity carried forward	19,324	23,330	28,059	33,557	39,873

Debt/equity calculations

Year	1	2	3	4	5
	$000	$000	$000	$000	$000
Outstanding debt at year end	62,000	59,000	56,000	53,000	50,000
Closing equity carried forward	19,324	23,330	28,059	33,557	39,873
Debt/equity ratio	321%	253%	200%	158%	125%
Maximum as per loan covenant	350%	250%	200%	150%	125%
Covenant breached?	No	Yes	No	Yes	No

Workings

(1) Current operating income before management fee

	$000
Sales revenue	60,000
Materials and consumables	(12,000)
Labour costs	(22,000)
Other costs	(4,000)
Operating income before management fee	22,000

Growth = 8% per annum

(2) Interest payable

Loan at start of year 1 = $81 million (market value of Tyche) - $12 million - $4 million = $65 million

Year	1	2	3	4	5
	$000	$000	$000	$000	$000
Loan outstanding at start of year	65,000	62,000	59,000	56,000	53,000
Interest at 9%	5,850	5,580	5,310	5,040	4,770

(c) **Implications of the results**

The covenant is breached in both years 2 and 4 and has only just been met in years 3 and 5. There are two issues to be considered as a result.

(i) How will the bank react to the breaches in covenant restrictions and will these breaches threaten Tyche's business?

(ii) Are the revenues and costs in years 3 and 5 likely to be achieved? Even a slight movement could cause the conditions to be breached. Tyche should carry out sensitivity analysis and put provisions in place to deal with any unexpected breaches in the covenant.

Possible actions (only two are required)

(i) Reduce the dividend payout ratio (although this would have to be agreed with the shareholders).

(ii) Pay off more of the loan from cash reserves (if available) to reduce the outstanding debt more quickly.

(iii) Ask the venture capitalists to consider taking on a higher equity stake for more funding at the start of the venture. This would have to be discussed and agreed.

(iv) Try to negotiate less restrictive terms with the bank or ask for greater flexibility when applying the restrictive covenant. It is unlikely that the restrictive covenant will be breached by a significant amount therefore the bank will probably be reluctant to enter into legal proceedings to cease Tyche Co's trading. It is likely to be open to negotiations.

BPP LEARNING MEDIA

(d)   **Reasons for management buy-out failure**

A major issue that a management buy-out may fail to overcome is that the managers may be able to run the business on an operational level, but they have **little or no experience** in business strategy, financial management and financial accounting.

The financial projections of the management team may not be realisable. In particular they may **fail to generate sufficient cash flow** to fund the business and the mandatory interest payments as a result of a leveraged buy-out, which most MBOs are.

Maintaining the **existing customer base** may be difficult. Some customers may take the change of ownership as a reason to reassign their supplier.

Suppliers may no longer be happy to supply the new business on the **same credit terms** as before, as it will be a new company with no trading history and may be seen as significantly riskier to do business with.

If the buy-out is as a result of **financial difficulties**, then the new management may not be able to address the issues as to why the business was struggling in the first place.

Some **key personnel** may remain with the disposing company. It may then be difficult for the new company to attract a similar calibre of employee.

46 BBS Stores

Text references. Unbundling is covered in Chapter 14. Financial strategy (including cost of debt, CAPM and ungearing/regearing betas) is dealt with in Chapter 2.

Top tips. There is a lot of information in this question and it is easy to become overwhelmed. Before delving into the detail, read the requirements. This will give you an idea about the detail you are trying to extract from the question and will focus your attention. You are required to carry out numerous calculations so label these clearly. It is very easy to get lost otherwise.

In part (a), don't forget that adjustments to the earnings for the EPS calculations will be net of tax. Part (b) involves a lot of calculations but remember to consider each option and don't forget what you are actually trying to achieve. You may find it easier to start from what you are required to find and work backwards. However you decide to do this part of the question, it is imperative that your workings are clear. Make use of the formulae in the formula sheet where you can.

Easy marks. This is a very involved question but you should be able to pick up some relatively straightforward marks in part (a) when constructing the comparative statements. You should also be able to gain at least a few easy marks in part (b) when calculating equity cost of capital (using CAPM) and WACC.

Marking scheme

		Marks
(a)	Comparative statement of financial position under the two alternatives (2 each)	4
	Revision of earnings figure for each alternative and calculation of EPS (3 each)	6
	Discussion of the unbundling impact upon the statements of financial position and earnings	3
		13
(b)	Ungearing of current beta and estimation of retail beta	2
	Estimation of the cost of equity under each alternative	4
	Estimation of the WACC under each alternative	2
		8
(c)	Note on problems of taking property assets off the statement of financial position	2
	Difficulty of predicting net impact of unbundling on shareholder value	2
	Conclusion	2
	Max	4
		25

(a) The proposal would involve the following:

	$m
Sell 50% of land and buildings	1,148.50
Sell 50% of assets under construction	82.50
	1,231.00

Impact on statement of financial position

Option 1 is the proposal to use the proceeds ($1,231m) to reduce medium-term borrowing and reinvest the balance in the business (non-current assets). The effect would be as follows:

	Borrowings and other financial liabilities $m	Property, plant and equipment $m	Sales proceeds received (used) $m
Balance at end 20X8 (before adjustment)	1,130	4,050	
Sales proceeds		(1,231)	1,231
Repayment of medium-term notes	(360)		(360)
Reinvestment in company		871	(871)
Balance after adjustment	770	3,690	Nil

Option 2 is the sale and rental scheme proposed by the company's investors on the assumption that this scheme would release substantial cash to them. The proposal would involve the repayment of the medium-term notes and the balance ($871m) used to execute a share buyback. This would involve ($871m/$4) **217.75m shares** with a nominal value of **$54.44m**.

	Borrowings and other financial requirements $m	Property, plant and equipment $m	Called-up share capital - equity $m	Retained earnings $m
Balance at end 20X8 (before adjustment)	1,130	4,050	425	1,535
Sales proceeds		(1,231)		
Repayment of medium-term notes	(360)			
Share buyback			(54.44)	(817)
Balance at end 20X8 after adjustment	770	2,819	370.56	718

Comparative statements of financial position

	20X8 (original) $m	Sales proceeds $m	Option 1 $m	Option 1 $m	Option 2 $m	Option 2 $m
Non-current assets						
Intangible	190			190		190
Property etc	4,050	(1,231)	871	3,690	(1,231)	2,819
Other	500			500		500
	4,740			4,380		3,509
Current assets	840	1,231	(1,231)	840		840
Total assets	5,580			5,220		4,349
Current liabilities	1,600			1,600		1,600
Non-current liabilities						
Borrowings etc	1,130		(360)	770	(360)	770
Other	890			890		890
	2,020			1,660		1,660
Total liabilities	3,620			3,260		3,260
Net assets	1,960			1,960		1,089

BPP LEARNING MEDIA

Equity

Called-up equity capital	425	425	(54)	371
Retained earnings	1,535	1,535	(817)	718
Total equity	1,960	1,960		1,089

Gearing is affected as follows:

	20X8 (Option 1)	20X8 (Option 2)	20X8 (before adjustment)
Long-term debt (borrowings and other financial liabilities)	770	770	1,130
Total capital employed (total assets – current liabilities)	3,620	2,749	3,980
Gearing ratio	21.27%	28.01%	28.39%

Gearing has been reduced substantially with option 1. Whilst gearing is also reduced slightly under option 2, it is considerably higher than the gearing ratio that would result from paying off the medium-term notes and reinvesting the balance in the company.

Impact on Earnings per Share (EPS)

Both options will result in a reduction in interest payable due to paying off the medium-term notes. In addition, credit spread on the 6 year debt would be reduced by 30 basis points with option 1. The sale of the property would reduce property rent with both options. Under option 1, the funds reinvested in the company would earn a return of 13%.

The total effect would be as follows:

	Current position $m	Option 1 $m	Option 2 $m
Earnings for 20X8	670.00	670.00	670.00
Add: interest saved on medium-term notes (net of tax): $360m x 6.2% x 65% (interest is charged at LIBOR 5.5% + 70 basis points)		14.51	14.51
Add: return on reinvested funds ($871m x 13% x 65%)		73.60	
Add: reduction in credit spread on 6 year debt (0.3% × $770m × 65%)		1.50	
Less: property rent foregone ($1,231m × 8% × 65%)		(64.01)	(64.01)
Adjusted earnings	670.00	695.60	620.50
Number of shares	1,700.00m	1,700.00m	1,482.00m
Adjusted EPS in cents per share	39.41	40.92	41.87

(b) **Impact of unbundling on the company's WACC**

Our starting point for this part of the report is to estimate the asset beta for the retail part of the business.

Current $k_e = 10.47\%$

Current WACC = 9.55%

We now ungear the current company beta using the formula:

$$\beta_a = \beta_e \times \frac{V_e}{V_e + V_d(1-T)} = \beta_e \times 1 - \frac{V_d(1-T)}{V_e + V_d(1-T)}$$

$\beta_a = 1.824 \times (1 - 0.09748)$

$\beta_a = 1.646$

The retail asset beta is the weighted average of the individual betas:

$$\beta_a = \left[\frac{V_R}{V_T} \times \beta_R\right] + \left[\frac{V_P}{V_T} \times \beta_P\right]$$

Where V_R = value of retail section β_R = beta of retail section

     V_T = total value of business β_P = beta of property section

     V_P = value of property

$$1.646 = \frac{4,338}{6,800} \times \beta_R + \frac{2,462}{6,800} \times 0.625$$

$V_T = \$4 \times$ no of shares $= \$4 \times (425 \div 0.25) = 6,800$,

$V_P = 2,297 + 165 = 2,462$,

$V_R = V_T - V_P = 6,800 - 2,462 = 4,338$

Rearranging the equation we find

$\beta_R = \mathbf{2.225}$

The beta of the company will be a combination of the retail beta (2.225) and the property beta (0.625). We can now calculate the cost of equity under each option as follows.

	Option 1	Option 2
Value of equity	$= 425m \times 4 \times 4$	$[(425m \times 4) - 217.75m] \times 4$
	$= \$6,800m$	$= \$5,929m$
Asset beta (adjusted)	$= \left[\frac{V_R}{V_T}\beta_R\right] + \left[\frac{V_P}{V_T}\beta_P\right]$	$= \left[\frac{V_R}{V_T}\beta_R\right] + \left[\frac{V_P}{V_T}\beta_P\right]$
	$= \frac{5,569}{6,800} \times 2.225 + \frac{1,231}{6,800} \times 0.625$	$= \frac{4,705}{5,929} \times 2.225 + \frac{1,231}{5,929} \times 0.625$
	$= 1.935$	$= 1.895$
Tax adjusted gearing	$= \frac{V_D(1-T)}{V_E + V_D(1-T)}$	$= \frac{V_D(1-T)}{V_E + V_D(1-T)}$
	$= \frac{770 \times 0.65}{(6,800 + (770 \times 0.65))}$	$= \frac{770 \times 0.65}{(5,929 + (770 \times 0.65))}$
	$= 6.856\%$	$= 7.784\%$
Equity beta (β_e)	$= \frac{1.935}{(1 - 0.06856)}$	$= \frac{1.895}{(1 - 0.07784)}$
	$= 2.0774$	$= 2.0550$
Cost of equity	$= 5\% + 2.0774 \times 3\%$	$= 5\% + 2.0550 \times 3\%$
	$= 11.23\%$	$= 11.17\%$

Option (1) WACC

$$= \left[\frac{6,800}{(6,800 + 770)} \times 11.23\%\right] + \left[\frac{770}{(6,800 + 770)} \times 5.9\% \times 0.65\right] = 10.48\%$$

(where 5.9% = LIBOR + 70bp – 30bp)

Option (2) WACC

$$= \left[\frac{5,929}{(5,929 + 770)} \times 11.17\%\right] + \left[\frac{770}{(5,929 + 770)} \times 6.2\% \times 0.65\right] = 10.35\%$$

Note that both options will increase the current WACC of 9.55% by a considerable margin.

(c) **Potential impact of each alternative on the market value of the firm**

It is difficult to assess the impact of unbundling on the value of BBS Stores. Although the equity beta will increase with the removal of part of the existing property portfolio, this will be countered by a reduction in

BPP LEARNING MEDIA

gearing. We have assumed that the balance of $871 million in Option 1 could be reinvested at the current rate of return of 13%. If we fail to do so then shareholders' value will be significantly reduced. To reduce this risk, shareholders appear to favour Option 2 where they are guaranteed a cash return through a share buyback.

Whether the property is owned or leased should have no effect on the company's value if we can assume that the current use of the assets and the resultant value gained remain unchanged. If a separate property company can be set up we may be able to remove ownership from the statement of financial position. However we must bear in mind that the ease with which this can be done will depend on accounting regulations in the country concerned.

A final observation is the assumption of a constant and known share price (400 cents). Share prices are not constant nor are they certain. In order to assess the potential impact of any movements in this variable, we should set up a simulation model and run the model for various share prices and equity betas.

47 Troder

Text references. Chapter 16.

Top tips. Remember in (a) that a cap is designed to benefit a lender, but a collar is used by both borrowers and lenders. The hint about not calculating the number of contracts in (b) indicates that you are meant to carry out the main calculations in terms of net interest rates rather than monetary amounts. Hence the first stage is to calculate the net interest rate that corresponds to receiving £6.75 million. The difference between (b)(i) and (ii) is that (b)(i) calculates the amount Troder is guaranteed to receive whereas (b)(ii) indicates how much leeway Troder has by letting its call option lapse, before the buyer of the put option exercises his rights. Your answer to (c) needs to bring out how these measures are used.

Easy marks. Good discussion in (a) could earn you 6 of the 8 marks you need to pass this question. Part (c) should be fairly easy if you have good knowledge of the Greeks.

(a)   **Advantages of caps**

(i)   For payment of a **premium**, caps provide an **insurance policy**, determining the **maximum level of interest** that a borrower will have to pay. By **buying a put option**, a borrower can deal in an agreed interest rate at a future date and will not need to go above that interest rate. Caps can provide **long-term protection** for up to ten years.

(ii)   If interest rates fall, the purchaser of the cap will not exercise the option and will thus take advantage of the **lower interest rates**.

Advantages of collars

(i)   Using a collar, a borrower can **buy** an **interest rate cap (put option)** and **sell** an **interest rate floor (call option)** at a lower strike rate. The main advantage compared with a **pure cap** is that the cost will be lower, since the borrower will **receive a premium** for **selling a call option**. However this advantage is tempered by the **borrowing company foregoing the benefit of movements in interest rates** below the floor.

(ii)   A collar for a lender would be **buying an interest rate floor (call option)** and **selling an interest rate cap (put option)**. The cost again would be **lower** than for a one-way option, and the lender would receive a **guaranteed minimum rate of interest**. However the lender would not be able to enjoy the benefit of receiving interest above the level at which the cap is set.

(b)   (i)   To earn $6.75 million, annual interest rate after premium costs would have to be:

$$\frac{\$6.75\,\text{million}}{\$400\,\text{million}} \times \frac{12}{5} = 4.05\%$$

Three possible collar combinations, using **December** options:

Call strike price	Put strike price	Interest rate %	Less 0.25% %	Less Call premium %	Add Put premium %	Net receipt %
95750	95500	4.25	(0.25)	(0.165)	0.170	4.005
95750	95250	4.25	(0.25)	(0.165)	0.085	3.920
95500	95250	4.50	(0.25)	(0.280)	0.085	4.055

Of the three the only combination that guarantees an interest rate above 4.05% is buying a call option at 95500 and selling a put option at 95250. The minimum return will be:

$$\$400,000,000 \times \frac{5}{12} \times 4.055\% = \$6,758,333$$

(ii)   The maximum interest rate that is possible under the selected hedge is 4.75%, equivalent to the put option exercise price of 95250. Troder will not have exercised its option, but taken advantage of the rate being above 4.5%.

Net return = 4.75 − 0.25 − 0.280 + 0.085 = 4.305%.

Maximum return = $\$400,000,000 \times \frac{5}{12} \times 4.305\% = \$7,175,000$.

(c)   **Delta**

$$\text{Delta} = \frac{\text{Change in call option price}}{\text{Change in price of the shares}}$$

Delta measures the gradient of the option value line at any point in time or price point. As the share price falls towards zero, delta should also fall towards zero. The delta calculation can be used to determine the **amount** of the **underlying shares** or other instruments that the writer of the option position **should hold** in order to hedge the risk of the option position.

Theta

Theta represents a change in an option's **price** (specifically its time premium) over **time**. The time premium element of an option's price will diminish towards zero. At the money options have the greatest time premium and thus the greatest theta. Theta can be used to judge how the **option price** will **reduce** as **maturity approaches**.

Vega

Vega represents the sensitivity of an option's price to a change in its implied **volatility**. It is measured as the change in the value of an option from a 1% change in its volatility. The Black-Scholes model is very dependent upon the accurate estimation of an option price's volatility, and vega is a measure of the **consequences of incorrect estimation**. Long-term options have larger vegas than short-term options; the longer the time period until expiration, the more uncertainty there is about the expiry price. Vega can be used to determine changes in value of both **put and call options**; these will **increase** as **volatility increases**, since there is an expectation of a potentially higher share price.

BPP LEARNING MEDIA

48 MJY

Text references. Chapter 16.

Top tips. Provided you recognised the importance of netting off transactions, part (b) is not as time-pressurised as many derivative questions. It is necessary to net off inter-group as well as external transactions though.

Possible problems are:

- Using the right forward rates; you wish to obtain dollars to settle the payment, so use the lower rate as you will obtain fewer dollars for each £ you spend. By contrast you need to use the higher rate on the € receipt as you will be sacrificing more of the € you have received to obtain the £ you ultimately want.
- Purchasing a put option as you have to **sell** £ contracts to obtain the dollars you require
- Translating the premium at the **opening** spot rate
- Because this is a single contract, and being compared with a forward contract, you should calculate the over-hedge and hedge the difference on the forward market.

Easy marks. Netting off the transactions inside and outside the group is quite straightforward. Discussing the advantages and disadvantages of centralised treasury management also offers some easy marks.

(a) **Advantages of centralised treasury management**

(i) Centralised management **avoids** having a **mix of cash surpluses** and **overdrafts** in different localised bank accounts. It facilitates **bulk cash flows**, so that lower bank charges can be negotiated and the subsidiaries that need to borrow can **borrow** from the **parent company** and hence **gain the benefit of lower rates**.

(ii) **Larger volumes of cash** are **available to invest**, giving better short-term investment opportunities (for example international money markets, high-interest accounts and CDs).

(iii) **Any borrowing** can be **arranged in bulk**, at lower interest rates than for smaller borrowings, and on the eurocurrency or eurobond markets. **Interest rate hedging** will be facilitated.

(iv) **Foreign currency risk management** is likely to be **improved** in a multinational group of companies. A central treasury department can match foreign currency income earned by one subsidiary with expenditure in the same currency by another subsidiary.

(v) A **specialist treasury department** will **employ experts** with knowledge of dealing in forward contracts, futures, options, eurocurrency markets, swaps and so on. Localised departments would not normally have such expertise.

(vi) The **centralised pool of funds** required for precautionary purposes will be **smaller** than the **sum of separate precautionary balances** that would be held under decentralised treasury arrangements.

(vii) A central function acts as a single focus, ensuring the **strategy** of the group is **fulfilled** and **group profitability** is **enhanced** by good cash, funding, investment and foreign currency management.

(viii) **Transfer prices** can be **set centrally**, thus **minimising the group's global tax burden**.

Disadvantages of centralised treasury management

(i) Local departments may find it easier to diversify sources of finance and **match local assets**.

(ii) Centralised management means that managers in subsidiaries and divisions are not motivated by being given the **autonomy to deal** with cash management and it may be **difficult to assess their performance** if the major decisions are being made centrally.

(iii) A decentralised treasury function may be **more responsive** to the needs of individual operating units.

(iv) A decentralised operation may find it **easier to invest** its own balances quickly on a short-term basis than a centralised function would.

(v) A central function may find it difficult to **monitor remote sites**; it may be difficult to **obtain information** from those sites.

(b) **Netting off**

We need to net off $ and € receipts and payments as far as possible inside and outside the group before hedging (ignore £ as MJY based in UK)

$ hedged amount = 90 + 50 + 40 + 20 + 30 − 170 − 120 − 50 = $110,000 payment
€ hedged amount = 75 + 85 + 72 + 20 + 52 + 35 − 72 − 35 − 50 − 20 − 65 = €97,000 receipt

Forward contract

Buy $ 3 months $\dfrac{110,000}{1.7835}$ = £61,676

Sell € 3 months $\dfrac{97,000}{1.4390}$ = £67,408

Option

Set up

(i) Contract date May

(ii) Option type Put as sell £ to buy $

(iii) Price Try $1.78 and $1.80

(iv) No of contracts Price 1.78

110,000 ÷ 178/62,500 = 0.99, say 1 contract

Over-hedge in forward market = (62,500 × 1.78) − 110,000 = $1,250

No of contracts Price 1.80

110,000 ÷ 1.80/62,500 = 0.98, say 1 contract

Over-hedge in forward market = (62,500 × 1.80) − 110,000 = $2,500

(v) Premium

1.78: 0.0420 × 62,500/1.7982 = £1,460
1.80: 0.0534 × 62,500/1.7982 = £1,856

Outcome

Assuming option exercised:

	1.78	1.80
	£	£
Amount paid through option	62,500	62,500
Premium	1,460	1,856
Forward market receipt 1,250/2,500 ÷ 1.7861	(700)	(1,400)
	63,260	62,956

Both options offer a worse outcome than the forward contract. However they will enable the company to use the spot market if the dollar weakens and hence the option be allowed to lapse.

However given that this is a small hedge for a multinational company, a forward contract would probably be used to **save time and costs**.

(c) **Hedging strategy for the MJY Group**

Netting inter-company transfers is a **common international cash management strategy** to **manage foreign currency risk**. The basis of netting is that, within a closed group of related companies, total payables will always equal total receivables. The **advantages** of netting are reduction in foreign exchange conversion fees and funds transfer fees and a quicker settlement of obligations reducing the group's overall exposure.

In the case of MJY Group it will be necessary to arrange for **multilateral netting** as it involves more than two companies. The arrangement can be co-ordinated either through the group's central treasury function or

BPP
LEARNING MEDIA

alternatively through the company's bankers. Given, that a group treasury function already exists it would be sensible to **use the in-house expertise** to carry out the multilateral netting.

It is also necessary to determine the **common currency** in which netting needs to be effected as well as the method of establishing the exchange rates to be used for netting purposes. In order to agree the outstanding amounts in time, but with minimum risk of exchange rate fluctuations, it may involve using exchange rates applying a few days before the date at which payment is to be made.

The **benefits** of netting are:

(i)   Reduced foreign exchange costs including commission and the spread between selling and buying rates as well as reduced money transmission rates.

(ii)   Less loss in interest from having money in transit.

However, it will be necessary to **check local laws and regulations** for these foreign countries to ensure multilateral netting is permitted.

It should be noted, however, that once netting has been accomplished then the **foreign exchange exposure** will need to be **hedged** in the normal way, ie through the use of:

- Forwards contracts
- Matching of receipts and payments within the individual company
- Currency options

49 KYT

Text references.   Foreign exchange hedging is covered in chapter 16, interest rate hedging is covered in chapter 17.

Top tips.   Part (a) is what can be generally expected from a futures currency hedging calculation question, make sure that you read all of the information and be careful not to make any basic error with the calculations.

Easy marks.   Part (c) is a fairly straightforward discussion requirement that could be attempted without having completed parts (a) or (b) first.

(a)   (i)   KYT can **hedge using futures** as follows:

- Use September futures, since these expire soon after 1 September, price of $1/0.007985 = 125.23$ ¥/$.

- **Buy** futures, since it wishes to acquire yen to pay the supplier, and the futures contracts are in Yen.

- Number of contracts $140m/12.5m = 11.2$ contracts ~ 11 contracts.

- Tick size

$0.000001 \times 12.5m = \$12.50$

(ii)   **Basis risk** arises from the fact the price of a futures contract may not move as expected in relation to the value of the instrument being hedged. Basis changes do occur and thus represent potential profits/losses to investors. Typically, this risk is much smaller than the risk of remaining unhedged.

Basis risk is the **difference between the spot and futures prices**.

Spot price = $1/128.15$
            = 0.007803

Basis   = $0.007803 - 0.007985 = 182$ ticks with 3 months to expiry

Basis with one month to expiry, assuming uniform reduction = $^1/_3 \times 182 = 61$ ticks

Spot price on 1 Sept = $1/120 = 0.008333$

Therefore predicted futures price = $0.008333 + 0.000061 = 0.008394$

(iii)   **Outcome**

Futures market

Opening futures price	0.007985
Closing futures price	0.008394
Movement in ticks	409 ticks

Futures market profit 409 × 11 × $12.50 = $56,238

Net outcome

	$
Spot market payment (¥140m , 120)	(1,166,667)
Futures market profit	56,238
	(1,110,429)

Hedge efficiency

$$\frac{56,238}{74,197} = 76\%$$

This hedge is not perfect because there is **not** an **exact match** between the exposure and the number of contracts, and because the **spot price** has moved more than the futures price due to the reduction in basis. The actual outcome is likely to differ since basis risk does not decline uniformly in the real world.

(b)   **Interest rate futures**

Hedging

A future is an agreement on the future price of a variable. Hedging with futures offers protection against **adverse movements in the underlying asset**; if these occur they will more or less be offset by a gain on the futures market. The person hedging may be worried about **basis risk**, the risk that the futures price may move by a different amount from the underlying asset being hedged.

Terms

The **terms, sums involved and periods** are **standardised** and hedge inefficiencies will be caused by either having too many contracts or too few, and having to consider what to do with the unhedged amount.

Deposit

Futures require the payment of a **small deposit**; this transaction cost is likely to be lower than the premium for a tailored forward rate agreement or any type of option.

Timescale

The majority of futures are taken out to **hedge borrowing** or **lending** for short periods.

Interest rate options

Guaranteed amounts

The main advantage of options is that the buyer cannot lose on the interest rate and can take advantage of any favourable rate movements. An interest rate option provides the **right to borrow a specified amount** at a **guaranteed rate of interest**. On the date of expiry of the option the buyer must decide **whether or not to exercise his right to borrow**. He will only exercise the option if actual interest rates have risen above the option rate.

Premium cost

However a premium must be paid regardless of whether or not the option is exercised, and the **premium cost** can be quite **high**, high enough not to make an option worthwhile if interest rate movements are expected to be marginal.

Types of option

Options can be **negotiated directly** with the bank (over the counter, OTC) or traded in a standardised form on the LIFFE. **OTC options** will be preferable if the buyers require an option **tailored to their needs** in terms

BPP
LEARNING MEDIA

of maturity date, contract size, currency or nature of interest. **OTC options** are also generally more appropriate if the buyer requires a **long time** to maturity or a large contract size. **Traded options** will be more appropriate if the buyers are **looking for options** that can be **exercised at any time**, are looking for a **quick, straightforward** deal, or might want to sell the options before the expiry date if they are not required.

(c) **Foreign exchange exposure risks resulting from overseas subsidiary**

If a wholly owned subsidiary is established overseas then KYT Inc will face exposure to foreign exchange risk. The magnitude of the resulting risk can, if not properly managed, eliminate any financial benefits we would be hoping to achieve by setting up the overseas subsidiary.

The **foreign exchange risks resulting from a wholly owned overseas subsidiary** are as follows:

(i) **Transaction risk**

This is the risk of adverse exchange rate movements occurring in the course of normal trading transactions. This would typically arise as a result of exchange rate fluctuations between the date when the price is agreed and the date when the cash is paid.

This form of exposure can give rise to real cash flow gains and losses. It would be necessary to set up a treasury management function whose role would be to assess and manage this risk through various hedging techniques.

(ii) **Translation risk**

This arises from fluctuations in the exchange rate used to convert any foreign denominated assets or liabilities, or foreign denominated income or expenses when reporting back to the head office and thereby impacting on the investment performance.

This type of risk has no direct cash flow implications as they typically arise when the results of the subsidiary denominated in a foreign currency are translated into the home currency for consolidation purposes. Although there is no direct impact on cash flows, it could influence investors' and lenders' attitudes to the financial worth and creditworthiness of the company. Given that translation risk is effectively an accounting measure and not reflected in actual cash flows normal hedging techniques are not normally relevant. However, given the possible impact the translated results have on the overall group's performance and the possible influence on any potential investment decision making process it is imperative that such risks are reduced by balancing assets and liabilities as far as possible.

50 Asteroid Systems

Text references. Foreign currency hedging is covered in Chapter 16.

Top tips. At first glance this appears to be a straightforward foreign currency hedging question but there is a twist involved. The money is being remitted to Asteroid Systems rather than the company making a commitment to pay – therefore a reverse money market hedge will be needed.

In part (a) you will have to calculate the two month rate using an average of the one month and three month rates. When using the interest rate parity formula for calculating the acceptable interest rate, remember that you are dealing with a reverse money market hedge – that is, the foreign currency is borrowed in the overseas market, converted at spot rate and then deposited in the domestic market. You are also trying to find the overseas country's interest rate (i_c) rather than the forward rate (f_0). Remember that you are trying to calculate a two month rate, therefore you will have to adjust the interest rate parity formula accordingly.

Easy marks. The effects of hedging on cost of capital should offer a fairly easy four marks and the discussion on the treasury department operating as a profit or cost centre should be fairly straightforward.

Examiner's comments. This was not a popular question and only a minority of candidates who attempted it were able to identify the money market requirements and the procedure for setting up a hedge of this type. Whilst straightforward, the calculations focused attention on identifying the minimum Swiss borrowing rate that would make the hedge worthwhile.

The discursive parts of the question asked candidates to discuss the relative merits of money market hedging compared with hedging through the use of exchange traded derivatives. Good answers focused on the range of hedging instruments available and commonly used in this type of business scenario (currency futures and forex options). Part (c) of the question asked candidates to consider whether hedging of this type would impact on the company's cost of capital. Good answers recognised that this depended on the significance of currency risk in the assessment of a firm's exposure to market risk (in the case of equity) and overall risk (in the case of debt). Many candidates ignored this part of the question.

Common errors in this question were:

(a)   Incorrect estimation of the appropriate forward rate.

(b)   Being unable to use the money market hedge in a situation where there is a remittance as opposed to a commitment in the foreign currency concerned.

(c)   Not recognising the role of the interest rate parity relationship in determining the minimum acceptable rate for borrowing.

(d)   Not appreciating the significance of the correlation between the domestic and the counter currency in determining the potential gains from hedging.

Marking scheme

		Marks	
(a)	Calculation of forward rates	4	
	Calculation of minimum rate at LIBOR + 7 through reverse money market hedge	5	
	Conclusion	1	
			Max 10
(b)	Advantages and disadvantages of OTC versus ET derivatives		
	Basis risk	2	
	Under/over hedging	1	
	Counterparty risk	1	
	Flexibility	1	
	Margin	1	
			6
(c)	Impact upon the cost of equity capital	2	
	Impact upon cost of debt capital	2	
			4
(d)	One mark per well explained point		Max 5
			25

(a)   **Money market hedge**

Calculate two month forward rate

Two month forward rate is the average of one month and three month rates

= (1.6223 + 1.6176)/2 = 1.6199 SFr/€

Exposure to transaction risk could be eliminated by entering into a forward contract to purchase Swiss francs at a rate of SFr/€1.6199 – that is, you would purchase SFr1.6199 x 1.5 million = SFr2.4299 million.

BPP LEARNING MEDIA

Use interest rate parity formula to calculate lowest acceptable Swiss borrowing or lending rate

Interest rate parity:

$$f_0 = s_0 \frac{(1+i_c)}{(1+i_b)}$$

where f_0 is the forward rate (calculated above as 1.6199)

s_0 is the spot rate (1.6244)

i_c is the interest rate in the country overseas (in this case, Switzerland)

i_b is the interest rate in the base country (Germany)

As we are looking for a two month interest rate, we have to multiply i_c by (2/12) in all cases.

$$1.6199 = 1.6244 \times \frac{1+i_c \times 2/12}{(1+0.03725 \times 2/12)}$$

$$(1 + i_c \times 2/12) = \frac{1.6199 \times (1+0.03725 \times 2/12)}{1.6244}$$

$$(1+ i_c \times 2/12) = 1.0034$$

$$(i_c \times 2/12) = 0.0034$$

$$i_c = 0.0204 \text{ or } 2.04\%$$

If Asteroid Systems can borrow at less than 2.04% in the Swiss market, the money market hedge will be preferable to selling Swiss francs in the forward market.

(b) **Relative advantages and disadvantages of a money market hedge versus exchange traded derivatives**

Money market hedge

A money market hedge is the **manufacture of a forward rate** using the spot exchange rate and interest rates of the home and overseas countries. It requires **preferential access** to the short-term money markets and can be a **substitute** for forward contracts.

The **main problems** with a money market hedge are that it is **difficult to reverse** and it can be **relatively expensive**. It is not always possible to construct a money market hedge depending on the currencies with which you are dealing, as you may not be able to get access to the short-term money market in the overseas country.

Exchange traded derivatives

Exchange traded derivates such as futures and options can be set up quickly and closed out easily.

Futures, for example, are normally closed out before maturity with the profit/loss being used to offset the gain or loss in the underlying. These derivatives tend to have **relatively low costs** for small deals and they are **marked-to-market**, they offer relatively low risk. **Options** offer flexibility in that the holder is **not obliged** to exercise the option on maturity if the market position is such that it would be more profitable not to do so.

However exchange traded derivatives are only available for **certain currencies** and offer **few maturity dates**. They are also only available in **fixed amounts** which may mean an **inexact hedge**. In the case of futures, there can also be **cash flow problems** as marking-to-market requires any daily shortfalls to be paid immediately. With exchange traded options, there will be a premium to be paid which could prove to be expensive for the privilege of flexibility.

Conclusion

For **small, infrequent hedges** the forward market may be more suitable for hedging risk. However you must take the **costs** of setting up loans and deposits into consideration before making a decision.

(c) **Currency hedging and cost of capital**

Cost of equity

As hedging reduces a firm's exposure to foreign currency risk, there should be a **favourable impact** on the company's **beta value** and hence its cost of equity. The extent of the impact will depend on **the size and**

importance of the potential foreign currency exposure and the **correlation of the currency with the market**. If the currency and the company have the same correlations with the market then the removal of currency risk would have **little or no effect** on the company's cost of capital, as the company's exposure to market risk would not change. The reverse would be true for different correlations with the market and the company's cost of equity would be affected by changes in levels of foreign currency risk.

Cost of debt

The reduction in foreign currency risk may have a **favourable impact** on the company's exposure to **default risk**. The risk of defaulting on debt payments is closely related to the volatility of the company's cash flows – the greater the volatility the greater will be the default risk. Reduction in foreign currency risk will have a **smoothing effect** on the company's cash flows which will therefore **reduce** the risk of defaulting on debt. This should have a downward impact on the cost of debt and hence the overall cost of capital.

(d) **Competence of staff**

Local managers may not have sufficient expertise in the area of treasury management to carry out speculative treasury operations competently. Mistakes in this specialised field may be costly. This would make a treasury department more likely to operate as a cost centre.

Controls

Adequate controls must be in place to prevent costly errors and overexposure to risks such as foreign exchange risks in a profit centre.

Information

A treasury department which acts as a profit centre would be competing with other traders employed by major financial institutions who may have better knowledge of the market. In order to compete effectively, the team needs to have detailed and up-to-date market information.

Attitudes to risk

The more aggressive approach to risk-taking may be difficult to reconcile with the attitude to risk that that the directors have. The recognition of treasury operations as profit making activities may not fit well with the main business operations of the company.

Internal charges

If the department is to be a true profit centre, then market prices should be charged for its services to other departments. It may be difficult to put realistic prices on some services, such as arrangement of finance or general financial advice.

Performance evaluation

Even with a profit centre approach, it may be difficult to measure the success of a treasury team for the reason that successful treasury activities sometimes involve **avoiding** the incurring of costs, for example when a currency devalues.

51 Multidrop

Text references. Netting is covered in Chapter 16.

Top tips. You should convert all amounts to the settlement currency first – it is important to have read the question thoroughly to pick up this point! A tabular approach makes finding the net amounts owing and owed much easier, both for you and for the marker. Don't forget to refer to both group and non-group companies in part (b) when discussing advantages and disadvantages of netting.

Easy marks. Part (c) should be a discussion using brought forward knowledge from F9.

BPP
LEARNING MEDIA

		Marks	
(a)	Set principal as European business	1	
	Conversion to Euros	3	
	Initial amounts owed and owing	2	
	Totals owed and owing	2	
	Net amounts owed	2	
	Conclusion: Payments and receipts to Multidrop (Europe)	2	
			12
(b)	Minimisation of number of transactions	1 – 2	
	Minimisation of cost of transacting	1 – 2	
	Avoidance of exchange controls	1 – 2	
	Minimisation of hedging costs	1 – 2	
	Limiting exposure to net	1 – 2	
	Taxation issues	1 – 2	
	Acceptance of liability	1 – 2	
	Re-invoicing and re-contracting	1 - 2	
			Max 9
(c)	Removal of transaction risk	1 – 2	
	Customers not willing to bear risk	1 – 2	
	Loss of gains on foreign exchange	1	
			Max 4
			25

(a)   **Netting**

There are several ways in which this question could be approached. We have shown what we believe to be the most straightforward approach – using a **transactions matrix**.

All settlements are to be made in Euros – the first step is therefore to convert all amounts owed to Euros.

Owed by	Owed to	Local currency (m)	€m
Multidrop (Europe)	Multidrop (US)	6.4	4.67
Multidrop (Singapore)	Multidrop (Europe)	16.0	7.75
Alposong (Malaysia)	Multidrop (US)	5.4	3.94
Multidrop (US)	Multidrop (Europe)	8.2	8.20
Multidrop (Singapore)	Multidrop (US)	5.0	3.65
Multidrop (Singapore)	Alposong (Malaysia)	25.0	5.01
Alposong (Malaysia)	NewRing (UK)	2.2	2.34
NewRing (UK)	Multidrop (Singapore)	4.0	1.94
Multidrop (Europe)	Alposong (Malaysia)	8.3	1.66

The next step is to determine how much is owed by (and owed to) each company and net the results off.

Owed to Owed by	Europe €m	US €m	Malaysia €m	Singapore €m	UK €m	Owed by €m
Europe		4.67	1.66			6.33
US	8.20					8.20
Malaysia		3.94			2.34	6.28
Singapore	7.75	3.65	5.01			16.41
UK				1.94		1.94
Owed to	15.95	12.26	6.67	1.94	2.34	
Owed by	6.33	8.20	6.28	16.41	1.94	
NET	9.62	4.06	0.39	(14.47)	0.40	

Net result

The amounts paid by Multidrop (Europe) are as follows:

US	€4.06m
Malaysia	€0.39m
UK	€0.40m
Total	€4.85m

Multidrop (Europe) receives €14.47m from Singapore.

The net result is a gain of €9.62m for Multidrop (Europe).

(b) **Advantages and disadvantages of netting arrangements**

Advantages

Netting reduces **foreign exchange exposure** as balances are offset between countries. This limits the number of foreign currency exchange **transactions** and thus reduces the transactions costs involved.

Transaction risks (and transaction costs) are also reduced as a result of fewer foreign currency exchanges and this will enable the group to focus their hedging activities on a smaller number of transactions. Fewer hedging activities mean **lower hedging costs** (such as arrangement costs, premiums, etc).

If **exchange controls** are in place (that limit cross-border currency flows), netting allows balances to be offset which minimises total exposure and helps to keep such currency flows to a legally acceptable level.

Disadvantages

One of the main issues with netting arrangements is making netting contracts **legally enforceable**. A netting system cannot operate effectively without resolving the legal status of contracts in numerous jurisdictions. As well as cross-border issues, there may be **taxation** problems to resolve before the netting arrangements can be approved.

There is also the issue of **liabilities** being accepted. This is a particular issue when external parties (in this case, Alposong and NewRing) are involved. The success of the netting arrangement depends on **acceptance of liabilities** by all parties, both internal and external to the group.

Costs in establishing the netting system have to be considered and compared with the savings. If there are no net benefits to be gained from the system then it should be abandoned.

Where third parties are involved, the netting arrangement may involve **re-invoicing** for the net amount or, in some cases, a completely **new contract** may be required.

(c) The main advantage of this policy is that Multidrop (Europe)'s foreign customers would have to translate their own currencies into Euro to pay Multidrop (Europe) and so they would have to bear the currency risk. This would mean Multidrop (Europe) **does not face transaction risk.** If there are time delays between the invoice and payment, the exposure could be significant.

The main disadvantage is likely to be loss of customers who are not prepared to bear the currency risk or possibly even the transaction cost of exchanging currency. These transaction costs will make Multidrop (Europe) less competitive than local companies which invoice in the local currency.

The removal of exchange rate risk also removes the chance for Multidrop (Europe) to make **gains on foreign exchange**.

BPP
LEARNING MEDIA

52 NTC

Text references. Chapters 16 on hedging techniques, Chapter 15 on treasury management.

Top tips. In (a) you would not have time to set out the workings of the exchange rates in full in the exam; you would have to put the figures straight in the multilateral netting table. In each case you should have divided the figure in the table in the question by the mid-market value eg 210 ÷ 1.4362 = 299.40. It would be perfectly legitimate exam technique to round the answers in (a) and subsequently to the nearest £'000.

You would not have been told that the Hong Kong dollar was fixed to the US dollar if you were not expected to make use of the information.

In (b) we have not carried out a full option calculation. Remember that we are trying to work out whether it would be advantageous to use options rather than the next best alternative. This involves considering what happens if the options are exercised, for which we need to know (i) the effect of hedging the amounts at the option price, (ii) the premium and (iii) what happens to the amount not hedged by the option contracts. Here it's best to assume that the amount not hedged by the option contracts is hedged on the forward market. Remember though you don't know in advance whether it will be necessary to exercise the option; hence the final calculation assuming options aren't exercised and trying to find the rate at which options are the best choice.
If you were short of time on (b) (ii) you could have passed that part by getting the money market and forward market calculations correct and correctly considering one of the possible option prices. However you would not have achieved full marks on this part without considering all of the option prices. Option outcomes should be considered at different exercise prices, and you should consider alternative exercise prices.

Don't worry if you didn't take into account the financing cost of the premium, it's a small issue.

Points to stress in (c) are costs, the difficulty of negotiating how much wheat to exchange and the potential problems of disposing of wheat (although it might be easier to dispose of wheat than other commodities).

Easy marks. In (b) about 5 out of 15 marks would be available for the forward and money market hedges, so provided you got those right and made some sort of an attempt at the option calculation (and drew a conclusion) you would have done enough to pass that part.

(a)

Receiving subsidiaries	Paying subsidiaries UK	SP	HK	US	Total
	£'000	£'000	£'000	£'000	£'000
UK		128.96	64.27	76.59	269.82
SP	100.00		49.13		149.13
HK	35.71				35.71
USA	299.40	73.69	26.78	–	399.87
Total payments	(435.11)	(202.65)	(140.18)	(76.59)	(854.53)
Total receipts	269.82	149.13	35.71	399.87	854.53
Net receipt/(payment)	(165.29)	(53.52)	(104.47)	323.28	–

Rather than have the UK, Spain and Hong Kong settle amounts owed amongst themselves, multilateral netting ensures the procedure is simplified by having each country make net payment to the US subsidiary.

(b)   The first stage is to work out what transactions need to be hedged.

Spain

As the balances are in different currencies, the full receipt of 210,000 Euros will be hedged.

US

The receipts and payments can be netted off.

430 – 110 = $320,000 payment

Hong Kong

The receipts and payments can be netted off.

720 – 400 = HK$320,000 receipt

As $HK is pegged to $US, the $HK can be converted to $US using the cross rate 11.2050/1.4358 = 7.8040. (There is little economic pressure to unpeg, since there is only a small difference in interest rates between US and Hong Kong.)

320,000/7.8040 = $41,005

Netting off against US payment

Hedged amount = 320,000 – 41,005 = $278,995 payment

Euros

(1) **Forward contract**

NTC should sell €210,000 three months forward at 1.6166 Euro/£

210,000/1.6166 = £129,902

(2) **Money market**

Borrow sufficient Euros now for three months at 5.3% per year in order to have a balance of €210,000 in three months' time. The net trading receipts will then be used to repay this loan. The interest rate for six months will be 1.325%.

To obtain €210,000, borrow now 210,000/1.01325 = €207,254.

The euros will be converted into £ at spot: 207,254/1.6292 = £127,212

£127,212 can then be invested in the UK for three months at 6.0% per year (1.5% for three months) to yield 127,212 x1.015 = £129,120

Dollars

(1) **Forward contract**

NTC should buy $278,995 at 1.4285$/£

278,995/1.4285 = £195,306

(2) **Money market**

Invest sufficient dollars now for three months in order to have a balance of $278,995 in three months' time. Since the annual dollar deposit rate is 5.4%, the three month rate is 1.35%.

To earn $278,995, invest now 278,995/1.0135 = $275,279.

Purchase dollars with pounds at spot rate of $/£ 1.4358

275,279/1.4358 = £191,725.

Borrow £191,725 in the UK for three months at 6.9% (1.725% for three months) to cost £191,725 x 1.01725 = £195,032.

Options

Dollars

Using currency options

Set up

(1) Date September

(2) Type of contract put as wish to buy $/sell £ with option contract in £.

(3) Exercise price 1.42/1.43/1.44

(4) Contracts and amounts hedged

	Number of contracts	Amount hedged 31,250 × 6 = £187,500	Amount not hedged, hedged on forward market
1.42	$\dfrac{278,995/1.42}{31,250}$ = 6.29, say 6	187,500 × 1.42 = $266,250	$\dfrac{278,995 - 266,250}{1.4285}$ = £8,922
1.43	$\dfrac{278,995/1.43}{31,250}$ = 6.24, say 6	187,500 × 1.43 = $268,125	$\dfrac{278,995 - 268,125}{1.4285}$ = £7,609
1.44	$\dfrac{278,995/1.44}{31,250}$ = 6.20, say 6	187,500 × 1.44 = $270,000	$\dfrac{278,995 - 270,000}{1.4285}$ = £6,297

(5) **Tick size**

$3.125

(6) **Premium cost**

As we are comparing the option with the money market hedge, we have to take into account the financing cost of the premium, 6.9% annual borrowing cost in the UK or 1.725% for the three months. Premium cost is translated at spot rate,

$$1.42 \text{ premium cost} = \frac{3.125 \times 215 \text{ ticks} \times 6 \times 1.01725}{1.4358} = £2,856$$

$$1.43 \text{ premium cost} = \frac{3.125 \times 312 \text{ ticks} \times 6 \times 1.01725}{1.4358} = £4,145$$

$$1.44 \text{ premium cost} = \frac{3.125 \times 435 \text{ ticks} \times 6 \times 1.01725}{1.4358} = £5,779$$

(7) **Total cost of exercising option**

	Amount hedged by option £	Amount hedged on forward market £	Premium £	Total £
1.42	187,500	8,922	2,856	199,278
1.43	187,500	7,609	4,145	199,254
1.44	187,500	6,297	5,779	199,576

Therefore the **money market hedge** will be **preferable** if any of the options have to be **exercised**. However we do not know in advance whether the option will be exercised. For each option price, the option will be advantageous if the option is not exercised and the dollar is weaker than a certain spot rate.

	Payment on money market £	Less: amount hedged on forward market £	Premium £	Required option cost £	Required spot rate $\dfrac{\text{Amount hedged in £}}{\text{Required option cost}}$
1.42	195,017	(8,922)	(2,856)	183,239	266,250/183,239 = 1.4530
1.43	195,017	(7,609)	(4,145)	183,263	268,125/183,263 = 1.4631
1.44	195,017	(6,297)	(5,779)	182,941	270,000/182,941 = 1.4759

For each option price, the dollar will have to **weaken to beyond the required spot rate** for the best choice to be to take out the option and then not exercise it. The cost of 1.42 and 1.43 options is similar, but the 1.42 option is preferable as the dollar will have to weaken less for that to become the best choice.

BPP LEARNING MEDIA

(c)   **Advantages of countertrade**

  (1)   Countries such as Russia **lack commercial credit** or **convertible foreign currency** to pay for imports, and so countertrade in wheat and other commodities is needed to finance imports.

  (2)   **Countertrade** may be the **best means** of **obtaining new business** in the Russian market.

  (3)   **Countertrade** will **eliminate the risk of foreign exchange movements**.

  (4)   The company may be able to take advantage of the **futures** market in wheat.

  Disadvantages of countertrade

  (1)   Countertrade may prove **costly** for NTC. As well as **transportation costs**, it can create **lengthy and cumbersome administrative problems** just to set up a countertrade arrangement. **NTC** might have to **increase the export price** to cover the extra costs, or it might try to **absorb the extra costs itself**.

  (2)   NTC may be **pushed into agreeing** to accept large quantities of wheat without being able to dispose easily of all of it, either because **lack of access to markets** or because the **wheat is of poor quality**.

  (3)   The importer may place an **unrealistically high value** on the wheat it wishes to countertrade.

  (4)   It may be difficult to obtain **bank guarantees or insurance** to combat the risks of countertrade.

53 Casasophia Co

> **Text references.** NPV is covered in Chapter 5 and currency hedging in Chapter 16.
>
> **Top tips.** In part (a) you are looking for the strategy that maximises receipts for the company. If you are faced with a fraction of a contract when dealing with options, round down and hedge the remainder using a forward contract. Note that the futures contracts will be closed out before expiry therefore you will have to estimate the futures rate (either of the two ways given is acceptable).
>
> Be careful in part (b) as the project is due to start in 6 months' time rather than the more usual 1 year's time. This means that you will have to calculate forward rates for 6 months' time and then go up in increments of 1 year.
>
> **Easy marks.** This is quite a challenging question but you should be able to pick up some marks in performing the forward contract and futures contract calculations and adding comments.
>
> **Examiner's comments.** This question was not done well. In part (a) many students presented adequate calculations of the cash flows using different derivative products but failed to advise adequately (for example although options are generally more expensive they do provide more flexibility). In some cases students had difficulty in calculating an estimate for the basis remaining and occasionally students tried to use money market hedges despite the necessary information not being available in the question.
>
> Few attempts were made to calculate future spot rates based on purchasing power parity for part (b) and some answers just discounted the project in the local currency rather than in Euro.

Marking scheme

		Marks
(a)	Forward contract calculation	1
	Forward contract comment	1
	Futures contracts calculations	3
	Futures contracts comments	2
	Option contracts calculations	4
	Option contracts comments	2 - 3
	Conclusion	1
		Max 15
(b)	Estimates of forward rates	3
	Estimates of present values and net present value in Euros	3
	Discussion	4 - 5
		Max 10
		25

BPP
LEARNING MEDIA

(a)   **Hedging strategy**

Forward contract

The company will be receiving US$ therefore we use US$1.3623 as the rate.

Receipt in € = US$20m/1.3623 = **€14,681,054**

The hedge fixes the rate at €1 = US$1.3623. This rate is legally binding.

Futures contract

A 2 month contract is too short for the required hedge period therefore we must use a 5 month contract. The contract will be closed out in four months' time.

Predicted futures rate = 1.3698 – [1/3 x (1.3698 – 1.3633)] = 1.3676

Using the predicted futures rate, **expected receipt** = US$20m/1.3676 = **€14,624,159**

Number of contracts = €14,624,159/€125,000 = 117 contracts

Alternatively you can estimate the futures rate using the 5 month price, the spot rate and the four-month forward rate:

We could estimate the number of contracts needed as:

$000s		€000s	contract size	no contracts
20000	1.3698	14601	125	117

Outcome

The outcome will depend on the spot and future prices, the futures price can be estimates as follows:

	now	4 months	
spot rate	1.3618	1.3623	assumed
5 month future	1.3698	1.3639	balance
basis	0.008 x 1/5 =	0.0016	
	5 months	1 month remaining	

Assuming that the spot rate in 4 months is the same as the forward rate, the outcome will be:

		$000		€000s
Actual		$20,000		
assumed spot in 4 months			1.3623	
in euros				€ 14,681
Future				
opening	1.3698	to buy		
closing	1.3639	to sell		
ticks	(0.0059)			
loss incurred by Casasophia		($86)	1.3623	(€ 63)
(117 × 125,000 × 0.0059)				
				€ 14,618
lock in rate			1.3682	

Comments

The futures rate is worse than the forward rate. Futures contracts are marked to market on a daily basis and require margin payments as a result. As with forward contracts, futures contracts fix the rates and are legally binding.

Options

With options the holder has the right but not the obligation to exercise the option (that is, the option will be exercised if it is beneficial to the holder). However there is a premium to be paid for this flexibility, making options more expensive than futures and forward contracts.

To protect itself against a weakening US$, Casasophia will purchase Euro call options.

Exercise price = $1.36

Receipts = $20m/1.36 = €14,705,882

Number of contracts = €14,705,882/€125,000 = 117.6 contracts (117 contracts)

With 117 contracts, receipts = €125,000 × 117 = €14,625,000

Premium payable = $0.0280 × 117 × 125,000 = $409,500 (or $409,500/1.3585 = €301,435)

Amount not hedged = US$20m − (117 × €125,000 × 1.36) = US$110,000

This amount can be hedged using a 4 month forward contract as follows:

US$110,000/1.3623 = €80,746

Total receipts = €14,625,000 - €301,435 + €80,746 = **€14,404,311**

Exercise price $1.38

Receipts = $20m/1.38 = €14,492,754

Number of contracts = €14,492,754/€125,000 = 115.9 contracts (purchase 115 contracts)

With 115 contracts, receipts = €125,000 × 115 = €14,375,000

Premium payable = $0.0223 × 115 × 125,000 = US$320,563 (or $320,563/1.3585 = €235,968)

Amount not hedged = US$20m − (115 × €125,000 x 1.38) = US$162,500

This amount can be hedged using a 4 month forward contract as follows:

US$162,500/1.3623 = €119,284

Total receipts = €14,375,000 − €235,968 + €119,284 = **€14,258,316**

The receipts from either of the options are considerably lower than those from either the futures contract or the forward contract. This is primarily due to the premiums payable to secure the flexibility that options offer. The US$ would have to move significantly against the € to allow Casasophia to cover the cost of the premiums.

Conclusion

Based on the calculations above, it is recommended that Casasophia uses forward contracts to hedge against the US$ depreciating against the € in order to maximise receipts. The company should be aware that once the contract is agreed, the price is fixed and is legally binding. In addition there is no formal exchange for forward contracts, thus giving rise to default risk.

(b) Project NPV

Expected forward rates (using interest rate parity)

$$F_0 = S_0 \times \frac{(1 + i_c)}{(1 + i_b)}$$

Year	Forward rate (€1 = MShs)
Half year	128 × (1.108/1.022) = 138.77
	128 + [(138.77 − 128)/2] = 133.38
1.5 years	133.38 × (1.108/1.022) = 144.60
2.5 years	144.60 × (1.108/1.022) = 156.77
3.5 years	156.77 × (1.108/1.022) = 169.96

NPV calculation (note that year 1 actually means 1.5 years from now as project starts in 6 months' time)

Year	1	2	3
Income (MShs, million)	1,500	1,500	1,500
Forward rate	144.60	156.77	169.96
Income (€m)	10.37	9.57	8.82
Discount factor (12%)	0.893	0.797	0.712
DCF	9.26	7.63	6.28

Total Present Value = €23.17m

Total investment required (from part (b)) = €21.84m

NPV = €1.33m

Will the swap be beneficial for Casasophia?

Forward rates based on interest rate parity show that MShs is depreciating against the € as interest rates are much higher in Mazabia (10.8%) than in the European country (2.2%). However even with a depreciating MShs the project is still worthwhile (positive NPV).

When forward rates are estimated using purchasing power parity, it is assumed that forward rates will change according to differences between the two countries' inflation rates. If Mazabia's inflation rate is greater than the European country's rate, the MShs will depreciate against the €.

We are told that Mazabia's inflation rate could vary between 5% and 15% over the next few years therefore a swap would appear to be advantageous (as it would fix the future exchange rates). Without the swap there will be uncertainty over the NPV of the project.

Default risk should also be taken into consideration and Casasophia may ask the government of Mazabia to act as a guarantor in order to reduce the risk.

The grant funding will currently be provided directly to the Mazabian government in MShs. It may be worthwhile for Casasophia to explore the possibility of receiving the grant directly in € as this would reduce currency exposure.

54 HYK

Text references. Chapter 17.

Top tips. Remember that the contracts are required for four months, and the fact that they're needed in two months time is irrelevant for calculating the number of contracts. In (a) the question does not give a suggested figure for the movement in the price of the futures contract. It is better to assume that basis risk narrows evenly over the life of the contract. Alternatively you may assume that there is no change in basis risk. In either case, state your assumption. Transparency, speed and flexibility are key considerations in (b).

For part (c) it is important to note that hedging reduces uncertainty which is a problem in business planning.

Easy marks. Make sure you get the easiest 5 marks first, for the basic interest rate calculations at the start of answers and the type and number of contracts in (a) and also leave enough time to earn the marks available in (b).

(a)   The cost for HYK plc of borrowing £18 million for 4 months at today's rate of LIBOR + 0.75% is 6.5% + 0.75% = 7.25%

or £18m × 4/12 × 7.25% = £435,000.

Maximum interest desirable = 7.5% or £18m × 4/12 × 7.5% = £450,000

Hedging the borrowing rate using futures

Setup

(i)   Either March or June contracts; use March

(ii)   Sell March futures (ie pay interest at 100 − 93.1 = 6.9%)

(iii)   Number of contracts

$$\frac{£18 \text{ million}}{£500,000} \times \frac{4}{3} = 48 \text{ contracts}$$

Estimate closing futures price

March contract expires in 4 months

LIBOR is 6.5% (93.50)

March contract basis risk = 6.90% − 6.50% = 0.40%

1 February 2 months to expiry = 0.40 × 2/4 = 0.20

⇒ If LIBOR rises to 8% (92.00) future price will be 8.20%

If LIBOR falls to 6% (94.00) future price will be 6.20%

Outcome

The results of the hedge under cases (i) and (ii) are shown below.

(i)   **Futures market**

	Rises	Falls
1 Dec: Sell 48 @	6.90%	6.90%
1 Feb: Buy 48 @	8.20%	6.20%
Tick movement: $\dfrac{\text{opening rate} - \text{closing rate}}{0.01}$	1.30%	(0.70)%

(ii)   **Net outcome**

	£	£
Payment in spot market (LIBOR + 0.75%)	(8.75)	(6.75)
Profit/(Loss) in futures market	1.30	(0.70)
Net cost of loan	(7.45)	(7.45)

BPP
LEARNING MEDIA

In both cases the net interest cost after hedging is below the target maximum of £450,000 (or 7.50%).

In practice **basis risk** may **not move evenly**. Potential futures gains or losses between December and February may be large if interest rates are volatile, because they are computed on a daily basis.

Hedging the borrowing rate using traded options

Setup

(i) March or June contracts can be used. Assume March, since this will have a lower time premium at close out on 1 March.

(ii) Buy put options

(iii) A strike price of 93.50 will be used since this is closest to today's LIBOR. (100 – 6.5 = 93.50)

(iv) Number of contracts 48

(v) Tick size £12.50

(vi) Option premium March Put = 0.60%

Closing prices

	(i)	(ii)
Spot	8.75%	6.75%
Futures	8.20%	6.20%

Outcome

(i) **Option market outcome**

On 1 February, the possibilities are:

	(i)	(ii)
	Rises	Falls
LIBOR		
Put option strike price (right to sell)	6.50%	6.50%
March futures price	8.20%	6.20%
Exercise option? (prefer to sell at highest price)	Yes	No
Gain (ticks)	170	nil

(ii) **Net position**

	%	%
Actual interest cost	(8.75)	(6.75)
Value of option gain	1.70	Nil
Premium	(0.60)	(0.60)
Net cost of loan	(7.65)	(7.35)

Similarly, the results of using options with the other two strike prices are shown below. (You would not be expected to analyse all options in the exam.)

Strike price	94.00		93.00	
Premium on setup	1.35%		0.20%	
	(i)	(ii)	(i)	(ii)
	Rises	Falls	Rises	Falls
LIBOR				
Put option exercise price	6%	6%	7%	7%
March futures price	8.20%	6.20%	8.20%	6.20%
Exercise option?	Yes	Yes	Yes	No
Gain	2.20%	0.20%	1.20%	–
	%	%	%	%
Actual interest cost	(8.75)	(6.75)	(8.75)	(6.75)
Value of option gain	2.20	0.20	1.20	–
Premium	(1.35)	(1.35)	(0.20)	(0.20)
Net cost of loan	(7.90)	(7.90)	(7.75)	(6.95)

If LIBOR rises, none of the options **allow** the **required maximum** of 7.50%. If LIBOR falls, the cheapest option (the 93.00 option) is the best, but this is, of course the situation where no hedge is needed. The futures hedge appears to be better.

However, the time value of the options sold, which still have 2 months to expiry, has been ignored in these calculations. This is likely to have a significant impact on the calculations.

(b) **Advantages of traded interest rate options**

(i) The **prices** are **clearly visible** and no negotiation is required.

(ii) The market place gives **quick access** to buyers and sellers.

(iii) The **options** can be **sold** if not required and there is still time to expiry.

(iv) **Gains or losses** are **computed** ('marked to market') on a **daily basis** and ability of counterparties to meet obligations is monitored.

(v) **Traded options** are **normally American-style** (ie can be exercised at any time). They are more flexible than many OTC options which are European-style (ie can only be exercised on maturity date).

(vi) The market is **more highly regulated** than the OTC market.

Advantages of OTC options

The main advantage of **OTC options** is that they can be **tailored more exactly** to the **needs** of the purchaser, in terms of maturity date, contract size, currency and nature of interest. **Contract sizes** are **larger** than on the traded markets and longer times to expiry are available. These complexities tend to mean that they are more expensive.

(c) The main **arguments for a firm to undertake hedging against risk** can be summarised as follows:

(i) Hedging reduces the risks imposed on the firm's managers, employees, suppliers and customers by reducing cost of capital. This is achieved by reducing the firm's volatility with regards to market risk (that is, exchange rates, interest rates and hence beta).

(ii) Hedging can control the conflict of interest between bondholders and shareholders, thus reducing the agency costs of debt.

(iii) Hedging can increase the value of a firm, if capital market imperfections exist, since it lowers the probability of the firm encountering financial distress - which in turn lowers the expected costs of financial distress and the cost of capital. In addition, hedging encourages investment by the firm. According to the agency theory between shareholders and bondholders, the issuance of bonds, which have higher priority than equity, creates incentives for the firm's equity holders to underinvest. Hedging reduces the incentive to underinvest since hedging reduces uncertainty and the risk of loss. Firms with more valuable growth opportunities and higher leverage are more likely to be affected by the underinvestment problem and so are more likely to hedge.

55 Phobos Co

Text references. Interest rate risk and hedging are covered in Chapter 17.

Top tips. If you are familiar with interest rate hedging using derivatives, this should be a relatively straightforward question. Use the BPP proforma for setting up futures and options to ensure you do not forget any of the steps. Make sure you answer the question in part (a) – you are asked for the effective interest rates for each type of derivative. For options, the effective rate will be the average of the two annualised rates for each possible interest rate.

In part (b) divide your answer into pros and cons to make it easier for you and the marker to identify key points.

Part (c) requires a good knowledge of the Black-Scholes model formula.

Easy marks. Part (a) allows you to pick up a number of easy marks such as in the calculation of the number of contracts. You can gain easy marks in part (b) if you are familiar with the pros and cons of derivatives for interest rate hedging purposes.

BPP LEARNING MEDIA

			Marks
(a)	Calculation of current interest rate		1
	Identification of appropriate future and hedge strategy		1
	Calculation of number of contracts		3
	(i)	Calculation of basis for interest rate futures	2
		Calculation of gain/loss on alternative close-outs	2
	(ii)	Identification of most appropriate option strategy	1
		Calculation of premium payable	1
		Calculation of loan cost under alternative payoffs	2
		Estimation of expected payoff given equal likelihoods	1
			14
(b)	Problems of making efficient match		1
	Hedge efficiency issues		1
	Default and basis risk		1
	Leveraged swaps and FRAs		2
	Dangers of leveraging		1
			6
(c)	One mark per fully explained point		Max 5
			25

(a) **Estimation of effective interest rate cost using different hedging techniques**

(i) **Futures**

Current interest = Length of exposure x amount of exposure × (LIBOR + 50 basis points)

= 4/12 × £30 million × 6.5%

= **£650,000**

Type of future = **March** future with an open price of 93.800 and a settlement price of 93.880

$$\text{Number of contracts} = \frac{\text{Amount of exposure}}{\text{Contract size}} \times \frac{\text{Length of exposure}}{\text{Contract period}}$$

$$= \frac{£30\,\text{million}}{£500,000} \times \frac{4\,\text{months}}{3\,\text{months}} = \textbf{80 contracts}$$

Basis = Current spot price – settlement price = 94.00 – 93.88 = 12 basis points (ticks)

Between the closure and maturity of the contract (one month), movement will be 4 ticks (12/3).

Close-out price if interest rate (a) increases, or (b) decreases by 100 basis points

	7%	5%
Interest rate at close-out		
Open price	93.88	93.88
Futures price at close-out	92.96	94.96
Number of ticks	92	(108)
Total value (80 contracts at £12.50 per tick)	92,000	(108,000)
Cost of loan in spot market	750,000	550,000
Less profit/(loss) on futures	92,000	(108,000)
Net cost of loan	658,000	658,000
Annual equivalent	**6.58%**	**6.58%**

(ii) **Traded options**

Type of option = March put option

Number of contracts = 80 (see above)

Premium = Number of contracts x premium on March put option x tick size
= 80 × 16.8 × £12.50
= £16,800

Basis = 4 ticks (see (a)(i) above)

Outcomes versus expected movements in interest rates

Interest rate at close-out	7%	5%
Futures price at close-out	92.96	94.96
Exercise price	94.00	94.00
Exercise option?	Yes	No
Option payoff (ticks)	104.00	Nil
80 contracts at £12.50 per tick	104,000	Nil
Cost of loan in spot market	750,000	550,000
Less option payoff	(104,000)	Nil
Less premium	16,800	16,800
Net cost of loan	662,800	566,800
Annual equivalent	6.63%	5.67%
Effective interest rate (average)	**6.15%**	

(b) **Pros and cons of using derivatives to manage interest rate risk**

Pros

In a climate of volatile interest rates, exposure to potential interest rate risk is more acute. Companies can use various financial derivative instruments to hedge against such risk, including futures, forward rate agreements (FRA), options and swaps.

The most obvious advantage of using derivatives is that the interest rate that will be applied in the future is **fixed** and there are no surprises. This helps with **financial planning** as companies know how much interest they will have to pay and can budget accordingly.

Futures and FRAs allow companies to **perfectly match** their hedged amounts with the amount of exposure as they can be tailored to the particular needs of the company in question. Whilst **traded options** do not offer this facility, they do offer **flexibility**. If the prevailing interest rate at the time at which options should be exercised is better than the 'locked-in' rate, companies can just let the options lapse – that is, options offer companies **the right but not the obligation** to accept the locked-in rate at the date of maturity.

To avoid the expensive premiums that come with the flexibility of options, companies may use **interest rate swaps** – for example, a company may swap a fixed rate stream of interest payments for a variable rate stream. This allows companies to take advantage of **favourable movements** in interest rates.

Cons

Traded options do not allow perfect hedging as they come in standardised amounts. This could lead to a company purchasing more options than required (expensive and unnecessary) or less than required (leading to some of the exposure being unhedged). In order to hedge the outstanding exposure the company may have to purchase **futures or FRAs**.

Options are **expensive** means of hedging as their flexibility comes at a high price. Regardless of whether the option is exercised, the company must pay a **premium** for the right (but not the obligation) to exercise.

Whilst **swaps** allow companies to exchange fixed rate interest payment streams for variable rate streams, it is often **difficult to gauge the extent of the risk exposure** and to ensure that the exposure (and the swaps) are effectively managed by the company. This can lead to companies suffering **losses** that may be on such a scale as to threaten their survival.

BPP
LEARNING MEDIA

(c) **Short-term nature of instruments**

The finance director's assertion about the nature of instruments is correct. Most are designed to hedge for interest rate changes over months rather than years. They are a form of **insurance** for the buyer, where the seller assumes the risk in return for a premium. They are not designed to deal with interest rate changes over a long period, where movements are less certain and the **risks to the provider of the option** would be **greater**.

Renewal of instruments

Costs to Phobos will become **less certain** if a succession of short-term instruments are used to hedge the risk. Phobos may find that once the term of the instrument has expired, an instrument offering the same rate is not available or only available at an **increased premium,** because **expectations about rate rises** have **changed**.

Pricing of instruments

The pricing of instruments will take account of **predicted interest rate movements, uncertainties in predictions** and build in a **profit element** as well. Every time Phobos buys a new instrument, it will be paying a premium to the sellers of the instrument that reflects these considerations. The cumulative cost of these premiums over the time period will be greater than the increased interest costs that Phobos will incur if it purchases the fixed interest rate swap.

56 Katmai Co

Text references. Interest rate risk and hedging are covered in Chapter 17. Value at Risk is covered in Chapter 5.

Top tips. In part (a), remember that 'doing nothing' is a viable option! In part (b), make sure you adjust for the fact that interest is payable at six-monthly intervals (as given in the question).

Easy marks. The Value at Risk calculations offer some easy marks as does the discussion of uses and limitations.

Marking scheme

			Marks
(a)	Enumeration and evaluation of the three choices (credit will be given for reasonable alternative choices)		
	Do nothing	2	
	Retire and reissue	2	
	Swap	2	
	Recommendation of appropriate course of action in the case	3	
			9
(b)	Calculation of 3.3%	4	
	Calculation of annual rate	1	
			5
(c)	Calculation of six-month volatility	1	
	Calculation of VAR	3	
	Comments on the results	2	
			6
(d)	One mark per well explained point	Max 5	
			25

(a) **Alternative choices available for managing interest rate exposure**

(i) **Do nothing**. This is a risky option and involves the company taking a gamble that future interest rates either stay the same or fall. Before taking such a decision the company should assess the degree of interest rate diversification on its overseas debt and the amount of any interest receivable.

(ii) **Move to fixed rate debt**. This would involve retiring the existing debt and issuing fixed rate bonds. This is a much less risky option than (i) above and protects the company against rising interest rates. However setting up such debt can be expensive.

(iii) **Enter into an interest rate swap**. The company would swap variable element (the LIBOR) for a fixed rate for the term of the loan. Such swaps are easy to set up but the company may find it has to reverse the swap if it wants to retire the debt early.

A movement from variable to fixed rate debt will reduce interest rate risk and will stabilise interest payments, thus making planning more straightforward. WACC is unlikely to change significantly. If managing interest rate risk is a core activity in the budgeting process then option (ii) should be considered. The fixed rate option would also be favourable for management and employees as it would stabilise the surplus from which any bonuses and other perks will be paid.

Equity investors may prefer option (i). Although this is the most risky of the three, the cost of setting up fixed rate debt or swaps may outweigh the perceived benefits from doing so.

From a cost viewpoint, option (iii) is most likely to be preferred by other stakeholders as it offers protection from interest rate movements but at a lower cost than (ii).

(b) **Estimation of six-monthly interest rate and effective annual interest rate**

Payments	LIBOR/2 + 0.6%
Receipt under vanilla swap	LIBOR/2
Payment on fixed element	(5.4/2) = 2.7%
Net payment	3.30%

Effective annual interest rate = $(1 + \text{six-month rate})^2 - 1 = 1.033^2 - 1 = 6.7\%$

(c) **Estimation of six-monthly Value at Risk (VaR)**

$\sigma_6 = \sigma_a \sqrt{N}$ where σ = standard deviation (volatility); N = number of time periods

$\sigma_6 = 1.5\% \times \sqrt{0.5} = 1.061$

This means that at the 95% confidence level, the interest rate will be 2.1% above or below current LIBOR.

At 95% confidence level:

VAR = Size of loan x σ_6 x 1.645

VAR = $150 million x 1.061% x 1.645

VAR = $2.62 million

The VaR figure above means that there is a 5% chance that the interest payments will exceed the interest expected by $2.62 million. For example, if LIBOR was 6%, interest payable for 6 months would be 3.6% x $150 million = $5.4 million. There would be a 5% chance that interest paid would exceed ($5.4 million + $2.62 million) $8.02 million.

(d) The **purpose** of VaR is to indicate the **potential scale of any loss of value** that may arise in extreme circumstances. What VaR gives is the **amount by which a value may fall over a given period of time at a given level of probability**, though perhaps this should say minimum amount. For example, if VaR is $1m at 5% over one week, then there is a 5% chance that, over a one-week period, we could lose $1m **or more**. As such, VAR does not place a limit on the scale of any potential losses, its aim is to quantify potential extremes.

To evaluate VaR we need to have:

- A unit of measure, eg $
- A specified time period
- A specified probability level (usually between 1% and 5%)
- A distribution for asset returns/values

BPP LEARNING MEDIA

Modelling the distribution is the most problematic and a number of different methods have been developed to deal with this, including

(i) **Parametric VaR** – where it is assumed that returns are normally distributed, making it relatively easy to assess. However share returns have not been observed to be normal and the returns from option type assets are far from normally distributed

(ii) **Historical simulation VaR** – where the distribution of returns is assessed using various financial models (eg Black-Scholes for options). This is again easy to understand and assess but requires extensive market data

(iii) **Monte Carlo simulation** – where returns from various assets are assumed to follow historical patterns and a series of simulations is run, combining various possibilities across all assets to get an overall distribution

None of these methods is foolproof and VaR appears to be **most effective** for **frequently traded assets** (for example, it is used to determine the initial margin on futures contracts).

VaR should not be viewed in isolation, rather it should be considered as just **one of many evaluation techniques**. VaR tells little about how large the amount of loss may be under extreme circumstances. The **application** of VaR ideas over different assets, classes and currencies, especially when overlaid with derivatives such as options and swaps, is very **problematic**.

57 Sembilan Co

Text references. Chapter 17 for interest rate hedging, chapter 13 for debt-equity swaps.

Top tips. For part (a) you need to use the forward rates rather than the current yield curve rates for years 2 to 4. Don't forget the second part of the requirement!

For part (b) (ii) it is important to note that the bank has guaranteed the swap.

Part (c) requires you to think about the implications of raising equity to pay off debt, including the willingness of the shareholders to participate.

Easy marks. Part (b) (i) is fairly straightforward, it just requires you to choose a higher and lower rate to use for the illustration.

Examiner's comments. Part (a) required the candidates to calculate the variable amounts received and the fixed amounts paid by Sembilan Co to Ratus Bank based on forward rates. A number of candidates incorrectly included the 60 basis points, which is part of the original loan contract but would not be part of the swap; and some answers used the spot rates instead of the forward rates. It is surprising that the responses contained basic errors when there was a recent article in the Student Accountant on how a swap contract can be valued based on forward rates and a fixed rate. Few candidates could explain why the fixed rate was lower than the 4-year spot rate.

In part (b) many responses gave explanations, rather than a demonstration, that the payment liability did not change. Many of the explanations lacked adequate detail. The requirement 'Demonstrate' means that the candidates should show, by examples or otherwise, that the payment does not change whether interest rates increase or decrease. Few managed to do this with any clarity.

			Marks	
(a)	Gross amount receivable by Sembilan Co		1	
	Gross amounts payable by Sembilan Co		1	
	Net amounts receivable or payable every year		2	
	Explanation of why fixed rate is less than the four-year yield curve rate		2	
				6
(b)	(i)	Demonstration of impact of interest rate changes	4	
		Explanation and conclusion	1	
				5
	(ii)	1 mark per relevant discussion point	Max 5	
(c)	1 – 2 marks per relevant discussion point		Max 9	
				25

(a) Gross amounts of interest receivable from Rabus Bank based on year 1 spot rate and years 2-4 forward rates.

Year 1 = 0.025 × \$320m = \$8m
Year 2 = 0.037 × \$320m = \$11.84m
Year 3 = 0.043 × \$320m = \$13.76m
Year 4 = 0.047 × \$320m = \$15.04m

Fixed gross amount of interest receivable from Rabus Bank in each of the years 1-4
3.7625% × \$320m = \$12.04m

Therefore the expected receipts / (payments) are:

Year 1 = \$8.00m – \$12.04m = (\$4.04m)
Year 2 = \$11.84m – \$12.04m = (\$0.20m)
Year 3 = \$13.76m – \$12.04m = \$1.72m
Year 4 = \$15.04m – \$12.04m = \$3.00m

The equivalent fixed rate of 3.7625% is less than the 3.8% four-year yield curve rate because the 3.8% represents a zero-coupon bond with one payment in the fourth year. The relevant bond here pays coupons at different time periods when the yield curve rates are lower, hence the fixed rate is lower.

(b) (i)

	% impact %	Yield interest 3% \$m	Yield interest 5% \$m
Borrow at yield + 60 basis points	(Yield + 0.6)	(11.52)	(17.92)
Receive yield	Yield	9.60	16.00
Pay fixed	(3.7625)	(12.04)	(12.04)
Fee 20 basis points	(0.2)	(0.64)	(0.64)
	4.5625	(14.60)	(14.60)

The receipt and payment based on the yield curve remove the fluctuating element, leaving the 60 basis points borrowing charge, the 20 basis points fee and the fixed payment rate. 0.6% + 3.7625% + 0.2% = 4.5625%

(ii) Sembilan Co is using the swap to manage its **interest rate risk** and is protecting against a rise in interest rates. This has been done without changing the initial debt of \$320 million, which is already in issue.

The interest rate payments are fixed, which means that it is much easier for Sembilan Co to **forecast its future cash flows** and also helps to budget accurately.

BPP
LEARNING MEDIA

The cost to Sembilan Co is relatively small, especially when compared to **potential losses** if interest rates are to rise. Other derivatives, such as options, are typically more expensive.

The swap will be relatively **straightforward**, with the bank undertaking all the relevant administration and organisation. Other derivatives would be more time-consuming to arrange.

The main disadvantage is that Sembilan Co will be unable to take advantage of a **favourable movement** in interest rates.

There is no **counterparty risk** involved as the bank is guaranteeing the swap and will make good any default.

(c) Issuing equity and using the proceeds to reduce the amount of debt will **change the capital structure** of Sembilan Co and there are a number of implications of this which needs to be considered.

As the proportion of debt compared to equity increases, **financial distress also increases** and associated costs along with it. Companies with high levels of financial distress may find that suppliers demand more onerous credit terms, they may have to give longer credit terms to attract customers and pay higher wages to attract employees. Also providers of equity may **demand a higher level of return** because financial risk has increased. In addition, there may be restrictive covenants that make it more difficult to raise funds (either debt or equity). On the other hand, there will be greater levels of tax relief from the higher interest payments. However this is only available while the company is making taxable profits or **tax exhaustion** will set in. Sembilan Co is assumed to have judged the relative benefits of high and low levels of financial gearing in making its original decision on debt and equity levels.

The proposed equity issue will change the existing balance and therefore the value of Sembilan Co may not be maximised. However a **lower debt level** would result in a **higher credit rating** for the company as well as reduce the scale of restrictive covenants. Increasing the level of equity would also increase the debt capacity of the company, which would help to raise finance for future projects more easily. Reduced financial distress may make it easier to deal with stakeholders such as suppliers and customers.

Changing the financial structure of a company can be expensive. There are likely to be costs for the early redemption of debt which can be found in the contractual clauses of the debt to be repaid. **A new issue of equity may also be expensive**, especially if shares are offered to new shareholders as there will be marketing costs and underwriting costs as well. Although a rights issue may be less expensive, the costs may still be significant.

If a rights issue is undertaken, Sembilan Co will need to decide on whether the current shareholders will be able to take up the rights and the level of discount to the current market price that should be offered to ensure a full take up of rights. The impact of the rights issue on the current price should be considered as well. Studies have shown that **typically markets view rights issues positively** and the share price does not reduce to the theoretical ex-rights price. However this is because the funds are usually spent on profitable projects and the reaction may not be so positive if the funds are to be used to repay debt.

The move will need to be justified to the market and so Sembilan Co will need to provide information to existing and any new shareholders which shows that one group will not be favoured at the expense of another. Sufficient information is required to **prevent issues with information asymmetry**, but if too much information is produced it may reduce the competitive position of Sembilan Co.

58 Lamri Co

Text references. Dividend capacity is covered in Chapter 18.

Top tips. The bulk of the marks relate to calculations in this question therefore it is important to show all your workings. However there is a lot to do for 14 marks so try to identify shortcuts where you can – for example, the cash from domestic activities both prior to and subsequent to the implementation of the proposal is the same so there is no need to calculate this twice.

Don't be afraid to state what you might think is the obvious. There are marks available for identifying the irrelevance of adjusting for depreciation so make sure you mention your reasons for not including this calculation.

In part (b) it is important to recognise that the implementation of the proposal would result in a shortfall in dividend capacity (don't forget to uplift existing dividend by 8%). By recognising this issue, you can then make suggestions as to how the problem can be overcome.

Easy marks. There are several easy marks to be gained in the calculations in part (a) – for example, calculating operating profit, interest and tax. Part (c) is a straightforward discussion of mechanisms to prevent transfer price manipulation.

Examiner's comments. This question required a logical and systematic approach as a lot was being asked (particularly in part (a)). Good attempts at part (a) achieved high marks but sometimes the answers were not appropriately structured which resulted in mixed-up answers. Few appropriate answers were received for part (b) and mostly reflected the disorganised approach to part (a).

Marking scheme

			Marks
(a)	Calculation of operating profit, interest and domestic tax	3	
	Calculation of investments in working capital and non-current assets (including correct treatment of depreciation)	3	
	Calculation of dividend remittance before new policy implementation	2	
	Calculation of additional tax payable on Magnolia profits before new policy implementation	1	
	Calculation of dividend remittance after new policy implementation	3	
	Calculation of additional tax payable on Magnolia profits after new policy implementation	1	
	Dividend capacity	1	
			14
(b)	Concluding comments and explanation of reason	2	
	Possible actions (1 mark per suggestion)	4	
			6
(c)	1 mark per valid point	5	
			25

BPP
LEARNING MEDIA

(a)   **Dividend capacity**

Prior to implementing TE's proposal

	$m
Operating profit (30% of $80m)	24.00
Less interest (8% of $35m)	(2.80)
Profit before tax	21.20
Less tax (28%)	(5.94)
Profit after tax	15.26
Less investment in working capital [15% of (20/120 x $80m)]	(2.00)
Less investment in non-current assets [25% of (20/120 x $80m)]	(3.33)
Less investment in new project	(4.50)
Cash flow from domestic activities	5.43
Overseas subsidiaries dividend remittances (W1)	3.16
Less tax paid on Magnolia's profits [(28 – 22)% of $5.40m]	(0.32)
Dividend capacity	8.27

Tutorial note. There is no need to add back depreciation to obtain cash flow as the investment that amounts to the total depreciation charged will cancel out this calculation. The effect is therefore neutral.

After implementing TE's proposal

	$m
Cash flows from domestic activities (see above)	5.43
Overseas subsidiaries dividend remittances (W2)	2.71
Additional tax on Magnolia's profits (6% of $3.12m)	(0.19)
Dividend capacity	7.95

Workings

(1)   **Overseas subsidiaries dividend remittances prior to TE's proposal**

	Magnolia $m	Strymon $m
Sales revenue	15.00	5.70
Less variable costs	(2.40)	(3.60)
Less transferred costs	(5.70)	Nil
Less fixed costs	(1.50)	(2.10)
Operating profit	5.40	Nil
Less tax	(1.19)	Nil
Profit after tax	4.21	Nil
Remitted to Lamri	(3.16)	Nil
Retained in company	1.05	Nil

(2)   **Overseas subsidiaries dividend remittances after implementing TE's proposal**

	Magnolia $m	Strymon $m
Sales revenue	15.00	7.98
Less variable costs	(2.40)	(3.60)
Less transferred costs	(7.98)	Nil
Less fixed costs	(1.50)	(2.10)
Operating profit	3.12	2.28
Less tax	(0.69)	(0.96)
Profit after tax	2.43	1.32
Remitted to Lamri	(1.82)	(0.89)
Withholding tax		(0.1)
Retained in company	0.61	0.33

(b)   **Comments on impact of TE's proposal**

If the proposal is implemented, Lamri's dividend capacity will fall from $8.27m to $7.95m. Whilst the dividend capacity prior to implementation of the proposal exceeds the dividend to be paid ($7.5m x 1.08 = $8.1m), the proposal would lead to a shortfall in dividend capacity. The shortfall arises due to the high tax rate paid on Strymon's profits that Lamri cannot obtain credit for. Not only does Lamri lose the withholding tax on the remittances (10%), it is also paying an additional 14% in corporation tax (42 – 28).

There are several ways in which the problem of this relatively small shortfall could be overcome. Lamri might consider reducing the growth rate of its dividends to a level that would be covered by the dividend capacity of $7.95m. However this might send adverse signals to the market given that a steady 8% growth has been maintained over the last few years.

Another alternative would be to borrow the shortfall. This may not be a popular option if Lamri wishes to avoid increasing its borrowings, particularly to fund dividend payments. Given that it would have to borrow to fund current shortfalls, there is a possibility that this problem would continue in the future, leading to even greater borrowings or the potential of having to reduce dividend growth.

Lamri might wish to consider postponing the project to a later date but the potential impact on company business would have to be evaluated. We are told in the scenario that a number of projects are in the pipeline for the future. Therefore postponing a current investment may not be feasible without impacting on future investments.

The final possibility would be to ask for a higher remittance from Strymon or Magnolia. The main problem with this would be the potential negative impact on morale of the subsidiaries' managers if they are required to pay over greater proportions of their profits (which may affect any profit-related benefits they may have).

(c)   Transfer price manipulation is said to occur where Lamri uses transfer prices avoid payment of taxes and tariffs, or other controls that the government of the host country has put in place.

The most common solution that tax authorities have adopted to reduce the probability of transfer price manipulation is to develop particular transfer pricing regulations as part of the corporate income tax code. These regulations are based on the concept of the arm's length standard, which states that all intra-firm activities of Lamri should be priced as if they took place between unrelated parties acting at arm's length in competitive market.

The arm's length standard is defined as the prices which would have been agreed upon between unrelated parties engaged in the same or similar transactions under the same or similar conditions in the open market. In the absence of the existence of data to allow a reasonable estimate of the arm's length standard then the alternative methods used to establish the arm's length transfer price include:

(i)   **Comparable uncontrolled price**
       This method looks for a comparable product to the transaction in question being traded by Lamri in a comparable transaction with an unrelated party or the same or similar product being traded between two unrelated parties.

(ii)   **Resale price method**
       This method focuses on one side of the transaction, either the manufacturer or distributor, to estimate the transfer price using a functional approach.

(iii) **Cost plus method**
       This method starts with the costs of production, measured using recognised accounting principles and then adds an appropriate mark up over costs. The appropriate mark up is estimated from those earned by similar manufacturers.

(iv)   **Comparable profit method**
       This method is based on the premise that companies in a similar industry to Lamri will tend to have similar financial performance and to have similar financial characteristics. This similarity in performance will be indicated by a similarity in financial ratios.

(v)   **Profit split method**
       This method allocates the profit earned on a transaction between related parties.

BPP
LEARNING MEDIA

59 Moose Co

Text references. The global debt problem and Islamic finance are both dealt with in Chapters 19. Credit risk is covered in Chapter 7a.

Top tips. This is a highly topical question and highlights the importance of keeping up to date with current issues in the financial markets. Part (a) in particular offers you the opportunity to demonstrate your knowledge and understanding of the global credit crisis. Throughout the question make sure you relate your answer to the company in the scenario. It would be very easy to get carried away here, particularly if you have a wide knowledge of the subject.

Easy marks. If you have knowledge of the issues surrounding the credit crunch, you should pick up some easy marks in part (a).

Marking scheme

		Marks

The mark ranges reflect the flexibility the examiner and markers use in assessing this question. The following points are indicative only.

(a) Origins of the credit crunch and its impact upon lenders — 1 - 2

Impact of the credit crunch on bank attitudes to borrowers and wider economy — 1 - 2

Importance of asset strength and default assessment — 2 - 3

Other relevant comments — 2 - 3

Max 7

(b) Loan syndication as a means of spreading load and risk — 1 – 2

Flexibility of syndication and possibility of cross-border finance — 2 – 3

Cost of loan syndication versus bond issues — 1 – 2

Flexibility of bonds in terms of repayments and size of issue — 1 - 2

Max 7

(c) Note on the significance of the real option to delay and the factors that might influence that decision. Other relevant points such as strategic and operational benefits of not delaying — Max 6

(d) One mark per relevant benefit or drawback — Max 5

25

(a) **Likely factors that a bank might consider in offering a $350 million loan**

The 'credit crunch' had its origins in years of lax lending by financial institutions. Funds were both easy and cheap to obtain, even to those with weak credit ratings (**sub-prime borrowers**) and were ploughed into property. The idea was that if such borrowers had difficulty in making repayments, the rising house prices would allow them to remortgage their property. However when interest rates started to climb, as they inevitably have to, house prices fell. Borrowers began to default on mortgage payments, leaving banks with huge losses, as the value of **collateralised debt obligations** plummeted.

Numerous banks came close to bankruptcy, many of which had to be bailed out by their respective governments. As a result there has been greater reluctance by banks to lend money. Banks with no government bail-out package were forced to raise additional equity capital in order to maintain their capital adequacy ratios which meant that liquidity was significantly reduced. More stringent requirements were put in place for potential borrowers, both corporate and individual, and the effects have been widely felt.

Lending rates, particularly to those seeking mortgages, **rose** and people found it more difficult to raise capital to buy property. The pessimism in the market in general has been felt by many industrialised countries in the form of slow-down or cessation of investment which has led to recession in numerous economies (including the UK). Interest rates remain low to try to stimulate economies back into growth and whilst banks are slowly increasing their willingness to lend they remain cautious.

Default risk remains a concern but as Moose Co is in a relatively strong liquidity position it may be looked on more favourably by the banks. Its highly profitable position, coupled with strong cash flows, suggests a high credit rating which will be more attractive to lenders. Despite this position however the company will no doubt be subject to a stringent credit risk assessment with particular emphasis on its cash flow position relative to its debt obligations.

As well as cash flow strength, asset strength will be a major factor in determining the likelihood of the company raising the necessary finance. Banks will be interested in the level of collateral the company can offer to support the loan as this will offer reassurance that they will be compensated in the event of default. If the value of the assets offered to support the loan exceed the value of the loan itself (known as **over-collateralisation**) the company is likely to be in a strong position to secure the necessary finance.

(b) **Loan syndication versus bond issue**

Loan syndication is the combination of several lenders to provide various proportions of a loan. One lender normally 'leads' the syndicate. One of the benefits of syndication is that it allows banks to **offer much higher loans** that would normally be feasible if acting singly, as several banks provide smaller portions of the total principal. Whilst the effective cost of a syndicated loan is likely to be higher than that obtained from a single lender, it is usually still lower than the cost of a bond issue. Loan syndication also makes **cross-border financing** more straightforward.

Bonds are where the amount is securitised and floated on the capital market, with a coupon rate and set redemption date. One of the disadvantages of bonds is the **high issue costs**. As with bank loans, some bonds may be syndicated with an investment bank managing the process. The size of the loan being sought is at the lower end of the scale of loan that might be raised through bond issue.

There is evidence to suggest that **large companies** with **high credibility** and performance (but fewer growth opportunities) prefer **syndicated loans**. Companies with higher levels of short-term debt and are perceived by the market to have more growth opportunities tend to favour bond issues.

The main advantage of syndicated loans over bond issues is the **lower issue costs**. However bonds tend to be more **flexible** in terms of coupon rate and date of redemption.

(c) **Advantages and disadvantages of entering capital market**

One of the issues to be considered is whether there is an **option to delay** on the project being financed. Options to delay (if they exist) can be appraised using the Black-Scholes model. If there is a positive option to delay then this should be taken up.

There are various uncertainties surrounding the economic climate which leads to numerous assumptions being made. This increases the **risk** of the project which could in turn increase the rate of return required. Moose Co should undertake sensitivity analysis on the project to determine the extent to which critical factors can change before NPV becomes negative.

There are also **strategic and operational factors** to consider. How will the company be perceived by the market if the project is delayed? Will this decision reduce confidence in the company's future success? Will potential investors increase the perceived risk attached to the company? Could a competitor take advantage of the delay by moving operations into South America first? All of these issues may have long-term effects on the company's continued success and development, including availability of future finance.

From an operational perspective, will the delay to development affect the day-to-day business of the company? Will it affect current products and customers? What about financial results? These issues must be considered before a final decision is taken on whether the project should be delayed.

(d) **Benefits of Islamic finance**

Islamic finance operates by the underlying principle that there should be a link between the economic activity that creates value and the financing of that economic activity. The main advantages of Islamic finance for Moose Co are that excessive profiteering is not allowed, only reasonable mark-ups are allowed, and that since Islamic banks cannot use excessive leverage they are less likely to collapse.

BPP
LEARNING MEDIA

Drawbacks of Islamic finance

The use of Islamic finance does not remove all commercial risk, indeed there may even be additional risk from the use of Islamic finance. There are the following drawbacks from the use of Islamic finance:

There is no standard Sharia'a model for the Islamic finance market, meaning that documentation is often tailor-made for the transaction, leading to higher transaction costs than for the conventional finance alternative.

Due to governmental and Sharia'a restrictions, Islamic finance institutions are subject to additional compliance work, which can also increase transaction costs.

60 GoSlo Motor Corp

Text references. Credit enhancement, credit default swaps and securitisation are covered in Chapter 19.

Top tips. The most challenging part of this question is probably where to start! Even if you are not confident about how to proceed, you can at least calculate the income from the loans (don't forget to account for the service charges) and the amounts owing on the A-rated and B-rated tranches. Remember to take account of the swap arrangement that will cancel out LIBOR in exchange for a fixed rate of interest.

If you have at least some knowledge of credit enhancement and securitisation, you should be able to answer parts (b) and (c). Don't forget to relate your answer to the particular scenario.

For part (d) you need to show the effect of GoSlo taking out a credit default swap under both situations and illustrate the reduction in risk from this.

Easy marks. There are a few easy marks to be picked up in parts (b) and (c).

Marking scheme

			Marks
(a)	Calculation of expected return from pool (inc service charge and over-collateralisation)	2	
	Role and impact of swap on A-tranche	2	
	Calculation of annual liabilities for tranches A-rated and B-rated	2	
	Estimation of return to subordinated certificates	1	
	Impact of marginal change and calculation of sensitivity	3	
			10
(b)	Explanation and purpose of securitisation	1 – 2	
	Methods of credit enhancement		
	Tranching		
	Ratings agency involvement		
	Over-collateralisation		
	Others	2 – 3	
			Max 4
(c)	Correlation risk	2 – 3	
	Timing and liquidity risk	1 – 2	
	Collateral risk	2 – 3	
	(Credit will be given for alternative, relevant points)		Max 6
(d)	Illustration of CDS if no default	3	
	Illustration of CDS if default after 3 years	2	
			5
			25

(a)   **Expected returns on investment**

The least complicated technique to employ here is the comparison of cash inflows and cash outflows.

Cash inflows

	$m
Loan income (10.5% of $200m)	21.00
Less service charges	(0.24)
Net cash inflow	20.76

Cash outflows

Note: 80% of collateral value at LIBOR + 140 basis points

This is the subject of a swap arrangement that exchanges LIBOR for a fixed rate of 8.5%. Net payments will be 1.4% of total A-rated loan notes plus 8.5% of total A-rated loan notes.

	$m
A-rated loan notes:	
1.4% of (0.8 × 0.95 × $200m)	2.13
8.5% of (0.8 × 0.95 × $200m)	12.92
B-rated loan notes: 11% of (0.10 × 0.95 × $200m)	2.09
Total cash outflows	17.14

Difference between the cash inflows and cash outflows goes to the unrated subordinated certificates.

Balance = $3.62m

Value of unrated subordinated certificates = 10% of (0.95 × $200m) = $19m

Return on investment = 3.62m/19m = 19.05%

Sensitivity analysis

If loan income fell by 1% (to $20.79), this would reduce net cash inflow from loan income to $20.55m – a reduction of $0.21m.

This would reduce cash available for unrated subordinated certificates from $3.62m to $3.41m (a fall of 5.8%).

Return on investment = 3.41m/19m = 17.95%

Summary – a 1% reduction in loan income leads to a 5.8% reduction in revenue for unrated subordinated certificates.

(b)   **Credit enhancement – purpose and methods**

Credit enhancement is the process of **reducing credit risk** by requiring collateral, insurance or other agreements to provide the lender with reassurance that is will be compensated in the event of default by the borrower.

Credit enhancement is a key part of the **securitisation** transaction in structured finance (such as mortgages and car loans).

A ratings agency will usually advise on the structure of the liabilities created. The A-rated tranche will attract such investors as banks and other financial institutions as they require low levels of risk exposure. The reduction in risk for such institutions is compensated for by the increase in risk for investors in subordinated certificates.

Other methods of credit enhancement include **over-collateralisation** and the issue of **credit default swaps** (CDS). Over-collateralisation occurs when the value of assets held to support a security exceeds the value of the security itself. Credit default swaps act in a similar manner to insurance policies whereby credit risk is transferred from the buyer of the swap to the seller (similar to house or car insurance).

(c)   **Risk to investors**

Correlation risk

The general assumption is that defaults on the part of the borrower are **uncorrelated**. However if there is a degree of positive correlation (for example, the number of defaults on car loans being positively correlated to the recession and unemployment) then there is likely to be **greater volatility** in the amounts received by the lenders.

BPP
LEARNING MEDIA

Collateral risk and default risk

The success of the securitisation process will depend on the **accuracy** of the assessment of quality of car loans made to purchasers. Car dealers are responsible for assessing the credit risk associated with purchasers and ensuring that loans are properly negotiated. There is **risk of default** and also risk attached to **the value of the vehicle** in the event of repossession.

Timing and liquidity risks

Timing of cash inflows is essential to ensure the fulfilment of commitments to the three tranches. If there is insufficient cash coming in from the loans at the right time, GoSlo Motor Corporation will be unable to pay its obligations to the tranche investors (that is, there will be **liquidity** problems).

(d) (i)   GoSlo would take out a CDS with a notional value of $5million and pay an annual premium to the bank of 450 basis points, or 4.5% which is $5 million × 4.5% = $225,000.

Therefore the total cost of the CDS will be $225,000 × 4 = $900,000 over four years.

In the event of no default, GoSlo will receive the $5 million, but will have paid $900,000 to hedge away the default risk.

(ii) If there is default after 3 years, GoSlo will stop paying the premiums, so only $675,000 will have been paid to the bank.

The loss will be limited to this amount as the bank will refund the $5 million in compensation. If no hedging had occurred, GoSlo would have lost the full $5 million in the event of a default.

61 Kilenc Co

Text references. International investment is covered in chapter 8, the global debt crisis is covered in chapters 4 and 19. Money laundering is also covered in chapter 19.

Top tips. Ensure that your answer to part (a) relates to the scenario rather than just a generic list of factors to consider for an overseas investment. Ensure that you comment on the economic situation as this is relevant to the decision.

For part (c) note that the actions to prevent money laundering should not change because Lanosia has a poor reputation. The steps should be in place anyway.

Easy marks. Part (b) offers easy marks if you are familiar with dark pool trading systems.

Examiner's comments. Part (a) of the question which asked candidates to discuss the key risks and issues of setting up an international subsidiary was done well and many responses gained high marks for this part. However, responses got relatively fewer marks for the mitigation of the risks and issues. Nevertheless, generally high marks were achieved in part (a).

On the other hand, few responses were able to provide adequate responses to part (b).

Marking scheme

			Marks
(a)	Discussion of key risks or issues (2 – 3 marks for each)	8 – 10	
	Suggestions for management or control of the risk or issue (1 – 2 marks each)	6 – 8	
			Max 15
(b)	Explanation of dark pool trading systems	2 – 3	
	Consequences and how these would affect Kilenc Co	2 – 3	
			Max 5
(c)	One mark per relevant discussion point		Max 5
			25

(a)   There are several risks and issues that Kilenc Co will need to consider in order to make a decision whether to set up a subsidiary company in Lanosia or not. It will then need to evaluate if these risks and issues can be mitigated or controlled.

Risks and issues

If the subsidiary is set up there is likely to be an impact on Kilenc Co's **current exports to Lanosia** and also to other countries in the same region. Assuming there are existing exports to the region, and that setting up the subsidiary will reduce these exports, there could be adverse effects on the employees and facilities currently supplying these exports. If there are to be redundancies this may damage Kilenc Co's reputation. In addition Kilenc Co needs to consider how the subsidiary would be perceived and whether the **locally produced products will be seen as the same quality** as the imported ones.

Lanosia is currently in **recession** and this may have a **negative impact on the demand** for the products. The costs of setting up a subsidiary will need to be less than the expected benefits from additional sales and cost reductions. The expected benefits may be less than forecast, especially if the recession continues. On the other hand, there may be additional opportunities from having a subsidiary once recovery from the recession has begun.

The Lanosian government offers support to pharmaceutical companies and Kilenc Co may find they are subject to restrictions if it is felt that the subsidiary is affecting local companies. For example they may impose repatriation restrictions or increase taxes that the subsidiary has to pay. Alternatively given the fact that 40% of the shares will be locally owned and 50% of the Board will be also be from Lanosia may mean that the **subsidiary is viewed as a local company** and the government support will also be available to the subsidiary.

Kilenc Co wants to raise debt finance in Lanosia. It needs to consider whether this finance will actually be available. Following the bailout of the banks there may be a shortage of funds for borrowing. Also the high inflation rate may mean that there will be pressure to raise interest rates which may in turn raise borrowing costs.

The Lanosian IPO is likely to result in a **number of minority shareholders**, which combined with the composition of the Board may create agency issues for the subsidiary. For example, the Board of the subsidiary may make decisions that are in local interests rather than those of the parent company. Alternatively the local Board and shareholders may feel that they are dictated to by the parent company and that local interests are not considered at all.

Cultural issues also need to be considered, which include issues arising from dealing with people of a different nationality and also issues of culture within the organisation. A good understanding of cultural issues is important, as is the need to get the **right balance between autonomy and control** by the parent company.

Other risks including foreign exchange exposure, health and safety compliance and physical risks all need to be considered and assessed. There are numerous legal requirements from health and safety legislation which must be understood and complied with. The risk of damage from events such as fire, floods or other natural disasters should also be considered.

Mitigation of risks and issues

The financial costs and benefits need to be fully analysed to establish the viability of the subsidiary. This should include techniques such as **sensitivity analysis** to assess the impact of changes in variables. Any real options should also be analysed to include the value of any follow-on projects in the appraisal.

A marketing campaign could be conducted to ensure that customers' perceptions of the locally produced products are the same as the existing products. Using the **same packaging as the existing products** can help with this. Communication, both external and internal, can be used to minimise any damage to reputation arising from the move to Lanosia. If possible, employees should be redeployed within the organisation to reduce any redundancies.

The Lanosian government should be negotiated with and communicated with regularly during the setting up of the subsidiary. This should help to **maximise any government support** and/or minimise any restrictions.

BPP
LEARNING MEDIA

This may continue after the establishment of the subsidiary to reduce the chance of new regulations or legislation which could adversely affect the subsidiary.

An economic analysis of the likely interest and inflation rates should be conducted. Kilenc Co may want to use fixed rate debt for its financing or use interest rate swaps to effectively fix their interest charge. The costs of such an activity also need to be considered.

The corporate governance structure needs to be negotiated and agreed on in order to get the right balance between autonomy and central control. All major parties should be included in the negotiations and the structure should be clearly communicated.

Cultural differences should be considered from the initial setting up of the subsidiary. Staff handbooks and training sessions can be used to communicate the culture of the organisation to employees.

Foreign exchange exposure can be mitigated through hedging. Health and safety and physical loss risk can be mitigated through a combination of hedging and legal advice.

(b)   Dark pools are **off-exchange facilities** that allow trading of large blocks of shares. They allow brokers and fund managers to place and match large orders **anonymously** to avoid influencing the share price. The transactions are only made public after the trades have been completed. Traders placing large orders on the transparent exchanges risk signalling that they are large buyers or sellers. Such signals could cause the markets to move against them and put the order at risk.

The main argument supporting the use of dark pools is that they **prevent artificial price volatility** that volume sales could cause on an exchange and so the market maintains its efficiency. The counter argument to this is that the regulated exchanges do not know about the transactions taking place until the trades have been completed. As a result, the prices at which these trades are executed remain unknown until after the event. Such a lack of information on significant trades makes **the regulated exchanges less efficient**. Dark pools also take trade away from the regulated exchanges, resulting in reduced transparency as fewer trades are publicly exposed. Such a practice could reduce liquidity in the regulated exchanges and hinder efficient price-setting.

Dark pools are unlikely to impact on the subsidiary company of Kilenc Co because the share price of the subsidiary would be based on the parent company which would not be affected by the Lanosia stock market. The **efficiency of the Lanosian stock market will be important though**.

(c)   It will be important for Kilenc Co to apply strict customer due diligence in all of its operations in Lanosia and also in the UK.

Applying this should mean the following steps are taken:

When establishing a **business relationship** it is likely that this will be an ongoing relationship. Therefore it is important to establish identify and credibility at the start. Kilenc Co will have to obtain information such as the source and origin of funds that its customer will be using, copies of recent and current financial statements and details of the customer's business.

Customer due diligence should also be carried out if there is a need to carry out an '**occasional transaction**' worth 15,000 euros or more – that is, transactions that are not carried out within an ongoing business relationship. Kilenc Co should also look out for 'linked' transactions which are individual transactions of 15,000 euros or more that have been broken down into smaller, separate transactions to avoid due diligence checks.

If there are any **doubts** about identification information that has been obtained previously, then additional checks should be performed.

When the **customer's circumstances change** – for example, a change in the ownership of the customer's business or a significant change in the type of business activity of the customer, then new checks should be performed.

Ongoing monitoring of your business

It is important that Kilenc Co has an effective system of internal controls to protect the business from being used for money laundering. Staff should be suitably trained in the implementation of these internal controls and be alert to any potential issues. A specific member of staff should be nominated as the person to whom any suspicious activities should be reported.

Full documentation of anti-money laundering policies and procedures should be kept and updated as appropriate. Staff should be kept fully informed of any changes.

Maintaining full and up-to-date records

Kilenc Co is required to keep full and up-to-date records for financial reporting and auditing purposes, but these can also be used to demonstrate compliance with money laundering regulations. Such records will include receipts, invoices and customer correspondence. European money laundering regulations require that such information be kept for each customer for five years, beginning on either the date a transaction is completed or the date a business relationship ends.

62 NRD Co

> **Text references.** Simulation and expected values are covered in Chapter 5. Islamic finance is covered in Chapters 7a and 19.
>
> **Top tips.** This question covers some parts of the syllabus that students typically struggle with.
>
> In part (a) you need to be able to summarise how an Islamic financial institution, such as a bank, can make money without charging interest. This may appear daunting unless you have a good knowledge of this area of the syllabus.
>
> Hopefully part (b)(ii) will simply be brought forward knowledge from *F9 Financial Management*.
>
> For part (c) don't forget about the non-financial factors that can also be important, particularly the potential conflict between shareholders and the use of Islamic finance.
>
> **Easy marks.** The calculations in part (b)(i) are straightforward for this level, but ensure you use the right discount rate.

(a) An Islamic finance institution makes money through investing in physical assets which are then used to generate a return, from which the Islamic finance institution gets a **share of the profit**.

The exact nature of the arrangement dictates the details, but investors/depositors will place funds with the institution (on which they are not guaranteed a return). The institution will find a **Sharia'a compliant investment** opportunity and will share in the returns for that investment. The return generated by the financial institution will then be **shared** with the original investors/depositors.

(b) (i) The discount rate to use is the discount rate associated with the project specific financing. This is 7% pre-tax.

The post tax discount rate is therefore

$7\% \times (1 - 0.28) = 5.04\%$ say 5%

Expected cash flow in year 1 = $(0.2 \times 84) + (0.3 \times 93) + (0.5 \times 105) = 97.2$ m Dinars

Expected cash flow in year 2 = $(0.2 \times 91) + (0.3 \times 102) + (0.5 \times 118) = 107.8$ m Dinars

Expected cash flow in year 3 = $(0.2 \times 97) + (0.3 \times 112) + (0.5 \times 130) = 118.0$ m Dinars

Expected cash flow in year 4 = $(0.2 \times 98) + (0.3 \times 114) + (0.5 \times 132) = 119.8$ m Dinars

Time	0	1	2	3	4
Cash flow	(375)	97.2	107.8	118	119.8
DF	1.000	0.952	0.907	0.864	0.823
PV	(375)	92.5	97.8	102.0	98.6

NPV = 15.9 million Dinars

NRD Co should proceed with the bid based on this evaluation.

BPP LEARNING MEDIA

(ii)   **Probability analysis**

The main advantage of using probability analysis is that it factors in **uncertainty** associated with the project cash flows.

There are a number of **disadvantages** with using probability analysis as in this scenario. As a one-off decision the expected value may not be a possible outcome. Also the expected outcome does not show the likelihood of the project having a negative NPV, which is a possible outcome, especially as the economy is in decline in each period.

The model used in this example is simplistic and unrealistic. The state of the economy in one period is likely to have a bearing on the state in the next period, but under the assumptions used here it doesn't. It is also difficult to assign accurate probabilities to these events when at best they can only be estimates.

Monte Carlo simulation

A great advantage of using Monte Carlo simulation is that a number of simulations can be run in a **short space of time** on a computer.

It is also possible to build a model with lots of variables and test changes in each of these variables.

The main disadvantage is in constructing a model that accurately reflects the real world. Although certain economic relationships can be predicted, it is unlikely that a detailed sophisticated model could be produced without significant **time and expense**. Even then, this may not accurately model the state of the economy.

(c)   **Financial factors**

Through using the Sukuk arrangement, the investment can be **financed** in the same currency (Dinars) as the related cash inflows. This then removes the currency risk that would be present if the US dollar denominated loan is used for the financing. For example if the US dollar weakens against the Dinar, the amount of capital to be repaid will increase in terms of Dinars.

Islamic finance can be more expensive than conventional debt such as a bank loan. This is due to the fact that there are **no standard contracts** for Islamic finance transactions which increases administration costs. There may also be **additional compliance costs** to ensure that the transaction complies with Sharia'a law. On the other hand, if the project does not make a profit, and there is a risk that this may happen depending on the state of the economy, then there is no profit share to be paid which would be **cheaper** than the case of a loss making project under a bank loan.

The use of debt finance and the associated **mandatory payments** can be seen to be a discipline on managers to ensure that they generate the necessary **cash flows** to enable the interest payments to be made. Under the Sukuk arrangement, there would be no mandatory payments and therefore this discipline will be lost.

Although NRD Co have been told it is possible to use Sukuk to fund the expansion, there is **no guarantee** that there is sufficient interest to generate the required funds. However the bank has already stated it is willing to lend the required amount. An unsuccessful attempt to issue Sukuk for this project could result in the project having to be cancelled or at least postponed with **damage** to the **reputation** of NRD Co.

Non-financial factors

The risk appetite of the shareholders and/or the board may influence the choice here. The profit share arrangement may appeal to more **risk averse** individuals who would accept the potentially higher cost of the Sukuk arrangement, if the project succeeds. Alternatively, other individuals may prefer the bank loan with **set interest payments,** which do not rise if the project is more successful than previously thought.

The use of Islamic finance could give rise to **stakeholder conflict**. It is assumed that existing shareholders will want to maximise their returns. Islamic finance cannot be used for investments that are not allowed under Sharia'a law. This may mean that the airport cannot include potentially lucrative retail opportunities such as the sale of alcohol.

63 Vadener

Text references. Chapter 2 covers performance analysis, and translation risk.

Top tips. To score well in (a) you needed to calculate for three years ratios under all the headings we use, though not necessarily all the ratios we have calculated. We have asterisked the ratios we think you should have included as a minimum, but have included other calculations as a check for you if you calculated those ratios as well. As these are simple calculations the examiner expects them to be done quickly.

Although it is unclear precisely how much time to spend on calculations and discussion, when planning your answer you should have allowed enough time to write a paragraph on each of the major areas of performance, plus one on the divisions – and enough time to make worthwhile comments in each paragraph about what the figures could signify.

The only calculation that can be done with the divisions is the required v actual return calculation (alpha values), and hopefully you picked up that you needed to do this (being given CAPM information and actual return is always a sign). (c) emphasises the importance of market efficiency– will the market be 'fooled' by translation losses or gains.

Easy marks. It should be possible to gain full marks in (b) by asking yourself certain questions when planning.

- Are there any figures in the group accounts that could usefully be broken down further? (operating costs)
- What information do we have for the group that we don't have for the divisions?
- What information do we need to carry out a fair valuation of the group? (cash flow data to assess its ability to generate cash flows)
- What other comparisons would it be useful to make? (competitor)
- What information do we need to assess financial performance in the light of Vadener's business strategy? (competitor, market and product information)

Report

To: The Board of Vadener plc

From: Senior Financial Manager

Re: Performance of Vadener plc

This report focuses on the performance of Vadener plc and its divisions. In considers the additional information which could help to provide a more accurate assessment and the implications of a £10million translation loss.

(a)   **Group performance**

The following commentary is based on the calculations provided in the appendix to this report.

Profitability

The company has expanded over the last two years, and the increase in revenue (23.1%) has outpaced the increase in operating costs (16.3%). It certainly appears as if there has been some expansion of business; the increase may also be due to Vadener being able to charge **higher prices**, but this raises the question of whether it can increase prices further. Alternatively, the increase in profit margins could be due to better purchasing terms or improved control of operating costs. However the explanation of improved operating cost control appears to be inconsistent with deteriorating working capital management discussed below.

Debt and gearing

The **gearing ratios** do not appear to be excessively high, although it would be helpful to know what the normal figure was for conglomerates like Vadener. However an interest cover of 8.6 times does not suggest that the group is over-geared.

Liquidity and working capital management

Working capital levels appear high, although Vadener's involvement in the construction sector may mean that levels are higher than if it was just involved in leisure or pharmaceuticals. Certainly all of the three measures have increased over the last two years, indicating **poorer control** over inventory and receivables,

		20X5	20X4	20X3

Debt and gearing

Debt ratio — $\dfrac{\text{Current liabilities} + \text{Long-term liabilities}}{\text{Total assets}}$

$\dfrac{1{,}269}{2{,}675} = 47\%$ | $\dfrac{1{,}138}{2{,}383} = 48\%$ | $\dfrac{965}{2{,}051} = 47\%$

* Gearing
(*BPP LM note.* Gearing could have been calculated excluding short-term loans) — $\dfrac{\text{Long-term liabilities} + \text{Short-term loans}}{\text{Long-term liabilities} + \text{Short-term loans} + \text{Equity}}$

$\dfrac{671}{2{,}077} = 32\%$ | $\dfrac{580}{1{,}835} = 32\%$ | $\dfrac{535}{1{,}621} = 33\%$

Interest cover — $\dfrac{\text{Operating profit}}{\text{Net interest}}$

$\dfrac{560}{65} = 8.6$ | $\dfrac{540}{56} = 9.6$ | $\dfrac{410}{40} = 10.3$

Liquidity

* Current ratio — $\dfrac{\text{Current assets}}{\text{Current liabilities}}$

$\dfrac{1{,}015}{799} = 1.3$ | $\dfrac{863}{728} = 1.2$ | $\dfrac{728}{565} = 1.3$

* Acid test ratio — $\dfrac{\text{Current assets} - \text{Inventory}}{\text{Current liabilities}}$

$\dfrac{525}{799} = 0.7$ | $\dfrac{453}{728} = 0.6$ | $\dfrac{388}{565} = 0.7$

Inventory days — $\dfrac{\text{Inventory} \times 365}{\text{Operating costs}}$

$\dfrac{490 \times 365}{930}$ | $\dfrac{410 \times 365}{870}$ | $\dfrac{340 \times 365}{800}$

= 192 days | = 172 days | = 155 days

Receivables' days — $\dfrac{\text{Receivables} \times 365}{\text{Turnover}}$

$\dfrac{510 \times 365}{1{,}490}$ | $\dfrac{438 \times 365}{1{,}410}$ | $\dfrac{378 \times 365}{1{,}210}$

= 125 days | = 113 days | = 114 days

Payables' days — $\dfrac{\text{Payables} \times 365}{\text{Operating costs}}$

$\dfrac{430 \times 365}{930}$ | $\dfrac{401 \times 365}{870}$ | $\dfrac{302 \times 365}{800}$

= 169 days | = 168 days | = 138 days

Market ratios

* Dividend yield — $\dfrac{\text{Dividend per share}}{\text{Market price}}$

$\dfrac{61.7}{1{,}542} = 4\%$ | $\dfrac{56.7}{1{,}417} = 4\%$ | $\dfrac{48.7}{1{,}220} = 4\%$

* Earnings per share — $\dfrac{\text{Profit after tax}}{\text{Number of shares}}$

$\dfrac{346}{300} = 115.3\text{p}$ | $\dfrac{339}{300} = 113.0\text{p}$ | $\dfrac{259}{300} = 86.3\text{p}$

* Price earnings ratio — $\dfrac{\text{Market price}}{\text{Earnings per share}}$

$\dfrac{1{,}542}{115.3} = 13$ | $\dfrac{1{,}417}{113} = 13$ | $\dfrac{1{,}220}{86.3} = 14$

* Dividend cover — $\dfrac{\text{Profit after tax}}{\text{Dividends}}$

$\dfrac{346}{185} = 1.9$ | $\dfrac{339}{170} = 2.0$ | $\dfrac{259}{146} = 1.8$

(d) **Objectives of transfer pricing strategies**

(i) The transfer price should provide a **selling price** that enables the transferring division to earn a return for its efforts, and the receiving division to incur a cost for benefits received.

(ii) The transfer price should be set at a level that enables **profit centre performance** to be **measured commercially**; thus the transfer price should be a **fair commercial price**.

(iii) The transfer price should encourage profit centre managers to **agree** on the **amounts of goods and services to be transferred**.

(iv) The transfer price should lead to a level **of goods and services being transferred** which is **congruent** with the **objectives** of the organisation, for example **generating retained earnings** in the most advantageous locations or **limiting remittances** of foreign currency between group members.

(v) **Transfer prices** can be used to **minimise the effect of import duties**; the lower the transfer price, the lower the level of import duty.

(vi) Transfer prices can also be used to **minimise tax levels** by ensuring that taxable income is earned in low tax economies.

(vii) **Transfer prices** can be used as a means of **remitting income** if restrictions on dividend remittances are in place.

64 International Enterprises

Text references. Dividend capacity is covered in Chapter 18; EVA is covered in Chapter 2.

Top tips. Being faced with the preparation of a cash flow statement in part (a) might throw you slightly but bear in mind that it doesn't have to be in a form that complies with accounting standards. You should be familiar with cash flow statements from earlier studies and this one is not so bad. Key things to remember are that the figures for interest, taxation and dividends in the cash flow statement will be the accrued figures at the end of the previous year and the treatment of changes in working capital components. Also, capital employed in the EVA calculation is the year-end figure, not the opening figure at the start of the year which is used in other examples. However, it is acceptable to use the opening figure.

The calculation of the maximum dividend capacity in part (b)(i) is complicated by the requirement to adjust working capital. As cost of sales is not fully funded, resources will have to be drawn from working capital to cover the shortfall. Ensure discussion in part (b) (ii) is related to the scenario and not just a generic list of points.

Part (c) looks daunting but make sure you follow the instructions to provide a report. Ensure your points are supported from the scenario and the calculations that are needed to support the performance judgement.

Easy marks. The preparation of the cash flow statement in part (a) is straightforward, as is the calculation of free cash flow before reinvestment in part (b).

Examiner's comments. Many candidates appreciated that this was a firm with substantial cash reserves, a low level of gearing and a relatively weak profit performance. The technical skills required by this question were largely drawn from earlier levels of study, reflecting the broad levels of competency required of the financial manager.

All but a small proportion of candidates knew how to extract a cash flow forecast but a substantial number made incorrect adjustments leading to cash changes which bore no resemblance to the movement in the statement of financial position. Most candidates understood the concept of free cash flow to equity although only a small minority were able to make reasonable adjustments for net reinvestment.

The estimation of WACC for the EVA™ calculation was generally well done although a number of candidates incorrectly applied the tax adjustment for debt. Relatively few candidates were able to explain the significance of this metric for investors and management.

(a) **Cash Flow Statement for the year ended 31 December 20X8**

	$m
Operating profit	108.8
Add: depreciation ($112.0 - 84.0m)	28.0
	136.8
Changes in working capital:	
Increase in trade payables	1.1
Reduction in inventories	0.5
Reduction in trade receivables	3.5
Operating cash flow	141.9
Less: Interest (20X7 figure paid in 20X8)	(2.3)
Less: Taxation (20X7 figure paid in 20X8)	(25.6)
Free cash flow before reinvestment	114.0
Less: Capital expenditure (note (ii) in question)	(80.0)
Less: Dividends (20X7 figure paid in 20X8)	(28.0)
Less: Financing (repayment of loan – note (i) in question)	(10.0)
Net change in cash	(4.0)

BPP
LEARNING MEDIA

(b) (i) **Dividend capacity**

International Enterprises' dividend capacity is determined by its free cash flow to equity holders after net reinvestment (where reinvestment is the level of investment required to maintain the required operating capacity of the business).

In this case, **free cash flow before reinvestment** is $114 million. **Capital expenditure** is $80 million; **repayment of loan** is $10 million. This would give a **maximum dividend capacity** of $24 million.

However, what about the **working capital requirement**?

International Enterprises appears to be funding working capital by reducing its inventories and the time it takes to receive money from its customers whilst at the same time increasing the time it takes to pay its suppliers. Total change in working capital is $5.1 million ($1.1 + 0.5 + 3.5 – see cash flow statement in (a) above). This should be taken out of the money available to pay dividends.

Dividend capacity is now reduced to $24 million – 5.1 million = $18.9 million.

(ii) International Enterprises' **actual dividend** is $28 million, which suggests that the company has over-distributed funds. The shortfall would need to be taken from its cash reserves. Clearly this is not a sustainable dividend policy in the long run.

There appears to be limited opportunity for International Enterprises to achieve further growth through introducing new products. Therefore, unless steps can be taken to increase free cash flow in the next few years then dividends will need to be reduced so that they are paid out of earnings.

International Enterprises appears to have a large cash balance which may not be required and therefore could be paid out to shareholders in the form of dividends. This would be better if it was done as a special dividend so as not to give shareholders **unrealistic expectations** about future dividend levels. However, if this cash balance is earmarked for future investment that can be used to increase shareholder wealth, then it should be used for this purpose and not distributed to shareholders.

In theory, the entire free cash flow to equity can be paid as dividends as this is the amount that is available for this purpose. In practice however only a portion of this figure will be given to the shareholders as dividends, as the management team tends to prefer a smooth dividend pattern.

(c) (i) (ii) **Report to Senior Management**

Report to Management of International Enterprises

From Chief Financial Officer

Review of potential performance for year ended 31 December 20X8

This report provides a review of how International Enterprises is projected to perform in the year to 31 December 20X8 and also considers the relative advantage and disadvantages for International Enterprises of growth by acquisition and organic growth.

Profit forecast and EVA

Detailed calculations can be found in the appendices to this report. Profit before tax is expected to increase by 7% from $100 million to $107 million. This is due mainly to revenue rising at a faster rate than cost of sales (10% compared with 8%).

EVA is projected to decrease slightly from the 20X7 figure of $49.6 million to $47.8 million, a decrease of 3.6%. This results from a combination of the expected NOPAT figure increasing from $71.6 million to $76.2 million and the increased capital charge arising from the rise in the cost of capital and the increase in the book value of capital employed.

As a percentage of capital employed, EVA in 20X8 is reduced to 16.5% from 22.1% in 20X7. This can be attributed to the increase of $9.1 million (33.7%) in Other operating costs.

Expected reaction of the market

The share price could fall as a result of these estimates, as the market is likely to view them as an indication of declining performance. Revenue has not increased in line with the increase in capital base – management should be investigating why this has occurred. Although gross margins are expected to increase from 49.36% to 50.3%, operating margins are projected to decline from 39.06% to 37.76%. This suggests that stricter operating cost control measures are needed.

Use of capital

The main issue appears to be the relative lack of revenue and value generation by the capital employed. There appears to be a large amount of cash being generated, the effective use of which will have to be reviewed, whether it is reinvested in new capital projects, used for paying off loan capital or perhaps for acquiring competitors with new products in the pipeline. If none of these are undertaken then the cash should be returned to the shareholders.

Organic growth

Organic growth for International Enterprises can come about in two ways. One is through introducing new products and the second method is through increasing sales of existing products. Since International Enterprises does **not have any new products in development**, organic growth would have to come from the second method.

Although there is a currently successful product, mobile communications is a fast-moving industry and technological advances could mean that the existing product becomes **obsolete** very quickly. Although upgrading the product may work in the short term, it is likely that new products would need to be developed for long-term growth. If there is no prospect of this, then organic growth does not appear to be a successful route for International Enterprises to take. Development of new products is likely to be expensive, involving an ongoing investment in a research and development function.

Organic growth is less disruptive than an acquisition and there will not be any issues with integration or cultural issues.

Growth by acquisition

Acquisition of another company is the alternative method of growth. An acquisition may be a **cheaper** way of acquiring productive capacity or new products in development than through organic growth. An acquisition can take place, for instance, through an exchange of shares, which would not have an impact on the financial resources of International Enterprises.

The acquisition of another company is a **quicker** way of implementing a growth business plan, as the company acquires another organisation that is already in operation. Acquisition as a strategy for expansion is particularly suitable for management with rather short time horizons.

An acquisition will acquire not only tangible assets but also **intangible assets**, such as brand recognition, reputation, customer loyalty and intellectual property, which are more difficult to achieve with organic growth.

If International Enterprises was to acquire another company, it would probably pay a premium over its present market value. This premium is normally justified as necessary for the benefits that will accrue from the acquisition. However, too large a premium may render the acquisition unprofitable.

If the acquired company is large relative to International Enterprises, International Enterprise's management may not have the experience or ability to deal with operations on the new larger scale, even if the acquired company retains its own management. If the acquisition of a large company took place through an exchange of shares, this would alter the relative shareholdings in International Enterprises significantly, possibly putting more pressure on international Enterprises management.

An acquisition would increase International Enterprises' business risk if the acquisition represents large investments by the bidding company and accounts for a large proportion of its financial resources. If the acquired company does not perform as well as envisaged, then the effect on International Enterprises may be catastrophic.

Conclusion on growth

Given the nature of the mobile communications industry and the significant disadvantages associated with growth by acquisition, the preferred method of growth for International Enterprises is organic growth.

If you have any questions about this report, please do not hesitate to contact me.

Appendices

1   EVA

EVA = NOPAT − WACC ×Capital employed

To calculate WACC, we need the cost of equity and cost of debt.

Cost of equity for 20X7 (using CAPM):

$E(r_j) = r_f + (E(r_m) − r_f) \beta_j = 3\% + 5 \times 1.4 = 10\%$

$$\text{Market gearing ratio (20X7)} = \frac{\text{Debt}}{\text{Debt} + \text{Equity}} = \frac{45m}{45m + (25 \times m4 \times 16.2)} = 0.027$$

WACC $= (1 − 0.027) \times 10 + 0.027 \times 5\% \times (1 − 0.3) = 9.82\%$

EVA (20X7) = $(102.3 \times 0.7) − 0.0982 \times (179 + 45)$

EVA (20X7) = $49.6 million (which is equivalent to 22.1% of capital employed)

EVA (20X8) = $(108.8 \times 0.7) − 0.0982 \times (253.9 + 35)$

EVA (20X8) = $47.8 million (or 16.5% of capital employed)

2   Return on Capital Employed

$$\text{ROCE} = \frac{\text{Profit before interest and tax}}{\text{Capital employed}}$$

$$\text{ROCE (20X7)} = \frac{102.3}{(179 + 45)} = 45.7\%$$

$$\text{ROCE (20X8)} = \frac{108.8}{(253.9 + 35)} = 37.7\%$$

65 McTee

Text references. This is really a question about strategic business planning, which is covered in Chapter 4. Chapter 2 covers financing strategy in general. Chapter 12 relates the discussion to different sources of finance. Chapter 7a gives guidance on the cost of capital calculations and Chapter 8 covers the issues involved in international investment.

Top tips. The requirements very clearly indicate that a combination of sources of finance is likely to be recommended.

As regards the costs:

- Equity – you are clearly given the details in the question to be able to carry out a dividend valuation calculation.
- Fixed rate loan – you need to do an IRR calculation as the debt is redeemable. Because you can draw up to £50 million, the net finance issued at time 0 after arrangement fees can match the finance required, although you have to gross up the eventual repayment. Interest payments are shown net of tax here and for the other forms of debt.
- Commercial paper – for one year, cost is interest paid, net of tax.
- Swiss Franc loan – again you need an IRR calculation which it's best to carry out in Swiss francs. Amount received at time 0 is SFr80 m − the initial costs, but you have to pay SFr 80m at time 5.
- Eurobond – interest paid is the US rate, net of tax. Again time 0 finance is taken after deducting the initial costs, and the full £42 m has to be repaid at time 10.
- US floating rate loan – easiest to estimate cost as current interest rate (3 + 3) %, net of tax.

The gearing calculation does not include other creditors. You are comparing debt with assets, so don't take into account the market value of shares. The extra debt will give rise to an asset of an equivalent amount, hence its appearance in both halves of the calculation.

As regards the rates to use, you use 1.7985 (the lower rate) to calculate the £ you will need as you will obtain fewer $ for each £ you pay to purchase the dollars you need for investment.

Part (c) is a good test of your knowledge of translation and economic exposures; if you struggled, our discussion covers the key points. You need to discuss the significance (ie the implications).

Easy marks. Provided you kept your answers focused on factors affecting finance, you can easily score 7-8 marks on (a). If you bore these factors in mind when answering (b), and clearly discussed the advantages and disadvantages, you can score enough on (b) to pass as well even if you didn't get any of the calculations right. Hopefully you got some right though, as you should have remembered to use an IRR calculation to calculate the value of redeemable debt.

(a)   **Foreign exchange risk**

It is possible to reduce foreign exchange risk by **matching**; using one of the dollar finance options to set against the dollar receipts.

Cost of finance

This covers not only any **annual interest payment costs,** but also arrangement fees, issue costs etc.

Availability

If the purchase is to take place rapidly, the finance should be **available quickly,** or (expensive?) **short-term bridging finance** will be required.

Flexibility

If the directors are expecting to use **different sources of finance,** they will prefer to use sources that can be changed without significant cost.

Period of investment

The length of time the finance is available should **match** the length of the investment period.

Tax

The **tax consequences** of the different sources of finance must be considered, as these may significantly affect their costs.

Desired debt-equity finance mix

The maximum amount of debt is limited by a covenant in any event, but the directors may have their own views about the **desired balance** and hence the **desired level** of **finance risk**. It will be determined by whether they believe that there is an **optimal level of gearing,** at which the company's **weighted average cost of capital** will be at its lowest.

Signalling

By issuing the maximum amount of debt, the directors may wish to demonstrate to the stock market their **confidence in the future**.

Interest rate expectations

The directors will **prefer floating rate finance** if interest rates are expected to **go down, fixed rate finance** if interest rates are expected to **increase**.

Maturity of debt

Directors will be concerned about when the debt is **due to mature**, and McTee's **likely cash position** around that date.

Security

Directors will be concerned about the **amount** of security required, also how any **restrictions over assets secured** might limit business decisions including the ability to raise loan finance in the future

Other sources

Other sources of finance such as **convertible** and **deep-discount bonds** may be appropriate.

(b)
To: Directors, McTee
From: Accountant
Date: 15 December 20X5
Subject: **Sources of finance**

Finance required

Amount required = $80 m = £80/1.7985 m = £44.48 m

If all raised by debt, gearing = $\dfrac{38 + 30 + 18 + 44.48}{117.8 + 8.1 + 98.1 + 44.48}$ = 48.6%

This would still be within the **terms of the covenant**, although it would not allow much scope for further investments to be financed solely by debt. There is also no indication that this is the **optimal mix of gearing** and hence **cost of capital** is at its **lowest**.

Rights issue

Amount raised = (80 × ¼ × 2.80)0.95 = £53.2 m

Cost of equity = $\dfrac{22.2(1.04)}{302}$ + 0.04 = 11.6%

Advantages

(i) The proposed rights issue would comfortably **exceed the amount required.**
(ii) The company's **gearing**, and thus **financial risk**, would decrease.
(iii) There would be **no change in control** if the current shareholders took up the rights issue.
(iv) McTee would not have a commitment to make **interest payments.**
(v) McTee would not face **exchange risk** on payments to providers of finance.

Disadvantages

(i) The **arrangement costs** are **higher** than for some of the other alternatives.
(ii) A **rights issue** is likely to take **longer to arrange** than the other alternatives.
(iii) The **cost of equity** is **higher** than the cost of debt because of the greater risk to equity shareholders and the company does not obtain the benefit of **tax relief.**
(iv) The **exchange risk** on the **income from the US investment** remains, as it cannot be matched against the payments to finance providers.

Fixed rate sterling loan

Amount issued = 44.48 × 100/99 = £44.93 m

Cost of debt

The cost of debt is calculated as 5.1% (see appendix 1).

Advantages

(i) Cost is **lower** than some of the other options.
(ii) There is a **further facility** available which has not been drawn.

Disadvantages

(i) Because the loan is in sterling, there will be **foreign exchange risk** as the finance is not matched with the dollar income.

(ii) Conditions may be attached to the security, that impose **restrictions** over and above the debt limit.

Commercial paper

Amount issued = $15m   **Cost** = 0.7 (3.0 + 1.5 + 0.5) = 3.5%

Advantages

(i) McTee will be able to take advantage of **short-term falls in interest rates.**

(ii) The cost looks **low** compared with other sources.

Disadvantages

(i) The commercial paper provides **less than 20%** of the finance required.

(ii) The **maturity** is wrong for the majority of the requirement; commercial paper is a short-term source to finance a long-term requirement of $72 m.

(iii) There are likely to be some **issuing costs.**

(iv) The **floating rate** is not attractive if interest rates are **expected to rise.**

Swiss franc loan

Amount raised = 80 (1 − 0.03)/2.298 = £33.77m

Cost of loan

The cost of the loan is 4.1% (see appendix 2).

Advantages

(i) The **cost of finance** is still **low** even after the swap fees.

(ii) McTee can pay interest in the currency in which it is obtaining returns, and thus **reduce exchange risk** by gearing.

Disadvantages

(i) The loan will not be enough to cover the **whole US investment**; approximately £10 million further finance will be required.

(ii) McTee would still be exposed to **foreign exchange risk** on the Swiss franc loan itself as against sterling.

(iii) McTee may be subject to **counterparty risk** although this will be minimal if it uses an intermediary such as a bank.

Eurobond

Assume the Eurobond is denominated in sterling as McTee has a relative price advantage in sterling.

Amount raised = £42m (1 − 0.02 − 0.017) = £40.45 million

Cost

The cost of the Eurobond is 4.0% (see appendix 3).

Advantages

(i) The interest payment can be **matched against the income** from the investment, reducing foreign exchange risk.

(ii) The cost is **reduced by undertaking** the **swap arrangement.**

(iii) **No security** is required, and McTee's assets could be used as security for additional loans.

(iv) The loan is for a **longer term** than the other financing.

Disadvantages

The Eurobond only raises $80m × 40.45/44.48 = $72.8 million, which is enough to cover the **longer-term financing requirement**, but not enough to cover the shorter term.

Floating rate loan

Amount provided = $40 million

LIBOR = 3%

Cost = (3 + 3) (1 − 0.3) = 4.2%

Advantages

(i)   The loan **matches** with dollar income, **reducing exchange risk.**
(ii) If **interest rates fall** during the duration of the loan, the **cost of the loan** will also **fall.**

Disadvantages

(i)   The loan only provides **half of the finance** required.
(ii)   The loan requires **security.**
(iii) The cost is **higher** at present than some of the other sources of loan finance.
(iv)   If **interest rates rise** during the duration of the loan, the **cost of the loan** will also **rise.**

Recommendation

The rights issue should be used if the directors are very concerned about gearing levels, and are prepared to accept a much higher cost of capital than is likely for any of the loan finance.

Of the longer term sources of debt finance, the Eurobond is recommended to cover the $72 million as it has the **lowest cost at present,** will **cover all of the long term investment**, does **not require security** and **matches foreign exchange. Commercial paper**, as the cheapest and best short-term source of finance, can be used to fund the shorter term working capital requirement of $8 m.

If you have any questions about the contents of this report, please do not hesitate to ask me.

Appendices

1   Cost of debt calculation

Year		Cash flow £m	Disc factor 7%	DCF £m	Disc factor 5%	DCF £m
0	Issue net of issue costs	(44.48)	1.000	(44.48)	1.000	(44.48)
1–5	Interest					
	44.93 × 7% × (1 − 0.3)	2.20	4.100	9.02	4.329	9.52
5	Repayment	44.93	0.713	32.04	0.784	35.23
				(3.42)		0.27

$$\text{Cost of loan} = 5 + \left[\frac{0.27}{0.27 - (3.42)} \right] [7 - 5] = 5.1\%$$

2   Cost of loan calculation

Year		Cash flow SFrm	Disc factor 5%	Disc cash flow SFrm	Disc factor 3%	Disc cash flow SFrm
0	Issue net of issue costs					
	(80 (1 − 0.03))	(77.60)	1.000	(77.60)	1.000	(77.60)
1–5	Interest: 80m × (2.5 +					
	2.3) % × (1 − 0.3)	2.69	4.329	11.65	4.580	12.32
5	Repayment	80.00	0.784	62.72	0.863	69.04
				(3.23)		3.76

$$\text{Cost of loan} = 3 + \left[\frac{3.76}{3.76 - (3.23)}\right][5 - 3] = 4.1\%$$

3 Cost of eurobond calculation

Year		Cash flow £m	Disc factor 5%	Disc cash flow £m	Disc factor 3%	Disc cash flow £m
0	Issue net of issue costs (42m × (1 − 0.037))	(40.45)	1.000	(40.45)	1.000	(40.45)
1–10	Interest: 42m × 4.95 % × (1 − 0.3)	1.46	7.722	11.27	8.530	12.45
10	Repayment	42.00	0.614	25.79	0.744	31.25
				(3.39)		3.25

$$\text{Cost of bond} = 3 + \left[\frac{3.25}{3.25 - (3.39)}\right][5 - 3] = 4.0\%$$

(c) Translation exposure

Translation exposure arises from **differences in the currencies** in which assets and liabilities are **denominated.** These effects are most obvious when **consolidated group accounts** are prepared and the values of assets and liabilities denominated in a foreign currency are translated into the home currency.

Implications of translation exposure

(i) **Effect on accounts**
The exact effect translation exposure has on the accounts will depend on the methods of translation used. **Legislation** or **accounting standards** will prescribe which methods should be used.

(ii) **Effect on cash**
Translation exposure is essentially an **accounting measure** and does not involve actual cash flows.

(iii) **Investors' and payables' attitudes**
However if markets are not strongly efficient, investors and payables may interpret losses on translation as a **reduction** in the **financial worth** and **creditworthiness** of the company. This risk can be reduced if assets and liabilities denominated in particular currencies are held in **balanced amounts**.

Economic exposure

Economic exposure is the risk that the **present value** of a company's future cash flows might be **reduced** by **unexpected adverse exchange rate movements.** Economic exposure includes **transaction exposure**, the risk of adverse exchange rate movements occurring in the course of **normal international trading transactions.**

Implications of economic exposure

(i) **Effect on international competitiveness**
This can affect companies through its **purchases** (where raw materials from abroad become more expensive because of a devaluation of the home currency) or its **sales** (where an appreciation in the home currency will mean that sales priced in foreign currencies will be worth less in home currency terms).

(ii) **Effect on remittances from abroad**
If a subsidiary is set up in an overseas country, and that country's exchange rate **depreciates** against the **home exchange rate,** the remittances will be worth less in home currency terms each year.

(iii) **Effect on accounts**
Investors will identify economic exposure as having an **adverse effect** on **accounts** if the markets are efficient.

(iv) **Effect on operations and financing**
In order to hedge the adverse effects of economic exposure, companies will consider **diversification**

BPP
LEARNING MEDIA

of operations, so that sales and purchases are made in a number of different currencies. The financing of operations can also be done in a **large number of currencies.**

(d) **Devaluation of the dollar**

(i) **Export sales from the US**

The US manufacturing operation will only supply the US market, so there is no issue with export sales.

(ii) **Production costs**

It is not clear whether materials will be imported for production in the US. If this is the case then production costs will rise as a result of the devaluation, which would squeeze profit margins.

(iii) **Remittances/charges made to parent company**

The parent company may impose management charges on the subsidiary. If these are priced in US dollars then they will be worth less to McTee, if they are priced in sterling then the charges become more onerous to the subsidiary. Hedging may be required to protect the value of expected dollar remittances to McTee. Decisions on the hedging methods used will depend on the decisions about financing discussed above.

(e) **Overall group capital structure**

The overall group capital structure should remain within **limits** that are **satisfactory** to the key financial stakeholders, in particular the **lenders** and **major shareholders.** These limits represent a constraint on the capital structure that can be adopted by the overseas subsidiaries.

Subsidiary capital structure

However, the subsidiary capital structure need not be the same as the group as a whole. The ideal capital structure for the subsidiary will depend on local conditions, in particular the **cost** and **availability of debt finance,** and whether McTee can provide any assurances that lenders require, such as security. If there are restrictions on the movements of funds from the US, this may also limit the appeal of equity finance.

66 Wurrall

Text references. Chapter 2 covers forecasts and ratio analysis, though you'll also need to look at Chapter 7b if you're unsure about free cash flow. Objectives are covered in Chapter 1.

Top tips. The question requires you to calculate proforma income statements and statements of financial position so you should use the same level of detail in your answer as you're given in the question. The way to approach this question is:

1   Copy out the proformas as per the question
2   Fill in all the figures that change by the percentages specified in the question for all of the four years (you need to show some figures for all of the four years; note the examiner's comment about giving limited credit for 1-2 years)
3   Work out the remaining figures for the income statement in 20X5 (interest, tax, dividends and retentions)
4   Calculate the reserves for year 1 and add up that half of the statement of financial position.
5   Calculate the short-term loan figures as the balancing figures
6   Repeat stages 3-5 for years 20X6 – 20X8

The key for the discussion of assumptions (ii) – (iv) is commenting on what relation these figures will or should have to sales. Assumption (ix) is a standard comment on dividend policy.

In (a)(iii) the change in assets represents the reinvestment figure you need to calculate free cash flow. Working capital = Total current assets – Total current liabilities.

For parts (b) and (c) make sure that the length of your answers is consistent with the marks on offer in each part.

Easy marks. The discussion in (a)(ii). The question requirement prompts you to discuss these points; however you would also have mentioned them if the discussion requirement had been more vague.

(a)   Report

   To: Board of Directors Wurrall Inc

   From: A N Accountant

   Date: 19 July 20X4

   Future performance

   This report looks at projected statements of financial position and income statements for the next four years and looks at the assumptions made in producing these. There is also a section considering whether the share price is likely to increase by 100% over the next four years.

   Pro forma accounts

   Pro forma income statement for the years ended March 20X5–20X8

	20X5 $m	20X6 $m	20X7 $m	20X8 $m
Revenue	1,787	1,929	2,064	2,188
Operating costs before deprecation	(1,215)	(1,312)	(1,404)	(1,488)
	572	617	660	700
Tax allowable depreciation	(165)	(179)	(191)	(203)
Earnings before interest and tax	407	438	469	497
Net interest payable (Note)	(63)	(65)	(66)	(70)
Profit on ordinary activities before tax	344	373	403	427
Tax on ordinary activities	(103)	(112)	(121)	(128)
Profit after tax	241	261	282	299
Dividends	(135)	(146)	(158)	(167)
Amount transferred to reserves	106	115	124	132

   Note. Interest = (8% × 580,000) + (7% × previous year's balance on short-term loans and overdrafts)

   Pro forma statements of financial position as at 31 March 20X5–20X8

	20X5 $m	20X6 $m	20X7 $m	20X8 $m
Non-current assets				
Land and buildings	310	310	350	350
Plant and machinery (net)	1,103	1,191	1,275	1,351
Investments	32	32	32	32
	1,445	1,533	1,657	1,733
Current assets				
Inventories	488	527	564	598
Receivables	615	664	710	753
Cash in hand and short term deposits	22	24	25	27
	1,125	1,215	1,299	1,378
Payables: amounts falling due within one year:				
Short term loans and overdrafts (balance figure)	266	287	332	320
Other payables	514	556	595	630
	(780)	(843)	(927)	(950)
Payables: amounts falling due after one year:				
Borrowings (Note)	(580)	(580)	(580)	(580)
	1,210	1,325	1,449	1,581

BPP
LEARNING MEDIA

Capital and reserves

Called up share capital (10 cents par)	240	240	240	240
Reserves	970	1,085	1,209	1,341
	1,210	1,325	1,449	1,581

Note. Repaid at end of 20X6 and refinanced with a similar type of loan in 20X6.

Implications of the assumptions

General assumptions

The pro forma accounts model treats **sales as the major variable** and makes forecasts of changes in several other factors dependent on sales. While this is basically a sensible approach where sales is the **limiting factor**, the relationships used are probably too simplistic and **not enough scenarios** of sales performance are considered.

Assumption (i)

The sales forecasts represent one possible scenario of the company's future performance. **Simulation analysis** could be used to generate other scenarios including best and worse cases, which may result in **different financing decisions** being made. The assumption that sales will continue to grow at 6% to perpetuity after 20X8 is over-optimistic.

Assumption (ii)

Presumably analysis of past data has shown that **cash operating costs** have been on average 68% of sales. This is too simplistic a formula, because costs will contain some **fixed elements** and some **variable costs** that **depend on a number of drivers**, not just sales. For example some variable costs are driven by number of employees and others by purchase quantities. Some costs are subject to price increases from inflation whereas others can be reduced as efficiency improvements take effect. A more detailed cost model, based on different categories of costs, would be more helpful in the forecasting process.

Assumption (iii)

The assumption that **plant and machinery** will **increase in line with sales** is unlikely to be **true even in the long term** and certainly not for the purposes of annual forecasts. Tax depreciation will not be a simple percentage of equipment value. Depreciation on new purchases of equipment will be higher than depreciation lost on old equipment. Any changes in tax depreciation rates and rules need to be reflected.

Assumption (iv)

Working capital does not need to increase in direct proportion to sales. For example according to inventory models, **optimum inventories** are likely to **vary with the square root of sales**. Receivables can be **controlled** so that they **grow less quickly than sales** whereas optimum use of payables implies obtaining as much finance as possible without harming trading relationships.

Assumption (ix)

A policy of paying dividends as a constant proportion of earnings each year could result in **volatile dividends**, and is less common than one of attempting to **maintain a steady growth of dividends** in line with the long run growth of profits. However, in the forecasts produced for the next four years there is no real difference between these policies because profit rises steadily.

Operating cash flow is estimated by EBIT(1-t) plus depreciation. To find free cash flow, this needs to be adjusted for changes in working capital and expenditure on non-current assets.

Changes in working capital and non-current assets

	20X5	20X6	20X7	20X8
	$m	$m	$m	$m
Change in land and buildings	–	–	40	–
Change in plant and machinery	91	88	84	76
Change in working capital	15	27	–	56
Change in assets	106	115	124	132

Free cash flow

	20X5	20X6	20X7	20X8
	$m	$m	$m	$m
EBIT (1 –T)	285	307	328	348
Depreciation	165	179	191	203
Change in assets	(106)	(115)	(124)	(132)
Free cash flow	344	371	395	419

Assuming growth to perpetuity of 6% per year after 20X8, the present value of free cash flow as at 31 March 20X8 is estimated as:

Free cash flow $(1 + g)/(WACC - g) = 419 \times 1.06/(0.11 - 0.06) = \$8,883$ million.

Loans at 31 March 20X8, as estimated in the pro forma accounts, will be $580 + 320 = \$900$ million. Subtracting this from the PV of free cash flow leaves $7,983 million as the value of equity. There are 2,400 million shares, so share price at 31 March 20X8 is estimated as $7,983/2,400 = 333 cents per share.

This represents an **increase of 59%** over the current share price of 210 cents. On the basis of these figures, and the fact that the projected growth rate of 6% is probably over-optimistic, the managing director's claim that the share price will double in four years appears to be unfounded. However a lot will depend on the performance of the stock market over the next few years.

If you have any questions about this report, please do not hesitate to contact me.

(b) The managing director believes that Wurrall Inc should have two financial objectives: the growth in profits before tax, and growth in share price. It is commonly felt that the principal objective for organisations is the maximisation of shareholders' wealth. The reasons for the suitability of this over the two objectives suggested by the managing director are as follows:

Growth in share price

Although capital gains from shares are a part of shareholder wealth, shareholder wealth also includes dividends received. It is thought that the share price should reflect the present value of all future expected dividends, but in reality the share price may be affected more by market confidence in the company.

Share prices can be affected by factors outside the control of the company, such as economic conditions. Therefore growth in share price is not the most suitable objective for a company to follow. Measures such as growth in earnings per share are generally felt to be better objectives for companies to pursue.

Growth in profits before tax

Profit before tax is a financial accounting figure that is reached after several accounting estimates have been made. If this is to be used as one of only two objectives for Wurrall Inc there is the possibility that manipulation of accounting policies could occur in order to achieve target growth percentages when in reality the performance has not improved. Similarly this measure does not take into account dividends paid to shareholders, although as Wurrall pays a constant percentage of earnings after tax, the link between profits before tax and dividends is currently strong.

In addition the focus on profit may encourage a short-term focus to increase this year's profits at the expense of profits in future years.

Other factors

Although maximisation of shareholder wealth is thought to be the main objective for a company, managers should not be pursuing this at any cost. They should not be taking **unacceptable business and financial risks** with shareholders' funds and must act within the law. Managers are aware that any actions that undermine their company's reputation are likely to be **very expensive** in terms of adverse effects on share price and public trust.

The managing director has only focused on financial objectives. Many companies have non-financial objectives too. These objectives may limit their ability to achieve their financial objectives. They do not negate the financial objectives but emphasise the need for companies to have other targets than the maximisation of shareholders' wealth. These objectives may take into account other stakeholders of the company, such as employees and the local community.

BPP
LEARNING MEDIA

(c)   EVA™ is an annual measure of performance based on historical figures. It measures the extent to which funds have been used to either increase or diminish shareholder value.

Advantages of EVA™

As the primary objective of any organisation is usually the maximisation of shareholder value, EVA™ should be the most relevant assessment of performance. The main advantages of this performance measure are:

Keeps the focus on shareholder value

Using EVA™ to monitor performance helps focus Wurrall's management's attention on shareholder value when making decisions. Wurrall's value depends on the extent to which the actual return to the shareholders exceeds their minimum required rate of return (cost of capital). An increase in EVA™ should lead to an increase in the value of Wurrall.

The most meaningful measure of profit for shareholders

Shareholders will only improve their wealth if the return they receive from their investment exceeds their minimum required rate of return. EVA™ recognises this fact by including all capital costs in its calculation and forces management to appreciate that when they use capital they must be expected to have a cost attached to it.

A single goal

There are numerous ratios that can be calculated to assess performance, each of which may have a target level. EVA™ links all these measures with a common focus – how to improve EVA™ and thus shareholder value.

Easy to understand

The calculation of EVA™ starts with the familiar operating profit and deducts a capital charge. It is similar to residual income which is a widely used and understood concept. EVA™ is also calculated periodically, unlike NPV, and its results show the extent of change in shareholder value.

Disadvantages of EVA™

The main disadvantages of using EVA™ are:

Easy to manipulate

The results could be manipulated by Wurrall's management choosing short-term projects with early (but low) yields, over long-term projects whose cash flows do not yield benefits for several years. This type of decision making may not be in the best interests of the company and its shareholders.

Short-term focus

EVA™ focuses only on the current accounting period, whilst ideally performance measures should have a longer-term focus.

Makes comparisons difficult

EVA™ is an absolute measure rather than a relative measure, which makes comparisons between Wurrall and other organisations difficult. Size adjustments would have to be made to make comparisons meaningful.

BPP
LEARNING MEDIA

67 Blipton International

Text references. MIRR and investment appraisal are covered in Chapter 5. Licensing and joint ventures are covered in Chapter 4.

Top tips. This is quite a straightforward question but a number of calculations are involved, making layout and labelling of workings very important. It is essential that you read the question carefully as the capital allowance rates are slightly unusual and tax is paid in the year of incurrence. The information is given in terms of nominal cash flows but the real cost of capital is given, meaning that you have to calculate the nominal cost of capital using the Fisher formula.

You are given information about the dollar/sterling spot rate. There are two issues here. Firstly, you are given cash flows in sterling but are required to produce a 'nominal dollar projection'. This means you will have to invert the spot rate to get dollars in terms of sterling. Also you have to project the exchange rate using the information about relative inflation rates.

As always with such questions, remember you are writing a report, therefore use the correct headings, language and layout. All three parts of your answer should be contained in the same report but make sure each part is clearly labelled to make it easy for the marker to spot.

Easy marks. Part (a)(i) offers some straightforward marks when determining the cash flows. Calculation of NPV and MIRR should not have posed any problems (you would have received 'own figure' marks for technique even if your cash flows and/or cost of capital were incorrectly calculated in part (i)).

(a)(i) **Report to the management of Blipton International Entertainment Group**

From: Financial consultant

Subject: 400 bedroom hotel in East End of London

This report focuses on the proposed building of a 400 bedroom hotel in the East End of London. It looks at the cash flows that are likely to arise from this project, together with an appraisal of whether it would actually be worthwhile to pursue the project further using the net present value (NPV) and modified internal rate of return (MIRR) methods. Finally the report considers the relative advantages and disadvantages of the two appraisal methods used.

Section 1 – after-tax cash flows

The after-tax cash flows have been distinguished between those arising during the investment phase and those that occur during the return phase. The analysis below has been prepared on the basis that room rental will remain as £60 per night (variable costs of £30 + 100% of variable costs) and that variable operating costs remain the same in real terms.

Investment phase

	20X3	20X4	20X5	20X6	20X7	20X8	20X9
	£'000	£'000	£'000	£'000	£'000	£'000	£'000
Initial investment		(6,200)					
Tax savings (Working 1)		930	310	310	310		
		(5,270)	310	310	310		
Exchange rate (Working 2)	0.6700	0.6552	0.6408	0.6267	0.6129	0.5994	0.5862
	$'000	$'000	$'000	$'000	$'000	$'000	$'000
Value of investment phase		(8,043)	484	495	506	Nil	Nil

BPP
LEARNING MEDIA

Return phase

	20X3	20X4	20X5	20X6	20X7	20X8	20X9
Occupancy rate (%)	0	0	40	50	90	60	60
	£'000	£'000	£'000	£'000	£'000	£'000	£'000
Contribution from rooms (Working 3)			1,752	2,190	3,942	2,628	2,628
Fixed costs			(1,700)	(1,700)	(1,700)	(1,700)	(1,700)
Real cash flows			52	490	2,242	928	928.00
Nominal cash flows			54.63	527.68	2,474.75	1,049.95	1,076.20
Tax at 30%			(16.39)	(158.30)	(742.43)	(314.99)	(322.86)
Nominal cash flows after tax			38.24	369.38	1,732.32	734.96	753.34
Terminal value of hotel ($6,200 \times 1.08^5 - 1,200$)							7,910.00
Total nominal cash flow			38.24	369.38	1,732.32	734.96	8,663.34
Exchange rate			0.6408	0.6267	0.6129	0.5994	0.5862

	20X3	20X4	20X5	20X6	20X7	20X8	20X9
	$'000	$'000	$'000	$'000	$'000	$'000	$'000
Nominal value of return phase			59.68	589.40	2,826.43	1,226.15	14,779.00
Total cash flow (investment + return)	Nil	(8,043)	543.68	1,084.4	3,332.43	1,226.15	14,779.00

Working 1 – capital allowances calculation

Year	Cost/WDV £'000	Tax saved at 30% £'000	Year of tax saving
20X4			
Initial cost	6,200		
50% FYA	(3,100)	930	20X4
WDV	3,100		
20X5			
Capital allowance	(1,034)	310	20X5
WDV	2,066		
20X6			
Capital allowance	(1,033)	310	20X6
WDA	1,033		
20X7			
Capital allowance	(1,033)	310	20X7

Working 2 – calculation of exchange rates

The spot rate is 0.6700 (1/1.4925). To calculate the exchange rate for subsequent years, we use the **purchasing power parity formula**.

$$S_1 = S_0 \times \frac{(1+h_c)}{(1+h_b)}$$

Year end	Exchange rate	
20X4	$0.6700 \times \dfrac{1.025}{1.048}$	$= 0.6552$
20X5	$0.6552 \times \dfrac{1.025}{1.048}$	$= 0.6408$
20X6	$0.6408 \times \dfrac{1.025}{1.048}$	$= 0.6267$
20X7	$0.6267 \times \dfrac{1.025}{1.048}$	$= 0.6129$
20X8	$0.6129 \times \dfrac{1.025}{1.048}$	$= 0.5994$
20X9	$0.5994 \times \dfrac{1.025}{1.048}$	$= 0.5862$

Working 3 – calculation of contribution from rooms

Room rate	= £60	(Variable cost + 100%)
Variable operating costs per room	= £30	
Contribution per room	= £30	

Contribution per annum = Contribution per room x no of rooms available x occupancy % x 365 days

For example:

20X5 = £30 × 400 × 40% × 365 = £1,752,000

The occurrence of leap years within the time frame being appraised has been ignored.

(ii) **Section 2 – estimation of net present value and modified internal rate of return**

As cash flows are in nominal terms and the cost of capital has been given in real terms, the cost of capital must be converted to a nominal rate using the **Fisher formula**.

$(1 + i) = (1 + r)(1 + h)$

$(1 + i) = (1 + 0.042)(1 + 0.048)$

$(1 + i) = 1.092016$

$i = 9.2016\%$ (say 9.2%)

The cash flows calculated in section 1 above can now be discounted using the **nominal cost of capital**.

	20X3 $'000	20X4 $'000	20X5 $'000	20X6 $'000	20X7 $'000	20X8 $'000	20X9 $'000
Total cash flow (investment + return)	Nil	(8,043)	543.68	1,084.4	3,332.43	1,226.15	14,779.00
Discount factors (9.2%)	1.000	0.916	0.839	0.768	0.703	0.644	0.590
Present value of cash flows	Nil	(7,367.39)	456.15	832.82	2,342.70	789.64	8,719.61

Net present value = $5,773,530

As NPV is positive this suggests that the project will increase shareholder value and is therefore acceptable.

Modified internal rate of return

MIRR can be calculated using the formula given in the exam formula sheet.

BPP LEARNING MEDIA

$$MIRR = \left[\frac{PV_R}{PV_I}\right]^{\frac{1}{n}} (1+r_e) - 1$$

PV_R is the present value of the return phase

PV_I is the present value of the investment phase

r_e is the cost of capital

	Total $'000	20X4 $'000	20X5 $'000	20X6 $'000	20X7 $'000	20X8 $'000	20X9 $'000
Present value of investment phase	(6,225)	(7,367)	406	380	356	Nil	Nil
Present value of return phase	13,010.07	Nil	50.07	453	1,987	789	9,731

$MIRR = (13,010.07/6,225)^{1/6} \times (1 + 0.092) - 1$

$= 22.4\%$

(iii) **Section 3 – Viability of the project**

Given the figures above, the hotel project is expected to increase shareholders' wealth by $5,773,530 which makes it a viable project. This figure has been established using the net present value (NPV) technique.

One of the advantages of NPV is that it takes into account the **time value of money** – that is, it recognises that money received today is more valuable than the equivalent amount received in the future. It therefore **discounts** each cash flow back to its present day value using the firm's appropriate cost of capital. If the present value of future cash flows **exceeds** the initial amount spent on the investment then the difference represents an **increase in shareholders' funds**. It also expresses this change in wealth as an absolute measure rather than as a percentage therefore there is no ambiguity regarding the monetary effect of the project on shareholders' funds.

There are however some **limitations** with NPV. The technique assumes that the **cost of capital does not change** over time which is not necessarily the case. Companies' circumstances change – such as change in risk perceptions, economic conditions – therefore the cost of capital must be adjusted to suit.

Another problem with NPV is that it is **based on estimates of future cash flows** which are often difficult to determine. If the estimates are significantly different from the reality, the project could result in a **reduction** in shareholders' wealth.

Although NPV does have some **limiting assumptions** it is still the method that is technically superior when appraising capital projects.

The **modified internal rate of return** method can also be useful for measuring returns on major capital projects. MIRR is the **rate at which the project breaks even** (that is, where the NPV is zero), **assuming that cash is reinvested at the firm's current cost of capital** (unlike IRR which assumes that cash is reinvested at the IRR). When there is conflict between NPV and IRR, the MIRR will give the same indication as NPV.

Although NPV is the main investment appraisal technique, MIRR is useful as it indicates the **maximum cost of capital** than the project could sustain before becoming financially non-viable. This information is particularly beneficial when trying to determine **how to finance** the project.

Should you require any further information on the above figures and analysis please do not hesitate to contact me.

(b) **Licensing**

Licensing is an alternative to foreign direct investment. It would mean a South East Asian company would be given rights to use Blipton's brand on a hotel, in return for royalty payments. It has a number of **advantages** for Blipton:

It can allow fairly **rapid penetration of** the South East Asian markets, as no new hotels need to be built and also does **not require substantial financial resources** for the same reason.

Political risks are **reduced** since the licensee is an established local company. This may help if the country in question restricts or prevents foreign direct investment.

The licensing agreement provides a way for **funds** to be **remitted** to Blipton in the form of licence fees.

The main **disadvantages** of licensing are:

The arrangement may give to the licensee **know-how** and **expertise** that it can use to compete with Blipton after the license agreement has expired.

It may be more **difficult to maintain quality standards**, and lower quality might affect the standing of Blipton's brand in international markets.

Although relatively insubstantial financial resources are required, on the other hand **relatively small cash inflows** will be **generated**, although this will depend on the royalty level. It will not be anywhere near as high as cash flows from Blipton operating its own hotels.

Joint venture

A **joint-equity venture** involves investment, is of no fixed duration and continually evolves. Depending on government regulations, joint ventures may be the **only** means of Blipton accessing a particular market.

The main advantages to Blipton of a joint-equity venture are:

There is a relatively **low-cost access** to new markets, although how much this is the case this will depend on how the costs of construction are split between the joint venture partners. It will still be lower than Blipton paying for the construction of the hotels itself.

Easier access to **local capital markets**, possibly with accompanying tax incentives or grants through the connection with the local joint venture partner.

Blipton will be able to make use of the **joint venture partner's existing management expertise**, local knowledge, supplier networks, and marketing or other skills.

There is a sharing of risk with the joint venture partner and also a sharing of costs, which provides economies of scale for Blipton.

The main disadvantages of joint ventures are:

Blipton's **managerial freedom** may be **restricted** by the need to take account of the views of the joint venture partners. Therefore it may not be able to have the same level of control over the look and feel of the hotels as it would under the licensing arrangement.

There may be **problems** in **agreeing on partners' percentage ownership**, transfer prices, reinvestment decisions, nationality of key personnel, remuneration and sourcing of suppliers.

Finding a **reliable joint venture partner** who understands Blipton's culture and who won't damage the brand image may take a long time.

Joint ventures are **difficult to value**, particularly where one or more partners have made intangible contributions.

(c) Large capital investment projects require a **significant proportion** of a company's monetary and human resources and their successful implementation is crucial for a company's performance.

Monitoring during the implementation stage can help Blipton to ensure that:

- The project **expenses** are within the budgeted limits
- Any **revenues** budgeted are achieved
- The completion **time schedule** is adhered to
- Any **risk factors** identified during the appraisal stage of the project remain valid.

Monitoring requires clearly defined roles and planning as well as recommendations for responding to any targets that are not achieved. Monitoring sets milestones for the assessment of the implementation process and the assessment of the various **risks** associated with the project implementation.

These risks may stem from industrial action, from changes in interest or exchange rates or other economic factors, which may affect the demand for Blipton's services and therefore its **revenues**.

Monitoring can also ensure that the **critical path** of the project is followed. The critical path is a series of linked activities which determine the completion of the entire project.

At any stage of the monitoring process, it can be decided whether risks, or even the financial viability of the project, need to be reassessed.

Once a project has been completed, a **post-completion audit** should take place to compare the income, costs and timing with the corresponding budgeted items. A valuable aspect of the post-completion audit is the attribution to specific and identifiable factors of any deviations between budgeted items and actual outcomes. Such attribution will be valuable for a company that may undertake similar projects.

However such attribution is not easy and it may be costly. It may not be easy to identify the causes of a delay, for example, in the execution of a project as there may several related and contingent factors. The **usefulness of an audit may also be limited,** especially for projects that are unique. It may also only be helpful in large projects where the benefits will **outweigh the costs** of the audit.

68 Jupiter Co

> **Text references.** Cost of debt, cost of equity, CAPM and WACC are covered in Chapter 2. Free cash flow to equity is covered in Chapter 7b. Sources of finance are covered in Chapters 2 and 7a.
>
> **Top tips.** On the face of it, this question appears to be quite straightforward as the scenario is quite short and the requirements seem to be clear. However there are some tricky calculations involved, particularly in parts (b) and (c). In part (b), the cost of equity calculations involve having to determine tax-adjusted gearing and equity beta.
>
> Part (c) is probably the most challenging part of the calculation sections. What the question is really asking for is the return required on the new to ensure that shareholders' wealth is not affected. You will have to calculate the current value of the firm and the free cash flow required to maintain shareholder value. Free cash flow is then compared to operating cash flow required to maintain shareholder value – the difference is the interest on the new debt.
>
> It is not very clear what part (d) is looking for. Although the requirement seems clear, you are given no direction on what you should be comparing bond issues to. Make sure you don't launch into the advantages and disadvantages of debt versus equity as means of finance, as the question clearly states that the comparison should be with alternative means of raising debt finance. Whilst the answer concentrates on syndicated loans, comparisons with alternative means of raising debt finance should be equally acceptable, given the lack of guidance.
>
> In (e) the requirement to evaluate means that you have to give some indication of how valid the argument is. The main issue that you need to bring out is that economic risk is less visible but has much more serious long-term consequences than translation risk. However shareholders' views need to be taken into account. You therefore need to explain in your answer what items translation gains and losses affect and how shareholders react to these.
>
> **Easy marks.** There are easy marks to be picked up in part (a) in the calculation of cost of debt, cost of equity and WACC.

Briefing note to Rosa Nelson, CFO

From Deputy CFO

Re Cost of capital

This briefing note assesses the effect of the proposed scheme to repay current debt and raise new capital through a bond issue on the firm's cost of debt and equity and the weighted average cost of capital.

(a) **Current cost of debt, cost of equity and weighted average cost of capital**

The current debt has an average term to maturity of four years. The cost of this type of debt is:

4.2% + credit risk premium of four year European government bonds

= 4.2% + 45 basis points = 4.65%

Cost of equity

Using the CAPM:

$E(r_i) = R_f + ß(E(r_m) - R_f)$

$E(ri) = 4\% + 1.5 \times 3\% = 8.5\%$

Weighted average cost of capital (WACC)

In order to calculate the WACC, we must value the current debt by discounting the average coupon rate at the current cost of debt.

$$\text{Market value of debt} = \frac{5.6}{1.0465} + \frac{5.6}{1.0465^2} + \frac{5.6}{1.0465^3} + \frac{105.6}{1.0465^4}$$

$$= \$103.40 \text{ for every } \$100 \text{ nominal of debt (or } 103.4\%)$$

Total market value of debt = $800 million x 103.4% = $827.2 million

Market value of equity = 500 million shares x 1,380 cents per share = $6,900 million

Gearing ratio = $827.2 million ÷ ($827.2 million + $6,900 million) = 10.7%

$$\text{WACC} = \left[\frac{V_e}{V_e + V_d} \right] k_e + \left[\frac{V_d}{V_e + V_d} \right] k_d (1 - T)$$

$$= (4.65\% \times 0.107 \times [1 - 0.25]) + (8.5\% \times [1 - 0.107])$$

$$= 7.96\%$$

(b) **Effect of redemption of existing debt and issue of new bonds**

New debt is in the form of 10 year fixed interest bonds (50% in the Yen market and 50% in the Euro market). This means that cost of debt will be a **weighted average** of 10 year risk free rate plus the credit premium in both the Yen and Euro markets.

Cost of debt = (50% of [1.80 + 0.5]) + (50% of [4.60 + 0.85])

= **3.875%**

Market value of debt is $2,400 million.

Cost of equity

Cost of equity will be affected by the change in gearing.

Tax-adjusted gearing ratio (based on market values)

$$= \frac{V_d(1-T)}{V_e + V_d(1-T)} = \frac{\$827.2 \times (1-0.25)}{\$6,900 + \$827.2 \times (1-0.25)} = 8.25\%$$

Asset beta = Equity beta x (1 – market gearing ratio)

= 1.5 x (1 – 0.0825)

= **1.376**

$$\text{Revised tax-adjusted gearing ratio} = \frac{\$2,400 \times 0.75}{\$6,900 + (\$2,400 \times 0.75)} = 20.69\%$$

$$\text{Revised equity beta} = \frac{ß_A}{(1 - \text{market gearing ratio})} = \frac{1.376}{(1 - 0.2069)} = 1.735$$

Cost of equity capital = Rf + ß(Rm – Rf) = 4% + 1.735 x 3% = **9.21%**

BPP
LEARNING MEDIA

Weighted average cost of capital

$$\text{WACC} = \left[\frac{V_e}{V_e + V_d}\right] k_e + \left[\frac{V_d}{V_e + V_d}\right] k_d (1 - T)$$

$$= \frac{6,900}{(6,900 + 2,400)} \times 9.21 + \frac{2,400}{(6,900 + 2,400)} \times [3.875 \times (1 - 0.25)]$$

$$= 7.58\%$$

(c) **Old value**

$$V_e = \frac{FCF(1+g)}{k_e - g}$$

where $g = 30\% \times 8.5\% = 2.55\%$

$$V_e = \frac{\overset{(b)}{400} \times 1.0255}{\underset{(r)}{0.085} - 0.0255}$$

$$= \$6,894m \text{ (approximately } \$6,900m)$$

New value

$$6,894 = \frac{FCF(1.02763)}{0.0921 - 0.02763} \qquad (g = 30\% \times 9.21\% = 2.763\%)$$

$$FCF = \$432.5m$$

	$m	$m
Free cash flow	400	432.5
Pre tax (divide by 0.75)	533.33	567.67
Add interest ($800m × 4.65%)	37.20	93.00 ($2,400m × 3.875%)
PBIT	570.53	669.67

PBIT increases by $99.14m and debt increases by $1,600m.

We therefore require a return of 6.2% on additional investment to maintain share price.

(d) **Comparison of proposed method of raising finance with alternative methods**

The use of bonds as a means of raising debt finance has considerable advantages. There is the obvious tax advantage related to interest payments. However as bonds are **tradeable** they may be issued at a **lower cost** than other forms of debt. Bonds open investment to a wider pool of subscribers who can sell the bonds to other investors if they choose.

Whilst **bonds issues** may appear to be an attractive means of raising large amounts of capital for investment purposes, they also carry significant risk. There are large issue costs involved and there is the risk that the issue will be **undersubscribed**. This risk may be mitigated somewhat by the process of underwriting (which comes at a price). Bonds issues tend to involve fairly rigid procedures due to the complex marketing procedures and regulatory requirements.

An alternative approach to raising the necessary debt finance is to use a **syndicated loan**. This type of loan involves a **group of banks** providing funds but without joint liability. There is normally a lead bank which then syndicates the loan to several other banks.

One of the main **advantages** of a syndicated loan is that **larger loans** can be arranged than through a single bank. This means that the company does not have to raise different loans from different banks. In addition, syndicated loans tend to be more flexible and can be tailored to the company's specific needs. However the lead bank may require a **higher interest rate** to cover its risk of one of the syndicate banks defaulting on the loan.

I hope this information helps but I am happy to answer any queries you may have on the proposed debt financing scheme.

(e)   **Maximisation of shareholder wealth**

The directors have a duty to **maximise shareholder wealth in the longer term.** This hedging policy is seeking to achieve this objective. Arguably, therefore, directors should not take into account, when establishing policy, the impact of temporary movements in exchange rates that do not have impacts upon cash flows for the period.

Impact of exchange rate changes on income statement

However, directors may be concerned about the impact on shareholders, because of the accounting requirements. This requires the euro bank balance to be translated at the exchange rate at the date of the statement of financial position, whereas the cost of inventory will be translated at the exchange rate at the date the inventory was purchased. In addition, the hedge is against future transactions as well as those reported in the accounting period. Thus the transactions and the hedge **do not fully match**. Also Jupiter has to **disclose the exchange gains or losses** arising from translating monetary assets at the accounting date. The impact of economic exposure need not be disclosed. Though it may result in a fall in profits as directors fear, shareholders will not be able to differentiate the impact of economic risk from other factors affecting the cost of sales.

Impact of exchange rate changes on statement of financial position (SOFP)

The retranslation of the euroaccount at the accounting date will also **affect its carrying value in the SOFP**. If the euro significantly weakens, the account will be included at a lower value, **worsening Jupiter's asset position and gearing**. This could impact on the financing of Jupiter, as finance providers require a higher cost of capital in return for higher perceived risks.

Shareholder reactions

Shareholders may be most interested in the income statement impact. They may be unhappy if a fall in euro value results in an exchange loss which has been disclosed and which has resulted in **lower earnings per share.** If an exchange gain arises on the euro account, the higher profits may result in shareholders **expecting a higher dividend**, although it would not be based on cash movements.

Disclosure

The company can provide more disclosure than is required by IAS 21 about exchange risks. Jupiter may be required, or it may be regarded as good practice locally, to include a **report on risk management within its annual report**. This would include an explanation of its hedging policy. This may help allay shareholder fears, although the fact that Jupiter **will not be able to quantify precisely the economic impacts** against which the hedge has been made may mean shareholders have problems judging the directors' actions.

(f)   (i)   If X = 5% and standard deviation = $650,000

Then Confidence level = 1.65 deviations from the mean

VaR = $650,000 × 1.65 = $1,072,500

(ii)   30-day SD = daily SD × $\sqrt{30}$ = 650,000 × $\sqrt{30}$ = $3,560,197

30-day VaR = $3,560,197 × 1.65 = $5,874,325

(iii) **Usefulness as indication for directors**

Risk appetite

The relevance of the decision to the directors will depend on how they relate to the decision to the risk appetite they have decided is appropriate. 5% is a widely-used measure, but it **may not match Jupiter's needs.**

Maximum loss

The VaR figure is a reasonable indication of the **maximum expected loss**, not the maximum *possible* loss. The directors may wish to consider whether there are extreme factors that could mean the maximum possible loss is significantly different, and try to estimate what it might be. This will be difficult. Generally the € and $ have been fairly stable, but a big shock, for example a country dropping out of the Euro, may be unprecedented and therefore have unpredictable consequences.

Historical figures

The value at risk model is **based on historical data,** which may not be a fair reflection of the future economic situation. The unprecedented shocks to the global financial system over the last few years have highlighted this weakness of VaR.

Other assumptions

The VaR model assumes that possible outcomes follow a **normal distribution** and that factors causing **volatility** are **independent** of each other. These assumptions may not apply in practice.

Usefulness as external indicator

The VaR is an **easy to understand and widely used figure** that directors can use to justify their decision to investors, particularly if the loss turns out to be higher than expected.

69 Trosoft

> **Text references.** Chapter 7a on WACC basics and adjusted present value. Financial synergies are covered in Chapter 9.
>
> **Top tips.** Do the NPV calculation first before looking at any of the APV adjustments as there would be ten or 11 marks for this.
>
> Complications included being given non-relevant costs (it's worth noting these in your answer, saying that you've ignored them) and the fact that you were given enough data to enable you to calculate six years worth of cash flows. You are expected to calculate flows for as many years as you are given data; though you will gain some marks for correct technique if you calculate for a limited number of years, you will limit the credit you are given.
>
> With the APV, the risk-free rate is chosen, as tax relief from a stable government is virtually risk-free provided the company has other profitable projects. The tax relief is only given for a limited number of years so you have to use the cumulative discount factor rather than the tax relief/risk-free rate perpetuity formula.
>
> For part (c) it is important to note that the question asks for sources of financial synergy, there are no marks here for talking about cost or revenue synergies.
>
> **Easy marks.** The discussion in the second part of the report brings in a number of points that are relevant in many other questions– data limitations, real options, whether in practice the company can cope with diversification and compatibility with strategy.

(a) To: Directors of Trosoft pte ltd
     From: Financial Management Consultant

Report on the proposed diversification into internet auctions

Introduction

Our assessment of the proposed investment takes into account **financial and non-financial factors** and considers the **effect of the diversification** on the **overall business strategy** of the company.

Time period of analysis

Four years of financial estimates were provided in your original brief. However, because the **IT infrastructure** underlying the project is expected to last six years before renewal is required, **the estimates have been extended to six years**, assuming that costs (apart from royalty payments and depreciation) and working capital rise at the current rate of inflation, 2% per year after year 4.

Method of analysis

The **adjusted present value** method has been used for the financial evaluation, first computing the base case NPV and then the PV of financial side effects.

Base case NPV

Using a cost of equity of 10%, the base case NPV is (S$2,810,000), see Appendix 1 for the full calculations.

Financing side effects

Tax shield (tax relief on interest payments)

The 6 year term loan covers IT infrastructure S$2.7 million plus working capital S$0.4 million = S$3.1 million.

The subsidised interest rate is 5.5% – 1% = 4.5%.

Annual interest = S$3.1m × 4.5% = S$139,500.

Annual tax relief = 24.5% × S$139,500 = S$34,177.

Discount this at the risk free rate 4%

The present value of tax relief for 6 years is: S$34,177 × 5·242 = S$179,156.

Alternatively the tax shield could be based upon the percentage debt capacity of the company.

Government interest rate subsidy

Annual interest saving net of tax is S$3,100,000 × 1% × (1 – 0.245) = S$23,405.

Present value for six years, discounted at the risk free rate, is S$23,405 × 5·242 = **S$122,689**.

Issue costs

Issue costs are S$3,100,000 × 1·5% = **S$46,500**.

Adjusted present value

The estimated APV of the investment is –S$2,810,000 + S$179,156 + S$122,689 – S$46,500 = **(S$2,554,655)**

Results of evaluation

On the basis of the financial estimates made, the **investment is not worthwhile**, having a large negative adjusted present value. Alternative investment opportunities are likely to produce much better results, and should be investigated. However, the negative APV of this project is subject to a **large margin of error**, as there are major potential benefits and uncertainties that have not been valued in the computation, such as **realisable value**, or **benefits after six years.**

Limitations of APV method

The APV method has a number of limitations which are as follows.

The discount rate used is based on the **capital asset pricing model**, which has a number of theoretical weaknesses. However, any errors in the discount rate are probably immaterial compared with **uncertainties in the cash flows** themselves. Some of the **cash flow estimates** may be **wrong** because of **lack of underlying information**. More information should be obtained to substantiate the forecast sales figures, and **sensitivity** and/or **simulation analysis** should be used to investigate the impact of different assumptions on net cash flows. It can also be difficult to identify all of the costs associated with the method of financing the project.

Other factors

Real options

There are several possible alternatives that have not been brought into the evaluation. These will add value as real options. They include the **option to sell the project as a going concern** at various points in its life (a **put option**), the **option to increase investment and market share**, and the **option to cross-sell other company products** to the project's clientele (**call options**). Although valuing these options is difficult, it is better to attempt an estimate rather than ignore their value altogether.

Lack of experience

The company has **no experience in this field of business** and may make **management mistakes** as it goes through the learning curve. For example, there may be **technological problems or legal regulations** that have not been fully explored. Also, **marketing and pricing** may prove **difficult** if existing suppliers decide to react to the **increased competition**.

Strategic considerations

Before engaging in a different market sector it is always wise to **revisit the company's overall business strategy**. A major risk is that this investment may divert management resources from the core business and cause long term problems.

If you have any questions about anything in this report, please do not hesitate to contact me.

Appendix 1 Base case NPV

Year	Working	0	1	2	3	4	5	6
		S$'000	S$'000	S$'000	S$'000	S$'000	S$'000	S$'000
Auction fees			4,300	6,620	8,100	8,200	8,364	8,531
Costs								
IT maintenance costs			1,210	1,850	1,920	2,125	2,168	2,211
Telephone costs			1,215	1,910	2,230	2,420	2,468	2,518
Wages			1,460	1,520	1,680	1,730	1,765	1,800
Salaries			400	550	600	650	663	676
Incremental head Office overhead	2		50	55	60	65	66	68
Marketing		500	420	200	200	–	–	
Royalty payments for Use of technology		680	500	300	200	200	200	200
Lost contribution From other activities			80	80	80	–	–	–
Rental of premises			280	290	300	310	316	323
Tax allowable depreciation	3		540	432	432	432	432	432
		1,180	6,155	7,187	7,702	7,932	8,078	8,228
Profit before tax		(1,180)	(1,855)	(567)	398	268	286	303
Tax (24.5%)		289	454	139	(98)	(66)	(70)	(74)
		(891)	(1,401)	(428)	300	202	216	229
Add back depreciation:			540	432	432	432	432	432
Other outflows:								
IT infrastructure		(2,700)						
Working capital	4	(400)	(24)	(24)	(25)	(26)	(10)	509
Net flows		(3,991)	(885)	(20)	707	608	638	1,170
10% discount factors	5	1	0.909	0.826	0.751	0.683	0.621	0.564
Present values		(3,991)	(804)	(17)	531	415	396	660

The expected base case NPV is (S$2,810,000)

Workings

1   The market research cost has been left out of the computation, as it is a sunk cost.

2   Only incremental head office overheads have been included. Other allocated overheads are irrelevant.

3   Depreciation $= \dfrac{2,700}{5} = 540$ year 1 and $\dfrac{(2,700 - 540)}{5} = 432$ in years 2–6.

4   Working capital in year 5 is assumed to increase by the 2% inflation rate. Accumulated working capital at year 4 = 400 + 24 + 24 + 25 + 26 = 499. 2% x 499 = 10. Total working capital at year 5 (509) is assumed to be released at the end of year 6.

5   **Cost of equity**

For the base case NPV the **ungeared cost of equity** has been used for the new project as the discount rate. To find this we ungeared the average equity beta of companies in the internet auction sector to find the asset beta:

Assuming corporate debt to be virtually risk free:

$\beta_a = \beta_e E/[E + D](1 - t)]$

$\beta_a = 1.42 \times 67/[67 + 33 (1 - 0.245)] = 1.035$

Using CAPM

$$k_{eu} = r_f + (r_m - r_f)\beta_a$$
$$k_{eu} = 4\% + (9.5\% - 4\%)\,1.035 = 9.69\%$$

We have approximated this result to 10% as the discount rate for the base case NPV computation.

(b)   It is sometimes argued that companies do not need to diversify since portfolio theory states that shareholders who hold a well-diversified portfolio will have diversified away the unsystematic or company-specific risk and are only left with systematic risk. Following this, a shareholder cannot reduce risk further by undertaking additional diversification in the same system or market.

Even if this is not the case, clearly an **individual investor** can diversify much more **cheaply** than a company can. All they have to do is buy shares in companies in different industries, whereas companies have to go through long, complicated and expensive processes in order to acquire other companies or develop new activities or products internally.

There are **specific factor relating to Trosoft** which may mean it makes sense for the company to diversify.

Trosoft is a **private limited company**. If the owners of Trosoft have all or most of their wealth invested in the company, then the owners will be exposed to all the risk of the company and therefore there is a greater case for diversification.

Since Trosoft is a software company, if it does not diversify there is a risk that due to **technological change** the existing products may become obsolete.

There may also be incumbent managers who have large amounts of their wealth invested in Trosoft. If these managers diversify, they will reduce their exposure to total risk. This opens up other arguments as to whether these managers are acting in the best interests of the other shareholders, if the other shareholders do hold well-diversified portfolios of other shares.

(c)   **Cash slack**

When an organisation with significant excess cash, such as Trosoft, acquires another organisation, with great projects but insufficient capital, the combination can create value. Managers may reject profitable investment opportunities if they have to raise new capital to finance them. It may therefore make sense for a company with excess cash and no investment opportunities to take over a cash-poor entity with good investment opportunities, or vice versa. The additional value of combining these two organisations lies in the present value of the projects that would not have been undertaken if they had stayed apart, but will now be because of the availability of cash.

Tax benefits

The tax paid by two organisations combined together may be lower than the taxes paid by them as individual entities. If one of the organisations has tax deductions that it cannot use because it is losing money, while the other has income on which it pays significant taxes, like Trosoft will have had in recent years, the combining of the two organisations can lead to tax benefits that can be shared by the two entities. The value of this synergy is the present value of the tax savings that accrue because of this merger. The assets of the organisation being taken over can be written up to reflect new market value, in some forms of mergers, leading to higher tax savings from depreciation in future years.

Debt capacity

By combining two organisations, each of which has little or no capacity to carry debt, it is possible to create an organisation that may have the capacity to borrow money and create value. Diversification will lead to an increase in debt capacity and an increase in the value of the combined organisation. When two organisations in different businesses merge, the combined organisation will have less variable earnings, and may be able to borrow more (have a higher debt ratio) than the individual entities could.

70 Your company

Text references. For parts (a) and (b), recent developments such as the emergence of the Islamic bond markets and the European Sovereign Debt Crisis are covered in Chapter 19. For part (c), CAPM is covered in the revision section at the beginning of the text. WACC and the cost of debt are covered in Chapter 7a.

Top tips. Parts (a) and (b) test your awareness of current developments in international finance and the financial markets. Part (c) is quite an unusual question which tests your knowledge by asking you to look for errors in the original 'guidance'. Remember to explain at all times what you are doing, as you are writing a guidance manual. The length of the question may put you off, but it is divided into sections to make it easier for you to deal with.

Easy marks. For part (c), the narrative guidance offers some easy marks as it covers areas that are fundamental to financial management.

(a) It is appropriate for an international company to consider ways of raising debt capital in foreign currencies, for two reasons. First, liabilities in a foreign currency may offset foreign currency investments, and reduce the exposures of the company to currency risk. Second, it may be possible to raise debt capital on more favourable terms than in the domestic bond market.

The suggestion that the company should use the **dim sum bond market** and the Islamic bond markets is unlikely to be appropriate however.

Unless the company has investments in China, there would be no benefit of currency risk hedging from a bond issue denominated in renminbi. The only potential benefit would therefore be any opportunity that may exist to raise debt on favourable terms.

A further problem is that the renminbi is not yet a fully internationalised currency. The company would need to ensure that it will be able to convert renminbi received from any bond issue into other currencies in which the company carries out its business operations.

The **Islamic bond markets** may also be inappropriate, unless the company has a strategic objective of attracting Islamic investors. Making new issues of Islamic bonds (sukuk) is more complex than issuing conventional bonds, because Islamic bonds must comply with Sharia'a law and principles, and new issues must be approved by a Sharia'a advisory council for the relevant bond market. This means that bonds take longer to issue.

In addition, the company may possibly be ineligible for Islamic bonds. The issue of sukuk would not be approved if the company is engaged in any business activities that are considered illegal or unacceptable in Shariah law.

Both the dim sum bond market and Islamic bond markets may be inappropriate for other reasons. The company may wish to issue bonds in a deep and liquid market, in order to attract investors. The dim sum bond market is not large or deep, and although Islamic bond markets are developing, they are not yet as large or deep as conventional bond markets.

In order to raise capital in financial markets, a company needs access to these markets. For either dim sum bonds or Islamic bonds, the company would need to identify financial institutions that could help it to attract investors in the market. Unless it has a very well-established international name, the company may well find that this is difficult.

(b) The European Sovereign Debt Crisis originated from the rapid growth in government debt in Europe, particularly the eurozone. Unlike the UK, where the central bank is able to print money and devalue the currency if necessary to pay back sterling-denominated debt, sovereign debt in the eurozone is denominated in euros, an international currency. Eurozone countries cannot get out of their debt problems by means of currency devaluation.

Efforts by governments to reduce their debt, or even their annual budget deficit, were hampered by very **low economic growth or economic recession**. Investors in the financial markets were alerted to the debt problem, initially in Greece but subsequently in other countries, mainly in Southern Europe. Yields on government bonds in troubled countries rose, bond prices fell and some governments found it difficult to issue new debt except at a high interest rate.

In Spain and Ireland, the financial problems of the government were **compounded by a property market crash**, causing large defaults of property loans and large losses for banks.

Banks were involved in the crisis partly because of loan defaults, but also because many European banks were large investors in government securities, and suffered losses from the falls in bond prices. They have also been required to increase their capital, to comply with the requirements of Basel III and their national regulators.

Because they have struggled to resolve their own financial difficulties, both solvency and liquidity problems, banks have restricted their lending. The shortage of capital for investment by business contributed to the problems of national economies.

Banks in countries such as Spain became **reliant on the European Central Bank** for liquidity.

The problems of sovereign debt have therefore had a knock-on effect for banks and the European economy in general.

The company should review its credit risk exposures to troubled European banks. It can do this by monitoring the credit ratings of banks, and may establish a policy of closing accounts and avoiding business with any bank whose credit rating is below an acceptable credit level. The financial position of banks can also be monitored by analysing new financial statements when these are issued and by checking the media for reports on banks.

The company should also review its banking policy and consider its dealings with European banks.

If the company is unable to avoid having an account with a bank in a country with debt problems, it should consider the imposition of limits on credit risk exposures to any bank in the country. This would involve limits on deposits and also limits on market transactions.

It may also be appropriate to transfer euro deposits from banks in the countries with debt problems to banks with stronger economies, such as Germany.

(c)   **Revised guidance manual**

(1)   **Discount rate**

The discount rate for a project should reflect the **cost of finance** for that project, taking into account its risk. There are two main ways of doing this.

(i)   The discount rate for a project should reflect the weighted average cost of capital for the company **only** if both the **business risk** and **financial risk** of the project are the same as the company's.

(ii)   If the project finance will change the company's gearing, the **adjusted present value method** should be used.

(2)   **Cost of debt and equity**

The cost of equity and cost of debt should always be estimated using **market values (no change from the original)**.

(3)   **Inflation**

If project cash flows include estimates for expected inflation, the **discount rate** should also **allow for inflation**. Discount rates calculated by the normal methods described in this manual will automatically contain this inflation allowance. If project cash flows are estimated in real terms (at today's prices), the discount rate will also need to be **adjusted** to real terms, by removing the expected inflation rate.

(4)   **Estimating cost of equity**

To estimate the cost of equity capital for a project we recommend the **Capital Asset Pricing Model** (CAPM), which relates the cost of capital to the project's systematic risk. The cost of equity capital for the whole company can also be estimated from the CAPM or from the **dividend valuation model** which relates the cost of capital to the company's share price and expected future dividend payments. Both models contain theoretical simplifications and require estimates which are subject to inaccuracies.

BPP
LEARNING MEDIA

(5) **Estimating cost of debt**

The company's cost of debt should be estimated from the **current market rate** it is paying. For some types of loan the market rate is quoted transparently. For others it is necessary to **compute** the **redemption yield**, taking into account **interest** and **capital payments** compared with current market value. In each case, the cost to the company is after allowing for **corporate tax relief** on interest. Where there are several forms of company debt, the weighted average can be taken.

(6) **Rounding**

There is **no need** to **round** the cost of capital to the nearest whole percentage, although it must be appreciated that the estimate is usually subject to a high margin of error. The practice of rounding *up* to be more prudent is wrong, as this may cause **potentially profitable projects** to be **incorrectly rejected**. It is good practice, however, to use sensitivity analysis to gauge the risk of accepting the project.

Revised illustrative examples

Illustration 1 – when the company is expanding existing activities

Cost of equity

Dividend valuation model

The model should be based on next year's dividend D_1. g should be estimated dividend growth, not earnings growth.

$$D_1 = D_0 (1 + g)$$
$$= 24 \times 1.06$$
$$= 25.44 \text{ cents}$$

Market price per share $= \$214m/50m = 428 \text{ cents}$

$$\text{Cost of equity} = \frac{D_1}{P} + g$$
$$= 25.44/428 + 0.06 = 0.119 \text{ or } 11.9\%$$

Capital Asset Pricing Model

The company's equity beta, not asset beta, should be used to estimate the cost of equity shares. Assuming that debt is risk free (and beta of debt is therefore zero):

$$\beta_a = \beta_e \frac{V_e}{V_e + V_d(1 - T)}$$

$\therefore 1.1 = \beta_e \times 214/[214 + 85(1 - 0.3)] = \beta_e \times 214/273.5$

and $\beta_e = 1.1 \times 273.5/214 = 1.41$

The cost of equity, Ke = 6% + (14% – 6%) 1.41 = 17.3%.

The two estimates of cost of equity are now very different. The CAPM estimate is used in the computation of WACC.

Cost of debt

The loan stock has a book value of $80m and a market value of $85m. Annual interest payments are 10% of $80m = $8m and result in tax savings of 30%, for which the timing difference is ignored, giving a net interest cost of $8m × 0.7 = $5.6m.

Assuming the debt is redeemed at par of $80 million:

$$\text{Rough cost} = 5.6/85 + \left[\frac{(80 - 85)}{85 \times 4} \right] = 5.1\%$$

For a more accurate answer, find the cost by estimating the IRR of the cash flows at 5% and 6% and interpolate:

Year	$m	Discount factor 5%	PV $m	Discount factor 6%	PV $m
0	(85.0)	1.000	(85.0)	1.000	(85.0)
1–4	5.6	3.546	19.9	3.465	19.4
4	80.0	0.823	65.8	0.792	63.3
			0.7		(2.3)

By interpolation, cost of debt $= 5\% + 0.7/(0.7 + 2.3) = 5.23$, say 5.2%

Weighted Average Cost of Capital (WACC)

$$\text{WACC} = Ke_g \left(\frac{V_e}{V_e + V_d} \right) + Kd\,(1 - T)\left(\frac{V_d}{V_e + V_d} \right)$$

$$= 17.3 \left(\frac{214}{214 + 85} \right) + 5.2 \left(\frac{85}{214 + 85} \right) = 13.9\%$$

The discount rate for the project is 13.9%. No further adjustment is needed because the market costs of equity and debt already allow for expected inflation.

Illustration 2 – when the company is diversifying its activities

Cost of equity

The asset beta of a similar sized company in the industry in which the company proposes to diversify is 0.90. This can be used as the asset beta of the new project. (**This does not need to be 'ungeared' as in the original example, as it is an asset beta not an equity beta**).

To estimate the equity beta for our company for the new project, we use the formula:

$$\beta_a = \beta_e \frac{E}{E + D(1 - t)}$$

$$\therefore \beta_e = 0.90 \times 273.5/214$$
$$= 1.15 \text{ (same computation as in illustration 1 with a different asset beta)}$$

Using the CAPM, $Ke = 6\% + 8\% \times 1.15$
$$= 15.2\%$$

Cost of debt

This is unchanged at 5.2%.

$$\text{WACC} = 15.2\% \times 214/299 + 5.2\% \times 85/299 = 12.4\%$$

BPP LEARNING MEDIA

71 Omnikit

Text references. Chapter 8 on international investment appraisal: Chapter 9 includes points that you could have discussed. Chapter 18 covers transfer pricing.

Top tips. Two foreign investment appraisals in one question! For this sort of question, which is relatively common and contains many computational techniques, you need to develop a standard approach and practice it hard, because a look at the marking scheme shows that not many marks are awarded for each computational element. Never miss out the discussion parts of a question like this: they are far better value for time than the computational parts. Our answer shows you the best sequence in which to tackle the problem, and provides further hints at the various key stages.

Part (d) requires detailed knowledge of transfer pricing methods and demonstrates the importance of knowing the whole syllabus.

Easy marks. The figures and workings at the start of each appraisal before you get onto the more complicated workings. The discussion part in (a) should be fairly straightforward, and the limitations of the assumptions are common to most questions of this type. Part (c) also offers some fairly easy marks.

(a) **Advantages of organic growth**

    (i)   It can be carefully planned to fulfil strategic objectives.

    (ii)   It is more likely to involve existing front-line managers than growth by acquisition and hence can be more motivating.

Disadvantages of organic growth

However, the costs of **entering new lines of business** can be high and the lead times involved might be too long to enable the business to gain competitive advantage. The new business has to researched, developed and planned, production facilities have to be acquired and suitable staff hired. The organisation then goes through a learning curve, often repeating the mistakes made by competitors.

Advantages of growth by acquisition

    (i)   It provides a **quicker method of entering new markets** or acquiring new technology or patents, sometimes enabling very rapid growth

    (ii)   **It enables increased market power** by eliminating competitors

    (iii)   **It provides economies of scale** by elimination of duplicated resources, combining complementary resources, etc

Disadvantages of growth by acquisition

By its nature, however, growth by acquisition cannot be **planned** in as much detail as organic growth. Quick decisions sometimes have to be made in response to acquisition opportunities, often without as much information as the acquiring company would like. Major acquisitions may change the company's strategic direction. Staff problems are more likely to arise as attempts are made to integrate or change the cultures of merged organisations.

(b)   To: Directors, Omnikit plc
        From: Accountant
        Date: 20 June 20X5
        Subject: **Proposed overseas subsidiary**

This report addresses the financial viability of the potential overseas subsidiaries in USA and Switzerland as well as addressing the uncertainties in the evaluation and detailing the assumptions made.

Contribution to organisational objectives

The evaluation of each of the two alternatives is made in terms of how well each one contributes to the **achievement of organisational objectives** and strategies. The information given enables a financial appraisal of each alternative to be made. This will only be part of the input to the final decision, albeit an important part. Many non-financial factors will also have to be taken into account.

Approach used

The financial appraisal is shown below. The basic approach is to estimate cash flows in the foreign currency, convert them to the home currency and discount them at a rate based on home country cost of capital.

Financial appraisal of the two alternative investments

The time horizon for appraisal of both investments is 7 years: six years of operation plus one further year to allow for the tax delay.

Appraisal of Swiss investment

The Swiss investment has a positive net present value of **£15.93 million** (See appendix 1 for calculations).

Appraisal of US investment

The net present value of the US investment is **negative £45,000** if the investment cost is the maximum $10 million.

If the cost is only $8m, the NPV is increased, giving a **positive NPV of £1.272m.**

(See appendix 2 for calculations)

Assumptions

The financial appraisals are based on several assumptions, which are stated during the course of the computation.

Uncertainties

Most of the estimates are subject to considerable uncertainty, for example:

(i)   Estimates of future exchange rates are based upon forecast inflation levels and purchasing power parity theory.

(ii)   Inflation is unlikely to remain at the levels given and may affect different types of costs and revenues in different ways.

(iii)   Tax rates may change.

(iv)   As in most financial appraisals, the most difficult figure to estimate is the residual value at the end of the time horizon of six years.

(v)   Estimates for the Swiss sales figures are more difficult to make than for the US investment, because it is a start-up business.

(vi)   The systematic risk of both investments is assumed to be the same as Omnikit's existing business. If this is not the case then project specific discount rates should be used.

(vii) Sensitivity analysis could be used to provide more information on which of the above uncertainties cause the most problems.

Conclusion

From the financial appraisal, the Swiss investment is the better alternative. If the US investment is thought to have a positive NPV, then both investments could be undertaken (they are not mutually exclusive) provided adequate funds and management resources were available.

If you have any queries about this report, please do not hesitate to contact me.

Appendix 1 - Appraisal of Swiss investment

Year	0	1	2	3	4	5	6	7
Production/sales units			2,000	2,500	2,500	2,500	2,500	
Cont. per unit, SFr (W1)			9,923	10,419	10,940	11,487	12,061	
	SFr '000	SFr '000	SFr '000	SFr '000	SFr '000	SFr '000	SFr '000	SFr '000
Total contribution			19,846	26,048	27,350	28,718	30,153	
Royalty(£750,000 ÷ exch.rate)			(1,806)	(1,841)	(1,877)	(1,914)	(1,951)	
Operating cash flow			18,040	24,207	25,473	26,804	28,202	
Tax at 40%				(7,216)	(9,683)	(10,189)	(10,722)	(11,281)
Tax saved by dep'n all. (W2)				1,120	360	270	202	152
Land	(2,300)							
Building	(1,600)	(6,200)						
Machinery		(6,400)						
After tax realisable value							16,200	
Working capital (W3)		(11,500)	(575)	(604)	(634)	(666)	(699)	14,678
Cash remitted to UK	(3,900)	(24,100)	17,465	17,507	15,516	16,219	33,183	3,549
Exchange rate SFr/£ (W4)	2.3175	2.3625	2.4084	2.4551	2.5028	2.5514	2.6010	2.6515
	£'000	£'000	£'000	£'000	£'000	£'000	£'000	£'000
Cash remitted from Switzerland	(1,683)	(10,201)	7,252	7,131	6,199	6,357	12,758	1,338
Royalty received			750	750	750	750	750	
Tax at 33% on royalty				(248)	(248)	(248)	(248)	(248)
Net cash	(1,683)	(10,201)	8,002	7,633	6,701	6,859	13,260	1,090
12.51% d.f. (W5)	1.000	0.889	0.790	0.702	0.624	0.555	0.493	0.438
Present value	(1,683)	(9,069)	6,322	5,358	4,181	3,807	6,537	477

Workings

1   Contribution per unit – Switzerland

At current prices (year 0):	SFr
Sales price	20,000
Variable costs	11,000
Contribution	9,000

This will increase by 5% per year. Contribution per unit in year 2 will be 9,000 x 1.05^2 = SFr 9,923.

2   Tax saved by tax-allowable depreciation (machinery only) in Switzerland

(Figures in SFr'000)

Year	1	2	3	4	5	6	7
Asset value at start of year	6,400	4,800	3,600	2,700	2,025	1,519	
25% depreciation	1,600	1,200	900	675	506	380	
Tax saved at 40%			1,120	360	270	202	152

It is assumed that, because the Swiss subsidiary earns no profits in year 1, the tax depreciation in year 1 cannot be claimed until year 2. The allowance in year 2 will therefore be 2,800, giving rise to a tax saving of 1,120 in year 3.

No **balancing allowance** has been shown, as the asset will still be in use after year 6 and its value is included in the after-tax realisable value of the investment, SFr16.2m.

3   Investment in working capital – Switzerland

It is assumed that total working capital requirement increases with inflation at 5% per year and is returned at the end of year 7. It is assumed that the amount of working capital at year 6 is *not* included in the value of the investment at that stage.

> **Top tips.** In the absence of clear instructions, reasonable assumptions have to be made, but clearly alternatives are possible.

(Figures in SFr'000)

Year	1	2	3	4	5	6	7
Total working capital	11,500	12,075	12,679	13,313	13,979	14,678	
Investment in WC	(11,500)	(575)	(604)	(634)	(666)	(699)	14,678

4. Computation of exchange rates for the next 7 years

For ease of computation, the spot rate will be taken as the mid-market exchange rate.

Spot rate for SFr = (2.3140 + 2.3210)/2 = 2.3175

Using purchasing power parity theory, each year the SFr/£ exchange rate is multiplied by 1.05/1.03

> **Top tips.** Alternatively multiply by $\dfrac{0.05 - 0.03}{1 + 0.03} + 1$

Year	SFr/£
0	2.3175
1	2.3625
2	2.4084
3	2.4551
4	2.5028
5	2.5514
6	2.6010
7	2.6515

5. Discount rate for the investments

Because both investment alternatives represent an expansion of the existing business, the company's existing weighted average cost of capital can be used as a discount rate.

The debt is borrowed in the UK where interest will save tax at the rate of 33%. Its after tax cost is 10%(1 − 0.33) = 6.7%

Market values should be used as weights.

WACC = 0.7 × 15% + 0.3 × 6.7% = 12.51%

Appendix 2 - Appraisal of US investment

Year	0	1	2	3	4	5	6	7
	$'000	$'000	$'000	$'000	$'000	$'000	$'000	$'000
Pre-tax cash flow		2,120	3,371	3,573	3,787	4,014	4,255	
Tax at 30%			(636)	(1,011)	(1,072)	(1,136)	(1,204)	(1,277)
Cost of acquisition (assume maximum)	(10,000)							
Machinery	(2,000)							
After tax realisable value							14,500	
Working capital (W2)	(4,000)	(240)	(254)	(270)	(286)	(303)	(321)	5,674
Cash remitted to/from USA	(16,000)	1,880	2,481	2,292	2,429	2,575	17,230	4,397
Exchange rate (W1)	1.5185	1.5627	1.6082	1.6551	1.7033	1.7529	1.8040	1.8565
Cash remitted to/from USA	(10,537)	1,203	1,543	1,385	1,426	1,469	9,551	2,368
Additional UK tax (3%) (W3) (See Note below)			(41)	(63)	(65)	(67)	(69)	(71)
Net cash	(10,537)	1,203	1,502	1,322	1,361	1,402	9,482	2,297
12.51% d.f. (as before)	1.000	0.889	0.790	0.702	0.624	0.555	0.493	0.438
Present value	(10,537)	1,069	1,187	928	849	778	4,675	1,006

Net present value = (£45,000)

BPP LEARNING MEDIA

1   **Computation of exchange rates for the next 7 years**

For ease of computation, the spot rate will be taken as the mid-market exchange rate.
Spot rate for $ = (1.5160 + 1.5210)/2 = 1.5185

Using purchasing power parity theory, each year the $/£ rate is multiplied by 1.06/1.03.

Year	$/£
0	1.5185
1	1.5627
2	1.6082
3	1.6551
4	1.7033
5	1.7529
6	1.8040
7	1.8565

2   **Working capital – US investment**

Year	0	1	2	3	4	5	6	7
	$'000	$'000	$'000	$'000	$'000	$'000	$'000	$'000
Total working capital	4,000	4,240	4,494	4,764	5,050	5,353	5,674	
Investment in WC	(4,000)	(240)	(254)	(270)	(286)	(303)	(321)	5,674

3   **Additional tax – US investment**

Additional tax of 3% (33% – 30%) is suffered in the UK on US taxable profits. This is computed by converting the pre-tax cash flow at the exchange rate for the year and then multiplying by 3%. eg Year 1: 2,120 ÷ 1.5627 × 3% = 40.69, rounded to 41.

The net present value of the US investment is **negative £45,000** if the investment cost is the maximum $10 million.

If the cost is only $8m, the NPV is increased by $2m/1.5185 = £1.317m, giving a **positive NPV of £1.272m.**

(c)   **Bad publicity**

Relocating to another country may lead to redundancies in the UK. This could mean adverse publicity for Omnikit plc, which may affect customer goodwill.

Quality of manufacturing

The quality of manufacturing will need, at least, to be maintained at the current level, as otherwise there may be a loss of custom due to customer dissatisfaction.

Strategic investments

Omnikit plc should consider whether this decision is sensible from the point of view of **business strategy**. Is there a particularly good reason for becoming involved in Switzerland or the USA, potential future markets possibly? Might investing in other countries with greater market potential and/or lower costs be better? Omnikit plc should also take into account the **PEST** factors affecting the business environment, including the legal and regulatory position, enforcement mechanisms, cultural influences on demand and methods of doing business.

Expertise and knowledge

Omnikit needs to assess whether it has the necessary expertise and knowledge to run an overseas subsidiary within its existing management team or whether local management will need to be brought in. The presence of local management may, particularly, help to address any cultural issues, but can lead to further complications, for example local managers being used to a different culture.

Agency problem

If local managers are used, they may take decisions that are in the interest of the subsidiary rather than for the group as a whole. To balance this, the degree of control from the parent company needs to be decided upon. Too much control from the parent company may demotivate the local management, though. An executive incentive scheme should help to reduce agency costs.

(d) **The comparable uncontrolled price (CUP) method**

The CUP method looks for a comparable product to the transaction in question, either in terms of the same product being bought or sold by the company in a comparable transaction with an unrelated third party, or the same or similar product being traded between two unrelated parties under the same or similar circumstances. The product thus identified is called a **product comparable**. All the facts and circumstances that could materially affect the price must be considered.

Tax authorities prefer the CUP method over all other pricing methods for at least two reasons. First, it incorporates more information about the specific transaction than does any other method. It is transaction and product specific. Second, CUP takes both the interests of the buyer and seller into account, since it looks at the price as determined by the intersection of demand and supply.

The resale price method (RPM)

Where a product comparable is not available, and the CUP method cannot be used, an alternative method is to focus on one side of the transaction, either the manufacturer or the distributor, and to estimate the transfer price using a functional approach.

Under the resale price method, the tax auditor looks for firms at similar trade levels that perform similar distribution function (ie. a **functional comparable**). The **RPM** method is best used when the distributor adds relatively little value to the product, so that the value of its functions is easier to estimate. The assumption behind the **RPM** method is that competition among distributors means that similar margins (returns) on sales are earned for similar functions.

The resale price method backs into the transfer price by subtracting a profit margin, derived from margins earned by comparable distributors engaged in comparable functions, from the known retail price to determine the transfer price. As a result, the **RPM** method evaluates the transaction only in terms of **the distributor**. The method ensures that the distributor receives an arm's-length return consistent with returns earned by similar firms engaged in similar transactions. Since the resale margin is determined in an arm's-length manner, but nothing is done to ensure that the manufacturer's profit margin is consistent with margins earned by other manufacturers, the adjustment is one-sided. Under the RPM method, having determined the distributor's arm's-length margin, all excess profit on the transaction is assigned to the manufacturer. Thus the resale price method tends to **overestimate** the transfer price, since it gives all unallocated profits on the transaction to the manufacturer.

The Profit Split Method (PSM)

When there are no suitable product comparables (the CUP method) or functional comparables (such as the RPM), the most common alternative method is the profit split method (PSM), whereby the profits on a transaction earned by two related parties are split between the parties.

The profit split method allocates the consolidated profit from a transaction, or group of transactions, between the related parties. Where there are no comparables that can be used to estimate the transfer price, this method provides an alternative way to calculate or 'back into' the transfer price. The most commonly recommended ratio to split the profits on the transaction between the related parties is **return on operating assets** (the ratio of operating profits to operating assets).

The profit split method ensures that both related parties earn the same return on assets.

BPP
LEARNING MEDIA

72 Intergrand

Text references. Adjusted present value is covered in Chapter 7a; investment appraisal techniques in Chapter 5. Failures of acquisitions are covered in Chapter 9. Valuation of companies is covered in Chapter 10. Eurobonds are covered in Chapter 4.

Top tips. The main calculation is the adjusted present value – debt calculation. Although the free cash flows is the most significant working, and the additional tax is dependent on the calculations of the free cash flows, it is better exam technique to work out the easier figures first before attempting the free cash flow calculations to make sure you get the marks for these.

The publicity costs are discounted at Intergrand's WACC because they are quoted at an equivalent figure for Intergrand.

You have to assume that the exchange rate in 20X6 applies in perpetuity.

The research is a sunk cost and should thus be excluded from the calculation.

There are several possible ways of calculating the tax shield on debt acquired. You can simply calculate the market value x tax relief, and assume that the loans similar to the current bonds will be available to infinity. More prudently, you can take the question at face value and assume that the tax relief on the bonds will be available until 20X9 when the bonds are redeemed, and that further bonds won't be issued. We have discounted the tax relief at the risk-free rate, but it would also be acceptable (though involve more calculations) to discount it at the cost of debt, calculating the cost of debt by an IRR calculation or using the interest yield.

It is definitely easier to round the base case cost of capital to the nearest whole number and thus be able to make use of discount tables.

The sale of assets and the extra investment both relate to Oberberg, so they should be discounted at its cost of capital, but they do not form part of the free cash flows. The interest should also be excluded from the free cash flows but the synergies should be included. The free cash flows and additional tax post 20X6 can be found using the dividend valuation model formula, but don't forget to discount these because they start from 20X7 (year 5).

Easy marks. Despite all the complications in the calculations, you can easily score marks on the discussion. Most of the discussion points will be raised in other investment appraisals.

(a)   To: **The Board of Directors**
        From: **AN Adviser**
        Subject: **Acquisition of Oberberg AG**

This report uses adjusted present value to appraise the proposed purchase of Oberberg AG and looks at the other factors to take into consideration before deciding to proceed with the acquisition.

Adjusted present value of investment

Using free cash flows and adjusted present value, the value of Oberberg is €116.3 million (see appendix for full calculations) which suggests an offer of €115 million is reasonable, although the estimate is subject to a large margin of approximation.

Other factors to be considered

Assumptions
The **assumptions** used in the forecasts need to be **examined carefully** and alternative forecasts prepared under different assumptions, for example the need for additional investment at a later date, tax changes or assuming that all the exports will be lost.

Risk
Further work needs to be done on **assessing risks**, as the risk assessments upon which the beta factor calculation is **based** may **not be accurate** and risks may change over time, particularly as we are looking at cash flows to infinity. Sensitivity analysis needs to be **undertaken** to see how much key figures may change before the decision is affected.

Timescale

The majority of the benefits from Oberberg will be **obtained after 20X6**, and the directors of Intergrand must **consider** whether this is **too long a timescale** for its investors.

Real options

The existence of real options, the **chance to take decisions** in the future that could **further enhance** the value of Oberberg should be considered.

Economic exposure

If inflation rates stay the same, the value of the euros and hence the value of the investment, will **continue to appreciate**.

Implications of acquisition

The board needs to consider the implications of diversification. Although the acquisition can **reduce risk by diversification**, it can also create **difficulties of integration**, particularly if Oberberg is significant in size relative to Intergrand. Intergrand's board needs to consider carefully any synergies involved and how reliable forecasts of these are, measured against the costs of changing the structure and culture of Oberberg. Intergrand's board should also consider carefully the attitudes of Oberberg's staff in the light of the planned redundancies, and what will be required to retain staff who are important for Oberberg's continued success.

Other strategies

Intergrand's board should try to **ascertain** whether there are other investments in Germany or elsewhere that offer **higher present values** or are **better strategic fits**.

If you have any questions about this report, please do not hesitate to contact me.

Appendix

Adjusted present value calculation

	Working	Euro m
Redundancy		(5.0)
Publicity	1	7.0
Lost exports	2	(4.3)
Tax shield	3	9.7
Sale of assets	5	7.3
Investment for expansion	6	(6.9)
Free cash flows	7	171.2
Additional tax	8	(10.5)
Adjusted present value		168.5
Value of outstanding loans (30 + ((1230/1000) × 18))		(52.1)
Value of Oberberg		116.4

Workings

1   **Publicity**

$$\text{Benefit} = \frac{\text{Annual cash flows}(1-t)}{\text{Intergrand's WACC}} = \frac{1(1-0.3)}{0.1} = €7 \text{ million}$$

2   **Lost exports**

Cost of lost exports = £800,000 × 0.5 × (1 − 0.3) = £280,000

However the exchange rate is not constant.

Under purchasing power parity, next year's euro/£ exchange rate is $\frac{1+0.02}{1+0.04}$ of this year's exchange

	20X3	20X4	20X5	20X6
Exchange rate	1.594	1.563	1.533	1.504
Cost of lost exports € million	0.45	0.44	0.43	0.42
Discount at Intergrand's WACC, 10%	0.909	0.826	0.751	0.683
Present value	0.41	0.36	0.32	0.29

BPP
LEARNING MEDIA

	€ million
Present value 20X3 – 6	1.38
Present value 20X7 – infinity ($\frac{0.42}{0.1}$) – (0.42 × 3.170)	2.87
	4.25

3 Tax shield

	€ million
Bank loans (Dt) (30 × 0.25)	7.5
Bonds: Annual interest charge × Tax relief × 4% Cumulative discount factor (18 × 0.08 × 0.25 × 6.002)	2.2
	9.7

The tax shield on the bonds has been discounted at the risk-free rate, on the assumption that tax relief is virtually certain to be received.

4 Discount rate

Discount at appropriate rate for Oberberg.

Use $\beta_a = \beta_e \dfrac{E}{E + D(1-t)} + \beta_d \dfrac{D(1-t)}{E + D(1-t)}$

Assuming debt is risk-free,

$\beta_a = \beta_e \dfrac{E}{E + D(1-t)}$

$E = 15 \times (300/100) = 45$

$D = 30 + (18 \times 1.23) = 52.14$

$\beta_a = 1.4 \dfrac{45}{45 + 52.14(1 - 0.25)} = 0.749$

Using CAPM

$K_{eu} = r_f + [E(r_m) - r_f]\beta_j$
$= 4 + (11 - 4)\,0.749$
$= 9.24\%$, say 9%.

This is used for the base case free cash flow calculation, before calculation of financing side effects.

5 Sale of assets

Present value = 8.0 × 9% Discount factor year 1
= 8.0 × 0.917
= €7.3 million

6 Investment for expansion

Present value = 9.0 × 9% Discount factor year 3
= 9.0 × 0.772 = €6.9 million

7 Free cash flows

	20X3 €m	20X4 €m	20X5 €m	20X6 €m
Sales	38.2	41.2	44.0	49.0
Synergies		2.0	2.0	2.0
Labour	(11.0)	(12.1)	(13.0)	(14.1)
Materials	(8.3)	(8.7)	(9.0)	(9.4)
Overheads	(3.2)	(3.2)	(3.3)	(3.4)
Tax allowable depreciation	(6.3)	(5.8)	(5.6)	(5.2)
Taxable profit	9.4	13.4	15.1	18.9
Taxation	(2.4)	(3.4)	(3.8)	(4.7)
Add back tax allowable depreciation	6.3	5.8	5.6	5.2
Working capital	(0.7)	(0.9)	(1.0)	(2.0)
Replacement investment	(4.2)	(4.2)	(4.2)	(4.2)
Free cash flows	8.4	10.7	11.7	13.2
Discount factor 9%	0.917	0.842	0.772	0.708
Present value	7.7	9.0	9.0	9.3

Free cash flows 20X3 – 20X6 = €35 million

Free cash flows post 20X6 $= 13.2 \dfrac{(1+g)}{k_e - g}$ × 9% Discount factor year 4

$$= 13.2 \frac{(1+0.02)}{0.09 - 0.02} \times 0.708$$

$$= €136.2 \text{ million}$$

Free cash flows = 136.2 + 35 = €171.2 million

8 Additional tax

Discount at Intergrand's cost of capital as relates to US liability.

Taxable profit	9.4	13.4	15.1	18.9
Extra tax at 5%	0.47	0.67	0.76	0.95
Discount factor 10%	0.909	0.826	0.751	0.683
Present value	0.43	0.55	0.57	0.65

Additional tax 20X3 – 20X6 = €2.2 million

Additional tax post 20X6 $= 0.95 \dfrac{(1+g)}{k_e - g}$ × 10% Discount factor year 4

$$= 0.95 \frac{(1+0.02)}{0.1 - 0.02} \times 0.683$$

$$= €8.3 \text{ million}$$

Extra tax = 2.2 + 8.3 = €10.5 million

(b) A number of alternative theories explain the failure of acquisitions through the fact that the main motive of the management of a company, when they bid for another company, may not be the maximisation of shareholder value but other motives.

Agency theory suggests that takeovers are primarily motivated by the **self-interest** of the acquirer's management. Reasons that have been advanced to explain the divergence in the interests of the management and the shareholder of a company include:

- Diversification of management's own portfolio
- Use of free cash flow to increase the size of the organisation
- Acquiring assets that increase the organisation's dependence on management.

BPP LEARNING MEDIA

The common idea of these explanations is that acquisition is a process that results in value being transferred from the shareholder of the acquiring company to the managers of the acquiring company.

The implication of agency theory is that, because the target knows that a bid is in the interest of the management rather than the shareholders of the acquiring company, it sees this bid opportunity to extract some of the value that would have gone to acquiring management. How much value the target company can extract depends on the bargaining power it has. The risk of this can be reduced by Intergrand carrying out robust investment appraisal and carrying out sensitivity analysis on key variables to see that shareholder value will be increased by the acquisition.

Errors in valuing a target company

Managers of the bidder may advise its company to bid too much, as they struggle to isolate the value of the target. A risk-changing acquisition cannot be valued without revaluing your own company on the supposition that the acquisition has gone ahead. The value of an acquisition cannot be measured independently. As a result, the merger may fail as the target's subsequent performance cannot compensate for the high price paid.

Alternatively, the expected synergies may not be realisable to the level that the target company was valued at, which means that the price paid is too high and ultimately the acquisition fails.

Window dressing

Another reason for the high failure rate is that companies are not acquired because of the synergies that they may create, but in order to present a better financial picture in the short term. This does not appear to be the case here, as Intergrand is looking for an operating subsidiary and has used APV to show that shareholder value will be increased by the purchase.

Poor integration management

In order to integrate two or more organisations effectively, there must be effective integration management and recognition that successful integration takes time. Where management is poor or there is an attempt to do too much too soon, potentially successful mergers can fail.

Inflexibility in the application of integration plans drawn up prior to the event can be damaging. Once the merger has taken place, Intergrand's management must be prepared to adapt plans in the light of changed circumstances or inaccurate prior information.

Poor staff-management can be detrimental to successful integration. Lack of communication of goals and future prospects of employees, and failure to recognise and deal with their uncertainties and anxieties, can lead to employees being unclear of what is expected of them. Hostilities may develop between the two groups of staff, with an unwillingness to adapt to new procedures and practices. Keeping staff informed is important for Intergrand.

(c) **Advantages of eurobonds**

There are a number of advantages of using eurobonds to finance an acquisition.

They are typically issued by companies with excellent credit ratings and are normally **unsecured**, which makes it easier for companies to raise debt finance in the future. Also eurobonds create a liability in a foreign currency to **match** against a foreign currency asset.

Eurobonds are often **cheaper** than a foreign currency bank loan because they can be sold on by the investor, who will therefore accept a lower yield in return for this greater liquidity.

Eurobonds are also extremely **flexible**. Most eurobonds are fixed rate but they can be floating rate or linked to the financial success of the company.

Eurobond issues are not normally advertised, because they are **placed** with institutional investors and this reduces issue costs.

Disadvantages of eurobonds

Like any form of debt finance there will be **issue costs** to consider (approximately 2% of funds raised in the case of eurobonds) and there may also be problems if gearing levels are too high.

A borrower contemplating a eurobond issue must consider the **foreign exchange risk** of a long-term foreign currency loan. If the money is to be used to purchase an organisation which will earn revenue in a currency different to that of the bond issue, the borrower will run the risk of exchange losses if the currency of the loan strengthens against the currency of the revenues out of which the bond (and interest) must be repaid.

73 Pursuit Co

Text references. Valuation of companies for acquisition purposes is covered in Chapter 10. Financing acquisitions is covered in Chapter 12. Environmental reporting is covered in Chapter 3c and the global debt crisis in Chapter 19.

Top tips. Your entire answer should be in report format so don't just produce a set of calculations with some explanations – you are expected to produce a professional-looking report with all the necessary details. It is up to you how you structure your report – for example, calculations could be in appendices – but make sure all the required elements are addressed.

There are numerous calculations required in part (a) before you can actually evaluate the benefits of the acquisition. If you are not sure where to start, ask yourself how benefits of acquisitions are calculated (the difference between the synergy benefits and any premiums paid to acquire the target company). You can then work back from there – synergy is the difference between the value of the combined company and the individual values of the separate companies. You are only given the value of Pursuit so you will have to start with trying to determine the value of Fodder.

The examiner's comments noted that many students struggled with finding a suitable discount rate. If you find yourself in this situation, assume a discount rate and carry on with the rest of the question (just state in your answer that you have assumed this rate). The marking scheme shows that there is only one mark available for this calculation – it is better to forego this mark than the rest of the marks in the question!

Easy marks. There are numerous straightforward calculations in part (a) where you can pick up marks. The implications of a change in capital structure should provide some easy discussion marks in part (iv).

Examiner's comments. Students generally answered part (a)(i) quite well, although common errors included putting interest in the cash flows (it is already built into WACC) and making mistakes in determining a suitable discount rate for the combined company using asset betas.

Answers were generally good for part (a)(ii) but students should study the range of factors from the solution as discussion was limited in some cases.

Parts (a)(iii) and (iv) were answered less well, with many students being unable to calculate whether capital structure could be maintained. Answers regarding the implication of the change in capital structure to the valuation method used were poor in most cases.

Part (a)(v) was answered well when students focused on the particular defence tactic. Poor answers included other defence tactics, which was not required by the question.

BPP
LEARNING MEDIA

		Marks
(i) Ignore interest in calculations	1	
Estimate cost of capital of Fodder Co	1	
Estimates of growth rates and profit margins for Fodder Co	2	
Estimate of intrinsic value of Fodder Co	3	
Equity beta of combined company	3	
Cost of capital of combined company	1	
Estimate of value of combined company	3	
Synergy benefits, value to Pursuit Co shareholders and conclusion	<u>2 - 3</u>	
		Max 16
(ii) 1 – 2 marks per point discussed (credit will be given for alternative, relevant points)		Max 4
(iii) Estimate of the increase in debt capacity after acquisition	1	
Estimate of the funds required to acquire Fodder Co	1	
Conclusion	<u>1</u>	
		3
(iv) Explanation of the problem of the changing capital structure	2	
Explanation of the resolution of the problem using the iterative process	<u>2</u>	
		4
(v) Assessment of suitable defence	2 - 3	
Assessment of viability	<u>2 - 3</u>	
(Credit will be given for alternative, relevant points)		Max 5
Professional marks		
Report format	1	
Layout, presentation and structure	<u>3</u>	
		4
(b) Up to 2 marks for each well explained point		Max 8
(c) Environmental policy	2	
Contents of environmental report	2	
Long-term increase in shareholder value	1	
Additional cost	<u>1</u>	
		<u>6</u>
		<u>50</u>

REPORT TO BOARD OF DIRECTORS OF PURSUIT CO

From: Strategic Financial Consultant
Date: June 20X1
Re: Potential acquisition of Fodder Co

Introduction

This report focuses on various issues related to the proposed acquisition of Fodder Co. It evaluates whether the acquisition would be beneficial to Pursuit Co's shareholders and estimates how much finance is likely to be needed to fund the acquisition. As the capital structure may change as a result of the finance required, the report highlights the potential implications of such a change and possible ways in which any issues could be resolved.

The Chief Financial Officer has recommended reducing Pursuit Co's cash reserves as a defence against a potential takeover by SGF Co. This report assesses the suitability of such a defence and whether it would be a viable option.

Valuation of Fodder Co

> **Tutorial notes**. This forms the answer to part (a). Remember to ignore interest as it is already included in the discount rate.

Year	1	2	3	4
	$000	$000	$000	$000
Sales revenue (W1) – growth rate 6%	17,115	18,142	19,231	20,385
Operating profit (6% growth rate)	5,479	5,808	6,156	6,525
Tax at 28%	(1,534)	(1,626)	(1,724)	(1,827)
Less additional investment (W2)	(213)	(226)	(240)	(254)
Free cash flow	3,732	3,956	4,192	4,444
Discount factor 13% (W3)	0.885	0.783	0.693	0.613
Discounted cash flow	3,303	3,098	2,905	2,724

	$000
Total discounted cash flows (years 1 – 4)	12,030
Terminal value (W4)	28,074
Total value of Fodder Co	40,104

Workings

(1) Sales revenue growth

Growth rate = $(16,146/13,559)^{1/3} - 1 = 0.0599$ or 5.99% (say 6%)

> Alternatively:
>
> Growth rate (20X8 – 20X9) = $(14,491 - 13,559)/13,559 = 6.87\%$
> Growth rate (20X9 – 20Y0) = $(15,229 - 14,491)/14,491 = 5.09\%$
> Growth rate (20Y0 – 20Y1) = $(16,146 - 15,229)/15,229 = 6.02\%$
>
> Average growth rate = $(6.87 + 5.09 + 6.02)/3 = 5.99\%$ (say 6%)

(2) Additional investment

Year	Sales revenue increase ($000)	22% of increase
1	$(17,115 - 16,146) = 969$	213
2	$(18,142 - 17,115) = 1,027$	226
3	$(19,231 - 18,142) = 1,089$	240
4	$(20,385 - 19,231) = 1,154$	254

(3) Cost of capital – Fodder Co

Using CAPM

Cost of equity $(k_e) = 4.5\% + 6 \times 1.53 = 13.68\%$

WACC = $(13.68\% \times 0.9) + [9\% \times (1 - 0.28) \times 0.1] = 12.96\%$ (say 13%)

(4) Terminal value

Growth rate is halved to 3% pa.

PV of cash flows in perpetuity = $4,444 \times [1.03/(0.13 - 0.03)] = \$45,773$

Discounted back to year 0 = $\$45,773 \times 0.613 = \$28,074$

Value of combined company

Year	1	2	3	4
	$000	$000	$000	$000
Sales revenue – growth rate 5.8%	51,952	54,965	58,153	61,526
Operating profit (30% of sales)	15,586	16,490	17,446	18,458
Tax at 28%	(4,364)	(4,617)	(4,885)	(5,168)
Less additional investment (W5)	(513)	(542)	(574)	(607)
Free cash flow	10,709	11,331	11,987	12,683
Discount factor 9% (W6)	0.917	0.842	0.772	0.708
Discounted cash flow	9,825	9,541	9,256	8,985

BPP LEARNING MEDIA

	$000
Total discounted cash flows (years 1 – 4)	37,607
Terminal value (W7)	151,566
Total value of combined company	189,173

Synergy benefits = Total value of combined company – total value of individual companies

= $189,173,000 – ($140,000,000 + $40,104,000)

= $9,069,000

Premium required to purchase Fodder Co = 25% of equity

Equity = 90% of $40,104,000 = $36,093,600

Premium = $9,023,400

Net benefits to Pursuit's shareholders = $9,069,000 – $9,023,400 = $45,600

Workings

(5) Additional investment

Year	Sales revenue increase ($000)	18% of increase
1	See note below	
2	54,965 – 51,952 = 3,013	542
3	58,153 – 54,965 = 3,188	574
4	61,526 – 58,153 = 3,373	607

Note – the additional investment for Year 1 is given in the question.

(6) Combined company cost of capital

Asset beta is calculated using the formula:

$$\beta_a = \left[\frac{V_e}{(V_e + V_d(1-T))} \beta_e \right] + \left[\frac{V_d(1-T)}{(V_e + V_d(1-T))} \beta_d \right]$$

Asset beta (Pursuit) = $1.18 \times (0.5/[0.5 + 0.5 \times (1 - 0.28)]) = 0.686$ (assume debt beta = 0)

Asset beta (Fodder) = $1.53 \times (0.9/[0.9 + 0.1 \times (1 - 0.28)]) = 1.417$ (assume debt beta = 0)

Asset beta (combined company)

= [(0.686 × $140m) + (1.417 × $40.095m)]/(140m + 40.095m) = 0.849

Equity beta (combined company) = 0.849 × [0.5 + (0.5 × 0.72)]/0.5 = 1.46

Cost of equity (k_e) = 4.5% + 1.46 × 6% = 13.26%

WACC = [13.26% × 0.5] + [6.4% × (0.5 × 0.72)] = 8.93% (say 9%)

(7) Terminal value

Growth rate is halved to 2.9% pa.

PV of cash flows in perpetuity = 12,683 × [1.029/(0.09 – 0.029)] = $213,948

Discounted back to year 0 = $213,948 × 0.708 = $151,566

Comments

The extent of the benefits to Pursuit's shareholders depends on the additional synergy from the acquisition of Fodder Co. The calculations above show the synergy to be $9,069,000. However once Fodder's debts have been cleared (as per the acquisition agreement) and equity shareholders paid there is only $45,600 left for Pursuit's shareholders. This amount is minimal and could be turned into a negative figure very easily if variables were changed even slightly. It is therefore unlikely that Pursuit's shareholders will see this acquisition as beneficial.

Limitations of the estimated valuations of Fodder and the combined company

Tutorial note. This forms the answer to part (a)(ii) of the question.

Whilst the valuation techniques used above are useful for providing estimates of company value, it is important to treat the results with caution. The valuation techniques use numerous limiting assumptions, such as constant growth rates both in the early years and for the remainder of the project – there is no way of guaranteeing that these growth rates will be sustainable. Other assumptions include those relating to debt beta (assumed to be zero), discount rates, profit margins and fixed tax rates. As the benefits from the acquisition are minimal, changes in any of these variables could lead to Pursuit's shareholders' wealth being **reduced**.

In addition no information has been given about **post-acquisition integration costs** or pre-acquisition expenses such as legal fees. These should be taken into consideration when trying to determine the net benefits to shareholders as such costs can be quite substantial.

Pursuit's ability to estimate such variables as sales revenue growth, additional investment required and operating profit growth for Fodder may be **limited** due to lack of detailed information. This means that the value of Fodder may be significantly **inaccurate** and thus synergy benefits will be more difficult to predict.

In view of the issues above, it would appear to be **unwise to rely on a single value**. It would be better to have a range of values based on different assumptions and the likelihood of their occurrence.

Amount of debt finance needed and likelihood of maintaining current capital structure

Tutorial note. This forms the answer to part (a)(iii) of the question.

Pursuit is currently valued at $140m – with a 50/50 split between debt and equity this means $70m debt and $70m equity. If this capital structure was to be maintained, the combined company (with an approximate value before payments to Fodder's shareholders of $189,173,000) would have debt of $94,586,500 and equity of the same amount. Debt capacity would thus have to increase by over $24.5m.

Amount payable for Fodder

	$000
Debt obligations (10% of $40,104,000)	4,010
Shareholders ($36,093,600 × 1.25)	45,117
	49,127

Part of the price for Fodder could be paid using the extra debt capacity of $24,586,500 and also the $20m cash reserves that Pursuit currently has. However there would still be a shortfall of $4,540,500. It is therefore impossible to maintain the current capital structure if Pursuit only uses cash reserves and debt finance to fund the acquisition.

Implications of changes in capital structure

Tutorial note. This forms the answer to part (a)(iv) of the question.

The use of either of the two proposals for funding the acquisition of Fodder (a combination of debt finance and cash reserves or the Chief Financial Officer's suggestion of debt finance only) will mean a change in capital structure.

Such a fundamental change will have significant implications for the combined company. The cost of capital will have to be recalculated, which will have an effect on the valuation of the combined company. As the valuation of the company changes, so will the market value of debt and market value of equity. This will have a subsequent effect on cost of capital and the cycle will continue.

This is the type of scenario that is consistent with a **Type III acquisition** (where both financial and business risk change).

The issue can be resolved by using an **iterative process** (which may be performed on an Excel spreadsheet). This process involves recalculating beta and cost of capital and then applying these to determine a revised company valuation. The process is then repeated until the assumed capital structure is close to the one that has been recalculated.

Another alternative would be to use **Adjusted Present Value** which first calculates a value assuming an all-equity financial structure and then makes adjustments for the effects of the method of financing used.

BPP LEARNING MEDIA

Suggested defence against a potential bid by SGF Co

> **Tutorial note.** This forms the answer to part (a)(v) of the question.

The Chief Financial Officer has suggested a distribution of the $20 million cash reserves to shareholders in the form of a special dividend in order to defend against the potential bid by SGF Co. This type of defence is known as the '**crown jewels**' approach, whereby a company dispenses with its most valuable assets (which may have been the main reason for the takeover bid).

Returning the cash to the shareholders may have a positive effect on the currently depressed share price. It may be that the shareholders do not agree with the Board's policy to retain large cash reserves and a reduction in these reserves may push up the share price and reduce the likelihood of a takeover bid.

A formal bid has not been made to date and it would be wise for Pursuit's Board to determine whether the large cash reserves are the attraction or if SGF has another reason for wishing to acquire Pursuit. In addition, before the cash is returned to the shareholders, it should be determined whether this is actually what the shareholders want. There would be no point returning the money to them if they would prefer it to be reinvested in the company.

If the cash reserves are returned to the shareholders this will have implications for funding the acquisition of Fodder. Even with the $20 million reserves to partially finance the purchase, the capital structure would have to change. If this money was not available then there would be a much more significant change in capital structure as an additional $20 million in debt finance would have to be found (if possible). This will have an effect on cost of capital and also on the value of the combined firm (see discussion above).

It may be the case that the amount of debt required is not feasible due to the considerable increase in gearing it would mean. The Board of Pursuit should consider whether the acquisition is worth pursuing due to its minimal benefit to shareholders.

Conclusion

This report has focused on the potential acquisition of Fodder Co and a possible defence against a takeover bid by SGF Co. There are numerous issues that must be resolved prior to making a final decision regarding going ahead with the acquisition, but it is clear that (if the valuations are correct) the capital structure cannot remain unchanged. The implications of this must be considered prior to a final decision being made. The Board should also consider whether the acquisition should go ahead at all, given the minimal benefit to shareholders.

Should you require any further information please do not hesitate to contact me.

(b)   The global debt crisis may affect Pursuit Co in a number of ways.

Lack of availability of debt finance for Pursuit Co

The global debt crisis has meant there is a lack of liquidity in the debt finance markets. This means that companies such as Pursuit Co find it more difficult to raise debt finance and as such may not be able to raise the debt finance required for the acquisition of Fodder Co.

Contraction in demand for Pursuit Co's product

The global debt crisis and ensuing lack of confidence in the economic system have meant that many consumers have restricted their spending and this may affect demand for electronic goods, or other products which have Pursuit Co's components in them. This will mean that the manufacturers of the end products reduced their purchases from Pursuit Co, meaning Pursuit Co's revenue will fall.

Supply chain disruption

The events described above to reduce the demand for Pursuit Co could also happen to reduce demand for members of Pursuit Co's supply chain. In the most extreme case members of the supply chain could go out of business, forcing Pursuit Co to seek new suppliers.

Positive aspects

If Pursuit Co is in a relatively strong position in its industry, it may still be able to obtain debt finance and may be able to acquire competitors in various countries that are struggling to achieve the level of financing they require to operate successfully. Alternatively Pursuit Co may be able to attract key personnel from competitors that are struggling as a result of the global financial crisis.

(c)   Many companies believe that development of a green environment policy will mean a **long-term improvement in profitability**. Environmental and social factors are seen to contribute to a sustainable business that will enhance long-term shareholder value by addressing the needs of its stakeholders – employees, customers, suppliers, the community and the environment.

Many companies are now including environmental performance as part of their annual reports. If Pursuit Co does the same, it could include the following items: what the business does and how it impacts on the environment, environmental objectives (eg use of 100% recyclable materials within x years), Pursuit Co's approach to achieving and monitoring these objectives, and any progress to date. If there are any measures used these should be backed by independent verification where possible.

The main advantage for Pursuit Co is that it can strengthen its corporate image and long-term shareholder wealth by portraying itself as an environmentally friendly company.

The main disadvantage for Pursuit Co is the additional cost of monitoring and reporting performance.

74 Laceto

Text references. Chapters 10 and 12 on the calculations, whilst Chapter 11 covers the merger discussion issues.

Top tips. The most important element of (a)(i) is the calculation of the free cash flows and the weight of the marks reflects this. The complications in this calculation are:

- The weighted average cost of capital calculation; we use Omnigen's equity beta (which reflects the systematic risk of Omnigen's activities) to calculate the cost of equity and the loan stock example to calculate the cost of debt.

- The post 20X5 position: the dividend valuation equation can be used to estimate the cash flows given the growth in earnings

Note that ACCA's marking guide highlighted the need for adjustment of debt values for the equity bid, a suggested minimum price and a reasonable range of prices.

In (b) we give more of the possible suggestions than you would need to gain full marks. We have excluded lobbying for a Competition Commission referral on the grounds that this is unlikely to succeed given the size of the company. We have also excluded the 'white knight', friendly bidder solution, as we have assumed that Laceto does not wish to be taken over. To gain high marks, you needed to mention the financial data in the report.

Easy marks. Although you are well rewarded for the calculations in (a), there are a number of marks available for discussion particularly in parts (ii) and (iii).

(a)   (i)   **Report**

To: The Board of Directors
From: AN Adviser
Subject   Purchase of Omnigen

This reports looks at the potential prices that Laceto could offer to purchase Omnigen. It also covers the factors that should be considered when deciding between a paper bid or a cash offer.

Minimum price

The minimum price that Laceto could possibly pay is the **current market price** of the shares, 410p. This would value Omnigen at $123 million. However unless Omnigen's shareholders were expecting the company's share price to fall in the near future, they are likely to be looking for an offer in excess of market price so Laceto will have to pay a **premium**. To decide what the company should pay, it is necessary to look at a range of valuation methods.

Realisable values

The realisable value of Omnigen's assets is **$82 million**. This is below the current market value of Omnigen's shares, reflecting market expectations of Omnigen's future profitability. The shareholders of Omnigen would clearly not accept an offer as low as this, but realisable value has some use of a measure of **comparison**, indicating the possible loss if Omnigen fails to make the necessary dividend payments.

P/E ratios

If the P/E ratios of Omnigen's two competitors were used to provide either end of a range within which the offer price would be located, then the offer price would be somewhere between earnings after tax, $14 million, multiplied by 13 and 15, to give a range of between **$182 million and $210 million**.

Problems with using P/E ratios

(i) Omnigen's **prospects** may differ substantially from both the companies used as comparisons, thus justifying its lower P/E ratio of 8.79 (123/14). The fall in the market price over the past few years may be an indication that a strong or semi-strong efficient market is taking a realistic view of Omnigen's future earnings.

(ii) We are not told anything of the **other factors** that may influence P/E ratios such as Omnigen's **asset backing**, **gearing** or **status** within the industry as compared with its competitors.

Cash flows

Basing the offer on the **present value of the future cash flows** of Omnigen is likely to be a more reliable method than realisable values or P/E ratios, since Laceto is offering to buy the company with a view to develop its operations and hence generate future cash flows. In particular use of **free cash flows,** which take into account plans for **asset replacement** and **future investment**, focus on the strategic aspects of acquisition.

	20X2 $m	20X3 $m	20X4 $m	20X5 $m
Net sales	230	261	281	298
Cost of goods sold	(115)	(131)	(141)	(149)
Selling/admin expenses	(32)	(34)	(36)	(38)
Capital allowances	(40)	(42)	(42)	(42)
Taxable profits	43	54	62	69
Taxation	(13)	(16)	(19)	(21)
Profits after tax	30	38	43	48
Add: Capital allowances	40	42	42	42
Less: Cash flow needed for asset replacement/growth	(50)	(52)	(55)	(58)
Net cash flow	20	28	30	32
Discount factors 14% (W)	0.877	0.769	0.675	0.592
Present values	18	22	20	19

Working

Cost of equity

Having Omnigen's predicted equity beta and assuming that any variation in gearing between 18% and 23% will not change equity beta,

$$K_e = r_f + [E(r_m) - r_f]\beta_j$$
$$= 6 + 1.3(14 - 6)$$
$$= 16.4\%$$

Cost of debt

Assume Laceto's cost of debt will remain unchanged on acquisition of Omnigen, as Omnigen currently has a lower gearing than Laceto.

Year		Cash flow	Disc factor	Present value	Disc factor	Present value
		$	5%	$	6%	
0	MV	(108.80)	1.000	(108.80)	1.000	(108.80)
1–3	Interest (1 – 0.3)	8.4	2.723	22.87	2.673	22.45
3	Redemption	100	0.864	86.40	0.840	84.00
				0.47		(2.35)

$$\text{Cost of debt} = 5 + \frac{(0.47)}{(0.47 + 2.35)}$$

$$= 5.2\%$$

Weighted average cost of capital

At 18% gearing

WACC $= (16.4 \times 0.82) + (5.2 \times 0.18) = 14.4\%$

At 23% gearing

WACC $= (16.4 \times 0.77) + (5.2 \times 0.23) = 13.8\%$

14% is near midway point, therefore use 14%.

Present values if growth is 3% after 20X5

$$\text{Present values} = \text{Present values (20X2-5)} + \frac{\text{20X5 earnings }(1+g)}{(r-g)} \times 0.592$$

$$= (18 + 22 + 20 + 19) + \frac{19(1 + 0.03)}{(0.14 - 0.03)} \times 0.592 = \$186 \text{ million}$$

Present values if growth is 5% after 20X5

$$\text{Present values} = (18 + 22 + 20 + 19) + \frac{19(1 + 0.05)}{(0.14 - 0.05)} \times 0.592 = \$212 \text{ million}$$

Value of shares

Present values are total values of equity. Assuming 3% growth, the value of shares will be between 77% and 82% of $186 million, between $143 million and $153 million. Assuming 5% growth, value will be between 77% and 82% of $212 million, between $163 million and $174 million.

Problems with value calculation

(i) **Predictions of operating cash flows** may not be accurate.

(ii) **Capital allowances** would not be less than **asset replacement flows indefinitely**.

(iii) Cash flow calculations have been based on an assumed investor time horizon of **infinity**, but in practice the time horizon may not exceed ten years.

Conclusion

Laceto must offer a premium, but must keep this premium as low as possible to **maximise the value to its own shareholders**. An initial offer of $160 million would be halfway between current market value and value of equity under the free cash flows assuming lower (3%) growth and maximum gearing. This would be a premium of about 30% on the current price, but does give Laceto reasonable scope to increase the offer should it initially be refused by shareholders.

(ii)   The choice between cash and paper offers depends on how the different methods are viewed by the company and its existing shareholders, and on the attitudes of the shareholders of the target company. Generally speaking, a company which believes that its stock is under-valued will not use

BPP
LEARNING MEDIA

equity for an acquisition. (Conversely, a company which believes that its stock is over- or correctly valued will use equity for an acquisition.) It should be noted that the premium paid is often larger when an acquisition is financed with stock rather than cash.

The following points should also be noted by Laceto when deciding on a method of financing:

A **fall in earnings per share** attributable to existing shareholders may occur if purchase consideration is in equity shares.

Use of **debt finance** to back a cash offer will attract tax relief on interest and therefore have a lower cost than equity.

A company with a **high level of financial gearing** may not be able to issue further loan stock to obtain cash for cash offer.

Control of Laceto could change considerably if a large number of new shares was issued in a paper bid.

The **authorised share capital** of Laceto may need to be **increased** if consideration is in the form of shares. This will involve calling a general meeting to pass the necessary resolution.

A general meeting resolution will be required if Laceto's **borrowing limits** have to change in order to fund the cash offer.

The following considerations about the shareholders in Omnigen are also important:

If the consideration is in the form of cash, many of Omnigen's shareholders may suffer **immediate liability to tax** on the capital gain.

If the consideration is equity, then the arrangement must mean existing **shareholder income is maintained**, or at least compensated by suitable capital gain or reasonable growth expectations.

Omnigen's shareholders who want to **retain a stake in the business** may prefer shares in the combined entity.

If consideration is in the form of shares, Omnigen's shareholders will want to be sure that the Laceto shares are **likely to retain their value.**

(iii)   Laceto could use any of the following methods to finance a cash offer

Cash retained from earnings

This is a common way when the company to be acquired is small, compared to the acquiring firm; but not very common if the target firm is large, relative to the acquiring firm. Currently it does not appear that Laceto has enough cash to finance the offer (it only has $122 million in current assets), but Laceto may be able to divest some of its own assets to accumulate cash in order to make the offer for Omnigen.

The proceeds of a debt issue

Laceto could raise money by issuing bonds. This is not an approach that is normally taken, because the act of issuing bonds will alert the markets to the intentions of Laceto to bid for another company and it may lead investors to buy the shares of potential targets, which would raise their prices and make the ultimate acquisition more expensive.

A loan facility from a bank

This can be done as a short-term funding strategy, until the bid is accepted; then Laceto is free to make a bond issue, which can then be used to pay off the bank loan.

Mezzanine finance

This may be the only route to raise cash for Laceto if it does not have access to the bond markets in order to issue bonds.

If you have any questions about the contents of this report, please do not hesitate to contact me.

(b) **Methods of defence**

Pre-acquisition

Improve asset utilisation

This may be achieved by **taking cash off low-interest deposit accounts**; by **selling redundant non-current assets** such as under-utilised property; **by rationalising operations** to make full use of business assets; or by **improving efficiency of working capital management** (eg reducing inventories and speeding up receivables' collections). In each case the cash released can be returned to shareholders. The effect may be to **boost share price** and persuade shareholders to vote against the bid.

Communicate information about Laceto

Release of information concerning **improved future cash flows** may persuade shareholders that the offer price is too low, and that they should not sell but retain their shares to benefit from future profits. Laceto should concentrate particularly on communicating with key shareholders such as institutional shareholders. A P/E ratio of 10.5:1, lower than other companies in its sector, suggests that Laceto may have scope to do this.

Poison pills

Laceto can grant **rights** to shareholders, to purchase shares at a discount or to exchange shares for **cash or debt securities** at a price in excess of what is likely to be offered by Agressa. It can also provide **golden parachutes,** expensive severance contracts, for directors and senior staff that Agressa would have to honour if they took Laceto over and made the directors or staff redundant.

Articles

The directors of Laceto can attempt to have the company's **articles altered** to require a large yes vote from shareholders to approve an acquisition.

Repurchase

Laceto could use any surplus cash to **re-purchase its own shares** and hence push the price up to a level that Agressa could not afford.

Strategic shareholdings

The directors of Laceto might arrange for a **friendly party to take a significant share** in the company.

Post-acquisition

Present a rational argument against plans

Documents justifying the **company's existing management and strategy** and criticising the bidding company's strategic plans are an important part of the defence procedures when a hostile bid is received. This could include a general analysis of Agressa's future prospects. Laceto's defence could **highlight the volatility of earnings** in the dot-com sector.

Counter-bid

Laceto could make a **counter-bid** for Agressa's shares; Agressa is a much smaller company than Laceto and is smaller than Omnigen. However its P/E ratio is a lot higher, and its activities may not fit well with Laceto's.

Acquisition of Omnigen

Successful acquisition of Omnigen by Laceto may make a successful takeover bid by Agressa less likely as the **combined market capitalisation** may be in excess of what Agressa can afford.

75 Anchorage Retail Co

Text references. Acquisitions and mergers are covered in Chapters 9 – 12. Risks associated with mergers are covered in Chapter 9, valuation of acquisitions is in Chapter 10 and impact of acquisitions on performance is covered in Chapter 12.

Top tips. Make sure you relate your answer to part (a) to the scenario in the question rather than making it generic. This will demonstrate that you can apply knowledge to particular situations.

Part (b) should not pose many problems but make sure you specify clearly which additional ratios you are using and the formulae used to calculate them. Remember to comment on the ratios and show all workings.

Part (c) requires a number of calculations in order to arrive at the answer. It might be useful to 'think backwards' – that is, determine what you are ultimately trying to do (calculate the required returns on equity pre- and post-acquisition) and the formulae you need to use. You can then determine what information you already have and thus the figures you have to find. Remember that Polar Finance does not pay tax on income therefore there will be no tax shield benefits from debt.

Part (d) suggests that you should be commenting on the efficiency of the market regarding pricing and also on whether the bid price is likely to be acceptable to Anchorage's shareholders.

Don't forget that there are 4 professional marks available so maximise your chances of gaining these marks by using a report format and making all your workings and explanations as clear as possible.

Easy marks. Part (b) offers some straightforward marks.

REPORT

To: Polar Finance management
From: Accountant
Subject: Anchorage Retail Company

This report covers various issues relating to the Anchorage Retail Company (Anchorage) in the light of your interest in this company as a potential acquisition target.

(a) **Principal general risks associated with a large acquisition**

Regulatory risk

This is a large acquisition and may therefore be subject to scrutiny from the government or other regulatory agencies if there is a threat to public interest. However, Polar Finance is not in the retail trade therefore is unlikely to attract attention from agencies regulating competition or restrictions to it. One potential issue is the lack of accountability of private equity funds and the background to Anchorage may result in scrutiny from regulatory authorities.

Disclosure risk

An acquisition of this size must be supported by reliable information that reflects the potential earning power and financial business of the company. It is essential to ensure that all supporting information, such as the financial statements, have not been manipulated to give a more favourable picture. The income statement must be supported by the relevant cash flow for example and all other supporting documents should be subject to scrutiny to verify their authenticity.

Valuation risk

This size of acquisition may change the risk of Polar Finance due to changes in exposure to financial risk or market risk. As a result, investors' or potential investors' perceived risk of Polar Finance may also be altered. Such changes to risk mean that the post-acquisition value of Polar Finance is unlikely to be a simple sum of its pre-acquisition value and the value of Anchorage.

(b)   **Performance of Anchorage in 20X8 and 20X9**

This section of the report compares Anchorage's performance in 20X8 with that in 20X9. Three measures have been used:

(i)   Return on capital employed (ROCE)
(ii)   Return on equity
(iii)   Economic Value Added (EVA®)

(i)   **Return on capital employed (ROCE)**

ROCE is a measure of the return that is being earned on shareholders' funds. Any reduction in the ratio indicates that funds are being used less efficiently than in previous years. There are numerous ways in which ROCE can be calculated but the following formula has been used for the purpose of this report:

$$ROCE = \frac{PBIT}{Capital\ employed}$$

Where capital employed = total equity + non-current liabilities

	20X9	20X8
	$m	$m
PBIT (operating profit)	1,250	1,030
Capital employed		
Total equity	2,030	1,555
Non-current liabilities	1,900	1,865
Capital employed	3,930	3,420
ROCE	31.8%	30.1%

ROCE has improved slightly, indicating that shareholders' funds are being used more efficiently than in 20X8. However, before this is taken as an indication of improved performance, further investigation should be undertaken of the information used in the ratio's calculation.

(ii)   **Return on equity**

This ratio measures the return on equity funds only – that is, the funds provided by the shareholders – and is calculated by dividing total equity funds by profit after interest and tax.

	20X9	20X8
	$m	$m
Profit after interest and tax	860	650
Total equity funds	2,030	1,555
Return on equity	42.4%	41.8%

Similar to ROCE, return on equity has shown a slight improvement in 20X9. Again further investigation of the accounting information behind this ratio should be carried out before assuming that Anchorage has improved the return it provides to its equity holders.

(iii)   **EVA®**

EVA is used to calculate the economic value or profit added each year and can be calculated as follows:

EVA = Net operating profit after tax (NOPAT) – (WACC x capital employed)

NOPAT	20X9	20X8
	$m	$m
Operating profit before interest	1,250	1,030
Less: Tax at 30%	(375)	(309)
Net operating profit after tax	875	721

BPP
LEARNING MEDIA

[Note NOPAT could also be calculated as PAT plus net interest, which would give different answers to those calculated above]

EVA	20X9	20X8
	$m	$m
NOPAT	875	721
Less: (WACC (6.12%) x capital employed)*	(241)	(209)
EVA	634	512

* Calculation of WACC is shown in Appendix 1.

There appears to have been a 24% increase in EVA in 20X9. However without further investigation of the accounting information, it is not possible to determine how accurately this depicts the true performance of Anchorage.

(c) **Impact of acquisition on the required rate of return of equity investors in Polar Finance**

One of the differences between Anchorage and Polar Finance is the fact that Polar Finance does not pay tax on its income. This means that there is no benefit to be gained from the tax shield on debt. In order to calculate the asset beta of Polar Finance we would use the following formula:

$$\beta_a = \beta_e \times \frac{V_e}{V_e + V_d}$$

The asset beta of Polar Finance is given as 0.285.

However as Anchorage gains benefit from the tax shield on debt, its asset beta should be calculated using the following formula:

$$\beta_a = \beta_e \times \frac{V_e}{V_e + V_d(1-T)}$$

$\beta_a = 0.75 \times [0.76/(0.76 + 0.24 \times 0.7)] = 0.614$

Anchorage's proportion of post-acquisition cash flows is expected to be 20%, meaning that Polar Finance will have 80%. The **combined asset beta** post-acquisition is therefore estimated as:

$(0.8 \times 0.285) + (0.2 \times 0.614) = 0.351$

Before we can determine the required return from investors in the combined company and compare it with that of investors in Polar Finance only, we need to calculate the **equity betas** of Polar Finance and the combined entity.

Polar Finance's debt is given as 85% of the total company, meaning that equity of $1,125 million makes up 15%. Debt can be calculated as:

($1,125 million/0.15) x 0.85 = $6,375 million

Post-acquisition level of debt = $6,375 million (Polar) + $2,500 million (additional borrowing)

= $8,875 million

Equity beta post-acquisition can be calculated using the following formula:

$$\beta_e = \beta_a \left(\frac{V_e + V_d(1-T)}{V_e} \right)$$

There is no benefit from the tax shield therefore $(1 - T)$ can be ignored.

$\beta_e = 0.351 \times [(1,125 + 8,875)/1,125] = 3.12$

Equity beta of Polar Finance is:

$\beta_e = 0.285 \times [(1,125 + 6,375)/1,125] = 1.9$

The CAPM can now be used to calculate the required return on equity pre- and post-acquisition.

Pre-acquisition:

$r_e = R_f + \beta_i(E(r_m) - R_f)$

$r_e = 5\% + 1.9 \times 2.224\%$ (calculated in Appendix 1)

$r_e = 9.23\%$

Post-acquisition:

$r_e = 5\% + 3.12 \times 2.224\%$

$r_e = 11.94\%$

As a result of the acquisition, shareholders in Polar will require an increase in return of 2.71%.

(d)   **Evaluation of argument that Anchorage may have been undervalued by the market**

The argument that the market may have undervalued Anchorage suggests **market inefficiency**. The **efficient market hypothesis** (EMH) suggests that this argument is unlikely. Further support for the EMH is given by the number of investors that operate in the market for a business such as Anchorage – it is unlikely that this number of investors would misprice the company. Although there is evidence of investors being deterred by Anchorage's reputation in the past, which may affect current investors' rational expectations about the company, the effect of such expectations is likely to be diversified away during the pricing process.

The current share price of Anchorage is $2.60. With 1,600 million shares in issue, this represents a market capitalisation of $4,160 million. Return on equity is 6.668% (see Appendix 1). If dividend payments were capitalised at this return on equity, this would suggest a market capitalisation of $4,049 million. The market appears to expect very little growth in Anchorage in the future, perhaps partly due to its reputation. As a result, a bid price of $3.20 should be attractive to Anchorage's shareholders.

I would be happy to discuss any aspect of this report with you so please do not hesitate to contact me.

Appendix 1

Anchorage – estimation of WACC

(a)   **Calculate the cost of equity**

    (i)   Calculate expected market return using dividend growth model:

$$P_0 = \frac{D_0(1+g)}{(r_e - g)}$$

Rearranging the formula to express in terms of r_e:

$$r_e = \frac{D_0(1+g)}{P_0} + g$$

$$r_e = \frac{0.031(1+0.04)}{1} + 0.04$$

$r_e = 7.224\%$

This result suggests that the market will have an expected return of 7.224%. The risk-free rate is given as 5% therefore the market risk premium is 2.224%.

    (ii)   Use the CAPM to calculate return on equity:

$r_e = R_f + \beta_i(E(r_m) - R_f)$

$r_e = 5\% + (0.75 \times 2.224\%)$

$r_e = 6.668\%$

(b)   **Calculate WACC** using $r_e = 6.668\%$ and $k_d = 6.2\%$

WACC $= 0.76 \times 6.668\% + 0.24 \times [6.2\% \times (1 - 0.3)] = 6.12\%$

BPP
LEARNING MEDIA

(e) (i) **Annual interest cost**

The **annual interest cost** to Anchorage of issuing a five-year sterling fixed rate bond is not known but we can use the cost of the existing bond as an approximation. This has been calculated above as approximately 9%.

Summary of swap transactions

	Anchorage	Swiss co
Borrowing (actual)	(9.0%)	(SFr LIBOR + 1.5%)
Payments		
Anchorage to Swiss co.	(SFr LIBOR + 1.0%)	SFr LIBOR + 1.0%
Swiss co. to Anchorage	9.5%	(9.5%)
Net payment after swap	(SFr LIBOR + 0.5%)	(10%)

Anchorage's viewpoint

If Anchorage were to enter into the swap, it would receive a fixed rate of interest from the Swiss company of 9.5% per year, which represents a net benefit of 0.5% (9.5% − 9%). At the same time it would pay the Swiss company at SFr LIBOR + 1.0% per year, making a net cost of SFr LIBOR + 0.5% per year. The alternative would be to borrow directly at SFr LIBOR + 0.75% per year (5.75% − 5.0%). Thus the swap offers Anchorage a gain over direct borrowing of 0.25% per year. Against this must be offset the annual fee to the bank of 0.20%, giving Anchorage a net gain of 0.05% per year.

Swiss company's viewpoint

From the point of view of the Swiss company, it can borrow directly at SFr LIBOR + 1.5%. Against this can be offset the annual interest payments from Anchorage of SFr LIBOR + 1.0%, making a net cost of 0.5% per year in addition to the 9.5% interest payment to Anchorage. This equates to an annual cost of 10%, to which must be added the bank fee of 0.2% giving a total cost of 10.2%. This compares with the cost to the Swiss company of borrowing fixed rate sterling at 10.5% per annum – a net annual benefit of 0.30%.

Thus both parties will benefit from the swap, although the Swiss company stands to gain more than Anchorage. However, if the SFr strengthens against the pound, then the benefits to Anchorage could be further reduced since the value of the sterling interest payments will fall relative to those denominated in SFr.

(ii) **Benefits of swaps**

(1) **Timing**

The companies may be able to **structure** the **timing of payments** so as to improve the matching of cash outflows with revenues.

(2) **Increased access to debt finance**

Each company gains **access to debt finance** in another country and currency where it is little known, and consequently has a poorer credit rating, than in its own country.

(3) **Hedging**

The swap provides a **hedge against currency risk** for the full five-year period.

(4) **Restructuring interest rate liabilities**

Swaps give the companies the opportunity to **restructure their interest rate liabilities** in terms of the relative proportions of fixed rate and floating rate debt, without the need to restructure the debt base itself.

(5) **Bank benefits**

The bank **benefits from the fees** from the swap; it may also gain the opportunity to undertake further business with the two parties if it is not already their first-line bank.

Risks of swaps

(1) **Default**

There is the **risk** of one of the parties **defaulting**.

(2) **Adverse movements**

There is the **risk** that **interest rates** and **exchange rates** could **move** in such a way that the net payments arising as a result of the swap are higher than they would have been had the swap not been undertaken.

(3) **Bank risks**

If the bank takes on a temporary role in the financing during the arrangement of the swap, it runs the risk that rates could **move during the delay** involved in completing the transactions.

76 Romage

Text references. Chapter 14 on sell-offs and demergers, Chapters 6 and 7a cover the more complicated calculations. Ethics are covered in Chapter 3b.

Top tips. It is easy to confuse sell-offs and demergers in (a). (b) is quite a thorough test of your financial appraisal skills, involving relevant cash flows, the correct risk, discounting over nominal cash flows and how real and nominal cash flows are used in investment appraisal.

In the workings, before going into the ungearing and regearing betas stage, you first have to confirm whether it is necessary by checking whether the capital structure of the divisions differs from the industry structure. Remember that you have to carry out IRR analysis to determine the cost of debt if it is redeemable.

Part (c) involves some thinking about the ethical aspects of the sale of a division.

Easy marks. The key to success in tackling this question is to make sure you score well on part (a). You can get a few easy marks on the calculations in (b) (central costs, correct treatment of depreciation, taxation) but the marking on the calculations is weighted towards getting the costs of capital right. However if you make a reasonable attempt at these you should be able to gain 3 or 4 marks for using the right techniques and getting the easier numbers even if your final answers are incorrect.

(a) Demergers, sell-offs and divestments are all means of **restructuring businesses**.

(i) **Sell-offs**

A **sell-off** involves the sale of part of a company to another company. A sell-off can act to **protect the rest of a business from a take-over,** by selling off a part that is particularly attractive to a buyer. It can also **provide cash**, enabling the remaining business to invest further without the need for worsening its gearing by obtaining more debt finance. It would also enable Romage to **concentrate** on what it perceives to be its core business, and **dispose of the more peripheral areas**.

(ii) **Demergers**

A **demerger** is the splitting up of a corporate body into two or more separate and independent bodies. It is **not** a **sale** of the separate bodies themselves, as the original shareholders have shares in both companies. The split does **enable analysts** to **understand** the two businesses fully, particularly when, as here, the two main divisions are in different fields. The two divisions are likely to have different risk profiles, and splitting them up enables **shareholders** to **adjust** the **proportion of their holdings** between the two different companies.

(iii) **Divestment**

A divestment involves selling off assets rather than a part of a company. It can be completed more quickly than either a sell-off or a demerger. It can be used to raise cash relatively quickly and can be used to ensure that Romage can focus on what it considers to be its **core business**.

Improvements in management

Both **sell-offs and demergers** can lead to improved **management and control**, and can enable management to **focus** on the **competencies** of the individual divisions rather than the varying considerations of both. These improvements may result in **reverse synergy**, where the combined value of the split-off divisions is more than the company would be worth if the divisions were still together.

Romage's position

The choice for Romage's management is therefore whether they wish to **retain control** of both divisions, or to relinquish control of one and just concentrate on the other division.

(b)   Report

To:	**The board of directors Romage Inc**
From:	**Financial Adviser**
Subject:	**Proposed floating of manufacturing and property sale divisions**

This report evaluates whether Romage Inc should pursue the option of floating the manufacturing and property sale divisions separately using both a 15-year and an infinite time horizon.

Summary of calculations

The results of the evaluation are summarised here, the full workings can be found in the Appendices to this report.

Total of two divisions to infinity   = \$364.4 + \$365.6 − \$125.5 (value of debt) = \$604.5 million

Total of two divisions to year 15   = \$269.1 + \$239.5 − \$125.5 = \$383.1 million

Current market value of equity is \$592 million.

Limitations of evaluation

The problems with using the geared and ungeared beta formula for calculating an equity beta from data about other companies are as follows.

It is **difficult to identify other firms with identical operating characteristics**.

Estimates of beta values from **share price information are not wholly accurate**. They are based on statistical analysis of historical data, and estimates using one company's data will differ from estimates using another company's data.

There may be **differences in beta values** between the industry average companies and the divisions of Romage caused by:

(i)   Different cost structures (eg, the ratio of fixed costs to variable costs)
(ii)   Size differences
(iii)   Debt capital not being risk-free

Perhaps the most significant simplifying assumption is that it must be assumed that the **cost of debt** is a **risk-free rate of return**. This could obviously be unrealistic. Companies may default on interest payments or capital repayments on their loans. It has been estimated that corporate debt has a beta value of 0.2 or 0.3.

The consequence of making the assumption that debt is risk-free is that the formulae tend to **overstate** the financial risk in a geared company and to **understate** the business risk in geared and ungeared companies by a compensating amount.

The decision to value the divisions using a 15-year time horizon and an infinite time horizon seems arbitrary. It may well be the case that a 10-year or 20-year time horizon may be more appropriate. It is suggested that further analysis using well thought out time horizons is performed.

Conclusion

The total of the two separate divisions to infinity is just higher than the current market value, but using a 15-year time horizon the total of the two separate divisions is lower.

As no replacement capital investment has been included in the calculation, it does not appear that Romage should float the two divisions separately.

If you have any questions about the content of this report, please do not hesitate to ask me.

Appendix 1 – Value of Manufacturing division

	1	2	3	4	5	6
	$m	$m	$m	$m	$m	$m
Net operating cash flow	45.0	48.0	50.0	52.0	57.0	60.0
Central costs	(6.0)	(6.0)	(6.0)	(6.0)	(6.0)	(6.0)
Taxable cash flows	39.0	42.0	44.0	46.0	51.0	54.0
Tax at 31%	(12.1)	(13.0)	(13.6)	(14.3)	(15.8)	(16.7)
Post tax cash flows	26.9	29.0	30.4	31.7	35.2	37.3
Tax credit on depreciation (depreciation charge × 31%)	3.1	2.5	2.2	2.5	2.5	2.5
One-off cost	(8.0)					
Net cash flow	22.0	31.5	32.6	34.2	37.7	39.8
Discount factors (10%) (W1)	0.909	0.826	0.751	0.683	0.621	
PV cash flow	20.0	26.0	24.5	23.4	23.4	

$$\text{PV to infinity} = \text{PV years 1–5} + \text{PV years 6–infinity}$$

$$= 117.3 + \left(\frac{39.8}{0.1} - (39.8 \times 3.791) \right)$$

$$= \$364.4 \text{ million}$$

$$\text{PV years 1 to 15} = 117.3 + (39.8 \times (7.606 - 3.791))$$

$$= \$269.1 \text{ million}$$

Working 1

Discount rate for manufacturing:

Gearing

MV debt = $60 million

$$\text{MV equity} = \frac{50}{0.25} \times 0.55 \times 2.96 = \$325.6 \text{ million}$$

Gearing level = (325.6/(325 + 60)) equity, (60/(325 + 60)) debt
= 84.4% equity, 15.6% debt

This differs from the industry gearing levels, and so we must ungear the industry beta and must regear the asset beta to take into account the differing capital structure.

$$\beta_a = \beta_e \left(\frac{V_e}{V_e + V_d(1 - T)} \right) \text{ (assuming debt is risk-free)}$$

$$= 1.3 \times \left(\frac{70}{70 + 30(1 - 0.31)} \right) = 1.00$$

Regearing

$$\beta_e = \beta_a \left(\frac{V_e + V_d(1 - T)}{V_e} \right)$$

$$P = 1.00 \times \left(\frac{84.4 + 15.6(1 - 0.31)}{84.4} \right) = 1.128$$

$$K_e = r_f + [E(r_m) - r_f]\beta = 5.5 + [14 - 5.5]1.128 = 15.09\%$$

For Kd, calculate redemption yield on loan stock as we are told that the cost of the term loan is virtually the same.

$$131 = \frac{13(1 - 0.31)}{(1 + k_d(1 - T))} + \frac{13(1 - 0.31)}{(1 + k_d(1 - T))^2} + \dots + \frac{13(1 - 0.31)}{(1 + k_d(1 - T))^{15}} + \frac{100}{(1 + k_d(1 - T))^{15}}$$

BPP
LEARNING MEDIA

Year		Cash flow $	Discount Factor 5%	PV $	Discount factor 6%	PV $
0	Market value	(131.00)	1.000	(131.00)	1.000	(131.00)
1–15	Interest	8.97	10.38	93.11	9.712	87.12
15	Capital repayment	100.00	0.481	48.10	0.417	41.70
				10.21		(2.18)

$$K_d\,(1-T) = 5\% + \left(\frac{10.21}{10.21+2.18} \times (6-5)\right) = 5.82\%$$

WACC for manufacturing division $= k_{eg}\left(\dfrac{V_e}{V_e + V_d}\right) + k_d\,(1-T)\left(\dfrac{V_d}{V_e + V_d}\right)$

$$= 15.09\left(\frac{325.6}{60 + 325.6}\right) + 5.82\left(\frac{60}{60 + 325.6}\right)$$

$$= 12.74 + 0.91$$

$$= 13.65\%$$

Real rate $= \dfrac{(1+\text{moneyrate})}{(1+\text{inflationrate})} - 1 = \dfrac{1.1365}{1.03} - 1 = 10.34\%$, say 10%

Appendix 2 – Value of Property Sale division

	1 $m	2 $m	3 $m	4 $m	5 $m	6 $m
Net operating cash flow	32.0	40.0	42.0	44.0	46.0	50.0
Central costs	(6.0)	(6.0)	(6.0)	(6.0)	(6.0)	(6.0)
Taxable cash flows	26.0	34.0	36.0	38.0	40.0	44.0
Tax at 31%	(8.1)	(10.5)	(11.2)	(11.8)	(12.4)	(13.6)
Post tax cash flows	17.9	23.5	24.8	26.2	27.6	30.4
Tax credit on depreciation	1.6	1.6	1.6	1.6	1.6	1.6
One-off cost	(8.0)					
Net cash flow	11.5	25.1	26.4	27.8	29.2	32.0
Discount factors (8%) (W2)	0.926	0.857	0.794	0.735	0.681	
PV cash flow	10.6	21.5	21.0	20.4	19.9	

PV to infinity $\quad= $ PV years 1–5 + PV years 6–infinity

$$= 93.4 + \left(\frac{32.0}{0.08} - (32.0 \times 3.993)\right)$$

$$= \$365.6 \text{ million}$$

PV years 1 to 15 $\quad= 93.4 + (32.0 \times (8.559 - 3.993)$

$$= \$239.5 \text{ million}$$

Working 2

Discount rate for property

MV equity $= \dfrac{50}{0.25} \times 0.45 \times 2.96 = \$266.4$ million

MV debt $= 50 \times 1.31 = \$65.5$ million

Gearing level $= \dfrac{266.4}{266.4 + 65.5}$ equity $+ \dfrac{65.5}{266.4 + 65.5}$ debt

$$= 80.3\% \text{ equity} + 19.7\% \text{ debt}$$

These are near enough industry averages (80 + 20) and thus there is no need to ungear and regear.

$k_e = r_f + [E(r_m) - r_f] \beta = 5.5 + [14 - 5.5]0.9 = 13.15\%$

$k_d (1 - T) =$ same as above, 5.82%

WACC for property division $= k_{eg}\left(\dfrac{V_e}{V_e + V_d}\right) + k_d (1 - T)\left(\dfrac{V_d}{V_e + V_d}\right)$

$$= 13.15\left(\frac{266.4}{266.4 + 65.5}\right) + 5.82\left(\frac{65.5}{266.4 + 65.5}\right)$$

$$= 10.55 + 1.15$$

$$= 11.70\%$$

Real rate $= \dfrac{(1 + \text{money rate})}{(1 + \text{inflation rate})} - 1$

$= \dfrac{1.1170}{1.03} - 1$

$= 8.44\%$, say 8%

(c) The issues that should be considered by Romage Inc will depend on its attitude to its **ethical** and **philanthropic** responsibility. Typically a company places its economic responsibility to its **shareholders** as its **main priority.** The ethical and philanthropic responsibilities may conflict with this, as they may be reducing the potential return to shareholders.

Romage's ethical responsibility will depend on whether the board feels there is a moral imperative for the company to be seen to operate in a fair and ethical manner. If there is, it will want to be seen to treat all parties involved in the sale fairly and won't want to attract adverse publicity.

There is a link between the ethical responsibility and the philanthropic responsibility where a company will try to improve the life of its **employees** and improve the **local community** as well. If Romage feels a sense of philanthropic responsibility then it will want to make sure that its employees are **protected** by the sale. Therefore it will need to assess the likely plans of the purchasing company.

For example, the purchaser may want to purchase the **networks and information** within the property sales division rather than looking to take over the division as a going concern. Therefore they may not want to keep the existing employees which could, in turn, have a significant effect on the local community. Romage Inc may wish to avoid the adverse publicity that may accompany the sale if it is seen to be favouring the shareholders at the expense of the employees.

77 Galeplus

Text references. Mainly Chapter 16. Chapter 15 for treasury department and money markets.

Top tips. As well as reducing borrowing costs, your answer to (a) needs to bring out other uses, effectively changing finance structure and hedging. (b) (i) is a starting point for all swap calculations. Note in (b) (ii) that the examiner regards purchasing power parity as a core technique and is pained by the number of students who don't use it.

The other key point was making sure to use different rates for the payment on which the swap was based and the rest of the monies. The key in (b)(iii) is expectations; do current economic indicators suggest that there will be a good enough chance that the option will be exercised for it to be worth paying the premium.

Easy marks. (a) should have been the easiest part and the answer is worth learning if you couldn't come up with many suggestions.

BPP LEARNING MEDIA

(a) Currency swaps

Currency swaps are agreements between two parties to **swap payments on each other's loans**, those loans being in different currencies. For example, a company may arrange to make the payments on a counterparty's US dollar loan, while the counterparty makes payments on the company's euro loan. The effect is to enable the company to **switch its effective interest payments from euros to dollars**. An equivalent effect could be achieved by terminating the company's euro loan and taking out a new loan in US dollars.

Advantages of swaps

(i) Companies may have a **comparative advantage borrowing in their own currency**. Doing this and agreeing a currency swap may produce a cheaper interest rate than trying to borrow directly in a foreign currency.

(ii) **Termination costs** for an existing loan may make it **prohibitively expensive** to change finance. A bank's service fee to arrange a swap may be lower than the termination charge. Also, if a company has long term borrowings in one currency but needs to switch to paying interest in another currency for a shorter period, a swap can enable this without having to terminate the original loan.

(iii) In some countries it is difficult or impossible for foreign registered companies to **borrow in the local currency**. A currency swap gets round these restrictions.

(iv) Borrowing in a foreign currency is an **effective method of hedging income** in that currency, and currency swaps are one way of achieving this. The **cost is often cheaper** than using the market for long term forward contracts. Currency swaps have also been used as a method of avoiding **exchange control restrictions**.

Problems of swaps

(i) The **counterparty** to the swap arrangement may **default** if it gets into financial difficulties. In this case the company is still liable to pay the interest on the original loan. In general, banks make less risky counterparties than many corporates.

(ii) If the swap is into a developing country's currency, there may be **significant risk of adverse government restrictions** being introduced.

(iii) If the swap has been entered into to **reduce currency risk** as with any hedging instrument, the exchange rate may move in a direction that means it would have been better **not to have undertaken the hedge**.

(iv) A swap between two floating rate loans may introduce **basis risk** if the interest rates are not referenced to the same base rate.

(b) (i) Report

To:	The board of directors Galeplus
From:	AN Adviser
Subject:	Currency hedging

This report looks at the potential interest saving that can make from the proposed currency swap and whether the communications centre should be purchased, assuming that the currency swap takes place.

The borrowing rates for Galeplus and its counterparty can be summarised as follows:

	Galeplus	Counterparty	
Wants	Floating	Fixed	
Pays with Swap	6.25%	PIBOR + 1.5%	PIBOR + 7.75%
Pays without Swap	PIBOR + 2%	8.3%	PIBOR + 10.3%
Potential gain			2.55%
Bank fee			– 0.75%
Potential gain			1.8%
Split 75:25	1.35%	0.45%	

BPP LEARNING MEDIA

(ii) Future currency exchange rates may be estimated using **purchasing power parity theory.**

Assuming the inflation rate in UK is zero the formula $(i_f - i_{uk})/(1+i_{uk})$ reduces to i_f. In other words the percentage increase in the exchange rate each year is the Perdian inflation rate, at best 15% and at worst 50%, as follows:

Estimated exchange rates, rubbits/£

	Inflation	Spot	Year 1	Year 2	Year 3
Best case	15%	85.40	98.21	112.94	129.88
Worst case	50%	85.40	128.10	192.15	288.23

The cash flows of the telecommunications centre are:

Million rubbits

Year	0	1	2	3
Purchase cost	(2,000)			
Fees		40	40	40
Sale price				4,000
	(2,000)	40	40	4,040

If the currency swap is used, 2,000 million of the year 3 cash flows will be translated at the current spot rate of 85·40 rubbits/£, giving £23.42 million and the remainder (2,040 million) will be translated at the year 3 rate. The net present values of the best and worst cases can be calculated using the 15% risk adjusted discount rate.

Cash flows

Year	0	1	2	3
	£m	£m	£m	£m
Purchase cost	(2,000)	40.00	40.00	4,040
Best case rate	85.40	98.21	112.94	
Best case £m	(23.42)	0.41	0.35	39.13
15% factors	1.000	0.870	0.756	0.658
DCF	(23.42)	0.36	0.25	25.75
NPV	2.95			
Worst case rate	85.40	128.10	192.15	
Worst case £m	(23.42)	0.31	0.21	30.50
15% factors	1.000	0.870	0.756	0.658
DCF	(23.42)	0.27	0.16	20.07
NPV	(2.92)			

$$\text{Year 3 cash flows} = 23.42 + \frac{2,040}{\text{Best/worst rate}}$$

$$\text{Best} = 23.42 + \frac{2,040}{129.88} = 39.13$$

$$\text{Worst} = 23.42 + \frac{2,040}{288.23} = 30.50$$

Results

Because the project receipts are fixed in Perdian rubbits, the net present value of the project depends entirely on the **rubbit exchange rate against the pound becoming worse** the **more the rubbit depreciates**. The currency swap provides some hedging, but this is for less than half the sum at risk in year 3. Galeplus should consider the availability of other hedging techniques to cover a greater proportion of the cash flows.

BPP
LEARNING MEDIA

On the basis of the figures used the expected value is approximately **break even**, but the **risk** of a **negative result** is high and on balance the investment does not appear to be worthwhile Other factors that also need to be considered include **default risk** of the Perdian government and liability of the project receipts to **taxation** in the UK.

(iii) **Swaptions**

A swaption is an **option to enter into a swap**. In this case Galeplus would exchange 2,000 million rubbits for pounds at today's spot rate and, on payment of a premium of £300,000, would have the option of swapping the money back at the same exchange rate. This option would be exercised if the rubbit depreciated against the pound over the next three years, but if it strengthened, the swaption would be abandoned and the pounds purchased on the prevailing spot rate.

Recommended course of action

The inflation rate in Perdia is so high compared with the UK's that it is highly unlikely that the rubbit would strengthen against the pound. The payment of £300,000 for the swaption's protection would therefore be unwise.

The European put option enables Galeplus to **sell the whole cash flow** at (and not before) the end of year 3 (4,040 rubbits) at 160 rubbits/£. On the basis of the forecasts provided, the option would be exercised under the worst case scenario (spot rate 288.23 > 160) but abandoned under the best case (spot rate 129.88 < 160).

Worst case scenario

Year 3 cash is 4,040 million rubbits, exchanged at the option rate of 160 r/£ giving £25.25 million. Discounted at 15% gives £25.25m × 0.658 = £16.61 million.

Years 0 to 2 present values are the same (see above, worst case), so discounted cash flows are – (23.42) + 0.27 + 0.16 +16.61 = (£6.38 million), less the option premium of £1.7 million gives **(£8.08 million)**.

Best case scenario

Spot rate of 129.88 r/£ is used: 4,040/129.88 = £31.11 million. Discounted at 15% gives £31.11 million × 0.658 = £20.47 million.

Discounted cash flows (best case) are (23.42) + 0.36 + 0.26 + 20.47 = (£2.33 million), less the option premium of £1.7m gives (£4.03 million).

Results

On the basis of these figures, the option **does nothing to protect Galeplus's investment** and should not be used.

In comparison with the swap its potential **advantage** is that it **covers the whole of year 3 proceeds**; the swap covers less than one half of this.

Its **disadvantages** are:

- It offers a **significantly inferior maximum exchange rate** (160 compared with 85.4).
- It has an expensive premium cost.

If you have any questions about the contents of this report, please do not hesitate to contact me.

(c) There are a number of advantages of having a treasury function which is **separate from the financial control function**, which are as follows.

A specialist department can employ staff with a **greater level of expertise** than would be possible in a local, more broadly based, finance department. Galeplus may also be able to benefit from the use of **specialised cash management software**.

The additional treasury expertise that Galeplus would have should help to **improve the quality of strategic planning and decision making** within the group.

Centralised liquidity management avoids mixing cash surpluses and overdrafts in different localised bank accounts, which should mean less banking charges for the group as a whole.

The central treasury department can pool all cash flows together. Bulk cash flows allow **lower bank charges** to be negotiated. These larger volumes of cash can be invested by the treasury department, giving **better short-term investment opportunities**.

Borrowing can also be agreed in bulk, probably at **lower interest rates** than for smaller individual locally-arranged borrowings.

Currency risk management can be improved, through **matching of cash flows in different currencies**. There should be less need to use expensive hedging instruments such as option contracts.

(d)   (i)   **Money markets** are the markets where **short-term instruments** are traded. Money markets are over-the-counter (OTC) markets and the transactions take place between **institutions** rather than individual investors. The main characteristic of money market instruments, apart from their short maturities (up to 12 months), is that they normally have only one cash flow.

Commercial paper is an example of a **discount instrument**. Discount instruments do not pay interest. They are issued and traded at a **discount to the face value**. The discount is equivalent to the interest paid to the investor and is the difference between the purchase price of the instrument and the price at maturity.

Commercial paper is **short-term unsecured corporate debt** with a maturity of up to 270 days. The typical term of this debt is about 30 days. Commercial paper can only be issued by large organisations with good credit ratings, normally to fund short-term expenditure.

A certificate of deposit is a coupon bearing instrument, meaning that it pays interest. A certificate of deposit is a certificate of receipt for funds deposited at a bank or other financial institution for a specified term and paying interest at a specified rate.

Certificates of deposit can be either **negotiable** or **non-negotiable**. The holder of a **negotiable certificate of deposit** has two options: to hold it until maturity, receiving the interest and the principal; or to sell it before maturity at the market price.

(ii)   The selling price formula is

$$\text{Selling price} = \left[1 + \left[\frac{\text{Days to maturity}}{\text{Days in a year}} \times \text{yield}\right]\right] \times \text{Purchase price}$$

$$= \left[1 + \left[\frac{57}{365} \times 0.07\right]\right] \times €1,000,000 = €1,010,932$$

78 Polytot

Text references. Chapter 16 on hedging techniques, Chapter 8 on raising capital overseas and Chapter 4 on international trade. Chapter 18 on transfer pricing.

Top tips. With the futures and options contracts, calculating the outcome is slightly different from some other questions:

(i)   With futures you are told enough about basis to work out the price in four months time, and you have to use that in this question to find the number of contracts. Strictly you should also take into account the over-hedge and take the difference to the forward market to make the results strictly comparable with the forward market result; however you are unlikely to be penalised for not doing so.

(ii)   With the options you use the 1.5250 to calculate the number of contracts but again should calculate the over-hedge. Remember the premium is translated at the opening rate. It would also be possible (although it would give you an extra calculation) to calculate the outcome using an option price of $1.55 as it is not that much worse than the forward market, and does mean the company can choose not to exercise the option if necessary.

(b) requires imagination as much as anything, but also note that it brings in government rules and reaction (tax).
(c) is a discussion of the key factors involved in the decision to borrow on the Euromarkets.

A proforma similar to the one we've used in (d) can help you ensure that you cover all relevant elements of transfer pricing calculations.

Easy marks. Hopefully the forward calculations and (c) if you have a good understanding of the Euromarkets.

BPP
LEARNING MEDIA

(a) **Report**

To:	The Board of Directors Polytot plc
From:	A Financial Adviser
Subject:	Currency hedging for Polytot plc

This report considers the alternative forms of currency hedge that are available to Polytot plc and calculate the expected sterling revenue that would be received as a result of the sale of good to Grobbia. The report also recommends the most appropriate hedging strategy.

Currency hedges available to Polytot

Polytot's receipt will be in four months' time, on 31 October.
60% of the sales price is $675 \times 60\% = 405$ million pesos.
Converted to dollars at the spot rate this is worth $405/98.20 = \$4,124,236$

From the information given, the company could try a forward market hedge, a currency futures hedge or a currency options hedge for this receipt of dollars.

The remainder of the sales price will in each case be converted at the unofficial rate of 1.15×156.30 pesos to the £, ie 179.745 peso/£, $\frac{675 - 405}{179.745}$ giving £1,502,128.

Forward market hedge

On 1 July, Polytot will enter into a contractual obligation to sell $\$4,124,236$ for £ on 31 October at a rate to be agreed on 1 July.

The 4 months $/£ forward rate will have to be interpolated between the 3 month and the one year rates.

$$\text{Interpolating, the rate for 4 months forward} = 1.5398 - ((1.5398 - 1.5178)/9)$$
$$= 1.5398 - 0.0024$$
$$= 1.5374$$

$\$4,124,236 / 1.5374 = £2,682,604.$

Futures hedge

Setup

(i) December £ futures
(ii) Buy futures
(iii) Number of contracts

The basis now is:

$$1.5510$$
$$1.5275$$
$$\overline{235} \text{ ticks}$$

If basis reduces evenly over the six month life of the contract, in 4 months' time basis will be $1/3 \times 235$ ticks = 78 ticks.

$1.5275 + 78$ ticks = 1.5353 (lock-in rate)

$$\frac{4,124,236/1.5275}{62,500} = 42.98, \text{ say 43 contracts}$$

(iv) Amount to be hedged on forward market = $(43 \times 62,500 \times 1.5353) - 4,124,236$
$$= 4,126,119 - 4,124,236$$
$$= \$1,883$$

Use interpolation to find rate (different forward rate to rate used above, as over-hedge).

$1.5362 - ((1.5362 - 1.5140)/9) = 1.5337$

(v) Tick size $0.0001 \times 62,500 = \$6.25$

Closing futures price

As an example, use forward rate of 1.5374 as predicted spot rate

Using basis of 78 ticks as above, closing futures price = $1.5374 - 0.0078 = 1.5296$

Hedge outcome

(i) Outcome in futures market

Opening futures price	1.5275 Buy
Closing futures price	1.5296 Sell
Movement in ticks	21 ticks profit

Futures profit 43 × $6.25 × 21 = $5,644

(ii) Net outcome

	£
Spot market receipt ($4,126,119/1.5374)	2,683,829
Futures profit, translated at closing rate ($5,644/1.5374)	3,671
Over-hedge on forward market ($1,883/1.5337)	(1,228)
	2,686,272

Basis risks

The basis calculation is subject to **basis risk**, which means that the basis of 0.78 cents is subject to a margin of error, which may give a better or worse result.

Initial margin

Unlike forward contracts, when Polytot enters into a futures contract, a deposit known as **initial margin** must be paid. Daily gains or losses on the futures market, known as variation margin, are then marked to Polytot's account and, in the case of losses, must be financed.

Impact of uncertainties

The futures market hedge aims to give the same locked-in exchange rate as is obtainable from the forward market, but a few more **uncertainties** are involved. For Polytot the exchange rate obtainable may be better than on the forward market, if it is prepared to accept the risks.

Currency options hedge

Currency options **provide protection against losses** in the event of unfavourable exchange rate movements, but allow the company to take advantage of exchange gains in the event of favourable movements. This is because an option does not have to be exercised unless it is to the investor's advantage.

Set up the hedge

(i)   December options

(ii) Call options as we need to buy £

(iii) Strike price 1.5250 as better than the forward rate

(iv) How many contracts

$$\frac{4,124,236 \div 1.525}{31,250} = 87 \text{ contracts}$$

Amount hedged on forward market = (31,250 × 87 × 1.525) − 4,124,236 = $21,858

(v)   Premium $= \dfrac{3.35}{100} \times 31,250 \times 87$

$= \$91,078 \text{ @ } 1.5475$

$= £58,855$

BPP LEARNING MEDIA

Outcome

	£
Option market (31,250 × 87)	2,718,750
Over-hedge on forward (21,858/1.5374)	(14,217)
Premium	(58,855)
	2,645,678

Effect of premium

As with all options, the **minimum guaranteed outcome** will be less than that obtainable on the forward or futures markets because of the cost of the option premium. However, if the dollar strengthens, the option can be allowed to lapse, enabling Polytot to make currency gains that would not be possible if the forward or futures contracts were used.

Recommendations

The hedge taken will depend on Polytot's **overall strategy** and **attitude towards currency gains and losses**.

Not hedging

Given that the forward markets are indicating that the dollar is likely to strengthen, Polytot may **decide not to hedge** at all, which is unwise, as an unexpected decline in the dollar could produce embarrassing losses

Forward and futures market

The forward and futures markets are effective at **eliminating losses**, which is the prime requirement for a risk averse policy. Of these two methods, the forward contract has **less risk** and requires **less administration**, though in this case it is predicted to produce slightly worse results.

Option

The option is a **compromise** between these two possible approaches, providing a degree of protection against losses but the opportunity of making a gain if the chance arises.

Conclusion

Assuming the company is reasonably risk-averse, the best hedge would probably be the simple, **risk averse forward contract**.

If you have any questions about this report, please do not hesitate to contact me.

(b) **Sale of strawberries**

Three million kilos of strawberries could be sold at between 50 and 60 pence per kilo, providing receipts of £1.5 to £1.8 million. This is in comparison with the receipt of £1,502,128 if the pesos are exchanged on the unofficial market.

Potential problems

The strawberries therefore can potentially provide a better income. However, there are important questions to be answered before the deal can be accepted.

(i) Does the import of strawberries **contravene food quotas** set under the European common agricultural policy?

(ii) How **reliable is the offer** to provide strawberries? Is it realistically possible to organise the supply? Will they be provided all at once, or in several lots?

(iii) What is the **general quality** of Grobbian strawberries? Are they likely to be rejected by large buyers? How will the quality be determined and inspected? What are costs of this?

(iv) Strawberries are perishable goods. How will they be **transported** and **insured**? Who will bear the cost of this?

(v) What **other additional costs** might be incurred?

(vi) How will the **receipt and sale** of strawberries be **taxed**?

(c) To: Directors of Polytot plc

From: Financial advisor

Briefing note

Using Euromarkets to raise international finance

Raising finance on Euromarkets has a number of advantages compared with domestic capital markets.

Regulation

Euromarkets are subject to fewer regulatory controls than domestic markets. This results in relatively low issue costs, smaller differentials between lending and borrowing rates and hence cheaper borrowing costs. Interest is usually payable gross of tax, which is attractive to some investors.

Range of products

The Euromarkets provide a flexible range of products, including interest rate swaps and currency swaps, and there is an active secondary market in many of the securities. They are capable of handling very large loan offers within a short lead time, compared with domestic markets that have queuing processes.

Need for high rating

In order to borrow on the Euromarkets the Grobbian company would need to achieve a high rating by an international rating agency or, as an alternative, would need to have any issue of funds guaranteed by the Grobbian government. Since the loan would be in a hard currency, the market will need to be sure that the company will have access to sufficient hard currency to pay interest and repay the principal.

(d) **Fixed plus variable cost**

	Umbaga $000	Mazila $000	Bettuna $000
Sales	8,200	16,000	14,800
Costs			
Variable costs	6,400	3,600	3,000
Fixed costs	1,800	700	900
Transfer price	–	8,200	8,200
Import duty	–	820	–
	8,200	13,320	12,100
Taxable profit	–	2,680	2,700
Tax	–	670	864
Profit after tax	–	2,010	1,836
Withholding tax	–	–	–
Remittance	–	1,206	1,101.6
UK tax on remittance (W)	–	(134)	–
	–	1,072	1,101.6
Retained (40% after tax profit)	–	804	734.4
Total profit	–	1,876	1,836.0

Total profit ($'000)

Umbaga + Mazila 0+ 1,876 = 1,876.0

Umbaga + Bettuna 0 + 1,836 = 1,836.0

Working

UK tax = (2,680,000 × 0.3) – 670,000 = 134,000

BPP
LEARNING MEDIA

Fixed plus variable cost plus 30%

	Umbaga $000	Mazila $000	Bettuna $000
Sales	10,660	16,000	14,800
Costs			
Variable costs	6,400	3,600	3,000
Fixed costs	1,800	700	900
Transfer price	–	10,660	10,660
Import duty	–	1,066	–
	8,200	16,026	14,560
Taxable profit	2,460	(26)	240
Tax	984	–	76.8
Profit/(Loss) after tax	1,476	(26)	163.2
Withholding tax			
(Umbaga 1,476 × 0.6 × 0.15)	132.84	–	–
Remittance			
(Umbaga 1,476 × 0.6 × 0.85)	752.76	–	97.92
UK tax on remittance	–	–	—
	752.76	–	97.92
Retained (40% after tax profit)	590.4	(26)	65.28
Total profit	1,343.16	(26)	163.2

Total profit ($'000)

Umbaga + Mazila 1,343.16 – 26 = 1,317.16
Umbaga + Bettuna 1,343.16 + 163.2 = 1,506.36

Conclusion

The best plan is to charge sales at fixed plus variable costs, and manufacture in Mazila. This avoids tax in the country of highest tax, Umbaga.

(e) **Likely government attitudes**

Umbaga

The government may query whether the **transfer price** is at a **commercial rate** and, depending on the tax laws, may be able to impart an artificial profit to the transaction and hence charge tax.

Mazila

The government's attitude is likely to be **favourable** as manufacturing is taking place in the country, and hence boosting its economy. Although the import duty is lower than under the markup scenario, this is more than outweighed by the company tax that the government will be able to collect.

Bettuna

The government can take **no action** against the company as the company is not doing anything. It can try to attract the company by offering a subsidy, which would only need to be greater than $40,000 (1,876,000 – 1,836,000) for the decision to be changed.

UK

The UK government would be happy with this arrangement, since it is the only arrangement of those considered that will mean that the company pays tax.

BPP
LEARNING MEDIA

79 FNDC

Text references. Chapter 17 on hedging techniques, Chapter 15 on the treasury function

Top tips. In part (a) ensure you answer the question that has been asked rather than just a general discussion of interest rate hedging.

For part (b) ensure that the effect of both the increase and decrease in interest rates are shown and don't forget to conclude on the best option for FNDC to choose.

Although it is only for a couple of marks, it should be easy to identify the correct FRA rate to use.

Easy marks. The illustration of the collar hedge in part (c) and both sections of part (d) offer some fairly straightforward marks.

(a)   **Interest rate futures**

Hedging

Hedging with futures offers protection against **adverse movements in the underlying asset market** (here the cash market and therefore changes in interest rates); if these occur they should be approximately offset by a gain on the futures market.

Basis risk

The person hedging may be affected by **basis risk**, the risk that the futures price may move differently from the amount that would be forecast from the change in interest rates.

Terms

The **terms, sums involved and periods** are **standardised** and hedge inefficiencies will be caused by either having too many contracts or too few, and having to consider what to do with the unhedged amount. Also the terms of the future may be based on **LIBOR**, which may not match with the basis of calculation of the interest rate being hedged.

Deposit

Futures require the payment of a **small deposit**; this transaction cost is likely to be lower than the premium for a tailored forward rate agreement or any type of option. However further payments of **variation margin** could be demanded if prices move in an adverse direction.

Interest rate options

Guaranteed amounts

The main advantage of options is that the buyer cannot lose on the interest rate and can take advantage of any favourable rate movements. An interest rate option provides the **right to borrow a specified amount** at a **guaranteed rate of interest**. On the date of expiry of the option the buyer must decide **whether or not to exercise his right to borrow**. He will only exercise the option if actual interest rates have risen above the guaranteed option rate.

Premium cost

However a premium must be paid regardless of whether or not the option is exercised, and the **premium cost** can be quite **high**, high enough not to make an option worthwhile if interest rate movements are expected to be marginal.

Choice of interest rates

Options offer a **wider choice of rate** to protect against adverse movements; the rate chosen may depend on **expectations of interest rate movements** and the **premium** for each option.

(b) To: The Board of Directors
From: AN Accountant
Date: 15 September XX
Subject: Hedging strategy

This report looks at the interest rate hedging strategy of FNDC plc and makes a recommendation on the preferred method.

Hedging the borrowing rate using futures

Setup

(i) June contracts as looking to borrow in five months time

(ii) Sell June futures as borrowing at 95.55 (or 100 − 95.55) = 4.45%

(iii) Number of contracts

$$\frac{\text{Exposure}}{\text{Contract size}} \times \frac{\text{Investment period}}{\text{Length of contract}}$$

$$\frac{£45,000,000}{£500,000} \times \frac{2}{3} = 60 \text{ contracts}$$

(iv) Tick size

£12.50

Estimate closing futures price

June contract expires in 7 months

LIBOR is currently 4.0% (96.00)

June contract basis risk 4.45% (futures rate) − 4% = 0.45% or 45 ticks, difference between current and futures price.

1 May: 2 months to expiry: $45 \times \frac{2}{7} = 13$ ticks

If LIBOR rises to 4.5%, the futures rate should be 4.5 + 0.13 = 4.63%
If LIBOR falls to 3.5%, the futures rate should be 3.5 + 0.13 = 3.63%

Outcome

The results of the hedge under cases (i) and (ii) are shown below.

(i) **Futures market**

	0.5% rise	0.5% fall
1 Dec: Sell 60 (ie pay interest) @	4.45%	4.45%
1 May: Buy 60 (ie receive interest) @	4.63%	3.63%
Profit/ (Loss)	0.18%	(0.82)%

(ii) **Net outcome**

	%	%
Payment in spot market (LIBOR + 1.25%)	(5.75)	(4.75)
Profit/(Loss) in futures market	0.18	(0.82)
Net cost of loan	(5.57)	(5.57)

In £ this is 0.0557 × £45 million × 2/12 = £417,750

However this rate is dependent on the assumption that **basis declines linearly**; this may not be the case if **basis risk exists**.

Hedging the borrowing rate using options

Setup

(i)   June as above

(ii) Buy put options

(iii) Consider all three possible prices (in the exam just analysing one would be sufficient)

(iv) Number of contracts 60

(v)   Tick size £12.50

(vi) Option premium

9500: 0.015%
9550: 0.165%
9600: 0.710%

Closing futures rates

4.63% and 3.63% as above

Outcome interest rates rise

(i) **Option market outcome**

	9500	9550	9600
Put option strike price (right to pay interest)	5.00%	4.50%	4.00%
June futures price	4.63%	4.63%	4.63%
Exercise option? (prefer to pay interest at lowest rate)	No	Yes	Yes
Gain	–	0.13%	0.63%

(ii) **Net position**

	9500	9550	9600
	%	%	%
Actual interest cost (as above)	(5.75)	(5.75)	(5.75)
Value of option gain	–	0.13	0.63
Premium	(0.015)	(0.165)	(0.71)
Net cost of loan	5.765	5.785	5.83

Outcome interest rates fall

At a closing futures price of 3.63% none of the options will be exercised

Net position

	9500	9550	9600
	%	%	%
Actual interest cost (as above)	(4.75)	(4.75)	(4.75)
Premium	(0.015)	(0.165)	(0.710)
Net cost of loan	(4.765)	(4.915)	(5.460)

Forward rate agreements

The correct forward rate agreement to use here is the FRA 5-7 which gives a rate of 5.85%.

Conclusion

Options will produce a better result if **interest rates fall**; the 9500 option appears to be the best choice if rates fall.

However if **interest rates rise**, as expected, the futures will produce a lower interest cost than the best option (the 9500).

If you have any questions on this report, please do not hesitate to ask me.

BPP LEARNING MEDIA

(c)   (i)   **Exercise prices**

If the company is seeking a **maximum rate** of 5.75%, this implies LIBOR of (5.75 – 1.25) = 4.5%, and a put option exercise price of 9550.

If the company is seeking a **minimum rate** of 5.25%, this implies LIBOR of (5.25 – 1.25) = 4.0%, and a call option exercise price of 9600.

FNDC will **buy put** and sell **call options**.

Premium

0.165% – 0.007% = 0.095%

If interest rates rise

Put option will be exercised, and calculation of outcome will be as in (b) with a different premium.

	%
Actual interest cost	(5.75)
Value of option gain	0.13
Premium	(0.095)
Net cost of loan	(5.715)

If interest rates fall

The put option won't be exercised, but the gain will be limited by the loss on the call option. The holder will be entitled to 3.63% futures rate less 4% (call option) = 0.37%.

	%
Actual interest cost	(4.75)
Premium and loss on option (0.095% + 0.37% = 0.465%)	(0.465)
Net cost of loan	(5.215)

The collar **saves premium cost**, but again it interest rates rise as expected the outcome is worse than **hedging with the futures**.

(ii)   **Advantages**

Upside risk – the company has the choice not to exercise the option and will therefore be able to take advantage of falling interest rates.

Over-the-counter options – these are tailored to the specific needs of the company and are therefore more flexible than exchange-traded options for a more exact hedge.

Disadvantages

Premium – the premium cost may be **relatively expensive** compared with the costs of other hedging instruments. It will be payable whatever the movement in interest rates and whether or not the option is exercised.

Collar – if the company has a collar, this will limit its ability to take advantage of lower interest rates to the lower limit set by the cap.

Liquidity – over-the-counter options are much less liquid than exchange-traded options, as they cannot be sold if not required.

(d)   (i)   Writing options will produce an income for the company. However option writers are **exposed to unlimited loss** unless the writer takes out a hedging transaction. Writing options is speculative and requires specialist financial expertise; it is not something that a manufacturing company such as FNDC would normally undertake.

(ii) **Centralised liquidity management** avoids having a mix of cash surpluses and overdrafts in different local bank accounts and facilitates bulk cash flows, so that lower bank charges can be negotiated.

Larger volumes of cash are available to invest, giving better **short-term investment opportunities** (for example, money market deposits, high interest accounts and Certificates of Deposit).

Any borrowing can be arranged **in bulk**, at lower interest rates than for smaller borrowings, and perhaps on the eurocurrency or eurobond markets.

Foreign currency risk management is likely to be improved in a group of companies. A central treasury department can match foreign currency income earned by one subsidiary with expenditure in the same currency by another subsidiary. In this way, the risk of losses on adverse exchange rate changes can be avoided without the expense of forward exchange contracts or other 'hedging' (risk-reducing) methods.

A specialist treasury department will employ **experts** with knowledge of dealing in futures, eurocurrency markets, taxation, transfer prices and so on. Localised departments would not have such expertise.

The centralised pool of **funds required for precautionary purposes** will be smaller than the sum of separate precautionary balances which would need to be held under decentralised treasury arrangements.

Through having a separate **profit centre**, attention will be focused on the contribution to group profit performance that can be achieved by good cash, funding, investment and foreign currency management.

Centralisation provides a means of exercising **better control** through use of **standardised procedures** and **risk monitoring**. Standardised practices and performance measures can also create productivity benefits.

80 Nente Co

Text references. Chapter 10 on valuation of acquisitions, Chapter 2 on performance measurement and Chapter 11 for defensive tactics in a takeover.

Top tips. In part (a) do all the calculations first as appendices and then write the report based on these calculations. Make sure you have read all of the information in the scenario. Spotting the risk free debt rate is difficult, but you are told 7% is 380 basis points over the government base rate so you can assume the risk free rate is 3.2%.

In part (b) you should perform a couple of easy calculations to show financial performance and comment on what these mean for Nente Co.

Easy marks. The discussion in part (c) offers some relatively straightforward marks.

Examiner's comments. Answers which gave a report title but then did not structure the answer appropriately gained few professional marks.

Part (i) was generally done adequately. A significant number of candidates calculated the growth rate, although some misread the question, and read the growth rate information as: 'by 25%' instead of 'to 25%'. In a number of responses, when calculating the free cash flow to firm, errors were made such as including interest and when calculating the tax impact. Many candidates did not deduct the debt value from the free cash flow to get to the value per share. Some candidates did not divide the total value by the number of shares to get a share price.

A significant number of candidates found difficulty with part (ii) and especially with obtaining a value for the combined company based on combined company earnings, which included synergies and a modified PE ratio. This is a fairly standard method of obtaining the value of the combined company and it was expected that most candidates should have been able to do these computations at P4 level.

BPP
LEARNING MEDIA

		Marks
(a) Appendix 1		
Based on PBIT, calculation of the growth rate	2	
Calculation of free cash flows	2	
Calculation of company value, equity value and value of each share	<u>3</u>	
		7
Appendix 2		
Cash offer		
Estimate of value of combined company	3	
Value created per share for Nente Co shareholders	1	
Share-for-share offer		
Expected share price for the combined company	2	
Value created for a Nente Co share	1	
Value created for a Mije Co share	<u>1</u>	
		8
Appendix 3		
PV of underlying asset	1	
Value of exercise price	1	
$N(d_1)$	2	
$N(d_2)$	2	
Value of call	1	
Value added to Nente Co share	<u>1</u>	
		8
Discussion		
Nente Co shareholders	2 – 3	
Mije Co shareholders	1 – 2	
Assumptions made	2 – 3	
Use of value of follow-on product	<u>2 – 3</u>	
		Max 8
Professional marks		
Report format	1	
Layout, presentation and structure	<u>3</u>	
		4
(b) Profit level discussion	1 – 2	
Financial gearing	2 – 3	
Growth rates and dividends	2 – 3	
Impact of follow on product	<u>1 – 2</u>	
		Max 8
(c) 1 – 2 marks for each defence covered		Max <u>7</u>
		<u>50</u>

(a) **REPORT**

> **To:** The Board of Directors of Nente Co
> **From:** A N Accountant
> **Date:** X/X/XX
> **Re:** Impact of the takeover proposal from Mije Co and the follow-on project

This report considers the value, to both Nente Co and Mije Co shareholders, based on a cash offer and also on a share-for-share offer. It discusses the potential reactions of these groups of shareholders to the alternative offers and how best to make use of the follow-on opportunity. All significant assumptions made in the assessments are also explained.

The appendices to this report show the detailed calculations for estimating an equity value for Nente Co, the value to shareholders of Nente Co and Mije Co of the acquisition under both a cash offer and a share-for-share exchange and the value of the follow-on product rights to Nente Co.

The results of the detailed calculations are shown here.

Estimated current price of a Nente Co share $2.90 (appendix 1)

Estimated increase in share price	Nente Co	Mije Co
	%	%
Cash offer (appendix 2)	1.7	9.4
Share-for-share offer (appendix 2)	17.9	6.9

Estimated value per share of the follow-on product   8.7% (appendix 3)

The cash offer is **unlikely to be accepted** by Nente Co shareholders because the estimated gains are only slightly higher than the current share price, although being unlisted Nente Co shareholders may not be able to realise the current price should they wish to sell. The share-for-share exchange gives a much larger increase of 17.9% and is much more likely to be acceptable to Nente Co shareholders. It is also **higher than the expected return** from the follow-on product and therefore based on the financial data the most attractive option for Nente Co shareholders is the takeover on a share-for-share exchange basis.

Mije Co shareholders are likely to **prefer the cash offer** so that they can maximise their own returns and not dilute their control of the company, but they may accept the share-for-share offer as this still offers an increase in value. Mije Co shareholders would need to consider whether these returns are in excess of any other investment opportunities that are available and whether the acquisition of Nente Co is the **best use of funds**.

There are a number of assumptions present in the calculations. For example, for calculating the current value of a Nente Co share the free cash flow model is used. This assumes that the growth rate and free cash flow exist in **perpetuity** and that the estimated cost of capital is appropriate. The takeover offer analysis is based on the assumption that the proposed synergy savings will be achieved and that the P/E **bootstrapping** approach is valid. For the calculation of the follow-on product value the option variables are estimates and an assumption is made that these will not change in the period before the decision is taken. The calculated value is based on the scenario that the option can only be exercised after two years, but it appears that the option can be exercised at any time within the two year period.

The follow-on product has been treated separately from the takeover, but Nente Co could ask Mije Co to **take this into account** in its takeover offer. The value of the rights to Nente Co is $609,021 (appendix 3) and adds around 25c or 8.8% to the value of a Nente Co share. If Mije were to increase their offer by this value, or the rights could be sold prior to the takeover, then the return to a Nente Co shareholder would be 17.9% + 8.8% = 26.7%.

In conclusion, the preferred outcome for Nente Co shareholders would be to accept the share-for-share offer and to convince Mije Co to take the value of the follow-on product into consideration. Nente Co shareholders will need to be assured of the **accuracy of the calculations** provided in the appendices before they accept the offer.

Appendices

Appendix 1

Estimate of current value of Nente Co's equity based on free cash flows

Total value = Free cash flows × (1 + growth rate (g))/(Cost of capital (k) – g)
k = 11%
Past growth rate = (latest profit before interest and tax (PBIT) / Earliest PBIT) $^{1/\text{no of periods of growth}}$ – 1
Past g = $(1{,}230/970)^{1/3}$ - 1 = 0.0824
Future g = 0.25 × 0.0824 = 0.0206

Free cash flow calculation

Free cash flow (FCF) = PBIT + non-cash flows – cash investment – tax

FCF = 1,230,000 + 1,206,000 – 1,010,000 – (1,230,000 × 20%) = $1,180,000

Total value = $1,180,000 × 1.0206/(0.11 – 0.0206) = $13,471,007

Equity value = $13,471,007 - $6,500,000 = $6,971,007

Number of shares = $960,000/$0.40 = 2.4 million

Equity value per share = $6,971,007/2.4 million shares = $2.90

Appendix 2

Cash offer

Gain in value to a Nente Co shareholder = ($2.95 – $2.90)/$2.90 = 1.7%

Additional earnings post-acquisition = $620,000 + $150,000 = $770,000

Additional earnings per share = $770,000/10m = 7.7c per share

Using the P/E ratio to calculate the increase in share price = 15 × 7.7c = $1.16

Additional value created = $1.16 × 10 million = $11.6 million

Less cost of acquisition = ($2.95 × 2.4 million) = $7.08 million

Value added for Mije Co shareholders = 11.6 million – 7.08 million = $4.52 million

Gain in value to a shareholder of Mije = $4.52m/10m = 45.2c

45.2c/480c = 9.4%

Share-for-share offer

Earnings of combined company = $770,000 (from above) + $3,200,000 = $3,970,000

Total number of shares in combined number = 10 million + (2.4million × 2/3) = 11,600,000

EPS of combined company = $3.97m/11.6m = 34.2c

Expected share price using P/E ratio = 34.2 × 15 = 513c = $5.13

Gain in value to a shareholder of Mije Co = ($5.13 – $4.80)/$4.80 = 6.9%

Current value of three shares in Nente Co = $2.90 × 3 = $8.70

Gain in value to a shareholder of Nente Co = ((2 × $5.13) – $8.70) /$8.70 = 17.9%

Appendix 3

Value of follow-on product

Present value of the cash inflows	2,434,000
Present value of the option cost	(2,029,000)
Net present value of the new product	405,000

Based on NPV, without considering the option to delay, the project would increase the value of Nente Co by $405,000.

Value of the option to delay

Price of asset (PV of future positive cash flows)	$2,434,000
Exercise price (initial cost - not discounted)	$2,500,000
Time to expiry of option	2 years
Risk free rate (government base rate = 7% – 380 basis points)	3.2%
Volatility	42%

$d_1 = [\ln(2,434/2,500) + (0.032 + 0.5 \times 0.42^2) \times 2]/(0.42 \times 2^{0.5}) = 0.359$

$d_2 = 0.359 – (0.42 \times 2^{0.5}) = -0.235$

$N(0.36) = 0.5 + 0.1406 = 0.6406$

$N(-0.24) = 0.5 – 0.0948 = 0.4052$

Value of option = $2,434,000 \times 0.6406 – 2,500,000 \times 0.4052 \times e^{-(0.032 \times 2)}$

= $1,559,220 – $950,199 = $609,021

This project increases the value of the company by $609,021 or 25.4c per share ($609,021/2.4m)

In percentage terms this is an increase of about 8.8% (25.4c/290c).

(b)   Nente Co has an **operating profit** margin of 14% (1,230/8,780) but the significant interest payments mean that profit after tax is approximately half of the profit before interest and tax figure. This profit after tax figure is less that the required annual investment in non-current assets and working capital.

Nente Co has a high level of **financial gearing**. When measured by book value, the gearing level is 73% (6,500/(2,360 + 6,500)). This high level of debt, coupled with rising interest rates, means that the interest payments are high and **interest coverage** is currently 2.7 times.

Given that future growth levels are only expected to be 2% (from part (a) above) profit after tax is unlikely to **increase significantly** unless interest rates fall dramatically. The low level of profit after tax means that **no dividend** has been paid in the most recent period. The business angels will want to see a **return on their investment**, which is unlikely to be in the form of future dividends given these prospects. Therefore they are likely to be attracted by the prospect of an exit route through a sale of their equity stake.

The **follow-on product** should help to increase Nente Co's growth rate, but with the limited scope for expansion and lack of other product development it would appear that the business angels would need to sell their equity stakes to generate significant returns.

(c)   There are a number of possible post-bid defences available to Mije Co.

Attempting to have the bid referred to the **competition authorities** seems unlikely to be successful, based on the size of Mije Co, and also that this is a vertical merger rather than a horizontal one - which means Tianhe Co is unlikely to significantly increase its existing market share.

If it is specifically the Tianhe Co takeover that Mije Co wishes to defend against, then a **white knight** defence could be a successful tactic. This involves finding a friendly company to join in the bidding process and eventually acquire Mije Co. The difficulty will be in finding a willing friendly company.

A **counter-bid** does not seem to be appropriate given the relative market capitalisation of Mije Co compared to Tianhe Co. Tianhe Co has a current market value of $245 million which is over five times the current market capitalisation of Mije Co of $48 million.

A **crown jewels** defence would involve selling off Mije Co's most valuable assets to make it less attractive as an acquisition. This may mean that Tianhe Co is uninterested in continuing the takeover bid, but it could compromise Mije Co's current operations and as such the existing shareholders may object to this.

A **poison pill** defence attempts to make a company unattractive, normally by giving the right to existing shareholders to buy shares at a very low price. This could be used by Mije Co, but the existing shareholders need to be willing to put additional funds into the business. The shareholders are unlikely to do this if the takeover is actually in their best interest.

A **golden parachute** involves offering large benefits to key management personnel who would lose their position in the event of a takeover. This would then make the takeover more expensive for Tianhe Co and acts as a deterrent. This could be a good option for Mije Co to take to defend against this takeover.

81 Seal Island

Text references. NPV, sensitivity analysis and simulations are covered in Chapter 5.

Top tips. Always make use of the NPV proforma when performing NPV calculations. You are given the annuity factor formula which makes things much easier when discounting the cash surpluses, but don't forget to discount them back to year 0 (the annuity formula will only discount back as far as the year of the first cash surplus).

It is tempting to write everything you know about project uncertainties in part (b) but relate your answer to the project in question.

Part (a)(iv) probably looks more difficult than it actually is. You are only required to write a basic summary of how simulations work.

Parts (b) and (c) test your knowledge of use of cost of capital.

Easy marks. There are numerous easy marks to pick up in part (a)(i) – you should be very familiar with NPV calculations by now.

Report

To: Seal Island Nuclear Power Company directors
From: Accountant
Subject: Advanced Boiling Water Reactor project

The purpose of this report is to appraise the Advanced Boiling Water Reactor project and to discuss various aspects surrounding its financial viability.

(i) **Net Present Value**

For the purposes of the NPV calculation it is assumed that 1st January 20X2 is the beginning of Year 1.

Value of cash inflows from electricity generation

Use the annuity factor formula to determine the annuity factor to be applied to the annual cash inflows of $100m.

$$A_n = \left[\frac{1 - \left(\frac{1+g}{1+i} \right)^n}{i - g} \right] (1+g)$$

Where

$g = 0.04$ $i = 0.10$ $n = 30$

$A_n = 14.11$

> **Tutorial note.** Be careful how you enter this complicated formula into your calculator. It is better to take the calculations one step at a time rather than trying to input the entire formula into your calculator at once.

	20X2	*20X3*	*20X4*	*20X5 – 20Y4*	*20Y4*
	$m	$m	$m	$m	$m
Construction costs	(300)	(600)	(100)		
Cash inflows				100	
Decommissioning costs (W1)					(2,189)
Discount factor (10%)	0.909	0.826	0.751	14.11 x 0.751	0.043
Present value	(272.7)	(495.6)	(75.1)	1,059.7	(94.1)

NPV = $122.2m

W1 Decommissioning costs = $600m x 1.04^{33} = $2,189m   ($1.04^{33}$ represents growth)

(ii) **Principal uncertainties associated with the project**

Capital expenditure

One of the main uncertainties of the project is the estimation of required capital expenditure. There are possibilities of delays which can cost both time and money, unexpected increases in labour costs that had not been factored in, and greater than expected increases in raw material costs (perhaps due to shortages). Incorrect estimates of timing of capital expenditures can have a significant effect on the NPV of the project, given that cash flows may have been discounted using an incorrect discount factor.

Discount rate

If the discount rate is incorrect, the results of the NPV calculations will be meaningless. Discount rates for projects of this size can be difficult to estimate. They are often estimated using various models and sources, all of which have their own uncertainties attached, therefore there is considerable scope for error. The project also has potential social and environmental elements that must be built into the discount rate - or example, the project is aiming to reduce emissions and Roseland's dependence on fossil fuels. There is a risk associated with securing a stable supply of energy which should also be accounted for in the chosen discount rate.

Cash surpluses

Given the length of the project, it is difficult to estimate cash surpluses to the end of its life. Such surpluses will also depend on the capacity of the reactor, the demand for the alternative energy and the prices charged for this energy. Such prices will be affected by preferences for other sources of energy (such as fossil fuels, which may be priced at a lower rate) and the continued availability of these sources.

Decommissioning costs

Such costs will depend on the effect the reactor has had on the environment (think of the decommissioning costs associated with such nuclear power stations as Dounreay on the north coast of Scotland). However such costs will occur far into the future and as such and errors in estimation will have very limited effect on the outcome of the project as a whole.

Real options

There may be a number of real options attached to such a project – the option to delay, the option to abandon at different points throughout the project's life or the option to expand or contract capacity. All of these options may add value to the project as they help to reduce the downside risk associated with it.

(iii)   **Sensitivity analysis**

If the project is to become infeasible the NPV must fall by $122.2m.

Changes in construction costs

Total discounted increase in construction costs = $122.2m

Increase per $100m in construction costs x (3 x 0.909 + 6 x 0.826 + 1 x 0.751) = $122.2m

Increase per $100m in construction costs = $122.2m/ 8.434 = $14.49m

This means that

20X2 costs must increase to ($300m + 3 x $14.49m) = $343.47m

20X3 costs must increase to ($600m + 6 x $14.49m) = $686.94m

20X4 costs must increase to ($100m + 1 x $14.49m) = $114.49m

before NPV becomes zero

This represents an annual increase in construction costs of 14.49%.

Changes in annual operating surplus

Annual operating surplus reduction = $122.2m/(14.11 x 0.751) = $11.53m

Surplus must reduce to $88.47m ($100m - $11.53m) before NPV reaches zero. This is a reduction of 11.53% per annum.

Changes in decommissioning costs

Decommissioning costs must increase by $122.2m/0.1571 = $777.8m (in January 20X2 prices) before NPV becomes zero.

This represents an increase of 129.6%.

(iv)   **Assessment of volatility**

Simulations (such as Monte Carlo simulation) can be used to estimate the volatility of the project's NPV. Such techniques amount to adopting a particular probability distribution for the uncertain (random) variables – such as cash surpluses – and then using simulations to generate values of these variables.

In this particular project, the decommissioning costs are not considered to be a random variable, but rather a variable with a limit value and a most likely value.

The simulation is performed in the first instance to obtain a 'trial value' but is then repeated thousands of times for the variables of interest to derive the NPV for each possible simulated outcome. A distribution of NPVs is then obtained which should estimate a normal distribution. This can be used to estimate project volatility.

The output from a simulation will give the expected NPV and other such statistics as the standard deviation of the output distribution. The output can also rank the variables in order of significance in determining the NPV of the project.

Should you wish to discuss any of the above in more detail, please do not hesitate to contact me.

(b) **WACC**

A company's weighted average cost of capital (WACC) is the **average of the after-tax costs** of the **different sources of finance** that it uses, **weighted in proportion to the market values** of **those funds**. WACC can be used as a **discount rate** to evaluate the company's potential projects provided that:

(i)   There is **no significant change in the capital structure** of the company as a result of the investment

(ii)   The **operating (systematic) risk of the new project** is the **same** as the **company's existing systematic risk**

If these conditions are true then a project whose return exceeds the WACC will be worthwhile and its NPV will indicate the expected increase in shareholder value if it is accepted.

Problems of WACC

(i)   One practical problem is whether to **include short-term debt** (eg overdraft) in the computation. This depends on whether the **short-term debt** is effectively used as a **long term source of finance**.

(ii)   If the new project has **different systematic risk** to the company's existing business (ie condition (ii) above is untrue) then a risk-adjusted version of the WACC must be computed if the method is to give reasonable results.

(iii)   WACC cannot be used if the finance for the new project would cause a **significant change to the company's capital structure** (ie condition (i) above is untrue).

(iv)   It is also difficult to use WACC if there are **specific financing opportunities**, for example subsidised loan finance, or complex tax allowances.

Adjusted present value

Adjusted present value (APV) is a more advanced method that can be used for any project appraisal exercise, but it is in the more complex cases (involving a **change in capital structure** and/or **other complex finance problems**) that it is the most useful.

(i)   The first stage is to **evaluate the base case NPV** of operating cash flows by discounting at the ungeared cost of equity.

(ii)   The **present value of each individual financing side effect** is then evaluated separately. The sum of the base case NPV and the PV of financing side effects is the APV.

The method has the advantage over basic net present value using WACC that it allows **each different type of cash flow** to be **discounted at a rate specific to the risk** of that cash flow. It also allows the effects of more complex financing situations to be considered.

Problems with APV

The main practical problem is to **identify correctly the financing side effects** and their appropriate discount rates. Theoretical weaknesses of the method stem from simplifications introduced by the Modigliani and Miller model of capital structure. For example:

- It is assumed that the only effect of debt issued at market rates is the tax relief on debt interest
- The computation of an asset beta assumes that **cash flows** are perpetuities

(c) (i) **No conversion: share price is 470 cents**

If no conversion takes place, the value of the convertible will be as debt with 4 years to maturity. Its value is found by **discounting interest** and **redemption** value at 9%, which is the company's pre-tax cost of debt.

Year		$	9% factors	PV $
1–4	Interest	8	3.240	25.92
4	Redemption	100	0.708	70.80
				96.72

(Note that the value per share for conversion to take place would need to be at least $96.72/20 = 484 cents).

Total market value of the loan stock = 96.72/100 x $20 million
= $19.34 million

Other debt has a market value of $23m, giving total debt value of $42.34m and a cost of 9%(1 – 0.3) = 6.3% after tax.

If the share price falls to 470 cents

Total market value of shares = 470/520 × $180m
= $162.69 million

The cost of equity is 15% because its systematic risk is the same as that of the market.

Total value of debt plus equity = $42.34m + $162.69m = $205.03 million
Weighted average cost of capital = 15% × 162.69/205.03 + 6.3% × 42.34/205.03
= 13.2%

(ii) **Conversion: share price is 570 cents**

Number of new shares issued = 20 × $20m/$100
= 4 million
Value of new shares issued = 4m × 570c
= $22.8 million
Value of existing shares = 570/520 × $180m
= $197.31 million
Value of all shares = $220.11 million
Debt remaining = $23 million
Total value of equity and debt = $243.11 million

Assuming the cost of equity and debt are unchanged

Weighted average cost of capital = 15% × 220.11/243.11+ 6.3% × 23/243.11
= 14.2%

The cost of capital is higher if conversion takes place because **cheaper debt** has been **replaced** with **more expensive equity shares.**

Conclusion

This calculation is unlikely to be correct because the **assumption** that the costs of equity and debt are unchanged by the conversion is probably **wrong**. When debt is reduced, the **financial risk** to shareholders **decreases**, causing a reduction in the cost of equity. However, it is unlikely that the cheaper equity will compensate for the loss of cheap debt in the capital structure because **debt interest** is **tax allowable** whereas dividends to shareholders are not.

82 Sleepon

Text references. Chapter 5 for the investment appraisal methods and complications.

Top tips. You should do the calculation first as an appendix for the report, aiming to spend about 50 minutes on it. The reference to costs being at current prices, and the fact that some costs were increasing at different rates, meant that you had to adjust most of the figures for inflation each year. The details given about the competitor should also have given you a big enough clue to identify the need to ungear and regear beta. Sleepon's current WACC and equity beta are not relevant.

The most complicated requirements are towards the end of the calculation, so you should be able to pick up enough marks on the earlier part and in the discussion to have a good chance of passing the question. It would have been acceptable to assume working capital was recovered in year 6 rather than year 5.

The strategic considerations are fairly basic – is diversification necessary (remember its disadvantages)? How will the competition respond? The bulk of the discussion consists of going through the major figures in the appraisal and considering how they might change or why they might not be accurate, also considering anything the appraisal may have missed out (real options).

Easy marks. The discussion should be fine if you questioned the figures given in the scenario. Most of the calculations though just consist of calculating the effect of inflation increases. Part (b) is also fairly straightforward.

(a)　**To:**　　　　**The board of directors**

　　　　From:　　　**Financial Adviser**

　　　　Subject:　　**Report on the theme park investment**

This report discusses the financial appraisal of the potential investment in the theme park, shown in an appendix, and other factors that the board of Sleepon should consider when making their assessment, including the further information required.

Financial appraisal

Net present value

The appraisal shows a negative net present value of $223.3 million, indicating that on financial grounds, the investment is not worthwhile. See appendix 1 for detailed calculations.

Modified internal rate of return

This supports the findings of the net present value appraisal, as the project would generate a negative rate of return of 13.6% per year. See appendix 2 for detailed calculations.

Project duration

The project duration (the amount of time it takes to recover half of the present value of the project) is 4.89 years. This is due to the fact that the vast majority of the returns are from the realisable value in year 5, not generated by the revenue from the project itself. See appendix 3 for detailed calculations.

Other factors

However there are a number of additional factors that Sleepon's board should consider.

Need for diversification

The board should asses whether the **strategic decision** to diversify is the correct one; it may be better to look for further investments in the hotel sector, in which Sleepon has experience. Sleepon is likely to have to **recruit managers and staff** with experience of running theme parks; this will be **costly** and successful recruitment is not completely certain.

Extent of diversification

Even if diversification is the best policy, there may be better investments in the theme park or leisure facility sector. The directors also need to investigate how much the theme park income is **correlated** with the hotel income. Will the factors causing a fall in demand for hotel accommodation (customers holidaying abroad for example) also affect the demand for theme parks.

Competition

Sleepon should not only investigate the current position of likely competitors, but also how the competition is likely to **respond** if the new theme park is opened.

Further information and calculations

The expected values given represent only one possible scenario. Appraisal is needed of other possible scenarios and information obtained about, or estimations made of:

- The effect on revenue of **different scales of admission charges**
- The effect on revenue of **different spending** within the theme park, if for example more attractions were offered
- The impact of **tighter control on working capital** as this is a major item of expenditure in the early years
- **Cost patterns** – is the assumption that all costs will increase in line with inflation too pessimistic
- The **accuracy of the realisable value estimate** in year 5 and what the effect would be on realisable value of extending the analysis beyond five years
- Whether disposal value would differ if the park was sold after 5 years as a **going concern** rather than its assets sold separately
- The **accuracy of the discount rate estimate – Thrillall's** activities may not be of the same risk, and maybe the future figures have been over-discounted
- The effect of extending the analysis beyond five years, calculating at what stage the park is likely to break even, and whether this **payback** period could be tolerated
- The impact of **scaling down** the **initial investment** on operating income and costs – would this decrease the payback period significantly
- The possibility of **real options** – further investment at a later date if the theme park proved more successful than expected

Simulations should be carried out under a number of different assumptions and **sensitivity analysis applied** to key figures in the scenario.

If you have any questions about the content of this report, please do not hesitate to contact me.

Appendix 1 – Net present value

	Working	0	1	2	3	4	5
		$m	$m	$m	$m	$m	$m
Receipts							
Adult admission	1			41.2	42.5	43.8	45.1
Child admission	1			34.4	35.4	36.5	37.6
Food	1			13.7	14.2	14.6	15.0
Gifts	1			11.5	11.8	12.2	12.5
Total receipts				100.8	103.9	107.1	110.2
Expenses							
Labour	2			42.4	43.7	45.0	46.4
Insurance	2			2.1	2.2	2.3	2.3
Maintenance				15.0	19.0	23.0	27.0
Capital allowances	3			62.5	46.9	35.2	26.4
Total expenses				122.0	111.8	105.5	102.1
Taxable profits				(21.2)	(7.9)	1.6	8.1
Taxation 30%				6.4	2.4	(0.5)	(2.4)
Capital allowances				18.8	14.1	10.6	7.9
Initial cost		(200.0)	(200.0)				
Realisable value							250.0
Working capital	4		(51.5)	(1.5)	(1.6)	(1.6)	56.2
Net cash flow		(200.0)	(251.5)	2.5	7.0	10.1	319.8
Discount factors 11%	5	1.000	0.901	0.812	0.731	0.659	0.593
Present value		(200.0)	(226.6)	2.0	5.0	6.7	189.6

Net present value = $(223.3) million.

Note. The market research, advertising and the apportioned overheads are not relevant cash flows.

Workings

1   Income

Estimated income $\times (1.03)^2$ year 2 etc

Estimated income is:
Adult admission $6,000 \times 360 \times 18$
Child admission $9,000 \times 360 \times 10$
Food $15,000 \times 360 \times 8 \times 0.3$
Gifts $15,000 \times 360 \times 5 \times 0.4$

2   Labour and insurance

Current costs $\times (1.03)^2$ year 2 etc

3   Capital allowances

Assume first allowance available for yr 1 for all expenditure $125,000 + $125,000 and benefit received in yr 2. Allowances available up to and including yr 4, no allowance claimable for yr 5 in yr 6 as after-tax realisable value given.
Assume allowances can be claimed against liabilities elsewhere in the group.

Year of claim	Written down value $m	Capital allowance $m	Tax saving $m	Year realised
1	250.0	62.5	18.75	2
2	187.5	46.9	14.07	3
3	140.6	35.2	10.56	4
4	105.4	26.4	7.92	5

4   Working capital

$50.00 \times 1.03 = 51.50$ yr 1, 3% increase yrs 2-4, assume repaid end of yr 5.

5   Discount factor

$E = 400 \times 3.86 = \$1,544m$
$D = 460 \times 0.93 = \$428m$

Ungearing Thrillall's equity beta

$$\beta_a = \beta_e \frac{E}{E + D(1-t)}$$

$$\beta_a = 1.45 \frac{1,544}{1,544 + 428(1-0.3)}$$

$$= 1.21$$

Regearing asset beta to reflect Sleepon's gearing

$$\beta_e = 1.21 \frac{61.4 + 38.6(1-0.3)}{61.4}$$

$$= 1.74$$

Using CAPM

$$K_e = r_f + [E(r_m) - r_f]\beta_j$$
$$= 3.5 + (10 - 3.5)1.74 = 14.8\%$$

$K_d = 7.5\%$

$$WACC = (14.8 \times 0.614) + (7.5 (1 - 0.3) 0.386)$$
$$= 11.1\%, \text{ say } 11\%$$

Alternative solution using M&M formula

Using Thrillall's beta k_e = 12.925% and M&M k_e formula and **assuming k_d for Thrillall is the risk free rate of 3.5%** (consistent with BPP solutions which use a debt beta of 0 – clearly other approaches are possible here):

$$12.925 = k_e^1 + (k_e^1 - 3.5)(0.7)(460 \times 0.93)/(400 \times 3.86)$$
$$12.925 = k_e^1 + 0.194k_e^1 - 0.679$$
$$13.604 = 1.194k_e^1$$
$$k_e^1 = 11.394\%$$

Then regear using Sleepon's gearing given as a percentage, again assuming that k_d = risk free rate (consistent with BPP solutions which use a debt beta of 0 – clearly other approaches are possible here):

$$k_e = 11.394 + (11.394 - 3.5)(0.7)(38.6/61.4)$$
$$k_e = 11.394 + 3.474$$
$$k_e = 14.868\%$$

WACC is calculated using the standard formula and k_d as given:

$$WACC = (14.868 \times 0.614) + (7.5 \times 0.7 \times 0.386)$$
$$= 11.16\% \text{ (say 11\%)}$$

Appendix 2 – Modified internal rate of return

Return phase

Present values are taken from Appendix 1

	2	3	4	5
	$m	$m	$m	$m
Present value	2.0	5.0	6.7	189.6
Multiplier at 11% p.a.	1.368	1.232	1.11	1.0
Reinvested value	2.7	6.2	7.4	189.6

Terminal value of return phase = 2.7 + 6.2 + 7.4 + 189.6 = $205.9m

Investment phase

PV of investment phase = year 0 + year 1 = 200 + 226.6 = $426.6m

$$MIRR = \sqrt[5]{\frac{205.9}{426.6}} - 1 = 0.864 - 1 = -0.136 \text{ or } -13.6\% \text{ p.a.}$$

Appendix 3 – Duration

	2	3	4	5	Total
	$m	$m	$m	$m	$m
Present value	2.0	5.0	6.7	189.6	203.3
Percentage of total PV	1.0%	2.4%	3.3%	93.3%	100%
Year number × percentage	0.02	0.07	0.13	4.67	4.89

Project duration is 4.89 years

(b)   As noted in part (a) there are issues to be resolved regarding the **correlation** of these two activities. The diversification would make sense from a business point of view if the two activities are negatively correlated, meaning that one activity prospers when the other activity is not doing as well. This would help to make cash flows more regular which in turn would help with budgeting.

It seems unlikely that the two activities are negatively correlated, unless the hotels are sustained by business customers instead of tourism. Even so there may be corresponding periods of low demand from both sectors.

BPP
LEARNING MEDIA

From a shareholder point of view the diversification is unlikely to bring any additional **diversification benefits** as the shareholders could invest in the theme park industry themselves if they wish to. The shareholders will not appear be getting additional value as claimed by the CEO since the investment has a negative NPV.

Given that Sleepon has no experience in running theme parks it could be argued that the diversification would actually increase the **business risk** of Sleepon. In additional the fact that the project will be financed by debt means that **financial risk** is increased too. Sleepon would have a higher debt percentage than Thrillall if it undertakes the project, which may make the gearing level high for the theme park industry.

The lack or expertise may also mean that the CEO's comments about a **stronger brand** are untrue. There is a risk that the lack of expertise will mean the venture could fail, generating adverse publicity for Sleepon. There is also a danger that the two activities are too dissimilar to create a coherent brand across both activities. The luxury hotels are likely to appeal to a different clientele than the family oriented theme parks. It would be better to operate these two activities under different brands.

83 Fuelit

Text references. Chapter 5 on investment basics, Chapter 7a on WACC and Chapter 6 on real options.

Top tips. In (a) ensure that you answer the question and present two separate computations of NPV. Split computations into operational cash flows, which can be handled by annuities, and specific one-off cash flows, which cannot. The discount rate should be a risk adjusted WACC for each project, in each case inflation-adjusted to real terms.

Don't be too depressed about getting aspects of the calculations wrong; instead carefully work through the answer to see why you went wrong and make sure you don't make the same mistake next time! Do also give yourself credit for the parts of the answer you got right; the marking scheme basically set down 1 mark for each correct figure.

The best answers will have correctly calculated WACC, real cost of capital and the discounted cash flows.

The discussion parts of the question are probably worth half the marks and you should make sure you spend enough time on these, as it should be easier to gain marks on (b) and (d) in particular than on the more difficult calculations. The assumptions discussed in (b) range from those that only affect certain figures to those that change the whole picture (political changes or a disaster). Alternative scenarios, using different assumptions, may be helpful.

(c) indicates how uncertainty can be incorporated; the key points were understanding that risk might be different and that the discount rate should be reduced. Make sure that you have a knowledge of real options, as there may well be a discussion part at the end of a compulsory question similar to (d). As well as the options described, the option to delay investments may also be significant.

Easy marks. The calculations listed above in (a) and particularly (b) of the written parts. (b) requires you to look closely at your assumptions, and also think about wider issues that might affect strategy (stakeholder interests for example).

(a)   **Report**

   To: **The board of directors**
   From: **AN Adviser**

   Subject:

   The purpose of this report is to analyse the financial suitability of the investment in a gas or nuclear fuelled power station. The report also covers factors that have not been covered in the initial financial assessment.

   NPV of the two investments

   The gas investment has a net present value of $859.6 million (See appendix 1 for full calculations)

   The nuclear investment has a net present value of $1,498.3 million (See appendix 2 for full calculations)

   Conclusion

   On the basis of net present values applied to the estimates given, the nuclear plant should be chosen.

(b)   **Other information required**

The most significant factors to affect the decision which have not been taken into account above are:

(i)   **Social and political acceptability of more nuclear powered station**

If **public opinion** is heavily **against** nuclear power, the government is unlikely to risk its political majority by deciding in favour of it. Even if a vocal minority is the only opposition, construction could be severely delayed by demonstrations and sabotaging actions. **Social and political intelligence** is therefore vital information.

(ii)   **Risk of a rapid change in political acceptability of nuclear plants**

Future political acceptability may be influenced by a number of events. For example a number of **small leakages** could cause a nuclear plant to abandoned at any time during its life because of a fall in public acceptability. Threat of **terrorist action** may also cause political opinion to change. **Risk scenarios** need to be constructed and **contingency plans** devised.

(iii)   **Risk of a large-scale nuclear accident or gas explosion**

Such risks are not easily analysed by expected values and NPV computations, but both events have actually happened in the past. Information needs to be collected to **model** these events as **scenarios**.

(iv)   **Technical information**

It would be useful to evaluate the **technical information** underlying the projected construction and operation of the plants to ensure that best practice, particularly in **safety testing,** is envisaged and that costs are realistic to achieve the necessary quality. This may indicate how likely delays are during construction. **Industry information** on current developments would aid an evaluation of **how long** the stations would be **in operation**, and the consequences if technology changes. It might also enable a narrower estimate of the rage of **decommissioning costs** to be made.

(v)   **Economic information**

More details and accurate estimates could be obtained on, for example, expected future **demand** for power, annual **inflation** rate estimates (both in general and for individual cost items), and **interest rate movements.** The likelihood of the United Kingdom **joining the euro currency zone** is also significant. If the UK does not join the euro zone in the near future, there may be **uncertainties** attached to the **cost of debt**, which is denominated in euros for both projects. Based on existing predictions of inflation levels, the **euro** is likely to **depreciate** against the pound, making the cost of debt cheaper.

(vi)   **Fiscal changes**

Expected **future tax rates** and **capital allowances** may have a significant impact, including the possibility of 'green' taxes or constraints on polluting industries and likely treatment of gas and nuclear power under these taxes.

(vii)   **CAPM implications**

It would be useful to get more information about the **systematic risk** of the power industry, and how **different gearing levels** would affect the assessment of other projects and the company's overall valuation.

(viii) **The value of real options associated with each project**

As discussed in part (d) below, these are likely to be **higher** for the gas fuelled power station.

On the basis however of the estimates made, the NPV of the nuclear power alternative is so much higher than the gas alternative that further information on the accuracy of other general cash flow estimates is unlikely to change the decision.

If you have any questions about the content of this report, please feel free to contact me.

BPP
LEARNING MEDIA

Appendices

Appendix 1 Gas investment

Discounted cash flow estimates

Annual operating cash flows	First 10 years	Last 15 years
Years	4–13	14–28
	$m	
Annual revenues	800.000	
Annual costs		
Labour	75.000	
Gas purchases	500.000	
Sales and marketing expenses	40.000	As for years 4–13
Customer relations	5.000	
Other cash outlays	5.000	
	625.000	
Incremental taxable	175.000	
Tax at 30%	52.500	
After tax cash flows	122.500	
Tax credit on depreciation	18.000	
Incremental cash flow	140.500	122.500
Annuity factors at 6% (W1)		
Years 4-13 (8.853 – 2.673)	6.180	
Years 14-28		
(13.406** – 8.853)		4.553
Present value	868.300	557.700

* Tax credit on building costs depreciation 600 × 10% × 30% = $18m.

** Using formula $\dfrac{1-(1+r)^{-n}}{r}$ for annuity 1-28.

Other cash flows

Year	1	2	3	4	28
After tax redundancy costs ($m)				4	
Building costs (2 instalments) ($m)	300	300			
After tax demolition of coal fired station ($m)			10		
After tax demolition of gas plant ($m)					25
6% factors	0.943	0.890	0.840	0.792	0.196
Present value of costs ($m)	282.9	267.0	8.4	3.2	4.9

Total net present value = 868.3 + 557.7 – (282.9 + 267.0 + 8.4 + 3.2 + 4.9) = **$ 859.6 million**

Note: Interest is ignored from annual cost estimates because it (and the tax relief it attracts) is included in the after tax discount rate.

Workings

1   We need to calculate a WACC and convert it to a real cost of capital to discount the real cash flows of the investments.

Gas

$K_e = r_f + [E(r_m) - r_f] B_j = 4.5 + [14 - 4.5] 0.7 = 11.15\%$

$K_d = 8.5 (1 - 0.3) = 5.95\%$

WACC = (Equity weighting × K_e) + (Debt weighting × K_d)
    = (0.65 × 11.15) + (0.35 × 5.95) = 9.33%

As WACC is a nominal rate, convert to real rate.

$$\text{Real rate} = \frac{(1 + \text{nominal rate})}{(1 + \text{inflation rate})} - 1 = \frac{1.0933}{1.03} - 1 = 6.15\%, \text{ say } 6\%$$

Appendix 2 – Nuclear investment

Discounted cash flow estimates

Annual operating cash flows	First 10 years	Last 15 years
Years	4–13	14–28
	$m	$m
Annual revenues	800.000	
Annual costs		
Labour	20.000	
Nuclear fuel purchases	10.000	as for years 4–13
Sales and marketing expenses	40.000	
Customer relations	20.000	
Other cash outlays	25.000	
	115.000	
Incremental taxable cash flows	685.000	
Tax at 30%	205.500	
After tax cash flows	479.500	479.500
Tax credit on depreciation	99.000	
Incremental cash flow	578.500	479.500
Annuity factors at 8% (W1)		
Years 4-13		
(7.904 – 2.577)	5.327	
Years 14-28		
(11.051** – 7.904)		3.147
Present value	3,081.700	1,509.000

* Tax credit on building costs depreciation
  3,300 × 10% × 30% = $99m
** Using annuity formula

Other cash flows

Year	1	2	3	4	28
After tax redundancy costs ($m)				36	
Building costs (2 installments) ($m)	1,650	1,650			
After tax demolition of coal fired station ($m)			10		
After tax decommissioning of nuclear plant ($m)					1,000
8% factors	0.926	0.857	0.794	0.735	0.116
Present value of costs ($m)	1,527.9	1,414.1	7.9	26.5	116.0

Total net present value = 3,081.7 + 1,509.0 − (1,527.9 + 1,414.1 + 7.9 + 26.5 + 116.0)
    = **$1,498.3 million**

Note: If the lowest estimate of nuclear plant decommissioning cost was used, the net present value would be $1,558 million.

BPP
LEARNING MEDIA

Workings

1   We need to calculate a WACC and convert it to a real cost of capital to discount the real cash flows of the investments.

Nuclear

K_e = 4.5 + (14 − 4.5) 1.4 = 17.8%

K_d = 10 (1 − 0.3) = 7%

WACC = (0.4 × 17.8) + (0.6 × 7) = 11.32%

Real rate $= \dfrac{1.1132}{1.03} - 1 = 8.08\%$, say 8%

(c) **Highest cost estimate**

Perhaps the simplest way of dealing with the range of options available is to use the **highest cost estimate.**

Discount rate

A further way of dealing with the high uncertainty attached to the cost of decommissioning is to **decrease the discount rate** for the cost figure used.

Risk free rates

An alternative method of handling risk is to **discount at the risk free rate** and to **convert all cash forecasts to certainty-equivalents**. The certainty-equivalent for this cost would be **higher** than the expected value.

(d) **Real options**

An option is a choice which need only be exercised if it is to the investor's advantage. A 'real option' is such a **choice or opportunity** which exists because of a capital investment. The choice may involve being able to change plans once the project is underway. The opportunity also may not have been envisaged when the original plans were made, but may arise later on.

Options associated with the project

Options associated with the projects are in the main more valuable for the gas fuelled than for the nuclear power project. They include the following:

(i)   **The option to abandon the project early**
      This may be needed for a variety of reasons, for example because of falling demand or because of the emergence of a new technology. High decommissioning costs make this a problem for the nuclear powered project.

(ii) **The option to expand if demand increases**
      This is easier for gas because of the lower investment costs.

(iii) **The option to switch power source in the future**
      This is more valuable for gas, because the technology could be adapted for other fossil fuels, such as oil. Nuclear power technology has no easy power source alternatives.

The significance of these options is that they **add value** to the project and should be taken into account in the **investment appraisal**. Although the valuation is difficult, even a rough estimate is better than no estimate at all. On this basis, the gas fuelled project is likely to be relatively more valuable than shown in the original calculations.

(e) Fuelit could develop an **environmental policy** to illustrate to the public that it is serious about not causing unnecessary damage to the environment. This could involve setting environmental objectives and goals.

Fuelit could also start producing **environmental reports** for its external stakeholders, to show the effect it is having on the environment and also its achievement or progress towards its environmental targets.

Since Fuelit currently uses a coal-fuelled power station it will emit CO_2. It may seek to cap these emissions or could alternatively participate in **carbon trading** or a carbon **offsetting** scheme. Carbon trading demonstrates that Fuelit is trying to reduce the overall level of emissions. A carbon offsetting scheme could involve planting trees to compensate for the CO_2 emitted by Fuelit.

An **environmental audit** could also be carried out to show that Fuelit is being transparent and is committed to its environmental policy. This involves having the environment policy independently assessed and checks on the environmental performance being performed. This level of scrutiny would bring greater reassurance for the public about Fuelit's intention.

84 Aggrochem Co

Text references. Company valuations are covered in Chapter 10, sources of finance and capital structure are covered in Chapter 7a and regulatory issues on acquisitions in Chapter 11.

Top tips. Follow the instructions to produce a report – there are 4 marks available for clarity and presentation.

It is important to state any assumptions you make in your calculations, particularly in part (a) (i) where they are specifically required. When using the FCF model, start with the FCF formula which will highlight the figures you have to calculate. Growth rate can be determined using the retention rate and the cost of capital – note that Aggrochem is financed entirely by equity therefore the cost of capital can be assumed to be the cost of equity.

In part (b) the borrowing rates are the rates to use when calculating the interest; the investing rates are a red herring. You should be comparing like with like, so you need to compare the 6.3% at which the factor provides credit with the 6.5% at which the bank provides credit.

With the forward contract you use the forward rate for the receipts but the spot rate for the other calculations.

With the factor the interest calculations need to take into account that Aggrochem will not receive the full amount that it is owed even if all the customers pay up; however you need to calculate interest on the amount not received for comparison with the other options. Even if the customers default, the interest and the fee are still calculated on the higher amount guaranteed by the factor, the $1,590,000.

Easy marks. There are some easy marks in parts (a)(ii) and (iii) if you know the regulatory devices and can make some sensible points about capital structure and sources of finance.

Report

To: **Senior management of Aggrochem**
From: **Accountant**
Re: **Acquisition of LeverChem Co**

This report focuses on the proposed acquisition of LeverChem by Aggrochem. It includes an estimate of the value of Aggrochem, the potential sources of finance for the acquisition and any regulatory issues that may affect the takeover.

Market value of Aggrochem using the free cash flow model

Aggrochem is financed entirely by **equity** therefore we can assume that its **cost of capital is the same as its cost of equity**.

Estimated market value = Free Cash Flow (FCF) $\times (1 + g)/(k_e - g)$

Where g = growth rate k_e = cost of capital

Free Cash Flow = NOPAT – net investment in assets

$$= \$580,000 - \$180,000 = \$400,000$$

Cost of equity $(k_e) = R_f + \beta(R_m - R_f) = 5 + (6 \times 1.26) = 12.56\%$

Growth rate = retention rate x cost of capital

$$= (180/580) \times 12.56 = 3.90\%$$

Estimated market value = $400,000 \times (1.039)/(0.1256 - 0.039) = \$4,799,076$

BPP
LEARNING MEDIA

Assumptions

(i)   Future growth is constant.

(ii)   Discount rate will not change in the foreseeable future.

(iii) Growth rate is based on the assumption that retained earnings can be reinvested at the cost of capital.

(iv)   Aggrochem is a going concern.

(v)   The Free Cash Flow model gives a fair estimate of the value of Aggrochem.

Capital structure and source of finance for the acquisition

Given the belief that the market is undervaluing shares in Aggrochem it is proposed that a cash offer, rather than a share-for-share exchange is used for the acquisition.

Although Aggrochem is completely funded by equity, the acquisition will lead to it **taking on the $3m debt** of LeverChem). This needs to be considered when taking into account the Chief Executive's view that the capital structure is not optimal at present.

It is unusual for a listed company to be funded entirely by equity. Modigliani and Miller theorised that, in a world with corporate taxation, a company should **borrow as much as possible** to increase its value due to the tax shield on the debt. However this does not occur in reality, due to factors including tax exhaustion and financial distress costs. Alternative theories such as static-trade off theory or traditional theory state that there is an optimal capital structure that gives a company its lowest WACC. The WACC will increase if the level of borrowing increases above this optimal point. It is suggested that the industry average gearing ratio may represent a capital structure that is close to the optimal one.

Traditional theory and static trade-off theory suggest that the firm should **increase its gearing** to capture further tax shield effects which are not currently being offset by increased default risk. Thus debt finance should be preferred to equity finance. Raising $2 million of debt by borrowing would represent a gearing level of 31% (2/(2+4.4)) for Aggrochem at the moment, which is generally seen as low, but it is difficult to comment on this without knowing the average financial gearing level for the industry. The only comparison that can be made is to LeverChem which currently has a gearing ratio of 71% (3/4.2). If this is typical across the industrythen Aggrochem would be able to borrow $2 million to fund the acquisition which would also mean it takes on an additional $3 million of debt and still has a sensible gearing level. This level of debt is likely to be generated through a bank loan as this amount would be very small for a bond issue.

Another potential source of debt finance is on the **sale and leaseback of assets**. If the assets are not owned but leased or rented then there are financial reporting implications, depending upon whether the leases are financing or operating leases. It is not clear from the information provided whether Aggrochem has assets that are suitable for sale and leaseback and so no further comment can be made on this.

Other sources of finance would be to raise equity capital by a **rights or new issue**. This would have the effect of increasing the weighted average cost of capital and would not provide any additional benefits of the tax shield.This would also be more expensive than any of the methods of raising debt, although a rights issue would be cheaper than a new issue of equity.

Recommendation

It is worth investigating the industry average gearing level before making any final decision, but if LeverChem's capital structure is representative of the industry then it is recommended that Aggrochem borrows $2 million to fund the acquisition and takes advantage of the tax shield from this borrowing and the loan that is currently LeverChem's.

Regulatory devices

There are seven main regulatory devices which can apply to a takeover situation. These are as follows:

Mandatory bid rule

Based on the UK threshold, Aggrochem Co would pass the mandatory bid limit level of share ownership when it acquires 30% of LeverChem, which would allow the minority shareholders to sell their remaining shares at a **fair price**. This means Aggrochem Co would have to make a bid for the remaining shares at a price that is not lower than the price paid for any of the already purchased shares.

The principle of equal treatment

The principle of treating all shareholders equally does not differ too much from the provisions of the mandatory bid rule. In general terms, the principle of equal treatment requires the bidder to offer to any remaining shareholders the **same terms** as those offered to the previous shareholders who have already sold their shares.

The squeeze-out rule and sell-out rights

The squeeze-out rule gives the bidder who has acquired a specific percentage of the equity (usually 90%) the right to force minority shareholders to sell their shares. The rule enables the bidder to acquire 100% of the equity once the threshold percentage has been reached and eliminates potential problems that could be caused by minority shareholders.

Sell-out rights would mean that the minority shareholders can **compel**   Co to buy all of the remaining shares, rather than leave them as a minority group who have no say in the new company. This prevents Aggrochem saving money by not buying out the minority group.

The one share-one vote principle

Where the one share-one vote principle is upheld, arrangements restricting voting rights are forbidden.

Differentiated voting rights, such as non-voting shares and dual-clan shares with multiple voting rights, enable some shareholders to accumulate control at the expense of other shareholders and could provide a significant barrier to potential takeovers.

The break- through rule

If differentiated voting rights exist which allow the remaining minority shareholders to control LeverChem once Aggrochem Co has purchased a majority of the shares in number, the break-through rule could be used to allow Aggrochem Co to **exercise control** by applying the one share-one vote principle.

Transparency of ownership and control

The disclosure of information about major shareholdings is an important element of investor protection and a well-functioning corporate market. The transparency enables the regulator to **monitor large shareholders**, minimise potential agency problems and investigate insider dealing. It also enables both minority shareholders and the market to monitor large shareholders who may be able to exercise undue influence or exact benefits at the expense of other shareholdings.

Board neutrality and anti-takeover measures

Seeking to address the agency issue where managersmay be tempted to act in their own interests at the expense of the interests of the shareholders, several regulatory devices propose board neutrality. For instance LeverChem's board would not be permitted to carry out **post-bid aggressive defensive tactics** (such as selling LeverChem's main assets, known as the crown jewels defence, or entering into special arrangements giving rights to existing shareholders to buy shares at a low price, known as the poison pill defence), without the prior authority of the shareholders.

Should you wish to discuss any of these issues, please do not hesitate to contact me.

(b)   (i)   **Forward market hedge and insurance policy**

                Advantages

                (1)   The hedge takes away any **uncertainty** involved in the **exchange rate** that will apply if the insurance company makes a **payment**.

                (2)   The insurance policy guarantees the **minimum amount** Aggrochem will receive.

                Disadvantages

                (1)   Aggrochem will have to pay a **premium** for the insurance policy that will take into account the cost of insurance and the **cost of a forward hedge**.

                (2)   The **insurance policy** may turn out to be unnecessary; Aggrochem may receive all monies on time.

                (3)   Aggrochem still has to bear a **residual risk**.

Net receipts if all monies are received on time

	$
Receipts $\dfrac{55 \text{ million}}{34.55}$	1,591,896
Interest $\dfrac{55 \text{ million}}{32.89} \times 6.5\% \times 3/12$	(27,174)
Insurance cost $\dfrac{55 \text{ million}}{32.89} \times 1.25\%$	(20,903)
	1,543,819

Net receipts if customers default

	$
Receipts $\dfrac{55 \text{ million}}{35.9} \times 90\%$	1,378,830
Interest $\dfrac{55 \text{ million}}{32.89} \times 6.5\% \times 6/12$	(54,348)
Insurance cost $\dfrac{55 \text{ million}}{32.89} \times 1.25\%$	(20,903)
	1,303,579

Expected value = (0.95 × 1,543,819) + (0.05 × 1,303,579) = $1,531,807

(ii) **Use of export factor**

Advantages

(1) Use of the factor **removes any foreign exchange risk** as the payments are in $.

(2) The factor guarantees that up to **80%** of the finance is payable immediately. The factor's terms for lending this money are more favourable than the current bank borrowing rate.

(3) The factor will apparently **take over the collection of debts** and the pursuit of slow payers. The factor's greater experience of collecting debts may mean it is more likely that monies will eventually be received.

(4) As the factor is non-recourse, the factor will **bear most of the risk of default** (although Aggrochem will receive a lower sum if there is default).

(5) Aggrochem may **save the administrative costs** of undertaking the debt collection itself.

Disadvantages

(1) The **administration fee** has to be **paid** whatever happens.

(2) The factor may not be **prepared to** offer a single deal, but will **require further business** to be undertaken.

Net receipts if all monies are received on time

	$
Receipts	1,590,000
Interest, amounts advanced (1,590,000 × 80% × 6.3% × 3/12)	(20,034)
Interest, remaining part of $1,590,000 not advanced (1,590,000 × 20% × 6.5% × 3/12)	(5,168)
Interest on amounts not factored (($\dfrac{55,000,000}{32.89}$ – 1,590,000) × 6.5% × 3/12)	(1,336)
Factor fee (1,590,000 × 2.5%)	(39,750)
	1,523,712

Net receipts if customers default

	$
Receipts	1,530,000
Interest, amounts advanced (1,590,000 × 80% × 6.3% × 6/12)	(40,068)
Interest, remaining part of $1,590,000 not advanced (1,590,000 × 20% × 6.5% × 6/12)	(10,335)
Interest on amounts not factored (($\frac{55,000,000}{32.89}$ − 1,590,000) × 6.5% × 6/12)	(2,673)
Factor fee (1,590,000 × 2.5%)	(39,750)
	1,437,174

Expected value = (0.95 × 1,523,712) + (0.05 × 1,437,174) = $1,519,385

(iii) **Documentary letter of credit**

Advantages

(i) Aggrochem can receive **immediate monies** from the **letter of credit** by discounting the bill in Xeridia and converting the proceeds.

(ii) The **ultimate receipt** is **unaffected** by whether the customer pays or not. If Aggrochem considers the risk of non-payment to be high, this is significant. The **guaranteeing banks** will bear the risk of non-payment.

(iii) The **terms of the letter of credit** might **appeal** to customers.

(iv) Because the letter of credit is **irrevocable**, the customers cannot change its terms.

Disadvantages

Documentary credits are **slow to arrange** and **administratively cumbersome**.

	$
Receipts ($\frac{55\ million}{32.89}$)	1,672,241
Discount on bill ($\frac{55\ million}{32.89}$ × 25% × 3/12)	(104,515)
Fees	(30,000)
	1,537,726

Conclusion

The letter of credit appears to be the best option, as it offers a higher net receipt than the best options of either of the other possibilities.

BPP LEARNING MEDIA

Mock exams

BPP
LEARNING MEDIA

ACCA Professional Level

Paper P4

Advanced Financial Management

Mock Examination 1

Question Paper	
Time allowed	
Reading and Planning Writing	**15 minutes** **3 hours**
Section A THIS question is compulsory and MUST be attempted Section B TWO questions ONLY to be attempted	
During reading and planning time only the question paper may be annotated	

DO NOT OPEN THIS PAPER UNTIL YOU ARE READY TO START UNDER EXAMINATION CONDITIONS

BPP
LEARNING MEDIA

SECTION A: THIS QUESTION is compulsory and MUST be attempted

Question 1

Daron is a listed public company located in a European country. Its senior management are reviewing the company's medium-term prospects. The company is heavily dependent on a single product. A general election will take place in the near future and the managers believe that the future level of inflation will depend upon the result of the election. Inflation is expected to remain at approximately 5% if political party A (the political party currently in government) wins the election, or will quickly move to approximately 10% per year if party B wins the election. Opinion polls suggest that there is a 40% chance of party B winning.

Projected financial data for the next five years, including expected inflation where relevant, are shown below.

Political party A wins, inflation 5% per year

	$million				
	20X7	*20X8*	*20X9*	*20Y0*	*20Y1*
Operating cash flows:					
Sales	28	29	26	22	19
Variable costs	17	18	16	14	12
Fixed costs	3	3	3	3	3
Other financial data:					
Incremental working capital*	–	(1)	(2)	(3)	(3)
Tax allowable depreciation	4	3	3	2	1
Replacement investment (not tax allowable)	10	–	–	–	5

Political party B wins, inflation 10% per year

	$million				
	20X7	*20X8*	*20X9*	*20Y0*	*20Y1*
Operating cash flows:					
Sales	30	26	24	20	16
Variable costs	18	16	15	12	11
Fixed costs	3	3	4	4	4
Other financial data:					
Incremental working capital*	1	(2)	(2)	(3)	(3)
Tax allowable depreciation	4	3	3	2	1
Replacement investment (not tax allowable)	10	–	–	–	5

* A bracket signifies a decrease in working capital.

Tax allowable depreciation will be negligible after 20Y1 in both cases. Taxable cash flows after year 20Y1, excluding tax savings from tax allowable depreciation, are expected to be similar to year 20Y1 cash flows for a period of five years, after which substantial new fixed investment would be necessary in order to continue operations. However no replacement investment will be necessary between 20Y2 and 20Y6.

Working capital will remain approximately constant after the year 20Y1. Corporation taxation is at a rate of 30% per year, and is expected to continue at this rate. Tax may be assumed to be payable in the year that the income arises.

Daron's current ordinary share price is 46 centos. (100 centos = $1).

The Finance Director has received a report from a consultancy firm which includes a prediction that whichever political party wins the election, the independent central bank will have to raise short-term interest rates as a monetary policy measure to prevent the rate of inflation from rising even higher than the 5% or 10% estimated for the investment appraisal. An increase in interest rates would have a significant adverse effect on consumer demand in the economy.

The company's remuneration committee has just come up with a new incentive scheme for senior executives involving the granting of company shares. The intention would be to create a pool of shares by repurchasing shares in the stock market, and awarding them to executives who meet performance targets. At the moment the company does not have any long-term incentive scheme for executives, but there are generous bonus schemes based on annual profit performance. The finance director, although a potential beneficiary from this scheme, is concerned about the possible reaction of major shareholders to an announcement of the scheme, and the possible financial implications for the company.

Summarised statement of financial position of Daron as at 31 March 20X6

	$m
Tangible non-current assets	17
Net current assets	12
Total assets less current liabilities	29
Loans and other borrowings falling due after one year	7
Capital and reserves:	
Called up share capital (25 cents par value)	5
Reserves	17
	29

The company can currently borrow long-term from its bank at an interest rate of 10% per year. This is likely to quickly rise to 15.5% per year if the political party B wins the election. The real risk free rate (ie excluding inflation) is 4% and the real market return is 10%.

Daron's equity beta is estimated to be 1.25. This is not expected to significantly change if inflation increases.

Three alternatives are available to the managers of Daron.

(i) Recommend the sale of the company now. An informal, unpublicised, offer of $10 million for the company's shares has been received from a competitor.

(ii) Continue existing operations, with negligible capital investment for the foreseeable future.

(iii) If the political party A wins the election, diversify operations by buying a going concern in the hotel industry at a cost of $9 million. The purchase would be financed by the issue of 10% convertible loan stock. Issue costs are 2% of the gross sum raised. Daron has no previous experience of the hotel industry.

Financial projections for the hotel purchase

	$million				
	20X7	*20X8*	*20X9*	*20Y0*	*20Y1*
Revenue	9	10	11	12	13
Variable costs	6	6	7	7	8
Fixed costs	2	2	2	2	2
Other financial data:					
Incremental working capital	1	–	–	1	–

Tax allowable depreciation is negligible for the hotel purchase. The after tax realisable value of the hotel at the end of year 20Y1 is expected to be $10 million, including working capital. The systematic risk of operating the hotels is believed to be similar to that of the company's existing operations.

Required

(a) Prepare a report advising the senior management of Daron which, if any, of the three alternatives they should recommend to the board of directors for adoption. Your report should include comment on any weaknesses/limitations of your data analysis. The report should also contain appendices that show relevant calculations, including:

  (i) Estimates of the present values of future free cash flows from existing operations, and
  (ii) The estimated adjusted present value of diversifying into the hotel industry

The book value and market value of debt may be assumed to be the same. State clearly any other assumptions that you make. **(30 marks)**

Professional marks for format, structure and presentation of the report for part (a) **(4 marks)**

(b) Discuss the possible financial implications for Daron of an increase in short-term interest rates by the central bank soon after the general election. **(6 marks)**

(c) Discuss the issues that the board of directors should consider before it asks the company's shareholders to approve the share incentive scheme for senior executives. **(10 marks)**

(Total = 50 marks)

BPP
LEARNING MEDIA

SECTION B: TWO QUESTIONS ONLY to be attempted
Question 2

(a) Retilon plc is a medium sized UK company that trades with companies in several European countries. Trade deals over the next three months are shown below. Assume that it is now 20 April.

	Two months time		Three months time	
	Receipts	Payments	Receipts	Payments
France	–	€393,265	€491,011	€60,505
Germany	–	–	€890,217	€1,997,651
Denmark	–	–	Kr 8.6m	–

Foreign exchange rates:

	Dkroner/£	Euro €/£
Spot	10.68 – 10.71	1.439 – 1.465
Two months forward	10.74 – 10.77	1.433 – 1.459
Three months forward	10.78 – 10.83	1.431 – 1.456

Annual interest rates (valid for 2 months or 3 months)

	Borrowing %	Investing %
United Kingdom	7.50	5.50
France	5.75	3.50
Germany	5.75	3.50
Denmark	8.00	6.00

Futures market rates

Three month Euro contracts (125,000 Euro contract size)

Contracts are for buying or selling Euros. Futures prices are in £ per Euro.

June	0.6964
September	0.6983
December	0.7013

Required

(i) Using the forward market, money market and currency futures market as appropriate devise a foreign exchange hedging strategy that is expected to maximise the cash flows of Retilon plc at the end of the three month period.

Transactions costs and margin requirements may be ignored for this part of the question. Basis risk may be assumed to be zero at the time the contracts are closed out. Futures contracts may be assumed to mature at the month end. **(15 marks)**

(ii) Successive daily prices on the futures market for a June contract which you have sold are:

Selling price	0.6916
Day 1	0.6930
Day 2	0.6944
Day 3	0.6940

Initial margins are £1,000 per contract. Variation margin is 100% of the initial margin.

Spot exchange rates may be assumed not to change significantly during these three days.

For each of the three days, show the effect on your cash flow of the price changes of the contract. **(4 marks)**

(b) Discuss the advantages and disadvantages of forward contracts and currency futures for hedging against foreign exchange risk. **(6 marks)**

(Total = 25 marks)

Question 3

Impex, a major food and beverage retailer, is considering a takeover of a small unlisted competitor in order to build market share. The business is, however, concerned about volatility, and the Chairman, who has been talking to the company's stockbrokers, wishes to monitor the value at risk for the business and make appropriate assessments for any investment opportunities.

Impex has 268m shares in issue on which it recently paid a dividend of 156c per share. Dividends have been growing steadily at 2.5% pa and the brokers have informed the chairman that the shares of the company have a beta of 0.98.

The company is geared with $3.26bn of 5.8% perpetual debt in issue which has an AA credit rating.

The target company, Elfix, generated earnings per share excluding interest (and tax thereon) of 80c last year and has a policy of distributing 60% of its earnings. Elfix has $220m of 15 year 7% debt in issue that is rated A2. Elfix has 57 million shares in issue.

General market statistics are that the risk-free rate is 6% and the market is returning 10% at a risk of 8%. The tax rate is 30%. Yield spreads for the wholesale sector in basis points are

Rating	5 yr	10 yr	15 yr	30 yr
AA	15	20	30	50
A2	80	95	107	120

Required

(a) Calculate the equity, debt and total market values of both companies along with the equity, debt and overall betas for both companies and an estimate of the share price for Elfix. **(17 marks)**

(b) Calculate the 3 month value at risk at a 1% level for shareholders, debt holders and the company overall for each company assuming zero unsystematic risk in each company. **(8 marks)**

(Total = 25 marks)

Question 4

A division of Reflator Inc has recently experienced severe financial difficulties. The management of the division is keen to undertake a buyout, but in order for the buyout to succeed it needs to attract substantial finance from a venture capital organisation. Reflator Inc is willing to sell the division for $2.1 million, and the managers believe that an additional $1 million of capital would need to be invested in the division to create a viable going concern.

Possible financing sources

Equity from management $500,000, in 50 cents ordinary shares.

Funds from the venture capital organisation

Equity $300,000, in 50 cents ordinary shares
Debt: 8.5% fixed rate loan $2,000,000
9% subordinated loan with warrants attached $300,000.

The warrants are exercisable any time after four years from now at the rate of 100 ordinary shares at the price of 150 cents per share for every $100 of subordinated loan.

The principal on the 8.5% fixed rate loan is repayable as a bullet payment at the end of eight years. The subordinated loan is repayable by equal annual payments, comprising both interest and principal, over a period of six years.

The division's managers propose to keep dividends to no more than 15% of profits for the first four years. Independently produced forecasts of earnings before tax and interest after the buyout are shown below:

	$'000			
Year	1	2	3	4
EBIT	320	410	500	540

Corporate tax is at the rate of 30% per year.

The managers involved in the buyout have stated that the book value of equity is likely to increase by about 20% per year during the first four years, making the investment very attractive to the venture capital organisation. The venture capital organisation has stated that it is interested in investing, but has doubts about the forecast growth rate of equity value, and would require warrants for 150 shares per $100 of subordinated loan stock rather than 100 shares.

Required

(a) Discuss the potential advantages of a management buyout of the division, compared to selling to a third party. Do not limit discussion to advantages for Reflator Inc. **(7 marks)**

(b) On the basis of the above data, estimate whether or not the book value of equity is likely to grow by 20% per year. **(7 marks)**

(c) Evaluate the possible implication of the managers agreeing to offer warrants for 150 ordinary shares per $100 of loan stock. **(4 marks)**

(d) Produce a short memorandum explaining the role of a venture capitalist in this management buyout. You should also mention the typical requirements the venture capital organisation will demand from the buyout team. **(7 marks)**

(Total = 25 marks)

BPP
LEARNING MEDIA

Answers

**DO NOT TURN THIS PAGE UNTIL YOU HAVE
COMPLETED THE MOCK EXAM**

BPP
LEARNING MEDIA

A plan of attack

You have no doubt been told to do it about 200 times and we know if we asked you you'd know that you should do it. So why don't you do it in an exam? 'Do what in an exam?' you're no doubt thinking. Well for the 201st time let's enlighten you. **Take a good look through the paper before diving in to answer questions.**

First things first

You are given 15 minutes' reading time before the exam begins. During that time you can obviously read the paper and make notes on the question paper *only*. You can also use your calculator to carry out preliminary calculations. The reading time most importantly allows you to carefully read and understand the question requirements and choose which optional questions you are going to attempt. You can also decide in which order you are going to attempt the questions. If you still have time after doing all that, you can start to plan how you are going to structure your answers.

The next step

When the 3 hours' writing time begins you will probably be in one of two minds – either still not knowing where to start or feeling reasonably confident about the questions.

Option 1 (if you don't know where to begin)

If you are a bit worried about the paper and not feeling overly confident about answering any of the questions, you might be as well to start at the beginning with the compulsory Section A question.

- **Question 1** is quite daunting as there is a large amount of information in the question. Start with the calculations first, ensuring that you take account of each of the two scenarios and remembering at all times that you are actually required to produce a *report*. Probably the best way to do this is to put the calculations into appendices (as per the model solution). As there are numerous calculations, make sure you label these clearly, as much for your own benefit as for the marker's. The discussion parts (b) and (c) could be attempted first as they do not depend on earlier answers.

- **Question 2** may look daunting, but the discussion in part (c) could be attempted first and pick you up some relatively easy marks. Also forward market and money market hedge calculations are easier than some other types of hedging and you should be able to pick up enough marks to pass this question.

- **Question 3** is a valuation question – if you are not comfortable with valuation calculations it would be a good idea to avoid this question.

- **Question 4** deals with management buy-outs. None of the calculations are particularly difficult, although a tabular approach to section (b) will save you some time.

What you should always remember is that you **must** answer the question in Section A but only **two** questions from Section B.

Option 2 (if you're thinking 'I can do all of these')

Whilst it is never wise to be over confident, if you feel you can answer all of the required questions reasonably well, start with the one you are most comfortable with. If you want to get the 50 mark compulsory question out of the way first then take that approach but don't feel you have to. However make sure you don't spend too much time on any particular question, regardless of how much you think you can write. If you are comfortable with the question and cannot answer it in the time allowed (remember 1.8 minutes per mark) then you are probably writing too much.

- **Question 1** – don't forget that you are required to write a *report* so make sure you use a suitable format. Calculations should normally be included in appendices with your commentary within the main body of the report. Don't spend too long on the calculations as the examiner is likely to be more interested in your ability to comment on the results. Also make sure your discussion is appropriate to the question.

- **Question 2** – it would be easy to spend too much time on the narrative parts of this question if you are familiar with the subject but these only account of 6 marks out of 25. Whilst you should obviously demonstrate your knowledge avoid writing pages and pages as you will just be wasting time. In part (a) (i) make sure you answer the question – that is, which hedging strategy is expected to maximise cash flows. Just calculating the figures won't gain you maximum marks.

- **Question 3** – remember to explain your calculations and to lay them out in a logical manner which is easy to follow. The key when calculating Elfix's values is to assume that the asset betas are the same for both companies.

- **Question 4** – make sure you read section (d) carefully as it asks you to specifically refer to the management buy-out in the question rather than just a general discussion.

No matter how many times we remind you...

Always allocate your time according to the marks for the question in total and for the individual parts of each question. Also **always answer the question you were asked** rather than the question you wished you had been asked or the question you thought you had been asked.

You've got free time at the end of the exam...?

If you have allocated your time properly then you **shouldn't have time on your hands** at the end of the exam. If you find yourself with some time at the end, however, go back to **any parts of questions that you didn't finish** because you moved onto another question.

Forget about it!

Don't worry if you found the paper difficult – if you did, no doubt other students would too. If this was the real thing you would have to forget about it as soon as you leave the exam hall and **think about the next one**. If it was the last one however – **celebrate!**

Question 1

Text references. APV is covered in Chapter 7a; NPV in Chapter 5; Financial strategy in Chapter 2; Conflicting stakeholder interests in Chapter 3a.

Top tips. In part (a), it is inappropriate to calculate expected values since the two scenarios are mutually exclusive. The only complex part of the present value analysis should be the calculation of the cost of capital. As we are told the financial data includes inflation but at varying rates, this means that the figures have to be discounted at the nominal cost of capital. Hence the real risk free rate and market return have to be adjusted for inflation.

The starting point for the adjusted present value calculation is calculating the base case NPV by ungearing the company's equity beta, in order to obtain a beta that can used in the CAPM equation to find the ungeared cost of equity. The ungeared cost of equity is in turn used in the base case NPV calculation.

Remember that Dt is only used to find the tax shield if interest is paid for an indefinite period (debt is irredeemable), Otherwise an NPV calculation has to be carried out.

In your discussion it is important to identify the strategic implications as well as the technical limitations of the calculations.

In part (b) you should think about the implications of an increase in short-term interest rates for a national economy, but you should then apply your understanding to the specific circumstances of the company in the question.

Similarly in part (c), although it is relevant to discuss agency theory, it is also important to consider the issues and the questions that arise for this company.

Easy marks. Base case NPV calculations are assumed knowledge from Paper F9 and should therefore present few problems. Some marks will be earned in parts (b) and (c) from a basic knowledge of monetary economic and agency theory.

Marking scheme

		Marks
(a)	Scenario 1 – taxable cash flows	1
	Scenario 1 – tax	1
	Scenario 1 – tax credit on depreciation	1
	Scenario 1 – working capital movement	1
	Scenario 1 – replacement investment	1
	Scenario 1 – calculation of discount rate	2
	Scenario 1 – Post 20Y1 cash flows	2
	Scenario 2 – taxable cash flows	1
	Scenario 2 – tax	1
	Scenario 2 – tax credit on depreciation	1
	Scenario 2 – calculation of discount rate	2
	Scenario 2 – Post 20Y1 cash flows	2
	Base case NPV – taxable income	1
	Base case NPV – tax	1
	Base case NPV – purchase cost / realisable value	1
	Base case NPV – working capital movement	1
	Base case NPV – calculation of discount rate	2
	Issue costs of debt	1
	PV of tax relief savings	2
	Discussion and assumptions	2
	Diversification discussion	3

30

Report format	1	
Layout, presentation and structure	<u>3</u>	
		4

(b)	1 mark per relevant point		Max 6
(c)	Conflict of interests	3 – 4	
	Current remuneration commentary	2 – 3	
	Dividend expectations	2 – 3	
	Conclusion	<u>1 – 2</u>	
			Max <u>10</u>
			<u><u>50</u></u>

(a)

REPORT

To: Managers of Daron
From: Company Accountant
Date: 14 December 20X6
Subject: **Long-term strategic options**

Strategic options

The purpose of this report is to evaluate the **strategic options** available to the company, namely an immediate sale of the company, continuation of existing operations, and diversification in the event of party A winning the forthcoming election.

Sale of the company

This option can be evaluated in terms of the value of the offer to the shareholders. The informal offer of $10m from the competitor compares with the current market value of the equity of $9.2m (20m × $0.46), a premium of 8.7%. However, it is perhaps more helpful to attempt a valuation of the company based on future cash flows, and figures illustrating this are included in Appendix 1 of this report. These suggest that if party A wins the election, the NPV of the future cash flows will amount to $18.8m, whereas if party B wins, the NPV will be $10.4m. Both of these are in excess of the competitor's offer, suggesting that if the shareholders do wish to sell they should seek a higher price for the company. However, these estimates are subject to a number of uncertainties which will be considered further in the next section of the report.

The shareholders will also need to consider some of the other implications of selling, such as the effect on the other stakeholders in the firm. For example, will many jobs be lost in redundancies? How will customers and the local community be affected by such a decision?

Continue existing operations

The figures contained in Appendix 1 represent a projection of performance for the ten year period up to 20Y6. However, when forecasting over such a long timescale the likelihood of inaccuracy increases, particular areas of potential error being as follows.

(a)   The assumption that the **cost of capital** will remain **constant** throughout the period
(b)   The assumptions made about the **inflation rate**
(c)   The **effect on economic conditions** of possible further elections beyond the one in the immediate future
(d)   The assumption that the **tax rate** will remain constant at 30%
(e)   Errors in the projections of sales revenues and costs

A further major assumption built into the figures is that there will be no significant additional capital investment throughout this period. This raises a number of questions, including the following.

(a)   Will **other opportunities** be **forgone** during this period if the company starts to lag behind its competitors in technology?
(b)   Will significant major new investment be required beyond 20Y1 to allow the company to continue operations?

(c) What is the realisable value of the company in 20Y1?

This final factor could also have a significant impact on the calculations in Appendix 1, and could mean that the true value of the future cash flows for the period in question is even higher than the figures suggest.

In view of the uncertainties described, it is proposed that further work needs to be done, particularly in investigating the sensitivities of the NPVs to changes in assumptions concerning the key variables.

Diversification into hotel industry

The figures relating to the diversification are contained in Appendix 2. These suggest that the project should yield a NPV of $0.56m. However, a major element in this forecast is the **terminal value** of $10m **on disposal** in 20Y1, and any variation in the amount realised is likely to have a significant effect on the projections. Again it is suggested that sensitivity analysis be undertaken to establish the impact of changes in this variable.

In addition to making the financial evaluation, Daron needs to consider the **investment** in the light of its **strategic objectives**. If the investment is essentially opportunistic with the diversification being for the benefit of the shareholders in terms of reducing their level of risk, this may be a mistaken goal. The shareholders can achieve diversification of their portfolios by themselves in their choice of other investments, and are unlikely to look to Daron to achieve this for them.

The key question is what the **company strategy** is to be in the face of the declining market for its core business. It may well be appropriate to seek **diversification** as a means for survival and growth, but the markets into which Daron seeks to diversify should be carefully chosen and should ideally be related in some way, be it **technological basis** or customer spread, to those in which it currently operates. The greater the departure from its existing experience, the greater the risk that the diversification will be less successful than anticipated.

Conclusions

Daron needs to consider its **long-term strategic objectives** and the **desires** of its **shareholders** before making any choices between the options facing it. If sale is perceived to be the best option, then the directors should seek to present the company to the market in the best possible light so as to **maximise the disposal proceeds**, and not just take the offer from the competitor because it is there. If continuing the existing business is desired, careful attention should be given to **long-term market conditions** and to the effect of alternative investment policies. If diversification is to be pursued then products and markets should be properly evaluated to obtain the best fit with the existing business.

Appendix 1: Estimates of the present value of Daron

Scenario 1: Party A wins the election

	20X7 $m	20X8 $m	20X9 $m	20Y0 $m	20Y1 $m
Sales	28.0	29.0	26.0	22.0	19.0
Variable costs	(17.0)	(18.0)	(16.0)	(14.0)	(12.0)
Fixed costs	(3.0)	(3.0)	(3.0)	(3.0)	(3.0)
Taxable cash flows	8.0	8.0	7.0	5.0	4.0
Tax at 30%	(2.4)	(2.4)	(2.1)	(1.5)	(1.2)
Post tax cash flows	5.6	5.6	4.9	3.5	2.8
Tax credit on depreciation					
(30% × tax allowable depreciation)	1.2	0.9	0.9	0.6	0.3
Working capital movement		1.0	2.0	3.0	3.0
Replacement investment	(10.0)				(5.0)
Free cash flow	(3.2)	7.5	7.8	7.1	1.1
13% discount factors (see Note 1)	0.885	0.783	0.693	0.613	0.543
PV cash flow	(2.8)	5.9	5.4	4.4	0.6

Total PV = $13.5 million (20X7 – 20Y1)

To these figures must be added the PV cash flow for the period 20Y2-20Y6. This can be found by applying the 13% annuity value for periods 6 to 10 (5.426 –3.517=1.909) to the annual cash flows. These cash flows will be similar to those for 20Y1 excluding tax credit on depreciation, working capital movements and replacement investment.

	$m
Sales	19.0
Variable costs	(12.0)
Fixed costs	(3.0)
Taxable income	4.0
Tax at 30%	(1.2)
Annual cash flow	2.8
Annuity value	1.909
PV cash flow	5.3

The NPV of the free cash flows for the period 20X7 to 20Y6 is therefore $13.5m + $5.3m = $18.8m.

Note 1. The discount rate to be used is the cost of capital. This can be estimated by finding the cost of equity using the CAPM, and then weighting the relative costs of debt and equity on the basis of market values.

The current market value of equity is 20m × $0.46 = $9.2m. It is assumed that the balance sheet value of the debt approximates to its market value ie $7m. Its cost (Kd) is taken as the current bank rate of 10%. The risk free rate of return including inflation is $(1.05 \times 1.04) - 1 = 9.2\%$. The market rate of return including inflation is $(1.10 \times 1.05) - 1 = 15.5\%$.

Using the CAPM: $E(r_j)$ = $r_f + [E(r_m) - r_f]\ \beta_j$
  = $9.2\% + [15.5\% - 9.2\%] \times 1.25\% = 17.075\%$

The WACC can now be estimated.

$$WACC = \left[\frac{V_e}{V_e + V_d}\right]k_e + \left[\frac{V_d}{V_e + V_d}\right]k_d\,(1\text{-}T)$$
$$= 17.075\% \times 9.2/(9.2 + 7) + 10\% \times (1 - 0.3) \times 7/(9.2 + 7)$$
$$= 12.72\%\ (\text{approx } 13\%)$$

Scenario 2: Party B wins the election

	20X7	20X8	20X9	20Y0	20Y1
	$m	$m	$m	$m	$m
Sales	30.0	26.0	24.0	20.0	16.0
Variable costs	(18.0)	(16.0)	(15.0)	(12.0)	(11.0)
Fixed costs	(3.0)	(3.0)	(4.0)	(4.0)	(4.0)
Taxable cash flows	9.0	7.0	5.0	4.0	1.0
Tax at 30%	(2.7)	(2.1)	(1.5)	(1.2)	(0.3)
Post tax cash flows	6.3	4.9	3.5	2.8	0.7
Tax credit on depreciation	1.2	0.9	0.9	0.6	0.3
Working capital movement	(1.0)	2.0	2.0	3.0	3.0
Replacement capital expenditure	(10.0)				(5.0)
Net cash flow	(3.5)	7.8	6.4	6.4	(1.0)
18% discount factors (see Note 2)	0.847	0.718	0.609	0.516	0.437
PV cash flow	(3.0)	5.6	3.9	3.3	(0.4)

Total PV = $9.4 million (20X7-20Y1)

The PV cash flow for the period 20Y2-20Y6 can be found by applying the 18% annuity value for periods 6 to 10 (4.494 – 3.127=1.367) to the annual cash flows. These cash flows will be as for 20Y1 excluding depreciation, working capital movements and replacement capital expenditure.

BPP
LEARNING MEDIA

	$m
Sales	16.0
Variable costs	(11.0)
Fixed costs	(4.0)
Taxable income	1.0
Tax at 30%	(0.3)
Annual cash flow	0.7
Annuity value	1.367
PV cash flow	1.0

The NPV of the free cash flows for the period 20X7 to 20Y6 is therefore $9.4m + $1.0m = $10.4m.

Note 2. The discount rate to be used is the cost of capital, which can be estimated by the same method as in Scenario 1.

The current market value of equity is again $9.2m. It is assumed that the balance sheet value of the debt approximates to its market value ie $7m, with its cost taken at the bank rate of 15.5%. The risk free rate of return including inflation is $(1.04 \times 1.1) - 1 = 14.4\%$. The market rate of return including inflation is $(1.10 \times 1.1) - 1 = 21.0\%$.

Using the CAPM: $k_e = r_f + [E(r_m) - r_f] \beta_j$

$$= 14.4\% + (21.0\% - 14.4\%) \times 1.25 = 22.65\%$$

The WACC can now be estimated.

$$WACC = \left[\frac{V_e}{V_e + V_d} \right] k_e + \left[\frac{V_d}{V_e + V_d} \right] k_d (1 - T)$$

$$= 22.65\% \times 9.2/(9.2 + 7) + 15.5\% \times (1 - 0.3) \times 7/(9.2 + 7)$$

$$= 17.55\% \text{ (approx 18\%)}$$

Appendix 2: Cash flow evaluation of diversification project

To estimate the **APV**, it is first necessary to find the **base case NPV**. This is calculated using the ungeared cost of equity. This can be found using the expression:

	20X6 $m	20X7 $m	20X8 $m	20X9 $m	20Y0 $m	20Y1 $m
Revenue		9.0	10.0	11.0	12.0	13.0
Variable costs		(6.0)	(6.0)	(7.0)	(7.0)	(8.0)
Fixed costs		(2.0)	(2.0)	(2.0)	(2.0)	(2.0)
Taxable income		1.0	2.0	2.0	3.0	3.0
Tax at 30%		(0.3)	(0.6)	(0.6)	(0.9)	(0.9)
Post tax income		0.7	1.4	1.4	2.1	2.1
Purchase cost	(9.0)					
Working capital movement		(1.0)			(1.0)	
Realisable value						10.0
Cash flow	(9.0)	(0.3)	1.4	1.4	1.1	12.1
14% discount factors (see Note 3)	1.000	0.877	0.769	0.675	0.592	0.519
PV cash flow	(9.0)	(0.3)	1.1	0.9	0.7	6.3

Total PV (base case NPV)= –$300,000

Note 3

$$\beta_a = \beta_e \frac{V_e}{V_e + V_d(1 - T)}$$

where: ẞ$_a$ = ungeared beta

ẞ$_e$ = geared beta (1.25)

V$_e$ = market value of equity ($9.2m)

V$_d$ = market value of debt ($7.0m)

t = tax rate (30%)

$$\text{ẞ}_a = 1.25 \times \frac{9.2}{9.2 + 7(1-0.3)} = 0.82$$

The ungeared cost of equity can now be estimated using the CAPM:

$k_{eu} = R_f + \beta\,(E(r_m) - R_f)$

= 9.2% + (15.5% − 9.2%) × 0.82 = 14.4% (say, approximately 14%)

This can be used to calculate the NPV of the project as if it were all equity financed.

Modigliani and Miller

The next stage is to use the **Modigliani and Miller formula** for the relationship between the value of geared and ungeared companies to establish the effect of gearing on the value of the project. The amount to be financed by debt will be the purchase cost of the hotel plus the issue costs: $9m/98% = $9.184m.

The present value of the tax shield on the debt interest can now be found.

Annual interest charge: $9.184m × 10%	$918,400
Tax saving: 30%	$275,520
Cost of debt (pre tax)	10%
PV of tax savings at 10% for 5 years: $275,520 × 3.791 (in round $'000)	$1,044,000

APV calculation

The APV is the base case NPV plus the financing side effects (including issue costs):

	$'000
Base case NPV	(300)
Issue costs	(184)
PV of tax savings	1,044
APV	560

This assumes firstly that all the funds required can be raised in the form of debt ie that Daron will have sufficient debt capacity, and secondly that the coupon rate of 10% is an accurate reflection of the risk of the convertible loan stock.

(b) The possibility of an initiative by the central bank to raise interest rates adds to the **uncertainty and risk** for the company. It would appear that Daron's business operations may be largely or wholly restricted to its own country, in which case the company will be exposed to shifts in **domestic economic conditions**.

An increase in short-term interest rates by the central bank will result in an immediate rise in the cost of bank borrowing, and it is probable that longer-term interest rates will also be affected. However the effect of higher short-term rates on longer-term rates may not be immediate. If there is an immediate increase in longer-term rates, the cost of debt finance for the diversification option will be higher than the estimated 10% cost of the convertible loan stock. This would **add** to the **cost of capital** for the diversification option and would reduce its present value.

An initiative by the central bank to raise interest rates would be intended to **reduce** the rate of **inflation**. Monetary policy initiatives by a central bank take time to have a noticeable effect, and it is therefore possible that the rate of inflation will be higher for a time than the estimate of 5% or 10%, depending on which political party wins the election. Without further information, it is not possible to assess the effect of revised expectations about inflation on the value of the company or the cash flows from a diversification strategy.

A **reduction** in **inflation** from a rise in short-term interest rates would be achieved through the effect on demand in the economy. Higher interest rates should eventually result in **lower demand** in the domestic

BPP
LEARNING MEDIA

economy. This in turn will affect sales and profits of businesses. When there is a fall in growth expectations and profit expectations, there will almost certainly be a general fall in share prices. Given that the systematic risk of Daron is measured by a beta factor of 1.25, Daron is likely to be affected by **more than the market average** by a general fall in returns.

The economic condition of the country appears **weak**, given concerns about the rate of inflation, and economic uncertainty is damaging for business. Investing becomes a much bigger risk, and the senior management of Daron should perhaps re-assess its investment options in the event of a faster-than-expected slowdown in the domestic economy.

(c)   When senior executives do not hold significant quantities of shares in their company, there is likely to be a **conflict** between the **interests** of shareholders and those of senior management. This is the basis of agency theory: senior management act as agents for their principal, the shareholders. An aim of corporate governance should be to minimise this conflict of interests, and one way of doing this is through the use of incentives in executive remuneration.

The current remuneration arrangements are **not satisfactory**. Senior management are incentivised through bonuses linked to the achievement of annual performance targets, without any longer-term incentive scheme. Inevitably the interests of senior management will therefore be to **maximise short-term** (annual) performance.

The interests of shareholders are to increase the value of their investment. According to the dividend theory of share valuation, the value of shares depends on expectations of future dividend payments on shares over the long-term. Dividend expectations depend in turn on expectations of future earnings and dividend growth. Shareholder wealth is therefore **dependent on long-term expectations** of performance, whereas senior management are incentivised entirely by shorter-term incentives.

The proposal to introduce a longer-term incentive scheme should therefore be welcomed in theory by shareholders, although the details of the scheme must be considered carefully. There are several issues to consider.

The incentive scheme should be based on **achievement** of challenging **targets** that are consistent with the objective of longer-term growth in the value of the company's shares.

The long-term incentive scheme needs to be sufficiently attractive to senior management to encourage them to give more consideration to longer-term objectives and in doing so give less emphasis to the short term. Unless the longer-term incentives are attractive, management will continue to focus on short-term performance. This means that the new incentive scheme must be a generous one, or that the short term bonus arrangements should be revised downwards.

The proposed scheme is a share grant scheme rather than a share option scheme, and the company will buy shares in the market to provide a pool of shares to award. If the company becomes a significant buyer of its own shares, this should have the effect of supporting, or even raising, the share price. Since existing shares would be used in the scheme, there should be no concerns about dilution in earnings per share.

In summary, the interests of senior executives and shareholders need to be **aligned** with each other, and the absence of a long-term incentive scheme is a drawback to this objective. A long-term incentive scheme is therefore desirable in principle, but the size of the scheme and the performance targets details must be appropriate in order **both** to win **shareholder support** and also to **incentivise management** to consider longer-term objectives and shareholder value.

Question 2

Text references. Foreign currency hedging is covered in Chapter 16.

Top tips. It is not necessarily clear how best to tackle the futures part of (a) (i) given the absence of spot rates at the end of the contract. You need to come up with an answer that can be compared with the results on the forward and money markets. Our answer does this by saying that for the amount hedged, the results on the spot and futures market will balance out to give a net payment at the current futures price. This leaves in both instances a certain amount unhedged which can then be hedged on the forward market. We demonstrate this by using an example although this may not be necessary to gain full marks. Most marks would be available for the money and futures market parts of the answer.

The caveat about the lack of basis risk is important. (a) (ii) illustrates the importance of variation margin.

Easy marks. The list in (b) represents basic knowledge in this area. Your answer needs to focus on cost, flexibility and risk of loss.

Marking scheme

				Marks
(a)	(i)	Calculation of net receipts/payments	1	
		Forward market hedge calculations	2	
		Money market hedge – two month payment calculation	2	
		Money market hedge – three month payment calculation	2	
		Money market hedge – three month receipt calculation	2	
		Type of futures contract	1	
		No of contracts	1	
		Calculation of gain/loss on future	2	
		Net position on futures	2	
				15
	(ii)	Calculation of Day 1	2	
		Calculation of Day 2	1	
		Calculation of Day 3	1	
				4
(b)		Advantages of forward contracts	Max 2	
		Disadvantages of forward contracts	Max 2	
		Advantages of currency futures	Max 2	
		Disadvantages of currency futures	Max 2	
				6
				25

(a)   (i)

	Receipts	Payments
Two months		€393,265
Three months	Kr8.6m	491,011 + 890,217 – 60,505 – 1,997,651 = €676,928

Forward market hedge

Two months

Payment $\dfrac{€393,265}{1.433}$ = £274,435

Three months

Payment $\dfrac{€676,928}{1.431} = £473,045$

Receipt $\dfrac{Kr8,600,000}{10.83} = £794,090$

Money market hedge

(i) **Two months payment**

We need to invest now to match the €393,265 we require.

Amount to be invested $= \dfrac{€393,265}{1+\dfrac{0.035}{6}}$

$= €390,984$

Converting at spot rate $\dfrac{390,984}{1.439} = £271,705$

To obtain £271,705, we have to borrow for two months.

Amount to be paid to lender $= 271,705 \times \left(1+\dfrac{0.075}{6}\right)$

$= £275,101$

(ii) **Three months payment**

Again we need to invest

Amount to be invested $= \dfrac{€676,928}{1+\dfrac{0.035}{4}}$

$= €671,056$

Converting at spot rate $\dfrac{671,056}{1.439} = £466,335$

Borrowing £466,335 for three months

Amount to be paid to lender $= 466,335 \times \left(1+\dfrac{0.075}{4}\right)$

$= £475,079$

(iii) **Three months receipt**

We need to borrow now to match the receipt we shall obtain.

Amount to be borrowed $= \dfrac{Kr8,600,000}{1+\dfrac{0.08}{4}}$

$= Kr8,431,373$

Converting at spot rate $\dfrac{8,431,373}{10.71} = £787,243$

Amount to be received $= 787,243 \times \left(1+\dfrac{0.055}{4}\right)$

$= £798,068$

Futures – 2 months

- Buy June futures as they mature just after the payment date
- Buy euro futures

- Number of contracts = $\frac{€393,265}{125,000}$ = 3.146 (say 3 contracts)

  This leaves (€393,265 − [125,000 × 3]) = €18,265 unhedged by futures contracts. This will be hedged on the forward market at 1.433.

- Tick size = 125,000 × 0.0001 = £12.50

Set up today (20 April)

1 Euros of cover needed = 393,265

2 Contract size   125,000
   Number of contracts   3 contracts

3 June future: Buy euros at 0.6964

Outcome (20 June)

4 **Actual transaction at June spot rate**

   Actual cover (393,265)

   Spot rate 1.433   £(274,434.80)

   Compare to April spot (1.439)

   = £273,290.50 ∴ bad news in June

5 **Futures – profit or loss**

   April – to buy   0.6964
   June – to sell   0.6978 [1]
                       0.0014 profit (14 ticks)

   Profit per contract = £12.50 × 14 = £175
   Total profit (3 × 175)   = £525

6 **Net position**

   Actual   £(274,434.80)
   Future   525.00
                             £(273,909.80)

[1]

	End of April	*End of June*
June future	0.6964	0.6978
Spot (1/1.433)	0.6978	0.6978
Basis	(0.0014)	NIL
	2 months' timing difference	0 months remaining

BPP LEARNING MEDIA

For the 3 month payment

Set up today (20 April)			**Outcome (20 July)**	
1	Euros needed =	676,928	4	**Actual transaction at July spot rate**

Set up today (20 April)

1   Euros needed =   676,928

2   Contract size   £125,000

    Number of contracts = $\dfrac{676,928}{125,000}$

           ≈ 5 contracts

3   September future: Buy euros at 0.6983

Outcome (20 July)

4   **Actual transaction at July spot rate**

    €676,928 @ 1.431 =   £(473,045.40)

    Compare to April spot:

    €676,928 @ 1.439 =

    = £470,415.60 ∴ bad news in July

5   **Profit or loss**

April – to buy	0.6983
July – to sell	0.7002 [1]
	0.0019 profit

    Profit per contract = 19 ticks × £12.50

                     = £237.50

    Total profit   = £237.50 × 5

                    = £1,187.50

6   **Net position**

Actual transaction at	
July spot rate	£(473,045.40)
Future	1,187.50
	£(471,857.90)

[1]

	End of April		End of July	
September future	0.6983		0.7002	
Spot (1/1.439)	9.6949		0.6988	(1/1.431)
	0.0034	× 2/5 =	0.0014	
	5 months' timing difference		2 months' timing difference	

Conclusion

For the three month Kr receipt, the money market will maximise cash flow. For the two Euro payments, the futures market should maximise cash flow assuming basis risk is negligible. If basis risk does have a significant impact, the forward market may be the best choice.

(ii)   **Day 1** movement 0.6930 – 0.6916 = 14 ticks loss. Extra payment of £175 (14 × £12.50) is required. If the extra payment is not made, the contract will be closed out. Therefore:

    Day 2 movement 0.6944 – 0.6930 = 14 ticks loss, extra payment of £175.

    Day 3 movement 0.6940 – 0.6944 = 4 ticks profit. Profit = 4 × £12.50 = £50; this can be taken in cash.

(b)   **Advantages of forward contracts**

(i)   The contract can be tailored to the user's **exact requirements** with quantity to be delivered, date and price all flexible.

(ii)   The trader will **know in advance** how much money will be received or paid.

(iii)   **Payment** is **not required** until the contract is settled.

Disadvantages of forward contracts

(i)   The user may not be able to negotiate **good terms**; the price may depend upon the **size** of the **deal** and how the user is rated.

BPP LEARNING MEDIA

(ii)   Users have to **bear** the **spread** of the contract between the buying and selling price.

(iii)   Deals can only be **reversed** by going back to the original party and offsetting the original trade.

(iv)   The **creditworthiness** of the other party may be a problem.

Advantages of currency futures

(i)   There is a **single specified price** determined by the market, and not the negotiating strength of the customer.

(ii)   **Transactions costs** are generally **lower** than for forward contracts.

(iii)   The exact date of **receipt** or **payment** of the currency does not have to be **known**, because the futures contract does not have to be closed out until the actual cash receipt or payment is made.

(iv)   **Reversal** can easily take place in the market.

(v)   Because of the process of **marking to market**, there is no default risk.

Disadvantages of currency futures

(i)   The **fixing** of **quantity** and **delivery dates** that is necessary for the future to be traded means that the customer's risk may not be fully covered.

(ii)   Futures contracts may not be **available** in the **currencies** that the customer requires.

(iii)   **Volatile trading conditions** on the futures markets mean that the potential loss can be high.

Question 3

Text references. Value at risk is covered in Chapter 5; cost of debt and cost of equity are covered in Chapter 7; valuations of acquisitions and mergers in Chapter 10.

Top tips. Method should help you to score well here. There are numerous calculations which should be laid out as clearly as possible otherwise you could miss something out. The key to the calculations for Elfix is being able to presume that its asset beta is the same as that of Impex.

Easy marks. Part (c) offers some easy marks if you are familiar with the theoretical aspects of value at risk.

Marking scheme

		Marks
(a)	Impex	
	Equity valuation using CAPM	2
	Value of the perpetual debt	2
	Market value of debt	1
	Debt beta	1
	Asset beta	1
	Overall beta	1
	Elfix	
	Equity valuation using earnings and growth	4
	Market value of debt (DCF calculation)	2
	Debt beta	1
	Asset beta	1
	Overall beta	1
		17
(b)	Use of VaR formula	1
	Impex calculations	3.5
	Elfix calculations	3.5
		8
		25

(a) **Impex**

$\beta_g = 0.98$, hence the **required return of shareholders** is

$r_e = r_f + \beta (r_m - r_f) = 6 + 0.98 (10 - 6) = 9.92\%$

From this we can calculate the **share price** as

$$E_{XD} = \frac{d_1}{r_e - g} = \frac{156 \times 1.025}{0.098 - 0.025} = 2,155c \text{ or } \$21.55$$

Given that there are 268m shares in issue, the **equity market value** is

$E = \$21.55 \times 268m = \$5,775.4m$

The debt of Impex is perpetual with a coupon of 5.8% and a credit rating of AA. Taking the 30 year bond as representative, this suggests a yield spread of 50bp or 0.5% giving a **required return to debt holders** of

$r_d = r_f + \text{spread} = 6\% + 0.5\% = 6.5\%$

And from this, the **value of the perpetual debt** can be calculated as

$$D_{XT} = \frac{c}{r_d} = \frac{5.8}{0.065} = \$89.23$$

Giving a **market value for the \$3.26bn of debt** as

$$D = 89.23 \times \left(\frac{3.26bn}{100} \right) = \$2,908.9m$$

Now, the required return to debt holders of 6.5% is above the risk-free rate of 6%. Since we are told there is no unsystematic risk, the 0.5% premium must be to compensate for systematic risk, ie the debt has a beta. The **beta of the debt** can be calculated by rearranging CAPM as follows.

$r = r_f + \beta\,(r_m - r_f)$

so

$(r - r_f) = \beta\,(r_m - r)$

hence

$$\beta = \frac{r - r_f}{r_m - r_f} = \frac{6.5 - 6.0}{10 - 6} = 0.125$$

we can use this to calculate the following

(i)   **Asset beta of Impex**

$$\beta_a = \left[\frac{V_e}{V_e + V_d(1-T)}\,\beta_e \right] + \left[\frac{V_d(1-T)}{V_e + V_d(1-T)}\,\beta_d \right]$$

$$= \left[\frac{5,775.4}{5,775.4 + 2,908.9 \times 0.7} \times 0.98 \right] + \left[\frac{2,908 \times 0.7}{5,775.4 + 2,908.9 \times 0.7} \times 0.125 \right] = 0.757$$

(ii)   **The overall beta of Impex (beta of the WACC)**

The overall beta can be calculated as the weighted average of the equity debt betas as follows

$$\beta_{WACC} = \frac{5,775.4}{8,684.3} \times 0.98 + \frac{2,908.9}{8,684.3} \times 0.125 = 0.6936$$

So for Impex we have

	Market value $m	Beta	$\sigma_s = \beta\sigma_m$ (needed below)
Equity (E)	5,775.4	0.98	7.84%
Debt (D)	2,908.9	0.125	1.00%
Total (V)	8,684.3	0.6936	5.5488%

Elfix

Since Impex and Elfix are competitors in the same sector it is reasonable to presume that their asset betas are identical at the 0.757 calculated above

If Elfix were ungeared it would, therefore, have a **required return to shareholders** of

$r_e = r_f + \beta\,(r_m - r_f) = 6 + 0.757\,(10 - 6) = 9.18\%$ which, in this situation, would be both its cost of equity and WACC.

Given that the policy of Elfix is to distribute 60% of earnings and retain 40% its **growth rate** would be

$g = rb = 9.18\% \times 0.4 = 3.672\%$

Here we are assuming that Elfix is also growing steadily in a highly competitive market so that the return achieved on reinvested earnings is simply the WACC.

We are given an EPS figure (excluding interest and tax thereon) of 80c. Given the distribution policy, the last dividend were the company ungeared would be 48c. From this we can determine the **ungeared share price** as

$$E = \frac{d_1}{r_e - g} = \frac{48 \times 1.03672}{0.0918 - 0.03672} = 903.46c \text{ or } \$9.0346$$

BPP LEARNING MEDIA

And with 57m shares in issue this gives an **ungeared equity value** of

U = $9.0346 × 57m = $514.972m

Now Eflix has $220m of 15 year 7% debt in issue with an A2 rating corresponding to a yield spread of 107bp or 1.07%.

As a result, the **required return for Elfix's debt holders** is 7.07% (6 + 1.07) and its **market value** is

Time	Cash flow	Discount factor	PV $
1-15	7.00	$\dfrac{1}{0.0707}\left(1-\dfrac{1}{1.0707^{15}}\right)$	63.474
15	100.00	$\dfrac{1}{1.0707^{15}}$	35.891
			99.365

And hence the **market value of Elfix's debt** is

$V_d = \$99.365 \times \dfrac{220m}{100} = \$218.603$

of which $139.643m represents the present value of the coupon.

In addition, as for Impex, the **beta of Elfix's debt** can be calculated as

$\beta_d = \dfrac{7.07 - 6.00}{10 - 6} = 0.2675$

Applying Modigliani and Miller we have

V = U + PV (tax shield) = 514.972 + 139.643 × 0.3 = 556.865

Giving

	$m
Total value of geared business	556.865
Debt value	218.603
Equity value of geared business	338.262

Which, when spread over 57m shares, gives a **share price** of $5.93 per share.

The **beta of the equity** in this geared company can now be found using

$\beta_g = \beta_u + (\beta_u - \beta_d)\dfrac{V_d}{V_e}(1 - T)$

$= 0.757 + (0.757 - 0.2675) \times \dfrac{218.603}{338.262} \times 0.7 = 0.9784$

And the **overall beta** established as

$B_{WACC} = \dfrac{338.262}{556.865} \times 1.9784 + \dfrac{218.603}{556.863} \times 0.2675 = 0.6993$

So for Elfix we have

	Market value $m	Beta	$\sigma_s = \beta\sigma_m$ (needed below)
Equity	338.262	0.9784	8.272%
Debt	218.603	0.2675	2.14%
Total	556.865	0.6993	5.8648%

(b)   The value at risk can be established as

$$VaR = S\phi\sigma\sqrt{t}$$

Where
S = current value
ϕ = normal distribution value corresponding to the described confidence level
σ = standard deviation
t = time

Since we are told that there is no unsystematic risk, then the total risk is the systematic risk calculated above. At the 1% level ϕ = 2.325, hence the three month value at risk for each component is

Impex

$$\text{Equity VaR} = \$5,775.4m \times 2.325 \times 0.0784 \times \sqrt{\frac{3}{12}} = \$526.4m$$

$$\text{Debt VaR} = \$2,908.9m \times 2.325 \times 0.01 \times \sqrt{\frac{3}{12}} = \$33.8m$$

$$\text{Total VaR} = \$8,684.3m \times 2.325 \times 0.055488 \times \sqrt{\frac{3}{12}} = \$560.2m$$

Eflix

$$\text{Equity VaR} = \$338.262 \times 2.325 \times 0.08272 \times \sqrt{\frac{3}{12}} = \$32.528m$$

$$\text{Debt VaR} = \$218.603m \times 2.325 \times 0.0214 \times \sqrt{\frac{3}{12}} = \$5.438m$$

$$\text{Total VaR} = \$556.865m \times 2.325 \times 0.058648 \times \sqrt{\frac{3}{12}} = \$37.966$$

Note. In this question the total VAR is the sum of the equity VAR and debt VAR. This will only be the case in situations like this where there is no unsystematic risk or where debt and equity risks are perfectly positively correlated.

Question 4

Text references. Chapter 14.

Top tips. Most of the advantages in (a) are for the investing company, although discussion of the other parties as well enhances your chances of scoring marks. Note in (b) the method for calculating the annual payment if a mix of interest and capital repayment is being made each year. The point of (c) is to focus on the number of shares being issued under the warrant in exchange for the loan stock, and not the price.

Easy marks. If you revised management buyouts, discussing their advantages in (a) should be straightforward.

Marking scheme

		Marks
(a)	Convenient disposal	1 – 2
	Reduced marketing and administration costs	1 – 2
	Speed of disposal	1
	Greater co-operation	1 – 2
	Future links	1
	Managers' position	1
	Venture capitalists' position	1
		Max 7

BPP
LEARNING MEDIA

Calculation of interest	2.5
Tax	1
Dividends	1
Asset beta	1
Growth rate calculation	<u>1.5</u>
	7

(c)
Original position	1 – 2
Revised position	<u>2 – 3</u>
	Max 4

(d)
Amount of finance provided	1 – 2
Required returns	1 – 2
Equity stake/ voting rights	1 – 2
Exit strategies	<u>2 – 3</u>
	Max <u>7</u>
	<u>25</u>

(a) (i) **Reflator Inc's position**

Convenient disposal method

A management buyout is a means of obtaining consideration for a division that is **peripheral** to the company's activities, is **loss-making** or in **severe financial difficulties** such as in this case.

Reduced marketing and administration costs

A willing purchaser is already known and there are no additional search and marketing costs for advertising the sale to prospective purchasers.

Speed of disposal

It may be **quicker** to dispose of the division to managers than to an external party.

Greater co-operation

If a parent company has decided to dispose of the division, it will probably get **more co-operation** from the managers and employees of the division if the sale is a management buyout as it will feel less under threat than if new owners came in.

Future links

The selling organisation is more likely to be able to **maintain beneficial links** with a segment sold to managers than to a third party. This may be more important if Reflator will need to continue business with the division once it is sold.

(ii) **Managers' position**

Because of their **expertise and knowledge of the company**, managers may have a better chance of making their acquisition succeed than an external party would. They may also be more **motivated** because of the possibility of the gains that they can earn.

(iii) **Venture capitalists' position**

Although venture capitalists may take **high risks** when investing in management buyouts, they will do so because of the possibility of **high returns** and the possibility of eventually being able to **realise their investment** by sale when the company is listed on the **stock market**.

BPP LEARNING MEDIA

(b) **Assume maximum dividend of 15% is paid.**

	Working	1	2	3	4
		$'000	$'000	$'000	$'000
EBIT		320.0	410.0	500.0	540.0
Interest 8.5% loan		(170.0)	(170.0)	(170.0)	(170.0)
Interest 9% loan	1	(27.0)	(23.4)	(19.5)	(15.2)
EBT		123.0	216.6	310.5	354.8
Tax 30%		(36.9)	(65.0)	(93.2)	(106.4)
EAT		86.1	151.6	217.3	248.4
Dividends 15%		(12.9)	(22.7)	(32.6)	(37.3)
Retained earnings		73.2	128.9	184.7	211.1
Book value of equity		873.2	1,002.1	1,186.8	1,397.9

Working

Annual payment required = 300,000/Cumulative 6 yr factor 9%
$$= 300,000/4.486$$
$$= \$66,875, \text{ say } \$66,900$$

	1	2	3	4
	$'000	$'000	$'000	$'000
Remaining value	300	260.1	216.6	169.2
Interest 9%	27	23.4	19.5	15.2
Capital	39.9	43.5	47.4	51.7

Annual growth rate in book value of equity = $\sqrt[4]{(1,397.9 \div 800)} - 1 = 15.0\%$

This is below the 20% claimed; however this growth rate is likely to be less significant to the investor than the growth rate of the **market value of equity**.

(c) **Original position**

Under the original suggestion managers would have 1 million shares and the venture capitalists 600,000. The warrants would give the venture capitalists 100/100 × 300,000 = 300,000 extra shares, bringing their total to 900,000, but still meaning that the managers owned the majority of shares.

Revised position

However on the revised terms suggested by the venture capitalists, they would gain 150/100 × 300,000 = 450,000 extra shares, bringing their total to 1.05 million and giving them **effective control** of the company if the warrants are exercised. The managers may not be prepared to accept this, unless they too have chances to increase their shareholdings.

(d) **Memorandum: The role of a venture capitalist**

Venture capitalists are organisations, such as 3i, willing to **provide venture (ie risk) capital** to a business organisation **normally in return for an equity stake in the organisation**. Venture capitalists are more inclined to **fund management buyouts**, as in this case, rather than the relatively riskier start-up situations. The minimum investment considered will normally be around $100,000 with the **average investment of $1 million to $2 million**, and so the additional finance requirements should present no problems to the venture capitalist.

The return required on venture capital for a well-established business with sound management (as in this case) is likely to be around the 25% – 30% mark. Clearly not all investments made by venture capitalists are successful and the **overall returns** on venture capital **average** out at around **10% – 15%**.

As in this case, the venture capitalist will not necessarily provide the majority of the finance. The **buyout** may be **funded by $300,000 venture capital, $2 million debt finance and $300,000 subordinated debt finance**.

The venture capitalist must **protect the interests of the investors** providing the venture finance. As a result, the venture capitalist will normally require an **equity stake**. This is normally between a 20% to 30% shareholding in the management buyout company. They may also wish to have **special rights** to be able to appoint an agreed number of directors. These directors will act as their representatives on the board and

BPP
LEARNING MEDIA

look after the interests of the venture capital organisation. The venture capitalist may require the company to seek their prior approval for any new issues or acquisitions. The venture capitalists will want the **managers** to be **financially committed**. This is not an issue in this situation as the management will hold 1,000,000 equity shares and the venture capitalists 600,000 equity shares.

The venture capitalist are generally likely to want a **predetermined target exit date**, the point at which they can recoup some or all of their investment in the management buyout. At the outset the venture capitalist will want to establish various **exit routes**. These include the sale of shares to the public or institutional investors following a flotation of the company's shares on a recognised stock market. Other exit strategies include the sale of the company to another firm, or the repurchase of the venture capitalist's shares by the company or its owners, or the sale of the venture capitalist's shares to an institution such as an investment trust.

BPP
LEARNING MEDIA

ACCA Professional Level

Paper P4

Advanced Financial Management

Mock Examination 2

Question Paper	
Time allowed	
Reading and Planning Writing	15 minutes 3 hours
Section A THIS question is compulsory and MUST be attempted Section B TWO questions ONLY to be attempted	
During reading and planning time only the question paper may be annotated	

DO NOT OPEN THIS PAPER UNTIL YOU ARE READY TO START UNDER EXAMINATION CONDITIONS

BPP
LEARNING MEDIA

BPP
LEARNING MEDIA

SECTION A: THIS QUESTION is compulsory and MUST be attempted

Question 1

Novoroast plc, a UK company, manufactures microwave ovens which it exports to several countries, as well as supplying the home market. One of Novoroast's export markets is a South American country, which has recently imposed a 40% tariff on imports of microwaves in order to protect its local 'infant' microwave industry. The imposition of this tariff means that Novoroast's products are no longer competitive in the South American country's market but the government there is, however, willing to assist companies wishing to undertake direct investment locally. The government offers a 10% grant towards the purchase of plant and equipment, and a three-year tax holiday on earnings. Corporate tax after the three-year period would be paid at the rate of 25% in the year that the taxable cash flow arises.

Novoroast wishes to evaluate whether to invest in a manufacturing subsidiary in South America, or to pull out of the market altogether.

The total cost of an investment in South America is 155 million pesos (at current exchange rates), comprising:

- 50 million pesos for land and buildings
- 60 million pesos for plant and machinery (all of which would be required almost immediately)
- 45 million pesos for working capital

20 million pesos of the working capital will be required immediately and 25 million pesos at the end of the first year of operation. Working capital needs are expected to increase in line with local inflation.

The company's planning horizon is five years.

Plant and machinery is expected to be depreciated (tax allowable) on a straight-line basis over five years, and is expected to have negligible realisable value at the end of five years. Land and buildings are expected to appreciate in value in line with the level of inflation in the South American country.

Production and sales of microwaves are expected to be 8,000 units in the first year at an initial price of 1,450 pesos per unit, 60,000 units in the second year, and 120,000 units per year for the remainder of the planning horizon.

In order to control the level of inflation, legislation exists in the South American country to restrict retail price rises of manufactured goods to 10% per year.

Fixed costs and local variable costs, which for the first year of operation are 12 million pesos and 600 pesos per unit respectively, are expected to increase by the previous year's rate of inflation.

All components will be produced or purchased locally except for essential microchips which will be imported from the UK at a cost of £8 per unit, yielding a contribution to the profit of the parent company of £3 per unit. It is hoped to keep this sterling cost constant over the planning horizon.

Corporate tax in the UK is at the rate of 30% per year, payable in the year the liability arises. A bi-lateral tax treaty exists between the UK and the South American country, which permits the offset of overseas tax against any UK tax liability on overseas earnings. In periods of tax holiday assume that no UK tax would be payable on South American cash flows.

Summarised group data

Novoroast plc, summarised statement of financial position:

	£m
Non-current assets (net)	440
Current assets	370
Less current liabilities	(200)
	610
Financed by	
£1 ordinary shares	200
Reserves	230
	430
6% Eurodollar bonds, eight years until maturity	180
	610

Novoroast's current share price is 410 pence per share, and current bond price is $800 per bond ($1,000 par and redemption value).

Forecast inflation rates

	UK	South American country
Present	4%	20%
Year 1	3%	20%
Year 2	4%	15%
Year 3	4%	15%
Year 4	4%	15%
Year 5	4%	15%

Foreign exchange rates

	Peso/£
Spot	13.421
1 year forward	15.636

Novoroast plc believes that if the investment is undertaken the overall risk to investors in the company will remain unchanged.

The company's beta coefficients have been estimated as equity 1.25, debt 0.225.

The market return is 14% per annum and the risk free rate is 6% per annum.

Existing UK microwave production currently produces an after tax net cash flow of £30 million per annum. This is expected to be reduced by 10% if the South American investment goes ahead (after allowing for diversion of some production to other EU countries). Production is currently at full capacity in the UK.

Other issues

The senior management of Novoroast are concerned about the risk that would be associated with an investment in South America.

The government of the country is in serious financial difficulties. The annual fiscal deficit is growing and may not be sustainable for much longer. The government has issued large amounts of bonds denominated in US dollars, and these now have a sub-investment grade credit rating from all the major credit rating agencies. There is a strong possibility that the government will have to ask the International Monetary Fund (IMF) for financial assistance to meet its debt obligations. The country's commercial banks are major holders of the government bonds.

There are also concerns about the possible actions that could be taken by the government of the South American company. It is possible that the government will introduce exchange control regulations, blocking the remittance of dividends from domestic companies to foreign parents.

Because of their concerns about the risk associated with the proposed investment, the senior management are considering an alternative option. This is to sell a license to manufacture microwave ovens to a public company in the South American country. This company has a stock market listing for its shares and has issued bonds that currently have a credit rating of BB+ from Standard & Poor's. The licensing agreement would be for five years.

BPP LEARNING MEDIA

Required

(a) Prepare a report advising whether or not Novoroast plc should invest in the South American country. Include in your report a discussion of the limitations of your analysis and suggestions about other information that would be useful to assist the decision process.

All relevant calculations must be shown in your report or as an appendix to it.

State clearly any assumptions that you make.   **(25 marks)**

(b) Prepare a separate report in three sections, providing an analysis of the following issues:

(i) the possible implications for the proposed investment in the South American company of a request by its government for financial assistance from the IMF.   **(7 marks)**

(ii) the imposition of exchange controls by the government, once the investment has taken place, imposing a block on the remittance of dividends to the UK, with suggestions about how Novoroast might try to avoid such a block on remittances.   **(5 marks)**

(iii) the financial implications for Novoroast of choosing a licensing arrangement for the manufacture of its microwaves by a company in the South American country.   **(9 marks)**

Professional marks for format, structure and presentation of the reports.   **(4 marks)**

(Total = 50 marks)

SECTION B: TWO QUESTIONS ONLY to be attempted
Question 2

The CEO of Autocrat plc is reviewing the company's interest rate and currency risk strategies for the next few months. There has recently been considerable political instability with some countries showing signs of moving towards economic recession whilst others are still showing steady growth. Both interest rates and currency rates could become more volatile for many major trading countries.

Autocrat is expected to need to borrow £6,500,000 for a period of six months commencing in six months' time.

The company also needs to make a US$ payment of $4.3 million in 3 months' time.

Assume that it is now 1 December. Futures and options contracts may be assumed to expire at the end of the relevant month, and the company may be assumed to borrow at the 3 month LIBOR rate.

LIFFE futures prices, £500,000 contract size

March	95.56
June	95.29

LIFFE options on futures prices, £500,000 contract size. Premiums are annual %.

	Calls		Puts	
	March	June	March	June
95250	0.445	0.545	0.085	0.185
95500	0.280	0.390	0.170	0.280
95750	0.165	0.265	0.305	0.405

Three month LIBOR is currently 4.5%.

Foreign exchange rates

Spot	$1.4692 – 1.4735/£
3 month forward	$1.4632 – 1.4668/£

Currency option prices

Philadelphia Stock Exchange $/£ options, contract size £31,250, premiums are cents per £.

	Calls		Puts	
	March	June	March	June
1.450	3.12	–	1.56	–
1.460	2.55	2.95	1.99	2.51
1.470	2.14	–	2.51	–

Required

(a) Using the above information illustrate the possible results of

  (i) Futures; and
  (ii) Options

  hedges if interest rates in six months' time increase by 0.75%. Recommend which hedge should be selected and explain why there might be uncertainty as to the results of the hedges. **(11 marks)**

(b) Illustrate and discuss the possible outcomes of forward market and currency options hedges if possible currency rates in three months' time are either:

  (i) $1.4350 – $1.4386/£
  or (ii) $1.4780 – $1.4820/£ **(8 marks)**

(c) Discuss and illustrate whether or not a currency straddle option with an exercise price of 1.460 might be an appropriate hedging strategy for Autocrat plc. Explain the circumstances in which straddle options could be a profitable strategy. **(6 marks)**

(Total = 25 marks)

BPP
LEARNING MEDIA

Question 3

The financial management team of Tampem Co is discussing how the company should appraise new investments. There is a difference of opinion between two managers.

Manager A believes that net present value should be used as positive NPV investments are quickly reflected in increases in the company's share price. It is also simpler to calculate than MIRR and APV.

Manager B states that NPV is not good enough as it is only valid in potentially restrictive conditions, and should be replaced by APV (adjusted present value).

Tampem has produced estimates of relevant cash flows and other financial information associated with a new investment. These are shown below:

$'000

Year	1	2	3	4
Investment pre-tax operating cash flows	1,250	1,400	1,600	1,800

Notes

(i) The investment will cost $5,400,000 payable immediately, including $600,000 for working capital and $400,000 for issue costs. $300,000 of issue costs is for equity, and $100,000 for debt. Issue costs are not tax allowable.

(ii) The investment will be financed 50% equity, 50% debt which is believed to reflect its debt capacity.

(iii) Expected company gearing after the investment will change to 60% equity, 40% debt by market values.

(iv) The investment equity beta is 1.5.

(v) Debt finance for the investment will be an 8% fixed rate debenture.

(vi) Capital allowances are at 25% per year on a reducing balance basis.

(vii) The corporate tax rate is 30%. Tax is payable in the year that the taxable cash flow arises.

(viii) The risk free rate is 4% and the market return 10%.

(ix) The after tax realisable value of the investment as a continuing operation is estimated to be $1.5 million (including working capital) at the end of year 4.

(x) Working capital may be assumed to be constant during the four years.

Required

(a) Calculate the expected NPV, MIRR and APV of the proposed investment.   **(15 marks)**

(b) Discuss briefly the validity of the views of the two managers. Use your calculations in (a) to illustrate and support the discussion.   **(10 marks)**

(Total = 25 marks)

Question 4

You have been asked to investigate the dividend policy of two companies, Forthmate Co and Herander Co. Selected financial information on the two companies is shown below.

Forthmate Co

	Earnings after tax ($'000)	Issued ordinary shares (m)	Free cash flow to equity ($'000)	Dividend per share (cents)
20X1	24,050	100	11,400	4.8
20X2	22,345	100	12,200	4.5
20X3	26,460	100	(3,500)	5.3
20X4	32,450	130	(2,600)	5.0
20X5	35,890	130	9,200	5.5

Herander Co

	Earnings after tax ($'000)	Issued ordinary shares (m)	Free cash flow to equity ($'000)	Dividend per share (cents)
20X1	8,250	50	6,100	10.0
20X2	5,920	50	(4,250)	10.0
20X3	9,140	50	10,300	10.3
20X4	10,350	50	4,400	10.5
20X5	8,220	50	3,140	10.5

A colleague has suggested that companies should try to pay dividends that are a constant percentage of a company's free cash flow to equity.

Required

(a)   Analyse and contrast the dividend polices of Forthmate Co and Herander Co. Include in your analysis estimates of dividends as a percentage of free cash flow, and any other relevant calculations.

Discuss possible reasons why the companies' dividend policies differ.   **(13 marks)**

(b)   Discuss whether or not a company should pay dividends that are equal to the free cash flow to equity.

(6 marks)

In both of the last two years Herander Co has considered the following potential investments with positive NPV

	NPV($'000)	Initial investment cost ($'000)	Undertaken
20X4	1,250	1,050	Yes
20X4	780	625	No
20X5	1,320	1,460	Yes
20X5	735	3,500	No
20X5	525	1,150	No

Required

(c)   Discuss the implications of your findings in (a) above for the financial strategy of Herander Co.   **(6 marks)**

(Total = 25 marks)

Answers

DO NOT TURN THIS PAGE UNTIL YOU HAVE
COMPLETED THE MOCK EXAM

BPP
LEARNING MEDIA

BPP
LEARNING MEDIA

A plan of attack

You have no doubt been told to do it about 201 times and we know if we asked you you'd know that you should do it. So why don't you do it in an exam? 'Do what in an exam?' you're no doubt thinking. Well for the 202nd time let's enlighten you. **Take a good look through the paper before diving in to answer questions.**

First things first

You are given 15 minutes' reading time before the exam begins. During that time you can obviously read the paper and make notes on the question paper *only*. You can also use your calculator to carry out preliminary calculations. The reading time most importantly allows you to carefully read and understand the question requirements and choose which optional questions you are going to attempt. You can also decide in which order you are going to attempt the questions. If you still have time after doing all that, you can start to plan how you are going to structure your answers.

The next step

When the 3 hours' writing time begins you will probably be in one of two minds – either still not knowing where to start or feeling reasonably confident about the questions.

Option 1 (if you don't know where to begin)

If you are a bit worried about the paper and not feeling overly confident about answering any of the questions, you might be as well to start at the beginning with the compulsory Section A question.

- **Question 1** is an overseas investment problem. Set up proformas for the calculations and work steadily through the information given in the question. Make sure you don't get too bogged down on individual figures. Ensure you leave enough time to answer the discursive part (b) and take care to make it relevant to the company in question.

- **Question 2** may not be as difficult as it first appears. Have a go at all the various calculations and remember that you are expected to consider a range of prices for options, and also situations where the option is exercised **and** when it is not exercised. Don't worry too much if you don't know what a straddle option is – it's only worth 6 marks.

- Although there are some marks for easy discussion in **Question 3**, if you struggle with cost of capital formula manipulation and APV calculations, you should avoid this question.

- The calculations in **Question 4** are quite straightforward (look at the relationships between dividends and earnings) and the bulk of the marks are available for discussion. However be warned that the marking scheme for (c) includes a warning not to reward waffle.

What you should always remember is that you **must** answer the question in Section A but only **two** questions from Section B.

Option 2 (if you're thinking 'I can do all of these')

Are you **sure** you are comfortable with all the requirements? If you are then that's encouraging. Tackle the question you feel most comfortable with first – that will settle you down and get you going. The questions are discussed in order here but you obviously don't have to tackle them in this order.

- **Question 1** – you may think you can handle all the complications in the calculations, but don't spend too much time on them. Part (a) is worth 25 marks so you have to allow yourself enough time to discuss your results rather than spending all your time calculating figures. Remember to use a report format, which includes a conclusion that actually answers the question!

- **Question 2** – apart from not knowing what a straddle is, the other most likely ways to lose marks in this question are not to consider a range of exercise prices, and also not to consider how the decision whether to exercise the option affects your analysis.

- **Question 3** – if you are comfortable with formulae manipulation and the various elements of APV, this question would be a good one to choose, as the discussion section is very reasonable.

- **Question 4** – the bulk of the marks in this question are for discussion, so if you choose it make sure you concentrate on relevant issues. In particular, make sure your answer in (a) clearly brings out the contrast.

No matter how many times we remind you...

Always allocate your time according to the marks for the question in total and for the individual parts of each question. Also **always answer the question you were asked** rather than the question you wished you had been asked or the question you thought you had been asked.

You've got free time at the end of the exam...?

Looks like you've slipped up on the time allocation. However if you have, don't waste the last few minutes; go back to **any parts of questions that you didn't finish** because you moved onto another task.

Forget about it!

Forget about what? Excellent – you already have!

Question 1

Text references. Chapter 8 covers international investment appraisal for the first report. Chapter 2 (political risk), Chapter 3b (ethics) and Chapter 4 (IMF, limitations on remittances and licensing) for the second report.

Top tips. For the first report, it is probably easier to place your calculations as part of the report rather than as an appendix at the end. Try to identify when reading through the question the figures that can be slotted in the NPV calculation with no or little workings (fixed costs, tax allowable depreciation here). However, remember that up to four marks are available for presentation and structure of the reports, so it is useful to consider the logic and clarity of your presentation.

Points to note in the calculation are:

- The treatment of working capital, (the increase is included each year and the whole amount released at the end of the period)
- The use of purchasing power parity to calculate exchange rates
- The additional UK tax (calculated on taxable profits, not on cash flows)
- The use of the existing WACC (as the company is still manufacturing the same products)

The discussion for the first report should include problems with the assumptions, and the limitations of only taking 5 years worth of cash flows. You also need to consider the risks and long-term opportunities of investing in South America.

For the second report, you need to be aware that IMF financial support is always associated with tough conditions, which normally include a requirement for the government to introduce severe austerity measures to reduce its fiscal deficit. Do not overlook the fact that government securities are denominated in US dollars, not domestic currency, so there is a considerable sovereign credit risk. The country's banks are major investors in government debt securities, so they are vulnerable to a government default on its debts. The second part of the report requires a thorough discussion on transfer pricing. Many government have however taken steps to discourage this technique. The company may gain most benefit from choosing the right method to finance its subsidiary. The final part of the report should be more straightforward, but your answer should demonstrate an awareness of the implications of a licensing arrangement for strategic risk for the company.

Easy marks. The discussion in the first report contains points that are normally relevant in foreign investment appraisals. In the second report, issues concerning licensing should be largely straightforward.

Marking scheme

		Marks
(a)	Total contribution	2
	Fixed costs	1
	Tax allowable depreciation	1
	Tax	1
	Add back depreciation	1
	Land and buildings	2
	Plant and machinery	2
	Working capital	2
	Exchange rates	2
	UK contribution	1
	Tax on contribution	1
	Additional UK tax	1
	Discount factors	2
	Negative NPV so do not proceed with project	1
	Limitations	2
	Other relevant information	2
	Recommendation	1
		25

(b) (i)   1 mark per relevant point   Max 7
    (ii) 1 – 2 marks per method discussed   Max 5
    (iii) 1 mark per relevant point   Max 9

    Professional marks
    Report formats   1
    Layout, presentation and structure   3
                                                                           ––
                                                                            4
                                                                           ––
                                                                           50
                                                                           ––

(a) To: Board of Directors of Novoroast plc
     From: Strategic Financial Consultant
     Date:

Proposed Investment in South American Manufacturing Subsidiary

1   Introduction

The proposed investment has been triggered by the imposition of a very **high import tariff** (40%) in the South American country. The effect of this tariff is that all sales from the UK to this country will be lost (10% of total UK sales). This loss of UK sales will occur whether or not the proposed investment is made, and has therefore been omitted from the financial evaluation which follows.

2   Financial evaluation

A financial evaluation of the investment, based on discounting the sterling value of incremental cash flows at the company's weighted average cost of capital, shows a **negative net present value** of £610,000, indicating that the investment is not expected to show high enough returns over the five year time horizon to compensate for the risk involved. Calculations are followed by workings and assumptions.

Year	0	1	2	3	4	5
Profit and cash flow – peso million						
Total contribution (W1)		5.80	44.20	92.82	97.04	100.92
Fixed costs (per year inflation increases)		(12.00)	(14.40)	(16.56)	(19.04)	(21.90)
Tax allowable depreciation		(12.00)	(12.00)	(12.00)	(12.00)	(12.00)
Taxable profit		(18.20)	17.80	64.26	66.00	67.02
Tax: from year 4 only at 25%					(16.50)	(16.76)
Add back depreciation		12.00	12.00	12.00	12.00	12.00
Net after-tax cash flow from operations		(6.20)	29.80	76.26	61.50	62.26
Investment cash flows						
Land and buildings (W3)	(50)					104.94
Plant and machinery (less 10% govt. grant)	(54)					
Working capital (W4)	(20)	(29.00)	(7.35)	(8.45)	(9.72)	74.52
Cash remittable from/to UK	(124)	(35.20)	22.45	67.81	51.78	241.72
Exchange rate P/£	13.421	15.636	17.290	19.119	21.141	23.377
UK cash flows (£m)						
Cash remittable	(9.24)	(2.25)	1.30	3.55	2.45	10.34
Contribution from sale of chips (£3 per unit)		0.02	0.18	0.36	0.36	0.36
Tax on chips contribution at 30%		(0.01)	(0.05)	(0.11)	(0.11)	(0.11)
Additional UK tax at 5% on S.Am. profits					(0.16)	(0.14)
Net cash flow in £m	(9.24)	(2.24)	1.43	3.80	2.54	10.45
14% (W5) discount factors	1	0.877	0.769	0.675	0.592	0.519
Present value £m	(9.24)	(1.96)	1.10	2.57	1.50	5.42
Net present value	(£610,000)					

Workings

1 | Year | 0 | 1 | 2 | 3 | 4 | 5 |
|---|---|---|---|---|---|---|
| *Contribution per unit* | | | | | | |
| Sales price (10% increases – pesos) | | 1,450.0 | 1,595.0 | 1,754.5 | 1,930.0 | 2,123.0 |
| Variable cost per unit in pesos | | | | | | |
| (previous year inflation increases) | | 600.0 | 720.0 | 828.0 | 952.2 | 1,095.0 |
| Chip cost per unit | | | | | | |
| (£8 converted to pesos – W2) | | 125.1 | 138.3 | 153.0 | 169.1 | 187.0 |
| Contribution per unit (pesos) | | 724.9 | 736.7 | 773.5 | 808.7 | 841.0 |
| Sales volume ('000 units) | | 8 | 60 | 120 | 120 | 120 |

2   **Prediction of future exchange rates**

Future exchange rates have been predicted from expected inflation rates, on the principle of Purchasing Power Parity Theory, eg Year 1 exchange rate = 13.421 × 1.20/1.03 = 15.636, etc or

$$13.421 \times \left(\frac{(0.2 - 0.03)}{(1 + 0.03)} + 1 \right).$$

	Inflation		
	UK	*SAm*	*Exchange rate*
Spot			13.421
Year 1	3%	20%	15.636
Year 2	4%	15%	17.290
Year 3	4%	15%	19.119
Year 4	4%	15%	21.141
Year 5	4%	15%	23.377

3   **Land and buildings**

Value after 5 years = P50m × 1.2 × 1.15⁴ = P104.94m. It is assumed no tax is payable on the capital gain.

4   **Working capital**

Value of working capital increases in line with inflation each year. The relevant cash flow is the difference between the values from year to year. Working capital is assumed to be released at the end of year 5.

End of year	0	1	2	3	4	5
Local inflation		20%	15%	15%	15%	
Value of Year 0 investment	20	24	27.60	31.74	36.50	0.00
Year 1 investment		25	28.75	33.06	38.02	0.00
Cumulative investment	20	49	56.35	64.80	74.52	0.00
Incremental cash flow	(20)	(29)	(7.35)	(8.45)	(9.72)	74.52

5   **Discount rate**

The company's WACC has been used as a discount rate, on the grounds that overall risk to investors is not expected to change as a result of this investment.

From the CAPM, k_e = 6% + (14% – 6%)1.25 = 16%.

k_d = 6% + (14% – 6%)0.225 = 7.8% pre-tax. After-tax rate = 7.8%(1 – 0.3) = 5.46%.

Market values: Equity: 200m × £4.10 = £820m. Debt: £180m × 800/1,000 = £144m.

Total = £964m.

WACC = 16% × 820/964 + 5.46% × 144/964 = 14.42%.

The discount rate will be **rounded** to 14% for the calculation.

6   **Limitations of the analysis**

The calculations are based on many assumptions and estimates concerning future cash flows. For example:

(i)   **Purchasing power parity**, used to estimate exchange rates, is only a 'broad-brush' theory; many other factors are likely to affect exchange rates and could increase the risk of the project.

(ii)   **Estimates** of inflation, used to estimate costs and exchange rates in the calculations, are subject to **high inaccuracies**.

(iii) **Assumptions** about future tax rates and the restrictions on price increases may be incorrect.

(iv)   **Cash flows** beyond the five year time horizon may be crucial in determining the viability or otherwise of the project; economic values of the operational assets at year 5 may be a lot higher than the residual values included in the calculation.

The calculations show only the medium term financial implications of the project. Non-financial factors and potentially important strategic issues have not been addressed.

7   **Other relevant information**

In order to get a more realistic view of the overall impact of the project, a strategic analysis needs to be carried out assessing the long term plans for the company's products and markets. For example, the **long term potential growth** of the South American market may be of greater significance than the medium term problems of price controls and inflation. On the other hand, it may be of more importance to the company to **increase its product range** to existing customers in Europe. There may also be further opportunities in other countries or regions.

Before deciding whether to invest in the South American country, the company should commission an evaluation of the **economic, political and ethical environment**. **Political risks** include the likelihood of imposition of exchange controls, prohibition of remittances, or confiscation of assets.

The value of this project may be higher than is immediately obvious if it opens up longer term opportunities in South American markets. Option pricing theory can be used to value these opportunities.

As regards the existing financial estimates, the **uncertainties** surrounding the cash flows can be quantified and understood better by carrying out **sensitivity analysis**, which may be used to show how the final result varies with changes in the estimates used.

8   **Conclusion**

On the basis of the evaluation carried out so far, the project is not worthwhile. However other opportunities not yet quantified may influence the final decision.

(b)

To: Board of Directors of Novoroast plc
From: Strategic Financial Consultant
Date:

Overseas investment risk

This report considers three separate issues relating to overseas investment risk for the company.

(i)   **Implications of IMF support for the national government**

Financial support for a government from the IMF is conditional on the introduction by the government of austerity measures to improve the fiscal position of the country. There would be a combination of higher taxation and reductions in government spending. Domestic demand would fall, and recovery in the economy may have to depend on export-led growth.

For a company such as Novoroast, which is considering inward investment into this country, the investment risk would be high. The estimates of sales volume for microwaves may be over-optimistic, and sensitivity analysis of the proposed investment should include assumptions of much lower sales than in the initial investment appraisal.

The government debt is denominated in US dollars. In view of the financial difficulties of the government, the risk of default on the debt may be high unless IMF support is obtained. This would have an immediate impact on the country's banking system, since banks are major investors in government securities and default by the government would result in large losses for the banks. Even if the IMF provides support, there may be some risk that the government will want to re-negotiate the terms of its debt with creditors and that bond investors may be forced to agree to a 'haircut' on their debt or an extension to the term of the debt.

If the company invests in the country, it will need to use a local bank for its banking operations. It will be necessary to consider the 'bank risk' or credit risk that the selected bank may become insolvent.

In view of the risks, whether or not IMF support is requested, the company should seriously reconsider its investment plans.

(ii) **Circumventing restrictions**

If the company nevertheless decides to make the investment it should consider measures to deal with the risk that the government may impose limitations on dividends to foreign investors.

Restrictions on the transfer of dividends from one country to another can be circumvented by two main methods:

(i)   **Adjusting transfer prices** for inter-company sales of goods or services between the subsidiary and other group companies; and/or

(ii)   **'Dressing up'** equity finance as debt finance.

Transfer prices

Under the heading of transfer prices, the following techniques can be used:

(i)   **Increasing prices** for the **subsidiary's purchases** from the parent or other group companies

(ii)   **Reducing** (or abolishing) prices for sales by the subsidiary to other group companies

(iii) **Charging the subsidiary** for head office **overhead and management charges**

(iv)   **Charging the subsidiary** for **royalties and patents** on processes used

The government of the South American country would probably attempt to prevent these arrangements from being effective.

Loan finance

If the company had foreseen the possibility of **dividend restriction**, it could have arranged for the subsidiary to be financed mainly by an inter-company loan, with equity investment nominally small. All expected returns could then be paid as inter-company loan interest.

Bank as intermediary

A less obvious way of achieving the same objective is for the parent to **lend the major part** of its **investment** to an independent international bank, which then lends to the South American subsidiary. Returns would be paid as interest to the bank, which would in turn pay interest to the parent company.

Parallel loans

If these financing arrangements have not already been made by the time dividend restrictions are imposed, the subsidiary may try to **lend its cash surpluses** to the **parent** (interest free) or, if this is prevented, to **lend** to the **subsidiary** of **another company** needing funds in the South American country, with an arrangement that the parent receives a corresponding loan from the parent of the other company. This device is known as a **parallel loan** and is, in effect, a currency swap.

(iii) **Licensing arrangement**

A licensing arrangement with a local company would have both advantages and risks.

In view of the weak state of the country's financial position, a major advantage with a licensing agreement is that there would be **little or no investment risk** for Novoroast. The company would not be required to commit a significant amount of resources to the arrangement, and the licensee would take on the investment risk.

A second advantage is that whereas the government may try to impose restrictions on dividend payments out of the country, it may **not restrict payments of licence fees**.

There would also be disadvantages and risks with a licensing arrangement.

The company would have no control over sales or production quality. Depending on the nature of the licence fee structure, the company may have to rely on the competence of the licensee in manufacturing microwave ovens to an appropriate standard and selling them successfully. If the operation runs into difficulty, there may be **nothing that Novoroast can do** to rectify the problems.

The **potential profitability** of a licensing arrangement will probably be much less than for the direct investment option. A licensee will not be prepared to pay a high price for what could be a risky investment. If the licence fee depends on sales volumes, the lack of control over sales, mentioned previously, could reduce future revenue prospects.

The company that has been identified as a possible licensee has a BB+ credit rating, which is two notches below investment grade level. The licensing agreement is for a five-year period. This suggests that there will be a fairly **significant credit risk**, and that the company may default on its licence fee payment obligations. Given the difficult economic situation in the country, there will also be a risk that the credit rating for the company will migrate downwards, and the risk of default would become greater.

A final consideration is that by allowing another company to obtain Novoroast's technology for its microwave ovens, the licensee may eventually, if successful, **become a competitor** and challenge Novoroast in its other sales markets.

The benefits and risks of making a licensing agreement should be assessed in more detail. Avoidance of investment risk, in view of the country's financial state, may be the safer, if less rewarding, option.

Question 2

Text references. Chapter 17 covers interest rate futures, and interest rate options.

Top tips. (a) and particularly (b) are very time pressured. The best use of time may be to carry out the full calculations in (a) and (b) for one of the exercise prices (the price nearest to today's interest/spot rate) and then to carry out the important elements of calculations for the other prices (no of contracts, premiums)

Other points in (b):

(i)   It is technically better to say the amount over or under hedged by the option contracts will be hedged on the forward market. If you are using the proforma, you would have to consider the impact of hedging on the forward market separately when considering the eventual cost of the option. However it would be simpler to assume the amounts unhedged are bought on the spot market and comment at the end that you could have hedged the amount unhedged on the forward market.

(ii) You can however use the alternative method below to deal with the option outcome calculations. This method does have the advantage of enabling you to deal with the amounts over or under hedged. If amounts are over hedged, you have enough dollars to fulfil the forward contract, and therefore can set the proceeds from fulfilling the forward contract against the cost of the option. However if the option is not exercised, you have to buy the dollars on the spot market to fulfil the forward contract. The reverse applies when the options under hedge the liability.

(iii) As you are given possible prices in the question, you do not have to consider at what spot rate options are the best choice, but it is worth commenting that if the spot price weakens beyond a certain level, options will have been the best choice.

Easy marks. The key point in (c) is that a straddle is used to hedge both ways by buying both a put and a call. A collar is where a put is bought but a call is sold (and vice versa). Straddles are unlikely to be used except in times of significant exchange rate volatility where hedging in **both** directions is required.

BPP
LEARNING MEDIA

			Marks
(a)	(i)	Type of contract	1
		Number of contracts	1
		Calculation of futures price	2
		Calculation of gain/loss	1
	(ii)	Calculation of premiums	2
		Calculation of market outcomes	2
		Calculation of net positions	1
		Recommendation	1
			11
(b)		Type of option	1
		Number of options	1
		Premium cost	1
		Calculation of gain/loss of option	3
		Conversion of option gain to £	1
		Forward market calculation	1
			8
(c)		Explanation of straddle	1 – 2
		Two premiums payable	1 – 2
		Only profitable for a given range	1 – 2
		Suitable for two-way exposure	1 – 2
			Max 6
			25

(a) **Hedging the borrowing rate using futures**

Setup

(i) June contracts as looking to borrow in six months time

(ii) Sell June futures as borrowing

(iii) Number of contracts

$$\frac{£6.5 \text{ million}}{£500,000} \times \frac{6}{3} = 26 \text{ contracts}$$

(iv) Tick size

$$(0.01\% \times \frac{3}{12} \times 500,000) = £12.50$$

Estimate closing futures price

June contract expires in 7 months

LIBOR is currently 4.5% (95.50)

June contract basis risk 95.50 – 95.29 = 21 ticks, difference between current and futures price

1 June 1 month to expiry $21 \times \frac{1}{7} = 3$ ticks

$\Rightarrow$ If LIBOR rises to 5.25% (94.75) 94.75 – 0.03 = 94.72

Outcome

The results of the hedge under cases (i) and (ii) are shown below.

(i) **Futures market**

1 Dec: Sell 26 @	95.29
1 Feb: Buy 26 @	94.72

Tick movement: $\dfrac{\text{opening rate} - \text{closing rate}}{0.01}$ 57

Profit/(Loss) 26 contracts × £12.50 × tick movement   18,525

(ii) **Net outcome**

	£
Payment in spot market 5.25% × £6.5m × 6/12	(170,625)
Profit/(Loss) in futures market	18,525
Net cost of loan	(152,100)

Effective interest cost is 152,100 × 2 /6,500,000 = **4.68%**

However this rate is dependent on the assumption that **basis declines linearly**; this may not be the case if **basis risk exists**.

Hedging the borrowing rate using options

Setup

(i) June as above

(ii) Buy put options

(iii) Consider all three prices

(iv) Number of contracts 26

(v) Tick size £12.50

(vi) Option premium

95250: 26 × 18.5 × 12.5 = £6,013
95500: 26 × 28 × 12.5 = £9,100
95750: 26 × 40.5 × 12.5 = £13,163

Closing price

94.72 as above

Outcome

(i) **Option market outcome**

	95250	95500	95750
Put option strike price (right to sell)	95.25	95.50	95.75
June futures price	94.72	94.72	94.72
Exercise option? (prefer to sell at highest price)	Yes	Yes	Yes
Gain (ticks)	53	78	103
Option outcome (26 × 12.50 × tick gain)	17,225	25,350	33,475

(ii) **Net position**

	95250	95500	95750
	£	£	£
Actual interest cost (as above)	(170,625)	(170,625)	(170,625)
Value of option gain	17,225	25,350	33,475
Premium	(6,013)	(9,100)	(13,163)
Net cost of loan	(159,413)	(154,375)	(150,313)
Effective interest cost (Cost × 2/6.5m)	4.91%	4.75%	4.63%

The 95750 option is the preferred hedging method, as it has a lower interest cost than the future. If interest rates fall, the option can lapse or be sold.

BPP LEARNING MEDIA

(b) **Forward market**

4,300,000/1.4632 = £2,938,764

Currency options

Set up

(i) March

(ii) Type of contract put as wish to buy $/sell £ with option contract in £

(iii) Consider all three exercise prices

(iv) Number of contracts

Number of contracts = $4,300,000 ÷ Exercise price/Contract price

$1.450: \dfrac{2,965,517}{31,250} = 94.8$ say 95 contracts

$1.460: \dfrac{2,945,206}{31,250} = 94.2$ say 94 contracts

$1.470: \dfrac{2,925,170}{31,250} = 93.6$ say 94 contracts

(v) Tick size = $0.0001 \times £31,250$

$= \$3.125$

(vi) Premium cost

$1.450: 95 \times \dfrac{1.56}{100} \times 31,250 = 46,312/1.4692 = £31,522$

$1.460: 94 \times \dfrac{1.99}{100} \times 31,250 = 58,456/1.4692 = £39,788$

$1.470: 94 \times \dfrac{2.51}{100} \times 31,250 = 73,731/1.4692 = £50,184$

Closing prices

$1.4350/$1.4780

Outcome

(i) **Options**

If the strike price is 1.4780, none of the options will be exercised.

If the strike price is 1.4350, all of the options will be exercised.

	1.4500	1.4600	1.4700
Futures price	1.4500	1.4600	1.4700
Strike price	1.4350	1.4350	1.4350
Tick gain	150	250	350
Outcome of option position			
No of contracts × 3.125 × tick gain	$44,531	$73,438	$102,813

(ii) **Net outcome**

	1.4500		1.4600		1.4700	
	1.4350	1.4780	1.4350	1.4780	1.4350	1.4780
	£	£	£	£	£	£
Spot market	(2,996,516)	(2,909,337)	(2,996,516)	(2,909,337)	(2,996,516)	(2,909,337)
4,300,000 ÷ 1.4350/1.4780						
Option outcome ÷ 1.4350	31,032	–	51,176	–	71,647	–
Premium	(31,522)	(31,522)	(39,788)	(39,788)	(50,184)	(50,184)
Outcome	(2,997,006)	(2,940,859)	(2,985,128)	(2,949,125)	(2,975,053)	(2,959,521)

All of these outcomes are worst than the forward contract. The spot price would need to weaken further for options to be the best hedge.

Alternative method – options

If strike price is $1.4350 all options will be exercised.

	1.4500 £	1.4600 £	1.4700 £
Costs of option contracts (£31,250 × no of contracts)	(2,968,750)	(2,937,500)	(2,937,500)
Amount hedged on forward market:			
$\dfrac{\text{(Cost of option contracts} \times \text{exercise price)} - 4{,}300{,}000}{\text{Forward rate}}$	$\dfrac{(4{,}304{,}687 - 4{,}300{,}000)}{1.4668}$	$\dfrac{(4{,}288{,}750 - 4{,}300{,}000)}{1.4632}$	$\dfrac{(4{,}318{,}125 - 430{,}000)}{1.4668}$
	3,195	(7,689)	12,357
Premium	(31,522)	(39,788)	(50,184)
	(2,997,077)	(2,984,977)	(2,975,327)

If the strike price is 1.4780, none of the options will be exercised.

	1.4500 £	1.4600 £	1.4700 £
Spot market 4,300,000/1.4780	(2,909,337)	(2,909,337)	(2,909,337)
$\dfrac{\text{Amount required to fulfil forward contract}}{\text{Spot rate}}$	$\dfrac{(4{,}304{,}687 - 4{,}300{,}000)}{1.4780}$	$\dfrac{(4{,}288{,}750 - 4{,}300{,}000)}{1.4820}$	$\dfrac{(4{,}318{,}125 - 4{,}300{,}000)}{1.4780}$
	(3,171)	7,591	(12,263)
Premium	(31,522)	(39,788)	(50,184)
Outcome	(2,944,030)	(2,941,534)	(2,971,784)

The conclusion remains the same.

(c) **Straddle option**

A straddle is made by **buying a put and a call** at the same time at the **same exercise price**. This provides **protection in times of exchange rate volatility** against exchange rate movements in either direction.

Because **two options** are **purchased, two premiums** will be **payable** (unlike with a collar where one option is purchased, one sold, and the two premiums are netted against each other.) The straddle will be profitable if the exchange rate is outside $1.46: £1 +/– the sums of the two premiums. (4.54 cents per pound) where a put option would suffice to cover exposure.

Straddles are suitable for **two-way exposures,** but would not be suitable for the **one-way exposure** in dollars that Autocrat has, where a simple put option will supply sufficient cover.

BPP LEARNING MEDIA

Question 3

Text references. Chapter 5 covers NPV and MIRR. APV is included in Chapter 7a.

Top tips. The key elements of the NPV calculation are the capital allowances and the CAPM-based cost of capital. You would not have scored well on the APV calculation if you didn't calculate the ungeared cost of equity.

The tax shield on debt has been discounted at the risk-free rate on the grounds that Tampern is virtually certain to receive tax relief on debt. Alternatively you could use the cost of debt to calculate the tax savings; this should have produced a positive APV of around £14,000.

In (b) a key point with NPV is that it assumes that risks will stay the same when investments are undertaken, although a key aim of major investments may be to change the risk profile of the company. APV takes into account the changes in financial risk.

Easy marks. The discussion in (b) about the advantages and disadvantages is quite straightforward.

Marking scheme

			Marks
(a)	Capital allowances/tax saving	1	
	NPV calculations	4 – 5	
	MIRR calculation	3	
	APV calculations		
	Base case NPV	3 – 4	
	Financing side effects	2 – 3	
	Give credit for technique		Max 15
(b)	Reward sensible discussion. Bonus mark for mention of real options		
			Max 10
			25

(a) **Expected NPV**

The NPV is found by discounting at the weighted average cost of capital, calculated as follows:

Cost of equity

Using CAPM

$Ke = r_f + [E(r_m) - r_f]\beta$
$= 4 + (10 - 4)\,1.5 = 13$

Cost of debt

After tax cost of debt $= 8(1 - 0.3)$
$= 5.6$

Weighted average cost of capital

Gearing after the investment has been financed is expected to be E = 0.6, D = 0.4

$$WACC = Ke_g \frac{E}{E+D} + Kd(1-t)\frac{D}{E+D}$$

$= 13(0.6) + 5.6(0.4)$

$= 10.04\%$, say 10%

Capital allowances

These are on the £4.4 million part of the investment that is fixed assets (not working capital or issue costs).

Year	Value at start of year	Capital allowance 25%	Tax saving 30%
	$'000	$'000	$'000
1	4,400	1,100	330
2	3,300	825	248
3	2,475	619	186
4	1,856	464	139

Year	0	1	2	3	4
	$'000	$'000	$'000	$'000	$'000
Pre-tax operating cash flows		1,250	1,400	1,600	1,800
Tax @ 30%		(375)	(420)	(480)	(540)
Tax savings from capital allowances		330	248	186	139
Investment cost	(5,000)				
Issue costs	(400)				
After tax realisable value					1,500
Net cash flows	(5,400)	1,205	1,228	1,306	2,899
Discount factor 10%	1.000	0.909	0.826	0.751	0.683
Present values	(5,400)	1,095	1,014	981	1,980

The expected net present value is **$(330,000)**

MIRR

Year	1	2	3	4
	$'000	$'000	$'000	$'000
Net cash flows	1,205	1,228	1,306	2,899
Multiplier	1.1^3	1.1^2	1.1	1
Reinvested amount	1,604	1,486	1,437	2,899

Total reinvested = 7,426

$MIRR = (7,426/5,400)^{0.25} - 1$

$MIRR = 1.083 - 1 = 8.3\%$

Expected APV

To calculate the base case NPV, the investment cash flows are discounted at the **ungeared cost of equity,** assuming the corporate debt is risk free (and has a beta of zero),

$$\beta_a = \beta_e \frac{E}{E + D(1-t)}$$

$$= 1.5 \times \frac{1}{1 + 1(1 - 0.3)} = 0.882$$

The ungeared cost of equity can now be estimated using the CAPM:

$Ke_u = r_f + [E(r_m) - r_f]\beta$

$= 4 + (10 - 4) \times 0.882$

$= 9.29\%$ (say, approximately 9%)

Year	0	1	2	3	4
	$'000	$'000	$'000	$'000	$'000
Net cash flows	(5,000)	1,205	1,228	1,306	2,899
Discount factor 9%	1.000	0.917	0.842	0.772	0.708
Present values	(5,000)	1,105	1,034	1,008	2,052

The expected base case net present value is **$199,000**.

BPP
LEARNING MEDIA

Financing side effects

Issue costs

$400,000, because they are treated as a side-effect they are not included in this NPV calculation.

Present value of tax shield

Debt capacity of project = $5.4m × 50% = $2.7m
Annual tax savings on debt interest = $2.7m × 8% × 30% = $64,800
PV of tax savings for 4 years, discounted at the risk-free rate 4%, is 64,800 × 3.630 = $235,224

	$'000
Adjusted present value	
Base case NPV	199
Tax relief on debt interest	235
Issue costs	(400)
	34

The adjusted present value is **$34,000**.

(b) **Validity of the views of the two managers**

Manager A

Manager A believes that the **net present value** method should be used, on the basis that the NPV of a project will be reflected in an **equivalent increase in the company's share price**. However, even if the market is efficient, this is only likely to be true if:

- The financing used **does not create a significant change** in gearing
- The project is **small relative to the size of the company**
- The project **risk is the same** as the company's average operating risk

The manager is correct that the NPV method is quicker than the MIRR (although this is only marginal) and APV methods. The main advantage of NPV over MIRR is that it gives an absolute measure of the increase in shareholder wealth.

Manager B

Manager B prefers the **adjusted present value method**, in which the cash flows are discounted at the ungeared cost of equity for the project, and the resulting NPV is then adjusted for financing side effects such as issue costs and the tax shield on debt interest. The main problem with the APV method is the **estimation** of the various **financing side effects** and the **discount rates** used to appraise them. For example in the calculation the risk-free rate has been used to discount the tax effect when the cost of debt of 8% could have been used instead and produced a different result.

Problems with both viewpoints

Both NPV and APV methods rely on the restrictive assumptions about capital markets which are made in the capital asset pricing model and in the theories of capital structure. The **figures used** in CAPM (risk-free rate, market rate and betas) can be difficult to determine. **Business risks** are assumed to be **constant**.

None of the methods considered attempt to value the possible **real options** for abandonment or further investment which may be associated with the project and could generate additional shareholder wealth. It is important to factor in these options to the initial evaluation of the project to ensure the correct decision is made.

Question 4

Text references. Chapter 18 for dividend policies.

Top tips. The calculations are the obvious comparisons between dividends and earnings, and dividends and free cash flows. The results demonstrate a very different picture depending on what comparisons are being made and the discussion needs to bring this out, and emphasise the importance of retaining cash in the business (which is **not** the same as retaining profits) for future investment. Despite the views of Modigliani and Miller, you need to mention that dividend policy is not normally set in a vacuum and takes no account of the views of shareholders; hence we need to know what shareholders want.

In (c) the chosen policy appears not to be maximising long-term shareholder value; however there may be real-world complications that our answer mentions.

Easy marks. The calculations are not complex, and centring the discussion round their results in (a) should ensure good marks.

Marking scheme

		Marks
(a)	Calculations, including payout ratio and dividends /FCFE	4 – 5
	Forthmate discussion	3 – 4
	Herander discussion	3 – 4
		Max 13
(b)	Reward sensible discussion. Look for benefits of the strategy and valid reasons not to use it	6
(c)	Look for problems and possible effect on shareholder wealth. Do not reward waffle	6
		25

(a) **Forthmate Co**

	Earnings after tax $'000	Free cash flow to equity $'000	Total dividend $'000	Dividend/ Earnings %	Dividend/Free cash flow %
20X1	24,050	11,400	4,800	20.0	42.1
20X2	22,345	12,200	4,500	20.1	36.9
20X3	26,460	(3,500)	5,300	20.0	(151.4)
20X4	32,450	(2,600)	6,500	20.0	(250.0)
20X5	35,890	9,200	7,150	19.9	77.7

Herander Co

	Earnings after tax $'000	Free cash flow to equity $'000	Total dividend $'000	Dividend/ Earnings %	Dividend/Free cash flow %
20X1	8,250	6,100	5,000	60.6	82.0
20X2	5,920	(4,250)	5,000	84.5	(117.6)
20X3	9,140	10,300	5,150	56.3	50.0
20X4	10,350	4,400	5,250	50.7	119.3
20X5	8,220	3,140	5,250	63.9	167.2

Both companies' dividend policies

Both companies have **consistent dividend policies**, indicating that the directors regard dividend policy as important. This is in contrast to some theories (eg Modigliani and Miller) that argue that the pattern of dividend payouts will not affect company value.

Forthmate's dividend policy

This has two factors.

(i) **Dividends are a constant percentage of earnings**

This policy is not common, as it could cause **dividends to vary widely** from year to year, as earnings vary, although in the case of Forthmate this has not happened between 20X1 and 20X5 (variation has been between 4.8c and 5.5c per share). It can also be argued that dividends should be **related to free cash flow**, rather than earnings (see below (b)).

(ii) **The dividend payout is low at 20% of earnings after tax**

This may be because the company's shareholders **prefer to make their gains from capital gains** (sale of shares at a profit) as opposed to dividends, probably for tax reasons. If the company has constant opportunities for growth and reinvestment, this is a common dividend policy to adopt.

Herander's dividend policy

The policy also has two factors, both different from those of Forthmate.

(i) **A nearly constant dividend of 10 cents per share is paid**

This has risen slightly, probably to allow for inflation. This has the advantage of allowing shareholders to **budget for their cash flows with more certainty**, but if profits fall, the **dividend** may have to be **reduced**, creating a possible loss of shareholder confidence.

(ii) **The dividend payout is high at over 50% of earnings after tax**

Shareholders may prefer a **higher payout**, but the **company's earnings fluctuate considerably** and there is some risk that in a bad year the dividend may have to be reduced.

(b) **Should a company pay dividends equal to the free cash flow to equity?**

Free cash flow

Free cash flow to equity is the annual cash that the company has available to pay dividends, after net investment in fixed and working capital and net debt financing flows have been taken into account.

Preference for lower dividends

Although payment of dividends equal to free cash flow is a sensible level for maximum dividends, there are reasons why companies often prefer dividends to be lower. For example:

- **Retaining cash** enables the trend of **dividends** from year to year to be **smoother**; this may increase shareholder confidence

- The company may be **accumulating cash** in order to make an **acquisition** or to hold as a **precautionary balance**

- **Legal restraints** (eg rules on distributable profits) may prevent a company from paying out all its free cash flows as dividend

Consequences of higher dividends

When companies pay out dividends that are more than FCFE (this happens in three of the five years for Herander plc) this is **financed by reducing cash reserves** (in the case of Herander) or alternatively by issuing new shares.

(c) **Herander's financial strategy**

Consequences of high dividends

In 20X4 and 20X5 Herander's FCFE has been significantly less than its equity earnings and its dividends have been 119% and 167% of FCFE. Also in those years Herander has had to reject three investments that would have increased shareholder wealth. These have a total inital cost of $5.275 million. It can be argued that if the dividend payout was less this would have allowed **further new investment in projects.**

Other issues

The investments may have been too **large to finance** even if the dividend had been significantly reduced. This is likely to be the case with the 20X5 project with an initial cost of $3.5 million. Herander may well be worried about the signalling effect of reducing dividends significantly even though shareholder wealth would actually be increased by this. **Further fund issues** (equity or debt) may have been required. However investors may be reluctant to contribute further equity. The directors may be unwilling to increase gearing or debt may not be available on acceptable terms. It may also be that the investment in additional projects would have placed **too large a strain** on the company's ability to **manage its project portfolio,** as each project is likely to have required separate management. It is assumed that these projects are **not divisible** or else it seems likely that some of them would have been undertaken in part.

ACCA Professional Level

Paper P4

Advanced Financial Management

Mock Examination 3

Pilot paper

Question Paper	
Time allowed	
Reading and Planning Writing	**15 minutes** **3 hours**
Section A	**THIS question is compulsory and MUST be attempted**
Section B	**TWO questions ONLY to be attempted**
During reading and planning time only the question paper may be annotated	

DO NOT OPEN THIS PAPER UNTIL YOU ARE READY TO START UNDER EXAMINATION CONDITIONS

BPP
LEARNING MEDIA

SECTION A: THIS QUESTION is compulsory and MUST be attempted

Question 1

Tramont Co is a listed company based in the USA and manufactures electronic devices. One of its devices, the *X-IT*, is produced exclusively for the American market. Tramont Co is considering ceasing the production of the *X-IT* gradually over a period of four years because it needs the manufacturing facilities used to make the *X-IT* for other products.

The government of Gamala, a country based in south-east Asia, is keen to develop its manufacturing industry and has offered Tramont Co first rights to produce the *X-IT* in Gamala and sell it to the USA market for a period of four years. At the end of the four-year period, the full production rights will be sold to a government-backed company for Gamalan Rupiahs (GR) 450 million after tax (this amount is not subject to inflationary increases). Tramont Co has to decide whether to continue production of the *X-IT* in the USA for the next four years or to move the production to Gamala immediately.

Currently each *X-IT* unit sold makes a unit contribution of $20. This unit contribution is not expected to be subject to any inflationary increase in the next four years. Next year's production and sales estimated at 40,000 units will fall by 20% each year for the following three years. It is anticipated that after four years the production of the *X-IT* will stop. It is expected that the financial impact of the gradual closure over the four years will be cost neutral (the revenue from sale of assets will equal the closure costs). If production is stopped immediately, the excess assets would be sold for $2.3 million and the costs of closure, including redundancy costs of excess labour, would be $1.7 million.

The following information relates to the production of the *X-IT* moving to Gamala. The Gamalan project will require an initial investment of GR 230 million, to pay for the cost of land and buildings (GR 150 million) and machinery (GR 80 million). The cost of machinery is tax allowable and will be depreciated on a straight-line basis over the next four years, at the end of which it will have a negligible value.

Tramont Co will also need GR 40 million for working capital immediately. It is expected that the working capital requirement will increase in line with the annual inflation rate in Gamala. When the project is sold, the working capital will not form part of the sale price and will be released back to Tramont Co.

Production and sales of the device are expected to be 12,000 units in the first year, rising to 22,000 units, 47,000 units and 60,000 units in the next three years respectively.

The following revenues and costs apply to the first year of operation:

- Each unit will be sold for $70;

- The variable cost per unit comprising of locally sourced materials and labour will be GR 1,350, and;

- In addition to the variable cost above, each unit will require a component bought from Tramont Co for $7, on which Tramont Co makes $4 contribution per unit;

- Total fixed costs for the first year will be GR 30 million.

The costs are expected to increase by their countries' respective rates of inflation, but the selling price will remain fixed at $70 per unit for the four-year period.

The annual corporation tax rate in Gamala is 20% and Tramont Co currently pays corporation tax at a rate of 30% per year. Both countries' corporation taxes are payable in the year that the tax liability arises. A bi-lateral tax treaty exists between the USA and Gamala, which permits offset of overseas tax against any USA tax liability on overseas earnings. The USA and Gamalan tax authorities allow losses to be carried forward and written off against future profits for taxation purposes.

Tramont Co has decided to finance the project by borrowing the funds required in Gamala. The commercial borrowing rate is 13% but the Gamalan government has offered Tramont Co a 6% subsidised loan for the entire amount of the initial funds required. The Gamalan government has agreed that it will not ask for the loan to be repaid as long as Tramont Co fulfils its contract to undertake the project for the four years. Tramont Co can borrow dollar funds at an interest rate of 5%.

Tramont Co's financing consists of 25 million shares currently trading at $2.40 each and $40 million 7% bonds trading at $1,428 per $1,000. Tramont Co's quoted beta is 1·17. The current risk free rate of return is estimated at 3% and the market risk premium is 6%. Due to the nature of the project, it is estimated that the beta applicable to the project if it is all-equity financed will be 0.4 more than the current all-equity financed beta of Tramont Co. If the Gamalan project is undertaken, the cost of capital applicable to the cash flows in the USA is expected to be 7%.

The spot exchange rate between the dollar and the Gamalan Rupiah is GR 55 per $1. The annual inflation rates are currently 3% in the USA and 9% in Gamala. It can be assumed that these inflation rates will not change for the foreseeable future. All net cash flows arising from the project will be remitted back to Tramont Co at the end of each year.

There are two main political parties in Gamala: the Gamala Liberal (GL) Party and the Gamala Republican (GR) Party. Gamala is currently governed by the GL Party but general elections are due to be held soon. If the GR Party wins the election, it promises to increase taxes of international companies operating in Gamala and review any commercial benefits given to these businesses by the previous government.

Required:

(a) Prepare a report for the Board of Directors of Tramont Co that

(i) Evaluates whether or not Tramont Co should undertake the project to produce the *X-IT* in Gamala and cease its production in the USA immediately. In the evaluation, include all relevant calculations in the form of a financial assessment and explain any assumptions made;

It is suggested that the financial assessment should be based on present value of the operating cash flows from the Gamalan project, discounted by an appropriate all-equity rate, and adjusted by the present value of all other relevant cash flows. **(27 marks)**

(ii) Discusses the potential change in government and other business factors that Tramont Co should consider before making a final decision. **(8 marks)**

Professional marks will be awarded in question 1 for the format, structure and presentation of the answer. **(4 marks)**

(b) Although not mandatory for external reporting purposes, one of the members of the BoD suggested that adopting a triple bottom line approach when monitoring the X-IT investment after its implementation, would provide a better assessment of how successful it has been.

Discuss how adopting aspects of triple bottom line reporting may provide a better assessment of the success of X-IT. **(6 marks)**

(c) Another member of the BoD felt that, despite Tramont Co having a wide range of shareholders holding well diversified portfolios of investments, moving the production of the X-IT to Gamala would result in further risk diversification benefits.

Discuss whether moving the production of the X-IT to Gamala may result in further risk diversification for the shareholders already holding well diversified portfolios. **(5 marks)**

(Total = 50 marks)

BPP LEARNING MEDIA

SECTION B: TWO QUESTIONS ONLY to be attempted

Question 2

Alecto Co, a large listed company based in Europe, is expecting to borrow €22,000,000 in four months' time on 1 May 2012. It expects to make a full repayment of the borrowed amount nine months from now. Currently there is some uncertainty in the markets, with higher than normal rates of inflation, but an expectation that the inflation level may soon come down. This has led some economists to predict a rise in interest rates and others suggesting an unchanged outlook or maybe even a small fall in interest rates over the next six months.

Although Alecto Co is of the opinion that it is equally likely that interest rates could increase or fall by 0.5% in four months, it wishes to protect itself from interest rate fluctuations by using derivatives. The company can borrow at LIBOR plus 80 basis points and LIBOR is currently 3.3%. The company is considering using interest rate futures, options on interest rate futures or interest rate collars as possible hedging choices.

The following information and quotes from an appropriate exchange are provided on Euro futures and options. Margin requirements may be ignored.

Three month Euro futures, €1,000,000 contract, tick size 0.01% and tick value €25

March	96.27
June	96.16
September	95.90

Options on three month Euro futures, €1,000,000 contract, tick size 0.01% and tick value €25. Option premiums are in annual %.

	Calls		Strike		Puts	
March	June	September		March	June	September
0.279	0.391	0.446	96.00	0.006	0.163	0.276
0.012	0.090	0.263	96.50	0.196	0.581	0.754

It can be assumed that settlement for both the futures and options contracts is at the end of the month. It can also be assumed that basis diminishes to zero at contract maturity at a constant rate and that time intervals can be counted in months.

Required:

(a) Briefly discuss the main advantage and disadvantage of hedging interest rate risk using an interest rate collar instead of options.

(4 marks)

(b) Based on the three hedging choices Alecto Co is considering and assuming that the company does not face any basis risk, recommend a hedging strategy for the €22,000,000 loan. Support your recommendation with appropriate comments and relevant calculations in €.

(17 marks)

(c) Explain what is meant by basis risk and how it would affect the recommendation made in part (b) above.

(4 marks)

(Total = 25 marks)

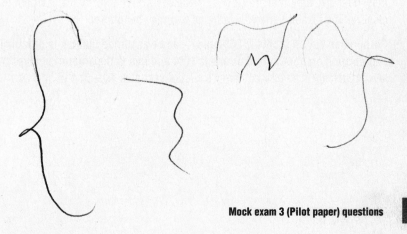

Question 3

Doric Co has two manufacturing divisions: parts and fridges. Although the parts division is profitable, the fridges division is not, and as a result its share price has declined to 50c per share from a high of $2.83 per share around three years ago. Assume it is now 1 January 2013.

The Board of Directors are considering two proposals:

(i)   To cease trading and close down the company entirely.

(ii) To close the fridge divisions and continue the parts division through a leveraged management buy-out. The new company will continue with manufacturing part only, but will make an additional investment of $50 million in order to grow the parts division after-tax cash flows by 3.5% in perpetuity. The proceeds from the sale of the fridges division will be used to pay the outstanding liabilities. The finance raised from the management buy-out will pay for any remaining liabilities, the funds required for the additional investment, and to purchase the current equity shares at a premium of 20%.The fridges division is twice the size of the parts division in terms of its assets attributable to it.

Extracts from the most recent financial statements:

Financial position as at 31 December 2012	$m
Assets	
Non-Current Assets	110
Current Assets	220
Share capital ($0.40 per share par value)	40
Reserves	10
Liabilities (Non-current and current)	280

Income statement for the year ended 31 December 2012

		$m
Sales revenue: Parts division		170
Fridge division		340
Costs prior to depreciation, interest payments and tax:	Parts division	(120)
	Fridge division	(370)
Depreciation, tax and interest		(34)
Loss		(14)

If the entire company's assets are sold, the estimated realisable values of assets are as follows:

	$m
Non-current assets	100
Current assets	110

The following additional information has been provided:

Redundancy and other costs will be approximately $54 million if the whole company is closed, and pro rata for individual divisions that are closed. These costs have priority for payment before any other liabilities in case of closure. The taxation effects relating to this may be ignored.

Corporation tax on profits is 20% and it can be assumed that tax is payable in the year incurred. Annual depreciation on non-current assets is 10% and this is the amount of investment needed to maintain the current level of activity. The new company's cost of capital is expected to be 11%.

Required

(a) Briefly discuss the possible benefits of Doric Co's parts division being divested through a management buy-out. **(4 marks)**

(b) An estimate of the return the liability holders and the shareholders would receive in the event that Doric Co is closed and all its assets sold. **(3 marks)**

(c) Estimate the amount of additional finance needed and the value of the new company, if only the assets of the fridges division are sold and the parts division is divested through a management buy-out. Briefly discuss whether or not the management buy-out would be beneficial. **(10 marks)**

(d) Doric Co's directors are of the opinion that they could receive a better price if the fridges division is sold as a going concern instead of its assets sold separately. They have been told that they need to consider two aspects when selling a company or part of a company; (i) seeking potential buyers and negotiating the sale price; and, (ii) due diligence.

Discuss the issues that should be taken into consideration with each aspect. **(8 marks)**

(Total = 25 marks)

Question 4

GNT Co is considering an investment in one of two corporate bonds. Both bonds have a par value of $1,000 and pay coupon interest on an annual basis. The market price of the first bond is $1,079.68. Its coupon rate is 6% and it is due to be redeemed at par in five years. The second bond is about to be issued with a coupon rate of 4% and will also be redeemable at par in five years. Both bonds are expected to have the same gross redemption yields (yields to maturity). The yield to maturity of a company's bond is determined by its credit rating.

GNT Co considers duration of the bond to be a key factor when making decisions on which bond to invest.

Required:

(a) Estimate the Macaulay duration of the two bonds GNT Co is considering for investment. **(9 marks)**

(b) Discuss how useful duration is as a measure of the sensitivity of a bond price to changes in interest rates. **(8 marks)**

(c) Among the criteria used by credit agencies for establishing a company's credit rating are the following: industry risk, earnings protection, financial flexibility and evaluation of the company's management.

Briefly explain each criterion and suggest factors that could be used to assess it. **(8 marks)**

(Total = 25 marks)

BPP
LEARNING MEDIA

Answers

DO NOT TURN THIS PAGE UNTIL YOU HAVE
COMPLETED THE MOCK EXAM

BPP
LEARNING MEDIA

A plan of attack

You have no doubt been told to do it about 201 times and we know if we asked you you'd know that you should do it. So why don't you do it in an exam? 'Do what in an exam?' you're no doubt thinking. Well for the 202nd time let's enlighten you. **Take a good look through the paper before diving in to answer questions.**

First things first

You are given 15 minutes' reading time before the exam begins. During that time you can obviously read the paper and make notes on the question paper *only*. You can also use your calculator to carry out preliminary calculations. The reading time most importantly allows you to carefully read and understand the question requirements and choose which optional questions you are going to attempt. You can also decide in which order you are going to attempt the questions. If you still have time after doing all that, you can start to plan how you are going to structure your answers.

The next step

When the 3 hours' writing time begins you will probably be in one of two minds – either still not knowing where to start or feeling reasonably confident about the questions.

Option 1 (if you don't know where to begin)

If you are a bit worried about the paper and not feeling overly confident about answering any of the questions, you might be as well to start at the beginning with the compulsory Section A question.

- **Question 1** requires a report that evaluates the proposed relocation of production facilities to an overseas country. The number of marks allocated to part (a)(i) might intimidate you but if you read the guidance in the requirement you are actually given some help on how to approach it. What it amounts to is an NPV calculation and the adjustments also suggest an APV calculation. If you feel more comfortable you could attempt some of part (a)(ii) first. You should be able to remember some factors that companies should consider when making overseas investment decisions (but make your answer relevant to the scenario you are given). Don't forget the report format – it is worth up to four marks! Parts (b) and (c) require some fairly straightforward discussion about triple bottom line and diversification.

- **Question 2** deals with interest rate hedging. You should choose this question if you are confident wit futures and options. Again the mark allocation in part (b) might seem intimidating but when you read the question you will find there are three hedging techniques you have to deal with (resulting in just over five marks each). You don't have to tackle the requirements in order so if you are more comfortable starting with the discursive elements (such as explaining basis risk) then do so. Try to remember the step by step approach in the Study Text for each of the hedging techniques and don't be afraid to make some assumptions about whether the company should buy or sell contracts if you can't remember the rules.

- **Question 3** focuses on divestment and management buy-outs. You should really only choose this question if divestments and management buy-outs are a strong topic for you. However if you are struggling to find a second option question to attempt you should at least be able to make a good attempt at parts (a) and (b).

- **Question 4** examines duration and credit ratings. If you don't know how Macaulay duration works then this question may not be a good choice. However part (c) offers some marks for knowledge taken straight from the Study Text if you need to choose a second optional question.

What you should always remember is that you **must** answer the question in Section A but only **two** questions from Section B.

Option 2 (if you're thinking 'I can do all of these')

Are you **sure** you are comfortable with all the requirements? If you are then that's encouraging. Tackle the question you feel most comfortable with first – that will settle you down and get you going. The questions are discussed in order here but you obviously don't have to tackle them in this order.

- **Question 1** – remember to present your answer in a report format (it is not enough just to include a heading entitled 'Report'!) Make sure your workings are laid out and labelled clearly and don't forget to reference the figures in your NPV and APV calculations to the correct workings. This will make it easier for the marker to find where the figures have come from (and hopefully award marks!)

- **Question 2** – this is quite a challenging question but on a key area of the syllabus. The majority of the marks are for the hedging techniques in part (b) but don't forget to leave enough time for the discursive elements. Also don't forget to make a recommendation in part (b) – it's easy to get immersed in the calculations and then not answer the question!

- **Question 3** – don't forget to answer both parts of the question in part (c). You are also asked to briefly discuss whether the MBO would be beneficial or not.

- **Question 4** – make sure you only talk about the criteria mentioned in the question. No credit will be available for discussing others.

No matter how many times we remind you...

Always allocate your time according to the marks for the question in total and for the individual parts of each question. Also **always answer the question you were asked** rather than the question you wished you had been asked or the question you thought you had been asked.

You've got free time at the end of the exam...?

Looks like you've slipped up on the time allocation. However if you have, don't waste the last few minutes; go back to **any parts of questions that you didn't finish** because you moved onto another task.

Forget about it!

Forget about what? Excellent – you already have!

Question 1

Text references. NPV is covered in Chapter 5, APV in Chapter 7 and international aspects (including purchasing power parity) in Chapter 8.

Top tips. It is very easy to feel daunted when you see the number of marks available for part (a)(i). However you are given guidance in the question regarding how to approach the financial assessment and you should follow this carefully. If you stop and think for a minute you will realise that you are dealing with a detailed NPV calculation and the requirement to adjust by the present value of all other relevant cash flows suggests an APV calculation will also be required. Once you have that clear in your mind the question should be more approachable.

There is a lot of information in the question but if you remember (and use) the NPV tabular approach the calculations should be more manageable. As Tramont is a US company you should expect to have to convert your results into dollars.

You are given inflation rates as part of the exchange rate information which suggests the use of purchasing power parity to forecast future rates. You are given the formula in the exam so this should give you some easy marks. Also make sure you use the correct inflation rate in your NPV and APV calculations – don't get the two countries' rates mixed up!

There are several interest rates given in the question – make sure you use the correct one at the correct time! For example, for the tax shield on borrowings in Gamala you are told that a 6% subsidised loan is available, therefore 6% is the rate you should use.

We have shown additional US tax, contributions and opportunity costs as part of one calculation – given that you have to discount all these figures at the same rate, this is the quickest way of doing so. You will gain full credit if you discounted all the figures separately but remember this is a time-pressured exam.

Easy marks. There are numerous easy marks to be picked up in part (i).

Examiner's answers. The examiner's answer to this question can be found at the back of this kit.

Marking scheme

		Marks	
(a)(i)	Estimated future rates based on purchasing power parity	1	
	Sales revenue, variable costs, component cost and fixed costs (in GR)	4	
	Taxable profits and taxation	2	
	Investment, terminal value and working capital	2	
	Cash flows in GR	1	
	Cash flows in $	1	
	Discount rate of all-equity financed project	2	
	Base case PVs and NPV	2	
	PVs of additional contribution, additional tax and opportunity cost	4	
	PV of tax shield and subsidy benefits	4	
	Closure costs and benefits	1	
	Initial comments and conclusion	1 – 2	
	Assumptions and sensitivity analysis	2 – 3	
			Max 27
(ii)	Implications of change of government	2 – 3	
	Other business factors (1 – 2 marks per factor)	5 – 6	
			Max 8
	Professional marks		
	Report format	1	
	Layout, presentation and structure	3	
			4
(b)	1 mark per relevant point		6

(c)	General commentary regarding benefits of risk diversification	2 - 3
	Relating specifically to Tramont Co and the Gamalan investment	2 - 3
		Max 5
	Total	**50**

(a)

To:	The Board of Directors of Tramont Co
From:	Accountant
Date:	XX/X/XX
Subject:	Evaluation of proposal to relocate production of X-IT to Gamala

The report considers the proposal to relocate production of X-IT from the USA to Gamala. The report includes an initial evaluation and then considers the key assumptions made in the evaluation, the potential effects of a change in the government of Gamala following the upcoming elections and also other business factors that should be taken into account before a decision is made.

The initial evaluation is a base case net present value calculation that assesses the impact of production in Gamala. This is then adjusted to show the impact of cash flows in the USA, including the impact of ceasing production, the impact of the subsidy and the tax shield benefits arising from the loan.

Based on the calculations, which can be found in the appendix, the move will generate a positive adjusted present value of just over $2.3 million. Based on these calculations it is recommended that production of X-IT should move to Gamala.

Assumptions

The **borrowing rate of 5%** has been used to calculate the present value of the tax shield benefits. The risk-free rate of 3% could have been used instead, but it was felt more prudent to use the 5% rate.
An adjusted present value calculation would normally use the debt capacity for the tax shield benefit calculation rather than the amount of debt finance used, but as this is not known it has been **assumed that the increase in debt capacity is equal to the debt finance used**.

There are a number of variables included in the calculations. It is assumed that these will change as stated over the four year period. Exchange rates have been forecast using purchasing power parity, which it is assumed will hold for the four year period. In reality these variables may not alter as has been assumed and therefore **it is recommended that sensitivity analysis is used** to calculate the effect of changes in these key variables on the overall conclusion.

Government change

A change of government in Gamala may have a significant impact on the project as a result of changes threatened by the opposition party. The **proposed tax increase may be significant** as this would reduce the total tax shield and subsidy benefits as well as creating higher cash outflows in years 3 and 4 of the project. An even more significant change may arise, however, from the review of 'commercial benefits.' Approximately 45% (1,033 / 2,317) of the adjusted present value comes from the tax shield and subsidy benefits. If these arrangements were to change then Tramont could lose a significant amount of value from the project.

The new government may also review whether remittances are allowed every year as has been assumed in these calculations. This issue may be fairly minor as the majority of the value comes from the final year of operation anyway.

Other business factors

Tramont needs to also consider whether being based in Gamala will lead to any **follow-on projects**. The real options that are present within any such projects should be factored into the assessment of whether to relocate.

Tramont also needs to ensure that this project **fits within its overall strategy**. Even if the decision to cease production in the USA is made there may be other, better alternatives than the Gamalan option. These other options should also be assessed.

BPP
LEARNING MEDIA

Tramont also needs to consider whether its **systems can be adapted to the culture in Gamala**. If Tramont has experience in international ventures then its directors may be surer of this. Tramont will need to develop strategies to combat any cultural differences. There may be further training costs as part of these strategies which have not been factored into this assessment.

Another factor to consider is whether the project can be delayed as this will reduce the opportunity cost of lost contribution, which is greater in years 1 and 2. Therefore **a delay could increase the overall value** of the project.

There are possible redundancies from the closure of production of X-IT in the USA. Since production will probably cease in the USA anyway the strategy should be clearly communicated to employees and other stakeholders in order to ensure its reputation is not damaged. As a result it may be even more important to consider alternatives to this plan.

Conclusion

The initial evaluation suggests that moving production of X-IT to Gamala would be beneficial. Before making a final decision, the Board should conduct a detailed sensitivity analysis, analysis of the effects of a change in government and the financial effects of the other factors identified above.

Appendix

Net Present Value of Gamalan project

Year	0	1	2	3	4
	GR '000	GR '000	GR '000	GR '000	GR '000
Sales revenue (W2)		48,888	94,849	214,442	289,716
Variable costs – local (W3)		(16,200)	(32,373)	(75,385)	(104,897)
Imported components (W4)		(4,889)	(9,769)	(22,750)	(31,658)
Fixed costs (inflating at 9%)		(30,000)	(32,700)	(35,643)	(38,851)
Profit before tax		(2,201)	20,007	80,664	114,310
Tax (W5)		0	0	(7,694)	(18,862)
Investment	(230,000)				450,000
Working capital	(40,000)	(3,600)	(3,924)	(4,277)	51,801
Total GR cash flows	(270,000)	(5,801)	16,083	68,693	597,249
Exchange rate GR/$ (W1)	55.00	58.20	61.59	65.18	68.98

Year	0	1	2	3	4
	$ '000	$ '000	$ '000	$ '000	$ '000
Total $ cash flows	(4,909)	(100)	261	1,054	8,658
$ discount factor (W6)	1.000	0.909	0.826	0.751	0.683
Present value	(4,909)	(91)	216	792	5,913

NPV = $1,921,000

Adjusted present value (APV)	$'000
Base case NPV	1,921
Additional US tax, opportunity cost and additional component contribution (W7)	(1,237)
Closure revenues and costs ($2.3m – $1.7m)	600
Tax shield and subsidy benefits (W8)	1,033
APV	2,317

Workings

1   Exchange rates

GR/$

Now	55.00
Year 1	55.00 × (1.09/1.03) = 58.20
Year 2	58.20 × (1.09/1.03) = 61.59
Year 3	61.59 × (1.09/1.03) = 65.18
Year 4	65.18 × (1.09/1.03) = 68.98

2 Sales revenue

Revenue = price × units × exchange rate

Year	1	2	3	4
	GR '000	GR '000	GR '000	GR '000
Sales revenue	70 × 12,000 × 58.20	70 × 22,000 × 61.59	70 × 47,000 × 65.18	70 × 60,000 × 68.98
	= 48,888	= 94,849	= 214,442	= 289,716

3 Variable costs - local

Unit cost × units × inflation after year 1

Year	1	2	3	4
	GR '000	GR '000	GR '000	GR '000
Cost	1,350 × 12,000	1,350 × 22,000 × 1.09	1,350 × 47,000 × 1.09^2	1,350 × 60,000 × 1.09^3
	= 16,200	= 32,373	= 75,385	= 104,897

4 Imported components

Price × units × inflation after year 1 × exchange rate

Year	1	2	3	4
	GR '000	GR '000	GR '000	GR '000
Cost	7 × 12,000 × 58.20 = 4,889	7 × 22,000 × 1.03 × 61.59 = 9,769	7 × 47,000 × 1.03^2 × 65.18 = 22,750	7 × 60,000 × 1.03^3 × 68.98 = 31,658

5 Taxation

Year	1	2	3	4
	GR '000	GR '000	GR '000	GR '000
Profit/(loss) before tax	(2,201)	20,007	80,664	114,310
Tax allowable depreciation	(20,000)	(20,000)	(20,000)	(20,000)
Revised profit / (loss)	(22,201)	7	60,664	94,310
Offset against previous losses	0	(7)	(22,194)	0
Losses carried forward	(22,201)	(22,194)	0	0
Tax base	0	0	38,470	94,310
Taxation @ 20%	0	0	(7,694)	(18,862)

6 Discount rate

Tramont Co equity beta = 1.17
MV_e = $2.40 × 25m shares = $60 million
MV_d = $40m × $1,428/$1,000 = $57.12 million

Tramont Co asset beta (assume debt is risk free)
1.17 × 60m/(60m + (57.12 × 0.7)) = 0.70

Project asset beta -= 0.70 + 0.40 = 1.10
Project discount rate if all equity financed = 3% + (1.1 × 6%) = 9.6% say 10%

7 Additional tax, additional contribution and opportunity cost ($'000)

Year	1	2	3	4
Additional tax *	0	0	(59)	(137)
Opportunity cost **	(560)	(448)	(358)	(287)
Additional contribution ***	34	63	140	184
Total cash flows	(526)	(385)	(277)	(240)
7% discount factor	0.935	0.873	0.816	0.763
Present value	(492)	(336)	(226)	(183)

Total present value = $(1,237,000)

* Taxable profits / exchange rate × 10%
**Units × contribution × (1 − tax rate)
***Units × contribution × inflation × (1 − tax rate)

BPP
LEARNING MEDIA

8   **Tax shield and subsidy benefits (GR'000 / $'000)**

Year	1	2	3	4
	GR '000	GR '000	GR '000	GR '000
Annual tax shield*	3,240	3,240	3,240	3,240
Annual subsidy benefit**	15,120	15,120	15,120	15,120
Total benefit	18,360	18,360	18,360	18,360
Exchange rate	58.20	61.59	65.18	68.98
	$'000	$'000	$'000	$'000
Cash flow	315	298	282	266
5% discount rate	0.952	0.907	0.864	0.823
PV	300	270	244	219

Total present value = $1,033,000

* Interest × loan × tax rate = 6% × 270m × 20% = 3.24m
** Interest gain × loan × (1 – tax rate) = 7% × 270m × 0.8 = 15.12m

(b)   Triple bottom line (TBL) reporting involves providing a quantitative summary in terms of social, financial and environmental performance.

The **underlying principle** is that in order to evaluate a company's true performance against its objectives, and assess the risk to the investor, the investor must consider all three areas.

Under the TBL approach decision-making should ensure that **each perspective is growing** but not at the **expense** of the others. That is economic performance should not come at the expense of the environment or society. The idea is that an organisation which accommodates all three areas will enhance shareholder value as long as the costs of producing the report are less than the benefits that arise from it.

In the case of Tramont and production of X-IT, reporting on the impact of moving production to Gamala, including the environmental impact, will show Tramont in a good light and improve its reputation. This should in turn make it easier to attract and retain the best employees.

(c)   Portfolio theory states that shareholders who hold a well-diversified portfolio will have diversified away the unsystematic or company specific risk and will be left with systematic risk. Following this a shareholder cannot reduce risk further by undertaking **additional diversification** in the same system or market. A company may be able to achieve further diversification for its shareholders by investing in a system or market that the individual shareholders do not invest in themselves. Some studies have shown that well-diversified investors **can benefit from risk diversification** when companies invest in **emerging markets**.

In the case of Tramont and X-IT, it is unclear whether there will be any diversification benefits from the Gamalan investment. Any benefits are dependent on the **size of the investment** and the **nature** of the business operations in Gamala. Another issue is whether the investment represents an investment in a different system or market. If the investment is large and the operations are similar to undertaking a Gamalan company then shareholders in Tramont who do not hold similar companies' shares **may gain risk diversification benefits** from the investment.

$$\beta_a = \beta_e \frac{E}{E + D(1-T)}$$

Question 2

Text references. Interest rate hedging is covered in Chapter 17.

Top tips. Remember that interest rate hedging involves finding the best interest rate whilst protecting yourself against interest rate movements. You are told that interest rates can move by 0.5% in either direction, therefore you really have six calculations to do in part (b) – three techniques with two interest rate movements. Use the tabular approach demonstrated in the Study Text as far as possible.

When tackling hedging questions on interest rates establish immediately whether the company is borrowing or lending. This will help when trying to decide whether it should be buying or selling contracts.

It is easy to get mixed up when deciding whether you should be buying or selling contracts. If you can't remember the rules (see Chapter 17 section 7.4 for a useful table of rules) just state your decision and base your calculations on this. Even if your decision is incorrect you should pick up marks for technique.

You do not have to tackle the hedging techniques in the order given in the question – just make sure you label your workings to make it clear which technique you are dealing with. Remember that the net cost of a future when the interest rate rises or falls should be the same (subject to rounding).

As the company is borrowing money and is using a collar, it should buy a put (the right to sell a future) and sell a call. The put will be at the higher interest rate (and the lower strike price) and the call will be at the lower interest rate (the higher strike price).

Whilst the calculations in part (b) may seem quite long, remember that you can use a number of the figures you calculated early on in your later calculations (such as expected futures price) – don't rework these calculations as you will just be wasting valuable time.

Easy marks. You should be able to pick up some relatively straightforward marks in part (c) – you should know what basis risk is.

Examiner's answers. The examiner's answer to this question can be found at the back of this kit.

Marking scheme

		Marks	
(a)	Discussion of the main advantage	2	
	Discussion of the main disadvantage	2	
			4
(b)	Recommendation to go short if futures are used and purchase puts if options are used	1	
	Calculation of number of contracts and remaining basis	2	
	Futures contracts calculations	4	
	Options contracts calculations	4	
	Collar approach and calculations	4	
	Supporting comments and conclusion	2 – 3	
			Max 17
(c)	Explanation of basis risk	2 – 3	
	Effect of basis risk on recommendation made	2 – 3	
			Max 4
			25

(a)   An interest rate collar involves the purchase of a **put option** and the **simultaneous selling of a call option** at different exercise prices. The main advantage is that it is **cheaper** than just purchasing the put option. This is because the premium received from selling the call option reduces the higher premium payable for the put option.

The main disadvantage is that the **benefit** from any upside movement in interest rates is **capped** by the sale of the call option. With just the put option, the full upside benefit would be realised.

(b)   **Futures**

As Alecto is looking to protect against a rise in interest rates it needs to sell futures. As the borrowing is required on 1 May, June contracts are needed.

No of contracts needed = €22,000,000/€1,000,000 × 5/3 months = 36.67

Need 37 contracts

Basis
Current price (1 Jan) – futures price = basis
100 – 3.3 – 96.16 = 0.54
Unexpired basis = 2/6 × 0.54 = 0.18

	Interest rates increase to 3.8%		Interest rates decrease to 2.8%	
Cost of borrowing	(3.8% + 0.8%) × 5/12 × €22m	€421,667	(2.8% + 0.8%) × 5/12 × €22m	€330,000
Expected futures price	100 – 3.8 – 0.18	96.02	100 – 2.8 – 0.18	97.02
Gain / loss on futures market	(9616 – 9602) × €25 × 37	(€12,950)	(9616 – 9702) × €25 × 37	€79,550
Net cost		€408,717		€409,550
Effective interest rate	408,717/22m × 12/5	4.46%	409,550/22m × 12/5	4.47%

The difference in interest rates comes from the rounding of the contracts.

Using options on futures

As Alecto is looking to protect against a rise in interest rates it needs to buy June put options. As before 37 contracts are needed.

Interest rates	Increase to 3.8%		Decrease to 2.8%	
Put option exercise price	4%	3.5%	4%	3.5%
June futures price	3.98%	3.98%	2.98%	2.98%
Exercise option?	No	Yes	No	No
Gain	-	0.48%	-	-
	%	%	%	%
Actual interest cost	(4.60)	(4.60)	(3.60)	(3.60)
Value of option gain	-	0.48	-	-
Premium	(0.16)	(0.58)	(0.16)	(0.58)
Net cost of loan	(4.76)	(4.70)	(3.76)	(4.18)

Using a collar

Buy June put at 96.00 for 0.163 and sell June call at 96.00 for 0.090. Net premium payable = 0.073. As before 37 contracts are required.

If interest rates increase to 3.8%

	Buy put	Sell call
Exercise price	4%	3.5%
June futures price	3.98%	3.98%
Exercise option?	No	No
	%	
Actual interest cost	(4.60)	
Value of option gain	-	
Premium	(0.07)	
Net cost of loan	(4.67)	

If interest rates decrease to 2.8%

	Buy put	Sell call
Exercise price	4%	3.5%
June futures price	2.98%	2.98%
Exercise option?	No	Yes

	%
Actual interest cost	(3.60)
Value of option loss	(0.52)
Premium	(0.07)
Net cost of loan	(4.19)

If the interest rate futures market is used, the interest cost will be fixed at 4.47%, but if options on futures or an interest rate collar is used the cost will change. If interest rates were to fall then the options hedge gives the more favourable rates. However if interest rates rise, then the futures hedge gives the lowest interest cost and the options hedge has the highest cost. If Alecto wants to fix its interest rate irrespective of the circumstances, then the futures hedge should be selected.

This recommendation does not include margin payments or other transaction costs, which should be considered in full before a final decision is made.

(c) **Basis risk** arises from the fact the price of a futures contract may not move as expected in relation to the value of the instrument being hedged. Basis changes do occur and thus represent potential profits/losses to investors. Basis risk is the **difference between the spot and futures prices** and so there is no basis risk where a futures contract is held until maturity. In this case however, the June contracts are closed two months before expiry and there is no guarantee that the price of the futures contract will be the same as the predicted price calculated by basis at that date. It is assumed that the unexpired basis above is 0.18 but it could be either more or less.

This creates a problem in that the futures contract, which in theory gives a fixed interest cost, may vary and therefore the amount of interest is not fixed or predictable. Typically, this risk is much smaller than the risk of **remaining unhedged** and therefore the impact of this risk is smaller and **preferable** to not hedging at all.

Question 3

Text references. Management buy-outs are covered in chapter 14.

Top tips. In part (c) don't forget to apportion the assets to each division in the two thirds to one third ratio. Also do not forget to conclude whether the MBO is likely to be beneficial or not.

In part (d) don't forget to address both aspects. There are a number of issues for both points so you should be able to produce a reasonable answer here.

Easy marks. There are some easy marks to be gained in part (a) as the comments are very generic and can almost be taken straight from Chapter 14 of the Study Text.

Examiner's answers. The examiner's answer to this question can be found at the back of this kit.

Marking scheme

			Marks
(a)	1 mark per benefit discussed		Max 4
(b)	Calculation of funds used to pay proportion of liabilities	2	
	Comment	<u>1</u>	
			3
(c)	Calculation of funds required from MBO	4	
	Calculation of value of the business	4	
	Discussion	<u>2 – 3</u>	
			Max 10
(d)	Due diligence	3 – 4	
	Apply formula	<u>4 – 5</u>	
			Max <u>8</u>
			<u>25</u>

(a) There are a number of possible benefits from disposing of a division through a management buy-out. These include: It may be the **fastest way of raising funds** compared to other divestment methods. It is likely that there would be **less resistance from the managers** and employees which would make a smoother process. It may also offer a **better price** to the selling company as the current management has knowledge of the division and is able to make it successful. Costs associated with a management buy-out may be less than other methods.

(b) If the company is closed, the net proceeds will be

	$m
Sale of all assets	210
Less redundancy and other costs	<u>(54)</u>
Net proceeds from sale of all assets	<u>156</u>

Total liabilities are $280m.

Therefore liability holders will receive $0.56 per $1 owing to them ($156m/$280m). Shareholders will not receive anything.

(c)   If the fridges division is sold

	$m
Sale of fridge division (2/3 × 210)	140
Redundancy and other costs (2/3 × 54)	(36)
Net proceeds from sale of all assets	104
Amount of current and non-current liabilities	280

	$m
Amount of MBO funds needed to pay current and non-current liabilities (280 – 104)	176
Amount of MBO funds needed to pay shareholders	60
Investment needed for new venture	50
Total funds required	286

Value of new company following buy-out

	$m
Sales revenue	170.0
Costs	(120.0)
Profits before depreciation	50.0
Depreciation (((1/3 × 100m) + 50m) × 10%) *	(8.3)
Profits before tax	41.7
Tax at 20%	(8.3)
Cash flows before interest payments *	33.4

* It has been assumed that depreciation is available on the revalued non-current assets plus the new investment. It is also assumed that no further investment in non-current assets or working capital is needed.

$$\text{Estimated value based on cash flows in perpetuity} = \$33.4m \times \frac{1.035}{(0.11 - 0.035)} = \$461 \text{ m}$$

This is about 61% over and above the funds invested in the new venture and therefore the MBO is likely to be beneficial. However, this assessment is based on estimates. Small changes in variables, particularly the growth rate, will have a large impact on the value. The assumption of growth in perpetuity may not be accurate either. Sensitivity analysis should be performed before a final decision is made.

(d)   The search for a potential buyer will either involve an **open tender** or the use of an **intermediary**. It may be that a single bidder is sought or maybe Doric Co will look to have an auction of the business among interested parties. Potential purchasers may be found amongst industry competitors as well as Doric Co's suppliers and distributors. A good deal of discretion will be needed to protect the value of the business for sale from adverse competitive action. If this did not happen a dominant competitor in the industry could start a price war which would reduce prices and also the value of the division prior to them making a bid.

Once a potential purchaser is found, it will want to conduct its own **due diligence** to ensure that **everything is as expected** / as it has been told. Access should be given to the potential purchaser for this, including up-to-date accounts and any legal documentation relating to the assets to be transferred. Doric Co should also perform some due diligence, on the ability of the potential purchaser to complete the transaction. It is necessary to establish how it will be able to finance the purchase and the timescale involved in obtaining this finance. Doric Co's lawyers will also need to assess any possible contractual issues relating to the sale, the transfer of employment rights, the transfer of intellectual property and any rights and responsibilities that will remain with Doric Co.

A sale price is likely to be **negotiated** and should be negotiated in a way that will maximise the return to Doric. **Professionals** should be used to conduct the negotiations and they must be fully informed of the situation around the sale, including any conditions and legal requirements. The consideration for the sale, the title deeds of the assets and terms for the transfer of staff and any accrued employment benefits (such as pension rights) will be **subject to agreement**.

Question 4

Text references. Duration and credit ratings are both covered in chapter 7a.

Top tips. To calculate the duration, you will first need to calculate the gross redemption yield using an IRR style calculation, which can then be used as the discount rate to determine the present value. Don't forget to then multiply the PV by the period number for the duration calculation.

In part (b) it is important to remember the limitations of duration, this is shown best by the inclusion of the diagram, as in the answer here.

Easy marks. There are some easy marks to be gained in parts (b) and (c) as the comments can almost be taken straight from the Study Text.

Examiner's answers. The examiner's answer to this question can be found at the back of this kit.

Marking scheme

		Marks	
(a)	Calculation of the gross redemption yield	2	
	PV of cash flows and the duration of bond 1	3	
	PV of cash flows and the duration of bond 2	4	
			9
(b)	Duration as a single measure of sensitivity of interest rates	3 – 4	
	Explanation of convexity	2 – 3	
	Explanation of the change in the shape of the yield curve and other limitations	2 – 3	
			Max 8
(c)	For each of the criteria – 2 marks for explanation and suggestion of factors		8
			25

(a) To calculate the duration of both bonds, the present value of the cash flows and the selling price of the bonds need to be calculated first. To obtain the present values of the cash flows they need to be discounted by the gross redemption yield. This requires an IRR style calculation.

The market price of the first bond, which is $1,079.68, can be used to find the gross redemption yield that is common to both bonds.

Period	Cashflow	Amount $	Discount factor 5%	PV	Discount factor 4%	PV
1-4	Interest	60	3.546	212.76	3.630	217.80
5	Interest plus redemption	1,060	0.784	831.04	0.822	871.32
				1,043.80		1,089.12

Gross redemption yield = 4% + [(1,089.12 – 1,079.68)/(1,089.12 – 1,043.80)] = 4.21% say 4.2%

Bond 1

Period	Cashflow	Amount $	Discount factor at 4.2%	PV
1	Interest	60	0.9597	57.58
2	Interest	60	0.9210	55.26
3	Interest	60	0.8839	53.03
4	Interest	60	0.8483	50.89
5	Interest plus redemption	1,060	0.8141	862.95
				1,079.71

Note: This should be the market price, difference is due to rounding.

Period	PV	Duration multiplier	
1	57.58	1	57.58
2	55.26	2	110.52
3	53.03	3	159.09
4	50.89	4	203.56
5	862.95	5	4,314.75
	1,079.71		4,845.50

Duration = 4,845.50/1,079.71 = 4.49 years

Bond 2

Period	Cashflow	Amount $	Discount factor at 4.2%	PV
1	Interest	40	0.9597	38.39
2	Interest	40	0.9210	36.84
3	Interest	40	0.8839	35.36
4	Interest	40	0.8483	33.93
5	Interest plus redemption	1,040	0.8141	846.66
				991.18

This is the market price of Bond 2.

Period	PV	Duration multiplier	
1	38.39	1	38.39
2	36.84	2	73.68
3	35.36	3	106.08
4	33.93	4	135.72
5	846.66	5	4,233.30
	991.18		4,587.17

Duration = 4,587.17/991.18 = 4.63 years

(b)   The sensitivity of a particular bond to a change in interest rates will depend on its **redemption date**. Bonds that have a later maturity date are **more price-sensitive** to interest rate changes.

Duration measures the average time that a bond takes to 'payback' its market price. The average time taken to recover the cash flow from an investment is not only affected by the maturity date of the investment but also by the coupon rate (which determines the interest payments). We want to be able to **compare bonds** quickly – this is where duration is useful.

Duration can be used to assess a bond's change in value following an interest rate change by using the following formula

$$\Delta P = -D/(1 + Y) \times \Delta Y \times P$$

Where:

ΔP = change in bond price   P = current market price of the bond

ΔY = change in yield   Y = gross redemption yield

D = duration

The main limitation of duration is that it **assumes a linear relationship** between interest rates and price. That is, it assumes that for a certain percentage change in interest rates, there will be an equal percentage change in price.

However as interest rates change the bond price is unlikely to change in a linear fashion. Rather, it will have some kind of convex relationship with interest rates (see below).

Relationship Between Bond Price and Yield

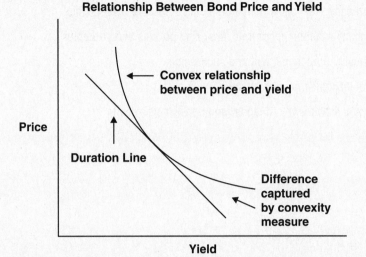

From the diagram above, the more convex the relationship the more inaccurate duration is for measuring interest rate sensitivity. Therefore **duration should be treated with caution** in predictions of interest rate/price relationships, for any interest rate changes that are not small.

Duration can only be applied to measure the **approximate change** in bond price due to changes in interest rates if the interest rate change does not lead to a change in the shape of the yield curve. This is because it is an average measure based on the GRY (yield to maturity).

(c) **Industry risk**

Industry risk is a measure of the resilience of the company's industry to changes in the wider economy. The following factors could be used to assess this:

- The strength of the industry measured by the impact of economic forces

- Cyclical nature of the industry and the scale of the peaks and troughs

- Demand factors within the industry

Earnings protection

Earnings protection is a measure of how well the company can maintain or protect its current level of earnings in changing circumstances. The following factors could be used to assess this:

- Sources of earnings growth

- Customer base

- Return on capital, pre-tax and net profit margins

Financial flexibility

Financial flexibility is a measure of the ability of the company to raise the finance it needs to pursue its investment goals. The following factors could be used to assess this:

- Relationships with banks

- Any existing debt covenants

- Evaluation of financing needs

- Plans and alternatives under stress

Evaluation of company management

Evaluation of company management is a measure of how well management is managing and planning the future of the company. The following factors could be used to assess this:

- The company's planning, controls, financing policies and strategies
- Overall quality of management and succession
- Merger and acquisition performance
- Record of achievement in financial and non-fiancial results

BPP
LEARNING MEDIA

ACCA Examiner's answers:
Pilot paper

Note. The ACCA examiner's answers are correct at the time of going to press but may be subject to some amendments before the final versions are published.

BPP
LEARNING MEDIA

1 (a) REPORT TO THE BOARD OF DIRECTORS, TRAMONT CO

EVALUATION OF WHETHER THE PRODUCTION OF X-IT SHOULD MOVE TO GAMALA
This report evaluates the possibility of moving the production of the X-IT to Gamala from the USA. Following the initial evaluation the report discusses the key assumptions made, the possible impact of a change in the government in Gamala after the elections due to take place shortly and other business factors that should be considered before a final decision is made.

Initially a base case net present value calculation is conducted to assess the impact of the production in Gamala. This is then adjusted to show the impact of cash flows in the USA as a result of the move, the immediate impact of ceasing production and the impact of the subsidy and the tax shield benefits from the loan borrowing.

Based on the calculations presented in the appendix, the move will result in a positive adjusted present value of just over $2.4 million. On this basis, the initial recommendation is that the production of X-IT should cease in the USA and the production moved to Gamala instead.

Assumptions
It is assumed that the borrowing rate of 5% is used to calculate the benefits from the tax shield. It could be argued that the risk free rate of 3% could be used as the discount rate instead of 5% to calculate the present value of benefits from the tax shields and the subsidies.

In adjusted present value calculations, the tax shield benefit is normally related to the debt capacity of the investment, not the actual amount of debt finance used. Since this is not given, it is assumed that the increase in debt capacity is equal to the debt finance used.

It has been assumed that many of the input variables, such as for example the tax and capital allowances rates, the various costs and prices, units produced and sold, the rate of inflation and the prediction of future exchange rates based on the purchasing power parity, are accurate and will change as stated over the four-year period of the project. In reality any of these estimates could be subject to change to a greater or lesser degree and it would appropriate for Tramont Co to conduct uncertainty assessments like sensitivity analysis to assess the impact of the changes to the initial predictions.

(Note: credit will be given for alternative relevant assumptions)

Government Change
From the facts of the case it would seem that a change of government could have a significant impact on whether or not the project is beneficial to Tramont Co. The threat to raise taxes may not be too significant as the tax rates would need to increase to more than 30% before Tramont Co would lose money. However, the threat by the opposition party to review 'commercial benefits' may be more significant.

Just over 40% of the present value comes from the tax shield and subsidy benefits. If these were reneged then Tramont Co would lose a significant of the value attached to the project. Also the new government may not allow remittances every year, as is assumed in part (i). However this may not be significant since the largest present value amount comes from the final year of operation.

Other Business Factors
Tramont Co should consider the possibility of becoming established in Gamala, and this may lead to follow-on projects. The real options linked to this should be included in the analysis.

Tramont Co's overall corporate strategy should be considered. Does the project fit within this strategy? Even if the decision is made to close the operation in the USA, there may be other alternatives and these need to be assessed.

The amount of experience Tramont Co has in international ventures needs to be considered. For example, will it be able to match its systems to the Gamalan culture? It will need to develop strategies to deal with cultural differences. This may include additional costs such as training which may not have been taken into account.

Tramont Co needs to consider if the project can be delayed at all. From part (i), it can be seen that a large proportion of the opportunity cost relates to lost contribution in years 1 and 2. A delay in the commencement of the project may increase the overall value of the project.

Tramont Co needs to consider the impact on its reputation due to possible redundancies. Since the production of X-IT is probably going to be stopped in any case, Tramont Co needs to communicate its strategy to the employees and possibly other stakeholders clearly so as to retain its reputation. This may make the need to consider alternatives even more important.

(Note: credit will be given for alternative relevant comments)

Conclusion

Following from a detailed sensitivity analysis, analysis of a possible change in the government and an evaluation of the financial benefits accruing from the other business factors discussed above, the BoD can make a decision of whether to move the production to Gamala or not. This initial evaluation suggests that moving the production of the X-IT to Gamala would be beneficial.

Report compiled by:

Date:

Appendix
Gamalan Project Operating Cash Flows
(All amounts in GR/$ 000's)

Year	Now	1	2	3	4
Sales revenue (w2)		48,888	94,849	214,442	289,716
Local variable costs (w3)		(16,200)	(32,373)	(75,385)	(104,897)
Imported component (w4)		(4,889)	(9,769)	(22,750)	(31,658)
Fixed costs		(30,000)	(32,700)	(35,643)	(38,851)
Profits before tax		(2,201)	20,007	80,664	114,310
Taxation (w5)		0	0	(7,694)	(18,862)
Investment	(230,000)				450,000
Working capital	(40,000)	(3,600)	(3,924)	(4,277)	51,801
Cash flows (GR)	(270,000)	(5,801)	16,083	68,693	597,249
Exchange rate (w1)	55.00	58.20	61.59	65.18	68.98
Cash flows ($)	(4,909)	(100)	261	1,054	8,658
Discount factor for 9.6% (w6) *(Full credit given if 10% is used as the discount rate)*		0.912	0.832	0.760	0.693
Present values ($)	(4,909)	(91)	217	801	6,000

Net present value (NPV) of the cash flows from the project is approx. $2,018,000.

Adjusted present value (APV)	$000s
NPV of cash flows	2,018
Impact of additional tax in USA, opportunity cost (revenues foregone from current operations) and additional contribution from component exported to project (net of tax) (w7)	(1,237)
Closure revenues and costs ($2,300,000 – $1,700,00)	600
Tax shield Benefit of subsidy (w8)	1,033
Total APV	2,414

BPP
LEARNING MEDIA

Workings

1   Exchange rates

Year	1	2	3	4
GR/$1	55 x 1.09/1.03 = 58.20	58.20 x 1.09/1.03 = 61.59	61.59 x 1.09/1.03 = 65.18	65.18 x 1.09/1.03 = 68.98

2   Sales revenue (GR 000's)

Year	1	2	3	4
Price x units x exchange rate	70 x 12,000 x 58.20 = 48,888	70 x 22,000 x 61.59 = 94,849	70 x 47,000 x 65.18 = 214,442	70 x 60,000 x 68.98 = 289,716

3   Local variable costs (GR 000's)

Year	1	2	3	4
Cost x units x inflation after year 1	1,350 x 12,000 = 16,200	1,350 x 22,000 x 1.09 = 32,373	1,350 x 47,000 x 1.09^2 = 75,385	1,350 x 60,000 x 1.09^3 = 104,897

4   Imported Component (GR 000's)

Year	1	2	3	4
Price x units x inflation after year 1 x exchange rate	7 x 12,000 x 58.20 = 4,889	7 x 22,000 x 1.03 x 61.59 = 9,769	7 x 47,000 x 1.03^2 x 65.18 = 22,750	7 x 60,000 x 1.03^3 x 68.98 = 31,658

5   Taxation

Year	1	2	3	4
Profits before tax	(2,201)	20,007	80664	114,310
Tax allowable depreciation	(20,000)	(20,000)	(20,000)	(20,000)
Profit/(loss) after depreciation	(22,201)	7	60,664	94,310
Taxable profits	0	0	38,470	94,310
Taxation (20%)	0	0	(7,694)	(18,862)

6   Gamala project all-equity financed discount rate

Tramont Co equity beta = 1.17
MVe = $2.40 x 25m shares = $60m
MVd = $40m x $1,428/$1,000 = $57.12m

Tramont Co asset beta (assuming debt is risk free)
1.17 x 60m/(60m + 57.12m x 0.7) = 0.70

Project asset beta = 0.70 + 0.40 = 1.10
Project all-equity financed discount rate = 3% + 6% x 1.1 = 9.6%

7   Additional tax, additional contribution and opportunity cost ($ 000's)

Year	1	2	3	4
Additional tax Taxable profits x 1/ exchange rate x 10%	0	0	38,470 x 1/65.18 x 10% = (59)	94,310 x 1/68.98 x 10% = (137)
Opportunity cost Units x contribution x (1–tax)	40 x $20 x 0.7 = (560)	32 x $20 x 0.7 = (448)	25.6 x $20 x 0.7 = (358)	20.48 x $20 x 0.7 = (287)
Additional contribution Units x contribution x inflation x (1–tax)	12 x $4 x 0.7 = 34	22 x $4 x 1.03 x 0.7 = 63	47 x $4 x 1.03^2 x 0.7 = 140	60 x $4 x 1.03^3 x 0.7 = 184
Total cash flows	(526)	(385)	(277)	(240)
PV of cash flows Discount at 7%	(492)	(336)	(226)	(183)

NPV is approx. $(1,237,000)

8   Tax shield and subsidy benefits ($/GR 000's)

Year	1	2	3	4
Annual tax shield (GR) Interest x loan x tax rate	6% x 270m x 20% = 3,240	3,240	3,240	3,240
Annual subsidy benefit (GR) Interest gain x loan x (1–tax rate)	7% x 270m x 0.8 = 15,120	15,120	15,120	15,120
Total tax shield + subsidy benefits (GR)	18,360	18,360	18,360	18,360
Exchange rate (GR/$1)	58.20	61.59	65.18	68.98
Cash flows ($)	315	298	282	266
PV of cash flows Discount at 5%	300	270	244	219

NPV of tax shield and subsidy benefit is approx. $1,033,000

(b) A triple bottom line (TBL) report provides a quantitative summary of performance in terms of economic or financial impact, impact on the environment and impact on social performance. TBL provides the measurement tool to assess a corporation's or project's performance against its objectives.

The principle of TBL reporting is that true performance should be measured in terms of a balance between economic (profits), environmental (planet) and social (people) factors; with no one factor growing at the expense of the others. The contention is that a corporation that accommodates the pressures of all the three factors in its strategic investment decisions will enhance shareholder value, as long as the benefits that accrue from producing such a report exceeds the costs of producing it.

For example, in the case of the X-IT, reporting on the impact of moving the production to Gamala, in terms of the impact on the employees and environment in the USA and in Gamala will highlight Tramont Co as a good corporate citizen, and thereby increase its reputation and enable it to attract and retain high performing, high calibre employees. It can also judge the impact on the other business factors mentioned in the report above.

(Note: credit will be given for alternative relevant answers)

(c) Shareholders holding well-diversified portfolios will have diversified away unsystematic or company specific risk, and will only face systematic risk, ie risk that can not be diversified away. Therefore a company can not reduce risk further by undertaking diversification within the same system or market. However, further risk reduction may occur if the diversification is undertaken by the company, on behalf of the shareholders, into a system or market where they themselves do not invest. Some studies indicate that even shareholders holding well-diversified portfolios may benefit from risk diversification where companies invest in emerging markets.

BPP
LEARNING MEDIA

In the case of Tramont Co and the X-IT, it is not clear whether diversification benefits will result in the investment in Gamala. The benefits are dependent on the size of the investment, and on the nature of the business operations undertaken in Gamala by Tramont Co. And whether these operations mirror an investment in a significantly different system or market. If the investment is large, the operations are similar to undertaking a a Gamalan company. Tramont Co's shareholders who do not hold similar companies' shares in their portfolios may then gain risk diversification benefits from the Gamalan investment.

2   (a)   The main advantage of using a collar instead of options to hedge interest rate risk is lower cost. A collar involves the simultaneous purchase and sale of both call and put options at different exercise prices. The option purchased has a higher premium when compared to the premium of the option sold, but the lower premium income will reduce the higher premium payable. With a normal uncovered option, the full premium is payable.

However the disadvantage of this is that, whereas with a hedge using options the buyer can get full benefit of any upside movement in the price of the underlying asset, with a collar hedge the benefit of the upside movement is limited or capped as well.

(b)   **Using Futures**

Need to hedge against a rise in interest rates, therefore go short in the futures market. Alecto Co needs June contracts as the loan will be required on 1 May.

No. of contracts needed = €22,000,000/ €1,000,000 x 5 months / 3 months = 36.67 say 37 contracts.

Basis
Current price (on 1/1) – futures price = total basis
(100 – 3.3) – 96.16 = 0.54
Unexpired basis = 2/6 x 0.54 = 0.18

If interest rates increase by 0.5% to 3.8%

Cost of borrowing funds = 4.6% x 5/12 x €22,000,000 =	€421,667
Expected futures price = 100 – 3.8 – 0.18 = 96.02	
Gain on the futures market = (9616 – 9602) x €25 x 37 =	€12,950
Net cost =	€408,717

Effective interest rate = 408,717 / 22,000,000 x 12/5 = 4.46%

If interest rates decrease by 0.5% to 2.8%

Cost of borrowing funds = 3.6% x 5/12 x €22,000,000 =	€330,000
Expected futures price = 100 – 2.8 – 0.18 = 97.02	
Loss on the futures market = (9616 – 9702) x €25 x 37 =	€79,550
Net cost =	€409,550

Effective interest rate = 409,550 / 22,000,000 x 12/5 = 4.47%

(Note: Net cost should be the same. Difference is due to rounding the number of contracts)

Using Options on Futures

Need to hedge against a rise in interest rates, therefore buy put options. As before, Alecto Co needs 37 June put option contracts (€22,000,000/€1,000,000 x 5 months/3 months).

If interest rates increase by 0.5% to 3.8%

Exercise Price	96.00	96.50
Futures Price	96.02	96.02
Exercise ?	No	Yes
Gain in basis points	0	48
Underlying cost of borrowing (from above)	€421,667	€421,667
Gain on options (0 and €25x48x37)	€0	€44,400
Premium		
16.3 x €25 x 37	€15,078	
58.1x €25 x 37		€53,743
Net cost	€436,745	€431,010
Effective interest rate	4.76%	4.70%

If interest rates decrease by 0.5% to 2.8%

Exercise Price	96.00	96.50
Futures Price	97.02	97.02
Exercise ?	No	No
Gain in basis points	0	0
Underlying cost of borrowing (from above)	€330,000	€330,000
Gain on options	€0	€0
Premium		
16.3 x €25 x 37	€15,078	
58.1 x €25 x 37		€53,743
Net cost	€345,078	€383,743
Effective interest rate	3.76%	4.19%

Using a collar

Buy June put at 96.00 for 0.163 and sell June call at 96.50 for 0.090.
Premium payable = 0.073

If interest rates increase by 0.5% to 3.8%

	Buy put	Sell Call
Exercise Price	96.00	96.50
Futures Price	96.02	96.02
Exercise ?	No	No
Underlying cost of borrowing (from above)		€421,667
Premium		
7.3 x €25x37		€6,753
Net cost		€428,420
Effective interest rate		4.67%

If interest rates decrease by 0.5% to 2.8%

	Buy put	Sell Call
Exercise Price	96.00	96.50
Futures Price	97.02	97.02
Exercise ?	No	Yes
Underlying cost of borrowing (from above)	€330,000	
Premium		
7.3 x €25 x 37	€6,753	
Loss on exercise (52 x €25 x 37)	€48,100	
Net cost	€384,853	
Effective interest rate	4.20%	

Hedging using the interest rate futures market fixes the rate at 4.47%, whereas with options on futures or a collar hedge, the net cost changes. If interest rates fall in the future then a hedge using options gives the most favourable rate. However, if interest rates increase then a hedge using futures gives the lowest interest payment cost and hedging with options give the highest cost, with the collar hedge in between the two. If Alecto Co's aim is to fix its interest rate whatever happens to interest rates then the preferred instrument would be futures.

This recommendation is made without considering margin and other transactional costs, and basis risk, which is discussed below. These need to be taken into account before a final decision is made.

(Note: credit will be given for alternative approaches to the calculations in part (b)).

(c) Basis risk occurs when the basis does not diminish at a constant rate. In this case, if a futures contract is held till it matures then there is no basis risk because at maturity the derivative price will equal the underlying asset's price. However, if a contract is closed out before maturity (here the June futures contracts will be closed two months prior to expiry) there is no guarantee that the price of the futures contract will equal the predicted price based on basis at that date. For example, in part (b) above the predicted futures price in four months assumes that the basis remaining is 0.18, but it could be more or less. Therefore the actual price of the futures contract could be more or less.

This creates a problem in that the effective interest rate for the futures contract above may not be fixed at 4.47%, but may vary and therefore the amount of interest that Alecto Co pays may not be fixed or predictable. On the other hand it could be argued that the basis risk will probably be smaller than the risk exposure to interest rates without hedging and therefore although some risk will exist, its impact will be smaller.

3 **(a)** Possible benefits of disposing a division through a management buy-out may include:

Management buy-out costs maybe less compared with other forms of disposal such as selling individual assets of the division or selling it to a third party.

It may be the quickest method in raising funds compared to the other methods.

There would be less resistance from the managers and employees making the process smoother and easier to accomplish than if both divisions were to be closed down.

It may offer a better price. The current management and employees possibly have the best knowledge of the division and are able to make it successful. Therefore they may be willing to pay more for it.

(Note: Credit will be given for alternative relevant benefits)

(b)

Close the company	$m
Sale of all assets	210
Less redundancy and other costs	(54)
Net proceeds from sale of all assets	156
Total liabilities	280

The liability holders will receive $0.56 per $1 owing to them ($156m/$280m). Shareholders will receive nothing.

(c)

	$m
Value of selling fridges division (2/3 x 210)	140
Redundancy and other costs (2/3 x 54)	(36)
Funds available from sale of division	104
Amount of current and non-current liabilities	280
Amount of management buy-out funds needed to pay current and non-current liabilities (280 – 104)	176
Amount of management buy-out funds needed to pay shareholders	60
Investment needed for new venture	50
Total funds needed for management buy-out	286

Estimating value of new company after buy-out	$m
Sales revenue	170
Costs	(120)
Profits before depreciation	50
** Depreciation ((1/3 x $100m + $50m) x 10%)	(8.3)
Tax (20%)	(8.3)
** Cash flows before interest payment	33.4

** It is assumed that the depreciation is available on the re-valued non-current assets plus the new investment. It is assumed that no additional investment in non-current assets or working capital is needed, even though cash flows are increasing.

Estimate of value based on perpetuity = $33.4 (1.035) / (0.11 – 0.035) = $461m

This is about 61% in excess of the funds invested in the new venture, and therefore the buy-out is probably beneficial. However, the amounts are all estimates and a small change in some variables like the growth rate or the cost of capital can have a large impact on the value. Also the assumption of cash flow growth in perpetuity may not be accurate. It is therefore advisable to undertake a sensitivity analysis.

(d) Potential buyers will need to be sought through open tender or through an intermediary. Depending upon the nature of the business being sold a single bidder may be sought or preparations made for an auction of the business. Doric Co's suppliers and distributors may be interested, as may be competitors in the same industry. High levels of discretion are required in the search process to protect the value of the business from adverse competitive action. Otherwise, an interested and dominant competitor may open a price war in order to force down prices and hence the value of the fridges division prior to a bid.

Once a potential buyer has been found, access should be given so that they can conduct their own due diligence. Up-to-date accounts should be made available and all legal documentation relating to assets to be transferred made available. Doric

Co should undertake its own due diligence to check the ability of the potential purchaser to complete a transaction of this size. Before proceeding, it would be necessary to establish how the purchaser intends to finance the purchase, the timescale involved in their raising the necessary finance and any other issues that may impede a clean sale. Doric Co's legal team will need to assess any contractual issues on the sale, the transfer of employment rights, the transfer of intellectual property and any residual rights and responsibilities to Doric Co.

A sale price will be negotiated which is expected to maximise the return. The negotiation process should be conducted by professional negotiators who have been thoroughly briefed on the terms of the sale, the conditions attached and all of the legal requirements. The consideration for the sale, the deeds for the assignment of assets and terms for the transfer of staff and their accrued pension rights will also all be subject to agreement.

4   (a) In order to calculate the duration of the two bonds, the present value of the annual cash flows and the price or value at which the bonds are trading at need to be determined. To determine the present value of the annual cash flows, they need to be discounted by the gross redemption yield.

Gross Redemption Yield (GRY)

Try 5%
$60 \times 1.05^{-1} + 60 \times 1.05^{-2} + 60 \times 1.05^{-3} + 60 \times 1.05^{-4} + 1060 \times 1.05^{-5} =$
$60 \times 4.3295 + 1000 \times 0.7835 = 1,043.27$

Try 4%
$60 \times 4.4518 + 1000 \times 0.8219 = 1,089.01$

GRY = 4 + [(1,089.01 - 1,079.68) / (1,089.01 – 1,043.27)] = 4.2%

Bond 1 (PV of cash flows)

$60 \times 1.042^{-1} + 60 \times 1.042^{-2} + 60 \times 1.042^{-3} + 60 \times 1.042^{-4} + 1060 \times 1.042^{-5}$

PV of cash flows (years 1 to 5) = 57.58 + 55.26 + 53.03 + 50.90 + 862.91 = 1,079.68

Market price = $1,079.68

Duration = [57.58x1 + 55.26x2 + 53.03x3 + 50.90x4 + 862.91x5] / 1,079.68 = 4.49 years

Bond 2 (PV of Coupons and Bond Price)

Price = $40 \times 1.042^{-1} + 40 \times 1.042^{-2} + 40 \times 1.042^{-3} + 40 \times 1.042^{-4} + 1040 \times 1.042^{-5}$

PV of cash flows (years 1 to 5) = 38.39 + 36.84 + 35.36 + 33.93 + 846.63 = 991.15

Market Price = $991.15

Duration = [38.39x1 + 36.84x2 + 35.36x3 + 33.93x4 + 846.63x5] / 991.15 = 4.63 years

(b) The sensitivity of bond prices to changes in interest rates is dependent on their redemption dates. Bonds which are due to be redeemed at a later date are more price-sensitive to interest rate changes, and therefore are riskier.

Duration measures the average time it takes for a bond to pay its coupons and principal and therefore measures the redemption period of a bond. It recognises that bonds which pay higher coupons effectively mature 'sooner' compared to bonds which pay lower coupons, even if the redemption dates of the bonds are the same. This is because a higher proportion of the higher coupon bonds' income is received sooner. Therefore these bonds are less sensitive to interest rate changes and will have a lower duration

Duration can be used to assess the change in the value of a bond when interest rates change using the following formula:

$\Delta P = [-D \times \Delta i \times P] / [1 + i]$, where P is the price of the bond, D is the duration and i is the redemption yield.

However, duration is only useful in assessing small changes in interest rates because of convexity. As interest rates increase the price of a bond decreases and vice versa, but this decrease is not proportional for coupon paying bonds, the relationship is non-linear. In fact the relationship between the changes in bond value to changes in interest rates is in the shape of a convex curve to origin, see below.

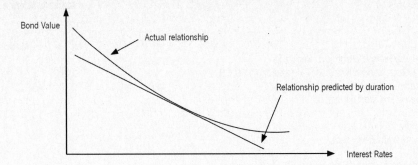

Duration, on the other hand, assumes that the relationship between changes in interest rates and the resultant bond is linear. Therefore duration will predict a lower price than the actual price and for large changes in interest rates this difference can be significant.

Duration can only be applied to measure the approximate change in a bond price due to interest changes, only if changes in interest rates do not lead to a change in the shape of the yield curve. This is because it is an average measure based on the gross redemption yield (yield to maturity). However, if the shape of the yield curve changes, duration can no longer be used to assess the change in bond value due to interest rate changes.

(Note: Credit will be given for alternative benefits/limitations of duration)

(c) Industry risk measures the resilience of the company's industrial sector to changes in the economy. In order to measure or assess this, the following factors could be used:
–   Impact of economic changes on the industry in terms how successfully the firms in the industry operate under differing economic outcomes;
–   How cyclical the industry is and how large the peaks and troughs are;
–   How the demand shifts in the industry as the economy changes.

Earnings protection measures how well the company will be able to maintain or protect its earnings in changing circumstances. In order to assess this, the following factors could be used:
–   Differing range of sources of earnings growth;
–   Diversity of customer base;
–   Profit margins and return on capital.

Financial flexibility measures how easily the company is able to raise the finance it needs to pursue its investment goals. In order to assess this, the following factors could be used:
–   Evaluation of plans for financing needs and range of alternatives available;
–   Relationships with finance providers, e.g. banks;
–   Operating restrictions that currently exist in the form of debt covenants.

Evaluation of the company's management considers how well the managers are managing and planning for the future of the company. In order to assess this, the following factors could be used:
–   The company's planning and control policies, and its financial strategies;
–   Management succession planning;
–   The qualifications and experience of the managers;
–   Performance in achieving financial and non-financial targets.

				Marks
1	(a)	(i)	Estimated future rates based on purchasing power parity	1
			Sales revenue, variable costs, component cost and fixed costs (in GR)	4
			Taxable profits and taxation	2
			Investment, terminal value and working capital	2
			Cash flows in GR	1
			Cash flows in $	1
			Discount rate of all-equity financed project	2
			Base case PVs and NPV	2
			PV of additional contribution, additional tax and opportunity cost	4
			PV of tax shield and subsidy benefits	4
			Closure costs and benefits	1
			Initial comments	1–2
			Assumptions and sensitivity analysis	2–3
			Max	27
		(ii)	Implications of change of government	2–3
			Other business factors (1 to 2 marks per factor)	5–6
			Max	8
			Professional Marks	
			Report format	1
			Layout, presentation and structure	3
			Total	4
	(b)		1 mark per relevant point	Total 6
	(c)		General commentary regarding benefits of risk diversification	2–3
			Relating specifically to Tramont Co and the Gamalan investment	2–3
			Max	5
			Total	50
2	(a)		Discussion of the main advantage	2
			Discussion of the main disadvantage	2
			Total	4
	(b)		Recommendation to go short if futures are used and purchase puts if options are used	1
			Calculation of number of contracts and remaining basis	2
			Futures contracts calculations	4
			Options contracts calculations	4
			Collar approach and calculations	4
			Supporting comments and conclusion	2–3
			Max	17
	(c)		Explanation of basis risk	2–3
			Effect of basis risk on recommendation made	2–3
			Max	4
			Total	25

					Marks
3	**(a)**	1 mark per benefit discussed		Max	4
	(b)	Calculation of funds used to pay proportion of liability holders			2
		Comment			1
				Total	3
	(c)	Calculation of funds required from MBO			4
		Calculation of value of the business			4
		Discussion			2–3
				Max	10
	(d)	Due diligence			3–4
		Potential buyers and sale price			4–5
				Max	8
				Total	25
4	**(a)**	Calculation of the gross redemption yield			2
		PV of cash flows and duration of bond 1			3
		PV of cash flows and duration of bond 2			4
				Total	9
	(b)	Duration as a single measure of sensitivity of interest rates			3–4
		Explanation of convexity			2–3
		Explanation of the change in the shape of the yield curve and other limitations			2–3
				Max	8
	(c)	For each of the four criteria – 2 marks for explanation and suggestion of factors		Total	8
				Total	25

BPP LEARNING MEDIA

BPP
LEARNING MEDIA

Mathematical tables and formulae

BPP
LEARNING MEDIA

BPP
LEARNING MEDIA

Formulae

Modigliani and Miller Proposition 2 (with tax)

$$k_e = k_e^i + (1 - T)(k_e^i - k_d)\frac{V_d}{V_e}$$

The Capital Asset Pricing Model

$$E(r_i) = R_f + \beta_i(E(r_m) - R_f)$$

The asset beta formula

$$\beta_a = \left[\frac{V_e}{(V_e + V_d(1 - T))}\beta_e\right] + \left[\frac{V_d(1 - T)}{(V_e + V_d(1 - T))}\beta_d\right]$$

The Growth Model

$$P_o = \frac{D_o(1 + g)}{(r_e - g)}$$

Gordon's growth approximation

$$g = br_e$$

The weighted average cost of capital

$$WACC = \left[\frac{V_e}{V_e + V_d}\right]k_e + \left[\frac{V_d}{V_e + V_d}\right]k_d(1 - T)$$

The Fisher formula

$$(1 + i) = (1 + r)(1 + h)$$

Purchasing power parity and interest rate parity

$$S_1 = S_0 \times \frac{(1 + h_c)}{(1 + h_b)} \qquad F_0 = S_0 \times \frac{(1 + i_c)}{(1 + i_b)}$$

7

BPP LEARNING MEDIA

Modified Internal Rate of Return

$$MIRR = \left[\frac{PV_R}{PV_I}\right]^{\frac{1}{n}}\left(1 + r_e\right) - 1$$

The Black-Scholes option pricing model

$$c = P_a N(d_1) - P_e N(d_2)e^{-rt}$$

Where:

$$d_1 = \frac{\ln(P_a / P_e) + (r + 0.5s^2)t}{s\sqrt{t}}$$

$$d_2 = d_1 - s\sqrt{t}$$

The Put Call Parity relationship

$$p = c - P_a + P_e e^{-rt}$$

BPP
LEARNING MEDIA

Present Value Table

Present value of 1 i.e. $(1 + r)^{-n}$

Where   r = discount rate
          n = number of periods until payment

Discount rate (r)

Periods (n)	1%	2%	3%	4%	5%	6%	7%	8%	9%	10%	
1	0·990	0·980	0·971	0·962	0·952	0·943	0·935	0·926	0·917	0·909	1
2	0·980	0·961	0·943	0·925	0·907	0·890	0·873	0·857	0·842	0·826	2
3	0·971	0·942	0·915	0·889	0·864	0·840	0·816	0·794	0·772	0·751	3
4	0·961	0·924	0·888	0·855	0·823	0·792	0·763	0·735	0·708	0·683	4
5	0·951	0·906	0·863	0·822	0·784	0·747	0·713	0·681	0·650	0·621	5
6	0·942	0·888	0·837	0·790	0·746	0·705	0·666	0·630	0·596	0·564	6
7	0·933	0·871	0·813	0·760	0·711	0·665	0·623	0·583	0·547	0·513	7
8	0·923	0·853	0·789	0·731	0·677	0·627	0·582	0·540	0·502	0·467	8
9	0·914	0·837	0·766	0·703	0·645	0·592	0·544	0·500	0·460	0·424	9
10	0·905	0·820	0·744	0·676	0·614	0·558	0·508	0·463	0·422	0·386	10
11	0·896	0·804	0·722	0·650	0·585	0·527	0·475	0·429	0·388	0·350	11
12	0·887	0·788	0·701	0·625	0·557	0·497	0·444	0·397	0·356	0·319	12
13	0·879	0·773	0·681	0·601	0·530	0·469	0·415	0·368	0·326	0·290	13
14	0·870	0·758	0·661	0·577	0·505	0·442	0·388	0·340	0·299	0·263	14
15	0·861	0·743	0·642	0·555	0·481	0·417	0·362	0·315	0·275	0·239	15

(n)	11%	12%	13%	14%	15%	16%	17%	18%	19%	20%	
1	0·901	0·893	0·885	0·877	0·870	0·862	0·855	0·847	0·840	0·833	1
2	0·812	0·797	0·783	0·769	0·756	0·743	0·731	0·718	0·706	0·694	2
3	0·731	0·712	0·693	0·675	0·658	0·641	0·624	0·609	0·593	0·579	3
4	0·659	0·636	0·613	0·592	0·572	0·552	0·534	0·516	0·499	0·482	4
5	0·593	0·567	0·543	0·519	0·497	0·476	0·456	0·437	0·419	0·402	5
6	0·535	0·507	0·480	0·456	0·432	0·410	0·390	0·370	0·352	0·335	6
7	0·482	0·452	0·425	0·400	0·376	0·354	0·333	0·314	0·296	0·279	7
8	0·434	0·404	0·376	0·351	0·327	0·305	0·285	0·266	0·249	0·233	8
9	0·391	0·361	0·333	0·308	0·284	0·263	0·243	0·225	0·209	0·194	9
10	0·352	0·322	0·295	0·270	0·247	0·227	0·208	0·191	0·176	0·162	10
11	0·317	0·287	0·261	0·237	0·215	0·195	0·178	0·162	0·148	0·135	11
12	0·286	0·257	0·231	0·208	0·187	0·168	0·152	0·137	0·124	0·112	12
13	0·258	0·229	0·204	0·182	0·163	0·145	0·130	0·116	0·104	0·093	13
14	0·232	0·205	0·181	0·160	0·141	0·125	0·111	0·099	0·088	0·078	14
15	0·209	0·183	0·160	0·140	0·123	0·108	0·095	0·084	0·074	0·065	15

9

Annuity Table

Present value of an annuity of 1 i.e. $\dfrac{1-(1+r)^{-n}}{r}$

Where   r = discount rate
             n = number of periods

Discount rate (r)

Periods (n)	1%	2%	3%	4%	5%	6%	7%	8%	9%	10%	
1	0·990	0·980	0·971	0·962	0·952	0·943	0·935	0·926	0·917	0·909	1
2	1·970	1·942	1·913	1·886	1·859	1·833	1·808	1·783	1·759	1·736	2
3	2·941	2·884	2·829	2·775	2·723	2·673	2·624	2·577	2·531	2·487	3
4	3·902	3·808	3·717	3·630	3·546	3·465	3·387	3·312	3·240	3·170	4
5	4·853	4·713	4·580	4·452	4·329	4·212	4·100	3·993	3·890	3·791	5
6	5·795	5·601	5·417	5·242	5·076	4·917	4·767	4·623	4·486	4·355	6
7	6·728	6·472	6·230	6·002	5·786	5·582	5·389	5·206	5·033	4·868	7
8	7·652	7·325	7·020	6·733	6·463	6·210	5·971	5·747	5·535	5·335	8
9	8·566	8·162	7·786	7·435	7·108	6·802	6·515	6·247	5·995	5·759	9
10	9·471	8·983	8·530	8·111	7·722	7·360	7·024	6·710	6·418	6·145	10
11	10·368	9·787	9·253	8·760	8·306	7·887	7·499	7·139	6·805	6·495	11
12	11·255	10·575	9·954	9·385	8·863	8·384	7·943	7·536	7·161	6·814	12
13	12·134	11·348	10·635	9·986	9·394	8·853	8·358	7·904	7·487	7·103	13
14	13·004	12·106	11·296	10·563	9·899	9·295	8·745	8·244	7·786	7·367	14
15	13·865	12·849	11·938	11·118	10·380	9·712	9·108	8·559	8·061	7·606	15

(n)	11%	12%	13%	14%	15%	16%	17%	18%	19%	20%	
1	0·901	0·893	0·885	0·877	0·870	0·862	0·855	0·847	0·840	0·833	1
2	1·713	1·690	1·668	1·647	1·626	1·605	1·585	1·566	1·547	1·528	2
3	2·444	2·402	2·361	2·322	2·283	2·246	2·210	2·174	2·140	2·106	3
4	3·102	3·037	2·974	2·914	2·855	2·798	2·743	2·690	2·639	2·589	4
5	3·696	3·605	3·517	3·433	3·352	3·274	3·199	3·127	3·058	2·991	5
6	4·231	4·111	3·998	3·889	3·784	3·685	3·589	3·498	3·410	3·326	6
7	4·712	4·564	4·423	4·288	4·160	4·039	3·922	3·812	3·706	3·605	7
8	5·146	4·968	4·799	4·639	4·487	4·344	4·207	4·078	3·954	3·837	8
9	5·537	5·328	5·132	4·946	4·772	4·607	4·451	4·303	4·163	4·031	9
10	5·889	5·650	5·426	5·216	5·019	4·833	4·659	4·494	4·339	4·192	10
11	6·207	5·938	5·687	5·453	5·234	5·029	4·836	4·656	4·486	4·327	11
12	6·492	6·194	5·918	5·660	5·421	5·197	4·988	4·793	4·611	4·439	12
13	6·750	6·424	6·122	5·842	5·583	5·342	5·118	4·910	4·715	4·533	13
14	6·982	6·628	6·302	6·002	5·724	5·468	5·229	5·008	4·802	4·611	14
15	7·191	6·811	6·462	6·142	5·847	5·575	5·324	5·092	4·876	4·675	15

10

Mathematical tables and formulae

Standard normal distribution table

	0·00	0·01	0·02	0·03	0·04	0·05	0·06	0·07	0·08	0·09
0·0	0·0000	0·0040	0·0080	0·0120	0·0160	0·0199	0·0239	0·0279	0·0319	0·0359
0·1	0·0398	0·0438	0·0478	0·0517	0·0557	0·0596	0·0636	0·0675	0·0714	0·0753
0·2	0·0793	0·0832	0·0871	0·0910	0·0948	0·0987	0·1026	0·1064	0·1103	0·1141
0·3	0·1179	0·1217	0·1255	0·1293	0·1331	0·1368	0·1406	0·1443	0·1480	0·1517
0·4	0·1554	0·1591	0·1628	0·1664	0·1700	0·1736	0·1772	0·1808	0·1844	0·1879
0·5	0·1915	0·1950	0·1985	0·2019	0·2054	0·2088	0·2123	0·2157	0·2190	0·2224
0·6	0·2257	0·2291	0·2324	0·2357	0·2389	0·2422	0·2454	0·2486	0·2517	0·2549
0·7	0·2580	0·2611	0·2642	0·2673	0·2704	0·2734	0·2764	0·2794	0·2823	0·2852
0·8	0·2881	0·2910	0·2939	0·2967	0·2995	0·3023	0·3051	0·3078	0·3106	0·3133
0·9	0·3159	0·3186	0·3212	0·3238	0·3264	0·3289	0·3315	0·3340	0·3365	0·3389
1·0	0·3413	0·3438	0·3461	0·3485	0·3508	0·3531	0·3554	0·3577	0·3599	0·3621
1·1	0·3643	0·3665	0·3686	0·3708	0·3729	0·3749	0·3770	0·3790	0·3810	0·3830
1·2	0·3849	0·3869	0·3888	0·3907	0·3925	0·3944	0·3962	0·3980	0·3997	0·4015
1·3	0·4032	0·4049	0·4066	0·4082	0·4099	0·4115	0·4131	0·4147	0·4162	0·4177
1·4	0·4192	0·4207	0·4222	0·4236	0·4251	0·4265	0·4279	0·4292	0·4306	0·4319
1·5	0·4332	0·4345	0·4357	0·4370	0·4382	0·4394	0·4406	0·4418	0·4429	0·4441
1·6	0·4452	0·4463	0·4474	0·4484	0·4495	0·4505	0·4515	0·4525	0·4535	0·4545
1·7	0·4554	0·4564	0·4573	0·4582	0·4591	0·4599	0·4608	0·4616	0·4625	0·4633
1·8	0·4641	0·4649	0·4656	0·4664	0·4671	0·4678	0·4686	0·4693	0·4699	0·4706
1·9	0·4713	0·4719	0·4726	0·4732	0·4738	0·4744	0·4750	0·4756	0·4761	0·4767
2·0	0·4772	0·4778	0·4783	0·4788	0·4793	0·4798	0·4803	0·4808	0·4812	0·4817
2·1	0·4821	0·4826	0·4830	0·4834	0·4838	0·4842	0·4846	0·4850	0·4854	0·4857
2·2	0·4861	0·4864	0·4868	0·4871	0·4875	0·4878	0·4881	0·4884	0·4887	0·4890
2·3	0·4893	0·4896	0·4898	0·4901	0·4904	0·4906	0·4909	0·4911	0·4913	0·4916
2·4	0·4918	0·4920	0·4922	0·4925	0·4927	0·4929	0·4931	0·4932	0·4934	0·4936
2·5	0·4938	0·4940	0·4941	0·4943	0·4945	0·4946	0·4948	0·4949	0·4951	0·4952
2·6	0·4953	0·4955	0·4956	0·4957	0·4959	0·4960	0·4961	0·4962	0·4963	0·4964
2·7	0·4965	0·4966	0·4967	0·4968	0·4969	0·4970	0·4971	0·4972	0·4973	0·4974
2·8	0·4974	0·4975	0·4976	0·4977	0·4977	0·4978	0·4979	0·4979	0·4980	0·4981
2·9	0·4981	0·4982	0·4982	0·4983	0·4984	0·4984	0·4985	0·4985	0·4986	0·4986
3·0	0·4987	0·4987	0·4987	0·4988	0·4988	0·4989	0·4989	0·4989	0·4990	0·4990

This table can be used to calculate $N(d)$, the cumulative normal distribution functions needed for the Black-Scholes model of option pricing. If $d_i > 0$, add 0·5 to the relevant number above. If $d_i < 0$, subtract the relevant number above from 0·5.

End of Question Paper

11

BPP
LEARNING MEDIA

BPP
LEARNING MEDIA

BPP
LEARNING MEDIA

BPP
LEARNING MEDIA

BPP
LEARNING MEDIA

BPP
LEARNING MEDIA

BPP
LEARNING MEDIA

Review Form – Paper P4 Advanced Financial Management (01/13)

Name: _____ Address: _____

_____

_____

How have you used this Kit?
(Tick one box only)

☐ Home study (book only)

☐ On a course: college _____

☐ With 'correspondence' package

☐ Other _____

Why did you decide to purchase this Kit?
(Tick one box only)

☐ Have used the complementary Study text

☐ Have used other BPP products in the past

☐ Recommendation by friend/colleague

☐ Recommendation by a lecturer at college

☐ Saw advertising

☐ Other _____

During the past six months do you recall seeing/receiving any of the following?
(Tick as many boxes as are relevant)

☐ Our advertisement in *Student Accountant*

☐ Our advertisement in *Pass*

☐ Our advertisement in *PQ*

☐ Our brochure with a letter through the post

☐ Our website www.bpp.com

Which (if any) aspects of our advertising do you find useful?
(Tick as many boxes as are relevant)

☐ Prices and publication dates of new editions

☐ Information on product content

☐ Facility to order books off-the-page

☐ None of the above

Which BPP products have you used?

Text	☐	Success CD	☐	Interactive Passcards	☐
Kit	☑	i-Pass	☐	Home Study Package	☐
Passcard	☐				

Your ratings, comments and suggestions would be appreciated on the following areas.

	Very useful	Useful	Not useful
Passing P4			
Planning your question practice			
Questions			
Top Tips etc in answers			
Content and structure of answers			
Mock exam answers			

Overall opinion of this Kit   Excellent ☐   Good ☐   Adequate ☐   Poor ☐

Do you intend to continue using BPP products?   Yes ☐   No ☐

The BPP author of this edition can be e-mailed at: andrewfinch@bpp.com

Please return this form to: Nick Weller, ACCA Publishing Manager (Professional papers), BPP Learning Media Ltd, FREEPOST, London, W12 8BR

Review Form (continued)

TELL US WHAT YOU THINK

Please note any further comments and suggestions/errors below.